THE
MURDER
OF THE
CENTURY

THE
MURDER
OF THE
CENTURY

THE GILDED AGE CRIME
THAT SCANDALIZED A CITY
AND SPARKED
THE TABLOID WARS

PAUL COLLINS

CROWN PUBLISHERS ☀ NEW YORK

Library of Congress Cataloging-in-Publication Data

Collins, Paul, 1969–
The murder of the century : the gilded age crime that scandalized a city and
sparked the tabloid wars / Paul Collins—1st ed.
p. cm.
Includes bibliographical references and index.
1. Nack, Augusta.   2. Murder—New York (State)—New York—Case studies.
3. Crimes of passion—New York (State)—New York—Case studies.
4. Tabloid newspapers—New York (State)—New York—History—19th century.
5. New York (N.Y.)—History—19th century.   I. Title.
HV6534.N5C66 2011
364.152'3092—dc22
2011009390

ISBN 978-0-307-59220-0
eISBN 978-0-307-59222-4

Printed in the United States of America

Book design by Gretchen Achilles
Jacket design by W. G. Cookman
Jacket photograph © Bettmann/Corbis

3   5   7   9   10   8   6   4   2

To Mom and Dad,
who let me read the mysteries from their bookshelf

IS ANY ONE YOU KNOW MISSING?

Send Any Information You May Possess to the Journal and It May Aid in Clearing Up a Mystery.

To the Public:

Do you know of a missing man? If you have a friend, a relative or an acquaintance who has disappeared, or if you have knowledge of the disappearance of any man, please send the information in detail to the Journal. Communications marked "Not for publication" will be held in strict confidence, and the information therein will be intrusted to none but the most reliable reporters, who will use it only to aid in solving the murder mystery that all society is interested in having cleared up. Do not assume that the missing man of whom you know cannot possibly be the victim. Send the facts to the Journal, and you may aid in bringing a murderer to justice.

THE JOURNAL.

CONTENTS

V. THE VERDICT   209

SOURCES   271

A NOTE ON THE TEXT

The tremendous press coverage of this affair, with sometimes more than a dozen newspapers fielding reporters at once—not to mention the later memoirs of its participants—allowed me to draw on many eyewitness sources. All of the dialogue in quotation marks comes directly from conversations recorded in their accounts, and while I have freely edited out verbiage, not a word has been added.

—P. C.

I.

THE VICTIM

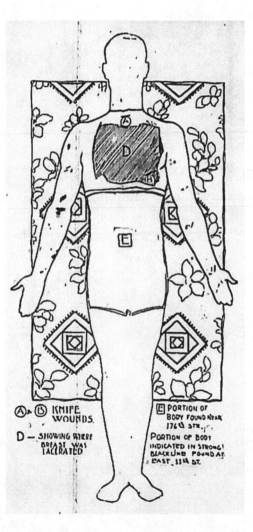

A - B KNIFE WOUNDS.

D — SHOWING WHERE BREAST WAS LACERATED

E PORTION OF BODY FOUND NEAR 176th STR.

PORTION OF BODY INDICATED IN STRONG BLACK LINE FOUND AT EAST 11th ST.

1.

THE MYSTERY
OF THE RIVER

IT WAS A SLOW AFTERNOON for news. The newsboys along the East River piers still readied themselves on a scorching summer Saturday for the incoming ferry passengers from Brooklyn, armed with innumerable battling editions of Manhattan's dailies for June 26, 1897. There were sensational "yellow papers" like Pulitzer's *World* and Hearst's *Journal,* the stately flagships of the *Herald* and the *Sun,* and stray runts like the *Post* and the *Times.* By two thirty, the afternoon editions were coming while the morning papers were getting left in stacks to bake in the sun. But there were no orders by President McKinley, no pitched battles in the Sudan, and no new Sousa marches to report. The only real story that day was the weather: OH! YES, IT IS HOT ENOUGH! gasped one headline. The disembarking ferry passengers who couldn't afford lemonade seltzer from riverside refreshment stalls instead downed the usual fare—unsterilized buttermilk for two cents, or sterilized for three—and then headed for East Third Street, where Mayor Strong was giving the dedication speech for the new 700-foot-long promenade pier. It was the city's first, a confection of whitewashed wrought iron, and under its cupola a brass band was readying the rousing oompah "Elsie from Chelsea."

Weaving between the newsboys and the ladies opening up parasols, though, were four boys walking the other way. They were escaping their hot and grimy brick tenements on Avenue C, and joining a perspiring crowd of thousands didn't sound much better than what they'd just left. To them, the East Eleventh Street pier had all the others beat; it was a disused tie-up just a few feet above the water, and surrounded by cast-off ballast rocks that made for an easy place to dry clothes. The boys took it over like a pirate's landing party, claiming it as their own and then lounging with their flat caps and straw boaters pulled rakishly low. It was a good place to gawk at the nearly completed boat a couple of piers over—a mysterious ironclad in the shape of a giant sturgeon, which its inventor promised would skim across the Atlantic at a forty-three-knot clip. When the boys tired of that, they turned their gaze back out to the water.

Jack McGuire spotted it first: a red bundle, rolling in with the tide and toward the ferry slip, then bobbing away again.

"Say, I'll get that!" yelled McGuire's friend Jimmy McKenna.

"Aw, will you?" Jack taunted him. But Jimmy was already stripped down and diving off the pier. A wiry thirteen-year-old with a powerful stroke in the water, he grabbed the bundle just before the wake from the Greenpoint ferry could send it floating away. They'd split the loot; it might be a wad of clothes, or some cargo toppled off a freighter. There was no telling what you'd find in the East River.

Jimmy dragged the parcel up onto the rocks with effort; the boys found it was the size of a sofa cushion, and heavy—at least thirty pounds, tightly wrapped in a gaudy red-and-gold oilcloth.

"It's closed," Jimmy said as he dripped on the rocks. The package had been expertly tied with coils of white rope; it wouldn't be easy for his cold and wet fingers to loosen it. But Jack had a knife handy, and he set to cutting in. As kids gathered around to see what treasure had been found, Jack sawed faster until a slip of the knife sank the blade into the bundle. Blood welled out from inside. He figured that meant they'd found something good; all kinds of farm goods were transported from the Brooklyn side of the river. It might be a side of fresh pork.

"I'm going to see what's in there," he proclaimed, and dug harder into the ropes. As they fell aside, Jack peeled back the clean new oilcloth to reveal another layer: dirty and blackened burlap, tied with twine. Jack cut that away too, and found yet another layer, this one of dry, coarse brown paper. Annoyed, he yanked it off. And then, for an interminable moment, the gathered boys stopped dead still.

On the rocks before them was a human arm. Two arms, in fact. Two arms attached to a muscular chest—and nothing more.

THE POLICE KNEW just who to blame.

Medical students, they muttered as they examined the sawn-off torso. The riverside boys had dithered for half an hour over the grisly and headless find, deciding what to do—though Jack had hastily tossed his knife into the river, afraid of catching any blame. But there was no real cause for alarm; a patrolman arrived and dragged the parcel up onto the dry pier, followed by two detectives from the Union Market station. In no great hurry, they eventually put in a call to the coroner's office to note that the med students were up to their usual pranks. The city had five schools that were allowed to use cadavers, and parts of them showed up in the unlikeliest places: You'd find legs in doorways, fingers in cigar boxes, that kind of nonsense. By the time the coroner bothered to pick up the parcel, it had been on the East Eleventh Street pier for three hours, exposed to the curious stares of the entire neighborhood. Meanwhile, boys had eagerly taken to diving into the water trying to find, as one observer put it, "every floating object that might by any possibility be part of a human body." They gleefully dragged waterlogged casks, boxes, and smashed timbers onto the pier, but alas, nothing more.

The morgue driver finally arrived. He wrapped the cloth back around their gruesome find, tossed the whole package aboard his wagon, and trundled it away with a signal to his horse. The city had yet to buy its first horseless carriages; it had been only two years since the first one had been seen in New York, and they remained such a rare sight that Manhattan still hadn't even recorded its first auto fatality. Every other kind of fatality, though, ended up where this one did, fifteen blocks north in Midtown, at the morgue's squat brick building on Twenty-Sixth Street.

They all came here: any skipping child struck by a dairy wagon, any organ grinder downed by apoplexy in the middle of Central Park, any wino found expired in a Bowery gutter, any sporting gentleman stabbed in a saloon. The Bellevue morgue was the haunt of the dead and the deadlined; newsmen were always around, because with about twenty unclaimed bodies a day thudding in—more during a good cold snap or a heat wave—you were always guaranteed some column inches for the late edition.

Even before the latest heat wave, Bellevue had been especially rich in news; its old morgue keeper had been arrested after twenty-seven years of illegally selling bodies to the local med schools at $5 a pop—selling so many, in fact, that he'd accumulated a $100,000 fortune on his morgue salary of $60 a month. The lowlier attendants were more cheaply bribed. A cigar or a pouch of shag tobacco would get a reporter the run of a windowless building some sixty by eighty feet wide, lined along one side with marble slabs, the other with chest-high tiers of cooled body drawers.

To wander through this library of corpses was a dubious privilege. The dead room's only respite from the gloom came from a single sky-light, and the occasional nudge from a resident tomcat. There were no fans, and flies buzzed constantly over the marble slabs where the latest deliveries reposed naked, awaiting identification. A thin mist of icy water was kept running over the slabs in an ineffectual attempt to keep the bodies fresh and to shoo the flies away. The effect was that of a dark, dripping cave filled with the broken bodies of Manhattan. It was, by universal assent, the most miserable place in the city. Worst of all were the mangled and bloated remains of bridge jumpers and failed swimmers pulled daily from the river.

"That horrible place—God!" novelist Theodore Dreiser would later recall of his days there as a *World* reporter. "Daily from the ever-flowing waters of New York there were recaptured and washed up in all stages and degrees of decomposition the flotsam and jetsam of the great city—its offal, its victims, its *what?*"

The *who* and *what* were always the questions for these nameless corpses. But the source of the oilcloth-covered bundle that had arrived that evening was not so hard to guess at.

"Medical students," an attendant seconded, noting its arrival in the ledger.

Probably cut from one of their own bodies here in the morgue, maybe off a cadaver sold just a day or two earlier. Well, now whoever it was had come back. They'd wait the obligatory seventy-two hours, of course, and then send it on to the coffin room, where another attendant hammered together cheap plank boxes. Anyone left unclaimed for three days went there—the body photographed, the clothes stored for laggardly friends or relatives to make a later identification, any money or jewelry on the body quietly pocketed—and then the newly filled coffins were disgorged out the back of the building onto the pier. Each day a dead-boat pulled up for a final stygian journey up the East River to a waiting trench in the potter's field on Hart Island.

That, no doubt, is where this misbegotten parcel would go, and nobody would ever hear of it again.

BY THE TIME Bellevue superintendent Dr. Thomas Murphy and city medical examiner Dr. George Dow arrived on their evening rounds, there were reporters from the *World*, the *Herald*, and the *Evening Telegram* all gathered in the morgue, waiting for their day's quota of Dreadful Cases and Awful Tragedies. They'd already gotten a good one out of Bellevue that day when Diamond Jim Brady forcibly checked his mother in to the insane ward next door. But the reporters could always hope for more, and as the two doctors made their obligatory check of the day's casualties, they froze before the river parcel, exchanging significant looks.

Dr. Murphy closely examined the oilcloth-wrapped package: the well-muscled chest and shoulders of a white man, its arms folded across in an X with the hands lying on its shoulders. The head, wherever it was now, had been rather raggedly hacked off at the larynx, while down below, the torso had been cleanly cut under the fifth rib.

"There is a mystery here," Dr. Murphy muttered cryptically.

Dr. Dow nodded. He felt the tone of the body's skin, and lifted the arms to reveal that an irregular horseshoe-shaped chunk had been sliced away from the chest. But it was the saw marks at the neck that most immediately caught his eye.

"No medical student would have done this," he announced. It was simple, Dr. Dow explained to the reporters: This body was no more a med-school cadaver than you or I. "A saw, and not a knife, was used to sever the head and the body," he explained. That was the mark of the untutored; professionals saw bone and slice flesh.

"I am pretty familiar with the methods employed by the different colleges," agreed Bellevue's superintendent. "None of them does this kind of work. The removal of the flesh from the breast has a very suspicious look." It might have been done, he ventured, to dispose of a telltale tattoo. But without a head or an identifying mark on the body, how could they describe it?

"Let me see . . ." Dr. Murphy brightened. "The height of the average man is that of arms extended and measuring from the tips of the fingers." He turned to a morgue assistant. "Measure the arms and fingers."

The assembled men watched as the orderly eased the headless trunk down from its drawer and laid it out at full length on the floor, then ran the measuring tape along the arms.

"Five foot eleven," the assistant announced.

Dr. Dow continued to examine the body and added his own guess. "I would not want to be quoted as expressing a positive opinion," he warned the reporters, "but I should think the man when alive weighed 190 pounds."

The muscular body the oilcloth enclosed, the *Herald*'s reporter wrote in some admiration, showed "a man of magnificent physical development." The hands were remarkably soft and uncalloused— genteel, even, with the nails carefully manicured. Dr. Dow pressed on the flesh of the arms and found it still soft and supple; he moved the fingers back and forth, and they yielded and straightened easily. Rigor mortis had not even set in.

Word spread quickly among the Bellevue buildings; a dozen physicians from the hospital piled into the morgue, each wanting to poke and prod the mysterious cadaver. The city's coroner was roused from his house. But as for Dr. Dow, he'd already seen enough. The medical examiner stood over the severed trunk and rendered his professional judgment.

"The man of which this formed a part," he informed the startled room, "was alive twenty-four hours ago."

2.

A DETECTIVE
READS THE PAPER

IT WAS A GLORIOUS Sunday morning. Julius Meyer was home in his Harlem tenement on 127th Street, enjoying a day off from his job as a mechanic.

"Papa, let's go cherrying!" pleaded his eight-year-old son. He could hardly say no, and so the father and his two boys—little Edgar and strapping teenaged Herbert—made their way up toward Ogden's Woods. Getting there meant a forty-block train ride north to the Highbridge station, and then a ten-block walk into the northern reaches of the borough—out toward the Bronx, that drowsy region of farms, apple orchards, and placid dairies.

Up here, between a densely wooded crescent bounded by Undercliff Avenue and the Harlem River on one side, 170th Street and the Washington Bridge on the other, one could forget the city altogether. These were the hinterlands, thick with pines and huckleberries and cherries but scarce in people; you could stand on Undercliff Avenue for an hour or more without seeing another soul. Just one house was visible along this lonely stretch of road, with nary another shack for a quarter mile around. As Julius and the boys wended their way into the woods—a good twelve-foot drop from the main road—it was as if they'd shimmied down into another country.

While Julius and Herbert pressed forward through the swatting tree limbs and the thick brambles, Edgar was able to snake through the tangled brush and scamper ahead of them—too far, almost. They'd entered down by Sedgwick and 170th Avenue, but Edgar, an ebullient boy, was charging into wild and thorny depths, far from any entrance.

Julius could no longer see his boy.

"Edgar!" he called out. "Edgar?"

SUNDAY AT the Highbridge station house was neither challenging nor especially rewarding police work—at least not for someone like Detective Arthur Carey. Once a rising star at HQ, he'd been caught in a department power struggle, knocked down a couple of pay grades, and exiled to the sticks. For two years Carey had been deprived of the murder cases he'd once landed downtown; testifying to packed courtrooms and seeing his name in the paper weren't part of his job in Highbridge. "I was walking a post," he'd explain without irony, "where, according to police tradition, a patrolman helped tend the goats."

That's what everyone in the department called it: Goatsville. It wasn't on any map, but every officer knew where it was. Goatsville was where you got sent when you shook down a gambling house too hard, or busted a local ward boss in a brothel, or when your service revolver discharged in an unfortunate direction. For Carey, it was for hitching himself to the wrong star; a few years earlier, a corruption scandal meant that some heads had to roll. Carey hadn't been implicated, but his mentor—the mighty Inspector Thomas Byrnes, the most famous police detective in America at the time—had stepped down, and another faction took over the Detective Bureau at the police headquarters on Mulberry Street. Carey had been in Goatsville ever since.

Inside his station were Julius Meyer, his sons, and the parcel they'd accompanied on the police wagon. It was turning into quite the Sunday adventure for the two boys.

Detective Carey listened carefully to their story. Little Edgar, they recounted, had yelled back excitedly to his father from the foot of Undercliff Avenue's steep retaining wall. He'd found a peddler's pack. There, on a small shaded ledge that jutted out just before the forest sloped away, was a tightly bound bundle, the sort that a linen or notions dealer might waddle under from one house to another, ready to untie it to lay out his wares. But it was heavy—easily a hundred pounds. A tug on one end had drawn out a putrescent waft. Meyer didn't know what it was, but he knew something was amiss. He left his boys to guard the find while he flagged down some mounted policemen. They'd needed a stretcher and towing ropes just to hoist the mass up from the ravine.

Detective Carey and Captain Thomas Killilea carefully appraised the package. The station captain was another Byrnes appointee sent up to Goatsville. He'd been on the force since the Lincoln administration and held a double claim to the precinct: He was also tangled in yet another corruption fiasco just a year earlier, accused of renting out on-duty police to work as security guards at football games. The former police commissioner Teddy Roosevelt had tried pushing Killilea and his cronies out altogether, getting so many top officers under indictment one year that the annual police parade was canceled. Still, even an old-timer like Killilea retained enough of a fondness for his old downtown beat to read of the latest doings beyond Goatsville. And to him, the red-and-gold-patterned oilcloth already looked plenty familiar; in fact, the captain knew exactly where he'd spotted it before. He'd seen it, he explained, in that morning's *New York Herald*.

Detective Carey cut the baling cords and pulled back layers of red oilcloth, burlap, and twine-secured brown paper. Inside was the midsection of a man—and it was very clearly a man—hewn between the ribs up top and about four inches below the hip joints at the bottom. *Medical students*, others at the station house shrugged. They figured the officers at Tenth Street had been right, and the morning's newspapers were just out to make something out of nothing.

Carey wasn't so sure.

The bundle would be sent onward to the morgue at Bellevue, of course—an officer was already making the phone call—but Carey

wanted a closer look. This wasn't the cat-up-a-tree work of his precinct that he had before him; and even if nobody else in the station
thought so, to Carey it had the feel of something big.

The detective examined the inside of the parcel. The layer of
dirty burlap was secured with faintly pink-colored string, and Carey
had seen spools of it before: It was a sort druggists used, a variety
called seine twine. Below that was a brown paper wrapping, and then
the body. The revolting smell was filling the station house. But Carey
wasn't quite finished: He wanted just one more look before they
loaded it up onto the wagon again. Carey rolled the limbless trunk
over for a better view.

There, in the small of the back, adhered another piece of brown
paper—a slightly different, smaller piece. He delicately peeled it
away and examined it. The paper bore a single, small ink stamp—
and the detective knew, in that moment, that he had to return to his
old precinct.

Murder, mused Carey darkly, *followed me here.*

THE TRIP from the cows and orchards of the north down to the corner of Houston Street and Bowery was only about ten miles, but
Arthur Carey might as well have been traveling to another world.
These were his old haunts from his rookie days on Byrnes's detective squad: a ramshackle and roiling retail polyglot of hagglers, banjo
players, dime museums, beer gardens, fruit stands, and discount
crockery shops. You could walk full blocks down Bowery and fill your
arms with newspapers hawked by newsboys, each one a different
title, and none of them in English. It was one of the city's oldest
streets, its name a mocking remainder of the land's old Dutch farms
or *bouwerij*—but now a cheap, noisy, and beery cacophony of drunk
bums and sober business.

If you didn't mind the occasional fisticuffs or dead body, it was
a swell place for an officer—a little too swell, maybe. Teddy Roosevelt had found the neighborhood so obliging to his men that he
went around pouncing on on-duty officers for quaffing pints in oyster

houses and dive saloons. In their place came recruits who had to pass fitness tests and undergo weapons training, and it was said that you could tell the old and new officers apart by sorting the fat from the slender. But the old sins remained, and then some; there was real money to be had in this neighborhood. The Bowery Savings Bank was improbably becoming one of the world's largest savings institutions, and for police the temptation to dip in at less reputable businesses was everywhere. Even Carey's well-regarded old boss retired with a fortune of $350,000—something not easily explained when a typical yearly salary on the force was $2,000. Some departmental accomplishments, perhaps, were better left unsung.

The Bowery's packed streets and low-slung tenements overflowed with Germans and Poles, and the storefront of Kugler & Wollens was emblematic of the changing neighborhood. John Jacob Astor IV owned the poky two-story brick building at 277 Bowery—in fact, the Astors owned much of the block, as their long-dead patriarch had made his first land buys a century earlier along this very street. For decades the building had been occupied by a clan of butchers and grocers, the Marsh family; but by the 1870s, as the neighborhood acquired umlauts at an impressive rate, it became a German beer saloon, and then a hardware retailer.

On this block of narrow brick buildings, hardware in every variety was hawked by Germans. The mighty Hammacher Schlemmer hardware shop held down one end, selling everything from mechanic's tools to piano fittings. At the other end was the domain of Ernst Kugler. Herr Kugler had been here more than twenty years, outlasting a previous partner, watching the passing of the Bowery Boy gangs, and seeing the latest immigrant wave turn the Bowery Theater into a Yiddish venue. Kugler and his employees knew their business well enough that when a detective turned up with a piece of paper stamped Kugler & Wollens, they knew exactly what it was for.

At some point, *someone* connected with that bundled body had been here. It might have been any time and for any purchase from a handful of wood screws to a brass keyhole escutcheon. Like every hardware store, they kept a large roll of brown paper, a stamp, and a reel of twine for wrapping up all manner of purchases. But the shape and condition of this piece was distinct.

It had been used to wrap a saw.

SO CAREY HAD ONE CLUE. The other—his only other, really—was the oilcloth that the trunk had been wrapped in. The fabric was still so new that it smelled of the store. But the piece found in Ogden's Woods had been about four feet wide and fourteen and a half feet long. Unless you had a baronial dining room table, you weren't buying sheets that long for a tablecloth. Someone had bought this with a task in mind—maybe, given its red color, for catching dripping blood. But where would they have bought it?

Finding someone in the Bowery who knew about oilcloth wasn't hard. The street was filled with exactly the kind of peddlers who used the stuff, people who immediately knew where to locate the nearest distributor: Henry Feuerstein, a sharp-eyed Hungarian who wholesaled yarns and fabric just three blocks away on Stanton Street. An Orthodox Jew, Feuerstein was contentedly working in his warehouse on the Christian sabbath; he personally examined the swatch and identified the maker of the brightly colored red-and-gold floral pattern. "A. F. Buchanan and Sons," he said. He even knew the pattern number. "Diamond B, number 3220."

It was a cheap and unpopular pattern—a leftover from last year's stock, in fact—and just too gaudy and vivid to sell well. He hadn't unloaded a roll of it to any store in four months. Most dry-goods customers for oilcloth, Feuerstein explained, preferred something a bit lighter in color.

Of course, the detective could check the other distributor that Buchanan & Sons used—there was also Claflin & Company, over on Church Street. But that wouldn't happen without a warrant; its proprietor, John Claflin, had been arrested weeks earlier after dodging a jury summons. He was not known to be overly fond of police. But Feuerstein, you understand, was a reasonable man.

The merchant threw open his ledgers, tracing out the network of dealers and distributors. And once they tallied up all the dry-goods shops and general stores they distributed this stuff to, it became clear: Carey would have something like fifty more shops to visit. Here, right in Feuerstein's books, you could see how far even an unpopular cloth went. There was a Mr. Bernstein on Belmont Avenue in Brooklyn; a Mr. Bratzenfelder on Avenue D; a Mr. Theimer uptown at Seventy-Second Street; a Mr. Prencky . . . It went on and on. A roll of Diamond B #3220 even went to the store of Ignatz Rucmark, over in Hoboken. You'd need to hit all five boroughs and then some to track this cloth down. That would take time—and men. Aside from Detective Carey, though, barely anyone else on the force had moved into action yet.

But if the police weren't on the case, Carey found, somebody was. Because someone *else* had been coming here and asking Feuerstein these very same questions.

Reporters.

3.

THE JIGSAW MAN

SUNDAYS WERE ALWAYS a bit slow at the *New York World*, and Ned Brown just about had the place to himself. Walking along a vast Park Row newsroom so crammed with rolltop desks that it was nearly barricaded, he read panel after panel on walls placarded with exhortations:

ACCURACY, ACCURACY, ACCURACY!

And:

WHO? WHAT? WHERE? WHEN? HOW?

And:

THE FACTS—THE COLOR—THE FACTS!

These continued around the perimeter of the room, so that in every direction a reporter looked, the *World* credo was shouted at him. But on this day the room was quiet; only the stale cigar smoke hinted at last night's fury in getting the June 27 *Sunday World* out.

From the windows between the placards, Ned could see out over the rooftops—over every rooftop, in fact—clear out to the East River. The teeming city below had nearly doubled in size over the last generation; it vaulted upward with newly invented elevators, and outward with hurriedly built elevated railways. Towering above it all were the eighteen-story offices of the mighty *New York World*, the crowning achievement of Joseph Pulitzer.

A lanky Hungarian immigrant, Pulitzer had enlisted in the Union army, ridden cavalry in Sheridan's Shenandoah Valley campaign, and then drifted into New York at the end of the Civil War. On the very site of this newspaper office had once stood French's Hotel, and Pulitzer, then a penniless veteran, was thrown out of it. Two decades later, in an almost operatic act of revenge, a wealthy Pulitzer returned from out west and razed the hotel to the ground, erecting on the spot the city's tallest building: *his* building. He'd lavished two miles of wrought-iron columns to support the world's largest pressroom and placed his offices on the soaring top floors beneath an immense 425-ton golden dome. The reflection of its gilded surface could be seen for miles out to sea; for immigrants coming to America, the first sight of their new land was not the Statue of Liberty but Pulitzer's golden beacon. Inside, his sanctum was decorated with frescoes and leather wainscoting; one of his first visitors, emerging from the elevator and into his office, blurted: "Is God in?"

But when Pulitzer had bought the paper from Jay Gould in 1883, the *World* was scarcely godlike at all. It was an arthritic operation with a circulation of twenty thousand, and it bled money. Pulitzer fired the old staff, bought a blazingly fast new Hoe press, and dragooned the best reporters and editors, pushing them mercilessly to reinvent the era's drab uniform columns into bold headlines and sensational woodcut illustrations. No longer would shipping news and market results count as front-page stories; as much a showman as a newsman, Pulitzer unapologetically courted women and immigrant readers with a heady mix of bombast, sentiment, and attention-grabbing promotions that rode on the latest fads. When Jules Verne was on everyone's nightstand, Pulitzer ordered daredevil reporter Nellie Bly to travel around the world in eighty days; she accomplished it in seventy-two. In the midst of the craze over Martian canals, Pulitzer even considered mounting a giant billboard visible to "readers" on Mars. Rather more pragmatically, the rags-to-riches immigrant seized the moment when the newly built Statue of Liberty lacked a pedestal: a flag-waving *World* campaign among housewives and schoolchildren raised more than $100,000 to buy one. And Emma Lazarus's "huddled masses" inscription? That came from a *World* contest.

The facts—the color—the facts! Circulation had risen fifteenfold since he'd bought it, making the *World* one of the largest dailies in the world. The paper itself had swollen, too, its immense three-cent Sunday edition becoming a thing of sensational beauty. Pulitzer had created the world's first color comics section, featuring the antics of a bald tenement kid with ears like jug handles: the Yellow Kid. His popularity inspired competing papers that year to scoff that the *World* was comic-strip journalism—*yellow journalism*, they called it. Perhaps, but it was an absolutely brilliant hue of yellow. Past the day's front-page grabber from the East Eleventh Street pier—BOY'S GHASTLY FIND—the paper was bursting with an exposé of a Chicago diploma mill, an account of a Maine aeronaut taking flight with a giant kite, fashion tips for women, and ads for everything from Hoff's Malt Extract to Dr. Scott's Electric Hair Brush. A thick periodical section promised "More Reading Material Than Any Four Magazines" and was fronted by a thundering headline on unregulated "baby farm" orphanages: NOTHING SO CHEAP IN NEW YORK AS HUMAN LIFE!

At the front of the newsroom was the ringmaster for this printed circus: the city editor, who regularly bellowed from a wooden platform for more copy. But today it was just the substitute editor enjoying the luxurious lull of Sunday afternoon.

And then the phone rang.

Ned Brown was motioned over. A second oilcloth-wrapped body part had been found up by the Bronx and was due to arrive at the Bellevue morgue any minute. Ned was to run over and meet up with Gus Roeder, the *World*'s crack morgue correspondent.

"Do whatever Gus tells you," the editor snapped. "The *Journal*'s probably got forty guys there already."

The competition! The newly launched *Evening Journal* had been nipping at the paper's heels for months, and here the emptied *World* offices would get caught flat-footed on the story. It could be a new victim, or a second helping of yesterday's East River find; either way, it was sizing up to be another front-pager, and the editor knew they'd have to grab it.

"If the pieces fit, it's the same stiff," he declared, and hurried his rookie to the door. "If it's part of a different stiff, then the guy with the red oilcloth has murdered them both."

RUNNING FROM THE EL STATION to the Bellevue morgue, Ned Brown was a sight: A short and stringy bantamweight, his blond hair swept up in a pompadour like his boxing heroes, he sprinted along Twenty-Sixth Street while dodging newsboys and Sunday strollers. The nineteen-year-old NYU student had been angling for any news assignments he could get over the summer. Today was his break, his first real story.

Gus Roeder was waiting for him when he flew into the morgue. So were Deputy Coroner Philip O'Hanlon's findings on the river bundle, the result of several hours of painstaking autopsy. Gus—a dour, red-faced German with a thick accent—bustled into the crowd of reporters to listen to Dr. O'Hanlon, while Ned went to examine the arms and shoulders found by the pier. By the skin he could immediately see that the victim was probably fair, about thirty-five years old; judging by his soft hands, he was not a manual laborer.

But who was he, and who had done this?

"At first," O'Hanlon admitted to the gathered reporters, "it looked to me as though it were the fore section of a body prepared for photography so as to show the position of the heart and lungs, as might be done in a medical college. But I do not believe so now."

Observe: not only did the torso still retain all its organs, the body contained no trace of any preservative. On the contrary: inside the broad chest of a powerfully muscled man, the tissue of the lungs was still spongy and the heart was filled with blood—the very blood that had stopped flowing after a knife was plunged between the victim's fifth and sixth ribs.

What?

The reporters looked closely at the body. The flesh stripped away from the chest—and, perhaps, an identifying tattoo along with it—had also quietly hidden two previously undetected stab wounds on the body. A casual observer would not spot them among the gore—but O'Hanlon had.

"They must have been inflicted *before* death," he flatly stated.

Making incisions around the stab sites, the deputy coroner found that blood had entered into the surrounding tissue—that is, it was pumped into them. That only happened in the living; a stab or incision made on a dead man created different internal damage than one on a living body. He'd also looked *inside* these stab wounds. A stab will typically show threads of clothing driven into the wound; but this one had none. So the victim, O'Hanlon concluded, had been alive and naked when stabbed.

"Both wounds were made with a long-bladed knife," O'Hanlon continued, "and both cuts were downward, as a man would strike while standing. One was above the left collarbone, and the other above the fifth intercostal space. The latter penetrated the heart . . . this alone would cause instant death."

Only, Dr. O'Hanlon realized, it *hadn't*. True, the fatal wound had been driven deep into the heart at a nearly perpendicular angle— plunged into the victim from above, possibly while he was sleeping. But the victim was a powerful man, and the assortment of nonfatal wounds—the other stab wound under the collarbone, a glancing cut to the left hand, blood under a fingernail, and boot-shaped bruises on the arm—these told the story of a horrific struggle. The victim had cut his hand in trying to grab the attacker's knife, the deputy coroner theorized, and had made an attempt to stand up and fight back in a terrifying but already doomed final effort.

"That he was knocked down I think is proved by the imprints of the boot," O'Hanlon theorized. "He struggled to his feet and was standing erect when someone, who I think must have been very muscular, stabbed him in the collarbone with a big knife. The blood under his nail shows that he struggled hard, or else that he clasped his hand to his bosom after he had been stabbed."

And with that, the deputy coroner—and the headless torso—had told their story.

The morgue doors slammed open. From outside, orderlies heaved in another load of cargo: a red-wrapped parcel that took two men to carry. Without the preserving cold of the East River, and after a spell sitting in a summertime forest, it was offensively rank. The morgue keeper ignored the smell to unwrap the bundle and lay it out: the midsection, male and muscular and circumcised. A mass of reporters watched as the two segments were pushed together on the marble slab.

They fit perfectly.

AT SIX P.M. on June 27, the body had its first claimant.

Bellevue was hardly the place to spend a Sunday evening, but Miss Clara Magnusson's friends and neighbors had been urging her to visit ever since the story in the previous night's *Telegram*. She lived just three blocks away, yet it had taken until now for her to make the journey over to this dismal place; her neighbor Gustav accompanied her to help with the identification and to provide a steady shoulder. She explained that her brother-in-law, Max Weineke, had been missing for a month: he was a thirty-four-year-old Danish scrap-metal dealer, and the descriptions of the morgue's find had her friends on East Twenty-Eighth Street wondering. Coroner Tuthill led the two over to the marble slab, and to the legless and headless segmented man who lay nude upon it.

There was a scar on Max's back, she recalled, and that would surely identify the body. But as she watched the attendant turn the body over, her heart sank; it had been sawed through *exactly* where the scar should be.

It's him, her neighbor Gustav decided. He was sure of it. Max had been a moody fellow—industrious, but he drank a bit at times— and . . . well, there's no telling what could have happened to him, really. He'd had $30 on him when he disappeared—more than a week's pay—and that right there was enough motive for a man to be killed.

And yet the body did not seem *quite* right. Max had been missing for more than a month, but this body was fresh. Then there was the matter of those strong but supple hands—so soft, so smooth and pampered. These were not the hands of a scrap-metal dealer. And there was a scar on the left hand—and an old fingernail injury where it had been partly cut away—that neither of them recognized or could account for.

For Bellevue's superintendent, it was the scar on the finger that did it. "If they had only been able to account for the scar on the finger." He sighed. "I should have thought the body was that of Weineke beyond a reasonable doubt."

Gustav and Clara stepped back out into the fading evening light, leaving just as much of a mystery as when they'd arrived.

WHILE THIS PUZZLING DRAMA played out, the morgue had received another visitor. A few among the reporters took notice: *Art Carey?*

They hadn't seen Byrnes's exiled protégé in ages. The detective was energized, back in his element. He walked briskly around the body—the segment he'd unwrapped earlier that afternoon now reunited like a jigsaw with its top half—and examined the matching red-and-gold oilcloth of both segments. He'd come to know it well, though maybe not as well as the newspaper reporters who'd scooped him on finding the fabric wholesaler. In fact, the newspapermen had been ahead of the police force all day.

I knew it was a murder all along, Captain Hogan had blustered earlier, claiming that he'd blamed it on medical students out of a concern for public safety—keeping the citizenry, you see, from panicking. The reporters were incredulous. Was Hogan joking? It took a *Telegram* reporter to actually get the first crime scene's facts right, since the patrolman's report claimed that the bundle included the abdomen but no organs—a patent falsehood to make it sound like a med-lab cut-up. And the police hadn't done anything since; it was a *Herald* reporter who had fetched the coroner the night before and escorted him to the morgue, and a *World* reporter who started knocking on doors even later that night to interview groggy oilcloth dealers around the city. The police hadn't secured the crime scene at the pier, hadn't assigned any extra men to the case, hadn't even admitted it was murder until the coroner telephoned and *insisted* they do something.

Well, Hogan ventured, the murder had probably been committed among a ship's crew, and so maybe it was out of their jurisdiction.

Wait, a *Herald* reporter had asked. Didn't the hands lack the kind of calluses a sailor would have?

Hogan didn't really have an answer on that one.

In fact, there was a lot the police didn't have answers for. They'd already been on the defensive all weekend, even *before* this case; one of their captains had led sweeps of women guilty of little more than walking along Broadway after midnight, filling the courts with the tragic injured respectability of sobbing baker's assistants and late-shift shopgirls. When one cop was asked for his evidence, he'd scarcely sputtered, "I saw her walk up and down the street a few times" before being cut off by a magistrate's bellow of "Discharged!" Reporters had been having a field day with it; a new murder was the last thing the department needed that day.

But Carey was different: He knew this was a homicide case, and he was making it *his* case. He even had his own pet theory. The murder, he mused aloud to a reporter, might have been committed in Long Island or Brooklyn. The killers—for it would have required more than one to cut up and dispose of the body so quickly—had taken a ferry and dumped the first piece. But then they'd panicked. Maybe they thought that they'd been seen. That's when they went back and fetched the larger piece with a wagon, drove over the Washington Bridge, and dumped it onto the loneliest stretch of road they could find. Of course, this was just a hunch—half a hunch, really. And as for who did it, or who the victim was . . . well, there was no way to tell yet.

Taking one last look at the body before he headed back to the World Building with Gus, though, young Ned Brown wasn't so sure about that. When he examined the headless corpse's hands, an unnerving sense of recognition crept over him. Those well-muscled arms and smooth fingers—they were like something he'd seen somewhere before.

But where?

4.

THE WRECKING CREW

ON MONDAY MORNING, New Yorkers awoke to find a hand shoved in their face. HAND OF THE HEADLESS MURDERED MAN—EXACT SIZE, crowed the June 28 *New York World*. There, above the fold, the life-sized fingers splayed across the morning paper—a dead man reaching out of the page to grab readers by the collar. RIVER MYSTERY GROWS IN HORROR, bellowed *Press* newsboys, while the high-minded *Herald* fretted over "the strangest and most brutal murder of the century." Even the immigrant sheets took notice, with the staidly Teutonic *New Yorker Staats Zeitung* trumpeting the latest on *Der Kopffabschneider*—"the Headcutter." But none topped the *World*'s engraving—procured, it boasted, "from a flashlight photograph made in the Morgue last night." The illustration irresistibly invited readers to place their own hand across the dead man's—to clasp their fingers across his—and wonder at his identity.

An overnight autopsy of the second parcel by Coroner Tuthill furnished some intriguing hints. The victim, as one reporter put it delicately, "may have been a Hebrew." He had no alcohol in his stomach, which discounted a drunken brawl. Nor was there food in there—so it had been at least three or four hours since his last meal. But among this minutiae, one of the coroner's consulting physicians had made a sensational finding: *The leg stumps had been boiled.*

"It appears to me," he'd confided to an *Evening Telegram* reporter, "that an attempt has been made to dispose of the body by boiling it. It is possible the murderers thrust the legs into a kettle hoping to boil the flesh off, but found they could not do it quickly or easily enough, and that they then cut up the remains."

Well, that was one way of looking at it.

CANNIBALISM SUGGESTED, the *Herald* announced. Or was it something more subtle—quicklime or a harsh deodorizer on the skin, the remains of a failed attempt at a hasty cover-up? The most fascinating solution offered up in the morgue came from a *Times* reporter: Weren't butchers in the habit of scalding stuck pigs to loosen up their skin? The suggestion was compelling; a butcher's handiwork might account for the curious quality of the murderer's saw cuts—more skilled than an amateur, yet cruder than a med student.

"A butcher may have done it," Coroner Tuthill mused aloud. "Or, perhaps, a carpenter."

Yet the scalding seemed to favor a butcher, and reporters and morgue employees alike could hardly keep from thinking of the Luetgert case—a recent Chicago murder where a local sausage maker dropped his wife into one of his factory's vats. Luetgert's case was a peculiar one, since there was no witness and no victim left to produce. But this Manhattan mystery provided a horrifying and neatly packaged clue—a body with skin, a *Herald* reporter marveled, that was "as white as marble." That, the coroner explained, was because "the body had been washed, and the blood removed before it was wrapped up."

But who would do such a thing? The victim might not have been drinking, a *Press* reporter suggested, but the killer surely had been. Not just to commit the deed, mind you, but to steel himself to venture into the Bronx woods at night. "His nerves must be of iron," he speculated, "and probably he fortified himself with liquor for the ordeal." Even just the sawing would have been exhausting, awkward work. On this the coroner spoke from some experience, after all—in cutting through the trunk, he explained, you'd need somebody to hold the arms so that they wouldn't keep getting in the way. And that meant an accomplice.

Or, perhaps, an entire gang.

The *World* knew just the man to ask about the case: Andrew Drummond, the former head of the U.S. Secret Service.

These days he was running a detective bureau at the foot of Newspaper Row, and he'd been following the case closely. "I believe that this most atrocious murder was committed by a foreigner," he huffed to a *World* reporter. Its ferocity, he deemed, was the work of men hailing from warm and lusty climes. "The murderer is a Sicilian, or possibly a Spaniard or Cuban. Maybe a Spanish spy has been put out of the way by the Cubans. The most likely one is that it is the result of a family feud among Sicilians. I know the ways of the Mafia."

To Drummond, the clincher was the oilcloth. What murderer would call attention to his deed by wrapping it in lurid red cloth? Ah, but attention was the *point* with a Mafia hit. And of course, as Drummond reminded readers—"Sicilians love bright colors."

Even as scores of reporters were fanning out across the city, beating the bushes and shadowing the police along the riverbanks and in the Bronx woods, Drummond was sure of one thing: Whether the head was burned, buried, or sunk in the river, they wouldn't like what they'd find. "When the head is found," he warned, "it will be seen to be horribly disfigured."

But where some saw horror, others sensed opportunity.

EVERY DAY OR SO for the last couple of years on Newspaper Row, a mob of mustachioed, derby-hatted men would come tumbling out of a low brick building, the first of them saddling up onto their squeaking bicycles even as they ran, and then careening wildly past City Hall; then a second group, more raggedly bohemian with their leather portfolios and wooden camera tripods, would clamber aboard carriages and go clattering madly after the bicycles. Behind them, editor Sam Chamberlain could be heard roaring from his desk.

"Get excited. God damn it, *get excited*!"

This was the Wrecking Crew.

The appearance of the Wrecking Crew meant just one thing: that a splendid story—a lover gunning his society sweetheart down on Broadway, a passenger ferry upending itself, or a rollicking downtown building collapse—was to appear in the next edition of the *New York Journal.*

You could tell when New York was having a peaceful day, it was said by friends, by how despondent *Journal* publisher William Randolph Hearst looked. But give him a murdered lad or tragic maiden, and Hearst joyfully revived. And a man dying at the hands of a maniac who scattered parts all around the city? He was ecstatic.

For their newly created *Evening Journal* edition—meant to be even saucier and more shameless than the morning *Journal*—it was pure homicide gold. What a way to launch! And so the word came down from the top: Do whatever it takes. Hearst editors sent reporters off to tail detectives and swipe evidence from the scene if necessary, the better to run it in the *Evening Journal* first. Photograph the Meyer boys, map the spot where they found it, show the twine and the knots and the pattern of the oilcloth around the torso. Get diagrams of the nude body. Get graphics and put it on page 1. That morning the Wrecking Crew seemed to be rushing in and out of the *Journal* almost nonstop; it was like nothing anybody had seen before.

"Events seem to indicate that men, like dogs, go mad at certain seasons," Hearst mused as he surveyed the day's news. There were race riots in Key West, idiots stealing electricity off high-voltage streetcar lines in Ohio, and two millionaires fighting over a $15 dog here in New York. But this story, *this* was something more than ordinary madness. It was already getting picked up by the wires and running across the country. And so the order came from Hearst's offices: Hire four launches, and set them to dragging the bottom of the East River—immediately.

Find that head, the chief wrecker commanded.

CAPTAIN O'BRIEN COULDN'T ward it off anymore, not with every newspaper headline on his way in to the Mulberry Street headquarters yelling at him. After two days of hopeless stalling by the police, several detectives were sent trudging over to the morgue in the early-morning hours to take down names and addresses.

They had a long day ahead of them. The steps and wooden porch leading into the death house were crowded with bereaved families—scores of people, all convinced their lost loved ones were inside—as well as local curiosity seekers, lounging surgeons from the neighboring hospital, and legions of reporters. The detectives and the coroner could barely make their way inside. The first two visitors to squeeze in gave their names to a detective as John Johnson and Adolph Carlson of 333 East Twenty-Eighth Street. They were fellow boarders with Max Weineke. As men living in close quarters, they'd seen Max nude a number of times; there was a mole on his shoulder, they said. There wasn't one on the body, so that settled that.

But then, marveled a *Herald* reporter, three "Japanese—or at any rate, Orientals" pressed their way to the front and were led to the slab. They announced that it *was* Weineke. Who were they, and how did the three of them know a Danish scrap-metal dealer? They wouldn't say. Another mysterious visitor correctly described, sight unseen, a surgical scar on the abdomen; the fact had not been announced to the public, and he was quickly led to the slab. He identified the body as Weineke; but the fellow wouldn't identify *himself*, and promptly melted back into the crowd. So now they had five positive identifications of Weineke—four by men who refused to name themselves—and three negative identifications of the very same body.

The morning had only just begun at the morgue.

Next came the presumptive widow of Mr. Robert Wood. She was regal in her floral-decked hat and dark mourning dress, waiting with her attending minister amid all the tumult and weeping outside. Wood, it seemed, was a Long Island City butcher who had gone missing after leaving his shop with a $150 bankroll in his pocket, and his empty wagon had been found abandoned in front of a Greenpoint saloon. His description, the location, the motive—they all matched the body pretty well. Mrs. Wood and the minister were led inside, and the headless and legless body—further decomposed and sliced into by two autopsies—was revealed to her. She fell into a dead faint.

It was too much—too much. She slumped into her minister's arms and was carried into a morgue office and revived. She wanted to try again. There was a scar on his left hand, she recalled, and so the morgue attendants covered up the remains, leaving only the forearm and hand undraped on the table. Mrs. Wood and the minister approached quietly, while the crowd inside kept keen watch from a close but respectful distance. She held the cold, lifeless hand in her own and examined the nails of the man she believed to be her husband—and a man with a distinctive scar on his middle finger. This body also had a scar on its finger . . . the index finger.

It is not him, Mrs. Wood announced.

It was also not missing Mafia murder witness Agguzzo Baldasano; neither was it a missing young Mr. Levaire of 106th Street, nor the Brooklyn gas engineer Charles Russell. But it *was* Brooklyn bartender John Otten, or Brooklyn printer John Livingston, or perhaps New Jersey carpenter Edward Leunhelt. The body also, apparently, belonged to a Manhattan bricklayer.

"It is surely George," his brother assured the morgue attendants.

On and on the identifications came, all day, like an endless handkerchief pulled from a magician's pocket. Watching outside was a young man dandling an infant; when asked by a *World* reporter what he was doing there, he refused to talk; all questions for him had to go through the gentlemen over *there*. The reporter turned to find himself face-to-face with the assembled forces of the *Evening Journal*. They were a formidable sight. Hearst was fond of giving his reporters bicycles, so that his crew were like another regiment of "scorchers"—the lunatics who barreled through city traffic on Sylph cycles, Lunol racers, and greased Crackajack bikes, their futuristic bronze headlights ablaze and slopping kerosene. There were enough of these wildmen riding up the sidewalks and getting horsewhipped by irritated carriage teamsters that Hearst retained a specially designated "bicycle attorney" on the paper's staff.

Cycles tossed aside, the Wrecking Crew pushed their way in. Their witnesses, they told detectives, were the nephew and niece of one Louis Lutz, a cabinetmaker who had disappeared from his Upper East Side home on Wednesday. His namesake nephew examined the left hand for a scar.

"I feel sure it is my uncle's body," he proclaimed.

The attending detective wasn't impressed.

"They are too willing," he muttered.

"The finger of the dead man looks like my uncle's marked finger," young Lutz insisted—whereupon a morgue attendant leaned in and wiped away the scar with a rag. It had been a streak of dirt. *Now* was Lutz sure?

He wasn't so sure.

As the Lutzes filed out, a hysterical woman passed them on the way in.

"Oh, Dick! Oh, Dick, why did you go away and leave me?" she wailed, and was led sobbing over to the body. It was her husband, she moaned—Richard Meggs, a retired liquor dealer of West Fifty-Second Street. He'd left on Thursday for a card game with $500 in his pocket, never to return. When shown the scarred finger on the left hand, she broke down again. "Dick had a scar right there," she sniffled.

The detectives and coroner's assistants weren't quite convinced. Did her husband have any other unique characteristics? Why yes, she recalled. Her husband had a very distinct scar on his groin. The attendants dutifully displayed it to Mrs. Meggs's full view.

It was not Dick.

IN THE DOORWAY of a redwood-paneled office at the *New York Journal*, a dapper young man could be seen dancing a little jig. Then, as page proofs were laid out over the floor of the war room, he'd indulge in another little dance—tapping over the day's stories, snapping his fingers like castanets. He might well dance: He was becoming the most powerful publisher in New York.

LOUIS A. LUTZ THE VICTIM? his evening edition demanded. Lutz wasn't, of course, but that hardly mattered. The important thing was that the *Journal* had a great story. "The public," he reminded his staff, "likes entertainment better than it likes information."

A generation younger than Pulitzer, William Randolph Hearst represented everything his Park Row neighbor was not: He was young, native-born, and the scion of a California senator and mining baron. Hearst seemed to have careless wealth written upon him, right down to the $20 gold piece he used for a tiepin. At Harvard he'd shown more interest in newsrooms than in his studies, and after presenting his professors with piss pots emblazoned with their portraits, he was booted out of the school. But no matter; he slummed around as a freelancer for the newly launched *World*, carefully observing the business. Pulitzer, he believed, had invented a whole new way to make a fortune from journalism.

"I am possessed of the weakness which at some time or other of their lives possesses most men," he wrote to his father. "I am convinced that I could run a newspaper successfully."

A decade later, he'd lifted Pulitzer's ideas to remake the scrawny *San Francisco Examiner* into the country's fourth-largest paper and bought the near-worthless *New York Journal*—"the chambermaid's delight," some called it—to turn it into a juggernaut of high-speed presses and color graphics and sensational headlines. He mocked rivals as doddering dinosaurs stuck "in the Silurian era." His comics pages were blazingly ornate and complicated print jobs; perfecting them chewed through equipment, though demolishing new presses was a price that Hearst was happy to pay. "Smash as many as you have to, George," he instructed his printer. Now Hearst had the best color Sunday supplement in the country—page after page of *The Yellow Kid*, the adventures of *The Katzenjammer Kids*, and *Happy Hooligan*—"eight pages of iridescent polychromous effervescence," his paper boasted, "that makes the rainbow look like lead pipe."

His headlines were equally colorful, especially for the wilder *Evening Journal* edition. THE MAN WITH THE MUSICAL STOMACH, proclaimed one, while a particularly fine science story announced that A GENIUS HAS CONCEIVED A PLAN FOR A MACHINE THAT WILL KILL EVERYBODY IN SIGHT. A good headline could always be ginned up; even a bizarre old 1856 French undertaker's patent for the "Application of Galvanoplating to the Human Flesh" might yield the splendid DROP DEAD AND HAVE YOURSELF PLATED. It wasn't the best quality journalism, granted, but it was the best *quantity* journalism. At an unheard-of cover price of one cent, the paper could proudly display its motto: "You Can't Get More News; You Can't Pay Less Than One Cent."

And that night, you couldn't get more on the river murder. Hearst proudly looked over an *Evening Journal* whose front page boasted lavish illustrations of both sides of a dead man's hand, the entire forearm—and a close-up of the wounded fingernail—*and* a "butcher's diagram" showing exactly how the body had been cut up. The next page was given over to a pictorial tour of the infamous Ogden's Woods and the East Eleventh Street pier, plus a complete list of current missing persons with their identifying marks. Column after column of crew reporting covered witnesses, the police chief, the coroner, and the invaluable Mr. Lutz.

Hearst barely had time to enjoy his grisly triumph when word arrived of the upcoming four o'clock *World*.

He had his spies in neighboring pressrooms, of course—he liked to know what his competitors were about to publish. But that evening's final edition of the *World*, stuffed with illustrations and columns about the case, had a real shocker right up front:

$500 REWARD

The *World* will pay $500 in gold for the correct solution of the mystery concerning the fragments of a man's body discovered Saturday and Sunday in the East River and in Harlem. All theories and suggestions must be sent to the City Editor of the *World,* in envelopes marked 'Murder Mystery', and must be exclusively for the *World*. Appearance of the solution in any other paper will cancel this offer of reward.

It was a jaw-dropping amount—a year's pay for the clerk who could recall selling the oilcloth; several thousand bottles of cheap claret for the proprietor in whose establishment the deed was hatched; a personal horse and carriage for the commuter who might have overheard it. It was $500, for that matter, to *any* reader who could deduce a solution, just like readers had been doing with the Arthur Conan Doyle stories that the *World* ran. Now they could do more than just read Sherlock Holmes; they could *be* him.

This was going to be a sensation.

Hearst ordered his pressmen into action: Run an Extra Final Edition, timed to appear just minutes after the *World*'s $500 reward. He had an utterly devastating headline to run atop his *Evening Journal*, and the words rolled deliciously off the tongue.

$1,000 REWARD . . .

5.

JILL THE RIPPER

ONE READER ALREADY KNEW who the culprit was: *Hearst.*

The body was the work, a *Journal* reader wrote in, of "some enterprising newspaper or group of men who wish to test the efficiency of the local detective force, which has been called in question quite often under its present management."

As letters piled into the *Journal* offices on Tuesday morning, other reader guesses included tramps killing a peddler (conveniently "using rope and oilcloth from the peddler's pack"); bickering butchers ("probably employed in one of the slaughter houses on the East Side or in Harlem"); a nefarious cabal ("I think the man was tattooed or branded with the marks of some secret society"); and, of course, "fiendish" Spaniards who "hacked him to pieces with their machetes." Some suspected a woman of the deed, since only "jealousy could have terminated with such terrible results." Still others invoked Sherlock Holmes, who seemed the best guide to such a baffling case. Alas, Arthur Conan Doyle had recently killed off his great detective. "If he were still alive," one reader mourned, "Sherlock Holmes would surely earn your thousand-dollar reward through deduction."

Still, the suggestion of Hearst himself topped them all. "It would be a comparatively simple matter," the reader insisted, "for a newspaper to secure through a physician a suitable cadaver and to dispose of the portions effectively, yet theatrically, so as to secure the widest possible publicity."

The *Journal* had a good laugh and ran the letter; if only they'd thought of it themselves! Hearst loved promotion; he'd already run bandwagon signs and sandwich-board men around the city and advertised his paper's one-cent price by mailing out sackfuls of pennies to New Yorkers. He'd invaded the city, as one editor put it, as quietly "as a wooden-legged burglar having a fit on a tin roof."

And the roof he most loved to dance on was the *World*'s. When he'd rolled into New York, Hearst stole his old paper's crown jewel by grabbing *Sunday World* editor Morrill Goddard, a daredevil journalist who'd made his name as a London correspondent covering Jack the Ripper. "Take all or any part of that," he'd told Goddard, tossing him a crumpled Wells Fargo bank draft for $35,000. Then, for good measure, Hearst immediately bought the rest of the *Sunday World* staff as well. An outraged Pulitzer purchased them back, only to find his repatriated *World* men emptying their desks yet again and walking back to the *Journal*. Hearst had stolen them *twice*. The Park Row sidewalk between the two papers, newsmen joked, was wearing thin.

Now, rallying his pirated staff from his barber's chair as he took his morning shave, the young millionaire was ebullient. "We must beat every paper in town," he declared.

His first blow for the *Journal* would beat them all—maybe even top the sensation created by the reward. It would be something nobody had ever seen before. He had his pressroom chief working up a special color illustration. Not for the Sunday comics supplement, mind you—but for that day, Tuesday.

And if that didn't knock the competition sideways, his next idea would: an elite band of Wreckers dedicated to homicide coverage. Backed by veteran crime reporter George Waugh Arnold, they'd be even *better* than the NYPD's rudderless Detective Bureau, which had been adrift ever since Inspector Byrnes was forced out. Not so George and his men. They'd carry their own badges, pack licensed pistols. They'd make arrests, they'd *get things done*. Hearst even had a dandy name for them, one that might have sent that suspicious letter writer into a tizzy: the Murder Squad.

CROWDS POURED into the morgue that morning, ready to identify the city's most famous body, but they were made to wait; the coroner had scheduled yet another autopsy. Three days had now passed since the body's first discovery, and reporters were growing jaded about the odds for any more would-be identifiers. "One might as well have tried to identify a particular Texas steer by the sirloin hanging in a butcher's shop," a Hearst man dryly observed.

Some guesses had certainly been less helpful than others. Occultists plied their way into the city morgue, including at least one phrenologist apparently undeterred by the absence of a head; that morning's *World* ran a palmist's not particularly edifying judgment: "Did love or jealousy have aught to do with the tragedy? Perhaps." Not to be outdone, the *Journal* hired the country's most famous palm reader, Niblo, who swanned into the morgue and performed a reading on the dead man's hands. Among his pronouncements: the victim had been murdered for love rather than money, and the killer might be a "female Jack the Ripper."

Oddly enough, it looked like Niblo might be on to something. Inside the Bellevue morgue, five men gathered around the dissecting table: Deputy Coroner O'Hanlon, three consulting physicians, and pathologist Frank Ferguson of New York Hospital. Dr. Ferguson had seen this kind of case before; three years earlier he'd been in this very same room, at this same table, examining the headless and limbless body of Susie Martin, an eleven-year-old girl who vanished from her Hell's Kitchen tenement. Twelve days later her remains were found in a cellar just blocks away, identifiable only by the clothes the killer had used to bundle her body into. The crime had gone unsolved; and now, reading the details of this new case in the papers, Ferguson sensed a chilling familiarity.

Look, he pointed to two stab wounds: one to the left lung, the other from a downward thrust to the collarbone. Both made with a long, narrow blade.

The same had been done to Martin.

The sawing along the neck and atop the legs?

The same.

Dr. Ferguson directed their gaze to a previously ignored wound—a faint cut into a rib, where the saw had glanced off the body. It was a crucial clue, for unlike the stumps, it was here that you could determine the width of the saw.

"The same kind of saw was used," he surmised after measuring the cut. "The blade of the saw is only a millimeter in thickness. A butcher's meat saw is about that thickness. A carpenter's saw is thicker." In fact, the angling of the cuts told a story of their own. "By examining the marks made by the saw and the knife," he said, "I can tell about how the murderer went at it to carve up the body." The body, disassembled under the terrible light of the dissecting room, bore mute witness as Ferguson envisioned its fate.

"I can almost see him in the room with his dead victim," he told his transfixed audience. "I can see him tearing off the clothing, if he had any on when he was slain. I can see him turn the body belly-down, so that the wild eyes should not stare at him. I can see him sever the flesh of the neck and then use the saw on the vertebrae. The murderer stood on the right-hand side. The marks of the teeth of the saw on the shoulder prove that there must have been a twisting motion as the sawing was finished."

The backbone had also been sawed from the right-hand side, and with the body still facedown; the left leg had been severed from the left side. The head had been sawn off not in one downward cut but rather around in a circle. These were the same actions the Martin killer had made. And there was an even more troubling similarity: the boiling of this body's legs. The body of Susie Martin had *also* been boiled, and a sliced-off bone fragment showed signs of at least some of its flesh having been consumed.

This, Ferguson announced, was the work of the same killer—a cannibal.

ALERTED BY FERGUSON'S FINDINGS about the saw, detectives coursed uptown to inspect the cellars of local butchers. But a lone cub reporter could be seen walking determinedly to Forty-Second

Street, notebook in hand, his blond hair pompaded high under his hat. Ferguson hadn't been the only one with an unnerving feeling that there was something familiar about that body in the morgue.

Those well-muscled arms and soft fingers: they were something Ned Brown had seen before—*felt*, even. It was a combination found in just one place, among the muscled masseurs of Turkish baths. The baths were where revelers would go after a night of hard drinking in Midtown; with rooms heated to 120 degrees, they were thought to evaporate the alcohol—and even to cure bites by mad dogs. Ned Brown had been known to work off a few shots in Murray Hill Baths, a long and narrow Times Square establishment on Forty-Second Street. A Romanesque space with white marble floors and a delightfully long swimming pool, it advertised itself as "the Most Handsome and Perfect Baths in the World." The locals had another name for it: "The House of a Thousand Hangovers." After signing up for a steam bath and massage there, Ned idly let a question drop. Had anyone slacked off from showing up for work that week?

That would be *Bill*, snapped an attendant.

"He took Friday off because he was going to look at a house in the country with his girl—or so he said . . . Guldensuppe is his name." He hadn't been back in since then, the attendant added, though someone had called him in sick on Sunday. "Drunk someplace, of course."

"I must have seen him around here," Ned ventured, "but I can't place him in my mind."

"He's just built like a big Dutchman. He has the upper half of a woman tattooed all over his chest—used to be a sailor on one of them Heinie windjammers when he was a kid."

If you see him, the baths' cashier warned as he rang up the $1 ticket, *tell him he's fired.*

Bill lived somewhere around Thirty-Third and Ninth Avenue, it was thought—a German and Irish neighborhood of low brick tenements. Ned joshed his way through the nearest bar there, knocking back a couple of beers and posing as a long-lost pal of Willie's. Had anyone seen his old buddy?

Not lately, the saloon's cook said, but try the apartment over Werner's drugstore, where he'd shacked up with his landlady.

"She got plenty of cash." He winked from behind the bar. "She treats him good."

"He's a hot sketch!" Ned quickly agreed. "Always after the dames."

"You bet!" The cook laughed. Strangely enough, though, he hadn't seen Willie around in the last few days.

Ned Brown knew he had to think fast.

How would he get inside the apartment? Pleading ten bucks from the *World*, he bought a suitcase of expensive twenty-five-cent soaps and made his way through the tenements around Werner's building, posing as a salesman with a five-cent trial offer. The air stung with the smell of cooking sauerkraut and the clatter of tin washtubs; hausfraus inside leaned out windows to gossip as they strung laundry over the fire escapes. They knew good sandalwood and verbena soap when they saw it, and at a nickel a bar, they didn't care if it was a trial offer or just plain stolen. Word was passed around quickly, and by the time Brown reached the apartment over Werner's, he was down to his last bars.

In the center of the apartment door was a brass nameplate:

AUGUSTA NACK
LICENSED MIDWIFE

That was rich: New York didn't license midwives.

He knocked and heard a faint commotion inside; the door opened to reveal the midwife herself, a dark-haired woman in her late thirties with a curiously sensual presence and the glow of an afternoon of exertions. Ned went into his spiel—wondrously soft, satisfaction guaranteed!—but she didn't wait to hear out his sales pitch.

"Give me the soap now," she demanded.

Well, it's a funny thing, Brown said—turned out he had used up all his cakes. But for *her* he did have two left, because he did need a testimonial for their next ad . . . "If you could give the soap a trial now, while I wait," he added, "I'd be glad to let you have one."

She regarded the bars; their fragrance brought release from the disorder of the apartment around her, which appeared to be halfway packed for a move; rugs lay rolled up on the floor.

"All right." She motioned him over to a black leather chair. "Give me the soap."

As Ned heard the water running in the next room, he continued his sales patter—"Let your hands soak in it! You will feel each finger separately caressed . . ."—and looked hungrily around the room. An object, any incriminating object, anything to set up as a chalk engraving and run in the next edition of the *World*. On a small side table, he spotted it: a portrait of a muscular beau, blond with a turned-up mustache. He quickly snatched the photo and thrust it into his jacket just before she reentered the room.

She liked the soap, she said, but she didn't want to be quoted for his ad.

Quite all right, quite all—

"Now you give me the other soap also," she demanded. "Here is a dime."

She hadn't noticed anything missing.

It was, perhaps, the sweetest single coin he had ever earned. He pocketed the dime, passed an angry-looking fellow on his way back downstairs—not the man in the picture—and noted the address: *439 Ninth Avenue.*

"IT WAS A GOOD DAY'S WORK, kiddo," Roeder admitted when young Ned returned to the World Building. "Thanks."

He'd gotten his first big scoop.

As he made his way to the El station that Tuesday evening, bound for home in Flatbush and a well-earned rest, the streets around Ned were strangely dotted with blotches of red—hundreds of them, *thousands* of them. It was the new issue of the *Evening Journal*. THE REAL CLEW TO THE MURDER MYSTERY, the front page proclaimed. "Facsimile in Colors of the Oilcloth Which Will Aid in Getting the $1,000 REWARD."

It was stunning—not the clue, but the *printing*. Hearst had out-done himself again: For the first time ever, color was being used on a breaking news story.

And yet everything else about the competition revealed them as safely clueless. Papers still fixated on Max Weineke, noting that his wife had insurance on him, and that she was a bad mother to boot: "I learned from some neighbors," a *Telegram* reporter huffed, "that Mrs. Weineke had gone out and left her babies alone many times." Rather inconveniently, though, a slender *Times* reporter attempted to try on one of Max's suits and couldn't struggle into it, so it certainly wouldn't fit the body in the morgue.

Ah, the *Times* theorized, that's because the secret of the crime was that two escapees from the state lunatic asylum had turned on each other—that "Mutilation Maniac" Olaf Weir had murdered his fellow maniac William O'Neill. Weir had been a carpenter with a suspicious talent for sawing. It was a fine theory, save for one problem: O'Neill's family didn't recall him having any markings on his chest or fingers.

As for the police, an afternoon's rummaging uptown in butchers' basements and along roadsides had netted but a single find. An aban-doned bag—without, alas, a head inside—was scooped up, emptied out for clues, and proclaimed THE DEAD MAN'S VALISE in the newspa-pers. The *Evening Journal* lavished a dozen illustrations on its mysteri-ous contents: writing slates, clothes, a thimbleful of tacks, a rolled-up newspaper. All terribly interesting, but none of it was Guldensuppe. The closest anyone had gotten was a chance comment to the *Journal* by William Pinkerton, musing that the use of dismemberment hinted at the killer's nationality: "The German seems to regard that as the best means of disposing of a body." If that was the best they could do, then Ned felt reassured; his find on Ninth Avenue belonged to just him and tomorrow's *World*.

THE COMPETITION'S COLOR PAGE was no gimmick at all.

Like Detective Carey, the head of Hearst's Murder Squad thought the oilcloth really *was* the clue to the mystery. "The solution of the whole matter hangs upon the oilcloth," the paper declared. Innumerable New Yorkers might lay claim to the body—and without a head, who was to disprove them?—but only one or two could claim that oilcloth. The body was one of two million New Yorkers, part of a constant and fluid population; the oilcloth was tangible, unequivocal, traceable: two sheets from just 6,000 yards manufactured upstate by A. F. Buchanan & Sons between June and December 1896. George Arnold knew Detective Carey had covered Manhattan and Brooklyn but hadn't made it to Queens or Long Island yet. So *Journal* men had swamped Newspaper Row saloons, hiring unemployed reporters on the spot as day labor, throwing *thirty men* into tracking the oilcloth. Thirty reporters—now armed with three hundred thousand color copies of the oilcloth.

They flooded across the boroughs as Ned Brown took his train home in innocent contentment. And before the sun set, a *Journal* team at the dry-goods store of one Max Riger had found an oilcloth purchase of Diamond B-3220. The name in the customer-accounts book pointed to just one address.

439 Ninth Avenue.

II.

THE
SUSPECTS

6.

THE BAKER IN
HELL'S KITCHEN

BY LATE MORNING Ninth Avenue was already getting hot and dusty, the first grim signs of another heat wave. A wagon from the Astoria Model Bakery threaded through the ice deliveries and brewers' trucks, its horses clip-clopping along the daily rounds to grocers with graham loaves, doughnuts, and raisin bread. The driver was an unshaven and tough-looking fellow, with a flat cap yanked low on his head, sweating as he guided his wagon team around a busy streetcar line and past the drunks staggering out of saloons. He was in the worst stretch of Hell's Kitchen, a couple of blocks from the hideout of gangster Mallet Murphy—so named after his favorite implement for braining victims. When two men clambered aboard at the corner of Fortieth and Ninth, Herman Nack knew it wasn't to buy pumpernickel.

One of them pulled himself up to the driver's seat. "Mr. Nack?" he inquired.

"What do you want?" the driver replied brusquely.

"Captain O'Brien wants to see you."

Nack gave him a violent shove, sending the man sprawling off the running board, then took off down Ninth Avenue. The loaded bakery wagon swerved wildly onto Thirty-Ninth, and then onto Tenth Avenue, loaf trays clattering as the driver looked back and swore. The two men were in hot pursuit on bicycles.

Stop! Stop! they demanded.

The mad trio flew past tenements and ash barrels, past the Salvation Army crowds on Thirty-Sixth Street, and straight toward the Garfield Drug Company on Thirty-Fourth, where regulars were already congregating for sodas to escape the heat. A patrol cop by the drugstore took chase after them, and in another block one of the pursuing cyclists leapt aboard.

You're under . . .

Nack slashed him with his horse whip, and the second cyclist vaulted on, trying to wrest control of the vehicle.

. . . arrest.

The cop came crashing in from the other side of the carriage, and the delivery driver roared and struggled desperately until the three men forced him down onto the ground. There the patrolman made his collar—not of carriage-jackers Oscar Piper and Walter McDevitt, who were Hearst reporters attempting a citizen's arrest—but of delivery driver Herman Nack, on suspicion of murder.

HE TRIED ESCAPING twice during the five-block ride to the precinct house.

"I have absolutely no idea why I have been arrested!" the driver yelled from the back of his own bakery carriage.

Walt and Oscar thought otherwise, and the officer wasn't buying it either. The night before, nine coworkers from the Murray Hill Baths—some brought on the sly by the *World,* the rest sneaked in equally secretively by the *Journal*—had identified the body as William Guldensuppe's. Why, all Nack had to do was look at one of that morning's papers: VICTIM THOUGHT TO BE THEODORE CYKLAM, declared the *World.*

Well, perhaps not at *that* paper.

Ned Brown's breakthrough piece for the *World* had been elbowed aside by Pulitzer's ace reporter Ike White, a man famous for once identifying a suicide bomber by a single charred button off the man's suit. Ike's pet theory this time centered on cabinetmaker Theodore Cyklam; he'd been missing from his job in Long Island since the previous Thursday. Cyklam owned a valise like the one found in the woods the day before, and the contents checked out. He'd owned two writing slates for charting shifts at his factory, and the can of tacks was common to cabinetmakers. And the injured index finger? A banged nail holder, the universal ailment of woodworkers. What was more, Ike tracked down one Diamond B-3220 oilcloth to a Mr. Cunningham, a peddler who also sold the same kind of cord used to tie the parcels. He worked a circuit near Cyklam—and, the *World* noted darkly, lived just a block from where little Susie Martin's body had been found three years earlier.

It was a splendid theory; everything fit perfectly. Except . . . except that it had no *motive*. And no witness. And no crime scene. And no time line to put Cunningham and Cyklam in the exact right place at the right time. Ike's story was beautiful—and useless.

Ned Brown's big scoop had been shoved into just a couple of inches of space at the bottom of page 2 under the deeply unremarkable headline ANOTHER IDENTIFICATION. Another indeed; in fact, there had already been a *Herald* reporter on this exact story. It was not unknown for reporters to tail detectives, for detectives to tail reporters, and for competing reporters and detectives alike to tail one another—anything for a good lead.

But this was different. The *Herald*, it seemed, had boozily stumbled into the Guldensuppe story all on its own. Several Murray Hill Baths coworkers had been drinking after work at a Third Avenue saloon, *also* idly wondering whether Willie Guldensuppe might be the guy in the morgue. They were overheard by reporter Joe Gavan, who dutifully reported the theory to the police, and in that morning's *Herald*: "Suspicion pointed to a jealous husband as the instigator of the crime. It was said that the man was a shampooer in an uptown Turkish bath. . . . This man, it is said, had been living with a baker's wife." But Gavan couldn't identify any of them; police detectives had immediately demanded secrecy to pursue the lead.

The *Journal* happily stole their thunder.

Incredibly, within hours three newspapers had all independently converged on the same victim. But Hearst alone made a personal visit to the Murray Hill Baths, and Hearst alone commanded a Murder

Squad to trail Herman Nack's morning delivery route. The *World* and the *Herald* had bobbled and dropped the lead of the year. Not only had Hearst's *Journal* nabbed the story, they'd nabbed the *man*.

THE DRIVER REMAINED ADAMANT. What did they want with him? He was just an honest immigrant delivering bread.

Nack was booked at the Twentieth Precinct station house and then quickly sent downtown with his *Journal* entourage to a building that was, as one police commissioner mused, "that antique and shabby palace, that sepulcher of reputations, that tomb of character, that morgue of political ambition, that cavern of intrigue and dissimulation—the Police Headquarters on Mulberry Street."

The *Journal* men had to be discreet going inside. The headquarters rose up four stories in a lopsided and grimy old marble hulk from Little Italy's labyrinth of cobbled alleys, tenements, and street vendors, and it was under constant watch by the competition. The *World* kept an apartment across the street, where reporters and photographers played cards to pass the hours between cases. One *World* reporter was always posted to the window to watch for colorfully agitated incoming suspects—or, better still, even more colorfully agitated police commissioners. That always meant a good story. Next door the *Tribune* kept an office that also spied through HQ's windows; so did most of the big papers, for that matter.

Their suspect was quietly hustled inside and through a lobby and dingy anterooms crowded with men in blue uniforms. Mulberry Street was a bewildering place, the nerve center for more than 100,000 arrests a year and uniformed officers issuing curt commands from the telegraph offices in the basement all the way up to the Lost Children Department on the top floors. The exterior of the building bristled with wires to every precinct house, firehouse, and hospital in the city; the interior was a constant flow of sour and sharp-looking hard cases—bunco men, badger schemers, wife stabbers. Shuffling newcomers were startled by the yells of "Mug him!" This, they would discover, meant they were to be photographed for the police files.

But today was different. Nack was not bound for the usual

fine-grinding wheels of mugs and glowering sergeants. He and the *Journal* reporters were led to the private office of Captain Stephen O'Brien, chief of the Detective Bureau.

O'BRIEN SAT PATIENTLY, letting his man sweat. The chief had more than 250 detectives serving under him, but a case this infamous required intervention from the top. O'Brien was the successor to chop-busting Inspector Byrnes himself—as famed for his honesty as Byrnes was for graft, and newly appointed by Teddy Roosevelt just before that reform-minded police commissioner left for a promising political career. The move had been so sudden that the paperwork for his new rank hadn't even gone through yet; he was a captain ordering other captains around, a downright comical situation to old-timers. And so the former inspector's presence lingered; the very walls and floors of the office had been carefully muffled on the old man's orders, the better to cuff prisoners around while interrogating with "the third degree"—a term the old inspector had coined himself. Captain O'Brien was more subtle than his predecessor but no less ruthless. He'd been on the force for more than twenty years, many of them spent breaking up waterfront gangs. A surly bakery driver was no match for what he'd dealt with.

Wasn't he married to Augusta Nack, of 439 Ninth Avenue?

Yes, the driver admitted, he had been—or rather, he still was on paper. They never divorced, but they'd lived apart ever since the last of their three children had died two years ago. She lived on Ninth Avenue, but he lived over in Astoria now—and he hadn't spoken to her since.

Did he know a Mr. William Guldensuppe?

Nack certainly did. Bill had been their boarder, back when he and Gussie lived together, just as things were falling apart, and she ran off with him. The *Journal* reporters wrote quickly and eagerly; a sketch artist busily drew Nack's sullen face and bushy blond eyebrows. The real question now hung pregnant in the air.

Where was he last Friday?

"I went to work at two o'clock on Friday morning," Nack said sullenly. "I got my load of bread and left the bakery at four o'clock. My work was finished by two thirty in the afternoon."

And then?

"I don't know where I went after that."

O'Brien was unimpressed.

"I guess I was drunk," Nack sneered—and his alibi for the next day was not much different.

"I get up at about 1 or 2 and go over the ferry to the bakery. I hitch up and then start to deliver bread. I get through about 4 p.m. Then I go on a spree."

"A spree?"

"Oh, I go to Strack's and I bowl with the boys and drink beer. I get back to my room in Eighty-Second Street about 10 o'clock. I had a good load on when I went to bed Saturday night. Haw! Haw!"

And the next day?

"I was so drunk that I had to stay in bed nearly all of Sunday."

"When did you last see the murdered man?"

"I don't remember exactly, but I guess it was three or four months ago. I saw him on the street at Ninth Avenue and Thirty-Fourth."

Captain O'Brien puzzled over the man before him. A brute, a drunk—yes, yes—a spurned husband with a perfect motive. But Nack didn't give a damn about his ex-wife, and bachelorhood seemed to suit him just fine.

"What the deuce do I care?" The suspect shrugged.

And it checked out: Word came in that not only could Astoria Model Bakery's owner vouch for Nack's working and drinking schedule but that on the fateful Friday night the bakery foreman and Nack had actually led Strack's saloon in belting out an entire set of drinking songs. *He's not it*, O'Brien quietly decided. Herman Nack's story just didn't fit the case.

But someone else's did.

AUGUSTA NACK WAS READY for the next steamer to Hamburg. She'd spent the previous afternoon with four hired men rolling rugs, packing furniture and bedclothes, and washing the curtains for the next tenant in her six-room flat over Werner's Drug Store. This was the last day on her $20 monthly lease; she'd given notice to Mr. Werner two days earlier, and with all the quarreling that had gone on in the place, the short notice didn't seem to trouble him. She'd even had to sleep in the apartment of her upstairs neighbor overnight, as nearly everything short of her portmanteau was packed.

The visit from the detective now sitting on her sofa was most inconveniently timed.

"Do you know William Guldensuppe?" he asked.

Mrs. Nack looked keenly at Detective Krauch, and then at the chair—which should have been readied for storage but was instead seating another detective. Then she shifted her gaze over to the doorway, where yet another detective stood with his back to the door, keeping any movers from coming in and Mrs. Nack from going out.

She hesitated. "Yes, I know him. He is my man. At least he *was* until Friday morning, when he came from the bath and made me give him fifty dollars. Then we quarreled over a woman, and he went away."

Detective Krauch watched her carefully as she spoke. She was not exactly a Gibson girl anymore, but she had dark eyes and the presence to fluster one observer into describing her "pleasing, yet repellant, appearance." Her man, she claimed, had been wooed away by the wanton widow of a grocer. She'd caught them in the parlor mirror the week before when they thought her back was turned. Why, just that very day that grocery hussy had come by to collect more of his worthless possessions.

"I gave her a bit of my mind," she snapped, "and told her she had stolen William from me." So now she was putting her own goods in storage and heading back to Germany and her mother, and—couldn't she just leave now?

No, they informed her, she could not.

For the detectives knew two things that Mrs. Nack didn't. First, that Detective Krauch had been watching her apartment, and neither the mistress nor anyone else had come up her stairs that morning. And now they also knew that she wasn't going to be making it to her Hamburg steamer that day.

SITTING IN CAPTAIN O'BRIEN'S OFFICE at the Mulberry Street headquarters, the midwife looked more like a wronged woman than a suspect in a murder case. Her chair was moved over to the window, suffusing sunlight over the fashionable tulle-trimmed hat that she'd quickly donned when detectives hustled her from the apartment over Werner's Drug Store.

"My name is Augusta Nack," she stated carefully for the record. "I am thirty-eight years of age. I have been living with William Guldensuppe for sixteen months."

She was, by her account and by her accent, a German immigrant. She'd married Herman Nack in 1883 in Lauenburg, on the Elbe. They'd moved here in 1886, whereupon Herman had squandered a series of jobs—in a pottery works, as a bologna-store proprietor, and finally as a grocer—all on account of his drinking. He was gone, their children were dead, and now she worked as a midwife and kept the occasional boarder, one of whom had been Guldensuppe.

What, O'Brien wanted to know, had happened to Guldensuppe after their argument the previous Friday, when he'd demanded money from her?

"The last time he was in the house Friday was about two p.m. He did not come home that night. Saturday morning between six and seven he came into the house." Mrs. Nack continued her account steadily, carefully choosing her words. "'Where did you come from?' I asked. 'None of your business,' he told me. 'Have you got that money?' . . . I then went to the Franklin Savings Bank at Forty-Second and Eighth Avenue and drew fifty dollars. This was about eleven o'clock Saturday morning. From the bank—"

Speak louder.

"*From the bank* I went to a confectionery store on Eighth Avenue and had some ice cream soda water. From there I went to the dry goods store of McPartland & Flaherty, and reached home about noon. I stayed until Willie came in, which was between three and four o'clock. The first thing he did was ask for the money. 'Here it is' I replied, throwing it on the kitchen table. Willie picked it up and went out, and I have not seen him since."

O'Brien and his detectives listened and took notes carefully. Home on Saturday afternoon; that was several hours after the first find in the East River. The implication was that Guldensuppe was still alive. Which, of course, he might be; after all, the body still didn't have a head or legs, and the morgue had filled again that day with people identifying the pieces as belonging to any number of other men.

So, can we talk with him?

Well, she explained, that's just it. Willie hadn't been back home since then. He'd sent notes asking for more money, though. Just yesterday, come to think of it. Probably spending it all on a woman somewhere.

"Monday afternoon I was convinced that Willie would not come back to me, and made up my mind to go to Europe—"

Louder.

"*Go to Europe* and see my mother, who was sick. Willie had asked me to draw my money from the bank and give it to him, saying he would accompany me to Europe, but this I had refused to do."

The last she'd heard from him, she said, was the day before—on Tuesday.

"About ten o'clock," she continued, "a man came to the house with a note from Willie asking for his clothes. I wrote on the back of the note, in German, *No; if you want your clothes come and get them yourself.* About two o'clock in the afternoon two other men, who were dirty and disreputable looking, and spoke English, came and said Willie wanted his clothes. . . . I put them in a brown valise and gave them to the men. That was the last I heard of him."

The room lapsed into an unnerving silence. O'Brien motioned to a woman he had hidden just outside his office door. It was Pauline Riger, dry-goods proprietress of Astoria, and she had been listening all along.

"This is the woman who bought the oilcloth," Riger said as she eyed Mrs. Nack. The proprietress had a hawklike countenance, and her face was sharp and pinched in concentration. "I am sure of her."

"You haven't the slightest doubt?" a *Journal* reporter pressed.

"No! It is the lady. I know it. . . . I remember her well because she was a fine looking lady, and better dressed than most people who come to my store."

Captain O'Brien maintained his disquieting gaze at Mrs. Nack. "This woman has identified you as having purchased oilcloth from her," he said evenly. "Which would seem to connect you to the murder of William Guldensuppe."

"That is impossible," the midwife shot back. Guldensuppe, she maintained, was still alive.

She didn't know where Willie was now, she didn't know this Mrs. Riger, she didn't even know any stores in Astoria. But as she spoke, word passed among the detectives that a new piece of evidence had arrived at headquarters; it had just been fished out of the Brooklyn Navy Yard after it came bumping up against the USS *Vermont*. And as they stood up to leave, Captain O'Brien coolly swung open the door for Mrs. Nack.

There, in the middle of his hallway, were two severed human legs—sawn halfway through, then snapped off.

"Do you know those?" he gloated.

They were hideous objects—rotted from five days in the river, and still nestled in an opened bundle of oilcloth. O'Brien waited for Mrs. Nack to faint, to shriek, to break down. But the midwife merely turned to him with a look to freeze the marrow.

"How should I know?" she asked coolly.

7

THE UNDERTAKER'S NEIGHBOR

WILLIAM RANDOLPH HEARST wheeled into action—literally.

Jumping onto a bicycle, Hearst sped up the fifty blocks from Printer's Square to Mrs. Nack's apartment building at Thirty-Fifth and Ninth. He marched past the peppermint-stick displays into Werner's Drug Store looking for the owner, and he was in luck: Franz Werner's indispensable assistant was vacationing in Larchmont, so Werner himself was in charge.

Didn't Mrs. Augusta Nack's lease run out today?

Indeed it did.

The young millionaire made the landlord an offer on the spot: He'd pay handsomely to rent out Nack's apartment—right now. Werner was delighted, and Hearst quickly conferred with the Wrecking Crew, which had finally caught up with him. Because he was such an upstanding new tenant, the publisher decided to post staff to all the entrances as complimentary doormen. Another group of Hearst reporters was sent out to the neighborhood hotels with instructions to take over every pay-phone booth. By the time Pulitzer's men caught on to the Nack arrest and arrived, they found a cordon of Wreckers around 439 Ninth Avenue that, as it so happened, allowed only the police and fellow Hearst reporters into the building.

It was only the latest indignity for the *World* men. The morning's triumphant Cyklam story was already being dethroned, and the kind of grandstanding that Hearst was doing here was exactly what Joseph Pulitzer would not and *could* not do. His eyesight and his nerves shot, over the past few years Pulitzer had increasingly taken to isolating himself in his Fifth Avenue mansion. All the day's papers were read to him, so that his presence remained constant and ghostly; nitpicking commands were brayed by telephone, telegraph, and memos. And with the *Journal* savagely attacking the *World*'s circulation, the messages from Pulitzer were getting harsher.

"We must smash the interloper," one memo commanded.

Other newspapers were looking endangered as well. The *Times* had briefly gone bust the previous year, and over at the stately *Sun*—the paper whose respectability the *Times* still only aspired to—an even more dire drama was now unfolding. It was being whispered that editor Charles A. Dana, after having helmed the *Sun* for more than fifty years, had stopped coming to his office in the previous week. Only imminent death could be keeping the old man from his desk in the middle of the year's biggest crime story. New York newspapers without Dana were nearly unthinkable—indeed, Pulitzer himself had trained under the *Sun*'s publisher before turning on him.

The irony was not lost on the denizens of Newspaper Row. Pulitzer had made his fortune by attacking his old colleagues at the *Sun* as dinosaurs, and he then went after James Gordon Bennett's equally celebrated *New York Herald* by undercutting its newsstand price. Now Hearst, trained in his college years at the *World*, was doing the exact same thing.

"When I came to New York," one editor heard Pulitzer say with a sigh, "Mr. Bennett reduced the price of his paper and raised his advertising rates—all to my advantage. When Mr. Hearst came to New York I did the same. I wonder why, in view of my experience?"

The *World*'s unmatched circulation of more than 350,000—an audited figure it proudly advertised atop its front pages by proclaiming CIRCULATION BOOKS OPEN TO ALL—was now in danger of being overtaken by the *Journal*. And as the two pulled perilously close in record-setting circulations, the city's other papers were getting shoved further aside. A future owned by yellow journalism was not one most reporters wished to contemplate. Some libraries had already barred the *World* and the *Journal* from their precincts, with one Brooklyn librarian sniffing that they attracted "an undesirable class of readers." Rival papers were quick to agree, and laid into the salivating coverage of what the *World* had dubbed the Missing Head Mystery.

· "The sensational journals of the city have now become scientific and publish anatomical charts and figures, solely in the interests of science, and to supply a want which the closing of the dime museums in the Bowery creates," mocked the *New York Commercial Advertiser.* A *Times* reporter bemoaned the sight of the yellow journals co-opting the case from a bumbling police force: "The freak journals, those startling and irrepressible caterers to the gross and savage side of human nature, are having a particularly fine time with their new murder mystery . . . and putting all the celebrated detectives of fact and fiction to shame." Worse still, he admitted, they were good at it: "Yet it seems that in an enlightened age criminals might be brought to justice in a manner less demoralizing to the whole community."

But it was another observation by the *Times*, one being quietly made all down Newspaper Row that day, that contained the real sting for Pulitzer's men.

"The *Journal*, by the way," they wrote, "is generally doing better nowadays. The pupil is taking the master's place now."

It was all too true. Ned and Gus and the rest of Pulitzer's newsmen were barred from the very crime scene that *they'd* been the first to uncover. Locked out of Nack's building while a joyous Hearst scampered about inside, infuriated *World* reporters marched off to the neighborhood pay phones to call the newsroom and complain. But when they picked up the earpieces, nothing happened.

Hearst's men had cut the cords.

WHILE PULITZER'S JOURNALISTS fumed in disbelief outside, the police carefully picked through Augusta Nack's apartment. Detectives Price, Krauch, and O'Donohue, the three who had taken Nack in, spent the next few hours unpacking and rifling through the hastily packed boxes. It wasn't easy. Nearly everything had been readied for storage, and by Nack's own account, she'd been busily brushing and sponging the apartment down before moving out. But was it to get her deposit back, or to wash away evidence?

Amid the crates of crockery and bedclothes there remained intriguing hints of life at 439 Ninth Avenue. Photographic albums immediately went into the evidence pile; so did a large number of letters, including the telegram that had arrived on Sunday, the day after the first bundle was found in the river. It was signed *Guldensuppe*, something that occasioned more than a little skeptical commentary among the detectives.

More policemen spread out onto the other floors of the building. There was, almost unnoticed in the fuss upstairs, a small trapdoor in the ground floor of the stairwell. It led to a basement, where their torches shone upon a motley assortment of barrels and stray wooden planks; against the wall stood a large wooden display cabinet, one of its doors fallen off onto the floor, filled inside with an array of bottles. An eerie spot, perhaps, and yet there was no particular sign of any scuffle or recent activity.

Upstairs was a different matter. Neighbors watched from the adjacent buildings to see a hatch atop Werner's roof thrown aside. Then, climbing a ladder from the top of the stairwell, officers and reporters emerged onto the roof, blinking in the sunlight. Normally the only noteworthy attraction up there was a small Werner's Drug Store billboard, but on this day a more humble object caught their attention: an overturned tub. It was exactly what one might need to boil a body. They grabbed it as evidence, though not before Hearst artists ran up a sketch of the suspicious tin hulk for the paper.

Looking down from the rooftop, they could see an avenue that was turning increasingly chaotic; word had gotten out, and police were holding back more than just competing reporters now. But in the neighboring tenements and stores, resourceful newsmen from the *World*, the *Times*, and the *Herald* were all conducting their own searches—and finding plenty. An undertaker's assistant up the block, George Vockroth, had rented a horse and surrey to Nack on Saturday morning; she'd come by at ten a.m. to arrange it, and then a mustachioed German stopped by at three thirty p.m. to pick it up. It wasn't Guldensuppe, though; this fellow was shorter, moodier, and darker-haired. Mrs. Nack's other neighbors had a notion of who that might be. They murmured that *another* boarder had lived in the apartment for while—a mysterious German barber known only as Fred, though that wasn't thought to be his real name. Mrs. Nack had been more than friendly with *both* of her boarders, until back in February when Guldensuppe had beaten his rival so badly that the barber was left with a black eye. He had moved out after that.

But if "Fred" was back, why was he picking up carriages on behalf of Mrs. Nack? Back inside her kitchen, the detectives had a good guess. One of them reached into the recesses of a cupboard and found that it was not empty. His hands emerged holding a butcher's knife, a broken saw, and then a revolver. And held up to the light, by the hammer of the pistol there appeared to be a dried spray of blood.

WORLD REPORTERS WERE TAUNTED all the way to Mulberry Street by Augusta Nack's visage staring out from below that evening's *Journal* headline:

MURDER MYSTERY SOLVED BY THE JOURNAL
Mrs. Nack, Murderess!

Crowds of commuters swarmed the pint-sized newsboys to grab precious copies of the *Evening Journal*. The paper, ginning up the publicity, ostentatiously sent out beefy guards to tamp down any riots by customers. To complement four full pages breaking open the case and the sensational find of the legs that afternoon, Hearst also whipped up portraits of everyone from Augusta and Herman Nack to William Guldensuppe and the oilcloth seller Mrs. Riger. That night he'd outdone the police, he'd outdone the *World*, and he'd very nearly outdone himself.

"When patting oneself on the back for a recent achievement, it is a reprehensible thing to boast," the tycoon began modestly. "But in an instance like an overwhelming victory over its rivals in the Guldensuppe murder case, the *Journal* comes to the front, sweeps the curtain away from the mass of doubt connected with the case, and exposes almost every detail of the crime." If his neighbors on

Newspaper Row still didn't get the message, Hearst was happy to elucidate: "All this was done, of course, with the main purpose of exhibiting the *Journal*'s superiority over its rivals."

Inside police headquarters, evidence kept piling up. The telegram in Mrs. Nack's apartment, dated from the day after the murder, was signed Guldensuppe, which was what *other* people called him—and not Gieldsensuppe, which was how the victim himself spelled it. Detectives poring over Mrs. Nack's bank account and purse couldn't find missing money she claimed to have given Guldensuppe just a couple of days earlier—it was all still on her, for a jail matron found it hidden in her corset.

The alibi literally didn't add up.

The matron also noticed bruises along Mrs. Nack's upper arm—signs of a struggle, perhaps—and called in a doctor to have a look. From their faded color, they were judged to be about five or six days old. Mrs. Nack couldn't account for those, either. Captain O'Brien made a great show of having her fingernails pared and scraped out—if there was any foreign blood or tissue there from a fight, he assured her, they'd find it.

Sitting in his office later that night with a crowd of reporters, O'Brien was pleased indeed. He had the putative murder weapons laid out on his desk, nearly a dozen identifications on the body in the morgue, and the prime suspect in a jail cell upstairs.

"Do you believe that Mrs. Nack killed the man whose body is now in the morgue?" one reporter asked.

"If that body belonged to William Guldensuppe, I believe she did, or is implicated."

It was a dramatic turnaround in just one day. That morning he'd had only two people in custody in connection with the case, and both were clearly useless. One was a Bowery waiter who'd seen two men carrying awkward packages on a streetcar—as if that were newsworthy in New York City—and the other was a babbling metal-polish peddler who'd led the police on a wild-goose chase after claiming to spot an eyeless and toothless severed head in a vacant lot. The "head" was nothing but an old hat. The peddler was booked purely out of pique, and returned the favor by giving a home address that proved to be a lumberyard.

"He is a freak," O'Brien had to explain earlier that day to an inquiring *World* reporter.

But now the chief of the Detective Bureau had a real suspect. And maybe, he mused contentedly, she was the only one he'd need.

"She has a temper—an awful temper, I believe," O'Brien said, though he hesitated to give specifics on her capacity for vengeance. He didn't need to: A *Herald* writer heard Herman Nack claim that his ex-wife had indeed once threatened to kill him.

"She is strong enough?" a *New York Press* reporter asked.

"Oh my, yes," O'Brien joked. "She has arms larger and more muscular than mine."

BUT MRS. NACK was not without friends.

Late that day, one of the city's top defense attorneys, Emanuel Friend, had marched into the Mulberry Street HQ. Manny was fond of asking awkward questions, and this case had plenty. Where was the victim's head, and how could they make a positive identification without it? Since none of Mrs. Nack's neighbors had heard or seen any struggle at all the week before, just where was the scene of this so-called crime? And what was her motive, exactly? Why hadn't they found this "Fred," who *did* have a motive?

In fact, it wasn't quite clear what *Manny's* motive was. Was he even Mrs. Nack's counsel, and who had hired him? He wouldn't say, but Murder Squad writers harbored their own suspicions about who might want to undermine the *Journal*'s case against their prime suspect. Badly burned by their bet on the Cyklam theory, the *World* editors were doubling down late that night with the next morning's headline:

THE MURDER MYSTERY IS A MYSTERY STILL
Not Sure of Identification
Police Losing Faith

"The detectives of the Central Office have very little faith in the case against Mrs. Nack," the paper insisted. The *World* found a few men who knew Guldensuppe—including drugstore owner Franz Werner, now profiting nicely by both papers—who were willing to testify that the body was not his. Alas, only one of them had actually been to the morgue to see it. A more serious challenge came from a woman identifying the headless body as belonging to *her* man, a soldier named Alpheus Clark, whom, she claimed, was killed "by a Spaniard named Julian." She seemed utterly certain of this, until a few probing questions were asked. Mrs. Clark, it turned out, had been caught up in a divorce with her now-missing husband and was trying very hard indeed to have him declared dead.

The coroner was not impressed by her story.

While the *World* kept rowing in circles, Hearst had more men shuttled over into the morgue to make positive identifications on the body, and blitzed the Murray Hill Baths with *Journal* reporters. A picture was beginning to emerge of Guldensuppe and his fate. He was a ladies' man, his boss said—"always mixed up in several affairs" with women, so much that it was a running joke that he'd get into trouble someday. But the man who really knew Willie's secrets—his best friend at work—was his fellow masseur, Frank Gartner. And when the *Journal* reporters sat down with Frank, a whole new story began to unfold.

THEY WORKED LONG HOURS there in the baths, nearly naked, sweating, feet calloused from the heated marble floors. And between jobs, they'd get to talking—especially about women and money. The previous Wednesday night, Frank said, Guldensuppe had a name on the tip of his tongue, and asked him if he'd ever heard of a Long Island town that sounded something like *Woods*.

"Well, there are three that I know of," Frank offered. "Woodbury, Woodhaven, and Woodside. Do you recognize any of those names?"

Guldensuppe wasn't sure, but he'd find out. On Thursday night, he told Frank just what *Woods* was about.

"I think," he confided, "that I am going to make something good out of that Long Island matter. A woman whom my wife performed an operation on about two years ago and for which she gave my wife four hundred dollars cash came to our house again this afternoon and told my wife that she would need her services again. She is a pretty little woman, twenty-two or twenty-three years old, and she's married to an old man."

Frank didn't need to read between the lines much. Everybody knew the illicit service that some midwives quietly provided: abortion. And in an old-fashioned May-December marriage, it wasn't hard to guess why the young wife needed one.

"This *voman* owns a small house on Long Island," Willie continued in his accented English, warming to the subject. "Her husband did not know that she owned the house, and I think she used it as a rendezvous. She told my wife that she had no ready money, but that she would sell her this house in Woodside for $1,500 cash. The remainder would, of course, be my wife's fee."

It was the deal of a lifetime, and Willie didn't have to do anything but go and look at the with his wife.

"How do you get out there?" he asked Frank. "I think my wife went there this afternoon. . . . If she likes it, why, I'll go out there tomorrow afternoon."

"I know a little about Woodside," Frank offered. "If your wife does not want to go with you Friday afternoon, I'll go over with you Saturday morning as soon as I get through here, and we'll see if the place is worth $1,500."

But in his mind, Willie was already buying the house. "This woman who owns the house is in a tight fix," he theorized. "I am only going to offer her *vun*-thousand dollars for the place. I'm tired of working here."

And with that, there was a call on the phone for him.

"Is that you, Gussie?" he answered. After a happy pause, Willie came back over to Frank, beaming. "It's all right," he said. "She was there today with a friend of hers, and says the house is well worth the money. I will take tomorrow night off and go there with her."

The masseur worked the rest of the night quietly, happily contemplating the new home awaiting him. When he finished his shift, he turned to Frank and the other masseurs on his way out: *"Vell, good-bye, gentlemens."*

And that, Frank said, was the last anyone ever heard from William Guldensuppe.

8.

THE WIDOW'S FRIEND

WHEN CAPTAIN O'BRIEN MADE IT to the office on Thursday, July 1, he found that he was a captain no more. Word had come down from the top: He'd finally been promoted to acting inspector.

It was a strange morning, amid all the backslaps. O'Brien wasn't born to the force like some men were; he'd spent his first few years out in the world as, of all things, a composer of novelty tunes. It was a local pol who talked him into trying for the police force. A life of patiently arranging notes and an easy familiarity with saloons had given him, oddly enough, just the right mindset for a good detective.

This morning he was orchestrating for an audience of one; on the table and chairs in O'Brien's office lay a revolver, a saw, a broken knife, and a washing boiler dismantled from a Ninth Avenue rooftop. Before these implements, sweating and tight-lipped in the rising heat, sat Augusta Nack. O'Brien had arranged the tools into an accusatory choir, facing her from whichever way she looked, while he questioned her about the events of Friday, June 25.

But Nack still wasn't budging.

"She is," marveled a *Brooklyn Eagle* reporter, "the most cold blooded woman in the world."

Her nerve was a thing of wonder, so much so that alienists wandered in and out of O'Brien's office to scrutinize Nack for telltale facial characteristics of criminal degeneracy. Doctors, after all, now looked for the devolution of mankind; they had neatly flipped Darwinism on its head, and then measured that head with craniometer calipers. They sought the inherited stigmata of criminal tendencies, and *Evening Journal* readers were treated to close-ups of Mrs. Nack's prominent chin, her ears, and her "dull and shifty eye."

Another doctor, though, observed the interrogations more quietly.

"I made an especial study of her facial and bodily peculiarities," Dr. Edward Spitzka told a *Herald* reporter. He was the city's top alienist, famed for discovering "masturbatic insanity" and for presiding over the electric chair's rather messy debut. And while Dr. Spitzka didn't know whether Mrs. Nack was guilty, he knew she had a guilty *look*. "A very coarse-minded animal creature," he pronounced. "Brutal, frozen and stolid, extremely selfish, with small mentality, yet with a certain amount of low cunning."

He listed the damning evidence: "Her ears are her most animal features. The lobules are of the short, stumpy, fleshy variety so often seen in state prisons and penitentiaries. . . . A pyramidal neck. . . . Her hands are remarkable for their breadth. In the old times an examiner in obstetrics would never have passed a medical student as being fit for that branch of medicine if the measurement of the hand at the finger line extended beyond three inches."

She had masculine hands, in other words—and bad ones at that.

"Did you know," a reporter ventured, "that she has never reported a live birth to the Bureau of Vital Statistics?"

Spitzka knew perfectly well what the reporter meant. "She might have been in the habit of disposing of the bodies of children stillborn or prematurely born in exactly the way in which she disposed of Guldensuppe's body," he agreed. Her likely sideline in abortions, he surmised, was why O'Brien's gambits were doomed. "I cannot understand how detectives could expect such a clumsy trick to succeed as showing the severed legs, the suspected tools and the wash boiler to a woman whose occupation has long deadened her."

But Inspector O'Brien was undeterred. He had detectives in hot pursuit of the *Journal* reporters headed for Woodside, and he still had one more surprise to spring on the midwife. A dignified gentleman in dark clothing was ushered in to the office, his bearing speaking of his profession; he was Mr. Streuning, the undertaker Mrs. Nack hired her surrey from. He'd identified her from a lineup and could point officers to the very carriage and horse that she'd used.

I did not hire a surrey, the lady insisted quietly.

Did she not even know who this gentleman was?

Not at all.

O'Brien was flabbergasted.

"She is a decided liar," he informed reporters afterward. She dissembled at every opportunity. Why, she'd returned the carriage the previous Saturday night with the complaint that the horse was balky—even though the animal was exhausted and sweating and the carriage muddy from a long run. And now she claimed that she'd never met the undertaker in her entire life? This very undertaker, the inspector explained, was a longtime neighbor and acquaintance of the Nacks, all the way back to when Herman and Augusta had lost their own five-year-old daughter to diphtheria. And he was not just any old acquaintance, either.

"Streuning buried a child of hers," he said incredulously.

HEADQUARTERS WAS the usual mess of cases the rest of the day: a servant girl who let burglars into a bandleader's house on Seventh Street, a would-be parachute inventor found dangling comically from a bridge arch, a severed black-stockinged leg netted from the East River. And there were the suicides—the druggist who hanged himself from a hotel transom, the lovelorn young man in Harlem who turned on the gas—there were always those.

The inspector paced his office and stayed focused on his subject.

"You will remember," he mused aloud to colleagues, "Mrs. Nack told me she had seen Guldensuppe three or four times on Friday, and that the last time he called to see her was on Saturday afternoon between three and four o'clock. That was the time she said she gave the man fifty dollars."

Before him in his office was a prim, dark-haired woman in her thirties and her angelic blond ten-year-old daughter, Amelia. And in these two witnesses, O'Brien saw the midwife's doom.

"My name," the mother began, "is Sophie Miller. I have known

Mr. and Mrs. Nack for about five years. I worked for the Nacks in their delicatessen store on Tenth Avenue."

After the Nacks' business and marriage both went under, Miller became a cook at Buck's Hotel but stayed close to Gussie. She knew Willie Guldensuppe well, and even knew about the fight he'd had with their boarder "Fred" back in February. The boarder was a silent and brooding sort, she said—a barber, apparently—and had been thrown out by Willie months ago.

"The last time I saw Willie was on Thursday," she recalled. "He came into Buck's and went upstairs with Mrs. Nack . . . . On Saturday night I went shopping in Eighth Avenue and took Amelia with me. We stopped at Mrs. Nack's house between 9 and 9:30 p.m. and rang her bell, but got no answer. A lady standing at the door of the house next door said . . . 'I don't think you will find her home. She has been out all day. I saw her shade down and her windows shut.'"

When she ran into Gussie later that evening at a grocer's down the street, Guldensuppe was nowhere to be seen.

"She said, 'Willie has not been home since Friday.' I said, 'What is the matter? Have you quarreled?' She said, 'No.' Between 1 and 2 p.m. on Sunday Mrs. Nack came to Buck's . . . . We were all at dinner when she came in and Mr. Buck invited her to join us. We all asked her did she hear anything from Willie. She said: 'No, not since Friday.'"

O'Brien was triumphant; he'd caught Nack in another lie. Better still, Sophie Miller knew the real name of the mysterious boarder called Fred. A lurking *Journal* reporter caught it, a scoop so close to press time that Hearst's print room hastily jammed the two crucial words into the one remaining opening in the layout—the front-page headline:

MARTIN THORN

THERE WAS NOBODY that night who needed a shave less than O'Brien's old partner, Detective James McCauley. The new inspector's right-hand man had spent the afternoon working barbershops for leads on Thorn, and barbers being the kind of fellows they were, the best way to really get them to talk was over a shave. By the time he reached Vogel's Barbershop on Forty-Seventh and Sixth, Mac had taken so many straight-edge shaves around Midtown that his face was raw with razor burn.

He took a deep breath and got into the barber's chair once again.

Vogel's was the sort of men's sanctuary one expected in a good Manhattan barbershop. It was redolent of cigars and bay rum, with leather-covered barber's chairs and a wall of long mirrors. The counter before them was well stocked with the myriad tools of the trade: Diamondine straight razors, Sanasack strops, tubes of Benitz's Waxine, bottles of Rezo Hair Tonic, jars of sweet-clover pomade, and heliotrope brilliantine. Nearby a shelf held dozens of enameled shaving mugs, elaborately emblazoned with customers' names and insignias of their professions: firefighters, bartenders, butchers. There were ruffled copies of the daily papers and the inevitable barbershop bible—the illustrated weekly *Police Gazette*—always full to bursting with boxing, murder, and cat-fighting dance-hall girls.

Listen, did he know of a barber by the name of Thorn?

Martin Thorn? Sure, Vogel knew him. He'd worked here, though he'd quit on the spot last week, and hadn't been seen in the shop since.

You don't say?

McCauley was in luck, though: Thorn's coworker Constantine Keehn was in that day. Keehn was a handsome, slicked-down Berliner, his mustache curled up like ram's horns in the German style—not unlike Thorn himself, actually. Keehn knew Thorn better than anyone else at the shop did. But, he mused as he slid a cold steel straight razor across the detective's face, their personalities could not have been more different.

And Keehn already knew why the detective was there.

"As soon as I saw in the papers that Nack had been arrested," he said, "I thought right away of Thorn."

Why?

"Martin was very *friendly* with Mrs. Nack," Keehn explained as he lathered. Thorn had been a brooding sort, but he was a first-rate barber, an even better pinochle player, and an absolute cad with women.

I always told him it would get him into trouble, another barber piped in.

"Thorn was a queer man," Keehn agreed. "He told me that for years he had been in the habit of hiring furnished rooms from women. If he learned that his landlady had money, he would make advances to her. If she repulsed him he would move away from her house and try someone else."

He had a particular fondness, Keehn said, for widows. He even used to advertise in German-language newspapers like the *Morgen Journal* for them. McCauley made a note of that. Mrs. Nack had taken to listing herself in the city directory with the notation *Widow*—a claim that would have been news to Herman Nack—and so she must have looked perfect to Thorn. There was just one thing in his way: her boyfriend.

"He used to laugh at Guldensuppe," Keehn recalled, "because for months Guldensuppe did not suspect his relations with Mrs. Nack." That changed when Thorn's suspenders turned up in her bedroom. Soon he was out of the house, and exiled to an apartment on Twenty-First and Third Avenue.

So why hadn't Nack just ordered Guldensuppe out instead?

"She was tired of him." The barber shrugged. "But he said the woman was afraid of the big fellow—that he was a powerful man, and that he threatened to kill both of them." They'd kept their trysts going until Guldensuppe caught on. "While they were drinking in there Guldensuppe rushed in and began to punch Thorn. Thorn had been expecting something like this for a long time, he said, so he always carried a revolver. He drew the revolver and tried to shoot Guldensuppe . . . "

Scrape—scrape—scrape.

" 'The damned pistol wouldn't go off,' Thorn said to me. 'I pulled and pulled and it wouldn't work. The rubber took it away and pounded me with it. That's how he blackened my eyes and smashed my nose. Then he threw me out. That taught me a lesson. No pistol for me after this. I'm going to get a dagger or a knife. I'll catch him some time when he isn't expecting me, and then I'll fix him.' "

It was an angry brag one might laugh off, except that Thorn wasn't the sort of fellow to laugh at, and he wasn't joking.

"He asked me if I knew where he could get a stiletto. I told him my brother-in-law, a police captain in Berlin, gave me one years ago. He wanted me to sell it to him. . . . For about three days he was at me all the time. One day he went downtown, however—I think it was in the Bowery—and bought a stiletto like mine. The stiletto had a yellow handle, and a yellow leather case."

A few months passed, but Thorn just couldn't let the idea go.

"Barbering is not my regular business," Keehn admitted. "I was a dentist in the old country. Thorn knew that, and he was always asking me about different poisons. He wanted to know how to give chloroform. I told him there were different ways. You could put it in a sponge, saturate a towel with it and put it up to the nose."

He'd gotten uncomfortable, Keehn said, when Thorn started asking about other poisons and then started showing up to work with little bottles in his vest. But how could Thorn think that he had any chance with Gussie, especially after that beating?

"Why, the man was always dreaming." The barber laughed. He'd even talked of marrying her. "Thorn had Mondays off. He used to talk about trips he made out to Long Island with Mrs. Nack, looking for a house where she could set up a baby farm and he would run a barber shop."

Really?

Mac kept a poker face. The *Journal* and the Detective Bureau had been sitting tight on Frank Gartner's story about a Woodside house—a lead that hadn't made it yet into any of the newspapers.

"He said," Keehn added innocently, "she had one thousand dollars in the bank and she would furnish the money for the whole business."

"He wanted to be a boss for himself," another barber agreed.

Thorn certainly had the ability to run a shop, the barbers concurred, if he just put his mind and a bit of money to it. But Detective McCauley had heard enough. He walked out into the summer evening, his face prickling painfully as theater-bound crowds swirled around him, emptying into and out of the multitude of tenements and houses of the teeming city. The detectives still hadn't found anything over in Woodside, but all the signs pointed to someplace across the river.

Thorn had fixed his rival, all right—but where?

9.

THE DISAPPEARING
SHOEMAKER

THE FARMER FROM WOODSIDE was insistent: Weren't the police interested in the extraordinary coincidence that he'd discovered in connection with their murder case?

"I noticed last Saturday morning," he explained earnestly, "that several of my ducks were sick."

Yes, of course he had.

The case was becoming a headache. Not only was it attracting curiosity seekers, but the newspapers were taking their circulation fight into the case itself. *Journal* and *World* reporters were tampering with witnesses, trampling crime scenes, and making wild accusations. The headline of yesterday's *World* bellowed, THE IDENTIFICATION UPSET—but the only dissenting identifier was unnamed and "refused to talk any further," the *World* claimed, "after being threatened by a *Journal* reporter." *World* reporters in turn humiliated Mrs. Riger, attacking her over accepting $30 in Hearst blood money, and rattling the Astoria storekeeper with a surprise lineup to identify a confederate who had just shopped there.

THE WORLD DESPERATE, the *Journal* shot back in a headline. "If Guldensuppe is dead, the *World* feels that it is going to be dead, too." One of Nack's neighbors signed an affidavit alleging overtures from the *World* for testimony favoring Mrs. Nack; outraged *Journal* reporters claimed that Pulitzer had a $10,000 slush fund dedicated to perverting the case. But it was becoming apparent along Newspaper Row that while Pulitzer and his editors were dictating hostile head-lines, their crime reporters had few doubts left about the murder. The denials from up top were becoming such an embarrassment that the *Journal* had taken to simply reproducing its rival's front page with the devastating caption STILL TWENTY FOUR HOURS BEHIND THE NEWS.

On this morning, July 3, just as they were gearing up for a blowout Sunday holiday that would see half the city tipsy and shooting off fireworks, the police were having to field questions about the lat-est stunt by the papers. After *World* editors wisely decided on a new strategy, a pair of their reporters hired Mrs. Nack's surrey and horse, promptly dubbed the Death Carriage, and galloped around asking if anyone recognized it. An impressionable young lady in Long Island said she did, and a nearby campsite offered up an old handkerchief and a few scraps of paper. This, the paper loudly announced on the front page, was surely where Guldensuppe's clothes had been burnt. It then helpfully directed the police to a "murder den," largely on the evidence of it being a frightful-looking old house.

And now this fellow wanted to talk about ducks. His name was Henry Wahle, and he lived in Woodside over by Second and An-derson. There was a two-hundred-foot-long field between his place and the next house, and his ducks had crossed it—toward Mrs. De-Beuchelare's dairy, you see, but not all the way down to the next street, where Mr. Jacobs kept that greenhouse, and . . .

Yes, they said. *Go on.*

"They had eaten something that they could not keep down," he explained with alarm. And it got worse. "I knew they had been swim-ming and paddling about in the open drain in Second Street, across the way. I went over to investigate . . . right at the end of the drain-pipe that comes from the house on Number 346, Second Street."

The cottage, Wahle said, was a vacant one. That's why it was so strange to see that ditch full on a hot summer day. "Water was run-ning out of the drain-pipe as if it had been left turned on in the empty house," he mused aloud.

Was that so? Officers took notice; maybe there was something to this. But Wahle still wanted to talk about his ducks.

Yes, the ducks. When they came out of that ditch, something had been running off their feathers—perhaps the very thing that had made them sick. A substance that was pooling into the mud by that drainpipe.

"Red stuff," the lamplighter confided.

FOUR MANHATTAN DETECTIVES marched off the New York & Queens County trolley at eleven that morning, accompanied by a sharp-eyed *World* reporter who'd at last gotten a jump on the Hearst men. It was hard for Woodside residents not to notice the group. They were out of their neighborhood, out of their jurisdiction, and out of the city altogether.

Detective Price surveyed the scene before him. He'd come from searching Mrs. Nack's place in Hell's Kitchen to . . . this?

Woodside was one of the sleepiest villages within reach of the city, a precinct of lonesome farmhouses and overgrown marshy lots, a place where churches were still the tallest buildings. A general store by the trolley stop sold hay and groceries, while up the street the local Greenpoint Avenue Hall offered wholesome rube entertainments like bowling and a shooting gallery. The city detectives swatted away insects as they strolled over to the village center, where the fire chief and a coroner were convenient neighbors. The local police captain was summoned as well—they were now in Queens County, after all, in his jurisdiction.

Did they know the way to 346 Second Street?

Sure, the detectives were told. *We'll walk you over there.*

Second Street held little more than a placid dairy and a flower nursery that supplied Broadway swells across the river with carnations for their lapels. Just up the street stood three cheap new wood-frame houses—two stories apiece, flat-roofed boxes with nearly windowless, unadorned sides. The eight men walking up to them hadn't gone unnoticed; a scowling woman was waiting in the nearest one, at number 344.

"Mrs. Hafftner," she introduced herself.

She was the caretaker for these three houses. The owners, the

Bualas, ran a wine shop over in the city. And yes, she said, someone had been in 346 recently—a couple from the city who had wanted to rent it—a Mr. and Mrs. Frank Braun. She'd warned them that it was a little desolate out here.

"On the contrary," Mrs. Braun had assured her, "I like to be where it is quiet."

The *World* reporter thrust a photo forward. *Is this her?*

Mrs. Hafftner examined the unlabeled photo of Augusta Nack. Yes, she said, that was the very image of Mrs. Braun.

The crew eyed the block around them. It was a good place to get in and out of quickly, if you were coming from the city. It *looked* rural, but near one end of the block was the stop for the NY & Queens County trolley line. A couple of blocks in the other direction was Jackson Avenue, which was a straight shot down to the East River ferries.

The couple had signed a year lease and paid the first month's rent, Mrs. Hafftner said, but after coming to their new house a few times, they'd disappeared.

"They promised me they were to move in yesterday or today," the caretaker fretted. "But I haven't seen them."

She unlocked the door of 346, and the detectives strode into the empty building, their footsteps echoing. It was a dreary little house, coated in cheap brown paint; its seven rooms sat vacant, the gloom unrelieved by the rays of light filtering in through the shutters. Someone *had* been here, it seemed, because crammed in among the ashes of a stove there lay the remains of a man's shoe. Just the steel shank was left, the leather having been consumed into fine ash. Someone had stoked the fire as hot as they could get it. Interesting. But that could have been the previous tenants, who'd left a couple of months before.

Detectives fanned out into the empty bedrooms upstairs, and one of the doors along the southeast side creaked open into a bathroom. There was nothing in the eight-by-ten room but a large zinc bathtub. It was spotless. Yet the pathologist, Frank Ferguson, had claimed there was some scalding on the body. Was this where it had happened?

The bathroom didn't look quite right, somehow. It was clean—*too* clean, for a place that had been vacant for nearly two months. There was no dust on the floor. Kneeling down, the detectives found a splatter of dark drips on the planking between the bath and the wall, and some hard-scrubbed sections of flooring around them; something had soaked into the wood, impervious to any effort at cleaning. They procured a carpenter's plane and, as the property's caretaker waited helplessly, shaved samples off the floor. Inspector's orders: that stuff was going to NYU's Loomis Laboratory for analysis. Another detective followed the drain line to the ditch outside and scooped up a bucket of the mud around the mouth of the drainpipe; it, too, would go the lab for testing.

As more men dug out the cellar and probed the cesspool in vain for Guldensuppe's head, a crowd gathered outside. Word had gotten out around the block and then back on Newspaper Row as well. Reporters were pouring over on the East River ferries, hungrily circling the local residents.

Why, yes, neighbors said, they *had* heard a strange cry last Friday. Something like—*"Help! Help! Murder!"* One of them had even poked his head outside to investigate. But he hadn't heard anything more, and, well, you hear all sorts of crazy things from neighbors' homes. But a trio of local busybodies—Mrs. Buttinger, Mrs. Ruppert, and Mrs. Nunnheimer—had indeed noticed when Mrs. Braun and another fellow stopped by here a week earlier.

"I clean my windows every Friday afternoon," recalled Mrs. Nunnheimer, "and somewheres about three o'clock, I noticed while at this work the trolley car stop at our corner. I turned my head and saw a nicely dressed man get off. He held his hand out and received a small yellow hand bag from the lady who sat next to him, and then he gave her his hand and helped her down. What fixes it in my mind is that he was so polite and nice about it.

"In *fact*," she added chidingly to her husband, "I said to my *husband* that night when he came home that I was jealous of such niceness and that I wished he had such *elegant* ways."

Another neighbor said she'd seen a second dapper gentleman enter the house the previous Friday, well before the couple arrived.

So *two* men had gone in there. Now that she thought of it, that seemed like a strange thing.

She'd only seen one come out.

WORLD WIDE HUNT FOR MARTIN THORN, the *Evening Journal* declared from the sidewalks as the detectives made their way back to the city. While they were gone, Inspector O'Brien had cabled Washington and asked the State Department to put out an alert for Thorn in all U.S. and foreign ports. Newspaper readers worldwide had been deputized into the dragnet:

> WANTED—For the murder of William Guldensuppe, Martin Thorn, whose right name is Martin Torzewski. Born in Posen, Germany; thirty-three to thirty-four years old; about 5 foot eight inches in height, weighs about 155 pounds, has blue-gray eyes, very dark hair, red cheeks, very light-brown moustache, thick, and curled at the ends; slightly stooped shoulders, small scar on the forehead, and red blotches around the lower part of the neck. He is a barber by trade. Speaks with a slight German accent. Wore, when last seen, a dark-blue suit of clothing, a dark-brown derby hat, and russet shoes; is an expert pinochle player and a first-class barber.

Suspicious that Thorn had already fled the country, the inspector had his eye on two ships in particular.

"Cable dispatches have been sent to Europe this afternoon," he explained, "for authorities to intercept the arrival of passengers on the steamers *City of Paris* at Southampton, and the *Majestic* at Liverpool, in order to cause the arrest of Martin Thorn, if by any chance he should have sailed."

But the detectives had a different destination that night: the hulking five-story building at 410 East Twenty-Sixth Street, where NYU maintained its newly built Loomis Laboratory. True, most police only resorted to a place like this when the third degree failed; tweezers were for the evidence that a nightstick couldn't reach. But the forensics lab represented the future. The first guide to preserving crime-scene evidence had been issued in Austria just a few years earlier, and the first book on cadaver fauna—the hatching of maggots and other bugs on a body—was issued not long afterward in Paris. New spectroscopes could find arsenic in blood, and high-powered optics could match the microscopic shells on a dead man's muddy boot with a specific ditch. A careful practitioner might even extract the wadding from a gunshot wound—that is, the paper used in a cartridge to tamp down the powder—for if some old incriminating scrap had been reused to pack a homemade cartridge, he could read the writing on it.

For reporters and cops alike, the Loomis Lab was an intoxicating blend of theoretical science and visceral practice. It was the kind of place that, crammed with the latest instruments of pathology and detection, also featured asphalt floors for easy hosing down after especially bloody cases. And for the expert on those cases, the detectives knew just where to take their evidence: the second-floor office of Dr. Rudolph Witthaus, professor of chemistry and toxicology.

With his round spectacles and an immense white mustache that drooped like tusks, he embodied one *World* reporter's judgment of him: "Witthaus looks like a sea-lion." But the man was a real-life Sherlock Holmes, and a Sorbonne scholar. Witthaus could discourse on book collecting while detecting cyanide hidden in some mail-order patent-medicine stomach salts, or a fatal dose of arsenic and antimony in the moldering exhumed remains of a dead husband. The author of the standard text *Medical Jurisprudence*, Witthaus had quite literally written the book on science and crime. And yet he owed much to his fictional counterpart; it was the immense popularity over the previous decade of Holmes and Watson, after all, that had nudged the public into expecting some scientific acumen in modern policing.

A trip to Witthaus was as good as a new Conan Doyle story, though, and detectives already knew his work well. Long before tracking down the oilcloth used to bundle Guldensuppe, Detective Carey had collared a physician suspected of poisoning his wealthy wife to feed his brothel-and-gambling habit. It was Professor Witthaus who'd gotten the goods on that one. He'd deduced that the wily doctor had poisoned his wife with morphine, and then applied atropine to her eyes to cover up the telltale dilation of her pupils.

But the professor was also, well . . . peculiar.

An ardent art and book collector, he was well known for possessing such gems as the original handwritten manuscript of Robert Louis Stevenson's *Strange Case of Dr. Jekyll and Mr. Hyde.* The story might well have been his own. Witthaus, it was whispered, could be a bit of a Mr. Hyde himself. Even as the detectives delivered their Woodside samples to the professor, Witthaus was battling an allegation of attempted murder. His wife was demanding a divorce because, she claimed, he'd been poisoning her. A bottle of malaria medicine he'd prepared for her was the damning proof: Under analysis, it had been found to contain a massively toxic concentration of quinine—a poison, as it happened, on which Professor Witthaus was the world's greatest authority.

But he was the best expert in the art of murder they had, even if he was a little *too* expert. They'd already brought him some suspected murder weapons the day before, and for starters, he could tell them that O'Brien had been going at it all wrong with his interrogations.

This is not blood.

The pistol, saw, and knife found at Mrs. Nack's flat on Ninth Avenue? There wasn't a speck of blood on them, he determined. The saw and knife weren't even the right fit for the cuts made on the body. It was no wonder that she had been so unimpressed when O'Brien made her sit in a room with the "evidence": He'd laid out the wrong weapons. He might as well have tried to frighten her with tea cozies.

The scrapings taken from under Mrs. Nack's fingernails might prove useful, though; that strategy had secured a conviction six years earlier in the East River Hotel disembowelment of Carrie Brown, a Bard-quoting prostitute nicknamed "Shakespeare." The case remained controversial. Inspector Byrnes had publicly dared Jack the Ripper to set foot in his precincts, and some suspected that the fellow had crossed the Atlantic to take up his challenge. With his career on the line, Byrnes roped in a hapless Algerian sailor nicknamed "Frenchy" and had his scrapings and clothing analyzed.

They revealed the telltale viscera of dismemberment—bile from the small intestine, tyrosol from the liver—plus roundworm eggs, blood, and stomach matter resembling the corned beef and cabbage that the victim had eaten earlier in a hotel bar. Frenchy was sent to Sing Sing for life, though more than a few observers had been left unconvinced by Byrnes's ulterior motives in using this strange new form of evidence. This time, though, there was less doubt; nobody was blaming the new inspector for this murder, and along with the mud and wood shavings from the Woodside house, such evidence might look convincing indeed.

Still, they'd have to wait for results, and the warm summer air and firecrackers outside hinted at why: An entire city was about to knock off work for July 4.

HOW COULD THEY BE ASKING these questions at a time like *this*?

Charles Buala was bustling around his wine shop on West Twenty-Sixth Street; it was where Parisian expatriates could still find an old-fashioned *cabaret*, the kind of place with sawdust floors and rickety tables, where you could split a bottle of cheap Spanish red with a neighbor and play dominoes into the hot summer evenings. But this was a Saturday, the busiest night of the week, and the eve of one of the busiest holidays of the year. New Yorkers stocking up for the next day's picnics and parades streamed in for bottles of champagne, sauterne, and sweet muscat; some were already well sauced.

Charles Buala didn't have time to talk, not about their new tenants or anything else. Mrs. Buala, though, was a kinder sort; her beauty and ready smile were not the least of the store's charms for its habitués.

"I do not remember these people very well. I thought they were German Hebrews," she said in her French accent. That's why the German caretaker, Mrs. Hafftner, had done so much of the talking with them. "The woman was fleshy, but I cannot remember more. If she was light or dark I do not know."

Talking in English was still a bit difficult for Mrs. Buala. Her thirteen-year-old niece was eager to help.

"Auntie says she couldn't even tell how the woman was dressed," the niece piped in.

"The woman was about thirty-five or thirty-six. The man the same. He was *good*-looking." Mrs. Buala smiled. "With a light-colored moustache, but I do not remember if it was straight or curly. He was a good-looking man, though—I remember that."

The trolley bells rang from the lines at either end of the block, and more customers piled in. Mr. Braun, she remembered, said he was a shoemaker in the next town over, on Jackson Avenue.

"They wanted a house to live in. The rent is fifteen dollars a month. They said they would take it. . . . They were nice looking people, and I thought it was all right. They said they might move in last Tuesday, if not, then Thursday."

She was still puzzled by the whole affair. "It is very strange," she added. "They said they would move in. Why did they not?"

But Mr. Buala had a pretty good idea why. Breaking away from his rush of shoppers, he dug out a letter and passed it over to the detectives. He'd received it that morning:

> *Mr. Buala:*
> *On account of sickness in my family I will not move into the house before another week or ten days.*
>
> > *Respectfully,*
> >
> > F. BRAUN

The handwriting was immediately recognizable to the detectives—it was the same as in the "Fred" letters to Mrs. Nack— the very ones they now knew to be Thorn's. And this one from "Frank Braun"? It had been postmarked only yesterday at the West Thirty-Second Street post office, six blocks from where they now stood.

Martin Thorn was still in the city.

10.

THE SILENT CUSTOMER

THE FOURTH OF JULY wasn't much of a holiday for Detective J. J. O'Connell. While his colleagues across the river were taking the Sunday off, going to church, or settling in for parade duty and fireworks accidents, he and his partner, Detective Boyle, were arriving in Queens for another search of the crime scene. Newsboys hawked thick Sunday editions the whole way over.

MURDER TRACED IN DUCK TRACKS, roared the *Herald*.

THE HOUSE OF DEATH! declared the *World*.

HAIR PULLING MATCH! added the *Press*. Well, some local news staples didn't change much.

Woodside had hung out its bunting for the holiday. A blazing sun rose over the village's preparations, promising a fine day in root beer and cider sales for the local merchants. But not, it seemed, on account of the Independence Day parade. Something strange was happening in the sleepy neighborhood of Woodside. It began slowly as the detectives walked up Second Avenue—a smirking urchin here, a girl screaming with hilarity there—and slowly gathered force. They came by ferries; they came by trolleys; they came up the roads with their flat caps and angelic curls, with penknives and cheap lockets, dusty rock candy in their pockets and blades of grass between their teeth.

The streets were filling with children.

Boys and girls, some brandishing their flags, thrashed around behind the house—the Den of Murder, the press called it—and into a field of cattails where cows grazed. Others went wading into the local pond, feeling for the mucky bottom. Still more beat the bushes and jabbed sticks into malarial ditches by the roadsides. A rumor had spread of a $1,000 bounty on William Guldensuppe's severed head, and the city's children were hooting with delight. A thousand dollars! It was Easter in July—a delightful, appalling Easter egg hunt.

O'Connell and Boyle forced their way forward to the Bualas' house, where a local constable struggled to keep the masses at bay.

Where's Mrs. Hafftner?

Nobody knew where to find the caretaker or the owner; the police didn't have a key to the place. The throngs of children and adults alike grew behind them. Scores became hundreds, their weight pressing against the fence around the property. If they didn't collect evidence now, they might never get it.

Let's go.

O'Connell and Boyle wrenched open a window and boosted themselves through. In a stroke of luck, the crowd was briefly distracted by a street show: Streuning's infamous "death carriage" and horse came trotting up to its old Second Avenue haunt. The police had lifted a page from the *World* and returned with the surrey to jog townspeople's memories. The duck farmer next door was one of the first to recognize it.

"Yes, that's the same rig those people had," Mr. Wahle said. "I remarked at the time on the black horse and the dark painted carriage, and thought it looked like an undertaker's rig."

The caretaker's husband, having belatedly arrived after the detectives, was quick to agree with his neighbor.

"That's the same carriage," Mr. Hafftner confirmed. "When I saw that man and that woman come here on Saturday in a carriage I was rather astonished, because Mrs. Buala had told us he was a shoemaker. It seemed strange that a shoemaker could afford to leave his business on a Saturday and hire a horse and carriage just to drive over from Jackson Avenue."

The house itself remained as vacant and unremarkable as ever, save for two previously unnoticed clues in an upstairs bedroom: an empty wine bottle and a small cardboard bullet box discarded in the back of the closet. Detective Boyle busied himself with testing planks to find any that might have been recently pried open to hide a body. But Detective O'Connell still had his mind on that ditch outside. Before landing a job on the force, he'd worked as a plumber, and the drainage described by the duck farmer gave him an idea.

I'm taking out the trap, O'Connell announced as he deftly exposed and disassembled the plumbing under the upstairs bathtub. There was a pastelike sediment in the drain—not hair, not black mildew, but a sticky mush with an awful, deathly smell. Another sample for the lab, O'Connell decided.

The bathroom window now looked out over a sea of children. More than a thousand of them were romping through the fields and ditches of Woodside, at least one for every dollar of the imagined reward. The borough was swarming with bicycling parties as well. Spurred by the fine weather and a day off, cyclists were getting drunk and crashing wildly into the undergrowth, all looking for the ghastly prize.

"Between drinks," a *World* reporter dryly observed, "this crowd dodged into the woods and sought for the head. Within the depths of these thickets are cat-briers that demand of each that passes through either blood or raiment. Profanity arose with the passage of each."

O'Connell tried to ignore the hubbub and stray fireworks outside and focus on the water. The drainage outside didn't look right. How could it have filled up like that in the middle of the summer? They called over Citizens Water Supply, a local supplier that pumped fresh water out from a spring in Trains Meadow. The water meter showed a whopping 40,000-gallon spike in the last month for the empty house.

"The amount of water," the utility's superintendent said incredulously, "is *three times* the amount that an ordinary family would use in a year."

There were no leaks in or around the premises, either; the water meter hadn't budged since they'd arrived that morning. As evening descended and the disappointed children and boozy holiday cyclists gently wended their way homeward, the inconspicuous device bore a mute testimony that no grisly find in the fields could have given.

"The only way I can account for it," the water representative said with a shrug, "is that all the faucets were open continually. For days."

BRING OUT THE BODY, came the order to the night-shift morgue keeper. Even after the tumult of Independence Day, a steady stream of identifiers still came to the morgue each day to view Gulden-suppe's remains. As Bellevue's superintendent stood nearby, the latest visitor's credentials were checked and an assistant sent to fetch the remains.

The staffer came back to the morgue's front desk, disbelief written over his face.

"The legs . . . ," he stammered to the superintendent, "are not in the morgue. The arms and trunk are, but . . . I don't know where the legs are."

The superintendent nearly fainted.

Morgue staff threw open paupers' coffins, while reporters took frantic notes. How could they just vanish?

"Guldensuppe has gained more fame by his death than he could gain by living a million years," one *Herald* writer reported drolly. "But for a pair of legs, detached and supposed on expert testimony to be dead, to make a clean escape from the Morgue—that was a mystery."

Maybe they were just out for a walk, one wag suggested.

"One of the theories," a reporter mused, "was that they had gone to help Acting Inspector O'Brien find Thorn."

In fact, the inspector's search was already going quite well. He'd even taken to praising the newspapers for the fine work they'd done. "I desire," he announced grandly, "to thank the newspaper men who during the past week have aided me so in bringing about the conclusions which I have reached."

It wasn't often that the Detective Bureau even grudgingly allowed that kind of praise, but it was true: The papers had outdone themselves. Hearst was already boldfacing praise from the coroner, police commissioners, and Mayor William Strong across his pages—"The *Journal* deserves credit" the latter admitted—and just that night announced the recipients of his $1,000 reward for identifying the body.

The case had been solved by many people at once, really, but half went to a Murray Hill Baths customer who'd overheard some attendants discussing Guldensuppe's absence; the fellow sent in what proved to be the first correct wild guess. The other half of the reward was split between Guldensuppe's coworkers, who had been key in the actual discovery. None, of course, would go to Ned Brown—or anyone else at the *World*.

But Pulitzer's paper was now basking in some fine publicity itself. After a week of humiliations by the Murder Squad, it had begun to regain its footing. The *World* was the first paper on the scene at Woodside, and lavished its first three pages on the case for the July 4 issue. And the next day the *World* once again had the best scoop—literally. They'd surreptitiously gouged a stain out of the floor in Woodside and rushed it to an analytical chemist ahead of the police.

BLOOD IN THE HOUSE OF MYSTERY, crowed its front page.

Their chemist, Dr. E. E. Smith of Frazer & Company, had cannily used the Teichmann test, one of the few ways to analyze a sample like this one. It was a tricky procedure: He dissolved the stain in an ammonia solution, then precipitated some brown crystals with common salt, acetic acid, and evaporation. Under the microscope, the rhomboid crystals revealed their telltale identity: hydrochloride of haematin.

"They are absolutely characteristic of blood," Dr. Smith announced.

Under the hammering of discoveries by both O'Brien's detectives and Hearst and Pulitzer reporters, Mrs. Nack was beginning to waver. She denied any murder—denied that Guldensuppe was even dead—but was now hesitantly admitting to O'Brien that, well, she *had* hired that surrey . . . and that she *had* been involved with Martin Thorn . . . and that she *had* seen him the week before. In fact, the two had been spotted at a saloon just before her arrest. Thorn had been spied reading about the case in a newspaper—purely as a disinterested party, you understand—and Mrs. Nack admitted that, yes, they had discussed Ferguson's theory on the then-unidentified victim's legs being boiled.

So Thorn was still in town, and in the habit of reading newspaper coverage of the case. Being friendly to reporters now made perfect sense: They were O'Brien's key to luring Thorn into the open. After flattering the journalists, the inspector fed them a steady stream of misinformation for the next two days. Thorn, he assured the *Journal* and the *Tribune,* had surely left the country on a steamship—probably, he added to the *Press* and the *Brooklyn Eagle,* escaping via Canada. To the *Mail and Express,* he was "positive" that Thorn had already fled.

Finding the murderer would still be harder than, say, finding Guldensuppe's legs. *Those* had turned up later that evening in the morgue's pickling vat; the afternoon shift had forgotten to mention that they were there to their hapless colleagues. The reporters had a fine wheeze over the incident, unaware that O'Brien was quietly laying out his bait in the columns of their newspapers. The inspector was lulling Martin Thorn into a false sense of safety; now all his fugitive had to do was make a mistake.

MY HUSBAND'S SEEN HIM, said a nervous woman the next day in the Central Office. Perhaps the beads of sweat on her brow were just due to the heat. It was getting past one in the afternoon, and with the hottest July 6 on record, the police were logging one sunstroke case after another: the ironworks owner who'd left his home that morning crying, "The heat! The heat!" who was later found raving in a cab for a ride "to the gates of heaven"; the fellow who went berserk on Broadway, hallucinating that he had turned into a cable car; the ladies who simply removed their flowered hats and crumpled out in the sun.

He's seen him, she insisted.

Of course he had. Thorn was everywhere and nowhere, a heat mirage. Two suspicious look-alikes had already been swept up from city streets, and they were indeed criminals, it turned out—a fugitive Louisville embezzler and a Brooklyn con man named Sleeping Jake—but, alas, neither was Thorn. A suicide found in a Jersey City cemetery, who'd swallowed acid and died in agony over a grave, surely *that* was Thorn. And what about the body that veteran stage actor George Beane found in the water while yachting off Staten

Island, its face blown off at close range? Headlines wanted to know: IS THIS MARTIN THORN?

Why should someone walking in off the street know any better? The suspect's own kin couldn't even be sure.

"I don't suppose I would know him if I saw him now," Thorn's younger sister Pauline told a *Journal* reporter who had tracked her down to an apartment on Forty-Second Street. The last time she'd seen Martin, she explained, was on July 4 . . . nine years earlier. "I have never heard from him to this day," she added. "He was at that time suffering nervous troubles, and he wrote to a doctor in Boston about it two or three times."

Not to be outdone, *World* reporters located Thorn's older brother John in Jersey City. Not only hadn't he heard from his brother Martin lately, he hadn't even heard from the police.

"I can only hope that the police are mistaken in their belief that Martin is implicated in it." He sighed. "But about that I have my misgivings. The description fits him."

He'd always despaired of his brother, he said.

"There are four boys and two girls in our family," the older brother explained. "Martin is the black sheep of the flock. As long as fifteen years ago I had trouble with him. I gave him money so that he could learn the trade of barber, but he did not appreciate my efforts to make a man of him. He preferred to loaf. . . . When I got married I forbade him from my house."

No, he didn't know where Martin was now. But his last encounter with him, after years of silence, made him fear the worst.

"I did not see him again until a year ago. He came into my store under the influence of liquor and I ordered him out. He had a revolver on him and he showed it to me.

" '*See that,*' he said. '*Well, some day you will hear of me using this on someone.*' "

The accounts in the paper that day made detectives look at one another significantly: Pauline had been married to one Ludwig Braun. And the shop that John Torzewski ran? It was a shoe repair. Pressed for a false identity, Martin Thorn had grabbed the closest materials at hand—his brother's profession and his brother-in-law's surname. And the disguise had worked well. The last confirmed sighting of Thorn was by a moving company that he'd tried to hire exactly one week earlier—the previous Wednesday, in the hours before Mrs. Nack's arrest. As soon as news of her arrest hit the streets, he'd vanished.

But the woman in the Detective Bureau's office seemed insistent. *My husband*, she explained, *is John Gotha.*

The detective on duty sat bolt upright. Gotha was a tall and lanky German barber, and one of Thorn's old pinochle friends. O'Brien had hauled him in on Saturday for questioning, to which the barber had innocently protested that he hadn't seen Thorn in a fortnight.

Well, Mrs. Gotha explained, that was true—he hadn't. But *now* . . .

They raced back uptown with Mrs. Gotha. She didn't want to make a scene at her husband's workplace, so detectives waited impatiently at the 125th Street El station while Mrs. Gotha walked over to Martinelli's Barber Shop. Her husband already knew what she was going to pester him about.

"I can't go back on a friend," he complained when he saw his wife.

"Put on your coat and hat and come with me," she said flatly. "I've told them everything."

Back downtown in Inspector O'Brien's office, his story came tumbling out. Thorn had come out of hiding to confide in him. He wasn't ratting out his friend—really, he wasn't!—but his wife had *made* him come down here.

When did you see him?

Yesterday, Gotha explained. He'd been waiting for a customer in Martinelli's when a man entered, sat in his chair, and uttered a single word: "Haircut."

Gotha looked up at the mirror and into the face of the country's most wanted murderer. Martin had changed his appearance a bit—shed his usual brown derby for a white fedora and shaved off his luxuriant mustache—but there was no mistaking the eyes or the old fighting scar along his nose. The barber clipped in absolute silence, neither of them breathing a word to the other, not even daring to lock eyes in the mirror. After the last clippings were brushed away, his silent customer stood up and pressed some coins into Gotha's hand. When Gotha opened his palm, it contained a note.

Meet me at the corner.

From there, the barber told Inspector O'Brien, they'd gone into the nearest saloon and talked for three hours—and Thorn spilled everything. At the end of it, they'd arranged to meet again.

When?

The barber sat under his wife's gaze and looked down at his shoes, as he was prone to do. He didn't want to turn his friend in; the man had trusted him.

Well . . .

IT WAS QUARTER PAST NINE that night, getting toward closing time, and the soda fountain at Spear's Drug Store ruled the busy Harlem corner of 125th and Eighth Avenue. Theodore Spear himself was manning the till, and his clerk Maurice was working the fountain. Like any drugstore, the gleaming bottles and tins of nostrums along Mr. Spear's shelves—Dr. Worme's Gesundheit Bitters, Telephone Headache Tablets, Kinner's Corn Cure—were window-dressing for the real profits, which lay in the slot telephone, in alcohol elixirs that skirted the liquor laws, in sen-sen gum to cover up that elixir breath, and in petty luxuries like Cosmo Buttermilk Soap and Tilford cigars. But on a sweaty July evening, the only part of the store that truly mattered was the soda fountain, with its gleaming chromium faucets and beautifully tinted bottles of orange phosphate, strawberry syrup, and violet *presse*. Harlem swells and their ladies fanned themselves at the counter seats, and Maurice watched the street scene outside.

Everybody knew it was too hot to work that day; city after city on the East Coast was reporting relentless heat. Laborers in soiled overalls had been shiftlessly waiting around for hours, escaping the sun under store eaves, and now whiled away the gathering dusk in the light thrown out by the shop windows onto the busy street. A gentleman stylishly dressed for the evening walked down the sidewalk, ignoring the workmen, and exchanged greetings with a friend.

"Let's go take a drink," his friend suggested, which was a fine idea indeed.

The gentleman demurred. "No, I don't want a drink. You go along by yourself."

What happened next came in a flash: The tall and lanky friend sank back into the gathering dusk, and a workman—a tough in a blue flannel shirt—seized the gentleman's arm and shoved him into Spear's drugstore.

It's a holdup, Maurice frantically signaled to Mr. Spear at the till.

In a fluid motion, the thief yanked out the gentleman's coat lining, gathered up its contents, pushed him down into a chair by the cigar counter, and withdrew his own weapon. A crowd of roughneck laborers came barreling in behind him. But rather than break up the robbery, they *also* seized the gentleman in a silent, desperate scuffle. Before Maurice and Mr. Spear knew it, the victim was pinned down, yet the drugstore till remained completely unmolested.

Nothing was what it seemed; the workmen had pulled out revolvers and slapped a pair of handcuffs around the fellow's wrists.

"He's shaved his mustache," one of them muttered.

"What's your name?" demanded a gruff foreman framed by the dusk.

"I am Martin Thorn," the handcuffed gentleman announced defiantly to the astonished store patrons.

The grizzled lurker in the doorway now also appeared transformed. The plain clothes of a slouch cap and dirty overalls no longer disguised a man that the startled druggist and his shop clerk knew from all the newspapers.

"And I am Inspector O'Brien," he replied.

III.

THE
INDICTMENT

SOLVED BY THE JOURNAL

MRS. NACK, MURDERESS!

She Bought the Oilcloth Found Around the Body of Her Mangled Lover, William Guldensuppe, the Turkish Bath Rubber.

11.

A CASE OF LIFE
AND DEATH

MARTIN THORN KNEW it was O'Brien all along—why, from the moment he'd walked into Harlem.

"I've thought so for five minutes," he said coolly.

The inspector was unimpressed. "Got anything else but your gun about you?"

"I've got a knife."

Thorn helpfully reached for an inner pocket before a detective seized his cuffed hands.

"Just keep it where it is," snapped Inspector O'Brien.

Along with the .32 revolver, a closer search of Thorn's pockets netted the knife and $6. Still in their plain clothes, the "laborers"—top detectives O'Brien, McCauley, and Price, along with the five beefiest backup officers from the precinct—whisked their suspect onto the 125th and Eighth El platform for the next train downtown.

Surrounded by police, Thorn sat stoically through more than a dozen stops on an elevated steam train that passed the second- and third-story apartments of Manhattan; he could glimpse the ordinary scenes of men and women settling in for the evening, washing dishes and hanging clothes for work. They reached Houston and Bowery just after ten p.m. As the El platform closest to HQ, the rowdy station was an honorary portal into the New York legal system. The lights of the Gaiety Theater and the towering Casperfeld & Cleveland jewelry billboard were among the last glimpses of everyday life a guilty man might ever have. Nightlife swirled below as newsboys clustered around the steel pillars of the station. AN ELECTRICAL EX-ECUTION, the *Evening Post* announced. It was not prescience, just the fate of a wife killer up in White Plains, but it abutted a front-pager of the day's latest news on Mrs. Nack.

A plainclothes scrum double-marched Thorn down Mulberry Street, so fast that the hindmost officer could barely keep pace. They hadn't gone unnoticed. Someone—from Spear's drugstore, or from an El platform on the way down—had called ahead to tip off the *New York Herald* to a big arrest; the *Herald* instantly relayed it to the round-the-clock watch post they kept across from the police HQ. A reporter and a sketch artist were waiting in the street to meet the grim-faced men.

Who'd you get?

Thorn, still unrecognizable in his new clothes and shaven face, was quickly hustled past them, through the heavy basement door and down a hallway. The reporter jumped up and shimmied his head into the transom, in time to see O'Brien and McCauley disappear with the prisoner up a stairway toward the inspector's office.

Who'd you get?

But he already knew.

"Pickpockets and *petit* larceny thieves are not hurried to Police headquarters at night, heavily shackled and guarded," he noted dryly. There was only one man it could be, and the lights burning brightly through the night in Inspector O'Brien's window were all the proof anyone needed.

THORN STARED OUT into the night, his fingers smarting from where they'd been scraped by forensics. Professor Witthaus himself had come in to collect the samples from under his nails; even though nearly two weeks had passed since the murder, they weren't taking any chance of losing evidence, and his scrapings were now en route to the Loomis Lab to be tested for blood or viscera. The rest of Thorn's body had been scrupulously measured, too; the station used a Bertillon card system, where each new arrest was mugged for the camera and then a card was filled in with the painstaking caliper measurements of M. Alphonse Bertillon's wondrous anthropometric system. Everything from the length of Thorn's ears and cheekbones to the length from the elbow to the tip of the finger was noted. All that was missing were Thorn's fingerprints: Bertillon did not approve of such dubious new notions. Just a few weeks earlier the royal governor in India had adopted a new system invented by one of his own administrators, one that annotated whorls and loops, but neither O'Brien nor anyone else in the United States was bothering with such exotic ideas.

Instead, the inspector worked quietly at his desk, saying nothing for hours, content to let his suspect stew in uncertainty. The clock ticked past eleven, then past midnight; Thorn's gaze fell upon the piles of letters on O'Brien's table, all rifled from Gussie's apartment. The useless tin heap of her washing boiler still lay in a corner of the room.

So, O'Brien began: Why had he shaved his mustache off?

Thorn glared back sullenly. He'd shaved it off the previous Wednesday—the same day, that is, that Gussie had been arrested—but he wouldn't explain why. Asked to account for his movements, he gave a carefully rehearsed story.

"I at present live in a furnished room at Number 235 East Twenty-Fifth Street. I have not seen William Guldensuppe since I was assaulted by him at the house of Mrs. Nack," he claimed. "I have been meeting with her two or three times a week ever since, up until Tuesday night. Mrs. Nack spoke to me about leaving Guldensuppe, and buying me a barber shop in the country. She told me that Guldensuppe had been using her badly the last six months, and that Guldensuppe wanted her to open a disorderly house. She agreed to leave Guldensuppe and live with me."

They'd still been planning for their future together, Thorn said, when he last saw her on June 29—the night before her arrest.

"We took an Eighth Avenue car at Forty-Third Street and went to Central Park," he recalled. "We sat on a bench in the park until about eleven o'clock at night. I told her I had seen in the newspaper that part of a human body had been found in the river, and that it stated it was a part of Guldensuppe's body. I told her how it was also mentioned in the newspapers that a part of the body found must have been boiled before being thrown in the river."

O'Brien eyed him intently.

"She said," Thorn continued, "she did not believe it was Guldensuppe's body, because she did not believe Guldensuppe was dead. She told me that he had not been home since Friday morning, and that she did not know where he was. Mrs. Nack went home after we made an appointment to meet the next day—Wednesday—but I saw in the morning newspapers that detectives were at Mrs. Nack's house, and I did not go there."

The inspector allowed one of his long, disconcerting silences to fill the room. But he was quietly pleased by this alibi. The times were wrong: They couldn't have discussed Guldensuppe's identification on the park bench that evening, because that revelation hadn't hit the streets until the following morning. And he had an even more unpleasant surprise for his suspect.

"Do you deny," he pressed, "that you were at Frey's saloon on East Thirty-Fourth Street on Tuesday morning, Tuesday afternoon, and Tuesday night playing cards with 'Peanuts' and Federer?"

"I don't exactly deny it."

"Do you remember being in Frey's saloon on Tuesday, June 29, when Federer was reading a newspaper in regard to the reward of one thousand dollars, and how Federer said to you, 'I guess that's you, barber,' and you said, 'Yes, that's right'?"

Thorn could see the darkened city out O'Brien's window; everyone was asleep but them.

"Yes," he admitted.

"Do you remember being in the saloon on Tuesday, June 29, and going out and coming back with a woman, and having one glass of beer each in this saloon?"

"Yes."

O'Brien paused, readying his knockout.

"Do you remember being in Frey's saloon on the night of Tuesday,

June 29, and telling Federer that you were going to meet a woman, and it was a case of life and death, and exhibiting to them a pistol?"

"I cannot say that I remember that," Thorn answered warily. "I had been drinking a good deal that day."

"Do you remember going back to Frey's saloon about eleven o'clock that same night, and playing pinochle with Federer and Gordon until nearly one o'clock in the morning?"

"Yes."

"Do you remember saying to them that by tomorrow night at this time you would be on the ocean?"

Thorn stared blankly at him. "I do not remember saying that."

He didn't need to; plenty of others at the saloon did.

The hours crawled onward until four in the morning, when O'Brien finally let his prisoner collapse onto a cot in his jail cell. Thorn had scarcely fallen asleep before he was awoken again, first to stand before a magistrate, then to drag himself back into O'Brien's office. The inspector was waiting for him, seemingly unaffected by the early hour, and invigorated by the fine day the Detective Bureau was having. And he wasn't alone.

That's him, said Mrs. Hafftner, looking the unshaven prisoner up and down. *That's who rented the house.*

Thorn kept a stony silence as another man was brought in.

That's him, said the undertaker's assistant. *That's who picked up the surrey.*

After they were led out, O'Brien turned his searching gaze back to Thorn. "Looks pretty bad, doesn't it?" the inspector remarked.

Martin Thorn fanned himself with his fedora, considering the situation.

"I don't fear death," he replied evenly.

"HIT HIM!" they roared down the cell block.

Thorn grabbed the bars of his jail cell and looked down the station's hallway; a man was being dragged in heavy shackles, shoved and smacked by jeering detectives.

It was John Gotha.

"I won't go in there!" he yelled. He looked exhausted and hollowed out. "I have done nothing, and you have no right to lock me up!"

"Go on, go on!" a detective yelled. "Hit him with your club!"

The mêlée continued down the hallway, and Thorn stared as his friend scuffled with the officers; he could hear yelling and the sounds of a solid police beating all the way into the next block of cells, until they finally disappeared.

The officers slung Gotha into an empty jail cell with a couple of final yells and dramatic groans, then waited a moment. And then, through Gotha's wan countenance, there flickered a sunny expression.

Thanks.

The detectives rolled their eyes. The whole ruse had been at Gotha's insistence; the lanky barber was still bitterly disappointed that he hadn't been arrested in Harlem alongside Thorn. *That was part of the deal*, he insisted. They'd been too busy with Thorn and had left Gotha there feeling like a fool. So now they were giving him the sham arrest that he'd wanted.

If they knew Thorn like he did, Gotha explained, they'd understand covering up his role as an informant. Gotha worried that their suspect could slip free or get turned loose, and he'd known Thorn too long to believe that any betrayal would go unpunished.

"I first met Thorn nine years ago," he recalled. "We were introduced in a saloon, where we played cards together."

They were a curious pair at the card table. Gotha was unmotivated and gawky, so tall that colleagues nicknamed him "Legs," and so unsuccessful in his barbershop trade that his wife had resorted to living in her parents' basement. Thorn was handsome and talented, and he always seemed lucky with women and money. Gotha couldn't help a sneaking admiration of his friend's life. But Thorn had a fierce temper when a card game didn't go his way, and Gotha was under no illusions about the murder charges against his old pinochle partner. Thorn, he admitted, "would be capable of such an act."

For now, his friend would stay in the dark about his betrayal; but as Gotha walked free from his untouched jail cell, he could no longer hide from the reporters.

JEFFERSON MARKET COURTHOUSE was less a municipal building than a misplaced Gothic castle, its bands of red and tan brick spiraling over the Sixth Avenue El and up into a great crenellated clock tower; far below, a heavy iron door swung open day and night to admit a ceaseless rabble that was, as one reporter put it, "old—prematurely old— and young—pitifully young." That Friday morning in a grand-jury hearing, the assistant district attorney led a procession of witnesses— Mrs. Riger, Frank Gartner, and a nephew of Guldensuppe's—through their statements, but then stopped short at John Gotha.

The terrible secrets entrusted to the man had kept him awake and unable to eat for days; reporters and jurors craned to watch the shaken man led to the stand. Martin Thorn was not present for this indictment, but that was of little comfort; John Gotha was clearly a haunted creature.

"He had the look of a man going to the electric chair," a *Herald* reporter marveled.

Laboring to keep his composure, the hapless barber spoke of drinking with Martin Thorn just three days earlier. "I met him at a saloon between 128th and 129th Streets, on the west side of Eighth Avenue. We had a couple drinks, and I said 'You made a botch job of that fellow.'"

Thorn had stared at him in terrible silence for a full minute.

"I know it," he finally said. "Have you read the newspapers? It is all the woman's fault."

Gotha struggled as he recalled his friend's next words. "I looked at him, and he said 'You are the only friend I've got, and I'll tell you all about it. I expect you to keep a closed mouth.'"

"Well, then," Gotha stammered, "he spoke about Guldensuppe, and said they wanted to get rid of him. He said: 'We talked the matter over, and decided to kill him. We looked about and rented the house at Woodside. We thought it was far enough out of the way and decided to do the thing on Friday. She bought the oilcloth at that place in Astoria, and bought the cheesecloth at Ehrich's.'"

"Thorn told me that he reached the house early and went upstairs and waited for Guldensuppe and Mrs. Nack to arrive, as she was to bring him. While waiting he took off all his clothing but his undershirt and socks. He did not want to get them bloodstained. About eleven o'clock he said he saw Mrs. Nack and Guldensuppe come up to the front gate. They entered the house."

The witness paused; the packed courtroom was dead quiet. Then, Gotha recalled, clad in underclothes and with a revolver in his hand, Thorn had hidden himself behind a closet door in an upstairs bedroom. He could hear the two talking downstairs.

"Go and see the rooms upstairs," he heard Gussie tell her boyfriend. "I think you'll like them."

Thorn cocked his pistol.

Guldensuppe's heavy footfall came up the stairs, step by step, growing closer. He could hear his rival whistling, walking room to room, looking out windows. Then, as the slit in the ajar door darkened, the hinges on the closet moved.

He fired point-blank into the face. The masseur had a moment of recognition—his hands flew up—but they never made it. Guldensuppe crashed to his knees, then slumped backward onto the floor.

Gotha swallowed hard, and what he said next made the jury gasp.

"*He was not dead*. Thorn dragged him into the bathroom and put him in the tub." Thorn slit his throat until a final breath came out of the hole he'd made. "*I heard a snore*," was how he put it.

The assistant DA stopped Gotha for a pregnant moment. "Are you *positive*"—he leaned forward—"that Thorn said Guldensuppe was 'snoring' or breathing when the razor was drawn across his throat?"

"Yes," Gotha said quietly. "He told me the man was 'snoring' when he cut his throat."

And Thorn kept cutting.

"He nearly severed the head from the body with the razor," Gotha told the jury. Then Thorn went downstairs to Mrs. Nack, who was waiting patiently for him.

"It's done," he said.

"I know," she replied. "I heard."

"He told her," Gotha continued, "to go away and come back at five that evening."

With hot water running at full blast, Thorn finished sawing off the head, then sliced away the chest tattoo. He sawed and bundled the legs, the midsection, and the chest—terribly strenuous work, really—then mixed up a basin full of quick-drying plaster and dropped the head in. When it was set into a smooth ball, he washed the tub and floor clean, lit his pipe, and waited for Mrs. Nack to return. They quickly carried their parcels out to the surrey and from there drove it onto the Tenth Street ferry.

"As the boat neared the slip the passengers walked to the front of the boat," Gotha explained. "Thorn remained behind with the bundle, and at a signal from Mrs. Nack that everything was all right, and as the boat was entering the slip, it was tossed from the stern."

The head went overboard as well. But ever the barber, Thorn now had second thoughts—not about the murder, but about his victim's *hair*. He fretted that he hadn't shaved off Guldensuppe's telltale mustache. But he wasn't really that worried, because the block of plaster sank instantly.

"They can't find it," he boasted to Gotha, adding dismissively, "I don't care."

But the bundled arms and chest were different: They *didn't* sink.

"I saw by newspaper reports that it was recovered fifteen minutes after I had dropped it from the boat," Gotha recounted Thorn saying. "Great God, what a fool I was! In the first place, we selected the house in which there was no sewer connection, and in the next place I permitted myself to be persuaded to hurry off to dispose of the bundles before having weighted them. If I had examined the house and seen where the drain led to, it never would have happened that way. I was a fool [in] every way. . . . I must have been blind, but the woman led me to do some things that I should not have done."

Among those things, Thorn didn't include the murder itself. No, Gotha's friend was angry at the *way* they'd murdered. "I should have weighted the bundles I threw into the river, but Mrs. Nack said no."

After disposing of the other portions uptown, Nack and Thorn parted. He pawned the dead man's clothes and watch for money to hide out, first in the Maloney Hotel, and then for $3 a week in an apartment on Twenty-Fifth Street.

The witness was spent, his story nearly told. The grand jury didn't need enough evidence to convict Thorn, just enough to determine that he could be tried—and now they'd heard plenty. They conferred while Gotha waited miserably on the stand.

"Mr. Gotha, I do not want to detain you, because I can see that you suffer," the jury foreman said in a kindly tone. "You should leave the city and take a long rest."

Gotha still looked terribly shaken, and he couldn't help it. His explanation before he was led away was simple and appalling: The murderer's parting words in the saloon still haunted him.

"Thorn said to me," he choked out, " '*I wish to God I had not told you all this.*' "

In that farewell in the saloon, a realization had crept over John Gotha—one that brought his anguished confessions to his wife, to Inspector O'Brien, and now to this grand jury. From the moment he became Thorn's sole confidant, he'd also become a marked man. Gotha had been horrified by his friend's insistence that they meet the next evening, because he'd instantly understood what it meant.

He was to have been Martin Thorn's next victim.

12.

HEADS OR TAILS

"GOING FISHING?" the small boy asked.

The crews swaggered past him and the swelling crowd along East Tenth Street, pulled their gear out from a tangled mass of ropes and hooks along the foot of the pier, then boarded the police launches gathered by the riverside. These were naphtha boats—steamboats that vaporized petroleum instead of water, which made for quick starts and fiery wrecks—and the men were grapplers, salvagers who worked the docks to drag the riverbed for dropped casks of wine, crates of oysters, and the occasional lost anchor.

This job was a little different. A couple of dozen grapplers had been rounded up, and policemen joined them on six launches. Rather than the usual draglines, they were deploying long rakes with splayed-out tines, and peculiar ice-tong implements that bristled with metal teeth. The riverside crowd knew exactly what these specialized tools were for.

"Three cheers for Guldensuppe!" yelled a spectator. "Rah! Rah! Rah!"

Captain Schultz of the harbor police ushered newsmen aboard his launch and maneuvered midstream to demonstrate his men at work. The imperturbable Schultz was in a droll mood. He liked reporters, and his grisly specialty in body dragging meant that he was always good for the darkest humor in town.

"Heads you win, tails you lose!" yelled a wag from onshore.

Schultz smiled and directed the reporters' attention to rivermen tossing lines into the water on the approach to the ferry slip. Finding a plaster-encased head would be no challenge for them.

"These men know how to find and pick up a gold watch," he boasted. "With their hooks down at the river's bottom, they can feel anything that they come in contact with as well as if they had their fingers on it."

A series of splashes echoed across the water; police looked up and shook their heads in exasperation. Street urchins were stripping off and swimming out from the riverbank, their gamine bodies diving among the rakes and hooks to try to touch bottom. The riverbed was a good twenty-five feet down, though, so all they were doing was getting in the way.

"Something's caught!" yelled a grappler. "I've got something!"

The mass of New Yorkers onshore whooped as the men on the launch swiftly and steadily pulled the line up to reveal . . . a water-logged black overcoat.

"Try a fine tooth comb!" jeered an onlooker.

The hooks and rakes had no sooner splashed back into the murky waters of the East River when the *William E. Chapman*, a wrecker steamboat, came chugging up the channel and dropped anchor. A man could be seen emerging onto the deck in a comically outsized diving suit, climbing over the gunwales onto a ladder, then pausing while two crew members rigged up a massive brass helmet.

The *World* was now conducting its *own* search.

The *Journal* had already run an operation with hooks a week earlier, an expensive stunt that hadn't yielded them much copy. But on this morning the *Journal* was completely upstaged. In a flash of brilliance, Pulitzer's crew had gone beyond mere grappling hooks and hired veteran deep-sea diver Charles Olsen. He was a survivor of the generation that had discovered the bends while doing underwater work on the pilings of the Brooklyn Bridge. The bottom of the East River, the grizzled diver explained to a *World* reporter on board the steamer, remained a treacherous place for divers.

"Unless you catch the tides just right, it is impossible to keep on your feet," he warned. Still, he thought the search might be a short one. "In my opinion, the head, in its plaster of paris casing, would sink just the same as a big, round stone. I don't think the tide would change its position."

If they followed the route of the ferry, Olsen suggested, they'd get Guldensuppe's head. Two assistants then screwed his helmet on tightly, checked the rubber hose leading into his suit, and set to work operating the air pump on deck. Olsen waited until the red Diver Down flag had been raised atop the steamer. Then he clumped down the ladder in his weighted boots, paused, and disappeared below the surface with a mighty splash.

Over on the police launches, the dredging proceeded at a painstaking pace; they were combing each inch of the riverbed. The grapplers might well have had the talent to find a sunken gold watch, but so far all they were pulling up were stones and tin cans. Meanwhile, the steamer crew paid out more and more of the 130 feet of rubber hose to Olsen's diving suit, receiving nothing in return but an occasional bubble of air on the surface. The prospect of finishing in mere hours was now fading.

But what the police didn't see as they toiled away was the slightest of movements on a signal rope leading up the *World*'s steamboat—a wordless series of tugs. Quietly, the *World* crew began raising Olsen as he relayed his message up the length of rope.

He'd found something.

THE DOOR of the narrow three-story brick boardinghouse on 235 East Twenty-Fifth Street opened to two Manhattan detectives waiting on the steps.

Stolen property, they explained to Mrs. Hoven, the pretty young widow who ran the home. They'd come to examine the room of a gentleman who had checked in the week before; he was believed to have pawned some ill-gotten clothing and possibly a watch as well. She knew exactly who they meant—though, she confessed with some embarrassment, she did not actually know his *name*.

"A week ago yesterday at about ten o'clock," she recalled, leading the detectives upstairs, "a stranger rang my doorbell and asked me if I had any furnished rooms to rent. I told him that I had, and invited him into the house."

But curiously, he had another question as he came inside.

"Do you recognize me?" he'd inquired rather searchingly.

"No, I can't say that I do," she'd admitted after a long pause.

"Why," he claimed airily as he stepped inside, "I was a great friend of your husband's."

Her late husband had known many people in his job as a hotel cook, she explained to the detectives. After his death three years earlier, Mrs. Hoven had resorted to managing a residence house where she and her two young children lived. She hadn't attached much significance to the question; the boarder, however, seemed unperturbed that she didn't recognize him—relieved, even.

"I showed him first a hall bedroom," she recalled. "He was not satisfied with it. It was too small. Then I took him to the front room on the second floor. He liked that one very much, and immediately engaged it. He paid me three dollars in advance."

By the time she thought to ask his name, though, he'd already locked his valise and his walking stick—his only apparent possessions— in his new room and left for the day.

She opened up the room to the detectives. He was a peculiar boarder, she admitted. When she went to clean his room, she couldn't help noticing that he was neat—a little *too* neat. Everything was always left packed and ready to go at a moment's notice.

"He never left a scrap, not so much as a hair brush around," she marveled. "You could only tell he had been in the room by the condition of the bed."

Unlike a hotel, where a fellow was far too easy to trace through the register, this sort of room was a fine place for hiding in and leaving quickly. Here, at one of the thousands of residence houses in Manhattan, one could be safely obscure. Even the landlady herself never saw him again after their first meeting.

"He used to come in late at night after the rest of us had gone to bed." She shrugged. "He would leave the home early in the morning before we were out of bed."

As promised, there was nothing inside the room but the walking stick and the valise. The detectives opened the latter carefully, as if wary that they might find something more than just clothing inside. Yet at the top of the case was an entirely ordinary and spartan set of possessions: a brush, a comb, trousers, socks, and shoes. But then, from the mysterious boarder's bag, there tumbled out something else: copy after copy of murder coverage from the *World*, the *Journal*, and the *Herald*.

THE NEWSPAPERS RELISHED their continuing role in the drama. When Augusta Nack's lawyer visited her cell with a newspaper announcing Thorn's arrest, her startled exclamation of "My God!" was gleefully illustrated by a *Journal* artist who showed her dropping the evening edition in horror. Now the *Journal* approvingly noted its presence in Thorn's valise, claiming that he had done little in his hideout but pore over the "morning, afternoon, and evening" editions of their paper.

Thorn would have plenty to read in the latest issues. A reporter accompanying Professor Witthaus and the coroner for yet another examination of the Woodside cottage witnessed them discovering a bullet hole in a baseboard, and claimed to find a second bullet that had entered into the lath of a wall. To top it all off, the paper ran an illustration of "Blood Spots on Martin Thorn's Undershirt," drawn so that Thorn himself appeared to be coming straight at *Journal* readers, thrillingly ready to decapitate them. Thankfully, Hearst declared, "the *Evening Journal*'s pen and pencil" had stopped him in his tracks. "And the police," he generously allowed, "for once deserve unstinted praise for having made Sherlock Holmes and Inspector Bucket look tardy."

The *World* played the skeptic; it complained that "a nail made the bullet hole" found by the *Journal* and inconveniently noted that Inspector O'Brien denied the bloody undershirt even *existed*. Yet among its plentiful complaints—and even more plentiful ads for Cowperthwait's Reliable Carpets and Dr. Pierce's Pleasant Pellets, for business was rolling in now—the *World* also boasted the best coverage of

O'Brien's interrogations and Gotha's ruse. Following up a disquieting comment by Gotha that Thorn had secretly joined the crowds at the morgue to admire his own handiwork, a *World* reporter discovered that Thorn did indeed resemble a man who'd walked up to Dr. O'Hanlon during the first autopsy.

"Horrible case, isn't it?" the man had said. And then, to O'Hanlon's surprise, the visitor had pointed out a collarbone stab wound—one so well hidden in the lacerated flesh as to be invisible to the untrained eye. But before the startled doctor could remark on this, the mysterious man had melted back into the crowd.

If Thorn couldn't help admiring his own handiwork in the morgue and in the press, then it was no accident that the *Herald* was the third newspaper found in his valise. A cut above the *Journal* and the *World*, it was the one quality newspaper to throw serious resources at the case. Before the arrival of Pulitzer, the *Herald* had been the city's colossus, with a circulation of more than 190,000. Under the boisterous editorship of celebrated bon vivant "Commodore" Bennett, it had cavorted with the best of them; along with a splendid 1874 hoax claiming escaped circus tigers were roaming Manhattan, it had also pulled off the greatest publicity coup in journalistic history when it sent reporter Henry Stanley in search of Dr. David Livingstone.

Those glories were long past, and *Herald* circulation had fallen to a distant third behind the yellow papers, but it could still land a scoop or two. Gotha's fears of Thorn, they discovered, were frighteningly justified. Another acquaintance had heard Thorn pondering aloud how one might lure, say, *some fellow* into Mount Morris Park, shoot him in the head, and then arrange the body to make it look like a suicide. Gotha was precisely the sort of depressive man whose apparent suicide would have evaded suspicion—and the park was just a few blocks from where Thorn had arranged to meet him. The plot was a chilling coda to Guldensuppe's murder, and the *Herald* had uncovered it before anyone else—including the police.

In fact, one could pretty well gauge a newspaper's health by how well it was covering the case. Galloping to the top of the circulation pile was Hearst's brash *Journal*, pulling ahead of Pulitzer's *World*; behind them, with still solid coverage, were the *Herald*, the *Staats*

Zeitung, and the quietly industrious *Times*. Lagging with lackluster stories were the ailing *Tribune* and the once mighty *Sun*, as well as scrappy but outgunned titles like the *Evening Telegram* and the *Press*; while the *Telegram* tried to lure readers with a Free Trip to the Klondike promotion, the latter was reduced to profiling the Woodside duck who broke the case. ("It is an ordinary duck," their hapless writer concluded.) At the bottom of the heap were the has-beens that could scarcely plagiarize yesterday's newspapers—the *Mail and Express*, the *Commercial Advertiser*, and the scrawny *New York Post*.

But buzzing along Newspaper Row late on the night of July 8 was a rumor that the *World* was about to leap ahead of them all with the biggest of breaks—one that might instantly upend the investigation.

IT WAS ONE A.M. when detectives marched into the *World* offices.

Where is it?

The rewrite and layout men, finishing their final late shifts for the next morning's July 9 issue, were the picture of innocence. Why, they were busy preparing a story on Mr. Valentine's turnip giveaway, where the local merchant gave away 171 barrels of last year's crop—lovely, fine specimens they were, too—because the vegetables just weren't selling. There'd almost been a riot on North Moore among paupers coming to get them; one poor man plain fainted on the sidewalk while trying to roll his barrel of turnips home, and . . . Where was what?

Where's the head?

Someone had seen the *World* diving crew draw a slimy white mass out of the water late the afternoon before. The *Herald* believed the *World* had the scoop of the day—literally scooping William Guldensuppe's head off the bottom of the East River—and that Pulitzer's henchmen were now concealing the ghastly thing in their editorial offices. In a burst of righteous indignation, the *Herald* called in the police.

Where is it?

The diver had indeed brought up a white chunk of stone the size of a human head, a *World* staffer patiently explained; but rather than the plaster-encrusted remains of William Guldensuppe, it had proven to be nothing more than a clump of barnacles that had dislodged from the hull of some passing ship.

"To reassure the gentlemen in charge of the *Herald*," a night reporter replied tartly, "*The World* has not the head of Guldensuppe and would not keep it if it had."

Yet there was no denying the head's importance. Old-timers in the newsroom still recalled "the Kelsey Outrage" of more than twenty years back, when Long Island poet Charles G. Kelsey unwisely wooed a very engaged woman named Julia. She'd set a candle in the window as their sign to meet, but he was seized in her yard by locals armed with tar and feathers, most likely led by Julia's fiancé, Royal Sammis. After turning the lovelorn poet into a scalding mass of tar, they sent him screaming out into the night, never to be seen again. Julia and Royal married three months later, freed of the bothersome suitor, and everyone lived happily ever after—at least until ten months later, when fishermen pulled Kelsey's tarred body from Huntington Bay. Or rather, they pulled out the bottom half of it; the top was gone, and his genitals had been hacked off.

As with Guldensuppe, the facts of the Kelsey case seemed clear: The identity of the victim, the perpetrators, and the motive all appeared obvious. There was even the same shock of betrayal: The candle that lured Charles Kelsey was lit deliberately by Julia, who then allegedly watched his tarring. But without a complete body, and with stories floated by the defense of live Kelsey "sightings," no jury had been able to convict a single person involved. The whole grisly affair was crudely preserved for decades in a popular turn of phrase—"as dead as Kelsey's nuts"—but Royal and Julia Sammis still walked free.

The assistant DA had been busy insisting to newspapers all day that, history aside, he didn't particularly need Guldensuppe's head to secure a conviction. Suspicious that the *World* had beaten the police to the punch, rival papers were glad to repeat the assertion that finding the final piece of Guldensuppe's body was a mere formality. HEAD NOT NECESSARY, the next morning's *Herald* headline assured readers.

But the small fleet of hired grapplers that gathered at the riverside again that next morning hinted otherwise. Reporters could already see that not all the other evidence would hold up; Mr. Buala, for one, now claimed he couldn't recognize Nack and Thorn as the couple who rented his Woodside house—because, detectives grumbled, he feared a conviction would keep him from being able to rent it out again. These suspicions were not exactly mollified when the annoyed wine merchant stubbornly attempted to keep the coroner from touching his precious baseboards to retrieve a spent bullet.

The longer Guldensuppe's head stayed missing, the more the questions would grow around the unthinkable. Could Nack and Thorn really get away with murder?

QUEEN OF THE TOMBS

THE CROWDS WERE ALREADY GATHERING outside of the Tombs that morning, milling below thick granite walls built to evoke the ancient Egyptian temple of Dendera but instead memorializing every form of corruption bred by modern Manhattan. There were always crowds here: bailsmen, lawyers, police, food hawkers, and fatherless urchins all lurking in and among massive columns carved to look like papyrus stalks.

It was hardly a welcoming spot to linger. Intended for a city of 300,000, the decrepit pile now served 1.8 million New Yorkers, with three and sometimes four men crammed into cells meant for one. But it had been a cursed place from the beginning, a heap on a swamp. The massive structure had instantly begun to settle, opening fissures from the roof to the foundation, throwing the stairways akimbo, and letting sewage ooze into the ground floor. Each of its cells measured only six by eight feet, with a single footlong slit facing outside; the darkness inside was perpetual, with gaslights left blazing at all hours, even on ferociously hot July days like this one. Each cell's narrow cot was shared by two inmates, sleeping head to foot, on sheets changed every six weeks. As prisoners lacked furniture, meals were eaten off tin plates perched on the rim of a malodorous toilet. Cold and rusty water dribbled from the single bathtub provided for each of its four floors. It was the largest jail in the country, and quite possibly the worst.

A prison commission had condemned the place as "a disgrace to the city of New York," which it certainly was, and recommended that "it ought to be immediately demolished"—which, to everyone's shock, it also was. Workmen were dismantling the fortresslike walls with derricks and tackles, even while the inmates still lived inside. Just a few days earlier a block of granite had tumbled into the streets below, nearly flattening a workman and two young boys. Not content with exerting its malevolence on those within its walls, the Tombs was now threatening those outside, too.

Inside the women's wing of the prison, amid the infernal clattering of demolition, a murmur passed among the inmates roaming the hallways and catwalks on their morning constitutionals.

"It's Mrs. Nack!"

The knots of prostitutes and shoplifters parted to gape as she passed by in a sort of regal procession. A blond-tressed inmate who had already befriended the midwife walked at her side. Carefully arranging the green ribbons atop her black hat, Mrs. Nack was led out by a side entrance and into a waiting streetcar, with reporters and citizenry in pursuit.

Across town, another carriage left police headquarters, followed down Mott Street by a second mass of hundreds of New Yorkers; they converged at the Jefferson Market Courthouse, where Martin Thorn was the first to stand before the crowded room for his arraignment. Dressed in a black coat and a straw boater, he didn't know quite where to put himself.

"Come on up the bridge, Thorn," the judge said, waving him over to the bar. "You can hear the proceedings better there."

The courtroom was sweltering and packed with the fan-flapping female curiosity seekers whom the case seemed to attract. With his back to the gallery as he ascended the platform, Thorn took no notice of them at all, or even of himself. The once-dapper barber now sported three days' stubble, the result of a suicide watch that barred him from shaving.

"Have you any counsel?" the judge asked.

"No sir," Thorn replied quietly.

"Do you wish for any counsel?"

"I don't know anybody."

It wasn't the usual response; most murder suspects had previous scrapes with the law to draw on. But Thorn was not a usual case.

"I will send for anyone you wish."

Thorn didn't know what to say. He twirled his hat on his finger and looked blankly at the floor.

The door at the back of the courtroom swung open, and the crowd turned to look—everyone, that is, except for Thorn himself. He heard a second prisoner led up to the table next to him, but he did not dare look to see who it was.

"We appear for Mrs. Thorn," her lawyer started before correcting himself. "I mean Mrs. *Nack*."

The courtroom tittered, and Thorn smiled quietly while still staring fixedly ahead. The two moved close together until few in the courtroom could see or hear what happened next: a quick squeeze of their hands. It was exactly two weeks since the alleged murder, and the first time they'd seen each other in more than a week. Mrs. Nack leaned in to her lover and whispered.

"*Shweige still*," she murmured to him.

OR PERHAPS SHE DIDN'T. A reporter for the *New Yorker Staats Zeitung*, a paper eminently qualified to eavesdrop on a German defendant, heard this instead: "*Halt den Mund und Spricht nicht!*" But both messages were the same: Tell them nothing.

"Mrs. Nack and Martin Thorn refuse to talk," Hearst mused over the proceedings. "All of which is very strange, considering that she is a woman and he is a barber."

They had already said plenty, of course, as had their witnesses; the mythologizing of the case had begun. Within hours of the indictment, Hearst had a team assembling *Journal* clippings and reporters' notes into a 126-page illustrated book titled *The Guldensuppe Mystery*. The instant book hit the streets just days later, as the first title by the newly launched True Story Publishing Company. Naturally, it heaped praise on the *Journal* as a "great newspaper" while calling for the miscreants to be electrocuted.

The city followed that prospect so avidly that New Yorkers even attempted trying Thorn themselves. One Lower East Side summer-school teacher found that his charges only wanted to discuss Guldensuppe, and he allowed his bookkeeping course to be turned into a mock trial. The result was covered in the *Times*, which noted that "the bookkeeping lessons quickly dwindled in interest and the full details of the cutting up and hiding of Guldensuppe's body were gone over by the boys with the greatest relish." Amid the blackboards and inkwells, "Thorn" and his "attorney"—two eleven-year-old boys—wilted under the aggressive questioning of a roomful of street urchins. Despite an impassioned half-hour-long closing argument by the diminutive attorney, his client was found guilty and sent to the electric chair—which, this being a Manhattan classroom, was simply a *chair*. School trustees were none too pleased when they learned of this extracurricular jurisprudence. Children were sent back to their bookkeeping texts with a stern admonition from the principal: *"I shall permit no more murder trials."*

But it was only to be expected in a city where masseurs were now slyly referred to as "Gieldensuppers" and where even local vagrants took a wild-eyed interest in the case. One unhinged man, chasing telegram messengers around William Street while shouting obscenities, was dragged off to Bellevue yelling: "That's not Thorn the police got! I'm the only original Thorn! I sliced Guldensuppe! I'm a holy terror! All others are imitations!"

In fact, there *was* an imitation Martin Thorn.

THE MURDER OF WILLIAM GULDENSUPPE, announced signs at the Eden Musée on West Twenty-Third Street. The Eden was the most upscale—or perhaps just the least downscale—of Manhattan's fabled dime museums. It was one of the city's most popular tourist destinations, and its elaborate waxworks could hold its own with Madame Tussaud's of London. Boasting the world's largest wax tableaus, and airy recital spaces for visiting Hungarian musicians and Japanese acrobats, it maintained a top-floor workshop that could whip up a body within twenty-four hours from wax, papier-mâché, wig hair, and costumes. Just days after Gotha's revelations, New Yorkers were lining up on Twenty-Third Street to hasten past old Ajeeb the Chess Automaton and beyond the impressive new re-creation of a Klondike gold-rush mining camp. Instead, they ventured down into the famed Chamber of Horrors. Along with its usual exhibitions of the Spanish Inquisition and a "Hindoo Woman's Sacrifice," it now housed the Woodside Horror; the infamous bedroom and bathroom had been painstakingly re-created, complete with Guldensuppe's decapitated body draining into a bathtub, and a waxen Martin Thorn industriously plastering the severed head.

Over at the Tombs, the prison matron couldn't help noticing that Augusta Nack was becoming something of a tourist attraction herself. She received a bewildering number of admirers, some bearing bags of oranges and bunches of flowers for the woman who had done away with her beau. One man sent her a letter professing undying love: "Your face possesses a charm that entrances me," it rhapsodized. "I wish I could make your acquaintance. . . . I should long to take you in my arms and give you a thousand kisses."

The object of his affections snorted in disgust and crumpled the note into a ball. When a group of curiosity seekers arrived begging the prison matron to see a *real* Mrs. Nack, one not made of wax, she became even less amused.

"I'm no freak," Mrs. Nack snapped at the matron. "Tell them they can't come in here and look at me. I'm not on exhibition."

But then she paused to reconsider. If Eden Musée and the *Journal* made good money off the case, why couldn't she? The Musée charged fifty cents admission, and surely she could beat their likenesses and their price.

"Wait a moment," she called to the departing matron. "Tell them they may come in and look as much as they like—*if they'll pay twenty-five cents apiece.*"

Gussie was back in business.

MARTIN THORN PASSED the days in cells #29 and #30, a double unit he was crammed into with five other men—all petty offenders, and all chosen to watch the star inmate for suicide attempts. Deprived of that pastime, Thorn resigned himself to tutoring cell mates in pinochle, a pursuit occasionally interrupted to watch newly arrived drunks hauled down the stifling cell block. The most entertaining was Johnny Boylan, who was found collapsed on the Bowery, so weighted down with stolen silverware that he couldn't walk; when the police collared him, dozens of pieces came crashing out of his jacket. Once Thorn tired of watching these new inmates arrive, he read the newspapers. His own story had traveled across the country and the ocean; even the *Aberdeen Weekly* in Scotland was carrying the headline THE HORRIBLE MURDER IN NEW YORK next to yet another announcement of INTENSE HEAT IN AMERICA. But there was other news to follow here at home: whisperings that Japan and Spain were considering an alliance to wrest Hawaii and Cuba from America, rumors of President McKinley allying with England and France to finish the Panama Canal, and reports of massive strikes by coal miners in Ohio and Indiana. It bothered Thorn that his own starring role on the front pages meant he'd miss the city elections in the fall; with the five boroughs set to consolidate for the first time under a single mayor, it looked like an entertainingly dirty race.

He'd settled into his routine for a few days when a new cell mate appeared, a smoothly polished businessman named Horton. It was said that he had been a lawyer, or perhaps an estate agent—nobody was quite sure. In any case, the genial old gent wanted in on the pinochle game.

After a few rounds, Horton looked squarely at Thorn. "Where's the head?" he asked affably.

Thorn continued regarding his flushes and his next bid. "What head?" he answered coolly.

Another minute passed, and more cards were exchanged.

"Where's the head?" Horton cheerfully repeated.

The accused murderer gave his opponent a withering look. *"What head?"*

Another minute of card play crawled by. Then: "Where's the head?"

This continued all day long.

And it was, to be fair, a very good question. Captain Schultz's crews were doggedly working their way up the East River from Tenth to Ninety-Second Street in the largest dredging search operation the city had ever mounted. "The new industry of finding William

Guldensuppe's head," a *Herald* reporter cracked, "is developing rapidly." Readers in the daily papers lobbed suggestions for locating it—floating mystically body-homing loaves of black bread with a candle inside, for instance—but the river workers remained as busy and as empty-handed as ever.

A steady stream of bewildering leads poured in throughout the summer. Children proved especially fond of claiming severed head sightings. A boy found a plaster-caked head in Branchport, New Jersey, panicked, and threw it into a local stream. Despite a welter of news stories about "little Tommy Cooper" and his ghastly find, the police couldn't turn it up again. It took an intrepid *Herald* reporter to discover why.

"The main fault with the Branchport discovery," the reporter ventured, "is that there is no such person as Tommy Cooper."

Three more boys spotted a head floating by the 117th Street Boathouse, but to no avail. Yet another "decomposed mass" frightened passing ferry passengers and was indeed found to be a head—but of "a large fish." A grisly find made in an Upper West Side boardinghouse by a janitor—he ran into the local precinct station screaming, "A head! A head! My god, the head!"—proved to be a med school's well-polished learning skull. But when a seven-year-old girl from Woodside found an actual chunk of plaster from a local ditch, matters began to look more promising. The police wasted no time in busting the plaster chunk open.

And it really did contain a head—of cabbage.

Another Woodside child promptly discovered a brown derby hat with a bullet hole in it—evidence curiously unnoticed by the one thousand other children who had thrashed Woodside's undergrowth on July 4. Hearst's and Pulitzer's men both immediately fell under suspicion of manufacturing the relics.

"Woodside is undergoing a boom in the agricultural line. They plant plaster casts with cabbage in them, blood-stained clothing, and bullet-perforated hats, and within a day or two they raise a crop of fakes," jeered the *New York Sun*. "There is more money grubbing for plaster in Woodside than for gold in the Klondike nowadays."

Another bonanza of plaster fragments found at the scene only made matters worse.

"It is impossible to dig anywhere in Woodside, if one is to take as evidence the results of recent excavations, without striking this product," the *Sun* continued. "All the town needs to do in order to get good roads is to clear away the upper surface, and there, only two feet or so below, will be found a complete Plaster of Paris pavement."

Allegations emerged that *someone*—and only two good guesses were needed as to who—had paid a couple of local utility workers a dollar an hour to salt the neighborhood with bogus evidence. It was a brilliantly unscrupulous investment. By the end of August, *Evening Journal* coverage of the case helped vault Hearst's newly debuted paper to more than half a million in circulation. It was more than every other evening newspaper combined in New York, and nearly double its circulation from before the first parcel had been hauled onto the Eleventh Street pier.

Yet for all their plaster jokes and deep-sea divers, every newspaper seemed to come to a dead end when it came to finding Guldensuppe's head. Nor, alas, did pinochle games lull Thorn into giving any hints. His cell mate "Horton" was none other than Perrin H. Sumner, a colorful con known in newsrooms as "the Great American Identifier." In his three-decade career Sumner had nearly bankrupted an Indiana college, run Florida real estate swindles, fleeced would-be fiancées, passed off worthless mining stock, and—in his finest moment—descended on the Bellevue morgue to identify an unclaimed suicide as a mythical Englishman named Edgar. Sumner and two confederates buried the fellow and wept over the grave of their "friend," while producing documents to prove they'd inherited his fabulous estate; the promised riches would presumably lure greedy women and gullible investors. Instead, the whole affair earned Sumner nothing more than his immortal nickname. Jailed for yet another con job, he'd talked the DA into putting him in Thorn's cell to pry out the location of the head.

That hadn't worked either.

The grapplers and Professor Witthaus's lab were the two lagging investigations left; the professor spent July embarrassingly tied up in divorce proceedings, and the crews continued to toil thanklessly in the East River. Witthaus was the first to announce a result: The spots on the floorboards in Woodside were human blood, he declared, and the grisly sediment in the house's plumbing was a mix of blood and plaster of paris. As for the grapplers, they had nothing to announce, but they still expected to get paid. That August the city was hit with a whopping dredging bill—and while the incorruptible chief of the Detective Bureau had gambled that finding the head would justify the heavy cost, he hadn't built a network of cronies willing to overlook an expensive failure. Lacking Guldensuppe's head, Acting Inspector Stephen O'Brien lost his own: He was relieved of his post the following week.

"I HAVE BEEN DESCRIBED in a paper as a 'murderess,'" the prisoner mused. She shot a significant look toward the *World* reporter visiting her cell. "Do you, young man, think that I have that appearance?"

No, he quickly assured Augusta Nack—she didn't look like a murderess at all.

"It did not seem," the reporter assured readers, "that her facial expressions were those of a fiendish woman." To the contrary: Manhattan's most famous prisoner had "a sparkle in her eyes," not to mention a "finely modeled neck" and "very fine white teeth." He complimented the low collar on her black wrap, and well he might; Augusta Nack was granting the *World* the first full interview since her arrest.

"Wait a moment and I will get you a chair." She ushered the reporter into her cell. "We can sit in this corner."

She'd agreed to talk, she explained as they sat down, because the *World* was the one paper that had treated her fairly. The rivalry between Pulitzer and Hearst was such that now they'd even taken opposing prisoners; thanks to the early doubts that *World* reporters had thrown on the *Journal*'s accusations against Mrs. Nack, they were the closest thing she had to a friend in the press. The quiet and brooding Thorn, on the other hand, was a confirmed *Journal* reader, and when he talked much at all, it was generally to Hearst reporters.

"I will cheerfully tell my life story to the *World*," Mrs. Nack announced. "All the others have condemned me."

The reporter joined in her indignation as he looked around her quarters. Mrs. Nack had settled into the Tombs over the course of the summer. True, she'd complained about the bad food in her first days there, and was shocked by the sight of women smoking—"a most degrading habit," she complained—but then she wised up fast. She was the undisputed queen of the cell block by one simple strategy: The quarters she charged from curious visitors and female well-wishers went to buying coffee and cake for her fellow prisoners. Short of a good lawyer, a berth alongside Augusta Nack was the best luck a Tombs woman could hope for.

She felt for these women, Nack wanted the *World* reporter to know—for she too had suffered a hard lot in life. She was a deeply wronged woman. Herman Nack, she claimed, was a drunkard who had abused her terribly.

"Shortly after my baby was born he seemed to become more abusive." She shuddered. In the few spare moments when he wasn't ordering her around their home in Germany, she'd bettered herself by studying for a midwifery degree. "A short time after I received my diploma, we decided to come to New York." This had only made matters worse.

"I first made the discovery that, in addition to being cruel and neglectful, he was unfaithful to me." She sighed. "I caught him several times in our house with strange women." In lieu of contrition, Augusta recalled bitterly, Herman beat her and made her sleep in the cellar.

"I made up my mind to leave him. I considered that living the life of a slave was paradise compared to living with that man."

And that, she pleaded, was why *World* readers—especially women readers—had to understand that her story was not about a murdered man, but about a wronged woman. "I ask those women who are happy and who have good, true husbands and pleasant families and happy homes, not to judge me too harshly," she pleaded. Her concern wasn't with the murder—*there had been no murder*—but with how people viewed her leaving her brutish husband. She was drawn to Guldensuppe because of his tenderness. Was that so wrong?

"He was kind and indulgent of me in every way," she declared passionately, "and I do not feel that I am deserving of blame that I grew to love him."

She did not mention Martin Thorn.

Mrs. Nack stood up and excused herself—it was time, she explained, for her to crochet. Also, she'd have to make time for her devotions; she was a pious woman, she explained, and "never a day goes by that I do not pray to God." But she knew those prayers would soon be answered. As long as the police and the DA couldn't find a head for the body in the Bellevue morgue, she could insist that it didn't belong to her boyfriend. Even if they'd argued and fallen out, Willie would surely come back to save her.

"There is no doubt in my mind that William Guldensuppe is alive today." She smiled. "I know he will turn up soon and clear me of this horrible suspicion."

The story of Augusta Nack's life, it seemed, was not a sordid crime drama; it was a love story.

14.

THE HIGH ROLLER

WHEN THE DELIVERYMAN SHAMBLED unannounced into the district attorney's office on Centre Street, it wasn't to drop off a package.

I'm going to tell you everything, Herman Nack told the astounded prosecutor.

Assistant DA Ed Mitchell hastily sent for a stenographer as he guided the gruff bakery employee into his office. Clutching his battered homburg, Herman Nack was none too pleased at spending a day off on anything besides beer or bowling, but Gussie's *World* interview had been nagging at him.

"She said lots of bad things about me," he groused. "I wanted to tell what I knew about her just to get square."

Herman was a man ill used by the case: attacked in the street by *Journal* reporters, briefly jailed as the prime suspect, his failed marriage paraded before the nation. Now the *World* was calling him a vicious brute. He'd just wanted to be left alone, but after biting his tongue for two months, he could keep silent no more. Still, he insisted he didn't want to get into any trouble.

"If I say anything," he hesitated, "I will be as liable as she is."

He would be safe, the prosecutors assured him. They were joined by Detective Samuel Price, who leaned in with keen interest; he'd staked out and arrested Augusta Nack at her apartment and harbored deeper suspicions about her.

"There isn't much to tell," the deliveryman stalled. "But what I know and remember I will tell."

"My wife left me in 1896," he began. "We had a scrap. I had been giving her $10 a week, and she wanted the whole business, which was the $17 that I received. I told her I would only give her *five* dollars a week."

The stenographer calmly transcribed the events of that violent evening.

"She came at me with a knife. I seized her by the arms, and she threw the knife on the ground. . . . Two or three days after that she moved the furniture. She said she did not want anything to do with me but wanted to live with Guldensuppe."

What was galling to Herman wasn't so much that his wife was leaving him, but that she already *had* money from her own sideline: abortions.

"Do you know whether your wife attended women at your house?" Detective Price asked sharply.

"Yes." He nodded. She charged her customers $25 each. "She had no diploma, either. She failed her examination in Europe."

Not surprisingly, some of her customers hadn't fared so well.

"Did any of them die?" Price pressed.

"I know two, for sure," Herman admitted. "Another case was a girl who came from the country."

"Do you know if any of these women ever died in your house?"

"No, not in my house. My wife told me that one girl died in Belle-vue Hospital. This was about five years ago."

Augusta was afraid of getting found out. Dr. Weiss of Tenth Av-enue, as well as her current landlord and pharmacist, F. W. Werner, quietly assisted in taking care of the women after their botched abor-tions.

"How would she dispose of the bodies of the infants?"

"Any child would be buried by an undertaker—Alois Palm."

Mitchell and Detective Price sat amazed. They knew that some doctors and undertakers treated botch jobs and buried fetuses with no questions asked, but Nack wasn't just making wild allegations now. He was naming names. Palm still ran a thriving undertaking business, just down the street from Mrs. Nack.

In fact, Herman admitted, not all the children were buried.

"My wife placed dead children in jars containing spirits," he recalled with some distaste—because she'd stored them in *his* bedroom.

"How many dead children did you see in your room?" an astonished Price asked.

"About a dozen," Nack shrugged.

"Did you ever see her cut up any of the bodies?" the detective asked pointedly.

"She told me"—he paused to think back—"*that she had burned some of them in the stove.*"

The sounds of Centre Street filtered in from outside; the Criminal Courts Building stood just across the street from the Tombs, and they could almost see Augusta Nack's cell window. As the stenographer scratched away, Price finally broke the silence.

"How many?" he asked.

"A whole lot," the deliveryman ventured. "She burned them for eight or ten years, two or three a month."

Assistant DA Mitchell quietly did the math in his head: two, maybe three hundred infants had been cremated in the kitchen of Mrs. Nack's apartment on Ninth Avenue. Herman Nack sensed he'd already revealed too much. Maybe he wasn't going to tell *quite* everything—such as, say, just why his wife had to leave the old country back in 1886.

"There is something at the back of that," the burly driver hinted darkly. "If she says anything more about *me*, maybe I'll say something else. She knows what I could say."

"IT'S A LIE!" Mrs. Nack roared from her cell. "It's a lie, every word of it!"

The *Evening Journal* for September 2 had landed the story, but the *World* was the first to get a reporter to Augusta Nack's cell. She spun away from the Pulitzer reporter and raged at her ex-husband from inside her cell.

"Fool!" she spat. *"Fool!"*

Her lawyer was quick to show up and ward off the reporters.

"I am not going to let Mrs. Nack see anyone about her husband's charges," he insisted, though the story had already slipped from his grasp. On the way over to the jail he'd been confronted by *World* front pages with the damning headline:

SAYS THE ACCUSED MURDERESS OUT-HERODED HEROD

"It is only natural," chimed in the *Evening Journal,* "that Mrs. Nack, in view of her record of baby killing, should place so little value on human life."

The papers had already been seizing on any death they could pin to the case. When a Woodside neighbor died in July, it was said to be from shock over the crime; so was the death of John Gotha's ninety-five-year-old father-in-law that same month, though a better theory was that the man had died at the shock of being ninety-five years old. But now there was the dizzying prospect of *hundreds* of deaths connected to the case. The Tenth Avenue doctors and undertakers named by Herman Nack found their shops invaded by reporters. Dr. Weiss claimed to have no idea what Herman was talking about; nor did Mrs. Nack's landlord, F. G. Werner.

"I do not think that Nack means me," the pharmacist demurred. "Surely I never aided Mrs. Nack in any way."

Alois Palm tried rather unsportingly to pin it all on his own brother, a fellow undertaker. But for all the perfunctory denials, none of them threatened to take Herman Nack to court. For those familiar with the city's thriving abortion business, it wasn't hard to guess why they didn't relish the prospect of testifying under oath.

Discussing the case with reporters, Assistant DA Mitchell found that Herman's charges made a great deal of sense indeed. Even Mrs. Nack's friends faulted her as avaricious, and there certainly was quick money to be made in illicit abortions. What was more, she *needed* quick money.

"We have found out," Mitchell announced, "that she was a high roller."

"What was her object," asked a puzzled *Journal* reporter, "in preserving the bodies of infants in jars?"

"Why, to sell them," the assistant DA answered. "Medical colleges and students pay well for good specimens of the kind."

Herman's charges also explained one of the oddest testimonies from the early days of the investigation: that of Werner, Mrs. Nack's landlord and the proprietor of the pharmacy on the first floor of her building. When the *World* was still trying to undermine the Guldensuppe identification, Werner had been one of the few to claim that he didn't see a resemblance in the body. Now that peculiar denial had a motive. A pharmacist could make good money providing abortifacients on the sly; perhaps Werner was desperately trying to steer attention away from his shop.

More important, Herman's accusation gave Mrs. Nack a *motive*. Martin Thorn's motive for the murder—revenge—had been clear all along, and vehemently voiced in front of fellow barbers and pinochle partners. But what of Mrs. Nack? Why hadn't she just left William Guldensuppe and moved in with Thorn? The logical answer was: she couldn't. Mitchell believed that Guldensuppe had kept Gussie from leaving with his damning knowledge of her abortion operations—and of the mothers who had died at her hands.

"Guldensuppe knew this," the *World* reported, "and threatened to tell."

It wouldn't be the first time, either. Herman's charges unearthed still another bombshell. Right after Augusta left him, he'd paid some angry visits to her—and, perhaps, made a few unwise threats about what he knew. So, Mitchell revealed, Mrs. Nack had gone to one Ernest Moring—the brother of her friend Mrs. Miller, who ran Buck's Hotel—*and tried to hire him to kill her ex-husband.*

He'd turned her down, and nothing had come of Herman Nack's threat anyway. But when she was ready to leave her next beau, Mitchell reasoned, Mrs. Nack was threatened with exposure once again. This time she found the right man for the job: a jealous lover with enough anger to do the deed, and to do it for free. And that was how she kept Guldensuppe from talking—forever.

THE *WORLD* REPORTER ascended the rickety stairs of a Grand Street tenement, wandered down a dark hallway, and passed through a doorway into a modest ten-by-twelve room. Before him sat Dr. Giuseppe Lapenta, director, president, secretary, and treasurer of the Italian School of Midwifery. Its entire campus consisted of this modest room.

How much do your degrees cost? the reporter demanded from the startled gentleman.

It was the oldest and surest of headline grabbers. Within a day of Herman Nack's revelations, Coroner Tuthill announced that he would lobby for new legislation to restrain midwives. The *World* promptly pursued local midwives with gusto. Reporters pounced on nursing schools for poor immigrant women, where degrees could be had in fifteen days for $50, and marched out with indignant headlines like A SCHOOL FOR BARBARITY and DIPLOMA MILL FOR MIDWIVES.

"Out of 55,000 live births last year, 25,000 and over were reportedly attended by women of this class," the newspaper warned. "No one knows how many midwives there are in New York City."

That, alas, was due to the *previous* midwife murder scandal: the death of Mary Rogers, the beautiful shopgirl whom Edgar Allan Poe barely fictionalized in his "Mystery of Marie Roget." After her body was found in the Hudson River in July 1841, Mary's despondent fiancé committed suicide, and suspicions ran strong that "Madame Restell," the city's wealthiest abortionist, had dumped her body after a procedure gone awry. She promptly became the designated villainess both for moralizing *Herald* journalists and for the American Medical Association, who cast midwives as a meddling and undertrained menace. The state criminalized abortion soon afterward, and a later wave of obscenity laws made it illegal to even discuss the procedure.

This, naturally, merely ceded the procedure to opportunists and criminals. Unregulated midwives still readily pierced the amniotic sac and then induced contractions with abortifacients such as pennyroyal, tansy, and black hellebore. The better practitioners were often immigrants from Bohemia, where stringent training was still available; the worse ones included anybody walking in from Grand Street with $50 to hand over to Dr. Lapenta. But for those with plenty of nerve and few scruples, there was money to be made. And it was a consensual crime that no woman—from chambermaid to heiress—was eager to volunteer information about.

"Their methods are so hidden and their ignorance so dense that they have no conception of law to restrain them," the *World* thundered against midwives. "Most can hardly sign their own names." But another anxiety shadowed the genuine concern over their scattershot training: namely, that it was women taking business away from men. Even as the *World* was pursuing midwives, it was running the headline WOMEN FARM, MEN COOK—a story noting that "the New Woman" was moving into traditionally male jobs in farming and manufacturing, while more men were taking domestic employment. Hearst's *Journal*, though generally sympathetic to women's labor, still ran headlines such as SHE'S PRETTY, EVEN IF SHE IS A LAWYER.

Yet the reporters could hardly fault their own motives in pursuing Mrs. Nack. After all, for a case initially written off as a prank, the Guldensuppe affair was now becoming an open sewer of murder, dismemberment, adultery, contract killing, false identity, gambling, illicit abortion, and medical malpractice. And as *World* reporters swarmed local diploma mills, all of it would have been curiously familiar to the blustery old editors of New York during the Mary Rogers case more than fifty years earlier.

"Really," the *Herald*'s publisher had mused during the throes of that scandal, "the newspapers are becoming the only efficient police, the only efficient judges that we have."

ACTUAL POLICE AND JUDGES, though, were now moving swiftly. With Martin Thorn and Augusta Nack in attendance at the Criminal Court on the morning of September 17, their indictment was dismissed. That wasn't exactly a victory for the defense, because another indictment had just been handed down from Queens County.

Guldensuppe was lured from Manhattan, murdered in Queens, and then scattered in Brooklyn, Manhattan, and the Bronx. The consolidation of the city's five boroughs was just months away; had the crime happened a bit later, there wouldn't have been any question of jurisdiction. As it was, with Inspector O'Brien off the case and with the murder scene firmly fixed in Queens, the lawyers and the DA's office had agreed to a move. The two prisoners were handed over to Undersheriff Baker of Queens County and led to gather their meager belongings from their cells at the Tombs. Then they said their good-byes to cell mates and slipped out the Leonard Street exit.

One thousand New Yorkers were waiting for them outside.

Undersheriff Baker quickly bundled Mrs. Nack and Martin Thorn into a waiting carriage. A phalanx of black cabs slowly pursued them, all filled with reporters ready to cover the pair's every move and scrambling for hotel accommodations by the Queens courthouse. "The line of carriages looked like a funeral procession," a *Sun* reporter marveled.

The crowd surged, gawking at the prisoners as they headed toward the ferry slip by New Chambers Street. It was only as the boat finally pulled away from its moorings that, with the expanse of the East River stretching out before them, Nack and Thorn could feel some measure of solitude. Any solace in the quiet journey was brief; the undersheriff was staring quite fixedly at them, trying to read their faces. The ferry was passing the East Eleventh Street Pier, where the first gory parcel had been discovered.

Martin and Gussie remained expressionless, watching as their adopted island of Manhattan slipped away for what might be the last time.

Anything was a welcome change after the Tombs. The Queens County Jail was everything the Tombs was not: quiet, modern, and brightly lit. Thorn, though, was uneasy. He'd become used to the sound of pile drivers and hammers at the Tombs; in the eerie silence of the Queens jail, he could ponder the steady drip of evidence against him.

"I rented the Woodside cottage under the name of Braun," he finally blurted out to *Journal* reporter Lowe Shearon. It was a stunning admission, but Thorn insisted that it was perfectly innocent. Sure, he'd rented it under a false name—"What of it?"—but that was no capital offense. And a new claim by a clerk that he'd bought seven cents' worth of plaster on the day of the murder left him unimpressed.

"That is all rot. I never bought plaster of paris in my life. I never even had a pinch of it," he insisted.

And with that, he retreated into the darkness of his new cell.

WHILE THORN WAS ASSIGNED to Murderers Row, Mrs. Nack had pulled an upper-floor unit with a vista of Long Island. The landscape was still pleasant and green; in a few weeks she'd be able to watch the foliage turn color. If she looked carefully, she could even make out the infamous Woodside cottage from where she stood. Gussie didn't care; she was delighted with her new cell.

She'd said little, though, since Herman's disastrous retaliation for her last interview. So while the *Journal* worked over the sullen Thorn, the *World* sent to Mrs. Nack's cell their star women's colum-nist: Harriet Hubbard Ayer. Gussie instantly relented.

"Come in if you want to see me," she heard herself saying.

Mrs. Ayer was startled to be welcomed; Mrs. Nack was even more startled by who she was letting in. For the first time since being jailed, she was face-to-face with a bigger celebrity than herself. Har-riet Hubbard Ayer was a household name, a glamorous riches-to-rags grand dame whose cosmetics empire had fallen apart in a messy di-vorce. After her ex-husband schemed, successfully, to commit her to an asylum, Mrs. Ayer made a sensational comeback as a beauty-and-manners columnist. Surely *she* would understand the terribly wronged Mrs. Nack.

"Must I be locked in?" Mrs. Ayer asked the jailer fearfully as she entered the cell. The memory of her own year in an asylum was never far away.

"Don't be afraid, you'll get out all right," Mrs. Nack assured her, clasping her hands in sudden sympathy. "I know just how you feel. *Ach, mein Gott!*"

Mrs. Nack's two cell mates fluttered about tidying the cell; they were so deeply in Gussie's thrall that they did all her washing and chores for her. As they fussed over the new arrival, Mrs. Nack led Harriet to a corner of the cell, where a table was festooned with one of the many bunches of flowers sent by admirers. She was, she confided to the columnist, still angry at how newly overthrown Inspector O'Brien had interrogated her.

"Fifty times or more already Inspector O'Brien tells me he knows just how the murder is committed. 'Ve know, *ve know*. Vill you tell or not?'" She punched her palm as she slipped into her old accent. "I say, screaming at him: 'Ven you know the story so well, vy in hell isn't that enough for you?'"

Mrs. Nack regained her composure and gazed intently into the columnist's face.

"Yes, I say just so," she continued. "Do you think if I have murder on my soul I could be as quiet as I have been? I sleep soundly all night—ask the Warden."

"It's a fact," her jailer piped up from outside the cell.

And, Harriet asked tenderly, had she lost her friends since being jailed?

"Yes." The midwife shook her head sadly. "My friends they all say, so Augusta Nack is a murderer, or if she isn't we better not have anything to do with her."

"Our friends want little to do with our troubles," Mrs. Ayer empathized.

Instead, Mrs. Nack had her cell mates and her sewing for company. Her dresses, already a sensation at her court appearances, would be even better for the trial. And Mrs. Nack was, of course, a woman you could trust with long needles.

"Have you seen in the papers that the Warden is afraid I am going to kill myself?" she scoffed incredulously. "Well now, I am going to show you how easily I could kill myself if I wanted to."

Nack crossed the room and pulled out a small basket from under the sink; it was filled with silverware. To Ayer's amazement, she drew five sharp steel knives and laid them out on the table before the columnist.

"You see"—the prisoner laughed—"if I want to cut my throat I have every convenience. I could take a knife in each hand and have some to spare. But I am not going to cut my throat. *I am going to be acquitted.*"

Every night before she went to bed, she admitted, she spun and twirled about her cell in anticipation: "When I think of how near the trial is, I dance around."

"If we had a piano," a cell mate chirped, "it would help so very much."

And then the heavy iron door was unlocked to Harriet once again, just as Mrs. Nack promised. But as she emerged, the beauty columnist was haunted by what she'd seen. Mrs. Nack's was a curious love story indeed, for the fates of Thorn and Guldensuppe had not even arisen once in the conversation.

"Augusta Nack knows nothing whatsoever about love," Harriet Ayer mused to her readers in the next morning's *World*. "That is to say, of the love which means self-abnegation. She loves herself." As for Martin Thorn, the columnist believed that to her he was merely a losing hand that she now wanted to fold—just as Herman Nack once was, just as William Guldensuppe had been.

"If she thinks of Martin Thorn at all," she wrote, "I believe she thinks of him to hate him."

15.

KLONDIKE WILLIE

BUT AUGUSTA NACK was thinking about Martin a great deal indeed. Even as Harriet prepared her article for the next day's October 3 edition of the *World*, Mrs. Nack motioned an inmate over to her cell.

Rockaway! came the summons as he strolled along the top floor of the jail. Rockaway Ed was a trusty, part of the peculiar prisoner hierarchy within Queens County Jail. Ascending to the rank of a trusty meant freedom: freedom to walk the halls and deliver messages and packages, freedom to walk the exercise yard, even the freedom to leave the prison when the sheriff wanted errands run. The trusty was second only to a "bum boss" in the underground ranking of prisoners, and when *Journal* men had first visited the jail, it was Ed who'd shown them around; he was considered the best guide. When, that is, he could be found there at all. He was on the last two months of a six-month sentence for pilfering some jewelry, and on a good streak he could stay clear of jail for the entire day, returning only to sleep on his hard pallet bed at night.

Ed came up close to the cell door.

"I believe I can trust you," Mrs. Nack whispered. "And if you will do what I tell you it's worth twenty-five dollars to you."

That sounded like escape money, and Ed's own sentence was going to end before Christmas. "Oh, that's all right," he assured her. "I'm not looking for pay."

"Well." Mrs. Nack hesitated. "I want to send a message to Thorn, and I want you to take it. I'll put it in a sandwich."

Food was a good medium of communication; Mrs. Nack was already known for securing cell-block friendships this way, so food handed through her cell door to a trusty wouldn't attract any notice.

Three days later when she'd saved up enough food and paper, the parcel passed through the barred door and into Rockaway Ed's hands. As he walked down the cell block, and then down the three flights of stairs to Murderers Row, he could see that there was more than just a sandwich in the parcel: Whether to hide the note, or simply out of a hostess's pride, Mrs. Nack had sent a side dish of potatoes as well.

At the bottom of the stairs, it was a straight shot through the iron cell-block door and to Thorn's room. But Ed bided his time; he knew that sooner or later he'd be wanted by the sheriff for an outside errand, and he was right. Sent out of the jail, he still held Mrs. Nack's parcel as he walked out through the locked doors, into the autumn sunlight, across the Court Square, and into the outpost of the *New York Journal*.

Whatever Augusta Nack could pay, William Randolph Hearst could pay better—much better.

I've got it, Rockaway Ed announced.

Journal staffers pounced. He'd slipped the lead to them days ago, and they'd been waiting with writers and artists at the ready to make a copy.

Rockaway Ed was hustled back out the door with the letter; he was to go immediately back to the jail and deliver it, they told him. If Thorn wrote a reply, they'd intercept that one, too.

A staffer who knew German quickly translated the note into the text that would appear in the next morning's paper:

Dear Martin
I send you a couple of potatoes. If you do not care to eat them, perhaps the others will. Dear child, send me a few lines how you feel. Dear child, I believe there is very little hope for us. I feel very bad this afternoon. Send me a letter by your sister or by your brother-in-law. I wish they could procure us something so that we could end our lives.

This would be best.

My attorney assures me the evidence against me is as strong as that against you, and that you have talked too much, which injures us, for the proofs are at hand.

Good night.

It was a puzzling note, because it was palpably false. The evidence was *not* as strong against her—she hadn't spoken publicly against Guldensuppe before his disappearance and hadn't unburdened herself to a friend about killing him. In fact, if it wasn't for

Thorn's presence, it might have been difficult to mount a murder case against Mrs. Nack at all.

It took a stunned moment to sink in: Mrs. Nack was trying to get her accomplice to kill himself.

"WHERE IS IT?" Sheriff Doht demanded as he burst into Thorn's gloomy cell. Jailer Jarvis barreled in behind him as Thorn grabbed for his clothing.

"Hand me the vest!" the sheriff yelled. Thorn yanked a sheet of paper out of a pocket and frantically tore it, stuffing pieces into his mouth.

"Don't let him, that's what I'm after!" the sheriff barked to the jail keeper. Jarvis closed his beefy hands around Thorn's neck, choking and rattling him as the writhing prisoner desperately tried to swallow the scraps.

"Give it up, Thorn!" they roared. "Open your mouth!"

The denizens of Murderers Row eagerly lined their cell doors, watching Thorn's eyes and face bulge; he was propelled backward over his cot until his head hung upside down, and Sheriff Doht pried his jaws open and reached into his mouth for the chewed scraps of paper. Jarvis at last released his grip on Thorn's throat, and the prisoner gasped in long drafts of air.

The fragments bearing Thorn's writing were reassembled on a table in District Attorney Youngs's office:

Some attending *Journal* reporters quickly translated it:

My dear—you wrote of self-destruction. That would be best. I had thought it over long ago and came to the conclusion that it would be best for me, but not before all is done to gain liberty. Perhaps it will be the better way, and I will, and it will be easy to accomplish it. I have a prescription for morphine that I can buy or get at any drug store. But have patience and endurance and say what I write to you. If it comes to extremes, then it is time, and I will arrange it so. It is not on account of living that I would like to get free, but to spite the people here.

The watch on Thorn's cell was instantly doubled, and his sister and brother-in-law were searched carefully whenever they entered the facility. As the only visitors Thorn deigned to see, they were almost certainly part of his plan for obtaining the morphine overdose.

"I am sorry," DA Youngs sighed. "The *Journal* did not give me Mrs. Nack's original letter. No scrap of her note has been found. He either threw the letter down a sink or tore it into fragments and swallowed it." The Hearst reporters shrugged it off; Doht's lousy security at the jail wasn't their problem.

"Bring the sheriff here," snapped the DA to a detective.

Sheriff Doht, led into the office, stammered out an excuse: Nack's letter was surely a fabrication by a German-speaking prisoner in the jail, or by the *Journal* itself.

"I don't blame you boys," he leered at the reporters. "I understand how you work."

The Hearst men scoffed at him; Doht just wanted to cover up his own missteps, which had been piling up. He had tried to induce vomiting in both prisoners by filling their soup with grease, with the ridiculous notion that he'd extract confessions out of them while they retched; then he'd hung a picture of a man's disembodied head over Mrs. Nack's cot while she slept. DA Youngs was unamused, and the sheriff quickly backed down.

Confronted at her cell, Mrs. Nack also tried denying the note—

"Oh, my God, I never write such a letter!"—before breaking apart in fury when the text was read back to her.

"To whom did you give the letter?" she was asked.

"Rockaway," she spat in disgust.

What kind of a world was it when you couldn't trust a jewel thief?

JOURNAL REPORTERS SWOOPED DOWN into Hell's Kitchen and up the block of brick tenements past the corner of Forty-Second and Tenth—past Stemmerman's grocery, past Mssr. Mauborgne's Mattress Renovating, past a stable and the neighboring blacksmith shop—and piled into the five-story walk-up at 521 West Forty-Second.

Where's Guldensuppe's head? they demanded.

Standing in the doorway was Paul Menker, a local butcher now better known to the world as Martin Thorn's brother-in-law. "I know nothing about this case at all," he said flatly to reporters.

Where's the head?

"Anybody who tries to drag me into it will get hurt," he said, his voice rising.

Come now, the reporters pressed—*we have his confession.*

Menker was enraged.

"I know nothing about the case," the mustachioed butcher sputtered, before reaching for a rather unfortunate turn of phrase. "Bring a man that says I do, and I'll knock his head off!"

Excellent; the *Journal* reporters made sure they got that quote down. They were on a roll, for their rivals at the *World* had fumbled yet another a priceless lead. The same day that the *Journal* revealed the lovers' suicide letters, Pulitzer's team had landed a tantalizing story: that one Frank Clark had heard a boozy confession back in late July. While laid up in the Tombs infirmary, Clark had been prescribed bitter quinine for his malaria, along with a ration of at least three shots of whiskey to wash it down. He wasn't a drinking man, though, and each day he gave his drams to the man in the next bed—Martin Thorn. Warmed by his first liquor in weeks, his neighbor talked about the mysterious fate of William Guldensuppe.

"He often boasted," Clark recalled, "that he was impossible to convict without the head."

And Thorn kept talking, lulled by the seeming nonchalance of his new friend. Clark was a talented forger—he could draw an exact replica of a dollar bill with nothing but a green pencil—but the man was no killer. What Thorn confessed next preyed on Clark's mind for months until he finally gave a 3,500-word affidavit to the district attorney.

"He told me that after he placed Guldensuppe's head in the plaster of paris, he threw it in a patch of woods," he testified. "He told me Gotha had erred when he said the head had been thrown into the East River. Thorn said he told Gotha it was his *intention* to so dispose of the head, but he was frightened off."

The attention being paid to the ferries and riverside in the days after the murder was discovered, not to mention the *Journal* hiring grapplers out on the river, simply made it too perilous for Thorn to come out of hiding to finish the job. Arrested with the head still on dry land, though, he'd found an even better solution.

"Two weeks after Thorn's arrest a man came to the Tombs to see him," Clark continued. "This was on July nineteenth."

It was on that visit, Clark said, that Thorn told his visitor exactly where to find the head. His accomplice promptly located it, packed the heavy chunk inside a tackle basket, and that very afternoon boarded a fishing excursion vessel, the *J. B. Schuyler*. With his rod and tackle, he didn't stand out from the other leisure fishermen on the side-wheel steamer. As the *Schuyler* floated among the fishing banks miles offshore, Thorn's accomplice simply tipped his basket's parcel into the water. Two days later, he returned to the Tombs to report the good news. "Thorn was very happy," Clark reported.

A visit to the ailing forger by the district attorney left prosecutors convinced of his story—but they refused to give the *World* the identity of Thorn's accomplice. And there things sat for the next six days, without much follow-up by Pulitzer's reporters—until the *Journal* came piling into Menker's hallway.

Is it true? Did you really do it?

Mrs. Menker, Thorn's sister, tried to fend off the reporters. Her husband was a good, hardworking man, she explained, and didn't know anything about the case.

Doesn't the prison record show he visited Thorn on the nineteenth and the twenty-first?

Paul Menker was a decent man, the wife insisted—and, she added, he will throw you down the stairs if you don't leave us alone. The *Journal* reporters quickly retreated, leaving the butcher quaking with anger.

"I tell you that Guldensuppe is alive!" he roared after them. "That Thorn is innocent! *That Guldensuppe will be found!*"

IN FACT, one official was wondering whether he just might be right. A letter had arrived in Coroner Hoeber's office back in early August, from a woman claiming to be the wife of an attendant at the Murray Hill Baths:

> *My dear sir:*
> *I cannot any longer keep quiet. Guldensuppe lives and keeps silent simply out of revenge against Thorn, of whom he is insanely jealous. He will only appear after Thorn has been sentenced to death. If the police would only look around Harlem they could easily find Guldensuppe. More I dare not say.*
>
> *Respectfully,*
> MRS. JOSEPHINE EMMA

Hoeber's staff was marveling over the newly arrived letter when they looked up to see an unannounced visitor peering at it: Mrs. Nack's lawyer, Manny Friend.

"I intended not"—the angry coroner slipped into his native German syntax—"that you should see that letter!"

They were old enemies, and Friend instantly accused the coroner of holding out evidence on him. Hoeber, the lawyer yelled, was "a dirty, insignificant little whelp." The two scuffled, and Hoeber's staff dragged them apart. Maybe the coroner wrote the letter *himself* to get attention from reporters, the lawyer yelled. "I believe," he jeered, "that he has resorted to this method to gain a little more advertisement for himself."

If so, then Hoeber was going through a lot of ink. A cascade of mysterious and often unsigned confidential letters now arrived at his office. One claimed that it was *Guldensuppe* who'd been hiding in the closet waiting to attack Thorn—and that he'd been killed in self-defense. At least two more claimed that Guldensuppe was alive and well, and seeking out his fortune prospecting in the Klondike.

The accused himself insisted that he'd be vindicated.

"I have always believed that he had gone to Europe," Thorn assured a *World* reporter about yet another Guldensuppe sighting in Syracuse, New York. "I am sure he will turn up in time to clear me of the charge of murdering him." Perhaps it was just as well that the reporter did not note that his own paper attributed the latest sighting to a Mr. "O. Christ."

Soon enough, another letter insisted that everyone else was wrong:

Kindly do not believe any of the cards being sent to you saying that Guldensuppe lives yet, as he does not. He was murdered at Woodside, L.I. and the head you can receive by looking sharp at the Astoria Ferry pier about near the point of the Ninety-first street dock. . . . Will let you know more. The party that killed him does not know that I saw this.

Yet another missive, sent by Mrs. Lenora Merrifield of 106th Street, claimed that Guldensuppe was working under an alias in a Harlem barbershop. When confronted by detectives, a puzzled Mrs. Merrifield didn't even recognize the letter; her teenaged son, however, showed a peculiar interest in the commotion it created.

But the most haunting notes were the anonymous ones penned in German and sent to Coroner Hoeber: *Guldensuppe is alive, and taking revenge on Thorn by setting him up to die.* No stock could really be put in these wild and unsigned allegations. But if William Guldensuppe was plotting retribution, it seemed he was about to get it: Thorn's trial was now set for October 18.

"THE POLICE DO NOT EXPECT to see Guldensuppe in this world," William Randolph Hearst joked. "In fact, they would be content to see his head."

It had been a splendid season for news. Along with this swell murder here in the north, Hearst also had a huge promotion to send a team of *Journal* cyclists eastward to Italy, an exciting gold rush out west, and from the south a bubbling Cuban rebellion against the dastardly Spanish. The latter had acquired a fine new angle over the summer: Evangelina Cisneros, the pretty eighteen-year-old daughter of a revolutionary, had been imprisoned for . . . well, depending on whom you asked, either for trying to break her father out of jail or for fending off the advances of a diabolical Spanish military governor. Hearst preferred the latter explanation.

Even as he sent reporters to run the gauntlet of Paul Menker's stairs, he'd sent another *Journal* operative—the hotshot reporter Karl Decker—to Cuba, to bribe a jailer, break into the prison with a ladder and a hacksaw, and chop out the iron bars of the damsel's jail cell. Disguised with a sailor's outfit and a cigar, "the Cuban Joan of Arc" was whisked away on a steamer bound for America. EVANGELINA CISNEROS RESCUED BY THE JOURNAL, his newspaper trumpeted the next day.

The rescue was not exactly *legal*. But Hearst was always pushing for more: Why just cover news when you could make it?

A NEW IDEA IN JOURNALISM, the *Journal* blared across a full-page illustration of a knight slaying octopus-like beasts: WHILE OTHERS TALK, THE JOURNAL ACTS. The paper was already launching city offensives against a gas trust and crooked paving contractors; now it would also shake the columns of national policy. Hearst lined up testimonials from the mayors of cities from San Francisco to Boston lauding his juggernaut, and even Secretary of State John Sherman delicately acknowledged the paper's rather tactless achievement.

"Every one will sympathize with the *Journal*'s enterprise in releasing Miss Cisneros," he admitted. "She is a woman."

The prime minister of Spain was more direct.

"The newspapers of your country seem to be more powerful than your government," he snapped.

Hearst was inclined to agree: The Guldensuppe case had paved the way for his paper to take it upon itself to shove aside any government, local or national, that moved too slowly to satisfy a pressroom deadline. The Cisneros rescue simply confirmed what he'd been claiming all summer.

"It is epochal," he announced from his office overlooking the city. "It represents the final stage in the evolution of the modern newspaper. Action—*that* is the distinguishing mark of the new journalism. When the East River murder seemed an insoluble mystery to the police, the *Journal* organized a detective force of its own. A newspaper's duty is not confined to exhortation, but that when things are going wrong it should set them right if possible."

He could afford to feel expansive in his powers, for his powers *were* expanding. The old order was literally falling away: *Sun* publisher Charles Anderson Dana was now on his deathbed, and Pulitzer's *World* was getting clobbered in the Guldensuppe case and in Cuba coverage. *Journal* sales were rocketing; a reader snapping it open to the latest revelations from Woodside or Havana would find them alongside a fine profusion of ads for everything from the Bonwit Teller department store to Seven Sutherland Sisters Scalp-Cleaner, or perhaps the Lady Push Ball Players—lasses in short garments who fought gamely over a giant medicine ball.

All this was laced with Hearst's own grand promotions. Just a day after raiding Thorn's brother-in-law's premises, Hearst was issuing new marching orders: Pull out all the stops for the arrival of Evangelina Cisneros.

"Organize a great open-air reception in Madison Square. Have the two best military bands," he barked to his managing editor. "Secure orators, have a procession, arrange for plenty of fireworks and searchlights. *We must have 100,000 people together that night.*" Rooms were hired at the Waldorf, reservations made at Delmonico's, and launches arranged to greet the bewildered ingénue as she arrived in New York Harbor. The story would then be splashed across the October 18, 1897, *Journal*—on the very day, in fact, that Martin Thorn's jury selection would begin. The *New York Journal* would yet again own the biggest local, national, and international stories for that day.

The *World*, one industry newsletter marveled, was now simply "scooped every day of its existence."

The paper wasn't just getting scooped, it was also getting hollowed out. Its star editor, Arthur Brisbane, was nettled by ceaselessly hectoring telegrams that Pulitzer sent from health retreats. In one the publisher cabled, THE PAPER SUFFERS AN EXCESSIVE STATESMAN-SHIP, yet in another he demanded the firing of a reporter for using the word "pregnant." He was stingy about the expenses for art—MAKE SALARIED ARTISTS EARN THEIR SALARIES, he warned—yet he kept constant tabs on the editorial page, perhaps the least commercial section of the paper. Just about the only relief the absentee owner's daily cables offered was this one: I REALLY DON'T EXPECT TO BE IN NEW YORK AT ALL THIS FALL. In fact, the *World* was perfectly capable of running without Pulitzer; instead, it would have to run without Brisbane, who jumped ship for the *Journal*. All it had taken, as usual, was a wave of Hearst's checkbook.

But amid these triumphs, just three days ahead of Thorn's jury selection, it was the *Brooklyn Eagle*—not the *Journal*—that carried the first word of a curious development in Germany. The call for jurors, it seemed, would have to wait: Carl and Julius Peterson, two "reputable merchants of Hamburg," were departing for New York via the ocean steamer *Fürst Bismarck* to personally testify about an unexpected old acquaintance they'd just recently run into.

The *Eagle* headline said it all:

GULDENSUPPE ALIVE?

IV.

THE
TRIAL

THORN DENIES THAT HE SHOT GULDENSUPPE.

16.

CORPUS DELICTI

A THICK FOG BLANKETED the Hudson, the cold seeping into the coats of the journalists huddling expectantly around the frigid Hamburg-American pier.

"The *Fürst Bismarck* has been sighted off Fire Island," confirmed a *Journal* reporter.

It wouldn't be long now; the *Bismarck* had broken transatlantic records more than once in its runs from Hamburg to New York. The November 5 arrival would boast the usual kingmakers and captains of industry, of course; Republican boss Hamilton Fish was on board for this voyage, as was a Pabst brewery scion. But that wasn't who the reporters were waiting for.

From the mist, the towering form of the *Bismarck* materialized on the river. It augured an entirely new identification in the case. Throughout the summer the coroner's office had turned away an array of disconcerting characters who wanted to view the body for no apparent good reason. The visitors who did have a reason were scarcely any better; one Josephine Vanderhoff had turned up, dressed in black and yelling at the top of her lungs that the body inside must be her husband, Marcus, a missing painter. It wasn't.

No, contended another helpful citizen. The body was surely the missing Virginia photographer William Edwards. When Edwards's minister visited to view the pickled body, he turned it into a family outing; reporters watched in undisguised fascination as the minister, his wife, and his thirteen-year-old daughter examined the hacked-up body and other clues. Remarkably, they immediately identified the abandoned valise found in the early days of the case; it had indeed belonged to Edwards. That made sense, as the clothes in it had been the wrong size for Guldensuppe. The minister could even explain the enigmatically marked-up slates found inside: Edwards was a spirit medium, and they were used for ghost writing. So perhaps he'd found a more direct line of communication with the dead—by joining them. But the minister's daughter examined the corpse's hands and shook her head; it wasn't him.

So the identification by the rubbers at Murray Hill Baths remained. But the problem of the missing head—the faint possibility that Guldensuppe was hiding abroad—remained a vexing one. And every journalist on the pier had another recent case in mind: Luetgert.

Just two weeks earlier, days after the Peterson brothers announced they'd be coming, a Chicago trial had concluded for the infamous sausage-maker Adolph Luetgert. Nobody had *seen* him kill his wife and throw her body into his factory's acid-rendering vat, and nothing but five bone fragments—some as little as a toe joint and a broken tooth—had been found in the vat, along with two incriminating gold rings. The defense claimed the police had planted the rings, though, and that the bone fragments were from pigs.

The jurors simply didn't know what to think.

The Luetgert trial ended in a hung jury, and Thorn eagerly read the wire reports that covered it. It was not hard to guess at the reason for his interest. And with the testimony of the Petersons—why, he might not even have to go to trial at all.

Slowly, carefully, the mighty S.S. *Fürst Bismarck* eased into its berth and the gangway was lowered. One by one, top-hatted gents and wives swathed in furs against the cold descended; reporters waited at the bottom, notebooks at the ready, and checked the manifest for the famous witnesses.

No Carl and Julius Peterson were listed.

SO SORRY, Thorn's lawyer explained. *We just received a cable, and it turns out the Petersons will be on the next transatlantic steamer.* It was an extraordinarily shameless excuse; but this was no ordinary case, and William F. Howe was no ordinary lawyer.

The office of Howe & Hummel was the best known in the city. Open twenty-four hours a day across the street from the Tombs, it was a cash-up-front operation that served as counsel for the Whyo Gang, the Sheeny Mob, the Valentine Gang, and every safecracker and pickpocket syndicate in Manhattan. When seventy-eight brothel madams were arrested in a one-night sweep, every one named William Howe as her attorney. He was a 300-pound whirlwind of indignation, a crusader in an endless array of loud green and violet waistcoats, checked pants, and diamond rings on every finger. In four decades Howe had personally defended 650 murder and manslaughter cases—and he was accustomed to winning.

"You cannot prove a *corpus delicti* by patchwork," he'd roar to anyone who listened. "And I shall prove that the body in the Morgue is *not* that of William Guldensuppe."

Publicly the DA's office laughed Howe off, but in private they feared their diamond-fingered foe. The Latin for "body of crime" meant the proof that a crime had actually occurred. The notion had originated with Lord Chief Justice Sir Matthew Hale, who pointed out that confessions alone were not trustworthy. It was powerfully revived in America in 1819 after the Boorn brothers case in Vermont, when a "victim" turned up alive shortly before a scheduled execution. But Howe was invoking a deliberate misreading—that a murder charge needed a *complete body*.

"They have not got the head," the lawyer needled. "And what is more, they can never find it."

Howe was enjoying the attention immensely. Reporters could come in and marvel at his Tombs office, a roughhouse operation where Howe cheekily kept the combination safe filled with coal for the furnace—actual money was hidden very quickly, and well away from the building—and where his staff amused themselves by serving one another with fake subpoenas. Beyond those, there was scarcely a scrap of incriminating paper in the place. Once, when his law offices were raided by police, they'd found nothing in the desks: no account books, no memoranda, no nothing. Howe and Hummel were the perfect gangsters' counsel, acting on nothing but their wits and a handshake.

Blessed with such a memory, Howe could reel off precedents for his defense of Thorn. "I cannot see how the District Attorney can get around the identification of the body," he insisted.

Take the case of the Danish preacher Soren Qvist, who smacked an insolent gardener with a spade and drove the fellow off his property— or so he said, until the man was found buried in his garden. At least, *someone* was found there, as the face was impossible to identify. The preacher professed amazement, but confessed after concluding that he must be guilty. It wasn't until two decades after his execution that a very alive vagrant was identified as the "victim"; the whole thing had been a revenge plot, he admitted, using a disinterred body seeded with suitably damning personal effects.

"Then there was the Ruloff case in this state," Howe noted, re- calling an infamous linguist suspected in at least eight murders in and around New York. "The prisoner was charged with having mur- dered his child. The body was missing altogether, and Ruloff was liberated."

True, he allowed, Ruloff was executed later—but only *after* he'd gone out again and murdered a store clerk.

Exasperated by such maneuvering, the police already had two hapless detectives on the next steamer to Hamburg to see whether Howe was up to his old tricks. This, after all, was the lawyer who had once scotched a murder case by secretly paying a witness to move to Japan. This was the lawyer who'd once gotten another murderer acquitted by blaming a stabbing on the man's four-year-old daughter.

"Well"—Howe smiled at any doubters—"when you see Gulden- suppe walk into the court room at Thorn's trial, you will all be might- ily surprised."

IF GULDENSUPPE *had* walked up to the Long Island City Courthouse that Saturday, he'd have had a hard time getting noticed; the place was abuzz with activity as carpenters added extra benches to the courtroom. More than 500 attendees were expected on Monday, and amid the lumber and dust, Sheriff Doht and DA Youngs were puzzling over how to rearrange the furniture.

Here.

They'd spent nearly two hours shifting tables and chairs around, trying to figure out how to cram everyone into the horseshoe-shaped courtroom. There'd be 200 people in the jury pool alone, not to mention reporters from every New York paper and national wire service, and witnesses, and legal teams, and officers of the court. Somewhere among all that, they'd have to fit in the accused, too.

No, over there.

William Howe's spot was a peculiar challenge; he had a table custom-built for the case, specially designed so he could be flanked by both his legal team and the mounds of evidence. At last, the sheriff and the DA had it worked out: The defense would be shoved up against the jury box, while the rest of the floor would be taken up by six tables accommodating seventy-two newsmen, including in the floor space directly in front of the judge. When the judge looked up from the bench, the first people he'd see would be the press; that would also be what he'd see when he gazed upward, as the first rows of the galleries were saved for sketch artists. The rest of the galleries would take the jury pool and a precious few spectator seats. Sheriff Doht was flooded with ticket requests—many of them, he noted, from women.

Pick your chairs! came the call to the news reps.

As the men scrambled for places, more sounds of construction filtered out from the courtroom's storage chamber. It was being converted into a newsroom bristling with telegraphs and typewriters; the prosecutor's thirty exhibits of clothing, oilcloth, and flesh that had been stored there were now instead overflowing from the desk and floors of Sheriff Doht's office.

There was scarcely any less commotion outside. Up and down Jackson Avenue housewives had cleared out guest rooms and hung Room for Rent signs for visiting reporters. Provision wagons were rumbling around the semicircular plaza in front of the courthouse, roasted-peanut vendors were staking out their territory, and sign painters were at hasty work: Four new saloons had opened across the street from the courthouse, including in the local butcher's shop.

"Preparations are being made as for a fair," mused a *Journal* reporter. "Everybody expects to make money."

Not least, naturally, was the *Journal* itself. Hearst had stolen a march on the *World* again by getting the courtroom wired. COURT TO PRINTING PRESS IN ONE MINUTE, crowed the *Journal* that weekend. For the first time ever, telephone wires from the courthouse plaza would instantly relay testimony—not just to the newsroom, but *directly into headsets worn by the Linotype operators*. Even if the *Journal*'s half million readers couldn't physically fit into the courtroom, they'd still be able to vicariously attend the trial.

"It is as though the words as they drop from the mouths of Gotha and other witnesses were by some magic instantaneously cast into type," the paper's front page promised rapturously. "It is as though some wizard had swept away the seven miles of tall houses and changed the course of the East River so as to bring the *Evening Journal* newsroom and the Long Island City Court House side by side." Testimony would hit the page, they boasted, before spectators could even tell their friends out on the courthouse steps.

Sharp-eyed saloon provisioners on the square could see another curious addition being made to the side of the courthouse: small cages. These, too, were a *Journal* idea. Hearst had hired three U.S.–record-holding racing pigeons—Aeolus, Flyaway, and Electra—so that courtroom sketches would arrive in minutes at the receiving cage set up in a *Journal* window on Newspaper Row. There a motion-detection circuit would ring a bell to alert editors and pressmen that the gallant birds had arrived with the latest cylinders.

There were, in fact, at least three other good trials scheduled for that same day: the prosecution of a recent Columbia graduate for highway robbery, the murder trial of a man who gunned down a police officer while raiding a church donation box, and the assault trial of a husband driven mad by his wife's incessant whistling of Sousa's "The Liberty Bell." Only Thorn's trial, though, would warrant the kind of attention that the *Journal* was paying.

"To the *Journal*," Hearst announced piously in a signed editorial, "Martin Thorn is the same as any other man brought to the bar of justice, presumably innocent until convicted. The *Journal* does not hound any man."

Observing Hearst's enthusiastic preparations for the trial, though, one sober *Times* reporter was feeling rather dour. "Every day there will be some fifty different pictures of scenes in the courtroom," he groused. "There is no lawful means of averting this disgusting visitation."

AS THE SUN ROSE that Monday, November 8, 1897, hundreds of potential jurors—nervous and excited, bleary-eyed and annoyed—waited on the courthouse steps, while newsboys, policemen, and journalists milled among them. The *World*'s fashionable Harriet Ayers was easy to spot, as was novelist Julian Hawthorne, fresh from reporting the grisly Luetgert trial for the *Journal*. At length a gray-haired janitor shuffled up and wrested open the courthouse doors; the great mass came coursing in, briskly shepherded by deputies into the galleries and onto the courtroom floor.

Sitting at the new defense table was William F. Howe, resplendent in a gray double-breasted suit, a yellow chrysanthemum in his lapel. He sported a cravat embroidered with a diamond medusa and doffed a yachting cap festooned with his initials in solid-gold buttons. His bejeweled fingers glittered under the gaslights as he waved to galleries filled with Long Island farmers. The attorney looked profoundly unworried, even as a police captain read that morning's newspaper with two-inch headlines proclaiming MURDERER over an engraving of his client.

Good morning! he boomed in his operatic baritone, startling DA Youngs. The district attorney was balding and bespectacled, wearing an off-the-rack suit; side by side, the barrel-chested defense lawyer and the knock-kneed prosecutor resembled a vaudevillian with his straight man.

Good morning, Youngs replied politely.

The defense attorney instantly decided he didn't trust the fellow.

"I rather fear Youngs, he's too infernally *polite*," he confided to a *Herald* reporter.

The courtroom quieted down as Judge Wilmot Smith took the bench, and his clerk called roll for the jury pool.

"William Hix," he began. There was a painful silence.

"He's dead," someone yelled.

The court briefly broke into a tumult—but the explanation, alas, was true. The clerk stolidly moved on until he'd called roll for all two hundred citizens. *Present,* rang male voices of every age and accent from the galleries. When the last was called, the clerk turned expectantly to the district attorney.

"Mr. Sheriff," Youngs ordered. "Bring up the prisoner."

A murmur and then a hush fell over the room. After a few minutes had ticked by, the tramp of three pairs of shoes could be heard echoing through marble hallways outside. The door handle turned, and a man in a sober black suit walked in with Sheriff Doht and Undersheriff Baker by his side.

"He's not so bad looking," a spectator observed.

Doht unshackled the shiny new irons and sat Thorn down by an ebullient Howe, who beamed at his slightly bewildered client. Thorn fussed with his pomaded hair a bit—he'd swept his cowlick up into an insouciant curl—and then smiled hopefully, a little nervously, at the crowds around him. The district attorney, though, was all business.

"We are here to open the case of *The People versus Martin Thorn*," Youngs announced to the judge.

"We are ready to go on for the defendant," Howe thundered back.

From the two hundred men called, Howe and Youngs would have to settle on twelve; they'd excuse some by mutual agreement and could peremptively challenge others on their own. There was careful strategy involved in that maneuver, though; each side only got thirty peremptory dismissals. As the clerk filled a lottery wheel with slips of paper bearing jury-pool names, nobody was sure which side would have to come out swinging first.

The clerk drew a name.

"L. E. Blomquist, of Woodside."
Woodside?

THE SPECTATORS WERE EXCHANGING significant looks when a rather alarmed-looking man shambled in. A deputy grabbed him and immediately began leading him toward the witness box, much to the fellow's consternation.

"Hold on," Judge Smith said to the erring court officer. "*That* is not Mr. Blomquist."

It was a reporter running late, and he quickly fled into the amused press corps. After some confusion and jostling of chairs in the crowded room, a slightly wild-haired and bearded man made his way up to the witness stand instead. It was Mr. Blomquist, and he confirmed that he was a citizen, though a native of France.

"How long have you lived in this country?" Youngs asked him.

"Since 1870," he answered. Recently he'd been working as a housepainter—and yes, in Woodside.

"Do you know Martin Thorn?"

The painter turned a stony gaze onto Thorn.

"I think I do."

There was a rustle from the crowd as people leaned forward.

"When did you meet Thorn?"

"I think I have seen him in Woodside."

A murmur rose up. Reporters nudged one another in recognition—they *had* interviewed Blomquist. He really was one of the neighbors, though he hadn't talked all that much.

"Have you an opinion as to the guilt or innocence of the accused?"

"I have," Blomquist said evenly.

"Have you any special scruples against capital punishment?"

"No." His eyes bored into the defendant. "*Not in this case.*"

"What's that?" Howe asked sharply. "When was it you saw him in Woodside?"

"June twenty-sixth," the painter responded.

Good Lord, what were the odds? Blomquist had just gone from the jury pool to a possible witness. Howe had to use his first peremptory dismissal already; the man was quickly excused. So were the next two jurors, who stated bluntly that they believed Thorn had done the deed. "I think he's guilty," one of them blurted to guffaws. A fourth—an elderly Swede—didn't understand English, or indeed why he was there. A fifth sounded perfect until, as he was being sworn in, he made a confession.

"I think I ought to say this, just here," he stammered. "I'm rather of too nervous a disposition to serve on this case. I've got nervous trouble. I've got vertigo—dizzy spells."

"I won't make you dizzy," Howe promised in a kindly tone, but it was not to be. Another two men confessed that they were over seventy years old, which was an instant disqualification. So was being a firefighter.

The air in the packed courtroom grew rank, even pestilent, so bad that the judge had to empty the room out twice. When at last a bell rang out lunchtime from the courthouse's downstairs canteen, the judge and staff rushed from the stifling room with alacrity. The rest of the crowd poured into the street; all the local establishments were out of food within minutes, before many patrons could make it to the counter.

Back at the courthouse, Howe dined in peace; he'd done enough celebrity trials to know the value of packing his own sandwiches. The peremptory challenges, he admitted to reporters, were following a pattern: Youngs knocked out jurors opposed to capital punishment and circumstantial evidence, while Howe knocked out anyone from the pool—known as talesmen, in court parlance—who were already convinced of Thorn's guilt.

"I'm going at every talesman with extreme care to see whether he has formed an opinion—whether he has read anything of the scores of hats, the hundreds of coats, and the tons of plaster of paris," he mused. Howe wouldn't bother asking them if they'd already discussed the case, of course. Finding a man in New York who hadn't was impossible. Even so, demanding a change in venue was never Howe's style; his firm's reputation in the city was so fearsome that it was like a baseball team playing to a hometown crowd.

After lunch the courtroom filled again. As the afternoon passed, the jury numbers finally crawled upward. The first approved juror was a retired oysterman named Jacob Bumstead; the next was a farmer; and the third bore an uncanny resemblance to Uncle Sam.

"Do you know the duties of a juror?" he was asked.

"I had ought to," he replied, beaming through his patriotic whiskers.

Amid all this sat Thorn, who could be observed twiddling his thumbs between his knees, then leaning back to stare up at the ceiling; he appeared to be counting the gaslights. With each change in position and each new juror, artists leaning against the gallery railing whipped out new sheets of paper; *Journal* men could occasionally be observed slipping out to run them to the pigeon cages. Meanwhile, the *World*'s beauty columnist took stock of the defendant's features.

"Thorn is a very average specimen of the type known as the degenerate," she warned readers. "He is not well made. His arms are too long for his legs. Thorn has no back to his head. A pair of deceitful, grayish eyes—the ears of epileptics and mental incompetents—a square chin."

But that chin, she admitted, *was* rather fetching.

"Cheap Don Juans, third-rate actors of melodramas, and Martin Thorns are frequently found with these highly attractive chins," she wrote.

By five o'clock, Thorn had the peers who would hear his case. They had run through sixty-four candidates to select a jury of twelve. *Journal* artists could be seen dashing out again—a *New York Press* journalist had wickedly spread the rumor that one of the paper's champion racing birds had fried itself on a power line—and William F. Howe strolled out onto the courthouse steps. He pronounced himself delighted with his case and with the jury.

"This," Howe bellowed expansively, "is magnificent."

17.

COVERED IN BLOOD

THE MEN WHO STEPPED OFF the Long Island Rail Road's special jury car the next morning held ordinary jobs; there were three farmers, three oystermen, a grocer, a saloon keeper, a janitor, a street contractor, a real estate agent, and a floor waxer. They weren't used to this sort of fuss, or to the courthouse crowds that parted before them and their escort of deputies. The twelve men trudged down a long marble hallway punctuated by a warning sign from the sheriff:

LOUD TALKING IN THESE HALLS

IS FORBIDDEN

While Court Is in Session

by order

HENRY DOHT, Sheriff

Led by their genially rotund foreman, Jacob Bumstead, the jurors were dutifully silent, if still a bit groggy. The farmers had stayed up until midnight talking crop forecasts and fretting over their livestock—"I'm afraid something'll happen to the brindle cow while I'm away," one said with a sigh. "Best milker for miles around, that cow." The others had warded off thoughts of the case by playing cards over cigars and cider, then puzzling over the newfangled electrical switches in their hotel rooms.

But now it was time.

The deputies pushed open the door, and twelve men filed into their jury box, their footsteps echoing in the nearly empty room. Bumstead settled in heavily against one front corner of the box; Magnus Larsen, a rather pained-looking road builder from Norway, took the other. The silence around them did not last for long: A janitor was still sweeping out clouds of dust when the first spectators poured through the gallery doors, clutching precious white slips that read "PASS ONE." The upper galleries filled with men and women talking excitedly, while down in the arena entered DA Youngs and Counsel Howe, along with their scores of accompanying journalists. Youngs was still looking a bit uncomfortable in his skin—he'd only just gotten over a neck rash—but Howe, in his yachting cap, helmed his custom-built table as if he were setting sail for the West Indies. The reporters duly noted the flower in Howe's lapel that day—a pink rose—and sat, as if at a county fair, guessing at the volume of gems on his person. "About a half-pint of diamonds," one *Times* reporter hazarded.

There was other guesswork going on, too: A *Herald* man was keeping track of the betting pools on whether or not Thorn would get the chair. But Howe wasn't having any of it. "Just you watch. Martin Thorn will be a free man," he grandly assured reporters, slapping his client on the shoulder. He wasn't worried at all, not even by an anonymous note that warned: *The yellow journals have a plant on the jury.* Well, just looking at the jury box quickly dismissed that theory. These were not exactly men of the world: One of them dealt with courtroom drafts by sitting with a handkerchief atop his bald head.

"*Hear ye! Hear ye!*" cried the court clerk. The old-fashioned formalities, it seemed, were still used in Queens. Howe and Youngs shook hands, and the DA promptly began his attack.

"This is one of the most remarkable crimes of the century," Youngs announced to the hushed room. "One of the most widely advertised in the world."

But now, he said, it was time to examine the facts.

"*Somewhere,* at *some* time, by *somebody* a most terrible tragedy has been enacted," he began. "Was this a crime? And if so, who were the actors in it?" Youngs paced the floor of the courthouse, looking searchingly at the jurors.

"The person alleged to have been murdered is William Gulden-suppe, the place a cottage in Woodside, the time June 25, 1897, and the man accused of the murder sits there." He swung out his arm and pointed at the prisoner, sitting just a few feet away. *"Martin Thorn."*

The accused returned his gaze coolly, with scarcely a flicker of his eyes.

"The evidence will be mainly circumstantial," Youngs continued. "A murderer of this kind does not seek the broad highway for the place of his crime, but we shall show you link after link of evidence that will bind Thorn in a fatal embrace.

"Mind you," he added, "the head is still missing."

Youngs gave the jury a quick recounting of the case—the love triangle, the fatal cottage in Woodside, the body cut in four, the head forever hidden in plaster—and he turned to the jury box.

"*Where* is Guldensuppe?" he asked warmly. "He was well known to many. The great newspapers of the country have published his pictures." The roomful of reporters basked in his momentary attention. "There are few people in the East that have not seen a picture of the missing man. If he were alive, hundreds of witnesses would be produced by the defense to prove it. *He has never been seen since he entered that cottage with Mrs. Nack.*"

And they, the jury, would not be fooled.

"You have been selected with great care," the DA assured them, at last returning to the prosecution team's table. All eyes turned to Howe and Thorn.

"I shall also prove"—here Youngs suddenly leapt back up from his seat like a billy goat—"that Guldensuppe 'snored' in the bathtub *even after Thorn had begun to turn the knife.*"

The men visibly shuddered. The trial of Martin Thorn had truly begun.

WHEN YOUNGS CALLED his first witness, the air in the room had already grown foul again, and it was about to get worse. Youngs slipped on black rubber gloves and produced a piece of red oilcloth. He hesitated before passing it to a court officer. The officer, he suggested, should wear gloves, too.

"It is *covered in blood*," Youngs explained, "and if you have a cut on your hand, it might be dangerous."

John McGuire was called to the stand; the fifteen-year-old boy had picked out some friends of his in the gallery and was grinning broadly at them. He'd already been signing autographs at just fifty cents a pop on their new copies of the latest Old Cap. Collier dime novel: *The Headless Body Murder Mystery*.

The prosecutor briskly turned the boy's attention to more serious matters.

"Where were you shortly after one o'clock last June twenty-sixth?" he asked.

"I was at the foot of Eleventh Street," the teenager replied. "East River."

"Did you see anything?"

"I seen a bundle a block away from there in the water," McGuire answered earnestly. "I showed it to Jack McKenna. He swam out and got it and brought it in. There was a wrapping of brown paper, and then a wrapping of oilcloth, and then a wrapping of cheesecloth with a bloodstain on it."

An attendant held a creased and fetid piece of red-and-gold oilcloth up to the boy.

"Was this the oilcloth?"

"Yes."

His friend Jack McKenna proved to be a saucer-eyed twelve-year-old with none of Johnny's bravado, and unsure whether Judge Smith or Counsel Howe was in charge of the courtroom.

"What was in the bundle?" the prosecutor asked him gently.

"The upper part of a human body, with arms and hands on it," the boy stammered. "There was no head."

The prosecution team shuffled through a stack of morgue photographs that lay on the exhibit table, one observer marveled, "like a ghastly pack of cards," and plucked out a grisly shot of the severed thorax.

"Is this the part of the body found by you?"

"Yes, sir."

His turn over, the boy gratefully bounded away, and Howe stood up to cross-examine Officer James Moore, the first policeman on the scene.

"Some portion of the breast was removed. How deep was the incision?"

"I can't say, exactly," the policeman replied modestly.

"Were any bones splintered?" Howe pressed.

"I can't say."

"How was the head severed?"

"I don't know."

"How was the lower part severed?"

"I can't tell that, either."

Wasn't it possible, Howe reasoned, that the head might have been eaten off by fish? There was surely a reasonable explanation for every-thing the boys found. The prosecution team was rather more skepti-cal; fish, after all, did not know how to bundle parcels and tie knots.

"A piece of rope was found by the oilcloth in the dock?" the DA asked.

"Yes," the officer replied.

"I object!" Howe pounced. "That's immaterial. There's plenty of rope around the docks, isn't there, Officer?"

"*I* object," the prosecutor snapped back.

"*Please* don't," Howe sighed theatrically, and his audience guf-fawed.

The witnesses proceeded at a brisk pace, with Herbert Meyer and his little brother, Edgar, called up to recount finding the second pack-age in the woods by the Harlem River. One *Telegram* writer dryly ob-served that the younger child, a towheaded boy still in knickerbocker pants, possessed "a voice entirely out of proportion to his size."

"He is a good little boy," Howe said, smiling indulgently at the bemused jury.

"Was there any one else there but your brother and your father?" the prosecutor dutifully went on to ask the older brother.

"*Yes,*" Edgar replied.

The defense and prosecution alike looked up, startled; nobody had heard *this* before. In the youthful logic of the two Meyer children, it may simply have been that nobody had ever asked them that precise question. Martin Thorn, whose foot had been swinging impatiently under his chair, suddenly froze.

"A man jumped out of the bushes," Edgar prattled on diligently, "and asked me about the blackberries, saying they weren't ripe. I told him they were *raspberries*, and—"

"Do you see that man in the court?" the prosecutor interrupted.

Edgar looked all around the room, sweeping his gaze back and forth several times as the crowd held its breath.

"No, sir," he said finally.

Martin Thorn exhaled and allowed his foot to fidget again.

Officer Collins of the Brooklyn Navy Yard stepped up to identify the legs, but the rows of newspapermen paid particular attention when a more familiar officer took to the stand: newly promoted Detective Sergeant Arthur Carey, the very first to track the oilcloth in the case. Carey was a sharp dresser: In his silk-faced Prince Albert jacket, left rakishly unbuttoned, he might have been the only witness to risk outshining Counsel Howe.

Carey nonchalantly handled the dirty piece of oilcloth. He'd carried another swatch all over the city while looking for fabric dealers and was unfazed by the grisly evidence.

"What did you subsequently do with the piece you retained?" the prosecutor asked.

I matched it to the other one at the morgue, Carey explained, waving the oilcloth about. A deathly stench wafted from the bloody scrap.

"Please, don't move it any more than you *have* to," Howe winced from the defense table. "You ought to have more consideration for our health."

Judge Smith agreed; the air was so bad that he adjourned for lunch. Or, at least, what lunch they still had an appetite for: Magnus Larsen, whose corner seat in the jury box was right next to the exhibit table, looked like he was about to turn green.

———

THE AFTERNOON'S FIRST WITNESS was a morgue keeper named Isaac Newton—a gaunt, severe fellow who failed to see anything funny about his name. He'd been in the job for more than a year and had handled some 7,000 bodies in that time. The DA's office, though, was only interested in one.

"Did you see these three portions together and take any measurements?" he was asked on the stand.

"Yes."

"Did the pieces fit?"

"*I object!*" Howe bellowed.

"This would seem to be a question for an expert, and this witness is hardly qualified," Judge Smith agreed.

"We intend, Your Honor, to show that this is a misfit," Howe explained, and Thorn nodded his vigorous agreement. The beaming defense counsel, his thick watch chain swinging around and his eyes alight, turned to Newton for cross-examination. "Have you these pieces of a body in your possession?" he asked.

"Yes."

"As I understand"—Howe leaned in—"they have been pickled, or whatever the process is, and are as yet intact?"

"Yes, sir."

"They could be *brought* here?" the lawyer asked with unfeigned delight.

"Oh yes, sir," the morgue keeper agreed, a little puzzled. "I suppose so."

"There!" Howe crowed. "I shall object to *any* evidence by this witness, or *any* identification of photographs, on the ground that the body itself is available and is the best possible evidence."

The crowd, packed into the airless courthouse, wasn't sure whether to be delighted or horrified by this prospect—or both. And, Howe reminded them, there had been false identifications at the morgue before; indeed, just recently a woman had identified her husband at the Bellevue morgue, only to have him turn up very much alive at home the next day.

"Many visitors have called at the morgue since you were there. . . .

Were you there when some persons from Virginia said the body was that of Edwards, a photographer?"

"*Object!*" Youngs cried.

"Overruled." The judge waved it off. "Proceed."

"I don't remember the circumstance," Newton replied.

"You see Mr. Moss here?" Howe pointed to another lawyer at the defense table. "You don't *remember* him coming with an order to show the body?"

"Yes," the morgue keeper admitted slowly.

"I see in this photograph—I don't know whether it is the *original*," Howe muttered contemptuously as he shuffled through the gory stack on the exhibit table, "that the great toe overlaps the next. Have you seen that condition in others?"

"Yes."

"How many?" Howe demanded.

"I don't *know*," Newton snapped.

"Fifty?"

"I never kept count."

"Then forty-nine? Thirty?"

"Well, very likely."

And then there were, Howe mused, the other famed distinguishing characteristics of the body—five in all, including a mole and a small scar from a finger infection, or a "felon."

"Now it is claimed"—Howe lifted his fingers—"that on the first finger of the left hand there is a scar left by a felon. You have seen it?"

"Yes."

Howe considered this for a moment. "By the way," he said offhandedly, "have *you* ever had a felon?"

"Yes," the morgue keeper replied innocently.

"Show it to me," Howe commanded.

Newton held out his hand from the witness stand, and the towering defense counsel took it in a curiously courtly gesture.

"Now, isn't that strange!" Howe eyed the morgue keeper's hand and turned triumphantly to the jury. "*Your felon was on the same finger of the same hand!*"

There was a gasp in the courtroom, then incredulous laughter as spectators considered their own hands. Why, some of them also had those scars on their fingers!

"No doubt," Howe boomed delightedly, "there are thousands of cases *precisely* similar."

The district attorney jumped up quickly to stem the courtroom's laughter. "You have other bodies with such strange features as twisted toes, or moles in certain spots or scars in other spots, or possibly one of the five peculiarities you mention. But did you"—Youngs paused dramatically—"did you ever see a body *bearing all five marks?*"

"No," Newton said plainly.

"That's all." Youngs smirked at Howe.

"One moment!" Howe bellowed as Newton stood up. The morgue keeper sank back down dejectedly. The defense counsel leveled his gaze at the official, and took his most serious tone. "Do you remember the case of . . . Aimee Smith?"

Newton recoiled slightly, as if struck. "Yes," he said, and swallowed hard.

It was an infamous local scandal: Back in March, a young woman had been left to die of a sudden illness in a Third Avenue hotel, but the "Mr. Everett" who signed the hotel register as her husband was nowhere to be found. After days passed, "Mrs. Everett" proved to be the pretty young Hackensack Sunday-school teacher Aimee Smith— and "Mr. Everett" was identified by a porter as her married Sunday-school headmaster, Nelson Weeks. Fearing scandal, he'd fled the hotel and left her to become a Jane Doe in the Bellevue morgue.

"How often was *she* falsely identified?"

"Not at all." The morgue keeper bristled. "I identified her as soon as I saw her."

Bring back Isaac Newton tomorrow, Howe demanded as the court let out for the day. He wasn't finished with him just yet.

AS THE COURTHOUSE EMPTIED OUT, *Journal* pigeon posts fluttered past the windows—the first four pages of tonight's issue would be devoted to the case, shoving aside every other national and international story, including a Spanish overture to President McKinley, a nearly unanimous vote by the Georgia legislature to ban the "brutal" sport of football, and word that infamous outlaw "Dynamite Dick" had been gunned down by lawmen in the wilds of the Indian Territory. With tomorrow's witnesses slated to be a parade of doctors and professors, the capital circumstantial case was turning historic.

"Interest in the case is not wholly that of a passing sensation," a *Brooklyn Eagle* reporter admitted. "The legal aspects of it are scientific and important, and may be cited for precedents in many trials of the future."

Howe, sparkling at the defense table, was quick to assure everyone that it would also be a historic *victory*. "We will disprove nearly all of the prosecutor's testimony," he announced flatly.

It wasn't just bluster, either: A *Herald* reporter had good word that betting on Thorn now ran at roughly even odds. Sure, the evidence looked bad for him, but Howe had an impeccable reputation for beating the rap. Yet as they left the courtroom, there was another presence—up in the gallery—that was altogether more surprising.

Maria Barberi?

The ranks of reporters crowded around her. Barberi had been the first woman ever sentenced to die in the electric chair—and just a year ago, she'd been at the defense table herself, appealing a murder conviction. But she'd been freed by reason of insanity, since Maria slit her lover's throat with a straight razor in what her lawyer argued was a "psychic epileptic fit"—a curiously selective fit, it must be said. The case was so sensational that it had already been turned into a Broadway play. And now Barberi was a free woman, sitting in the gallery right beside the lawyer who had saved her from the chair: none other than Manny Friend, who was now representing Mrs. Nack.

In her round spectacles and a white floral hat tied under her chin with a wide bow, Maria looked for all the world like a schoolmistress. "I did not see the use of showing those awful pieces of cloth so many times," she complained to the *Evening Journal*. It made her feel especially sorry for Thorn. "Every time they were held up my heart thumped, and I know that his did."

Sitting in the courtroom with Barberi was cheap advertising for

Manny, and the message about Mrs. Nack's case was clear: *If I got Barberi off the hook, I can get Nack off, too.* William F. Howe was less impressed as he walked over and, towering over his fellow lawyer, sized up Manny Friend.

"What are you *doing* here, anyway?" he asked.

It was a good question—and when the answer came later that night, the case would be turned upside down.

18.

CAUGHT IN THE
HEADLIGHT

MANNY FRIEND SIMPLY HAD no time for drama that night.

He'd tried. Shadowed on the Long Island Rail Road by reporters, Mrs. Nack's lawyer was followed into the city and to the Harlem Opera House. As rain and wind whipped outside the theater, Mr. Friend and his pursuers strode down 125th Street, past Hurtig & Seamon's music hall, and then disappeared under a marquee reading THE FIRST BORN.

It was a melodrama set in Chinatown—a tragedy of honor and revenge—but as the houselights dimmed, Friend fretted about the real revenge tragedy that had just played out before him back at the jail. The reporters out in the ornate lobby were surprised to see Friend walking purposefully away, leaving before the show had even really started; his face was flushed, his movements nervous, his affect that of a man who simply couldn't stay still.

Is it true? they yelled as they ran after him. *Has she confessed?*

Friend stopped in the lobby, stunned; but on second thought, it shouldn't have been any surprise at all. Of course the jail staff couldn't keep their mouths shut.

"She has made a full confession," Friend stammered, looking deeply ill at ease. "I shall go home, disconnect my phone, and refuse to see any one or answer any questions. She has made a full confession. That's all I can say."

Within minutes on Newspaper Row, reporters from the *Times*, the *Herald*, the *Journal*, and the *World* were jumping onto streetcars to wake up everyone from Captain O'Brien to Sheriff Doht for reaction quotes. When reporters descended on William Howe's house on Boston Avenue, though, they found it darkened and quiet; he wasn't home.

But the *Herald* knew where to find him. Howe was still in his pajamas and nightcap when the *Herald* arrived at the lawyer's room in the Park Avenue Hotel. Howe had allies at the paper—including, it was said, a reporter secretly on his payroll—and they knew that during big cases he worked out of the Park Avenue. The luxury hotel off Thirty-Third was an immense cast-iron castle painted a blinding white and lit up at night—precisely where one would expect William F. Howe to hold court. The imperial-sized lawyer waved the reporters into his suite, then paused to draw out a metal flask from his luggage.

"Yes, I've heard the news," he sighed. "We got the message from Friend. I was in bed and asleep—dreaming of the ultimate acquittal of Thorn—when I was awakened by a boy pounding on the door. There is no doubt about it. Look at this." He passed a *Herald* reporter a note sent up by the hotel's phone operator: *Mrs. Nack has confessed and will be a witness for the state.*

Another knock came at the door—this time it was a *World* reporter, scarcely seconds behind his rivals. Stirred by his growing audience, Howe passed around the flask, lit a cigar, and soliloquized to the reporters.

"I had the *most perfect case* that was ever worked up for a jury. Only today I had Dr. Huebner, a medical expert, go to the Woodside cottage and take the measurements of that bathtub. The doctor found that the tub was only two-thirds as long as the body of the murdered man—*if* he was murdered. Had he been placed there, only an expert in anatomy could have cut up the body."

And there was his coup de grâce: Howe had quietly been serving, it just so happened, as counsel . . . *for Nelson Weeks.* The disgraced Sunday-school supervisor was up on a manslaughter charge, and Howe happened to know that morgue keeper Isaac Newton was a *friend* of Weeks's. The body in the Aimee Smith case had *not* been quickly identified by Newton; it was identified by two detectives based on a notebook in the body's possession. It was assumed to be stolen until they visited Smith's family, found the daughter absent, and matched the family's photos to the unclaimed body at Bellevue. So when the morgue keeper said that he immediately identified Aimee Smith— his fugitive friend's dead mistress—Howe knew the man was lying under oath. And if he could discredit Newton, then Howe could discredit *all* the physical evidence in the morgue keeper's possession, for he had cannily established during cross-examination that Newton was in direct charge of the Thorn case's body parts.

Tomorrow, at one swipe, he'd have knocked the legs right out from under the prosecution—*if only Manny Friend had been patient.*

"I cannot understand one thing." Howe shook his head, after a long pause. "And that is how a lawyer who has a client with so little against her could permit his client to make a confession."

"Were you surprised when you received the news?" a *Herald* reporter asked.

"I had a suspicion she might tell a pack of lies to save her own neck," Howe replied grimly.

There was a stir at the door, and in staggered Howe's assistant, Frank Moss, disheveled from a nighttime sprint to the hotel; he'd been bowling down on Seventeenth Street when he got the news. A glance at the reporters in the room told him everything.

"Well," Moss panted, "I suppose you have heard."

"Yes." Howe regarded his cigar thoughtfully. "What are we going to do?"

But it seemed a mere formality to even ask. Even as the sounds of the night ebbed away outside, the old lawyer was already working out his next move.

HOWE AND HIS TEAM arrived at the courthouse the next morning amid a mad rush for seats; the confession was all over the papers. The wire services had picked it up, so that Californians and even Londoners woke that morning to the news about Mrs. Nack. Spectators were pressing to get in, and when the doors were finally thrown open, the men in the crowd sprinted for the best seats, in the Right Gallery; fashionably attired women, slowed by their long skirts, took the Left Gallery. Reporters and artists gawked at these "specimens of womanhood"—many of them being, a reporter noted dryly, "young . . . and not ill-looking." Some had brought their opera glasses, and one beaming pair of beauties wore identical plaid frocks for the occasion. Their gallery bloomed with so many fancy hats that a *World* reporter dubbed it the Flower Garden.

Whispers flew around the women's gallery that a heartbroken Thorn had committed suicide overnight, but this romantic rumor was dashed when the young barber was led in. Only Martin Thorn, in all the courtroom, had not yet heard the news; as he sat down at the defense table, Howe wordlessly handed him the *World*, opened to that morning's front-page headline:

MRS. NACK HAS CONFESSED THE MURDER

Thorn went pale and stiffly passed the newspaper back.

"Augusta Nack," announced the court clerk.

A roar rose over the courtroom as the side door opened.

"Augusta Nack!" the clerk yelled over the commotion, and the star witness was guided through the packed room's maze of chairs and tables. Mrs. Nack swept by Thorn without a glance, smoothing her skirt as she sat down in the witness chair. She was clad in black— black dress, black lace, black straw hat, black ostrich feather—with sleek apple-green banding and silk gloves. Her appearance, the *Times* sniffed, was "cheap and tawdry"—and yet, it confessed, "strong and sensual."

"State your name," the prosecutor began.

"My name is Augusta Nack," she said in accented English, and verified that she was a German immigrant married to one Herman Nack.

"Were you living with Herman Nack in June?"

"No." Mrs. Nack flushed slightly.

"With whom?"

Thorn stared at her from the defense table, his gaze as fixed as hers was averted.

"With William Guldensuppe," she answered.

"When did you become acquainted with Martin Thorn?"

"I advertised a furnished room, and he came and took it in June 1896—I think until January of this year."

It had ended badly, of course; Guldensuppe had landed Thorn in the hospital for four days. Then, she said, Thorn began visiting when Guldensuppe was away at work.

"What passed between you and Thorn?"

A hint of a smile began to cross Martin Thorn's face, but Mrs. Nack continued looking away from him.

"He always told me to leave Guldensuppe and live with him. I refused."

"Why?"

"I told him from the first night I was a married woman," Mrs. Nack replied earnestly. There were titters in the courtroom, and she added, "He said, 'It is not so. I know your husband lives in Astoria.'"

The prosecutor quickly stepped in. "Now in March, what did Mr. Thorn say to you about Guldensuppe?"

"I told Thorn I couldn't live with him, and I gave him twenty dollars. A couple of days later he wanted more, but I said I could not give it to him. Then . . ." She paused, and her words echoed out over the horrified crowd. "He said—*I don't want money. I want Guldensuppe's head.*"

There was a commotion in the gallery; a transfixed spectator leaned so far past the railing that she nearly toppled over. The courtroom fell silent again as the prosecutor led Mrs. Nack's recollections forward.

"Wanted his head?"

"He wanted his head," Nack nodded. She was becoming animated; the ostrich feather atop her hat bobbed with each motion. "I got scared. Then he says he will kill Guldensuppe and put his body in a trunk and lock it, and I should send it express to where he is going to hire a room. I say—*I won't do it.*"

"Go on."

"I said, *Kill me.* He said, *That will give me no satisfaction.*"

Her face darkened as she kept it turned away from Thorn.

"He came one evening in my house, and said *Do you love me?* And

I said, I told you I can't love nobody, and he took me on my neck, here," she pointed at her throat. "He strangled me till I was half dead and the blood come out of my mouth."

By Nack's telling, her role was curiously passive: *She* had been the victim, too.

"I want to say that I always did what the man wanted me to because I was afraid," she added. "When the house was hired, Thorn told me that I should bring Guldensuppe over and he will kill him. I had to do everything that man told me."

"What did you say to William Guldensuppe?"

"I told Guldensuppe that he should come with me, I got the house where I am going to open a baby farm."

As if to protest this very notion, an infant briefly squalled from the women's gallery.

"A baby farm?"

"Well, he always told me I should do something," she shrugged.

At about nine on Friday morning, June 25, they took the Thirty-Fourth Street ferry and then a streetcar out to the cottage.

"I had the key, and I went inside and I was so excited I went out into the back yard," Mrs. Nack told the courtroom. There was not another sound in the room save for the furious *scritch scritch* of reporters' pencils. "Guldensuppe went upstairs, and when I was in the yard I heard a shot. After a while Thorn came out and called me. He said—*I shot Guldensuppe. He's dead.*"

She'd never hurt Guldensuppe, she explained, never even saw his body; she left for the afternoon, and when she returned, Thorn had wrapped him up in parcels.

"Was there anything bought for the purpose of wrapping up parcels?"

"I bought oilcloth."

"Look at that." The prosecutor held up a foul swatch of the red-and-gold cloth.

"Yes." Mrs. Nack nodded. "That is it."

They'd thrown the plaster-encased head off the ferry on the way back, and she disembarked with another package under her arm—Guldensuppe's clothes—and burnt them that night in her apartment's stove. The next day they hired the undertaker's carriage to dispose of the larger parcels.

"Now, state what happened on Saturday the twenty-sixth, when you went over there with the wagon."

"He had a bottle of ammonia," she explained, the better to clean the blood spots. "I cleaned the bathtub. There was some white stuff in it, I suppose."

"Don't *suppose*," Howe snapped from the defense table.

"It was the plaster of paris," Nack added apologetically. After dumping the parcels and meeting again Monday night, she said, they parted until their arraignment.

"Here is a photograph." The prosecutor held up a portrait. "Who does it represent?"

"William Guldensuppe," her voice trembled.

"Here is another photograph—do you recognize it?"

"Yes," Nack said quietly. "It is the cottage in Woodside."

The prosecutor paused thoughtfully, then leaned in. "Mrs. Nack," he asked softly. "Why do you make this confession?"

Her eyes began to well up.

"I make it to make my peace with the people." She began to sob and reached for her handkerchief. "And with God."

Augusta Nack burst into tears, and for a moment everyone in the courthouse was speechless—everyone, that is, but the counsel sitting by Martin Thorn.

"*God?*" Howe's incredulous voice rang out in disbelief.

THE DEFENSE COUNSEL drew himself up to his full height and towered before the witness box. Across William F. Howe's chest hung his favorite diamond pendant, a massive creation known among court reporters as "the Headlight"—and Mrs. Nack began blinking nervously, as if blinded by its rays. But then, Howe's sartorial splendor was always more than mere vanity: It was a warning, a proof of enemies bested before.

"Mrs. Nack," he said gravely. "You have told us that on June twenty-fifth, after Guldensuppe was killed, you took his clothes to your home. Is that true?"

"Yes."

"And the clothing was saturated with blood?" Howe asked.

"Y-yes."

"This was the day you say Guldensuppe was killed?"

"Yes."

"And you knew it?"

"Yes, I knew." Her voice grew quieter.

Howe lowered his own voice to a stage whisper. "Did you cry, Mrs. Nack? When you burned Guldensuppe's clothes?"

"No." She appeared confused. "I didn't."

"You cried today, didn't you?" Howe asked in mock surprise.

"I have often cried . . . ," she began.

"*Today!* In the court room!" Howe yelled. "Yes or no?"

"Yes?"

"You bought the oilcloth?" Howe continued briskly.

"Yes."

"And you bought it for purposes of wrapping his body in it, didn't you?"

"Yes." Augusta blinked nervously.

"Did you cry then?"

"No."

"Did you cry when you heard the shot that killed him?"

Mrs. Nack was catching on.

"Yes," she now replied.

Howe looked at her queerly, his face a mask of puzzlement. "You knew *perfectly well* that Guldensuppe was taken to Woodside to be killed, didn't you?"

"Yes," she stammered.

The lawyer mused on this, looking at the jury to share his confusion.

"Did you *love* Guldensuppe?" he finally asked.

"No," she insisted stoutly. "I didn't love anybody but my husband."

The silence was broken by a bitter laugh of disbelief—Thorn's. It was nearly his first utterance of the trial.

"You still loved your husband while you lived with Guldensuppe?"

"I stopped loving my husband then and began to love Guldensuppe," she stammered.

Howe smiled; he'd caught the witness in her first contradiction.

"You plotted to kill the man you loved?"

"No," she shot back. "I did not."

"But you paid the money for the rent?"

"Yes."

"And bought the oilcloth?"

"Yes," she snapped.

"And the house was rented for the purpose of killing Guldensuppe?"

"Yes." Mrs. Nack's eyes teared up again. "You must excuse me."

"No, *I won't*!" Howe roared, and leaned into the witness box as the crowd laughed nervously. "When did you begin to love *Thorn*?"

"I don't know."

"How long before the killing?"

"I never loved him until he choked me. Then I had to."

"He choked you into loving him?" Howe asked incredulously.

"Yes," she insisted. "I was afraid of him."

"How long did this frightful love continue?"

"Always." Nack reached quickly for an explanation. "Thorn told me if I didn't leave Guldensuppe, he'd buy some stuff and a syringe and squirt it into Guldensuppe's eyes and into my eyes—and that then we wouldn't be able to see each other. And that *then* I could have Guldensuppe."

Acid attacks were not unknown among jilted lovers, yet Howe looked puzzled.

"It was fear of this syringe," he intoned, "that made you buy oilcloth before this man was dead, and fear of this syringe after he was dead made you burn his clothes?"

"Yes," she insisted.

"Why, Mrs. Nack, did you go back to the house again?"

"Thorn told me so."

"Ah—fear of the syringe again?"

"Yes," she nodded earnestly.

The courthouse was stifling; more spectators had crept in past the guards, and they were now spilling out into the aisles and sitting on the steps.

"You prepared to go to Europe, didn't you?" he asked after a long pause.

"No," she said loudly. "I did not."

"Did you not intend to go to Europe?"

"I did not know what to do," she said blandly.

Howe smiled broadly, amiably.

"No, of course you did not know what to do. I know that. I understand that very well." Howe spun around and roared: *"Did you not intend to go to Europe?"*

"Well, er—yes."

"Were you going away or were you not?"

"No," she now said. She was reversing herself on one question after another, and Manny Friend watched helplessly as the rival lawyer enmeshed his client.

"What do you mean by saying that you *did not know what to do?*" Howe demanded.

"I did not want to remain," Nack said, struggling to explain her testimony. "I could not pay the rent."

"Didn't you have $300 in your corset when you were arrested?"

"Yes."

"Yet you couldn't pay your rent?"

"Well . . ." Mrs. Nack hesitated and decided to try a new story. "Thorn told me I should skip," she began brightly, and added piously, "I said no. Truth is truth and—"

"Mrs. Nack," Howe interrupted to guffaws, "we don't want any homilies on truth from *you.*"

The defense counsel paused to have his team search for an old copy of the *New York Journal,* then turned back to his witness. "Mrs. Nack, when you were before Judge Newberger in New York, did you say to Thorn, 'Hold your mouth, keep quiet'?"

"No," she insisted. Now it was the reporters' turn to look astonished: They had *heard* her. "Nothing of the sort."

An old copy of the *Journal* was passed forward, bearing the facsimile of her intercepted jailhouse letter to Thorn. Howe read the English translation out loud: *"Dear Martin—I send you a couple of potatoes. If you do not care to eat them, perhaps the others will. Dear child, send me a few lines how you feel . . ."*

He then passed the newspaper to her.

"That your writing?"

"Yes."

"You call him 'Dear child' and 'Dear Martin.' What do you mean by that?"

"I never loved him," she sputtered. "But I did . . . *show* him I loved him. Since he choked me."

"You only *pretended* to love him?" Howe gasped in understanding. "Make believe?"

"Yes."

"And that letter was only a *make-believe letter?*"

"Yes," she insisted as laughter bubbled from the courtroom.

"Did your fear continue while you were in jail?" Howe pressed.

"No."

"Then why did you write the letter?"

Nack kept her eyes averted from Thorn, even as he broke into a quiet grin.

"Because I thought he was hungry?" she ventured.

"Then it was for sweet charity's sake?" Howe swept his arms grandly.

"Yes," she eagerly agreed, to a new blast of laughter from the court. Howe beamed at the crowd, the gems glittering from his fingers.

"Now regarding the potatoes . . ." He turned back to his witness. *"—Is it not true that you shot Guldensuppe!"*

"No!" she cried, starting from her chair.

"Is it not true that you cut the body in pieces?"

"No!"

"Didn't *somebody,*" Howe thundered, "tell you to deny that you shot Guldensuppe and cut up his body?"

"No," Mrs. Nack laughed in disbelief.

"Don't *laugh*, Mrs. Nack," Howe shook his finger. "This is an awful matter."

But Mrs. Nack could not stop laughing; her testimony was falling apart, and she was becoming hysterical.

"Answer me!" he demanded.

"No!" she yelled.

Howe handed her photographs of her lover's mutilated body. *Not your handiwork, then?* But he wasn't finished—he'd also had a little talk with her ex-husband about her business as a midwife. Didn't she also help women . . . *avoid* birth?

"How many *children* did you kill?" he crowed.

"None," she shot back, then wavered. "So far as I know."

Didn't she have a chute in her old apartment for disposing of fetuses straight from the stove grate into the sewer? No? And hadn't she tried hiring Thorn to kill her husband?

"No," Mrs. Nack replied, her expression hardening. Howe narrowed his eyes back at her and tapped a table impressively.

"This is too important a case to mince matters, and I'm going to ask some direct questions. I want you to think before you answer. Mrs. Nack, don't you remember a place in New York in which you lived with Thorn for two entire weeks before the killing?"

"Lived with Thorn?" she stalled.

"You heard the question!" Howe bellowed. "Answer it."

"No, I did not."

"I call your attention now to a house on East Twenty-First Street. . . . Didn't you visit Thorn again and again at this place?"

"I did."

"Did you not remain in the house with Thorn at night several times?"

"No, I was there a couple of hours."

"Yes, when he wanted you to be as a wife to him."

"No, never," she stated primly. "I never was a wife to him. That was the reason I loved him. He was always a gentleman."

Howe exulted, buoyed by the rising tide of incredulity from the crowd. Now she loved Thorn, and called him a gentleman?

"Hasn't Thorn been as a husband to you?"

"No," she insisted.

But Howe had one question prepared for her like a dagger.

"Is this as true as any other answer you've given?"

"Yes," she declared.

The packed courtroom erupted into laughter and whoops; her testimony ended, a *Commercial Advertiser* reporter marveled, in "a scene of disorder in the court room which, in all probability, has seldom if ever been equaled in this state." DA Youngs and Manny Friend stared on miserably through the chaos as the judge gaveled the room to order; their star witness was pinned between lying to beat the rap and lying to stay respectable. Howe knew this, and he'd destroyed her on the stand with it.

Yet one man scarcely paid attention to Howe and Nack at all; he was collapsed in a far corner of the jury box, doubled over and in pain.

Magnus Larsen?

Judge Wilmot Smith quickly called a halt to the proceedings, and reporters and the crowd had a sudden shock of realization: In the middle of their murder trial, another man was dying before their very eyes.

19.

SCYTHE AND SAW

THE JURORS SPENT the night disconsolately gathered around the Garden City Hotel billiard table, not even bothering to pick up the cues, just aimlessly rolling the balls. They couldn't focus while Magnus Larsen was at death's door; he was doubled over with appendicitis by the time the train pulled up, and had to be carried to the hotel, where doctors decided to operate on the spot. Injected full of morphine, Larsen was now laid out on his bed upstairs in room 27, slipping miserably in and out of consciousness.

At the empty courthouse the next day, disappointed crowds scoured the floors for souvenirs, and locals pointed out the chairs in which Nack and Thorn had sat. When the trial reconvened two days later, the matter of life and death was not Thorn's but Magnus Larsen's. A scrum of reporters ran after Howe on the way in, cutting one another off with overlapping questions: *Will you—? Can you—? Have you—?*

"Yes, yes, yes—no, no, no," Howe joked from atop the courthouse steps, then marched inside. The artists were already after him, sketching his rose-and-scarlet scarf; fastened across his chest by a weighty gold cable shone a diamond-encircled moonstone pendant. It was the size of an egg, and carved with the figure of a young maiden.

"The gallery was nearly full of Long Island folks," one *Times* reporter smirked, "who, as this blazing, scintillating apparition flashed up, leaned forward and gasped and gazed."

Thorn soon followed him in, looking rather reinvigorated himself.

Howe jokingly shook a fist under his client's nose: *Bah, look at all the trouble you've caused this week!* The prosecutor and Judge Smith, though, had a more pressing concern to attend to: When, exactly, could their missing twelfth juror report back to the courthouse?

"Larsen had a very narrow escape," an attending physician explained. Upon opening the juror's abdominal cavity, they'd discovered that it was already filling with pus. "We found a perforation of the appendix. It is certain that he will be unable to leave his bed for three weeks, and I am not prepared to say that he will recover—though the indications are that he will."

Continuing without Larsen was mulled, but to Howe it was out of the question.

"No!" he said sharply. "Such a proceeding would be against all legal precedent." In the Cancini case of 1857, he noted, a man accused of killing a policeman had agreed under similar conditions to continuing on with a jury of eleven. After he was sentenced to the gallows, though, his conviction was thrown out: Even Cancini himself hadn't the right to waive his guarantee under the state constitution to trial by a jury of twelve peers.

"The judge would censure me if I consented to any such arrangement and I would deserve to be censured," Howe added stiffly. "The court would very properly ask me if I had ever read the law." Restarting the trial from the beginning, but with the eleven remaining jurors and one newly selected one, was a slightly less shaky idea—but only slightly.

Prepare for a brand-new trial, Judge Smith decided, in ten days' time, on Monday, November 22. *Journal* reporters dashed for their telephones and their pigeons; and on his way out of the courthouse, Howe suddenly cut in as Manny Friend chatted with a cluster of men from the *World* and the *Times*.

"*You!* You insignificant little imp!" Howe roared at Mrs. Nack's counsel on the courthouse stairs. "You *insect*! I ought not to notice you! You are not worthy of being considered a respectable rival of Howe & Hummel!"

It was more, perhaps, than just his usual grandstanding. The master of legal escapes, William F. Howe knew there was one final rap that he couldn't beat—and that at seventy-one, his career was already longer than his famed appetites augured. Falling quiet as he walked away, he turned suddenly to a *Times* reporter.

"This," Howe said plainly, "is the case of my life."

HOWE ARRIVED at his office on Centre Street to cheers and congratulations from his staff, with a coterie of reporters following as he settled back into his lair. The usual huddle of gangsters and madams awaited appointments, but Thorn was still on Howe's mind. The lawyer had instantly—without the least discomfort—abandoned his theory about Guldensuppe being alive and was now instead pouring all his effort into pinning the murder on Mrs. Nack. The black-clad femme fatale, Howe added, was "a damnable spider" sinking her fangs into the love-struck Martin Thorn.

"From my first interview I found him *saturated* with chivalry," he rhapsodized, "ready, if necessary, to yield his life to this Delilah who has placed him in this present position."

Yes, Thorn was chivalrous—"too chivalrous for his own good," the lawyer lamented. For William F. Howe himself was the city's great defender of virtue; he and Abe Hummel ran a million-dollar operation in breach-of-promise cases, where comely showgirls settled with wealthy men who'd wooed them without intent of marriage. A private communication from Howe & Hummel was all that was needed for the firm and the showgirl to evenly split five or ten thousand in hush money. It was extraordinarily lucrative, and extraordinarily *moral*, and just about the only man it hadn't worked on was the actor John Barrymore, because he didn't give a damn about his reputation. But Martin Thorn was no Broadway rake, Howe insisted. The humble immigrant barber was the victim of "this modern Borgia" and her venomous lawyer.

"She is the biggest liar unhung," Howe snapped. "And I want to say, for publication, that the conduct of Mr. Friend is the dirtiest piece of unprofessional work I have heard of in all my experience."

All that dirt would stick to her, Howe promised—for his firm had dug up plenty more. They now had the names, he declared, of the two women she'd killed with botched abortions—and he'd have Herman Nack himself on the witness stand to back it all up.

"Mrs. Nack admitted that she herself had cremated Guldensuppe's clothes—she must have been skilled at the art of cremation," Howe mused aloud. "Apropos of all this cremating, it is just possible—mind you, I say possible—that Guldensuppe's head was cremated instead of having been dropped overboard."

And if that wasn't damning enough, sitting in Howe's office was a brand-new witness: a stern, bespectacled Bronx landlady named Ida Ziegler. A full three months before Mrs. Nack claimed the plot had begun, Ziegler had received a curious response to her home-rental ad for 1671 Eastburn Avenue.

"On one Sunday," she began, "I believe it was prior to the fifteenth of March, a woman in the company of a man called upon me and wanted to see the room that I was advertising. The gentleman, after examining the rooms, said they were all very comfortable, and suited him just fine; but to the lady they were not at all suitable." Mrs. Ziegler, a little wounded, enumerated all the alleged faults of her lovely home. "Because there was not any *sewer conduit* leading from the house; the neighborhood was *too lively*; the house was *somewhat conspicuous*; because the bathtub was *too small*, although an average man could bathe himself with ease. She also became displeased with the rooms upon learning that I was not in the habit of going out during the day."

The prospective tenant, the landlady recalled, also had a very peculiar question. "We had a garden in the back of the house. She asked me whether I would *strike water* if I were to dig three feet down."

The woman, she said, was a midwife who had given her name as Mrs. Braun. Ziegler was shown a photograph of Augusta Nack. *That's her*, she said.

THORN READ THE NEWSPAPERS that Howe sent him, played pinochle, and tried to lose himself in a volume of Emerson's essays left in the jail. He was not feeling very high-minded, though: For days the accused barber had been left unshaven, much to his professional disgust. When his jailers finally deigned to break out his shaving cup, the undersheriff and a barber showed up at Thorn's cell with manacles.

"What are you going to do with those things?" the prisoner asked.

"Just put them on, that's all," the undersheriff replied.

"I never put handcuffs on a customer when I shaved him," Thorn shot back.

"Look here, Martin," his jailer said, pulling Thorn's arms behind the chair back and slapping the cuffs shut, "we are going to run no chances."

Thorn fumed as he was shaved—they kept missing the stubble over his lip. It only took a look in the mirror after he was unshackled to see why. DA Youngs had directed the jail to bring back Thorn's mustache for the trial—to grow it in, inexorably, against his will—so that soon he would look precisely like the man their witnesses had seen entering the Woodside cottage.

And yet his days were not without some strange rewards. As Thorn sulked over his treatment at the jail, a Howe associate led a short impresario and a willowy actress through the heavy clanging door to the Flats, up to the bars of Martin's cell. Florenz Ziegfeld, Broadway's showgirl master, was not particularly used to visiting jails. But even stranger was the presence of his star talent and personal mistress, newly acquired from the Folies of Paris—Miss Anna Held, whose famed dark eyes stared out from promotional posters all over town.

Thorn greeted Howe's assistant warmly, while eyeing the actress with caution. He'd seen her soak up publicity by sitting in on some of the trial, but she was strangely out of place here on Murderers Row. Still, the sympathy of a famous starlet was not a bad thing for an accused man to have, especially with *World* reporters watching nearby.

What do you think of Mrs. Nack's confession? she asked breathlessly.

"She lies!" He shrugged. "All lies."

Anna watched as Martin Thorn sat in his cell, nuzzling the stray dog he'd adopted; a brindle-and-black bulldog-pug mix, it had recently wandered into the jail and unaccountably attached itself to him, refusing to leaving his side. Thorn cheekily dubbed it "Bill Baker," after the jailer who'd shackled him. The mutt, he mused aloud, was his only real friend anymore—since Mrs. Nack certainly wasn't.

"Would you have died for her?" the actress asked.

"Yes, I would," he replied evenly. "But she has killed my faith in all women. She killed Guldensuppe herself. I have loved that woman, and she has ruined me."

Miss Anna Held leaned dramatically against the cell door; she felt so dreadfully sorry for him. *New York World* artists frantically sketched her mooning through the cold bars of the prison cell.

"Were you . . . happy with her?" She lowered her voice.

"Yes," he paused. "I was, once."

The *World* artist tore off his sheet; it was a minor publicity coup for Howe and a fine morning front-pager, with the glamorous starlet providing an appropriately dramatic quote to accompany it: "Thorn is a man of impulse, a man of passionate temper," she explained to readers, "and such men are but easy prey in the hands of women they love." It was good copy, and—taking a page from the *Journal*'s favorite strategy for humiliating them—*World* editors even put together an accompanying montage of competitor's pages, to show how the *World* had been the first to discover that Mrs. Nack was about to make her treacherous confession on the stand.

But the *World* had already blown the scoop.

Blurted out in Thorn's conversation with Held were four startling words about Mrs. Nack—"*She killed Guldensuppe herself*"—his first public acknowledgment that there *was* a murder, and that it was of Guldensuppe. Not one of Pulitzer's editors recognized its importance, but Hearst's men did. As the *World* fussed over its showgirl-in-prison illustrations for the next morning, the *Evening Journal* trumped them with a late-edition headline: THORN CONFESSES HIS PART IN THE MURDER.

The *World* just couldn't get it quite right. It still managed innovations, such as running women's fashion plates with actual photographed faces superimposed on the pen-and-ink dress drawings; the result looked comical, but reproducing an entire photo in the newspaper was quite difficult. Still, it hinted at the future. Soon all nineteenth-century news would be distinguishable from that of the looming twentieth century at a glance: The old was monochromatic and engraved, the new, color and photographic. And while Hearst hadn't sprung his attack with photography yet, he was busy opening up a widening lead on color printing. Pulitzer anxiously telegraphed from Maine about the headlines he was seeing in Hearst's paper: not about Nack and Thorn, but about the *Journal* itself—or, as he called it in a coded cablegram, "Geranium":

I AM EXTREMELY INTERESTED TO KNOW WHETHER THAT STORY ABOUT GERANIUM ORDERING TWO MORE COLOR SEXTUPLES IS TRUE—ABSOLUTELY TRUE.

It was. Hearst had ordered up more color presses, and his *Evening Journal* was punishing other competitors so badly that for one precarious night, until it got its finances in order, the *Evening Telegram* ceased publication altogether. The *New York Times,* itself barely recovered from bankruptcy, was trying to beat back at the tide of yellow journalism by running a pointed new motto on its front page: "All the News That's Fit to Print." But other papers were inexorably drifting with Hearst's powerful current. On the same day that the *Evening Journal* boasted such edifying stories as COCAINE PHANTOMS HAUNT HIM and HYPNOTISM NEARLY KILLS, one could also find all these headlines on a single page of the more respectable *New York Herald*:

ABSINTHE HIS BANE

ITALIAN FATALLY STABBED

INQUIRY ABOUT POISON GAS

FEROCIOUS DOG MANGLES A BOY

SINGER ENDS LIFE

THEY TRIED TO DIE TOGETHER

New York papers now ran far more column inches on crime and accidents than other cities did, and the *Journal* ran so much "bleed" copy in combination with women's-interest stories and comics that business, labor, and religion were nearly crowded out altogether.

Hearst knew his readers, and he knew what they liked.

"The two stories of Nack and Thorn have reached an equilibrium of contradiction," he announced to readers in a column. The real question, his paper now asked, was *Which one's more guilty?* They tallied some 1,147 letters from readers: 713 found Augusta Nack the guiltier party, 329 blamed both equally, and just 105 laid the blame on Thorn.

"He is no more guilty of the murder of Guldensuppe than a babe," a hypnotist wrote in. "Mrs. Nack forced him to do it by the power she exerted over him." Another reader begged to differ, offering up the novel theory that Thorn *and* Guldensuppe were the real conspirators: "It was a plot of Guldensuppe and Thorn to convict Mrs. Nack of murder," he wrote. "Guldensuppe got out of the way, and Thorn cut up a body that he palmed off on Mrs. Nack as Guldensuppe's." Nine-year-old Helen Weiss of Princeton, on the other hand, was ready to wholeheartedly condemn Nack and Thorn alike: "I think they are both guilty."

But an even more telling sign was tucked away in the latest ad for the Eden Musée waxworks, where the scene of Thorn cutting up Guldensuppe was no longer the main attraction. It had been replaced by a slightly different pair of deadly combatants: *Augusta Nack and Martin Thorn.*

ON SUNDAY MORNING BEFORE DAWN, newsboys hauled off fat bundles of the *Journal*. They were going to be sure sellers. The paper had produced an alarming scenario headlined THE INVASION OF NEW YORK, complete with "a thrilling description by an expert of what would happen with the Spanish Fleet in New York Harbor." But even that took a backseat to what they'd used to headline the entire front page: THE STORY OF MY LIFE—BY AUGUSTA NACK. Along with a sober-looking portrait of Mrs. Nack taking pen to paper in her prison cell, Hearst's front page was given over to her melancholy and remorseful account of life before she became New York's most notorious woman, back when she was still young Augusta Pusat. "I was born in the little village of Oskarweischen, in Posen, Germany," she wrote, remembering the poverty of her family there. "When I was a girl I used to tend the geese and drive them down to the water in the morning. . . . In Germany idleness is considered not the right thing for either girls or women, and when I was tending my geese and looking after the kettles to make sure that they did not boil over, I made my lace."

After moving to the United States, she was soon earning more money than the rest of her family in the old country—"I had everything—and they had nothing," she marveled—but after she begged her mother to save the family's prayers for their own needs, she received a stern response. *"My daughter,"* the elder Mrs. Pusat wrote back, *"you don't know. Everything you have may be taken from you in a twinkling of an eye."*

Mrs. Nack often thought upon that letter.

Her confession in the case, she told *Journal* readers, was inspired by the visits of the Reverend Robert Miles to her cell. At first she'd spurned him and his Bible, but then one day the minister had brought his four-year-old son, little Parker Miles, and as he prattled on and jumped up into her lap, asking her to tell him a story, her steely re-serve cracked. She broke down in sobs and confessed to the loving God of Reverend Miles. The *Journal* had a fine portrait of the cler-gyman too, and of his angelic son on Mrs. Nack's lap; it was a heart-warming story for a Sunday paper, and it would fly off the stands.

But one person wasn't buying her story yet: the DA.

As the newsboys fanned out into the still-darkened streets of the city, Augusta Nack was quietly let out of her cell and joined the dis-trict attorney, Detective Sullivan, and Captain Methven in a waiting carriage outside the Queens County Jail. It was a private hire, with the passenger veiled so that nobody on the street could spot her. She arranged a shawl around herself in the bitter predawn air, and they headed up Jackson Avenue.

"Can you point out the place?" Youngs asked her again.

"Yes," she promised.

"If you do," he said significantly, *"then* we shall be prepared to believe what you say."

Youngs eyed her carefully as they made their way along the muddy avenue. His star witness had already been terribly undermined on the stand—it wasn't for nothing that William Howe was considered the best trial lawyer in the city. Youngs still hadn't offered her a plea deal, and before he did, he wanted more from Mrs. Nack, some solid evidence that Howe wouldn't be able to bully and balderdash his way out of.

Woodside, announced their driver.

The trio of lawmen stepped out of the carriage, and as the sun rose they watched Mrs. Nack wander aimlessly in the garden of the Woodside cottage—hesitating here, stopping there. She hadn't been back in five months, since just after the murder, and the gardens that had been lush in that dangerous time were now barren and frosted.

Well? Youngs demanded.

She couldn't remember . . . but . . . perhaps she *could* remember. Yes, what they were looking for was surely in an entirely different place.

Youngs snorted in disgust and sat heavily back in the carriage. He kept a peeved silence as they made their way through Flushing toward College Point, past a series of scrubby, empty lots.

"That's the place!" yelled Mrs. Nack.

The carriage stopped by a crumbling stone wall on a vacant lot; it was an African American neighborhood, and the party's presence was becoming uncomfortably conspicuous to passersby. The veiled prisoner pottered in the weeds a bit—Was it here? Perhaps it was there?—until the DA finally lost all patience. The carriage promptly left with a jolt, hauling the humiliated prisoner back to Queens County Jail.

"Did you find the saw?" Detective Sullivan was asked as he returned from the jaunt.

"No," he snapped. "We didn't."

The rest of Augusta Nack's story wasn't holding up much better. Within hours after she and Manny Friend paraded her newfound piety to the papers, a familiar figure turned up at the *World*'s editorial offices: Herman Nack. The bakery driver was upset—deeply upset. He'd already lost his job at the Astoria Model Bakery from the bad publicity, couldn't sleep at night from the worry it had caused. He appeared, one reporter remarked, like nothing so much as a sleepwalker.

"I can only think of her," he sighed.

With the *Journal* getting Augusta's childhood, the *World* ventured into Herman's.

"Where did you first meet Mrs. Nack?" the paper asked.

"In Kiel, in Germany. She was a servant girl then. The family she worked for was a very fine family. I was working in a pottery. I loved her, and that's all." He paused, then admitted thoughtfully: "By and by Guldensuppe, he loved her. He was not a bad man either. I always liked him, but he loved her—that was the matter with him."

"What do you think of the strange course the trial has taken?"

"What do I think about it?" he mused, and fell silent. "I think so much that I do not know what to think. It is with me think, think, all the time. Maybe she killed that fellow, maybe Thorn did. I do not know. If she did, I hope they will"—he stumbled over the language, and then over the emotion—"how do you call it? Put her in the chair of electricity."

He was growing animated. There was something else, he said, that had truly made him upset: her confession.

"I am sure of one thing: it was not from religion or fear of God that she tells about the death of Guldensuppe. She was *not* religious. She was *not* good. Sometimes she used to go with one of her customers to church—but when she comes home she laughs at such things." Herman Nack's expression was becoming anguished. "I want to tell you, sir, that woman will not go to heaven. She is bad—*she is bad*."

And a bad liar as well, by the look of it. The newspapers gloated after word of her failed carriage trip leaked out. But two days later, as laborers worked with scythes to clear a salt-hay field in College Point, a call came in to the DA's office. Just by the spot Mrs. Nack had pointed out, they'd discovered a rusting eighteen-inch surgeon's saw—a Richardson & Sons model for slicing through bone. It was found jammed blade first into the ground, as if someone had tried to murder the dirt itself.

20

A WONDERFUL MURDER

MALWINE BRANDEL CLUTCHED a bouquet of red roses. Barely eighteen years old, with lustrous blond hair and blue eyes highlighted by her most stylish high-collared velvet jacket, she was begging Sheriff Doht to let her inside to that morning's retrial. *I want to give these to Martin Thorn*, she pleaded.

The sheriff regarded her with sheer disbelief. "No, I can't do that," he finally managed. "As long as I am in charge of these proceedings, Thorn will never receive any flowers in the courthouse."

But I must, she begged. Mrs. Brandel had recently lost her husband, and already had her heart stolen by the newspaper pictures of Thorn.

"Thorn is a fearfully *interesting* fellow," she said breathlessly. "I cannot believe him guilty of such a fiendish crime. The more I look at him and his honest eyes, the more I like him."

The sheriff shook his head.

"Don't you know," he mocked gently, "that you are subject to imprisonment if you send flowers to Thorn? He might *poison* himself with them."

"Then I'll give them to Mr. Howe," she insisted. "He'll give them to Thorn."

Sheriff Doht held out his hand; if she was going inside, she'd have to give up the roses. The heartsick young widow reluctantly parted with the bouquet, and he tossed it aside as she pressed past.

"I wish women with these sort of ideas would stay in New York," he muttered.

But they wouldn't. The ferries and streetcars coming over from Manhattan that morning were crowded with wave after wave of spectators. Women poured into the galleries, chatting and carrying the de rigueur accessory of the trial—opera glasses. "I came here out of curiosity—woman's curiosity, if you want to call it that," one devotee explained. Her name was Tessie, and she'd come up from Greenpoint early that morning to get the best front-row gallery seat. "I think that every woman that has heard of this case is interested in it."

"It is a woman's case, a story of a woman's troubles," another agreed.

"It's a wonderful murder," Tessie enthused. "Oh, but Mrs. Nack is an awful creature."

"I came here just to see Mrs. Nack," a neighbor chimed in.

"So did I," another offered. "I'd have given my last $5 and gone without breakfast to see that woman."

But on this day Mrs. Nack was nowhere to be seen; there were only platoons of journalists, newly installed justice Samuel Maddox on the bench—the last judge having excused himself on account of malaria—and, at the center of it all, the famed defense table. Howe was dressed in his usual splendiferous manner, and Thorn presented a fine sight, with his mustache now grown to full luxuriousness. One woman in the gallery admitted that she'd actually *sung* to him.

"I go to the Tombs to sing to the prisoners," she explained. "It was there that I became interested in Thorn and Mrs. Nack. I go to nearly *all* of the big trials."

And this one promised to be the biggest yet. A swift jury selection—LOOK MORE INTELLIGENT THAN THE FORMER LOT, ran one headline—drew together a group made up of two farmers, a florist, a property agent, an oyster dealer, and fully seven builders, for the November frost had left construction crews free to fill the jury box.

After quickly recalling the children and police witnesses of the first trial, they soon came to the first of the new witnesses: Mrs. Clara Nunnheimer, a Woodside neighbor. A fresh-faced and beaming young woman, she seemed to brighten the gaslit room as she took the stand.

"Do you recall the 25th of June?" the prosecutor asked her.

"Yes, sir." She nodded cheerily. Fridays, she explained, were her day for chopping wood. At around eleven she'd seen Mrs. Nack and a man in a light suit step out of a trolley car, then go inside the house next door. She never saw him come back out—but she did soon see a different man in an upstairs window—one in blue shirtsleeves.

"The fellow between the two officers there?" the prosecutor asked, pointing at a poker-faced Martin Thorn.

"Yes, sir."

Howe wasn't having any of it. "From where you were standing chopping wood in your back yard, you could see the features of a man who got off the trolley car?"

Mrs. Nunnheimer broke into a dazzling smile.

"Well," the Woodside neighbor explained, "I *watched* them."

The courtroom broke into laughter, and no amount of interrogation by Howe could dim the woman's sunny disposition. Nor could he rattle a thirteen-year-old girl who'd seen Thorn buying plaster at the local shop, the undertaker who'd rented out the carriage, or the neighbor who explained that he lived "kind of diagonally across from Mr. Buala's property."

"Are you the man who owned the ducks?" Howe asked dubiously.

"Yes, sir," Henry Wahle nodded from the stand.

"That ditch was a little slimy—that which you call blood, you say you saw it on top of the slime?"

"I suppose if I had a quart can I could have filled it up," Wahle said.

Howe looked triumphantly out at the crowd. "How can you say that the drainpipe from *that* cottage drained into *that* ditch?"

"Because," the witness said, instantly deflating him, "I was there when the plumbing was put in."

But Wahle wasn't the only one privy to a hidden clue. And as the women in the galleries focused their opera glasses on the stand, the truth of how the case was cracked—one that no newspaper had dared to reveal—now came to light.

THE DA HAD the same question for each of the victim's colleagues: "Did you ever see William Guldensuppe naked?" he demanded.

"I have," masseur Philip Krantz answered warily.

"Frequently?"

"Yes, sir." They'd worked in the Murray Hill Baths, after all.

"Did you notice any particular distinguishing marks upon the body of William Guldensuppe during his lifetime?"

Why, yes, Krantz replied—a tattoo of a girl on his chest, a mole on his right arm . . .

"Any *other* mark?" Youngs pressed.

"The scar on the left finger?" the coworker ventured.

"Anything *else*?"

Philip Krantz shifted uncomfortably in his chair.

"There was his . . . " And then he mumbled something.

"What?" Youngs called out.

Krantz mumbled again and looked down.

"Speak so the jury can hear," Youngs demanded, as courtroom spectators leaned forward.

"*His penis,*" Krantz said.

Guldensuppe, it seemed, was a memorable fellow.

"He had very *peculiar* privates," another coworker, Herman Specht, struggled to explain.

"This peculiarity of the penis," the DA went on, turning to the crowd and then back to the masseur, "was that so noticeable as to attract the attention of the other bath rubbers?"

"Yes," Specht admitted. "*Many* times."

"What can you say"—here Youngs drew out one of the morgue photographs—"as to the penis of Exhibit Number Five?"

That's the one, he replied.

"The most peculiar thing *was* his penis," a third coworker reminisced. "Like where he was circumcised on the head of the penis, underneath from the head he had a lump of skin hanging. Which he could *stretch.*"

Ladies in the gallery gasped, but the masseur had only just started.

"I saw him stretch it at least *two and a half inches,*" he added brightly.

All this was just too much for the defense attorney's dignity.

"Yes, a circumcision," Howe scoffed dismissively, and tried steering the testimony back to the mole and the tattoo.

"Mr. Howe dropped the subject of the penis very quickly," the district attorney jeered. But he wasn't about to let go so easily. As

Coroner Tuthill took the stand and held forth on the mole—"a warty growth under the right arm, just at the lower border of the axilla"— the prosecutor cut in impatiently.

"Did you notice the penis?" he demanded.

"Yes," the coroner sighed. "I am coming to that. A *very* peculiar penis. The peculiarity consisted in the fact that the upper portion of the foreskin was absolutely denuded down to the body of the organ, leaving no foreskin on top, but a long pendulous foreskin beneath it." He produced a drawing that he'd made and held it out. "I have a piece of paper here to illustrate that with—"

"I object!" bellowed Howe.

The galleries burst out into laughter, and Judge Maddox gaveled the crowd to order; he'd expel them *all* from the courthouse if he had to. Put the penis schematic away, he told the coroner.

"*Describe* it," the judge said wearily.

"The under portion of the foreskin," Tuthill replied, a little hurt, "extended down very long, an inch and three-quarters in length."

"Now, what was done with this body after your examination?"

"It was placed in formalin to preserve it," Tuthill said, indicating a container on the exhibit table. It was a small one-quart fruit jar, sealed with red wax; inside an alcohol solution suspended, one *Times* reporter recounted, "something looking much like small sections of tripe."

"Has that changed its appearance?"

"Very much so." Tuthill nodded. "The action of formalin is to harden and practically tan the skin. The penis has practically shrunken up and is as hard as a bone now."

Reporters were almost snapping their pencils. They couldn't print *this*. What the courtroom ladies now knew—and what the rest of the world would not hear a word of—was that back in July, the papers fibbed about how Murray Hill Baths employees so conclusively iden- tified Guldensuppe. The papers claimed, rather metaphorically, that it was by his peculiar finger. But bathhouse attendants and morgue staff alike, when asked, agreed that of the thousands of naked men they'd seen, this one was *special*.

The judge wisely called a recess.

—————

"CHURCH—OR GOLF?" demanded the jury foreman over breakfast the next morning. They'd all been sequestered from their families for the Thanksgiving holiday in the Garden City Hotel; when Judge Maddox had broken the news back at the courthouse, the crowd visibly pitied the twelve crestfallen men.

But perhaps Thanksgiving at the hotel wouldn't be so bad: the Garden City had been designed by Stanford White, and it was the most luxurious hotel for miles around. They came downstairs that morning to find preparations already being made for an impressive spread of turkey and roast duck. One juror promptly hit the breakfast table and stuffed buckwheat pancakes into his pockets.

"I wish there were *more* murders in this county," another cracked between mouthfuls.

But, alas, they were already a hung jury. *Church*, a stout minority of five argued. *Golf*, responded the other seven, noting that as they were sequestered, and many sermons of late referred to the Thorn case, it was their civic duty to stay far from baleful public influences. Such isolation could only be guaranteed by standing in the middle of an open field . . . with a caddy.

It was fortunate that the men were nowhere near the jail that day, for the inquisitive public had turned out in battalions. Just as when children flooded Woodside on Independence Day, the enforced idleness of Thanksgiving seemed to bring out the amateur detective in New Yorkers. Hundreds milled about, hoping to gain an audience with Nack or Thorn, only to have Sheriff Doht turn them away.

For Thorn, the day inside at first passed much like any other, with a marathon session of pinochle, albeit with the happy interruption of turkey and potatoes. His faithful dog, Bill Baker, fared well, and the jailers presented Thorn with a precious commodity indeed: a Havana cigar. As Thorn watched the smoke curl away through the bars of his cell, only a *Journal* correspondent managed to dampen his holiday spirits. What, the reporter asked, did he think of Adolph Luetgert's comments on the trial?

Luetgert? Thorn had avidly followed the Chicago sausage maker's retrial—it had begun the same day as his own, even—but he didn't know Luetgert had been following *his* retrial as well.

A newspaper was handed to the prisoner with a headline blaring across the front page: LUETGERT PREDICTS THORN'S CONVICTION. "I believe the jury will convict them both," the accused acid-vat killer told the press. "Nothing, I believe, can save them, unless the state has made an agreement with Mrs. Nack to let her off with imprisonment."

"Luetgert is guilty, *I* think, and ought to be hanged," Thorn snapped back. But the comment aggravated him. Picking up the *Evening Journal* later that day didn't help. After a day of reading religious books, his co-conspirator had issued a statement that a suspicious mind might read all sorts of deal making and betrayal into.

"I can say," Mrs. Nack announced to the press, "that I really knew what Thanksgiving is today."

BY FRIDAY the crowds had turned ruthless.

"Show your passes!" the courthouse deputies barked. Forged tickets had been showing up among those trying to get in. Bickering women seized seats in the courthouse galleries, refusing to go even when caught with bad and expired papers. "Out!" one guard yelled across a row, while another collared a spectator—"*He means you!*"

"It's a disgrace to have women in attendance," the DA complained bitterly from the courthouse floor, appalled that he'd had to present testimonies about Guldensuppe's foreskin in front of so many women.

Hearst, though, was unrepentant: "To show crime in its vulgarest and most revolting aspects," he announced piously to his readers, "is to perform a service."

Reporters eagerly telegraphed across the river what lurid details they could: BRAZEN WOMEN AND BAD AIR, one headline announced. For the courthouse was indeed suffocating again; the malodorous atmosphere, a *New York Press* reporter complained, was now "more offensive than ever, if possible." The district attorney himself was demanding an investigation into the courthouse's ventilation, and more than a few suspected that the first judge's malaria attack had been brought on by the evil-smelling miasma.

And yet the crowd pressed forward into the seats, nearly bowling one another over the railings, arguing and gossiping in equal
measure—then breaking into a low murmur as the suspects were led
in. Nearly lost in the commotion was the strangely familiar face of a
rather dapper gentleman; the guards almost hadn't even let him in
until he produced a subpoena from his soft camel-hair overcoat.

Herman Nack?

The subpoena was courtesy of Mr. Howe—and so, the press pool
surmised, was Herman's new wardrobe. Before calling in the delivery driver as a battering ram against Mrs. Nack, the lawyer had first
bought him a good shave and a fitting at his tailor. And so here it
was, then: Herman, Gussie, and Martin glowering at each other from
across the courtroom floor, along with some remnants of Willie floating in an old alcohol-filled fruit jar. The four principals of the tragedy
were together in one room at last.

The bakery driver remained bewildered by it all.

"Just a crazy barber," Herman muttered to a reporter as he sized
up Thorn. He peered over at his wife, whom he'd last seen the morning they were both arrested. "She looks pale," he said with a hint of
concern, before quickly adding, "I don't know whether to feel sorry
for her or not. She is nothing to me now."

With everyone finally seated, the testimony proceeded through a
cross section of New York life: the newsboy who recognized Thorn at
the ferry; the saloon keeper who saw Gotha and Thorn together; a pinochle player who spotted a pistol in Thorn's vest. Detective Sullivan
identified the bullets from Woodside's walls, and an NYPD pistol instructor noted that their caliber matched Thorn's blue nickel-plated
.32. Detective O'Donnell, the former plumber, identified a vial of the
foul-smelling plaster he'd found in the Woodside sink trap. Thorn
watched with mild interest, occasionally narrowing his eyes at Mrs.
Nack; she refused to return his glances. But the man they all awaited
was John Gotha.

As the tall and jittery witness was led in, Thorn smiled at the sight
of his old friend. Gotha, though, locked his eyes on the floor. Thorn's
informant looked puffy and tired, like a man who had been gaining
weight but losing sleep.

"State your name."

"John Gotha."

The prosecutor walked him through Thorn's affair with Nack and the fight with Guldensuppe. Thorn listened with a faintly indulgent smile, as if his hapless friend was confused yet again. But Gotha's recollection of Thorn's confession sounded all too precise.

"I asked him if he done the murder, and first he denied it," Gotha recounted steadily. "And then he said yes, he did it. Told me how he went into the house about half past nine, and while he was waiting for Mrs. Nack and Guldensuppe he took out his pistol and tried it out. He said it didn't work at first. He snapped it several times before it discharged, and fired it off a couple times to make sure it was all right."

It made sense now. Thorn's first brawl with Guldensuppe was lost by a misfire; these test shots explained why two bullets were found buried in the plaster lath of the Woodside cottage.

Gotha made sense to Howe, too—but not quite in the same way.

"Were you not," the lawyer demanded, rising up, "a confirmed inebriate?"

"No, sir," Gotha replied indignantly.

"Were you not taken to the Inebriates' Home at Fort Hamilton?"

"No," the barber insisted.

Howe eyed his prey for a long moment, his gold-fretted scarf glimmering under the gaslights.

"How much *money*," he rang his words out slowly, "had you in your pocket at the time of the arrest of Thorn?"

"Well," Gotha said, shifting uncomfortably. "I didn't have much money."

"How—much—*money?*"

"About twenty dollars," Gotha admitted.

"Where have you been since Thorn's arrest?" Howe pressed.

"Been up in the country."

"Paid your board there?"

"I did."

"With what money?"

"My wife's money."

"Do you know the *police* paid your board there? Yes or no?"

Gotha looked over at the prosecutor helplessly, then back at Howe.

"Yes," he said in a small voice.

Howe directed the crowd's attention to Gotha's next residence, on West 122nd.

"Who paid for *that*?" he demanded.

"I paid for that," Gotha insisted.

"Where did you get the money? From Mr. Sullivan?"

"Yes, sir."

"The district-attorney's officer, is he not?"

"Yes, sir," Gotha mumbled.

"Yes or no!" Howe bellowed.

Gotha was perspiring freely now.

"Yes."

"How much did Sullivan give you?"

"Well," the barber stuttered, "he gave me enough to—"

"How much?" Howe roared. *"You understand the English language?"*

"I couldn't get no work!" Gotha blurted.

"One hundred dollars?" Howe pressed mercilessly.

"Couldn't tell you."

"You mean that, do you Gotha?" Howe yelled. He was towering over the barber now, quaking with indignation.

"If Mr. Howe wants to save time, I will put in the records of—" the prosecutor interrupted.

"Allow me to conduct my cross-examination!" Howe belted, and turned back to his cowering witness. "Sullivan has given you the money on which you have lived?"

"Not *all*," Gotha protested.

"Nearly all?"

Gotha sank down farther in his seat. "Nearly all," he replied quietly.

"Have you earned *one penny*"—Howe banged his fist down— "from the time you went to the police headquarters? Yes or no?"

"I have not *earned* it," Gotha stumbled, "but I got it from my wife's people . . ."

"Haven't done a day's work, have you?"

"No," he mumbled.

"You know"—Howe motioned at the teeming press tables—"there

was one thousand dollars offered by the *New York Journal* for the discovery of the perpetrator of this murder, do you not?"

"Yes, sir."

Howe turned back to him. "Is it not true that Thorn told you that it was *Mrs. Nack* who shot Guldensuppe?"

"No," Gotha insisted.

No further questions, Howe scoffed.

The whole thing, Howe declared, was a flimsy farrago to get a reward when the real murderer was already under arrest. With Gotha reduced to rubble, the lawyer now had Herman Nack at the ready to demolish his ex-wife's credibility. "I'll tear her apart," Howe assured a reporter.

But the district attorney had a surprise for him.

"The people rest," Youngs announced.

What?

The crowd was stunned. No Mrs. Nack? A capital case without the star witness? But they were hardly as amazed as the glimmering figure who stood before them on the courtroom floor. Howe was thunderstruck for what seemed the first time in his life, as the realization dawned on him.

In a single instant, the prosecution had just outflanked his entire defense.

CROWD MAY BREAK RECORDS, the headlines warned that Monday. Over the weekend Sheriff Doht's office had been flooded with thousands of applications, including a bar association's worth of lawyers; attorneys were making a pilgrimage to see how the Great Howe would magically free his client. But another constituency was not admitted.

"No women," Sheriff Doht told an uproarious crowd gathered outside. He was taking no chances; the mistake of allowing women to hear about Guldensuppe's anatomy would not be repeated this week. Newspapers couldn't even hint at the reason; they had to settle for informing their readers that the testimony was simply too shocking even for modern-minded ladies. Scores of women promptly laid siege to the sheriff's office and overflowed into hallways, all hoping to glimpse either Nack or Thorn.

But behind the courtroom's heavy oak doors, Martin Thorn was staring too—at the jury.

"I have been watching them pretty closely, though some think I take little interest in the trial," Thorn confided to a *Herald* reporter as the room filled up. He nodded toward the ever-smiling Valentine Waits, a perpetually cheerful farmer who had become a favorite of courtroom cartoonists. He appeared particularly well fed and jolly that morning. "I notice many of them are getting rosy cheeks."

The rest of the jury filed into the jury box, with the out-of-season builders looking almost as crisply groomed that morning as Thorn himself.

"Some of them have had a hair cut," he observed quietly. "I suppose I notice that because I'm a barber."

Thorn's voice, the *Herald* reporter mused, retained the same calm register of the barbershop—as "if he had been discussing freaks of weather with favored customers." His lawyer, though, was more boisterous: Howe slapped his client's back, prepared his papers, and then stood up before the quieted courthouse.

Gentlemen—his voice rang out. For they were indeed gentlemen, save for seven or eight canny women who had gotten in under the pretense of being newspaper artists; their sketch pads sat unused on their laps. "Gentlemen of the jury," he began impressively. *"Martin Thorn is innocent of the murder of William Guldensuppe."*

He strode up to the jury box, looking with great meaning at each man sitting in it.

"The killing of Guldensuppe germinated in the mind of the assassin—Mrs. Nack. She is a perjurer as well as a murderess. It was *she* who hired the cottage for the purpose of converting it to a slaughterhouse in which to take the life of her lover. Guldensuppe had been pestering this woman and she wanted him no longer—she wanted Martin Thorn. And so this Lady Macbeth of modern times came to Woodside and hired a cottage. *She* bought the oilcloth, while Guldensuppe was yet alive. *She* took him there to have him killed. *She* was the murderer. This anatomist who could carve a body as well as you could carve a turkey—this Lady Macbeth and all the Borgias rolled into one—then proceeded to cut that body up. After his butchery *she* put his clothes in a cooking stove, gentlemen, and watched the fire do its work. That's the creature that talks of confessing through God and her conscience."

Howe paused and turned pensive. His white hair glowed against the somber black of his suit, and now he spoke in a low, tremulous voice.

"In a long career in the court, I am in—*yellow* leaf," he confided. After days of vigorous bluster, Howe was turning old and kindly. "But I believe that justice will be done."

Summoning his strength, Howe turned to the packed house. "Martin Thorn!"

Captain Methven loosened Thorn's handcuffs and then led the prisoner behind the jury box, through the narrow passage, to the stand.

"Will Your Honor pardon me if I sit down during this examination?" the old lawyer asked, turning to Judge Maddox. "Out of respect to the court I prefer to stand, very much—but I ask that I may sit down."

"Yes," the judge nodded.

The effect was curiously intimate: Howe and Thorn were two men now, sitting and talking.

"Thorn," Howe asked genially, "what is your proper name?"

"Martin Thorzewsky."

"When did you first meet Mrs. Nack?"

"A year and a half ago."

A glance around the courtroom showed that she had not been brought in by the prosecution; their feint had already succeeded. He was on his own, even if their entire defense relied on attacking her.

"Did Mrs. Nack make love to you—or you to her?" Howe asked delicately.

"She made love to me."

"And did you love her in return?"

"I did," he smiled.

"Very fondly?"

"Very," Thorn replied quietly.

Soon, Thorn explained earnestly, she talked of leaving Gulden-suppe, so they could run off together to start a lucrative orphanage in Woodside. But on the morning of June 25, when he visited the house they'd secretly rented, he had the shock of his life.

"I came there a little after eleven, and soon as I came up the stoop, the door came open and Mrs. Nack stood inside, a little excited. I asked her—'What is the matter?' She said, 'Oh, I just left Guldensuppe upstairs.' I said, 'What's he doing up there?' She said, 'I just shot him, and I am glad of it; I am rid of all my trouble now.'"

Thorn shook his head in disbelief: The woman had immediately tried pinning it all on *him*. "She said, 'We'll have to get rid of the body now—*you* have to. If you don't suspicion will fall on you because you had a fight with him, and you got the receipt in your name for the cottage.' So we proceeded to take the body, undressed him and put him in the bath tub, and I went out and bought the plaster of paris."

"Where did you go?"

"Fourth Street—I don't know, the corner." He shrugged. "When I got back Mrs. Nack had her hat and dress off, and I got hold of the body. Mrs. Nack took a big knife and cut his throat. When she came to the back of the neck she took a saw and cut it, and then she commenced to count his ribs. I said, 'What are you doing that for?' She said, 'So I won't cut the body too far down, so as not to open any of the bowels.'"

The crowd squirmed a little, but the detail rang true: The fairly expert carving of the body attested to great deliberation in the cut lines, and to someone with a knowledge of anatomy.

The courtroom was dead quiet as Howe rose and walked to the jury box. "Thorn," he inquired gravely, "were you ever convicted of any offense?"

"Never."

"Look at that jury, Thorn." Howe swept his arm out. *"Did you shoot William Guldensuppe?"*

Martin Thorn looked up from the chair: out over the courthouse, at scores of men scribbling in steno pads, at errand boys sliding telegraph dispatches under the door, at disheveled artists scrolling pictures into pigeon tubes, at hundreds of New Yorkers staring fixedly upon him from the galleries.

Then the defendant leveled his gaze squarely at the twelve men who would decide his fate.

"I did not," he said.

V.

THE
VERDICT

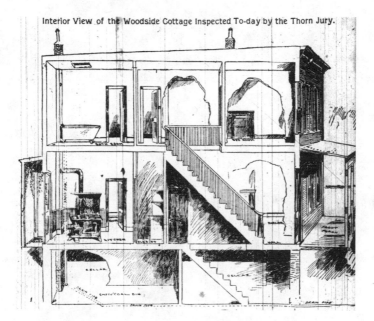

Interior View of the Woodside Cottage Inspected To-day by the Thorn Jury.

21

MRS. NACK'S OFFICE

NOT EVERYONE WAS TRANSFIXED by Martin Thorn's stare. True, there were newspaper reports of his "evil eye"; Hearst even joked that its baleful power had caused that week's unraveling of Paddy Gleason, the Long Island City mayor caught trying to use the Woodside Water Company to scoop up a $60,000 windfall for himself. But the evil-eye rumor was taken seriously enough by District Attorney Youngs's daughter that she loaned him her lucky piece of coral; this, she told her father, was to be carried in his pocket for protection against Thorn. In his other pocket William Youngs dutifully carried a rabbit's foot—a present from his wife. But he knew Thorn had no unearthly power now, and scarcely even earthly power; why, the man could be undone by a schoolgirl.

"Clara Pierce," Youngs called out into the packed courthouse.

The prosecution, allowed a final rebuttal to Thorn's testimony, had tantalized the press with the lure of an appearance by Mrs. Nack; but alas, they would not give Howe the satisfaction of attacking her. "The case for the people was complete without her," one of Youngs's team insisted. Instead, wending past the jury box and up to the stand was a slender and neatly attired girl, her eyes wide before the murmuring crowd.

Who is that? the whisper ran.

"Where do you live?" Youngs asked her after she was sworn in.

"439 Ninth Avenue."

"Do you go to school?"

"Yes, sir." Clara nodded earnestly.

"How old are you?"

"Thirteen."

Her manner was a curious contrast to Thorn's or indeed nearly every adult who had taken the stand—her voice small and precise, free of artifice.

"Do you remember"—Youngs measured his words carefully—"Friday, the twenty-fifth of June?"

"Yes," she nodded. "I got home at two o'clock."

"How do you know it was Friday?"

"Because I got home early."

"Friday is the only day you get home early?"

"Yes, sir," she explained, adding that it was her time to visit Mrs. Stewart, a neighbor in the building, to babysit the woman's infant.

"What did you do with it?"

"I was bringing it down in its carriage."

"Did you take it to see Mrs. Nack?"

"Yes," the girl said plainly.

"You know Mrs. Nack?"

"I didn't just know her," the schoolgirl smiled. "She *lived* in 439 Ninth Avenue."

"Did you see her that day?" the prosecutor asked.

"Yes—between half past two and three o'clock."

"What was Mrs. Nack *doing* at that time?" he asked significantly.

"Trimming her hat," Clara replied.

A murmur arose in the courtroom. The girl was with Mrs. Nack—at a sewing table, calmly banding ribbons around a brown hat—at the precise moment Thorn claimed she was miles away cutting up a body.

No further questions, Youngs said as he walked back past Howe. It was a child on an East River pier who had begun the case one balmy June day; now, five months later and in the winter darkness of a courtroom, another child had ended it.

"IS THAT ALL YOUR EVIDENCE?" Howe scoffed.

"I believe it is," Youngs replied with a slight bow.

Pacing before the bench the next morning, the defense counsel had one last request for Judge Maddox.

"I ask"—Howe leaned forward—"that the jury be permitted to view the bath tub in which it is claimed the body was cut up—with a view to showing that no one person alone could have put that body in the bathtub without indentation of the tin."

"These premises are now in the same condition that they were at or about the twenty-fifth of June?" Judge Maddox asked.

"Practically the same," the DA cut in. "There are certain marks on the walls and things of that kind, but the premises are practically in the same condition."

"The district attorney cut out little pieces to have it analyzed with respect to the blood," Howe added. "Our point is that the bath tub should be viewed."

The judge did not look entirely convinced. "What say you, Mr. Youngs?"

"We have nothing to conceal at all," the DA shrugged. "The key is in the custody of Detective Sullivan."

"How long will it take to go from here to the cottage?"

"About twenty minutes."

After nearly thinking better of it, the judge decided to let them go ahead; Martin Thorn, not surprisingly, wasn't interested in joining them.

"Gentlemen of the jury"—Judge Maddox turned to the twelve men—"you will be conducted to this house."

With that, he sent them to fetch their hats and overcoats. Captain Methven and the rest of their police escort cut a path through the crowd as the jurors filed out into the cold air of the courthouse steps and down to the streetcar stop. While a private trolley was requisitioned for the jurors, reporters jockeyed to hire their own. An *Evening Journal* artist stood nearby and hurriedly sketched the scene in pen and ink.

It won't fit, a colleague informed him. *One bird can't carry a sheet that size.* The chagrined artist, realizing his mistake, promptly sliced the drawing down the middle. The two halves were sent across the river by different pigeons.

The jurors themselves wouldn't see the drawings; Captain Methven made sure of that. He hadn't allowed his charges to read anything in their off-hours—"nothing but hotel menu cards," he declared. But the twelve men climbing aboard the trolley had taken it all good-naturedly, and had even amused themselves the day before by forming a fraternity. After considering calling it the Thorny Club, they settled upon the Good Thing Club—good things, of course, coming to those who wait. They'd passed around cigars to make it official, made an appointment for a group photograph, and genially hazed their police escort by loading his rifle with blanks on the hotel's trap-shooting range. *Same time next year,* the jurors promised the officers after dissolving into hilarity. *We'll treat you to dinner.*

But now, it was all business.

The procession—the jurors and police sequestered in their one drafty streetcar, and a parade of reporters and spectators following them—rolled at a stately pace, beyond the saloons selling hot rum, past cart horses shaking off the cold, by greenhouses fogged with winter. When the convoy reached the sleepy corner of Second Street, a crowd was already gathered around the house that locals jovially referred to as Mrs. Nack's Office.

"All off here for Woodside cottage!" the conductor called back to his passengers, and the twelve men stepped out of their streetcar and into the scene of the crime.

THE PLACE had hardly changed at all.

The trees were bare now, the grass in the backyard high and un-mown, but otherwise it remained recognizable from last summer's front pages. The house's windows slumbered under closed wooden shutters, heedless of the men treading through the mud and ice up to the creaking wooden front porch. There the jurors paused while Detective Sullivan fished out a key and slid it into the lock.

Back, back, they could hear the police yelling behind them, shoo-ing gawkers to a perimeter around the property line.

The door groaned awake on its hinges, and they quietly filed into the darkened parlor. The air in the unheated house was frigid, leaving their breath visible in white clouds; with the power long shut off, Detective Sullivan busily threw open the shutters to let in the subdued light of the winter morning. *This way,* he motioned them downstairs. He'd been one of the first in the house back in the summer, and he knew it well. Down in the cellar lay the smashed remains of a chimney, a hole still gaping where detectives in search of Guldensuppe's head had attacked the brickwork with sledgehammers. A peek inside the hole revealed why that search had failed: The aperture inside was scarcely four inches wide.

Back upstairs and through the parlor, they paused in the kitchen to peer into the black iron stove that had held the ashes of the dead man's shoes, then trod up the steep flight of stairs to the house's second story. Their footsteps echoed loud and hollow through the hallways. It was a modest home, cheaply made and of small proportions, with just two bedrooms and a bathroom upstairs. The jurors barely fit into the front bedroom. Its walls still bore neatly penciled forensics notations and small scars down to the wooden lathing—specimens pried away by detectives extracting the two bullets that Gotha said Thorn had test-fired from his revolver.

At the next room, the men paused.

The second bedroom remained as it had been—without a hint of trouble, save for subtle shavings planed off sections of the floorboards for blood analysis. The closet was empty, its door ajar, waiting. With a rug over the nicked-up floor, one could imagine a tidy little boarder's room being made of such a space. Yet the murder had been perpetrated in *one* of these two bedrooms, for according to Nack and Gotha, Thorn had fired from this very closet, while Thorn contended that Mrs. Nack had done the deed herself in the front room.

The bathroom's back here. Sullivan waved them along.

The jurors inspected the metal bathtub, leaning down one by one to examine its surface. As Howe had promised, there was neither a dent nor a saw mark to be found. It would indeed have been difficult for one person to do the dismembering alone. But if both hands had grasped that terrible saw, which one had leveled the revolver or grasped the dagger—and in which bedroom?

Walking back downstairs, Foreman Morse led his jury into the weedy backyard, the ground furrowed with the diggings of detectives and treasure hunters. Then they strolled out front to the roadside ditch, where ducks cavorted in half-frozen water. It was the same flock that had turned pink with Guldensuppe's draining blood, and the jurors watched the ducks waddle past them and across the yard of the emptied house.

In a few hours, the jurors would have to decide just what had happened inside that cottage.

JUDGE MADDOX HADN'T YET finished his cigar when the jurors returned; the justice was gazing out over the packed room with a thoughtful look. It was too bad they hadn't taken a bit longer; cigars were just about the only way to make the room's air fit to breathe.

Quiet! He gaveled the tumultuous crowd, and he motioned for Howe to come up. The defense had elected to give the first closing argument, and it was time for him to make his last stand. The old lawyer tugged down on his pin-striped vest—a favorite gesture of his—and then turned to the hushed room with great seriousness.

"May it please Your Honor and gentlemen of the jury," Howe began quietly. "I firmly believe that the woman with a pistol taken from her apartment and brought here into this court is the one who shot William Guldensuppe. Mrs. Nack, the vile thing that left her husband, tells Thorn that she loves *him* dearly: *'I love Thorn and would die for him.'* Instead she made another man die—Guldensuppe."

Howe's voice climbed in indignation as he paced before the jury box.

"Yet you're asked to place the blame on this man! He was no more the murderer of Guldensuppe than you were. The District Attorney was too astute to have dared a second ordeal of that woman on the stand. He was afraid to have her confronted. He feared she would go to pieces on the rack of truth, and you would see into the recesses of her murderous heart. Thorn is on trial for what *she* did— and I say, God forbid that murderess should go free, and Thorn pay the penalty."

Howe paused before one juror and then the next—hovering,

one reporter mused, like an immense bee before each blossom in a flower box.

"Gotha is the *only one* who testified that Thorn confessed. *Gotha.* Judas was a saint compared to this *Gotha.*"

Howe turned and swung out his arm.

"Who is *Gotha?*" he barked. "Thorn was a hard-working barber until he fell in with this vile creature, this harridan. *Gotha* left his wife and lived alone. And then he came here, with blood money in his pocket, to swear away the life of this *man.*"

The courtroom was electric with silence, the crowd almost holding its breath.

"He had read about the one thousand dollar reward. He had Detective Price's one hundred dollars. But we don't stop with Sam Price's one hundred dollars. We have him going to the New York District Attorney's office. This barber, who from his looks couldn't earn ten dollars a week by shaving, gets one hundred dollars in a lump and then *lies* to you. He was acting a lie from the time he put on the handcuffs until he went on the stand."

Howe glanced between the jury box and the prosecution team.

"Suppose the evidence of Gotha were out of the case. What evidence is there that Thorn fired the shot or did any killing? Can they find anything besides that? No—and I can't conceive of your believing *Gotha.*"

As for the innocent schoolgirl from Mrs. Nack's building, well— surely she told the truth, Howe admitted, but she or Thorn merely had their times confused. No, he declared, the schoolgirl's testimony made the case against Nack even worse.

"Trimming a ha-aat!" He banged down his fist. "Trimming a hat, *just after she trimmed her lover's body!*" Howe's voice, marveled a reporter, roared so loud that the chandeliers jangled. In the startled silence that followed, he stopped and mopped the perspiration from his brow.

"Now, as to your visit to the cottage just now—you didn't find a single indentation in that tub, did you? The body could not have been cut unless *two* people had helped with it. Under this indictment it is perfectly reasonable that you could find a verdict of murder in

the second degree—punishment worse than death itself. Imprisonment for life in a tomb of stone! Never leaving that tomb until the
dead body is carried out. Some of you"—he motioned to the jurors—
"may have been sick in your comfortable houses, and the very paper
on the wall begins to punish you with weariness. But picture *twenty
years* in a cell."

His voice dropped low, and he pulled up close to the jury-box
railing.

"To take the life which God has given—unjustly—is an awful
thing. Remember that the scenes of this day will never, ever leave
you. They will follow you to your farm"—he eyed Valentine Waits,
and then the builders—"to your carpenter's shop. These scenes will
sleep by you on your pillow. If it should transpire that this man is
innocent after you have judged him guilty, this man will haunt you
through your lives. If you find him guilty, at the final accounting *that
man's spirit will rise to condemn you before the judgment seat of God.*"

Youngs's summation was plodding and methodical: Thorn had the
weapons, had the motive, had been placed at the scene, and confessed to a friend. They had unprecedented circumstantial evidence,
and testimony by detectives and a firearms expert allowed the jury
to draw its own conclusion. "Put these things together in a mosaic,
gentlemen," he invited. "And see the picture they form."

The defense, Youngs noted tartly, changed its story with each
passing day—first it was Guldensuppe's body, then it wasn't; Thorn
hadn't been at the scene, then he had.

"Gentlemen of the jury"—the district attorney smiled faintly—
"the eloquence of Mr. Howe is world-wide in its reputation, standing
as he does at the head of the criminal bar of the city of New York. The
eloquence you have listened to today has been thrilling. And"—he
glanced at Howe—"through its exertion, no doubt more than one
guilty man has escaped."

Thorn stared ahead stonily, while Howe glared back in fine indignation.

"We lay no claim to any greatness of oratory," Youngs continued.
Balding and bespectacled, the very diminutiveness of the DA now

turned against the defense counsel. "He has given you that, but we have given you something stronger than oratory, more powerful than eloquence: *evidence.*"

The district attorney paused before the jury box. He wanted them to also consider their solemn duty as Long Islanders—as the bulwark that honest tradesmen like them kept up against the depredations of the big city across the river.

"Gentlemen of the jury, he has appealed to your heart, your passions. I appeal to your common sense, to your heads. Don't let it go out that men and women can come over *here* from neighboring cities and conspire to commit crimes."

The crowd of reporters rolled their eyes; they'd be going back to that great corrupting city tonight—and be glad of it, too. But it was not the reporters that Youngs had turned toward.

"I know," the DA concluded as he gazed earnestly at the carpenters and farmers, "that I can leave the matter in *your* hands."

THE COURTROOM WAS RAVENOUS; closing arguments had taken so long that it was 2:25 p.m. by the time the twelve men left for the jury room. Judge Maddox had lunch sent in to the jurors, while the courtroom itself broke out sandwiches and bottles of ginger ale in a flurry of wax paper and napkins; the spectators, not wanting to lose their seats, had packed their own lunches. It was a masculine affair, with women still hopelessly crowded out on the courthouse steps and in hallways. Their only representative inside was a single black-veiled woman nearly hidden behind one of the spectator gallery pillars. *It's Thorn's sister*, the murmur went.

Thorn himself was led downstairs to a holding cell for lunch, while at his defense table Howe assumed a philosophical look. He was delighted with their case, he declared, but then his expression darkened. He'd torn down every major witness on the stand as an inebriate, a busybody, or an outright criminal—all of them, that is, except one.

"The *one thing* is the testimony of little Clara Pierce," he confided quietly to his associates. The schoolgirl's placement of Mrs. Nack in the city could undermine Thorn's entire alibi. "It may turn the jury against us."

Howe's sheer oratory, reporters and spectators agreed, had expertly maneuvered around the prosecution. "So long as Mr. Howe kept in a sphere above the actual evidence, he soared triumphant," the crime novelist Julian Hawthorne telegraphed from his post at the *Journal* table. Along the way, Howe had deftly rolled back his defense from brashly denying Guldensuppe's death to admitting that someone had caused the fellow to never be seen reemerging from that Woodside cottage.

But who?

"It is not believed that he cut *himself* up," a *Brooklyn Eagle* reporter wrote tartly. "It is not supposed that he took a saw with him into the cottage for the purpose of separating himself from his arms and his legs and incidentally his head."

And yet many clues to who *had* done the deed were not used. Gotha's testimony was a necessary gamble, but every other marginal witness had been ruthlessly excluded. Youngs saw in the first trial that Howe's specialty was in demolishing any witness with an ulterior motive or the least vulnerability in character. Mrs. Nack's testimony was left out, of course; but so was Mrs. Riger's account of the oilcloth purchase. It was said that the poor woman had suffered a breakdown over all the publicity. Frank Clark's old allegation from the Tombs of an infirmary confession was also left untouched; Youngs had planned to use it in the first trial, but now a con like Clark was clearly easy prey to Howe. But so, remarkably, was the analysis of blood spots on the floors. With poisoning charges and money troubles now hanging over Professor Witthaus's divorce, the forensics expert's character would have been mauled by the defense—and in any case, while forensics evidence might have worked in Manhattan, Long Island farmers and carpenters had no truck with chemistry professors.

How quickly would such a jury weigh a secondhand confession to an unemployed barber and a series of circumstantial clues from friends and neighbors? Not too quickly, it seemed. As the cigars and flasks were swapped among the denizens of the galleries, the courtroom's pendulum clock ticked slowly forward to three o'clock, and then to four. Passing by the guarded jury-room door a half hour later, reporters could make out raised voices.

Sitting at the jury room's table, among the picked-over remains of their lunches, one builder was demanding that the jury vote remain by secret ballot. And after six votes in a row, the foreman had opened the slips of paper, counted them, and hit the same result each time.

Eleven to one.

One hour later—after demanding and then poring over the intercepted jailhouse correspondence between Nack and Thorn—the twelve men filed back into the courtroom through the side door, and drowsy spectators scrambled to their feet.

"Remove your hats!" deputies bellowed up into the galleries as Judge Maddox returned from his chambers and then as Martin Thorn was led back in. Actually, it was Thorn doing the leading: He was so nervously eager that he was nearly dragging in Captain Methven with his handcuffed arm.

The twelve solemn men looked to the judge and waited.

"Gentlemen of the jury, have you agreed upon a verdict?"

"We have," their foreman replied.

"Defendant, rise," the court clerk commanded Martin Thorn. "Jurors, look upon the defendant. Defendant, look upon the jurors. What say you?"

The men locked eyes, and Thorn knew his fate.

"We find the defendant guilty," the foreman announced—"of murder in the first degree."

22.

THE SMOKER
TO SING SING

MARTIN THORN KNEW they were out to kill him.

"I suppose Howe will get a new trial, but it won't do any good in this county," he snorted to the *Herald* reporter waiting back at his cell. "You can't get a jury in this county who wouldn't hang you for stealing a loaf of bread."

There wasn't much left to cheer Thorn up other than wrestling with his adopted mutt—the only creature on earth uninterested in judging him.

So, did you do it?

Thorn sat down and looked pensively around his cell; the room had been freshly whitewashed the day before in anticipation of the press, and it still smelled of paint.

"I had no motive to kill Guldensuppe," Thorn said quietly, and then eyed the *Herald* reporter. "He did *exactly* what I would have done under the circumstances. What could he have done? I never had any ill will against the man for striking me."

So then . . .

"Mrs. Nack had a motive," he snapped. "I didn't."

But when Thorn's sister Pauline and her husband came to visit, his defiance was to no avail: They both looked thunderstruck.

"Martin!" his sister sobbed, and grasped his hand. "Martin!"

The husband stood by, eyes welling up, also unable to speak. Thorn sat his sister in a corner of the tiny cell, a rather melancholy gesture toward privacy.

"Martin!" she wept.

"Well," he motioned cheerfully outside. "Pretty cold out today, ain't it?"

She was not fooled by his nonchalance.

"Poor fellow!" Pauline dabbed her eyes and finally composed herself a little. Her expression turned indignant. "It's a shame that they should make a deal with Mrs. Nack. It's a shame. She—"

"Hush, hush." Thorn held his hand up. "I don't want you to say anything about her. I wouldn't care if she were turned loose tomorrow. I don't care what becomes of her."

His sister looked astounded—as did everyone else in the cell.

"Yes, I mean it," the prisoner insisted. "I do mean it."

His sister and brother-in-law left the cell as distraught as when they'd arrived, unsure whether they'd ever see him alive again.

Do *you mean it?* a *Herald* reporter asked.

"It doesn't make any difference to me what they do with her." Thorn shrugged. But he was struggling with his feelings, because it wasn't just the jury or the State of New York that he knew was out to kill him. "I am convinced," he said slowly, "that these letters that Mrs. Nack sent to me are part of a scheme—to commit *suicide*. She thought I would carry out my part of the contract, and then she'd change her mind. Then I would be out of the way, and she would have nothing to fear."

It's true, one of the jailers admitted quietly—they hadn't told the press at the time, but before the trial they found a smuggled dose of morphine in Thorn's vest—enough for an overdose. They'd had an extra guard on him ever since.

"You needn't trouble yourself about me trying to commit suicide," Thorn laughed. He wasn't going to die for Mrs. Nack—not *now*. And he wouldn't die for the people of New York, either. "I'm not going to do anything to save the county or the state the expense of killing me."

The prisoner's expression darkened.

"I'll make the state pay," he said.

HOWE WASN'T WORRIED about their case at all.

"I am smoking a cigar in contentment," he informed reporters the next morning. He'd file an appeal, and he expected to win it. "My mind is in a state of peace and tranquility. I shall take lunch in a dress suit and drink a quart of white."

"On what ground will you base your appeal?" asked a reporter for the *Eagle*.

"I do not wish"—Howe smiled enigmatically—"to unmask any battery."

His first salvo came just one day later, and from an utterly unexpected source: the jury's hotel bill. The Garden City Hotel dutifully filed an itemized list with Queens County's board of supervisors: $2,049.90 for both juries. It was steep, but it was a long trial and retrial, after all, and it included hundreds in private jury streetcars and in attending physician's bills for Magnus Larsen's appendicitis. The supervisors were relieved: Some had feared that, along with misadventures like Detective Sullivan's fruitless trip to Hamburg to find Guldensuppe, the entire cost of the case might balloon to $40,000 or $50,000. Instead, it was looking like everything might come in at less than $20,000.

But they hadn't anticipated William Howe.

Much of the hotel bill consisted of the usual pettiness—a ten-cent charge marked "Listerine," a twenty-five-cent charge when a juror borrowed a quarter for a poker game—and a few luxuries as well. Thorn's trained eye had also been right about the jury's newfound grooming; they'd run up an impressive $30 barber bill. But it was something else that caught his defense counsel's eye. The jurors had mown down more than $80 worth of booze and cigars in a single night—and many other evenings as well. The Good Thing Club, it seemed, was a little too much of a good thing.

Intoxication! Howe bellowed. The jury was incompetent to render a verdict, he declared, on account of their disgraceful state of inebriation. District Attorney Youngs, flabbergasted, quickly rounded up the jurors and their guards in his office and demanded affidavits.

"I saw no wine drunk," insisted Captain Methven. "They were allowed to have a bottle of beer or ale and cigars for dinner, but that's all."

One juror allowed that maybe they *did* have wine—but just a single glass.

"I saw only *one* glass of wine while I was there, and that was when I was sick," a much-recovered Magnus Larsen said primly before quickly adding, "I don't care for it anyway." The other jurors admitted to a little more. Maybe there were some other drinks, too—a glass or two—some Bass beer, a blackberry cordial, maybe Jamaican ginger for a bad stomach. But they'd absolutely been quite sober in the courtroom.

When Martin Thorn reported back to the courthouse on Friday, December 3, several jurors joined the crowd of reporters and spectators to hear his sentencing. It took all of eight minutes, for the county still pointedly regarded the entire matter as settled.

"Prisoner, arise," commanded the court clerk.

Judge Maddox gazed solemnly on his audience, then read slowly from his finding.

"Thorn," he began, "you are indicted for having deliberately designed and caused the death of William Guldensuppe. You have had a fair trial—defended most ably by an astute lawyer; by counsel, indeed, who could not have done more than they did for you." Howe's expression remained stoic; his fight was not over yet. "A jury found you guilty of murder in the first degree," the judge continued. "The punishment for that crime is death."

Thorn's face paled slightly, but he remained motionless.

"*Reflect upon it*," Judge Maddox instructed, his voice lowered. "Reflect upon your past. Reflect upon the death of him who you have slain."

From the press tables, the reporters maintained a steady whisper of pencil points against paper and telegraph forms, and the crowd held its breath as Maddox straightened himself for the final pronouncement.

"The judgment of the court," he announced, "is that you shall be taken to the place from whence you came, and thence to the state prison in Sing Sing. There judgment shall be executed, and you shall be put to death according to law, in the manner provided by law, in the week beginning January tenth."

Martin Thorn had just five weeks left to live.

WHEN THE CONDEMNED MAN opened his eyes the next morning, it was still dark outside.

Six o'clock.

Thorn sat up on his jail cot, padded the short distance across the cold floor of his cell, and began smoothing out the creases in his trousers and brushing clean the only outfit he had left—a black coat, a shirt with a standing collar, and his blue polka-dotted cravat.

Breakfast, his jailer announced, and slid in his tray.

Thorn didn't much feel like eating; he dangled the morsels above his dog, and watched as Bill Baker snapped and pranced at them. When Captain Methven and Sheriff Doht arrived at the cell at seven-fifteen, Thorn was ready. He pulled on his thin summer coat, asked for his fedora—they couldn't find it, and gave him an old battered alpine hat instead—and then he turned to his dog. Bill Baker paused from pouncing repeatedly at a steam grate and tilted his head quizzically as his master was led away from the cell. "Good-bye, Bake," the man called back.

It was the only farewell Thorn made that morning.

There were two inches of slush and snow on the ground outside, and as the trio walked out to the Jackson Avenue streetcar in the darkness, Thorn slid on the ice; only Methven's beefy hand, manacled to his, kept him from hitting the sidewalk. He hadn't been outside much in the previous five months, and he had no winter clothes. When they reached the Thirty-Fourth Street ferry, he was shivering. The cabin of the boat was warmer but no more welcoming: The morning commuters immediately recognized the chained passenger, and once they reached the other side of the river a growing crowd was following him.

It's him, word shot across Grand Central Depot. The vast space—the marble colonnades, the luggage wagons being loaded for the Waldorf Astoria, the morning shoppers clutching Charles & Company praline bags—it all seemed to contract around the three men. The crowd was pressing on Thorn and his two jailers and into the scrum of *World, Journal,* and *Telegram* reporters that already surrounded them. *You must intervene,* they beseeched the station police, who then pushed the mob back into the onrush of commuters. But as Methven and Doht picked up smoking-car tickets for the next train—*three for the 8:05 smoker*—the masses cascaded wildly into adjacent lines, buying ticket after ticket to Sing Sing.

"They all want to see you," a *World* reporter marveled aloud. Thorn allowed himself a small smile as he was yanked by a manacled hand toward the train platform.

Inside the smoking carriage, the seats were crammed with onlookers, and there was nothing the conductor could do about it; they had bought tickets, after all. Even more were pressing their faces up against the glass where Thorn took a window seat on the left side of the carriage; it took another sweep of patrolmen to clear the unticketed gawkers off the platform. Thorn stared down, his hat pulled nearly over his eyes.

Cigar? Captain Methven offered.

Thorn shook his head; he wasn't interested. The train pulled forward with a jerk as the couplings tightened, and the last of the pursuing crowd pulled away; here, among the smaller crowd of gawkers who had bought their smoker tickets, Thorn at last looked up and watched as the landscape of the Hudson Valley slid by.

The reporters and sketch artists, sitting across from Thorn and his jailers, tried drawing him out: What were his thoughts on Mrs. Nack? But the prisoner wouldn't respond. Another tried a more clever opening: What did he think of the city elections a few weeks earlier?

"I wish that Tammany won," Thorn admitted. "I'd have voted for that ticket."

The thought seemed to depress his spirits further as he stared back out the train window. Captain Methven made a gruff attempt to cheer him up.

"Say, Martin." Methven nudged his prisoner. "Wouldn't you like to have your dog up here? He'll be lonely in jail."

"Yes." Thorn brightened a little. "If you will send him."

A *World* reporter quietly shook his head; maybe Methven and his prisoner didn't know Sing Sing well, but he'd accompanied condemned men there before, and he knew they'd never let Bill Baker into that place.

The train pulled up to Ossining station, where a second crowd had gathered. Thorn was hustled into a waiting hackney cab and past the onlookers, through the outskirts of the small town, and to the great stone gate that marked the entrance of Sing Sing. On the road in, crews of convicts in striped outfits worked in the freezing cold, breaking rocks and raking gravel under the gaze of men holding Winchester rifles.

His journey was almost over.

THERE WERE HUNDREDS of them out in the cold the next morning in Manhattan—and then thousands. They'd all read the newspaper accounts of Thorn's trip to Sing Sing, and then caught the notice beneath: *William Guldensuppe's viewing to-day, 115 East Third Street.*

The block of Third Street between First Avenue and Avenue A had never lacked for strange stories: At one end, a piano maker's wife had thrown herself from the top of a building; at the other was the home of a man recently arrested for assisting a high diver's illegal leap from the Brooklyn Bridge. The diver, as it happened, had not fared any better than the piano maker's wife. Conveniently, in the middle of this block sat the obliging funeral home of Herr Franz Odendhal. True, even this establishment had a bit of local infamy—an employee had once run off with the florist's wife, which made for some rather awkward moments in ordering memorial bouquets. But this Saturday morning they had a fine display ready for their latest casket.

At 10 a.m., Franz threw the doors open and the mourners poured inside. Facing them was a burnished oak coffin, and leaning against it, a photograph from life of the handsome, mustachioed masseur whom everyone in the city now recognized. At the back of the coffin rose a four-foot-high floral arrangement, ordered by his eight coworkers from the night shift at Murray Hill Baths, its blossoms spelling out a single word: COMRADE.

By now there were so many waiting outside that each was given about one second to view the body—they had to walk through the parlor briskly. It was just enough time to glance at the flowers, the photograph, and the brass plate at one end of the coffin. It bore the full name that the man himself had never used:

Christian W. Guldensuppe.
Died June 25, 1897.
Age, Forty-two Years.

As each New Yorker walked up, the glass top that Franz had placed over the coffin revealed the contents: a cleansed and carefully dressed man, wearing a suit and with his right hand laid upon his breast—protecting, it seemed, his stilled heart.

The body had no head.

Some ten thousand New Yorkers had filed past by two o'clock, and hundreds more lingered to follow a carriage procession to a ferry at the foot of Houston Street. The waiting boat soon slipped away from its mooring, its cargo bound for the Lutheran Cemetery across the river. And there, so long after that phone call to the bathhouse one warm June evening, Willie Guldensuppe finally got the Long Island home that Mrs. Nack had promised him.

THE ALLEGATIONS were terribly unfair, Mrs. Nack insisted to the *Journal* women's page reporter who visited her on Christmas Day. Having turned State's evidence in the first trial, she was still waiting for what she hoped would be a reduced sentence. In the meantime, she wanted the world to know that the crime wasn't her fault at all—it was the fault of her husband.

"Then Herman Nack was cruel?" the reporter pressed.

Mrs. Nack looked up and burst into tears.

"If he had not been, I would not be here now," she sobbed. "I would still be with him, for I loved him. If I did not, I would not have married, for my people didn't like him. But he said we need not mind that—we could be in this new country, and he would earn good wages, and I could learn a new business, and we would get rich.

"We both worked, but we didn't get rich." She dabbed her eyes. "We only got poorer."

And now, she sighed, she was here. Weeks had passed since Thorn was sent to Sing Sing, and on this day—Christmas Day—she was still in Queens County Jail, still assailed in the newspapers. Though the common wisdom among legal experts was that Mrs. Nack's confession meant that she'd escape the chair, the *Eagle* still pronounced her the "head devil" of the case, and Howe's office had been even blunter to the *Journal*.

"They should place her in the electric chair with Thorn," one of Howe's team snapped, before quickly adding, "*if* Thorn is to be placed there."

But for Mrs. Nack, passing her hours in jail making handcrafts, every page of the newspaper was trying reading. It wasn't just the cartoon in the *Evening Telegram* that showed the Woodside ducks proclaiming: *"Once again the town is ours!"* It was that the world outside was passing her by, what with the holiday and the coming of the New Year. One Christmas ad in the *World* rode the craze for Professor Röntgen's new discovery—*"Imagine Santa Throwing an X-Ray,"* it announced—with an illustration of the jolly old man irradiating the Third Avenue façade of Bloomingdale's to reveal the bounty of toys within. Beyond the *Herald*'s usual headlines of FIRE IN A MATCH FACTORY, the future beckoned with a proposal to put bike racks on trolley cars, and a promise that an eccentric British scientist had developed a photographic brain scanner: THOUGHTS PICTURED, it announced. The *Journal* had kept its headline circus running, too: Microscopic shrimp in the water supply inspired the headline FISH CHOWDER POURS FROM THE FAUCETS OF BROOKLYN HOUSES. But for the holiday season Hearst's men topped themselves with a new contest—the Prophecy Prize, which had readers stopping by the office to drop their predictions for 1898 into giant ironbound boxes in the lobby.

"Perhaps at the end of 1898 Queen Victoria will have passed away," editors helpfully suggested on the front page. "The problem of aerial navigation may have been solved, America may have annexed Cuba, a great war may have begun between European nations."

When the boxes were opened in a year's time, the best prediction would win $1,000. Yet there would surely be no prize for guessing the likely fate of Martin Thorn.

"Poor Martin," Gussie sighed. She could not help him now; and the paper flowers and lace heaped upon her cell's table would be of no comfort to the man.

Suddenly, her face brightened with an idea: "I cannot wish him a merry Christmas, but I can wish him a happy Christmas." She quickly jotted down a note on a sheet of paper, then puzzled over a second notion. "*And* I would like to send him a basket of fruit. Do you think they'll let me send it? . . . How will he get it?"

"I will see that he gets it," the *Journal* reporter assured her. "Then, if there is any answer I'll bring it back to you—"

"There won't be," Mrs. Nack cut her off.

"There *may* be."

Mrs. Nack shook her head slowly.

"I know him better than you," she said.

The *Journal* reporter picked up a basket of apples, bananas, and grapes from a fruiterer's near Grand Central, then promptly boarded the next train to Sing Sing. When she arrived, the warden reluctantly allowed her onto the cell block—but insisted on handing over the note and the basket himself.

"Martin," he called into the cell. "Here is a message from Mrs. Nack. A Christmas greeting."

He held out the envelope, and the prisoner emerged into the doorway to take it. He was not wearing the striped uniform of ordinary convicts; instead he wore the solid black outfit of a condemned man. The reporter watched as he ran his eyes over the words:

Dear Martin:

It is Christmas time. I send you greeting to your lonely cell at Sing Sing. I have found great peace with my own heart since I put my whole case in the Lord's hands. Let me say this to you, Martin, that I can send you no better gift than that you seek the Lord while he has given you time. Martin, it is determined by law that you must die . . .

His hands began to tear the sheet apart.

. . . Find peace before you go—then, you are not afraid what man can do.

AUGUSTA NACK

Thorn tossed the shredded pieces onto the floor.

The warden, unfazed, extended his other arm.

"And some fruit from her, too," he added.

The prisoner hesitated for a moment, and then, with a philosophical shrug, he took the basket.

"Any answer?" the reporter called from the hallway.

For a moment Thorn opened his mouth, as if to respond. But then, without a word, he shook his head and withdrew into his cell.

23.

A JOB FOR
SMITH AND JONES

THE FRUIT FROM MRS. NACK was the only splash of color in Martin's
cell. He had windowless walls on three sides, a fourth of iron bars, and
the constant glare of electric bulbs. To be here, one inmate mused,
was "like living, eating, sleeping, and bathing in a search-light." It il-
luminated the barest of existences: a steel cot, a lumpy straw mattress
with a single pillow and a blanket, a tin cup, a basin, and a bucket.

Guards, soundless on their crêpe-soled shoes, constantly patrolled
the Death Row hallway, so that the only escape was to be found in
books from the prison library. Thorn had already devoured *The Old
Curiosity Shop* and then more Dickens volumes, day after day. He had
to—because he didn't have a table or pinochle cards, didn't even
have a cell mate. But he was not alone. Though they couldn't see one
another, by talking between the cells, Martin knew he was sharing
Murderers Row with just two other men.

Hadley, said one.

Fritz, halloed the other.

Hadley Sutherland was a West Indian in for shooting his wife in
their Brooklyn home; Fritz Meyer had gunned down a patrolman
while robbing a church poor box on East Third Street. Hadley and
Thorn were both scheduled to die in the electric chair on January 10.
There were no clocks here, but the bananas in the fruit basket had
scarcely ripened when the warden stopped by with a message from

Howe. It was New Year's Eve, he told Thorn, and he had a holiday present of sorts.

Your execution is delayed on appeal.

Hadley was not as fortunate. On what had been their appointed day, Thorn awoke to a thick curtain being pulled over his cell door, and then the sound of a manacled man shuffling past. The execution chamber was so close that it shared a wall with Martin's cell. A few minutes later, there was the distant hum of three electrical dynamos suddenly building up speed, then slowing back down into ominous silence.

Fritz? he called out.

Martin? the other answered.

But now there was no third.

Soon Mrs. Nack's basket would be gone, along with the torn note: *"I have found great peace with my own heart since I put my whole case in the Lord's hands."* But he didn't want to talk about the case, didn't want to think about her, didn't want to consider what her betrayal had probably bought—not even when the warden stopped by later that day with more news for him.

Manslaughter, he told the condemned man.

Thorn could see into the hallway behind the warden, where the keepers were clearing out Hadley's cell.

Fifteen years, the warden reported. *With good behavior, she'll be out in nine.*

Gussie had made her deal.

"I NEVER COULD EAT off *that* table," one woman in the crowd declared.

"I never could look at *that* clock," another added.

"Look at them!" cried the auctioneer, sweeping his arm over a table heaped with laces. "All elegantly knit by Mrs. Nack!"

The house was packed that Saturday morning. Scarcely three blocks from the Harlem drugstore where Thorn had been arrested, hundreds of women pressed into the ground-floor premises of the Standard Auction House. It had been given over that day to the property of one Augusta P. Nack, with the ground-floor sales-rooms on 125th Street magically transformed, fitted up to precisely resemble her newly vacated apartment on 439 Ninth Avenue. Here in the reconstituted parlor was a suite of red velvet furniture and a zither and a music box; there in the kitchen, cabinets clattered with the glassware from which Mrs. Nack and her lovers had once drunk. In her bedroom stood her white-and-gold-painted bedstead, and beside that a dressmaker's dummy attired in a rather garish gown with a crêpe waist of "crushed strawberry."

The sign in front of it read:

COSTUME

WORN BY

MRS. NACK

ON THE DAY OF THE

MURDER

Her outfit for dismembering her lover possessed, reporters dryly noted, "a low cut."

The second bedroom was occupied by the plain and melancholy wooden bed of Guldensuppe; and although his estate was supposed to have been sent on to his relatives in Philadelphia, the masseur's suspenders had gotten mixed up in the lot. So had one of his green neckties.

"The famous necktie!" an auctioneer bellowed. Nobody was sure why that item was famous, until one woman ventured that surely Mrs. Nack had thought of strangling him with it.

Circulating among the crowd were dime-museum managers, the sort of fellows immediately identifiable by loud suits and cigars. It was dime-museum men in Chicago who, a few weeks earlier, had very nearly gotten hold of Luetgert's sausage vat for display. New York promoters would not be so easily shaken off, and they were taking auction-house officials aside.

Five hundred dollars for everything, one offered.

The auctioneer shook his head. *Go higher.* Why, the *Journal* itself had already said it all in a headline: MURDER DEN A KLONDIKE. It was gold! The kitchen alone contained the stove—THE FAMOUS STOVE, they'd placarded it—where Mrs. Nack had burned her lover's bloody clothes.

"A message from Mrs. Nack, ladies and gentlemen!" yelled a staffer, waving a scrap of paper to the crowd as it surged forward. "A *real message* from Mrs. Nack, currently in Queens County Jail!"

This proved to be an old draft of a mail order for more corsets. But the crowd was happy and garrulous, clutching the favors that everyone had been handed at the entrance—business cards addressed from the apartment over Werner's Drug Store and inscribed with words that everybody now knew by heart: AUGUSTA NACK, LICENSED MIDWIFE.

THAT SAME WEEKEND, the owner of those cards was preparing for her departure from Queens County Jail. The cards, she insisted, had been for a respectable business.

"Those are terrible things my husband told about me. I want to ask you—" she demanded of a reporter, "how is it possible I had only three hundred dollars to draw from the bank at the time of the murder? Do you think if I had burned one baby's body, not to speak of more, I should not have been well paid? Go to the neighborhood and ask whether I could have done such things! The children all knew me—I was 'Nanty Nack'—the fairy who brought the last baby to their house. Go, ask their parents."

She shook her head at the injustice of it, and passed out the last of her paper flowers and lacework to her fellow prisoners. The humble earnings of her honest labor, she explained, was also what Thorn was after on the day of the murder. In fact, her entire conduct in the case had been an elaborate way to save herself from certain death at Thorn's hands.

"Explain to me why"—she jabbed a finger into the air—"when Thorn distinctly told me to go over to New York to buy the oilcloth,

I went to the nearest store and talked with the people, so that there was no doubt of identifying me?"

The reporter hid his amazement: Did she mean to say that this fiendishly complicated trail of circumstantial evidence was actually a distress call to detectives? That she *meant* to get arrested?

"I would have surely died but for *one thing*," she continued. "I had not brought money with me. You see, he had told me to draw the money from the bank and always carry it in my bosom. He thought I had done this, but I had not. He led me up stairs and when we reached there he told me to sit on the edge of the tub." She allowed the image of the headless Guldensuppe already draped into the tub to sink in with her listener. "I could only sit and sob until he suddenly said, *Did you bring money with you?* When I told him it was not drawn from the bank he was furious. That saved my life."

And that, she said, was when she managed to get the crime traced back to her.

"He said, *Very well, take the ferry over to New York and get some oilcloth, but don't go to any store on this side.* You know the remainder of the story."

The reporters did indeed know it. And they also knew that Mrs. Riger's sales register in Astoria showed that Augusta Nack bought the oilcloth on June 23—two days before the murder.

EIGHT MONTHS PASSED at Sing Sing. Winter turned to spring, with appeals piled up like dirty snow. They'd melted away in the summer until there was nothing left behind but a condemned man in a sweltering cell. Governor Black had refused to stay the execution.

"This is good news," Thorn said through the bars of his cell. "It's the best news I've had for months."

The warden was taken aback: This wasn't how most prisoners reacted to the governor turning them down.

"I *want* to die," Thorn explained with a shrug.

They'd tried every ploy already. Howe was known, after all, for disrupting courtrooms and wearing opponents out, and even the fetid air had seemed to conspire with him during the trial. So perhaps it was not entirely a surprise in May that a renovation crew opening the courtroom's ventilation ducts found one hundred dead rats crammed inside.

Howe didn't have much to say about that.

The rats hadn't worked. Neither had the intoxication claim. And the jury's visit to the Woodside cottage that Thorn had so nonchalantly neglected to join? Howe had claimed a mistrial, because *the defendant was not present during a presentation of evidence.* That argument had tied up the execution for months, though at length the superior-court judges didn't buy it; in fact, they didn't buy Howe, either. His $427 legal bill was cruelly knocked down to $127 by the state. Howe talked grandly to the press of taking the case to the U.S. Supreme Court, but with final appeals exhausted in the broiling heat—one year since the first mysterious parcels were found in the East River—a date of August 1 was now set for Thorn's execution.

And now Martin Thorn had one day left to live.

The day began with some measure of inconvenience. As soon as he finished his breakfast, his keepers called him out of his cell.

"Take all your clothes off, Martin," one of them directed.

It was a standard precaution, the same they'd used on Hadley on his last day. After Thorn stripped, they led him down to his final home, cell #1. It was slightly larger than the other cells, and arranged on the bed were black execution trousers and a new shirt. For once, the shirt wasn't also black. Thorn had always dressed well, and his pleas to the warden had been heard: Folded neatly atop the trousers was a crisp dress oxford—white, with light pink stripes. Thorn was delighted with it.

"My last clean shirt!" he yelled in mock triumph to the other inmates.

There were five condemned prisoners on the cell block now. Among them was Adrian Braun, a paranoid cigar maker whose domestic-assault charge turned capital after he stabbed his wife to death in the Sing Sing visitors' room. In Braun's lucid moments, Thorn found him fine company.

Thorn's neighbors weren't quite sure how to answer, though.

"Good luck!" Braun finally blurted.

Turning his attention to the rest of his new cell, Thorn also noticed what was missing.

"I want my books," he pleaded to a guard through the bars. It was the first time that morning that he'd actually sounded upset, and his relief was palpable when the guards moved the pile to his new cell.

"They are my friends," Thorn said as he hefted his books. He'd developed a fierce love of reading while on Death Row and even had managed to snare a coveted title from the prison library: *"There's a cold-blooded scoundrel!" said Holmes, laughing as he threw himself down into his chair once more. "That fellow will rise from crime to crime until he does something very bad, and ends on a gallows."*

Well, if Sherlock Holmes wasn't quite a comfort on this day, at least he was entertaining. Thorn paused occasionally to chat across the cell walls with the other prisoners. One was reciting Heine poems, another chimed in with a dirty story, and a third started talking politics—namely, anarchy and socialism.

"I don't believe in it," Thorn shook his head. "Let a man keep what he earns."

"And what a man doesn't earn, let him steal," cracked Braun from his cell, before turning more serious. "Have you seen your mouse yet, Thorn?"

"No," Thorn called back. He'd caught one earlier in the summer and tamed it with portions of his prison ration. When the pet went missing earlier that week, it had nearly brought him to tears. "Smart little fellow, too—he'd eat out of my hand and all that."

But now Thorn was alone again in his cell.

"Rats desert a sinking ship," he added dryly to Braun and said a salutary set of prayers—for while religion had come slowly to him, he was covering his bets now. At six there arrived a final meal of roast beef, turnips, rye bread, and pudding—the foods of Thorn's youth in Prussia—and as the night finally fell outside, Thorn turned talkative with the priest dispatched to his cell as spiritual counsel. One of the keepers brewed a pot of coffee at the guard station, and cups were passed between the keepers, the priest, and Thorn. The prisoner didn't want to talk about his case; instead, he mused upon his childhood in his hometown of Posen. Those were happy days. Why dwell on the present?

I still remember, he said as midnight closed in. *I remember the sound of my father's hammer as he worked on shoes.*

"You must get some sleep, Martin," the priest said gently.

Thorn clasped his hand, then hung his clothes for the morning and settled into his cot. Soon he was so soundly asleep that the guards were startled when he suddenly sat up bolt upright at 4:30 a.m.

Fritz? he called out. *Adrian?*

The other inmates were still asleep.

"What are you doing, Thorn?" a keeper asked.

"Thinking about Posen," the prisoner mumbled—and then collapsed back into his slumbers.

THE NEXT MORNING, the curtains were drawn across the other inmates' cells. Warden Sage was bustling around his office, making preparations and welcoming his guests: the visiting physicians, electricians, and newspaper artists clutching thick pads of paper. All wore black for the occasion, and they mingled with nervous solemnity. More than two thousand applications had poured into the warden's office in the last week, but state law dictated that only twenty-eight observers were allowed at the death chamber. These men were the elite of the New York press and medical establishment. The old-timers could spot the yellow-press men by the sheer flash of their presence: *They've sent Smith and Jones.*

Hearst had deployed Langdon Smith, one of the *Evening Journal*'s top correspondents, and a man once famed as the country's fastest telegrapher. Standing by him was rival Haydon Jones, the *World*'s own speed artist. Barely out of art school, he'd been scooped up by Pulitzer's crew from the *Mail and Express* when it became clear that he was the best quick draw in town.

Follow me, the warden motioned the crowd. Smith and Jones tagged behind them, observing the location. The artist readied his favorite Blaisdell pencil and rakishly square Steinbach pad for the *World* litho crew, while Smith took notes for the *Journal* even as they crossed Sing Sing's grounds: *"The procession, black-clad and quiet, fol-lowed the Warden across the prison yard, where the dumb convicts were work-ing: through the engine-room, where three noiseless dynamos were running, and on to the death chamber. An empty, high-ceilinged room, with broad glazed glass windows, a room without the softening effect of curtains or pic-tures, a room bare and spartan-like and well-fitted for the rigors of death."*

To the *World*'s man, the room was reminiscent of a small chapel— its only ornamentation a subtle Grecian meander painted around the walls, like a funeral urn, its totality bathed in the glare of sunlight. A few colored panes had been placed in the high skylights, giving the walls a ghostly green tint. As they sat down on the room's perimeter of hard pine benches, the crowd was already beginning to perspire under the rays of an August morning.

"Gentlemen"—the warden stood before them as the revving dy-namos became faintly audible—"you will oblige me if you will not leave your places until after the physicians have declared the execu-tion complete."

Before them, at the center of the far end of the room, stood the instrument of that execution: a heavy, plain-hewn oak chair with leather straps dangling idly from its sides. Above it spread black cables—"the tentacles of an electrical octopus," one awed reporter wrote—that snaked down and around the front legs, before creeping up to the screw cap at the back of the empty chair. Nearby, the state's electrician pointed to a board with a stark arrangement of three rows of six naked lightbulbs.

"By these lamps," the electrician explained, "we will test the cur-rent and see that we have the necessary power."

He tapped five bells to the dynamo room, then threw the switch. The lights rose in a row, each in succession, their filaments turning from a cherry-red glow to a blinding white radiance; the empty chair was coursing with electricity, the room ablaze with incandescent light. *1,750 volts at ten amperes*, he read from his gauge. When the power was cut, it took nearly thirty seconds for the angry glow of the test lights to finally die away.

The electric chair was ready.

Warden Sage opened the iron cell-block door and stepped out of the room with a guard. Reporters could hear the squeal of an iron door in the adjoining hallway and the low mutter of voices.

"The hour has come," the warden said.

"All right," they heard Thorn answer. "I want to thank you for your kindness."

The men appeared in the doorway: the warden, the guards, Father Hanselman, and the prisoner, who greeted his old newspaper acquaintances with a quick half smile. Thorn's gratitude to the warden showed on his sleeve, for Warden Sage had allowed a concession to the man's vanity: Thorn was wearing his best frock jacket and a white cambric tie. He sat down in the chair without any prompting, as if he were taking breakfast on an ordinary Monday morning.

"Dear God, this will be the birthday of a new life," intoned Father Hanselman. "Christ have mercy."

"Christ have mercy," Thorn dutifully repeated as his feet were lashed to the chair legs.

His eyes followed the guards as they placed sponges soaked in salt water against his calves and then against the base of his neck, the better to increase conductivity; over these they firmly buckled the cable fittings and the headpiece. A long black rubber sash was stretched across his face and around the back of the chair to hold his head in place; only his mouth was visible through a slit. Scarcely two minutes since he'd been led out of his cell, Thorn was now immobile and blindfolded.

"Christ, Mary, Mother of God," the priest chanted as he slid a small wooden crucifix into Thorn's right hand. "Christ have mercy."

The warden silently nodded to the electrician.

"Chri—" The prisoner's lips moved.

He never finished the word. Thorn's body was thrown into the straps by a massive shock. For ten seconds, then another twenty, then thirty more, his limbs convulsed and his neck swelled as the powerful current coursed into him, the amperage needle nearly twisting out of its gauge. A thin curl of smoke rose from his right calf, and when the electrician pushed the lever back up, Thorn's body slumped. White foam dripped from the slit of the faceless rubber mask.

The prison's physician stepped forward, stripped open Thorn's shirt, and lay the cold medallion of his stethoscope against the con-demned man's chest. The only sound in the room was a pencil mak-ing quick slashing and cross-hatching across a sketch pad—for of all the newspaper artists there, only Haydon Jones had the presence of mind to catch Thorn in the moment before the lever was pulled. The others sat stunned and breathing in air that, a *Herald* writer noted, smelled "like an overheated flatiron on a handkerchief."

The doctor turned to the witnesses.

"The man is dead," he said.

24.

A STORY OF LIFE
IN NEW YORK

SMITH AND JONES hustled to get their stories and pictures out, and the other reporters followed hard on their heels. While the *Evening Telegram* announced MARTIN THORN GOES CALMLY TO HIS DEATH, and the *New York Sun* chimed in with THORN MET DEATH CALMLY, *Herald* readers were treated to a different execution altogether: MARTIN THORN DIES IN ABJECT TERROR. The *World*, always solicitous of its female readership, declared WOMAN MEDIUM COMMUNES WITH THORN JUST AS HIS SPIRIT WINGS ITS FLIGHT.

"It was all for thy sake, Augusta," they reported him calling out from the astral plane, "but I have forgiven and I died happy."

One man, though, was not so sure of that. As the reporters quickly exited the stifling death chamber, a different sort of witness pressed past them to the front of the room. Dr. Joseph Alan O'Neill was a surgeon with the New York School of Clinical Medicine, and he looked keenly at the lifeless body still slumped in the chair. It smelled of singed flesh, for one of the saltwater sponges had dried out, causing a burn hole nearly an inch deep under the electrode on Thorn's right calf. The body was still warm from the departed electrical current.

O'Neill opened his medical bag, revealing syringes and a ready supply of restoratives: nitroglycerin, strychnine, and brandy.

Shall I administer them? Dr. O'Neill asked the warden.

No, the prison official shot back. *You may not.* The law, the warden insisted, did not allow for resuscitation measures, but if Dr. O'Neill insisted on ascertaining that the patient was indeed dead, there was no language in the statute against that.

Then I will, Dr. O'Neill replied, and produced a stethoscope from his bag.

It was a tense moment. O'Neill was raising a delicate matter that few of the doctors still lingering in the room wished to acknowledge: that nobody was quite sure whether the electric chair actually worked. It had been introduced with great fanfare by the State of New York just eight years earlier, promising a new era of humane and instantaneous execution. But on the chair's first use, condemned prisoner William Kemmler had been left still breathing, with brown froth pouring from his mouth; some said he'd also caught fire. The nine-minute ordeal left witnesses so shaken that one deputy sheriff emerged in tears. Thorn, only the twenty-seventh man to go to Sing Sing's chair, faced a procedure that had hardly been perfected yet.

O'Neill bent over and rested the stethoscope on Thorn's skin. There was a motion underneath—a faint thrill in the carotid artery. That, he suspected, might just be blood draining from the head down to the trunk. But there were other disturbing signs. With swift and practiced movements, the doctor examined the cremasteric reflex, which retracted or loosened the testes; it was still working. O'Neill then lit his ophthalmoscope and pulled back Thorn's left eyelid; the pupil contracted beneath the blaze of light.

"If required, I should be very reluctant to sign his death certificate," the surgeon announced.

It was an admission many physicians made in utmost privacy after these executions—but not in front of the public. The prison doctor pointedly ignored O'Neill and directed two attendants to carry the body to an autopsy room. Thorn's skull and chest were quickly opened to reveal little of note.

Aghast, Dr. O'Neill fired off a dispatch titled "Who's the Executioner?" to the *Atlantic Medical Weekly*. "The law requires post-mortem mutilation," he noted. "It is, in fact, part of the penalty; for, as it reveals no cause of death and teaches nothing of interest to science, it is evident that *its purpose is to complete the killing*."

Thorn suffered nothing less than a modern drawing and quartering, the surgeon charged, and another medical journal scorned the autopsy as "the prostitution of science." But the debate remained a quiet disagreement among colleagues. Reading the afternoon papers, one might never have guessed this most appalling irony of the case: that carried into an autopsy room and cut apart while faintly alive, Martin Thorn had met the same fate at Sing Sing that William Guldensuppe once suffered in a Woodside bathtub.

THE *EVENING JOURNAL* lavished attention that night on the execution, right down to helpful anatomical close-ups of Thorn's "Degenerate Ear" and "Pugnacious Nose." It was the end of an affair that had been very good to them: The Guldensuppe case had pushed Hearst's circulation past the *World*'s. He'd capitalized on this success with front-page attacks on crooked dealings in local trolley and gas franchises, stoked his paper's capacity even further with a baroquely engineered Hoe dectuple multi-color half-tone electrotype web perfecting press, and then trumpeted the serial debut of "the most startling and interesting novel of modern times"—something called *The War of the Worlds*. But it was freeing the comely Evangelina Cisneros that had shown William Randolph Hearst that *Journal* readers needed more than just Martian invaders to root against. They needed a real war.

THE WORST INSULT TO THE UNITED STATES IN ITS HISTORY, his paper had declared after obtaining a leaked letter from a Spanish diplomat that described President McKinley as weak and easily led. "A good war," the newspaper thundered, "might free Cuba, wipe out Spain, frighten to death the meanest tribe of money-worshipping parasites that has ever disgraced a decent nation." But a good war needed a good excuse, and early in 1898 Hearst had gotten it: a mysterious explosion that ripped open the USS *Maine* while docked in Cuba, sending the battleship and most of its men to the bottom of Havana Harbor.

"Have you put anything else on the front page?" Hearst demanded in a dawn phone call to his newsroom.

"Only the other big news—" his editor began.

"There is no other big news," Hearst replied. "This means war."

WAR! SURE! MAINE DESTROYED BY SPANISH, the *Journal* announced. Neither war nor the culprit was a sure thing—many suspected a coal fire belowdecks had doomed the ship—but Hearst was not to be deterred. THE WHOLE COUNTRY THRILLS WITH WAR FEVER, his paper insisted, and he proudly coined a national rallying cry: *"Remember the* Maine! *To hell with Spain!"* When McKinley finally declared war that spring, Hearst and his headlines left no doubts about their proud role in the matter:

HOW DO YOU LIKE THE JOURNAL'S WAR?

William Randolph Hearst liked it very much indeed. Having already issued his Murder Squad badges to pursue Thorn, he thought nothing of the next logical step: He offered the U.S. military $500,000 to raise a *Journal*-sponsored army regiment. His offer spurned, Hearst spent the money anyway: the Wrecking Crew poured out of his Park Row offices, this time headed for the next boats to Cuba. The paper's circulation, already the highest in the country when it had hit 300,000, now rocketed up to a dizzying half million, then a million, and then a million and a half.

It was now the greatest newspaper juggernaut the world had ever known.

Pulitzer was obliged to keep up, of course; he duly matched Hearst star Frederic Remington with his own Stephen Crane. The *World* charged that the *Journal*'s "war news was written by fools for fools." The *Journal* jeered that the *World* was so jealous that it stole the *Journal*'s wire reports. To prove it, the *Evening Journal* ran news of the death of one Colonel Reflipe W. Thenuz; the next morning's *World* ran a similar story on the ill-fated officer. Hearst's editors gleefully revealed that there *was* no Colonel Thenuz; reversing the colonel's first name and middle initial, though, revealed this message inadvertently run by the *World* "in cold type—in its own columns":

We Pilfer the News

Hearst had yet another humiliating trump card, which he knew the frail and nervous Pulitzer could not match: He sent *himself.* Soon the U.S. Navy was treated to the sight of the newspaper publisher tearing around Havana Harbor in a convoy of chartered yachts.

MUST FIND THAT FLEET! he roared in giant front-page headlines draped in patriotic red, white, and blue bunting, while inside, his paper offered up summer dessert tips for homemakers that included such "warlike dainties" as Ice Cream Soldiers and Lemon Ice Cannons. ("You will swallow bullets—of chocolate," it promised.) Hearst himself took to dodging actual bullets; after blithely ignoring press restrictions and taking some Spanish prisoners of war, the young publisher was spotted at the Battle of El Caney. A *Journal* correspondent, struck to the ground by a bullet to the shoulder, opened his eyes to see his own boss leaning over him, a ribboned straw hat on his head and a revolver strapped to his belt.

"I'm sorry you're hurt," Hearst beamed as the enemy rounds whistled past them. "But wasn't it a splendid fight? We must beat every paper in the world."

BACK IN NEW YORK, the Eden Musée was busy adding a score of patriotic new waxworks of Rough Rider charges and Manila Bay victories, and setting up pride of place for the latest in entertainment: the cinematograph. It had been scarcely a year since the first public cinema screenings in Paris and New York; not only did the Musée now have one of its own, its sign also announced the most eagerly awaited films of all: CINEMATOGRAPH WAR SCENES. While the war scenes were moved and spooled into place, other Musée staffers prepared a more familiar mannequin for a new scene down in its Chamber of Horrors. The Musée's old star wax attraction would now be seated in an oak chair festooned with ominous wiring and leather restraints convincingly riveted to its frame. The exhibit bore a stark caption: "The Electrocution of Martin Thorn."

Not many blocks away, the Empire Limited pulled in to Grand Central Depot bearing the genuine article; its baggage car disgorged a plain pine box, and handlers quickly moved it to a side entrance of the station, all under the watchful eye of a detective. There were worries that freak-show promoters might try stealing the remains, but so far the arrival of Martin Thorn had passed unnoticed and unannounced.

As a carriage bore the coffin toward Christian Herrlich's funeral parlor off Eighty-Third and First Avenue, though, word raced ahead: *He's here.* A thousand disappointed spectators had appeared at Herrlich Brothers' doors the night before, only to find that Thorn hadn't arrived yet. Even as the hearse drew quickly up the street, hundreds of onlookers were already gathering again. A dozen policemen from the Twenty-Seventh Precinct station house labored mightily to clear a path into the funeral home.

Out of the way! they yelled as the coffin passed through. *Move along.*

The undertaker barred the door to the surging crowd. Inside, sitting in the cool and darkened funeral parlor, was Martin Thorn's sister with her daughter and husband; alongside them stood three barbers from Thorn's old shop. They'd raised the money for their coworker's burial, and Thorn was quickly moved from his prison-issued pine box into a more respectable casket with silver handles. Beneath his dark curls, his head still bore red electrode marks; his young niece wept at the sight, and bent over to kiss his face.

After a few minutes, the brother-in-law leaned over for a word in the undertaker's ear. Herrlich open the door, and a boisterous line of New Yorkers poured in to view the executed man. As much as his exposed face, though, they gawked at the massive and luxuriant display of lilies of the valley decorating one end of the bier. It was a $45 delivery order—hardly the sort of expense the family or the barbers could have paid for. Who, then, had arranged for it to be delivered?

"Probably a woman," theorized a *Journal* reporter.

The undertaker just smiled, and an explanation became clear.

"Mrs. Nack?" a *Herald* reporter ventured.

"I will neither affirm," the undertaker replied, "*nor* deny your question."

And then he smiled again.

MRS. NACK had been busy indeed. As inmate #269 at Auburn Prison, she woke up each morning at seven sharp to find herself alone in a cell that was secured not with the usual iron bars but instead with a three-inch-thick oak door with a peephole—for the building still bore some touches of its origins as a hospital for the insane. After dressing in a blue-and-white-striped uniform of coarse awning cloth, the former midwife then spent her day in the prison's sewing room, where she labored quietly with other prisoners on a huge government order for 6,000 haversacks. She'd been a model prisoner, and for good reason: Soon she'd be able to earn the privilege of a bedside rug on her cell floor.

Word was leaking out, though, that while Thorn in his final days hadn't wanted to talk about his crime, he did admit one thing: Mr. Nack's wild charges about Gussie were *true*. She really had been disposing of fetuses in a kitchen stove and then dumping remains down a chute into the sewer system.

"He added," a reporter noted, "that it was very profitable. It was practically all profit."

A week after Thorn's burial, the *Journal* pounced on a damning discovery: Augusta Nack was quietly trying to arrange from behind bars the sale of two parcels of land in Cliffside, New Jersey. It was hardly the work of a poor midwife who had claimed to have only $300 to her name.

"Detectives have always believed that Mrs. Nack burned the bodies of babies," Hearst's paper charged. "Now, after Thorn's execution, like a confirmation of his charges, comes proof that Mrs. Nack is a woman of means." The imprisoned midwife maintained a stony silence, though not before another newspaper wittily nominated her for a Hall of Fame statue under the sardonic inscription of AUGUSTA NACK, SURGEON.

Some, though, were studying Nack and Thorn's methods more seriously. Mutilation murders now occurred with such alarming frequency that one medical journal declared that the Guldensuppe case had induced "Epidemic Hypnotic Criminal Suggestion." When a sawn-off trunk bobbed up in the East River the summer after Thorn's execution, the *Times* headline SECOND GULDENSUPPE CASE hardly covered it; there were also third, fourth, and fifth Guldensuppe cases. Still another trunk appeared on October 8, 1899: That morning, a woman's leg was found carefully wrapped in recent issues of the *World* and the *Journal* and tossed into the gutter in front of 160 West Seventeenth Street. Soon her midriff bumped up against the Thirtieth Street pier, and her chest washed ashore on Staten Island, where it was discovered by a boy out gathering driftwood.

Station houses around the city emptied out as the NYPD threw 200 detectives on the case. The discovery of coal dust on the wrappings quickly led to a house-to-house rifling of coal cellars.

"Everybody that shows the slightest hesitancy will regret it," one officer barked to a *Sun* reporter. "I will kick the door in and search every house on the block."

Newspapers roared to life again with offers of reward money, and Bellevue's morgue filled with would-be relatives; newspapers ran lists of missing women, and papers leapt at the clue that one of the newspaper wrappers had borne the small pencil notation of *16c*. That traced the paper to a dealer named Moses Cohen, the "C" newspaper concession on Sixteenth Street. Another witness, the captain of the barge *Knickerbocker*, reported a chillingly familiar sort of suspect fleeing the scene near the Thirtieth Street pier: a German male, aged about thirty-five. It was looking like the efforts of the police and the newspapers would bust open an insoluble case once again.

"The methods are largely those which would have appealed to Sherlock Holmes," the *Brooklyn Eagle* exulted. "The killers of Guldensuppe have paid the penalty for their crime and it is probable that within a few days we shall know who killed this woman."

The comparison was turning startlingly apt, for it looked like another German midwife might be the accomplice. The Prospect Place coal cellar of Alma Lundberg was found filled with bloody rags and quicklime, and she'd abandoned the house hurriedly after the first clues were found—perhaps running from a botched abortion. But the lead went nowhere, and other clues proved to be the usual nonsense—an overexcited servant girl, a missing beauty who turned up alive in Scranton, and an encore appearance by "the Great American Identifier," who this time gravely informed the police that the crime had been committed by two women.

There was also a more troubling development in the case. Examining the body, Deputy Coroner O'Hanlon determined that the cuts precisely matched those on Guldensuppe. Whoever had done this, he theorized, had been one of the many who had gawked at Guldensuppe's body in the Bellevue morgue.

"I believe that the persons who committed this murder saw the body of Guldensuppe more than once," the doctor warned. "The cutting up of this body is identical. These murderers copied Mrs. Nack and Thorn in everything."

OTHER CURIOUS REMEMBRANCES of the crime surfaced in the years after Thorn's execution. One of the first was a novel, *Three Men and a Woman: A Story of Life in New York*, by none other than the Reverend Robert Parker Miles, the minister whose young child had inspired the jail-cell confession of Augusta Nack. Along with the rushed-out *Guldensuppe Mystery* and the dime novel *The Headless Body Murder Mystery*, this became the third book on the case. Now living in Iowa, Miles restyled the crime a bit for his version; in his novel, the hard-drinking delivery driver Herman Nack became an earnest Viennese physician. But the story of a faithless wife who "plunges into a sea of gaiety" and then murder remained perfectly recognizable.

The real Herman Nack, though, was suffering even more than his fictional counterpart. "The death of Guldensuppe preyed upon his mind," one reporter noted; he found it hard to hold down delivery jobs whenever his name was recognized. In 1903, almost six years to the day after Guldensuppe's murder, Nack calmly abandoned his delivery wagon at the foot of Canal Street and drowned himself in the Hudson River.

The Woodside cottage proved nearly as ill starred. The modest home at 346 Second Street sat vacant for years after the last visit of the jury during Thorn's trial, for the building's reputation was so fearsome that the hapless Bualas were unable to rent it to anyone. The old bedroom upstairs where Guldensuppe was shot never quite recovered from the crime, either, for the district attorney had carelessly thrown the Bualas' baseboards into a bonfire during a fit of evidence-room housecleaning—though not before saving the two extracted bullets for himself and turning them into a jaunty pair of scarf pins.

At least one other man was determined to remain unfazed by the house.

"We have already put one haunted house out of business," Bill Offerman boasted to a *Tribune* reporter. As the president of the Brooklyn Society for the Extermination of Ghosts and Dispelling of Haunted House Illusions, Offerman and his fellow members—"thirty young men between the ages of seventeen and twenty-three"—had already rented and then camped out in a vacant Brooklyn home where a butcher had committed suicide. Armed with revolvers and lanterns, the Society held a weeklong stakeout to prove to fearful locals that the butcher did not, in fact, return each night to slit his own throat. Toward the end of the vigil, the bored debunkers amused themselves by testing out some new recruits.

"A skeleton in the dark hall, rigged up on wires, with electric lights for eyes, was enough to demonstrate that one young man was unfit for membership," Offerman noted drolly.

Now, he declared, his tried and tested group was ready to take on the infamous Woodside cottage. Their efforts did not rid the house of its reputation for bad luck: A few years later, a new tenant set up a pet shop in the house, only to die of rabies from a dog bite. A wine seller named Peter Piernot had fared little better after preserving the bathroom upstairs "as it was on the day of the murder" for curious customers. In the dead of a November night, Piernot ran half-naked and screaming from the premises and leaped aboard the next train out of Woodside. Before being placed in an insane asylum, Piernot babbled in horror to the police.

He was running, he told them, from the ghost of William Guldensuppe.

CARRY OUT YOUR
OWN DEAD

"WHAT DO YOU WANT?" the frightened train passenger demanded. "I am not this woman you are looking for."

She was in the last seat of the third carriage on the Metropolitan Express—an unassuming country matron in a simple dress with white lace and a sensible black hat trimmed with fresh violets. But the crowd of reporters who boarded at Poughkeepsie wouldn't leave her alone. A tall, long-haired artist ostentatiously pulled out his sketch pad and drew on it rapidly.

"Why does he draw my picture?" she snapped. "I am the wife of a farmer named Ross, of Buffalo. Is my face of interest to any one? I hate newspapers, and I shall not say anything to them."

A glance at the latest *New York Journal* for July 19, 1907, explained everything. The papers had their usual horrors that day—CUT HIS THROAT BY ACCIDENT and SHE HEARD VOICES; LEAPED TO DEATH—and reporters were scrambling on the story of a Civil War vet in Central Park who threw hundreds of coins into the air; as they rained down on delighted children, the man pulled out a revolver and blew his head off. There was even another heat wave to report on. But there was no question at the *Journal* about the day's biggest story. A single gigantic headline roared out over the top half of their front page:

MRS. NACK
SET FREE

"Oh, Mrs. Nack," the farmer's wife said distantly. "What did she do? I never heard of Mrs. Nack."

"There are some here," a reporter in the train carriage answered tartly, "who remember you very well."

"Oh, you do? Well, I am not the same woman. I tell you I am not Mrs. Nack at all."

She arranged herself primly in her seat, hands folded across her purse, looking away from her tormentors. But it was no use; a train crewman stopped in the middle of his rounds, startled, and spoke volubly to her in German. His passenger was thinner now, with a few streaks of gray in her hair, but he'd recognized her immediately—because he'd been a spectator at Thorn's trial ten years earlier.

Mrs. Nack slumped back into her seat, defeated.

"I am glad to be out," she finally said. "I spent a long time in that awful prison. I have served my time, and I guess that pays my debt to the state."

So where was she going now?

"New York," she shrugged. "Because it is the only place I know. I do not quite know what I shall do. Maybe get a place as a seamstress or a housekeeper."

She considered what awaited her. The three men she had loved were all gone: one murdered, another executed, and the third a suicide.

"I have no family now," she said plainly. "My children are dead too."

When reporters asked about the murder, though, she pursed her lips into a tight frown and stared back out the train window. As the Metropolitan Express slid into Grand Central Terminal some ten minutes late, the platform boiled over with hundreds of people jostling in the July heat for a better look.

"Mrs. Nack!" reporters outside yelled. *"Mrs. Nack!"*

It was chaos. Mrs. Nack clutched her bags as she pressed forward into the crowd, swarmed by reporters and gawking New Yorkers. *Mrs.*

Nack! they yelled, jockeying for position. As the crowd pressed her up against an iron railing, she grew terrified.

"Go away!" she yelled. "I am not this Nack woman that you say I am! Go away!"

A lithe women's-page reporter scrambled to the front of the crowd and tried to whisper in her ear.

"Get away from me!" Mrs. Nack recoiled. "I know you all. You are bad, bad, bad. . . . Shall I scream? *Police!*"

A station policeman shoved through the crowd, clearing a path for her across the terminal. Near the entrance, a trio of women accosted her.

"We are friends of yours," they began. "You must remember—"

"I have no friends," she cut them off, then rushed away.

Outside was even worse: Ranks of tripod cameras lying in wait on Lexington Avenue went off all at once like lightning in her face. She began to run. "Reporters by the score," marveled a *Sun* reporter, "pestiferous kodakers, idlers, curiosity seekers, and fifty varieties of rubbernecks chased a pale faced, frightened woman in black in and among the trolleys, trucks and hansom cabs."

In front of the Grand Union Hotel, the frantic woman spotted an empty horse-drawn carriage.

"*Keb?*" the driver asked in a clipped accent.

"Yes!" cried Mrs. Nack as she clambered aboard. "Drive away from here quick!"

The cab jerked away with a snap of the driver's whip, followed by ten more reporter-filled carriages in hot pursuit.

"Go away!" she could be heard yelling from her carriage. "Get away!"

THE WORLD her cab galloped into was not the one she'd left ten years earlier. The Victorian era had ended, and a new century had begun. Humans had learned to fly. The police station where she'd been interrogated was gone; the courthouse and the jury's hotel were both burnt out. Along the stretches where she and Thorn had hurried in a horse-drawn funeral carriage, the streets of New York were now giving way to gleaming automobiles, and they rushed to a new entertainment called *cinema*.

The reporters didn't have autos, but it wasn't easy to get rid of them; she'd had to pay the driver six dollars to urge him on. Their cab rattled down to Thirty-Second Street, threw a hard right to Fifth Avenue, cut back up to Thirty-Eighth, then to Broadway, and then toward Hell's Kitchen. As her pursuers got lost in the traffic, Mrs. Nack relaxed a little and asked to see her old neighborhood.

"I suppose I shall find things a great deal different than they were when I was free in New York before," she had mused earlier to the *Herald*.

Many of the blocks by her old home were already gone, demolished to make way for Penn Station. There was little familiar left for her, just mocking echoes. Even the lawyer who had defended her, Manny Friend, had been gone for three years now. He died on the very afternoon he'd sent his premium check over to his life insurance company, after jovially instructing his clerk, "You'd better take it over now, as I might drop dead this afternoon."

Her legal tormentor was gone, too, for William Howe had passed away in 1902. In fact, he and Mrs. Nack had rather more in common than anyone realized. Before his career as America's top attorney, Howe had spent a stretch in the penitentiary himself. Recalled in obituaries as the son of an American minister, he was in fact the English child of a brothel keeper. Howe's first appearance before a judge had been not as a lawyer but as a defendant. In 1848 he was hauled before the bar as a young law-office clerk in London, accused of forging admission tickets to the Lyceum Theater. He narrowly escaped the charge by claiming it had been a practical joke, but he was less lucky the next time around. While employed as a clerk in Blackfriars, he was convicted in 1854 of impersonating a lawyer. Tossed into prison for eighteen months with hard labor, Howe emerged to reinvent himself across the ocean as the person he'd once only pretended to be: not just a real attorney, but one of the greatest in the country.

But for Mrs. Nack, starting over would not be so easy.

Her cab pulled up to the Forty-Second Street entrance to the

Hotel Markwell, where the manager recognized her. She wasn't welcome there. A few blocks and one alias later, the Hotel Rand was hardly an improvement: Its proprietor was Wilson Mizner, a colorful character whose lobby sign read CARRY OUT YOUR OWN DEAD. Mizner had a fighter's battered knuckles—"I got those knocking down dames in the Klondike," he claimed—but the quiet woman who signed in as "Mrs. A. Ross, Buffalo" was too much even for him. As reporters descended on his hotel late that night, Mizner ordered "Mrs. Ross" to leave first thing next morning. *I don't want your money,* he told her. *Just get out.*

"I have had enough misery for one woman," she sobbed, and collapsed in the hallway with her bags. "What interest can anyone have in the past? Are they not satisfied?"

But by the next day, Augusta Nack was beginning to see the value of the past.

"I am selling this story," she informed the *New York Times* as she marched into its offices. "What arrangements is your paper making to pay me?"

To her chagrin, she was told that this was not how the *Times* operated. It was, however, how the *Journal* did. Some things hadn't changed. Even so, Hearst's paper had become almost unrecognizable to Mrs. Nack in her decade away. Along with the downright futuristic sight of newspaper photographs, the *Journal* now carried such inconceivable captions as "Remarkable Photograph Showing Fatal Crash Between Autos Going 50 Miles Per Hour." Life outside prison, it seemed, had gotten faster while she was gone—and louder. Hearst's paper was now more squat and squarish in shape, and some already believed an outright tabloid format would be "the 20th Century newspaper." Pulitzer's *World* had already tested out an issue in this potent new form; tabloids were cheap to print, after all, and easier to read on the crowded new subways. Hearst hadn't quite made the shift yet, but he was halfway there: His paper already looked coarser, its front-page headlines a Klaxon call of massive type, sometimes in crude wooden-type letters that were seven inches tall. In the *Journal*'s early days, only the beginning of a war could summon up crude and gargantuan typesetting; but in this new century every day was a conflict, every day a panic. BUILDING FALLS; 40 KILLED, blared one copy from that week. WOMAN KILLS MAN IN UNION SQUARE, roared another.

There were far more subtly disturbing stories out that day, too—such as word that Kaiser Wilhelm was becoming fascinated by the notion of sending armed zeppelins across the English Channel. ("The young German Emperor gets peevish sometimes," the paper mused.) But after Mrs. Nack's visit, she had booming type of her own on the *Evening Journal*'s front page:

MRS. NACK CONFESSES!

Readers looking inside the paper discovered that indeed she had confessed . . . to her love for William Guldensuppe.

"Guldensuppe and I were happy until Martin Thorn came," she insisted. "He was younger and extremely good looking, but I had no love for him. I told him I could never love him. God knows I did not dream of what was going to happen. I should have given him over to the police as a dangerous man. But I did not think of it."

The entire crime from start to finish, she continued, had been his doing. In fact, she hadn't even known Thorn was upstairs in the Woodside cottage.

"I heard a shot, an exclamation of pain, and a fall. Then it flashed over me in an instant that Thorn had killed the man I loved. He slowly came down the stairs and towards me. I shut my eyes because I thought he was going to kill me. He thought I had fainted and went to get me a glass of water. When he came with the water he said: *Gussie, darling, I did it for you.*"

Her tale sounded curiously theatrical—which indeed it was.

"A theatrical company has made me an offer to go on stage," she admitted, "but I don't think I shall accept. I am going to write a book of my life, and when people read that they will see."

But first she'd have to find a place to live, a place where she could be left alone—"anywhere—everywhere—just so I can lose my identity," she explained. Maybe, she wondered aloud, she'd have to pull together enough money to move back to Germany. The $300 the

police seized when arresting her was presumably still in a bank somewhere, but with her lawyer long dead, she wasn't sure where to start
looking.

Instead, she was busy seeking lodging; the very next place she'd
gone to after the Hotel Rand also rejected her. Visiting the towering
World Building to hawk her story again that day, she looked out over
the sprawling city that spurned her. Augusta Nack no longer knew
New York, but New Yorkers still knew her.

"This," she muttered, "is worse than prison."

ONE YEAR LATER, a call came upstairs to the head matron of the
Tombs; there was, one of the jail staff informed her, "a lady wearing diamonds" waiting for her on a bench in the lobby. The matron
puzzled over who it might be as she walked down to the entrance of
the jail.

"How do you do, my dear?" her visitor called out as she rose. "Oh,
it is so good to see you again!"

The head matron stood back, mystified. Her visitor was a
respectable-looking middle-aged woman, finely adorned with a gold
watch and a diamond brooch, and utterly unfamiliar to her.

"Who are you?" she finally asked.

Her visitor looked about a little conspiratorially, then leaned in. "I
am Mrs. Nack."

The matron was startled, and quickly led her former star prisoner
into her office. It had been some eleven years since she'd last seen
her—so long, in fact, that the entire jail had been rebuilt since she left.

"I have just returned from Germany, where I went to see my old
mother," Mrs. Nack explained as they sat down. "I had a good time
in the old home, but I wanted to come back to America. I wouldn't
live in Europe if you paid me. This is the place to make money."

Mrs. Nack had seen the takings at the Tombs and at Auburn
Prison; the first was almost mythically corrupt, and a state audit later
found Auburn a "brutal" place of "wanton waste and extravagance."
Mrs. Nack had already been on the receiving end of that cruelty
and graft. "You do not have enough to eat," she recalled of Auburn.

"When I was in solitary confinement I received one slice of bread and two ounces of water a day. I thought I would commit suicide, and I tried to open a vein in my arm with a pin. I sucked out the blood and it moistened my lips, and I did not die."

But as long as you were the one standing outside the cell, it was clearly a good business to get into.

"I would like to get a place as a matron or a head keeper in a prison," Mrs. Nack earnestly explained to the flabbergasted jailer. "I know something about the business. Such a place would just suit me."

The matron, a reporter dryly noted, "made no offer to help."

For others, though, the Guldensuppe case launched new careers. Both Judge Smith and Judge Maddox went on to state supreme court appointments soon afterward. For District Attorney William Youngs, the case was followed by a plum promotion: He became Teddy Roosevelt's private secretary, and later the U.S. attorney in New York. After retiring, he even tried the other side of the reporter's notebook and ran a newspaper himself. He drew upon his experience in the first Thorn mistrial to urge the adoption of an alternate-juror rule. The state government in Albany being what it was, it only took another thirty-three years for his sensible proposal to become law.

The chemist whose forensic evidence was spurned for Thorn's trial, Professor Rudolph Witthaus, also went on to great success. Witthaus was brilliant, disturbing, and arrogant to the end, testifying in major murder cases over the next two decades, including such star-studded scandals as the shooting of Stanford White. It was his expertise in poisons, though, that made his fame. He could view stomach membrane under a microscope and pick out the dazzling crystals of arsenic poisoning—or "inheritance powder," as it was dubbed. That same flesh could be minced and boiled and mixed with lye and benzene; if the slurry fluoresced under an ultraviolet light, that was chloroform poisoning. Blasted with the rotten-egg stink of hydrogen sulfide, it would also turn yellow for mercury poisoning. Witthaus's skills were in such demand that in one 1900 case he charged the city a dizzying $18,550 for his services. He could have used some of that consulting himself, as his heirs would later claim that a paramour had kept the dying professor in a chemical haze while filing three conflicting wills. Witthaus, it turned out, died leaving a poisoning case probably only he could have solved: his own.

At least one vital advance was already being made for his successors, though. For all of Witthaus's tools, he had often been frustrated by the evidence ruined by drunk and incompetent coroners, who were still appointed out of political patronage. Emil Hoeber had been one such appointee—and a man not opposed to being bribed with, say, a nice gold watch. The office proved so hopelessly corrupt that in 1915, the year of Witthaus's death, the coroner's job was abolished altogether and replaced by a trained medical examiner. With that, New York City forensics had finally stepped—a little belatedly—into the modern era. Were a Guldensuppe case to come to trial again, no DA would need to feel embarrassed to call forth a coroner or a chemistry professor to testify.

Among police officers, the old "river mystery" remained legendary: Whenever a head was found buried in a basement or a vacant lot, it was promptly dubbed "Guldensuppe's head." Those who really had searched for his head, though, went on to upstanding careers. The first officer to interrogate Mrs. Nack, Captain Samuel Price, rose to become one of the most recognizable detectives in the city and eventually the head of the Detective Bureau in the Bronx. Another key officer at the Harlem find, George Aloncle, became one of the city's top safecracking experts. And even Captain Stephen O'Brien— who lost his Detective Bureau post after triumphantly wrapping up the case—went on to address the bewildering rise of automobiles by founding the city's Traffic Squad. Fittingly enough for the man famed as "the honest cop," after first observing traffic squads in London, Paris, and Berlin, O'Brien submitted a travel-expense report so scrupulously penny-pinching that he was ribbed about it on the force for years afterward.

But the man most marked by the Guldensuppe case was Arthur Carey, the demoted police officer who'd opened the package found in the bushes near the Harlem River. His pursuit of the oilcloth provided a key break in solving the case; his star rose again, and he was made the first head of the NYPD's newly formed Homicide Bureau.

For three decades he was New York City's "Murder Man," famed for being so relentless that he once questioned a suspect in the middle of the funeral of the man's murdered wife. In one Chinatown murder case, he interrogated a suspect for thirty hours, until they both nearly broke down. Carey became a city institution, teaching the homicide course in the NYPD's detective academy. Along with training in weapons and crowd control, the police academy also imparted to recruits a new lesson: Never run roughshod over a crime scene. Spurred by the meticulous new methodologies developed in Austria, police were now exhorted to leave them untouched, and to neatly number and photograph each piece of physical evidence wherever it had fallen. They weren't to touch anything if they could help it; though fingerprints were still ignored in New York City back in 1897, by the time of Mrs. Nack's release, dusting for them had become a standard procedure. The identification of Guldensuppe's body and the murder scene—once so precarious that Howe had nearly used them to overturn the whole case—would in this new era have been clinched by Carey through fingerprints from the body and at Woodside.

By the time Carey retired, he'd personally overseen more murder investigations than possibly any police officer before or since—more than ten thousand, by a *Times* estimate. But it was the Guldensuppe case that stayed with him. Carey always recalled what his first big case and its "hundred different sources" taught him.

"In a murder case there is no one obvious clue," Carey mused, "but all clues are good."

And it was just one such murder case, as it turned out, that would bring Augusta Nack into the news again.

IT WAS A WARM JUNE EVENING in 1909 when a man—a European immigrant, perhaps thirty-five years old—approached a young boy not far from the newsrooms of the *Journal* and the *World*.

"Do you want to make five cents?" the man asked.

The boy was to guard two large parcels wrapped in black oilcloth, then wait for the man to come back to pick them up. Minutes ticked by, then an hour; there was no sign of the man or the nickel. Just as the boy was losing hope, a passing dog caught a scent and began frantically trying to tear at the packages.

Inside them, sliced cleanly in two, was a freshly murdered man with no head.

As Officer Carey hurried over from his newly formed Homicide Bureau, newspaper reporters dashed out of their offices and onto the scene unfolding just down the street. Written in blood on the inside of the oilcloth were the words *Black Hand*; but this, it was surmised, was a murderer's ruse to fool the police into blaming an Italian gang. Before a day had passed, the head was discovered under the Brooklyn Bridge, and newspapers had their real victim: a Russian housepainter named Samuel Bersin.

VICTIM CARVED UP LIKE GULDENSUPPE, one paper announced, while the *Evening Journal* declared CASE MOST PUZZLING SINCE GULDENSUPPE. This time the police were ready. Scores of detectives tracked the distinctive oilcloth pattern and piled into pawnshops, where they soon found Bersin's missing jewelry. Reporters followed in hot pursuit, pouncing on the latest theories: Sammy was murdered by a jealous husband; Sammy was robbed for his diamond rings; Sammy was a Russian Jewish anarchist caught in a political squabble. But the most palpable clue was also the most alluring one: Everyone who knew Sammy knew that he had romantic rivals for the hand of a comely Russian émigré named Jennie Siegel.

Among those swept up in the dragnet around the case was one unexpected bystander: Augusta Nack. With memories of the Guldensuppe case revived, reporters discovered the infamous Mrs. Nack hiding in plain sight just blocks from her old apartment.

"Mrs. Nack has taken the name of Augusta Huber," a wire-service article revealed, "and now manages and owns a small fancy goods store at No. 357 Ninth Avenue." Within hours, Mrs. Nack's new identity had been exposed to both her neighbors and to newspaper readers across the country; within a month of the Bersin murder, she was in bankruptcy court, her business in ruins. And with that, Augusta Nack vanished from public view again—this time, it seemed, for good.

But for old-timers on the force, the memory of Gussie Nack was not so easily lost. Still working the streets of New York decades later, they'd recognize her face with a start, then pass quietly onward. Even so, Chief Inspector Ernest Van Wagner admitted that there'd never been any question among these detectives that it was Nack herself "who actually designed and planned" the murder of William Guldensuppe.

But had she also carried it out?

It is worth considering why the detectives in the case remained insistent on Mrs. Nack's equal guilt, even decades later. *Neither Thorn's explanation nor hers fit the evidence.* The medical examiner, in examining Guldensuppe's body, found signs of a desperate fight: a deep stab wound from a knife plunged straight down, wounds to the hand from where he'd grabbed at a blade, and additional glancing or angled stab wounds. These wounds were clean of any fibers, indicating that he'd been attacked while naked. And upon Mrs. Nack's arrest, the jail matron had discovered bruises on her arm that corresponded in age to the day of the crime. Finally, there was one last humble piece of physical evidence left unaccounted for in the Woodside bedroom. It was the only thing there, in fact, other than the two bullets and a discarded cartridge box: an empty cabernet bottle.

None of these clues were explained in the trial, in Thorn's story to Gotha, or in either murderer's testimony on the stand. But it *is* possible to conceive of one explanation of what happened that afternoon—one that accounts for all of the evidence. Guldensuppe was stabbed while naked, and stabbed from above when he least expected it. Only one person could have led Guldensuppe to the bedroom of a vacant house, offered him wine, stripped him naked, straddled atop him—and then plunged a knife straight down into his chest.

That person was not Martin Thorn.

Guldensuppe would have reached out and grabbed at his assailant's arm and hand, leaving bruises—and was stabbed across the palm and clumsily in the chest. That is when Martin Thorn would have stepped out from a closet to finish his rival off with a gunshot to the head.

Neither Mrs. Nack nor Thorn could admit to this. Thorn's story to John Gotha—the hapless friend who admired his way with cards and women—would quietly omit that he'd triumphed over Guldensuppe by watching him tryst with Gussie. And once Thorn and Mrs. Nack went to trial, each was determined to establish that *only the other had been upstairs to commit the murder.* If they'd acted in concert, neither could breathe a word of the actual plot. And if DA Youngs suspected the truth, there was nothing to be gained by airing it; he lacked hard evidence against Mrs. Nack. As it was, the prosecution managed to keep the salacious details of Guldensuppe's anatomy away from the public. The appalling way he was killed would also remain safely distant from Victorian eyes and ears.

Those who knew better couldn't quite shake off the chill of seeing Mrs. Nack walk free. She had never really left her old streets—the place where she'd considered herself to be the beloved "Nanty Nack" of young mothers and their families alike. There, Chief Inspector Van Wagner wrote in 1938, she could still be found, covered under the cloak of passing decades.

"I last saw her a few years ago," the old detective wrote, "smilingly selling cheap candy in her little store to the unsuspecting and innocent children of her neighborhood."

EPILOGUE: THE LAST
MAN STANDING

REPORTERS RECALLED the Nack and Thorn case for years to come, but by the time Walter Winchell hailed it in 1948 as "the first of the great newspaper trials," he was already speaking of events from his own infancy. The star reporters were long gone: George Arnold, who traced the famed red-and-gold oilcloth for the *Journal*, had one of the more peaceful retirements by capping off his long newspaper career with a venture into writing novelty songs. The *World*'s crack reporter, Ike White, went on to expose dozens of Wall Street fraud operations, and courthouse correspondent Julian Hawthorne landed in prison himself for promoting a nonexistent silver mine.

The yellow-journalism era had taken a toll, though, on Joseph Pulitzer. At the end of the mighty battles over Guldensuppe and Cuba, his advisors estimated that the *Journal* had burned through about $4 million in Hearst's family coffers—but that another $5 million was left. That was more than enough to throw knockout blows at the *World*. The blind and ailing Pulitzer wavered, and finally emerged from the soundproofed mansion where he had ruled by the dictates of a telegraph. He and Hearst met quietly—their one face-to-face meeting—and negotiated a deal. What if they split up the market? The *Journal* could become the carnivalesque one-cent paper of the masses, and the *World* would return to being a more respectable two-cent paper, bent once again on bloodying the *Sun* and the *Herald*.

Just as important, the two papers would band together to fight labor unrest in their ranks.

The *World* and the *Journal,* famed for their crusades against cartels, were now secretly plotting one of their own.

After a year of delicate maneuvering, their resulting agreement went unsigned. Ultimately, though, the *World* inched away from sensationalism of its own accord. Joseph Pulitzer never was very happy playing against Hearst's one-upmanship; in his final years, he quietly came to admire the sober reliability of the *New York Times.* After Pulitzer's death in 1911, the *World'*s proprietor was rehabilitated in historical memory; the yellow-journalism wars faded away, replaced by the rosy glow of bequests to Columbia University and to the writing awards that still bear his name.

Hearst, though, remained unrepentant. He had always delighted in the blockbuster Sunday editions that the yellow revolution fostered—"a Coney Island of ink and wood pulp," as one contemporary put it—and he relished the sensational headlines that made them sell. But just as he challenged his spiritual godfather in Pulitzer, and Pulitzer had turned on James Bennett, so too was Hearst attacked. Now it was by Joseph Patterson, a young Chicagoan that Hearst had once hired as a China correspondent. Patterson's founding in 1919 of the New York *Daily News* upped the stakes in newspaper journalism once again; printed in a bold tabloid format, the paper made its fame by sneaking a shoe-mounted camera into the electrocution of murderess Ruth Snyder and snapping a picture at the moment the switch was thrown. And like Pulitzer and Bennett before him, Hearst seemed rather appalled by his own journalistic progeny. He tried buying out Patterson, and when that didn't work, he launched his own version—the *New York Daily Mirror.* The tabloid war long fomented by Hearst had now truly begun, with square front pages and fist-high headlines socking New Yorkers as they stepped out of the subway.

William Randolph Hearst had always cut a bigger figure than just his newspapers, though. Yet even after parlaying his populism and grandstanding into runs for mayor, then governor, and inevitably for president—he finally settled for a couple of terms in Congress—he never quite recaptured the youthful excitement of his Murder Squad. As the media baron's holdings expanded into dozens of newspapers, and his persona grew to the mythical proportions immortalized in *Citizen Kane*, one contemporary mused that the Guldensuppe case remained "a lark and a triumph which he enjoyed more keenly" than any party nomination.

"Ah well, we were young," he later reminisced. "It was an adventure."

IT SEEMED AS IF that final word on the Guldensuppe case might remain with Hearst himself. But when the media baron died in 1951, there was still another man who hadn't forgotten about the case— one man still standing. That man was Ned Brown.

The cub reporter who first found Mrs. Nack's apartment rose in time to write the *World*'s "Pardon My Glove" boxing column. He outlasted the newspaper itself; Ned worked in its newsroom until its final hours in 1931, then graduated to a long career handling publicity for Jack Dempsey and editing *Boxing* magazine. But he never stopped filing ringside newspaper reports, and when his fellow boxing writer A. J. Liebling profiled him in 1955, it was as much in admiration of an era as of a man: Ned was the last Victorian holdout in the New York sports pens.

"Being a newspaperman gave you stature then," the old man fondly recalled. "Everywhere except in society. It didn't cut any ice there."

Ned then went on to outlive Liebling, too. In fact, he also outlived nearly every New York newspaper. After the *World* went under, it combined with the *Evening Telegram* to become the *New York World-Telegram*. Then it swallowed the *Sun* to become the *New York World-Telegram and Sun*. Then it was mashed together with the remnants of the *Journal*, the *Herald*, and the *Tribune* to become the *New York World Journal Tribune*. And then it died.

But Ned Brown lived on.

Nothing could knock Ned to the mat; the same inquisitive blue eyes that searched Mrs. Nack's mantelpiece for a picture of

Guldensuppe would go on to witness the Manson trial and Watergate. In an age of *Kojak* and *Dirty Harry*, he still recalled the days when *journalists* carried badges. Yet although news evolved from carrier-pigeon dispatches to satellite broadcasts, the business remained curiously familiar; when Rupert Murdoch started his chains, and Ted Turner bought his first TV stations, it was already old news to Ned Brown. He'd seen it all before. Hearst's saturation coverage of sensational local crime—creating a suspenseful narrative out of endless news updates from every angle, whether there was anything substantive to cover or not—had already anticipated the round-the-clock cycle of broadcast news.

When Ned Brown died in 1976, he was well into his nineties— nobody was quite sure how old he was anymore. It wasn't long since he'd made a final bow to the public; evicted from his apartment by the Hudson River, the one possession the old man had bothered to retrieve was his tuxedo.

"I need that suit for my social life," he explained to a reporter.

With him ended the living memory of Augusta Nack and Martin Thorn. Even the case files had been destroyed years earlier by the Queens County Courthouse in a fit of housekeeping. As they were on their way to the incinerator, though, one curious reporter picked out a yellowed evidence envelope and opened it up.

It held little inside—just six duck feathers and a mystery.

SOURCES

PRIMARY SOURCES

Newspapers may be the first draft of history, but most of what they cover never gets a second draft. This book is the first on the entire Guldensuppe affair, and it's indebted to the several thousand newspaper articles about this case that I gathered by examining each day's reporting from more than a dozen daily newspapers:

Brooklyn Daily Eagle (BE)
New York Commercial Advertiser (NYCA)
New York Evening Post (NYEP)
New York Evening Telegram (NYET)
New York Herald (NYH)
New York Journal (NYJ)
New York Evening Journal (NYEJ)
New York Journal and Advertiser (NYJA)
New York Mail and Express (NYME)
New York Press (NYP)
New York Sun (NYS)
New York Evening Sun (NYES)
New York Times (NYT)
New York Tribune (NYTR)
New York World (NYW)
New Yorker Staats Zeitung (NYSZ)

I'm also fortunate to have both court records and memoirs written by the journalists and detectives from the case:

Carey, Arthur. *Memoirs of a Murder Man*. New York: Doubleday, Doran, 1930.

Collins, Frederick L. *Homicide Squad: Adventures of a Headquarters Old Timer*. New York: Putnam, 1944.

Court of Appeals of the State of New York: People of the State of New York Respondent, Against Martin Thorn, Appellant. Jamaica, NY: Long Island Farmer Print, 1898.

Edwarde, Charles. *The Guldensuppe Mystery: The True Story of a Real Crime*. New York: True Story, 1897.

O'Neill, Joseph Alan. "Who's the Executioner?" *The Atlantic Medical Weekly*, vols. 9–10 (September 17, 1898): 184–85.

Pulitzer, Joseph. *Joseph Pulitzer Papers, 1880–1924.* Washington, D.C.: Library of Congress.

Van Wagner, Ernest. *New York Detective.* New York: Dodd, Mead, 1938.

ADDITIONAL SOURCES

Annual Report of the Committee on the Fire Patrol to the New York Board of Fire Underwriters. New York: Economical Printing, 1894.

Ashley, Perry J. *American Newspaper Journalists, 1873–1900.* Detroit: Gale Research, 1983.

Baldasty, Gerald. *The Commercialization of News in the Nineteenth Century.* Madison: University of Wisconsin Press, 1992.

Bell, Suzanne. *Crime and Circumstance: Investigating the History of Forensic Science.* New York: Praeger, 2008.

Bleyer, Willard. *Main Currents in the History of American Journalism.* Boston: Houghton Mifflin, 1927.

Blum, Deborah. *The Poisoner's Handbook: Murder and the Birth of Forensic Medicine in Jazz Age New York.* New York: Penguin Press, 2010.

Brandon, Craig. *The Electric Chair: An Unnatural American History.* Jefferson, NC: McFarland, 1999.

Branigan, Elba. *The History of Johnson County, Indiana.* Indianapolis: B. F. Bowen, 1913.

Brian, Denis. *Pulitzer: A Life.* Hoboken, NJ: Wiley, 2001.

Brodie, Janet Farrell. *Contraception and Abortion in Nineteenth Century America.* Ithaca, NY: Cornell University Press, 1997.

Bromley, G. W. *Atlas of the City of New York, Borough of Queens.* New York: G. W. Bromley, 1909.

Brown, Henry Collins. *In the Golden Nineties.* Hastings on Hudson, NY: Valentine's Manual, 1928.

Byrnes, Thomas. *Professional Criminals of America.* New York: Cassell, 1886.

Cahn, Julius. *Julius Cahn's Official Theatrical Guide,* vol. 9. New York: Julius Cahn, 1904.

Campbell, W. Joseph. *Yellow Journalism: Puncturing the Myths, Defining the Legacies.* New York: Praeger, 2003.

———. *The Year That Defined American Journalism: 1897 and the Clash of Paradigms.* New York: Routledge, 2006.

Churchill, Allen. *Park Row: A Vivid Re-Creation of Turn of the Century Newspaper Days.* New York: Rinehart, 1958.

Cole, Simon. *Suspect Identities: A History of Fingerprinting and Criminal Identification.* Cambridge: Harvard University Press, 2001.

"Conspiracy Charge Against William Howe, William Thompson, Gavin Rickards." *Proceedings of the Old Bailey,* September 18, 1854. Old Bailey Online, oldbaileyonline.org, Ref #t18540918–997.

Copquin, Claudia Gryvatz. *The Neighborhoods of Queens.* New Haven, CT: Yale University Press, 2007.

Creelman, James. *On the Great Highway: The Wanderings and Adventures of a Special Correspondent.* Boston: Lothrop, 1901.

Crouthamel, James. *Bennett's New York Herald and the Rise of the Popular Press.* Syracuse: Syracuse University Press, 1989.

Dennett, Andrea. *Weird and Wonderful: The Dime Museum in America.* New York: New York University Press, 1997.

Dicken-Garcia, Hazel. *Journalistic Standards in Nineteenth-Century America.* Madison: University of Wisconsin Press, 1989.

Douglas, George H. *The Golden Age of the Newspaper.* Westport, CT: Greenwood Press, 1999.

Dreiser, Theodore. *Newspaper Days.* Edited by T. D. Nostwich. Philadelphia: University of Pennsylvania Press, 1991.

Eden Museé: Monthly Catalogue. N.d.

Flint, Austin. *Collected Essays and Articles on Physiology and Medicine.* New York: Appleton, 1903.

Ford, James L. *Forty-Odd Years in the Literary Shop.* New York: Dutton, 1921.

Forrest, Jay W. *Tammany's Treason.* Albany, NY: Fort Orange Press, 1913.

Gilfoyle, Timothy J. "America's Greatest Criminal Barrister." *Journal of Urban History* 29, no. 5 (July 2003): 525–54.

Gregory, Catherine. *Woodside, Queens County: A Historical Perspective, 1652–1994.* Woodside, NY: Woodside on the Move, 1994.

Harlow, Alvin Fay. *Old Bowery Days: The Chronicles of a Famous Street.* New York: Appleton, 1931.

Houck, Max. *Forensic Science: Modern Methods of Solving Crime.* New York: Praeger, 2007.

Hughes, Rupert. *The Real New York.* New York: Smart Set, 1904.

Important Events of the Century. New York: United States Central Publishing, 1876.

Ingersoll, Ernest. *Handy Guide to New York City.* New York: Rand McNally, 1897.

Ireland, Alleyne. *An Adventure with a Genius: Recollections of Joseph Pulitzer.* New York: E. P. Dutton, 1931.

James, W. I. *The Headless Body Murder Mystery, or Old Cap. Collier Searching for Clews; Old Cap. Collier Library #711.* New York: Munro's, 1897.

Jeffers, H. Paul. *Commissioner Roosevelt: The Story of Theodore Roosevelt and the New York City Police, 1895–1897.* New York: John Wiley, 1996.

Johnston, Alva, and Reginald Marsh. *The Legendary Mizners.* New York: Farrar, Straus and Young, 1953.

Juergens, George. *Joseph Pulitzer and the New York World.* Princeton, NJ: Princeton University Press, 1966.

King, Moses. *King's Handbook of New York City.* Buffalo, NY: Moses King, 1893.

Kobbé, Gustav. *New York and Its Environs.* New York: Harper & Brothers, 1891.

Korom, Joseph. *The American Skyscraper, 1850–1940.* Branden Books, 2008.

Lardner, James, and Thomas Reppetto. *NYPD: A City and Its Police.* New York, Henry Holt, 2000.

Lee, Alfred McClurg. *American Journalism, 1690–1940.* New York: Routledge, 2000.

Lee, James Melvin. *A History of American Journalism.* Boston: Houghton Mifflin, 1917.

Liebling, A. J. *Liebling at* The New Yorker: *Uncollected Essays.* Albuquerque: University of New Mexico Press, 1994.

Loerzel, Robert. *Alchemy of Bones: Chicago's Luetgert Murder Case of 1897.* Champaign: University of Illinois Press, 2007.

Lofton, John. *Justice and the Press.* Boston: Beacon Press, 1966.

Longworth, Thomas. *Longworth's American Almanac, New York City Register, and City Directory.* New York: Thomas Longworth, 1834.

Marcuse, Maxwell. *This Was New York.* New York: LIM Press, 1969.

McAdoo, William. *Guarding a Great City.* New York: Harper & Brothers, 1906.

McKerns, Joseph P. *Biographical Dictionary of American Journalism.* Westport, CT: Greenwood Press, 1989.

Miles, Robert Harrison Parker. *Three Men and a Woman: A Story of Life in New York.* New York: G. W. Dillingham, 1901.

Molineaux, Roland. *The Room with the Little Door.* New York: G. W. Dillingham, 1903.

Moran, Richard. *The Executioner's Current.* New York: Random House, 2002.

Morgan, Wayne, and Charles Lincoln Van Doren. *A Documentary History of the Italian Americans*. New York: Praeger, 1974.

Morris, James McGrath. *Pulitzer: A Life in Politics, Print, and Power*. New York: HarperCollins, 2010.

Moss, Frank. *The American Metropolis: From Knickerbocker Days to the Present Time*. New York: Collier, 1897.

Mott, Frank Luther. *American Journalism: A History, 1690–1960*. New York: Macmillan, 1962.

Nasaw, David. *The Chief: The Life of William Randolph Hearst*. New York: Houghton Mifflin, 2000.

"Note: Proof of the Corpus Delicti Aliunde the Defendant's Confession," *University of Pennsylvania Law Review*, 1955: 638–49.

O'Brien, Frank Michael. *The Story of the Sun: New York, 1833–1918*. New York: George H. Doran, 1918.

Palmer, Frederick. "Hearst and Hearstism." *Collier's*, September 22, 1906. In *A Calvacade of Collier's*. New York: A. S. Barnes, 1959.

Prison Association of New York. *Annual Report of the Prison Association of New York for the Year 1895*. State of New York, 1896.

Procter, Ben. *William Randolph Hearst: The Early Years, 1863–1910*. Oxford: Oxford University Press, 1998.

Reel, Guy. *The National Police Gazette and the Making of the Modern American Man, 1879–1906*. New York: Palgrave Macmillan, 2006.

Researches of the Loomis Laboratory of the Medical Department of the University of the City of New York. No. 1. New York: Douglas Taylor, 1890.

Rovere, Richard R. *Howe & Hummel: Their True and Scandalous History*. New York: Farrar, Straus & Giroux, 1947.

Seitz, Don. *Joseph Pulitzer: His Life and Letters*. New York: Simon & Schuster, 1924.

Spitzka, E. C. "Cases of Masturbation (Masturbatic Insanity)," *Journal of Mental Science* 33 (1887): 238–54.

Srebnick, Amy Gilman. *The Mysterious Death of Mary Rogers: Sex and Culture in Nineteenth-Century New York*. Oxford: Oxford University Press, 1997.

Stashower, Daniel. *The Beautiful Cigar Girl: Mary Rogers, Edgar Allan Poe, and the Invention of Murder*. New York: E. P. Dutton, 2006.

Stevens, John D. *Sensationalism and the New York Press*. New York: Columbia University Press, 1991.

Swanberg, W. A. *Citizen Hearst: The Monumental and Controversial Biography of One of the Most Fabulous Characters in American History*. New York: Scribner's, 1961.

Sweetser, M. F. *How to Know New York City*. New York: J. J. Little, 1898.

Tifft, Susan, and Alex S. Jones. *The Trust: The Private and Powerful Family Behind the New York Times*. New York: Back Bay Books, 1999.

Trow's New York City Directory. 1860, 1879, 1890 eds. New York: Trow City Directory.

Turner, Hy. *When Giants Ruled: The Story of Park Row, New York's Great Newspaper Street*. Bronx, NY: Fordham University Press, 1999.

Villard, Oswald. *Some Newspapers and Newspaper-Men*. New York: Alfred A. Knopf, 1926.

Waldman, Bette S., and Linda B. Martin. *Nassau, Long Island, in Early Photographs, 1869–1940*. New York: Dover, 1981.

Warren, Samuel. *Famous Cases of Circumstantial Evidence*. Jersey City, NJ: Frederick D. Linn, 1879.

Whyte, Kenneth. *The Uncrowned King: The Sensational Rise of William Randolph Hearst*. Berkeley, CA: Counterpoint, 2009.

Wilson, James Harrison. *The Life of Charles A. Dana*. New York: Harper & Brothers, 1907.

Winkler, John K. *W. R. Hearst: An American Phenomenon.* New York: Simon & Schuster, 1928.

———. *W. R. Hearst: A New Appraisal.* New York: Hastings House, 1955.

Witthaus, Rudolph, and Tracy Becker. *Medical Jurisprudence, Forensic Medicine and Toxicology.* New York: William Wood, 1894.

Wood, Francis Carter. *Chemical and Microscopical Diagnosis.* New York: Appleton, 1905.

Wyeth, John Allan. *With Sabre and Scalpel: The Autobiography of a Soldier and Surgeon.* New York: Harper & Brothers, 1914.

NOTES

1. THE MYSTERY OF THE RIVER

3 *"OH! YES, IT IS HOT ENOUGH!"*   *NYET*, June 25, 1897.

3 *riverside refreshment stalls . . . the new 700-foot-long promenade pier*   "Large Public Pier Opened," *NYET*, June 26, 1897.

3 *a confection of whitewashed wrought iron*   "New Public Pier," *NYW*, June 27, 1897.

3 *tenements on Avenue C*   Edwarde, *Guldensuppe Mystery*, 9.

4 *flat caps and straw boaters*   "River Gives Up a Murder Mystery," *NYH*, June 27, 1897.

4 *a mysterious ironclad in the shape of a giant sturgeon*   "Flyer for the Sea Afloat," *NYH*, June 26, 1897.

4 *Jack McGuire spotted it first*   Edwarde, *Guldensuppe Mystery*, 10.

5 *The police knew just whom to blame*   "River Gives Up A Murder Mystery," *NYH*, June 27, 1897.

5 *five schools that were allowed to use cadavers*   "Boy's Ghastly Find," *NYW*, June 27, 1897.

5 *The city had yet to buy its first horseless carriages*   Lardner and Reppetto, *NYPD*, 152.

6 *morgue keeper had been arrested*   See *New York Times* coverage of March 23, 1896, January 10, 1897, and April 2, 1897.

6 *tobacco would get a reporter the run*   Dreiser, *Newspaper Days*, 492.

6 *resident tomcat*   "Bellevue Cat a Prisoner," *NYT*, January 15, 1900.

6 *"That horrible place"*   Dreiser, *Newspaper Days*, 492.

7 *obligatory seventy-two hours . . . . Each day a dead-boat pulled up*   King, *King's Handbook*, 461.

7 *the coffin room, where another attendant hammered*   Wyeth, *With Sabre and Scalpel*, 362.

7 *Brady forcibly checked his mother*   "Wealthy Woman Committed," *NYT*, June 27, 1897; and "Rich Woman Insane," *NYEJ*, June 26, 1897.

7 *"There is a mystery here"*   *NYW*, June 27, 1897.

2. A DETECTIVE READS THE PAPER

9 *his Harlem tenement on 127th Street*   "Fragments of a Body Make a Mystery," *NYW*, June 28, 1897.

9 *"let's go cherrying!"*   Ibid.

9 *Just one house was visible . . . twelve-foot drop*   "Strange Murder Mystery Deepens"   *NYH*, June 28, 1897.

10 *Sedgwick and 170th*   *NYH*, June 28, 1897.

10 *he called out*   *NYW*, June 28, 1897.

10 *"I was walking a post"*   Carey, *Memoirs*, 49.

10 *everyone in the department called it: Goatsville*   Lardner and Reppetto, *NYPD*, 63.

10 *Carey had been in Goatsville ever since*   "Detectives in New Jobs," *NYT*, July 20, 1895.

11   *easily a hundred pounds. . . . They'd needed a stretcher and towing ropes*   "River Mystery Grows in Horror," *NYP,* June 28, 1897.

11   *captain was another Byrnes appointee . . . . renting out on-duty police*   "The Killilea Fiasco," *NYT,* May 17, 1896.

11   *the annual police parade was canceled*   Lardner and Reppetto, *NYPD,* 112.

11   *in that morning's New York* Herald   *NYH,* June 28, 1897.

12   *It was a sort druggists used*   *NYW,* June 28, 1897. NB: This *World* report was the only one to specifically note the use of druggist's seine twine, a telling minor detail that others—including their own reporters—then overlooked or forgot.

12   *adhered another piece of brown paper*   Carey, *Memoirs,* 49. NB: The piece of paper bearing the stamp of Kugler & Wollens is noted in Carey's account, and *it is only in his account.* The stamped paper is not cited in any newspaper, or indeed in the trial. Given the insatiable hunger newspapers had for reproducing illustrations of any clue in the case, the reasonable supposition is that they never saw this one. The exiled Carey was clearly hungry for a real case, and he was by far the earliest to make a good guess—startlingly so—at where the crime had been committed and how the body had been disposed of. I can't help but wonder whether, rather like the newspaper reporters, Carey wasn't above pocketing a hot lead for himself.

12   *ramshackle and roiling retail polyglot*   Marcuse, *This Was New York,* 54.

12   *pouncing on on-duty officers*   Lardner and Reppetto, *NYPD,* 112.

13   *you could tell the old and new officers apart*   "Conlin Leads a Long Line," *NYTR,* June 2,1897.

13   *one of the world's largest*   "The Bowery Savings Bank," *World's Work* 4 (1902): 2229.

13   *retired with a fortune of $350,000*   Lardner and Reppetto, *NYPD,* 83.

13   *John Jacob Astor IV owned*   "The Building Department," *NYT,* December 30, 1899.

13   *For decades . . . the Marsh family*   Longworth, *Longworth's American Almanac* (1834), 471; and *Trow's New York City Directory* (1860), 571.

13   *it became a German beer saloon*   Important Events, *132.* NB: John Volz's short-lived saloon is featured in an ad on this page.

13   *Ernst Kugler*   *Trow's New York City Directory* (1890), 163.

13   *outlasting a previous partner*   Ibid. (1879), 115.

14   *used to wrap a saw*   Carey, *Memoirs,* 49.

14   *it smelled of the store*   *NYP,* June 28, 1897.

14   *four feet wide and fourteen and a half feet long*   "East River Mystery," *NYT,* June 28, 1897.

14   *nearest distributor: Henry Feuerstein*   *NYH,* June 28, 1897.

14   *other distributor that Buchanan & Sons used*   "A Queer Murder Mystery," *NYTR,* June 28, 1897.

14   *Claflin, had been arrested*   "Will Arrest Mr. Claflin," *NYT,* May 27, 1897.

15   *something like fifty more shops to visit*   *NYW,* June 28, 1897.

3. THE JIGSAW MAN

16   *Ned Brown just about had the place to himself*   Liebling, *Liebling at* The New Yorker, 169.

16   *walls placarded with exhortations*   Dreiser, *Newspaper Days,* 625.

16   *clear out to the East River*   Ibid., 632.

17 *ridden cavalry in Sheridan's Shenandoah Valley campaign*   Morris, *Pulitzer,* 24.

17 *Pulitzer, then a penniless veteran, was thrown out of it*   Bleyer, *Main Currents,* 334.

17 *two miles of wrought-iron columns to support the world's largest pressroom*   Morris, *Pulitzer,* 286.

17 *425-ton golden dome*   Ibid., 287.

17 *its gilded surface could be seen for miles out to sea*   Ibid., 272.

17 *"Is God in?"*   Brian, *Pulitzer,* 153.

17 *a circulation of twenty thousand*   Churchill, *Park Row,* 27.

17 *attention-grabbing promotions*   Ibid., 39. NB: The idea of the Mars billboard was slightly less loony than it may sound; astronomers like Thomas Dick proposed decades earlier that a giant geometric ditch could be dug out in Siberia, and perhaps be set aflame, the better to send a signal of intelligent life to our fellow astronomers on Mars. The *World* scheme of sending an actual message to Mars was shelved, alas, when someone at a promotion meeting asked: "What language shall we print it in?"

18 *Circulation had risen fifteenfold*   Liebling, *Liebling at* The New Yorker, 165.

18 yellow journalism, *they called it*   Campbell, *Yellow Journalism,* 25.

18 *the day's front-page grabber*   *NYW,* June 27, 1897.

18 *today it was just the substitute editor. . . . Ned was to run over*   Liebling, *Liebling at* The New Yorker, 169. NB: The description of Ned Brown, as well as his conversations with editors and other reporters, is drawn entirely from Liebling's September 24, 1955, *New Yorker* article "The Scattered Dutchman," reprinted in *Liebling at* The New Yorker. Although the article contains a few errors and chronological inconsistencies, it was by far the most ambitious account ever attempted regarding the Guldensuppe case. That it's a Liebling piece makes it a joy to read—he writes tartly of the victim's "brisket" arriving "in installments"—and he conveys what it was like to be a denizen of Newspaper Row in the old days. The article focuses largely on the opening stages of the case, and in particular on revealing Ned Brown as the *World*'s near-miss reporter.

19 *"At first," O'Hanlon admitted*   *NYW,* June 28, 1897.

19 *lungs was still spongy and the heart was filled*   *NYT,* June 28, 1897.

19 *between the victim's fifth and sixth ribs*   *NYW,* June 28, 1897.

20 *blood had entered into the surrounding tissue*   Ibid.

20 *alive and naked when stabbed*   *NYT,* June 28, 1897.

20 *"Both wounds were made"*   *NYH,* June 28, 1897.

20 *The victim had cut his hand*   *NYP,* June 28, 1897.

20 *"That he was knocked down"*   *NYW,* June 28, 1897.

21 *the two segments were pushed together*   Edwarde, *Guldunsuppe Mystery,* 17.

21 *Magnusson's friends and neighbors had been urging her to visit*   *NYTR,* June 28, 1897.

22 *"If they had only been able to account"*   *NYW,* June 28, 1897.

22 *A few among the reporters took notice*   *NYT,* June 28, 1897.

22 I knew it was a murder all along   "River Gives Up a Murder Mystery," *NYH,* June 27, 1897.

22 *the patrolman's report claimed . . . a patent falsehood*   *NYW,* June 27, 1897.

22 Herald *reporter who had fetched the coroner*   *NYH,* June 27, 1897.

22 World *reporter who started knocking*   *NYW,* June 27, 1897.

22 *hadn't secured the crime scene*   Ibid.

22 *Hogan ventured. . . . out of their jurisdiction*   NYH, June 27, 1897.

23 *sweeps of women . . . walking along Broadway*   "Moss Gets on Chapman's Trail," *NYET,* June 28, 1897.

23 *his own pet theory*   *NYT,* June 28, 1897.
23 *an unnerving sense of recognition*   Liebling, *Liebling at* The New Yorker, 186.

4. THE WRECKING CREW

24 *"may have been a Hebrew"*   "River Mystery Grows in Horror," *NYP,* June 28, 1897.
24 no alcohol in his stomach. . . . Nor was there food   "Louis A. Lutz the Victim?" *NYEJ,* June 28, 1897.
24 *"It appears to me"*   "Dr. Weston Says Body Was Boiled," *NYET,* June 28, 1897.
25 CANNIBALISM SUGGESTED   *NYH,* June 30, 1897.
25 *"A butcher may have done it"*   "Strange Murder Mystery Deepens," *NYH,* June 28, 1897.
25 *a recent Chicago murder*   Loerzel, *Alchemy of Bones.*
25 *"as white as marble. . . . body had been washed"*   *NYH,* June 28, 1897.
25 *a* Press *reporter suggested*   *NYP,* June 28, 1897.
25 *The* World *knew just the man to ask*   *NYW,* June 28, 1897.
26 *scores of reporters were fanning out*   "World Men Find a Clue," *NYW,* June 29, 1897.
26 *"God damn it, get excited!"*   Churchill, *Park Row,* 86.
27 *You could tell when New York was having a peaceful day*   Ford, *Forty-Odd Years,* 260.
27 *sent reporters off to tail detectives and swipe evidence*   Liebling, *Liebling at* The New Yorker, 166.
27 *"Events seem to indicate"*   signed W. R. Hearst editorial, *NYEJ,* June 29, 1897.
27 *race riots in Key West*   "Inviting a Race War," *Boston Daily Globe,* June 28, 1897.
27 *stealing electricity off high-voltage streetcar lines*   "Up-to-Date Burglars in Ohio Tap Trolley Wires for Electricity"   *NYH,* June 29, 1897.
27 *a $15 dog*   "Millionaires War Over a $15 Dog," *NYEJ,* June 27, 1897.
27 *Hire four launches*   "Picture of the Murder," *NYJ,* June 29, 1897.
27 *crowded with bereaved families*   "Undurchdringlithes Dunkel," *NYSZ,* June 29, 1897.
28 *could barely make their way inside*   *NYW,* June 29, 1897.
28 *John Johnson and Adolph Carlson*   "The Body Not Identified," *NYCA,* June 29, 1897.
28 *"Japanese." . . . Another mysterious visitor*   "Dark Crime of River and Wood," *NYH,* June 29, 1897.
28 *presumptive widow of Mr. Robert Wood*   *NYH,* June 29, 1897.
29 *Brooklyn gas engineer Charles Russell*   "No Clew Yet Found," *NYTR,* June 29, 1897.
29 *bartender John Otten*   "No Light on Murder Mystery," *NYP,* June 29, 1897.
29 *printer John Livingston, or . . . Edward Leunhelt*   *NYH,* June 29, 1897.
29 *Manhattan bricklayer:*   *NYCA,* June 28, 1897.
29 *he refused to talk*   *NYW,* June 29, 1897.
29 *"bicycle attorney"*   "Drivers in Trouble," *NYJ,* June 29, 1897.
29 *"I feel sure it is my uncle's body"*   *NYEJ,* June 28, 1897.
30 *"Oh, Dick!"*   *NYW,* June 29, 1897.
30 *dancing a little jig . . . as page proofs were laid out*   Winkler, *W. R. Hearst,* 71.
30 *"The public . . . likes entertainment better"*   Stevens, *Sensationalism,* 87.
31 *$20 gold piece he used*   Churchill, *Park Row,* 46.

31 *piss pots emblazoned with their portraits*   Winkler, *W. R. Hearst*, 58.
31 *"I am possessed of the weakness"*   Procter, *William Randolph Hearst*, 41.
31 *"chambermaid's delight"*   Ibid., 78.
31 *"in the Silurian era"*   Campbell, *Yellow Journalism*, 3.
31 *"Smash as many as you have to"*   Winkler, *W. R. Hearst*, 110.
31 *"polychromous effervescence"*   Whyte, *Uncrowned King*, 187.
31 MAN WITH THE MUSICAL STOMACH   Stevens, *Sensationalism*, 84.
32 *word arrived of the upcoming four o'clock* World   Liebling, *Liebling at* The New Yorker, 178.
32 *$500 REWARD*   *NYW,* June 28, 1897.
33 *Run an Extra Final Edition*   Liebling, *Liebling at* The New Yorker, 179.
33 *$1,000 Reward:*   *NYEJ*, June 28, 1897.

5. JILL THE RIPPER

34 *reader guesses included*   "Theories of the Multitude," *NYEJ*, June 29, 1897.
35 *Hearst loved promotion*   Turner, *When Giants Ruled*, 124.
35 *"a wooden-legged burglar"*   Lee, History of American Journalism, *373.*
35 *"Take all or any part of that"*   Turner, *When Giants Ruled*, 123.
35 *Park Row sidewalk . . . was wearing thin*   Swanberg, *Citizen Hearst*, 83.
35 *"We must beat every paper"*   Churchill, *Park Row*, 87.
35 *Wreckers dedicated to homicide coverage*   Procter, *William Randolph Hearst*, 99.
36 *"One might as well have tried"*   Edwarde, *Guldensuppe Mystery*, 30.
36 *"Did love or jealousy have aught"*   *NYW*, June 29, 1897.
36 *five men gathered around the dissecting table*   "Light on the Murder Mystery," *NYW*, June 30, 1897.
36 *Ferguson sensed a chilling familiarity*   "May Be Cyklam's Headless Body," *NYP*, June 30, 1897. NB: The quotes from Ferguson that follow are from this account.
37 *detectives coursed uptown*   Ibid.
37 *a lone cub reporter could be seen*   Liebling, *Liebling at* The New Yorker, 186.
38 *bites by mad dogs*   "Hints for Dog Bites," *NYCA*, June 29, 1897.
38 *A Romanesque space with white marble floors*   Advertisement in Cahn, *Theatrical Guide.*
38 *"The House of a Thousand Hangovers"*   "Miscellany," *Time,* December 7, 1925. NB: The baths' demolition occasioned the magazine's recollection of its old days. These same baths, incidentally, also figured in the infamous Becker-Rosenthal murder case of 1912.
38 *Ned idly let a question drop*   Liebling, *Liebling at* The New Yorker, 187. NB: Liebling's article is the sole source for the account in this section of Brown's exploits.
40 *It was the new issue of the* Evening Journal   "The Real Clew to the Murder Mystery," *NYEJ*, June 29, 1897.
41 *For the first time ever, color was being used*   Stevens, *Sensationalism*, 92.
41 *"I learned from some neighbors"*   "Saw Two Men with Package in a Saloon," *NYET,* June 29, 1897.
41 *a slender* Times *reporter attempted to try on one of Max's suits*   *NYT,* June 29, 1897.
41 *the* Times *theorized . . . that two escapees*   *NYT,* June 29, 1897.
41 THE DEAD MAN'S VALISE   "Police Work on a New Clue," *NYEJ*, June 29, 1897.
41 *"The German seems to regard"*   "Theories of Prominent Persons as to How the Murder Was Committed," *NYJ*, June 29, 1897.

41 *"The solution of the whole matter hangs upon the oilcloth"*   "The Rest of the Roll," Ibid.

42 *Carey . . . hadn't made it to Queens or Long Island*   *NYT,* June 29, 1897.

42 *throwing* thirty men *into tracking the oilcloth*   Bleyer, *Main Currents,* 368.

42 *a* Journal *team at the dry-goods store of one Max Riger*   "Murder Mystery Is Solved by the Journal," *NYEJ,* June 30, 1897.

6. THE BAKER IN HELL'S KITCHEN

45 *another heat wave*   "Scorching Heat for the Freshmen," *NYET,* June 30, 1897.

45 *unshaven and tough-looking fellow*   "Mr. and Mrs. Nack Under Arrest; Guldensuppe's Legs Found in Brooklyn"   *NYET,* June 30, 1897.

45 *gangster Mallet Murphy*   Marcuse, *This Was New York,* 63.

45 *two men clambered aboard*   *NYEJ,* June 30, 1897.

45 *"Mr. Nack?"*   "Murder Charged to a Midwife," *NYP,* July 1, 1897.

46 *Garfield Drug Company on Thirty-Fourth*   *American Druggist and Pharmaceutical Record* 30 (1897): 22.

46 *carriage-jackers Oscar Piper and Walter McDevitt*   *NYEJ,* June 30, 1897.

46 *tried escaping twice . . . .*   *"I have absolutely no idea . . . "*   Ibid.

46 *nine coworkers from the Murray Hill Baths*   "May Be Guldensuppe," *NYT,* July 1, 1897.

46 VICTIM THOUGHT TO BE THEODORE CYKLAM   *NYW,* June 30, 1897.

46 *elbowed aside by Pulitzer's ace reporter Ike White*   Liebling, *Liebling at* The New Yorker, 191.

46 *Ike's pet theory*   *NYW,* June 30, 1897.

47 *not unknown for reporters to tail detectives*   Liebling, *Leibling at* The New Yorker, 166.

47 *The* Herald, *it seemed, had boozily stumbled*   "Police Say Murder Mystery Is Solved," *NYH,* July 1, 1897.

47 *overheard by reporter Joe Gavan*   Collins, *Homicide Squad,* 55.

47 *Hearst alone made a personal visit*   Ford, *Forty-Odd Years,* 260.

48 *"that antique and shabby"*   McAdoo, *Guarding a Great City,* 3.

48 *under constant watch by the competition*   Jeffers, *Commisioner Roosevelt,* 87.

48 *more than 100,000 arrests a year*   "New York at Its Best and Worst," *NYW,* July 1, 1898.

49 *chief had more than 250 detectives*   "Police Chief's Suggestion," *NYT,* December 1, 1897.

49 *new rank hadn't even gone through . . . . on the force for more than twenty years*   Lardner and Reppetto, *NYPD,* 114.

49 *walls and floors of the office had been carefully muffled*   Ibid., 88.

49 *"I went to work at two o'clock"*   *NYEJ,* June 30, 1897.

50 *"I get up at about 1 or 2 and go over the ferry"*   *NYP,* July 1, 1897.

50 *I was so drunk that I had to stay in bed"*   *NYEJ,* June 30, 1897.

50 *"What the deuce"*   *NYP,* July 1, 1897.

50 *Bakery's owner vouch . . . Nack had actually led Strack's saloon*   *NYP,* July 1, 1897.

51 *$20 monthly lease; she'd given notice*   *NYP,* July 1, 1897.

51 *detective now sitting on her sofa . . . . another detective stood*   Edwarde, *Guldensuppe Mystery,* 62.

51 *"pleasing, yet repellant, appearance"*   *NYT,* July 1, 1897.

51 *"I gave her a bit of my mind"*   *NYET,* June 30, 1897.

51 *Krauch had been watching her apartment*   *NYH*, July 1, 1897.
52 *fashionable tulle-trimmed hat that she'd quickly donned*   *NYET,* June 30, 1897.
52 *"My name is Augusta Nack"*   Edwarde, *Guldensuppe Mystery*, 69.
52 Speak louder   Ibid.
53 *Pauline Riger . . . had been listening all along*   "Mrs. Nack Will Be Formally Charged with Murdering Guldensuppe"   *NYEJ*, July 1, 1897.
54 *bumping up against the USS* Vermont   *NYT,* July 1, 1897.
54 *in the middle of his hallway, were two severed human legs*   Edwarde, *Guldensupe Mystery*, 77.

7. THE UNDERTAKER'S NEIGHBOR

55 *Werner's indispensable assistant was vacationing*   *NYH*, July 1, 1897.
55 *The young millionaire made the landlord an offer*   Churchill, *Park Row*, 90.
56 *Pulitzer had increasingly taken*   Ibid., 57.
56 *"We must smash the interloper"*   Procter, *William Randolph Hearst*, 85.
56 *The* Times *had briefly gone bust*   Tifft and Jones, *The Trust*, 36.
56 *Dana . . . stopped coming to his office*   Wilson, *Charles A. Dana*, 513.
56 *"When I came to New York"*   Juergens, *Joseph Pulitzer*, 350.
56 *The* World*'s unmatched circulation*   Stevens, *Sensationalism*, 86.
57 *"undesirable class of readers"*   "Views of New Journalism," *NYT,* March 4, 1897.
57 World *had dubbed the Missing Head Mystery*   *NYW,* July 2, 1897.
57 *"The sensational journals of the city"*   "The Sensational Journals of the City," *NYCA*, June 29, 1897
57 *"The freak journals"*   "Vociferous Journals," *NYT,* June 30, 1897.
57 *Hearst's men had cut the cords*   Churchill, *Park Row*, 90.
57 *Price, Krauch, and O'Donohue . . . spent the next few hours unpacking*   *NYEJ*, July 1, 1897.
58 *small trapdoor in the ground floor . . . motley assortment*   Ibid.
58 *Neighbors watched from the adjacent buildings*   Ibid.
58 *avenue that was turning increasingly chaotic . . . police were holding back*   *NYH*, July 1, 1897.
58 *Vockroth, had rented a horse and surrey to Nack*   "More Murder Clues," *NYME*, July 1, 1897.
59 another *boarder had lived in the apartment*   *NYEJ*, July 1, 1897.
59 *in February when Guldensuppe had beaten his rival*   *NYT,* July 1, 1897.
59 *knife, a broken saw, and then a revolver . . . a dried spray of blood*   *NYEJ*, July 1, 1897.
59 *that evening's* Journal *headline*   *NYEJ*, June 30, 1897.
59 *sent out beefy guards*   Stevens, *Sensationalism*, 93.
59 *"When patting oneself on the back"*   Editorial, *NYEJ*, July 1, 1897.
60 *signed Guldensuppe . . . not Gieldsensuppe*   "Fear and Strain Weaken Mrs. Nack," *NYP,* July 2, 1897.
60 *couldn't find missing money she claimed*   "Now Formally Accused," *NYTR,* July 3, 1897.
60 *a jail matron found it hidden in her corset*   "The Murder Mystery," *NYTR,* July 2, 1897.
60 *The matron also noticed bruises*   "Murder Will Out," *NYEP,* July 1, 1897.
60 *having her fingernails pared and scraped*   "Police Couldn't Weaken Her," *NYET,* July 2, 1897.
60 *"If that body belonged to William Guldensuppe"*   "The Identification Upset," *NYW,* July 2, 1897.

60 *One was a Bowery waiter . . . other was a babbling metal-polish peddler*   *NYT,* July 1, 1897.

60 *home address that proved to be a lumberyard*   *NYP,* June 30, 1897.

61 *"He is a freak"*   *NYW,* June 30, 1897.

61 *"She has a temper"*   *NYP,* July 1, 1897.

61 Herald *writer heard Herman Nack claim*   *NYH,* July 1, 1897.

61 *"She is strong enough?"*   *NYP,* July 1, 1897.

61 *Friend, had marched into the Mulberry Street*   "To Protest Her Innocence," *BE,* July 2, 1897.

61 World *editors were doubling down*   "Murder Mystery Is a Mystery Still," *NYW,* July 1, 1897.

62 *willing to testify that the body was not his*   "The Identification Upset," *NYW,* July 2, 1897.

62 *Mrs. Clark, it turned out, had been caught up in a divorce*   "Police Seeking Thorn," *NYT,* July 2, 1897.

62 *"always mixed up in several affairs"*   "Mrs. Nack Spends Hours on Detective Chief O'Brien's Rack," *NYEJ,* July 2, 1897.

62 Journal *reporters sat down with Frank*   Ibid. NB: The remainder of this chapter's dialogue is drawn from this account.

63 *the illicit service that some midwives quietly provided*   Brodie, *Contraception and Abortion,* 54.

8. THE WIDOW'S FRIEND

64 *finally been promoted to acting inspector*   "More Murder Clues," *NYME,* July 1, 1897.

64 *a composer of novelty tunes*   "Ex-Inspector O'Brien Dead," *NYT,* July 3, 1913.

64 *on the table and chairs . . . O'Brien had arranged the tools*   *NYET,* July 2, 1897.

64 *"the most cold blooded woman"*   "Trying to Trace Thorn," *BE,* July 3, 1897.

64 *alienists wandered in and out*   "An Expert Alienist Studies Mrs. Nack," *NYH,* July 4, 1897.

65 *readers were treated to close-ups*   *NYEJ,* July 1, 1897.

65 *"I made an especial study"*   *NYH,* July 4, 1897.

65 *"masturbatic insanity"*   Spitzka, *Cases of Masturbation,* 238.

65 *presiding over the electric chair's rather messy debut*   Moran, *Executioner's Current,* 19.

65 *"Did you know . . . she has never reported a live birth"*   *NYH,* July 4, 1897.

65 *"I cannot understand how detectives could expect such a clumsy trick"*   "World-Wide Hunt for Martin Thorn," *NYEJ,* July 3, 1897.

66 *"She is a decided liar. . . . Streuning buried a child of hers"*   "Looks Black for the Midwife," *NYH,* July 2, 1897.

66 *lost their own five-year-old daughter to diphtheria*   *NYP,* July 1, 1897.

66 *a servant girl who let burglars*   "A Servant's Intelligence Suspected," *NYEP,* July 1, 1897.

66 *a would-be parachute inventor*   "Hung by One Foot in Midair," *NYH,* July 1, 1897.

66 *a severed black-stockinged leg*   "Found a Woman's Leg," *NYEJ,* July 1, 1897.

66 *the druggist who hanged himself*   "Rope His Last Resort," Ibid.

66 *"My name . . . is Sophie Miller"*   "Mrs. Nack at the Bar of Justice," *NYH,* July 2, 1897.

67 *Hearst's print room hastily jammed the two crucial words*   "Mrs. Nack Will Be Charged with Murdering Guldensuppe," *NYEJ,* July 1, 1897.

67 *spent the afternoon working barbershops . . . over a shave*   Collins, *Homicide Squad*, 61.
68 *he'd quit on the spot last week*   NYH, July 2, 1897.
68 *"As soon as I saw . . . I thought right away of Thorn"*   NYW, July 2, 1897.
69 *a particular fondness, Keehn said, for widows*   NYH, July 2, 1897.
69 *"He used to laugh at Guldensuppe"*   NYW, July 2, 1897. NB: The dialogue in the remainder of this section is all drawn from this *World* account.
70 *his face prickling painfully*   Collins, *Homicide Squad*, 61.

9. THE DISAPPEARING SHOEMAKER

71 THE IDENTIFICATION UPSET   NYW, July 2, 1897.
71 World *reporters in turn humiliated Mrs. Riger*   NYW, July 2, 1897.
71 THE WORLD DESPERATE   NYEJ, July 2, 1897.
71 *One of Nack's neighbors signed . . . that Pulitzer had a $10,000 slush fund*   Ibid.
72 STILL TWENTY FOUR HOURS BEHIND THE NEWS   Ibid.
72 *reporters hired Mrs. Nack's surrey and horse*   "Murder Will Out," NYW, July 3, 1897.
72 *His name was Henry Wahle, and he lived in Woodside*   "Mrs. Nack's Confession," NYW, July 4, 1897.
72 *Mrs. DeBeuchelare's dairy*   Gregory, *Woodside*, 77.
72 *Mr. Jacobs kept that greenhouse*   Ibid., 75.
73 *Four Manhattan detectives marched*   NYW, July 4, 1897.
73 *A general store by the trolley stop*   Gregory, *Woodside*, 84.
73 *Greenpoint Avenue Hall . . . rube entertainments*   Gregory, *Woodside*, 89.
73 *fire chief and a coroner were convenient neighbors*   "Murder Traced in Duck Tracks," NYH, July 4, 1897.
73 *"Mrs. Hafftner," she introduced herself*   NYW, July 4, 1897.
74 *near one end of the block was the stop for the NY & Queens County trolley*   Copquin, *Neighborhoods of Queens*, 207.
74 *a dreary little house, coated in cheap brown paint*   NYH, July 4, 1897. NB: Second Street has since been renamed Fifty-Fifth Street; its northern intersection of "Anderson Avenue" is now Thirty-Seventh Avenue. The location of the cottage, based on a graphic from the September 20, 1897, NYEJ (which pinpoints the cottage), as well as a 1909 Bromley map of Queens (plate 13), would place the crime scene on the west side of Fifty-Fifth Street, roughly a quarter of a block south of the intersection with Thirty-Seventh Avenue. This side of Fifty-Fifth is now completely covered by warehouses; a single old house wedged in across the street is the sole indication that it was once a residential block.
74 *the remains of a man's shoe*   "Murder Still a Mystery," NYT, July 5, 1897.
75 *The bathroom . . . shaved samples off the floor*   NYW, July 4, 1897.
75 *scooped up a bucket of the mud*   NYT, July 4, 1897.
75 *Reporters were pouring over on the East River ferries*   Edwarde, Guldensuppe Mystery, 87.
75 *Something like—"Help! Help! Murder!"*   "Is Thorn in New York?" BE, July 4, 1897.
75 *"I clean my windows every Friday afternoon"*   Edwarde, *Guldensuppe Mystery*, 89.
76 *She'd only seen one come out*   "Dying Screams Heard by Three," NYH, July 5, 1897.
76 WORLD WIDE HUNT   NYEJ, July 3, 1897.

76 WANTED—*For the murder*   "Heard Murder Cried," *NYT,* July 4, 1897.

76 *NYU maintained its newly built Loomis Laboratory*   *Researches of the Loomis Laboratory,* 7.

77 *first guide to preserving crime-scene evidence*   Bell, *Crime and Circumstance,* 192.

77 *the first book on cadaver fauna*   Ibid., 216. NB: Specifically, the two books are Hans Gross's *Handbuch für Untersuchungsrichter als System der Kriminalistik* (1893) and Jean Pierre Mégnin's *La faune des cadavres* (1894).

77 *match the microscopic shells on a dead man's muddy boot*   Witthaus and Becker, *Medical Jurisprudence,* 353.

77 *A careful practitioner might even extract*   Ibid., 354.

77 *featured asphalt floors for easy hosing down*   *Researchers of the Loomis Laboratory,* 70.

77 *"Witthaus looks like a sea-lion"*   "Dr. Witthaus Found Deadly Poison," *NYW,* January 11, 1900.

77 *Carey had collared a physician . . . . Witthaus who'd gotten the goods*   Carey, *Memoirs,* 42.

78 *original handwritten manuscript*   "Witthaus Bought Copies as Real Art," *NYT,* July 16, 1916.

78 *Witthaus was battling an allegation of attempted murder*   *NYT,* January 24, 1898.

78 *There wasn't a speck of blood*   "Mrs. Nack's Oilcloth," *NYME,* July 2, 1897.

78 *saw and knife weren't even the right fit*   *NYME,* July 2, 1897.

78 *strategy had secured a conviction*   *NYET,* July 2, 1897.

78 *Byrnes had publicly dared Jack the Ripper*   Lardner and Reppetto, *NYPD,* 88.

79 *telltale viscera of dismemberment*   Flint, *Collected Essays,* vol. 2, 516.

79 *Buala was bustling around his wine shop*   *NYW,* July 4, 1897.

79 *"I do not remember these people"*   *NYW,* July 4, 1897. NB: The remainder of the dialogue in this section is drawn from this *World* account.

80 *same as in the "Fred" letters*   Ibid.

80 *It had been postmarked only yesterday*   "Den of Murderers Located," *NYP,* July 4, 1897.

10. THE SILENT CUSTOMER

81 *Detective J. J. O'Connell . . . . and his partner, Detective Boyle, were arriving in Queens*   "Dying Screams Heard by Three," *NYH,* July 5, 1897.

81 MURDER TRACED IN DUCK TRACKS   *NYH,* July 4, 1897.

81 THE HOUSE OF DEATH   *NYW,* July 4, 1897.

81 HAIR PULLING MATCH   *NYP,* July 4, 1897.

81 *Den of Murder*   Ibid.

82 *rumor had spread of a $1,000 bounty*   "Blood in the House of Mystery," *NYW,* July 5, 1897.

82 *constable struggled to keep the masses at bay*   Ibid.

82 *Nobody knew where to find the caretaker*   *NYH,* July 5, 1897.

82 *O'Connell and Boyle wrenched open a window*   Ibid.

82 *"Yes, that's the same rig"*   *NYW,* July 5, 1897.

82 *"That's the same carriage"*   Ibid.

82 *wine bottle*   "Mrs. Nack May Be Indicted," *NYT,* July 6, 1897.

82 *small cardboard bullet box*   "Queens County Wants Mrs. Nack," *NYEJ,* July 6, 1897.

83 *he'd worked as a plumber. . . . exposed and disassembled the plumbing*   "Murder Still a Mystery," *NYT,* July 5, 1897.

83 *a sea of children. More than a thousand of them*   *NYH*, July 5, 1897. NB: This remarkable figure is also given in the same day's *Evening Telegram.*

83 *cyclists were getting drunk and crashing wildly . . . . "Between drinks"*   *NYW*, July 5, 1897.

83 *water out from a spring in Trains Meadow*   Gregory, *Woodside*, 78.

83 *meter showed a whopping 40,000-gallon spike . . .* "The amount of water"   Edwarde, *Guldensuppe Mystery*, 92.

84 *"The legs . . . are not in the morgue"*   "Guldensuppe's Legs Gone," *NYTR*, July 6, 1897.

84 *"Guldensuppe has gained more fame"*   *NYH*, July 6, 1897.

84 *"One of the theories"*   *NYT*, July 6, 1897.

84 *"I desire"*   *NYP*, July 4, 1897.

84 *announced the recipients of his $1,000 reward*   "These Men Got the $1000," *NYEJ*, July 5, 1897.

85 *gouged a stain out of the floor*   *NYW*, July 5, 1897.

85 *BLOOD IN THE HOUSE OF MYSTERY*   Ibid.

85 *Teichmann test*   Wood, *Chemical and Microscopical Diagnosis*, 17.

85 *Mrs. Nack was beginning to waver*   *NYW*, July 4, 1897.

86 *Thorn, he assured the* Journal   "Heard Victim's Appeal," *NYEJ*, July 5, 1897.

86 *and the* Tribune   *NYTR*, July 6, 1897.

86 *he added to the* Press   "Thorn May Be Caught in Canada," *NYP*, July 5, 1897.

86 *and the Brooklyn Eagle*   "Is Thorn in New York?" *BE*, July 4, 1897.

86 *To the* Mail and Express, *he was "positive"*   "No News of Thorn," *NYME*, July 5, 1897.

86 *turned up later that evening in the morgue's pickling vat*   "Guldensuppe's Legs Vanish," *NYH*, July 6, 1897.

86 *logging one sunstroke case after another*   "Heat in the City," *NYW*, July 7, 1897.

86 *Louisville embezzler and a Brooklyn con man*   "Nack Hearing Postponed," *NYT*, July 7, 1897.

86 *A suicide found in a Jersey City*   *NYT*, July 5, 1897.

86 *body that veteran stage actor George Beane found*   Ibid.

87 *IS THIS MARTIN THORN?*   *NYT*, July 5, 1897.

87 *Pauline told a* Journal *reporter*   "Queens County Wants Mrs. Nack," *NYEJ*, July 6, 1897.

87 World *reporters located Thorn's older brother*   "Saw Thorn on Wednesday," *NYW*, July 6, 1897.

88 *last confirmed sighting of Thorn was by a moving company*   *NYW*, July 6, 1897.

88 *woman in the Detective Bureau's office*   "Thorn Has Confessed to the Murder," *NYEJ*, July 7, 1897.

88 *detectives waited impatiently at the 125th Street El station*   *NYEJ*, July 7, 1897.

88 *"I can't go back on a friend"*   *NYEJ*, July 7, 1897.

88 *uttered a single word: "Haircut"*   "Martin Thorn Is a Prisoner," *NYH*, July 7, 1897.

88 *shed his usual brown derby for a white fedora and shaved*   Edwarde, *Guldensuppe Mystery*, 96.

89 *quarter past nine that night*   *NYH*, July 7, 1897.

89 *Spear's Drug Store ruled the busy Harlem corner*   *NYW*, July 7, 1897.

89 *Spear himself was manning the till, and his clerk Maurice*   "Martin Thorn Is Captured," *NYW*, July 7, 1897.

89 *the real profits, which lay in the slot telephone*   *American Druggist and Pharmaceutical Record* 31 (1897): 113.

89 *city after city on the East Coast was reporting relentless heat*   "The Whole Country Overheated," *NYW*, July 7, 1897.

89 *Laborers in soiled overalls*   *NYH*, July 7, 1897.
90 *"Let's go take a drink"*   *NYEJ*, July 7, 1897.
90 It's a holdup, *Maurice frantically signaled*   *NYW*, July 7, 1897.
90 *"I am Martin Thorn." . . . "And I am Inspector O'Brien"*   Edwarde, *Guldensuppe Mystery*, 109.

11. A CASE OF LIFE AND DEATH

93 *"I've thought so for five minutes"*   "Thorn Indicted with Mrs. Nack," *NYP*, July 9, 1897.
93 *Along with the .32 revolver, a closer search*   "Indicted for the Murder," *NYT*, July 9, 1897.
93 *O'Brien, McCauley, and Price, along with*   *NYH*, July 7, 1897.
93 *They reached Houston and Bowery just after ten p.m.*   *NYH*, July 7, 1897.
94 AN ELECTRICAL EXECUTION   *NYEP*, July 6, 1897.
94 *A plainclothes scrum double-marched Thorn*   *NYH*, July 7, 1897.
94 *they'd been scraped by forensics*   "Thorn Murdered Guldensuppe," *BE*, July 7, 1897.
94 *Witthaus himself had come*   "Thorn's Friend Betrays Him," *NYW*, July 8, 1897.
94 *Thorn's body had been scrupulously measured*   "Thorn Says He Alone Is Guilty," *NYH*, July 9, 1897.
95 *Bertillon's wondrous anthropometric system*   Houck, *Forensic Science*, 26.
95 *India had adopted a new system*   Cole, *Suspect Identities*, 87.
95 *inspector worked quietly at his desk, saying nothing for hours*   *NYH*, July 7, 1897.
95 *Thorn's gaze fell upon the piles of letters*   *NYW*, July 8, 1897.
95 *"I at present live in a furnished room"*   *NYH*, July 9, 1897. NB: The remainder of this scene's conversation is from this *Herald* account.
97 *four in the morning, when O'Brien finally let his prisoner collapse*   *NYW*, July 8, 1897.
97 That's him   Ibid.
97 *"Looks pretty bad." . . . "I don't fear death"*   Ibid.
97 *"Hit him!"*   "Gartha [*sic*] Tells of the Murder," *NYH*, July 8, 1897. The remainder of the description of Gotha's ruse is drawn from the *Herald* account.
98 *"I first met Thorn nine years ago"*   "Thorn Warns Mrs. Nack in Court," *NYEJ*, July 9, 1897.
99 *"old—prematurely old"*   Rheta Childe Dorr, "The Prodigal Daughter," *Hampton's Magazine* 24 (1910): 526.
99 *"He had the look of a man going to the electric chair"*   *NYH*, July 9, 1897.
99 *"I met him at a saloon"*   Edwarde, *Guldensuppe Mystery*, 100.
100 *"He nearly severed the head"*   Ibid., 103.
100 *"It's done"*   *NYH*, July 8, 1897.
101 *"He told her"*   Edwarde, *Guldensuppe Mystery*, 103.
101 *With hot water running at full blast*   *NYW*, July 8, 1897.
101 *"As the boat neared the slip"*   Edwarde, *Guldensuppe Mystery*, 105.
101 *He fretted that he hadn't shaved*   "Lured to His Death," *NYME*, July 7, 1897.
101 *"I saw by newspaper reports"*   "Gartha Tells of the Murder," *NYH*, July 8, 1897.
102 *"Mr. Gotha, I do not want to detain you"*   "Thorn Says He Alone Is Guilty," *NYH*, July 9, 1897.
102 *"'I wish to God I had not told you'"*   Edwarde, *Guldensuppe Mystery*, 106.
102 *he'd instantly understood what it meant*   *NYEJ*, July 9, 1897.

12. HEADS OR TAILS

103 *"Going fishing?"*   "Mrs. Nack Sees Martin Thorn," *NYET,* July 9, 1897.
103 *These were naphtha boats*   *NYEJ,* July 8, 1897.
103 *grapplers, salvagers who worked the docks*   "How the Grappler Earns His Bread," *NYT,* May 5, 1901.
103 *A couple of dozen grapplers . . . on six launches*   *NYEJ,* July 8, 1897.
103 *"Three cheers for Guldensuppe!"*   "Still Seeking the Head," *NYT,* July 12, 1897.
103 *Captain Schultz . . . was in a droll mood*   *NYET,* July 9, 1897.
103 *"Heads you win, tails you lose!"*   Ibid.
104 *"These men know how to find"*   *NYEJ,* July 8, 1897.
104 *Street urchins were stripping off . . . diving among the rakes*   Ibid.
104 *The riverbed was a good twenty-five feet*   "Diver Hunts Head," *NYW,* July 9, 1897.
104 *"Something's caught!"*   Ibid.
104 William E. Chapman . . . *came chugging up*   Ibid.
104 *already run an operation with hooks*   "Valise and Clothes of the Murdered Man Found," *NYJ,* June 29, 1897.
104 *veteran deep-sea diver Charles Olsen*   *NYW,* July 9, 1897.
105 *all they were pulling up were stones and tin cans*   "Mrs. Nack Faces Martin Thorn," *NYP,* July 10, 1897.
105 *130 feet of rubber hose to Olsen's diving suit*   *NYW,* July 9, 1897.
105 *The door of the narrow three-story brick boardinghouse*   *NYEJ,* July 7, 1897. NB: The remainder of this scene is drawn from this *Evening Journal* account, except for the quote that follows.
106 *"Do you recognize me?"*   *NYH,* July 8, 1897.
107 *copy after copy of murder coverage*   "Lured to His Death," *NYME,* July 7, 1897.
107 *from the* World   *NYW,* July 7, 1897.
107 *the* Journal   NYEJ, July 7, 1897.
107 *the* Herald   *NYH,* July 8, 1897.
107 *"My God!" was gleefully illustrated*   *NYEJ,* July 7, 1897.
107 *witnessed them discovering a bullet hole*   *NYEJ,* July 8, 1897.
107 *"Blood Spots on Martin Thorn's Undershirt"*   *NYEJ,* July 8, 1897.
107 *"the* Evening Journal's *pen and pencil"*   Editorial, Ibid.
107 *"a nail made the bullet hole"*   *NYW,* July 9, 1897.
108 *Thorn did indeed resemble a man who'd walked up to Dr. O'Hanlon*   Ibid.
108 Herald *had been the city's colossus, with a circulation of more than 190,000*   Reel, *The National Police Gazette and the Making of the Modern American Man,* 48.
108 *1874 hoax claiming escaped circus tigers*   Ibid.
108 *Thorn pondering aloud how one might lure*   *NYH,* July 9, 1897.
109 *reduced to profiling the Woodside duck*   "Thorn Said to Have Confessed," *NYP,* July 8, 1897.
109 *detectives marched into the* World *offices*   *NYW,* July 9, 1897.
109 *Mr. Valentine's turnip giveaway*   "Turnips Free for All," Ibid.
110 *Old-timers . . . recalled "the Kelsey Outrage"*   *NYEJ,* July 9, 1897.
110 *no jury had been able to convict*   *NYT,* "The Kelsey Murder Mystery," November 6, 1876.
110 *"as dead as Kelsey's nuts"*   Carol Richards, "The Kelsey Outrage Gets More Outrageous," *Newsday,* February 3, 2001.
110 *assistant DA had been busy insisting . . . didn't particularly need Guldensuppe's head*   "Mrs. Nack Warns Thorn in Court," *NYH,* July 10, 1897.

111   *he couldn't recognize Nack and Thorn . . . detectives grumbled, he feared a conviction*
      "Mrs. Nack May Be Indicted," *NYT,* July 6, 1897.

111   *attempted to keep the coroner from touching his precious baseboards*   *NYW,* July 8,
      1897.

13. QUEEN OF THE TOMBS

112   *Intended for a city of 300,000 . . . now served 1.8 million*   "Tombs an Unfit
      Prison," *NYT,* June 29, 1895.

112   *throwing the stairways akimbo, and letting sewage ooze*   Gilfoyle, "America's
      Greatest Criminal Barrister," 528.

112   *tin plates perched on the rim of a malodorous toilet*   "A Disgrace to the City of
      New York," *Annual Report of the Prison Association,* 79.

113   *murmur passed among the inmates . . .* "It's Mrs. Nack!"   "Thorn Warns Mrs.
      Nack in Court," *NYEJ,* July 9, 1897.

113   *Dressed in a black coat and a straw boater*   "Mrs. Nack Sees Martin Thorn,"
      NYET, July 9, 1897.

113   *"Come on up the bridge, Thorn"*   *NYEJ,* July 9, 1897.

113   *stubble, the result of a suicide watch*   *NYET,* July 9, 1897.

113   *"Have you any counsel?"*   *NYEJ,* July 9, 1897.

114   *"We appear for Mrs. Thorn"*   "Mrs. Nack Meets Thorn in Court," *NYW,*
      July 10, 1897.

114   "Schweige still"   *NYEJ,* July 9, 1897.

114   "Halt den Mund und Spricht nicht!"   "Im Anklagezustand," *NYSZ,* July
      10, 1897.

114   *"Mrs. Nack and Martin Thorn Refuse to Talk"*   Signed editorial, *NYEJ,* July
      13, 1897.

114   The Guldensuppe Mystery. . . . *hit the streets just days later*   Edwarde, *Gul-
      densuppe Mystery.* NB: The Library of Congress's copy of *The Guldensuppe Mys-
      tery* bears a Received stamp of July 24, 1897. The last dated event noted in the
      text is July 8, so the book was completed, printed, and shipped to Washington,
      D.C., within this astonishingly short interval.

115   *Lower East Side summer-school teacher . . . turned into a mock trial*   "Murder
      Trial in School," *NYT,* July 24, 1897.

115   *masseurs were now slyly referred to as "Gieldensuppers"*   "A Gieldensupper Ar-
      rested," *NYS,* September 14, 1897.

115   *"That's not Thorn the police got!"*   "The Question of Jurisdiction," *NYTR,*
      July 18, 1897.

115   THE MURDER OF WILLIAM GULDENSUPPE   Advertisement, *NYT,* July 18, 1897.

115   *one of the city's most popular tourist destinations . . . a top-floor workshop that
      could whip up a body within twenty-four hours*   Dennett, *Weird and Wonder-
      ful,* 115.

115   *the Chess Automaton . . . a Klondike gold-rush mining camp*   "Notes of the
      Stage," *NYTR,* July 25, 1897.

116   *Woodside Horror*   *NYTR,* July 25, 1897.

116   *"Your face possesses a charm"*   *NYW,* July 7, 1897.

116   *"I'm no freak," Nrs, Nack snapped*   "Howe's Move for Thorn and Mrs. Nack's
      Novel Charity," *NYW,* July 16, 1897.

116   *Thorn passed the days in cells #29 and #30*   "Dredging for the Head Hope-
      less," *NYEJ,* July 10, 1897.

116   *tutoring cell mates in pinochle*   "Martin Thorn's School for Card Players,"
      NYEJ, July 14, 1897.

117 *Boylan . . . so weighted down with stolen silverware*   "John Boylan Laden Down with Silver," *NYEJ*, July 8, 1897.

117 THE HORRIBLE MURDER IN NEW YORK   *Aberdeen Weekly* (Scotland), July 9, 1897.

117 *Japan and Spain were considering an alliance*   "Japan and Spain May Be Allies," *NYP*, July 16, 1897.

117 *reports of massive strikes by coal miners*   "Strike Battle on Ohio River," *NYH*, July 9, 1897.

117 *his own starring role . . . he'd miss the city elections*   "Thorn's Vanity Betrayed Him," *NYW*, December 5, 1897.

117 *businessman named Horton. . . . "Where's the head?"*   "Thorn and Mrs. Nack in Court," *NYTR*, July 22, 1897.

117 *"The new industry of finding William Guldensuppe's head"*   "Guldensuppe's Head," *NYH*, July 14, 1897.

118 *mystically body-homing loaves of black bread*   "Says Tombs Fare Makes Her Ill," *NYP*, July 13, 1897.

118 *an intrepid* Herald *reporter to discover why*   *NYH*, July 14, 1897.

118 *Three more boys spotted a head floating*   "Italian Boys Find a Head," *NYT*, July 27, 1897.

118 *"decomposed mass" frightened passing ferry passengers*   "A Head, Not Guldensuppe's," *NYT*, September 2, 1897.

118 *A grisly find made in an Upper West Side boardinghouse*   "Not Guldensuppe's Skull," *NYTR*, July 20, 1897.

118 *girl from Woodside found an actual chunk*   "Guldensuppe Death Mask," *NYT*, September 20, 1897.

118 *Woodside child promptly discovered a brown derby*   *BE*, September 22, 1897.

118 *"Woodside is undergoing a boom in the agricultural line"*   "Yellow Sleuth's Work," *NYS*, September 23, 1897.

119 *Allegations emerged that* someone *. . . had paid a couple of local utility workers* *BE*, September 22, 1897.

119 *more than half a million in circulation*   "It Breaks All Records," *NYEJ*, August 23, 1897.

119 *Perrin H. Sumner . . . "the Great American Identifier"*   "Habeas Corpus for Martin Thorn," *NYH*, July 16, 1897.

119 *nearly bankrupted an Indiana college*   Branigan, *History of Johnson County*, 293.

119 *run Florida real estate swindles*   "Perrin H. Sumner Sued," *NYT*, November 13, 1907.

119 *fleeced would-be fiancées*   "Perrin H. Sumner Dies in the Subway," *NYT*, March 20, 1914.

119 *passed off worthless mining stock*   "Telegraphic Brevities," *Harvard Crimson*, May 18, 1883.

119 *descended on the Bellevue morgue to identify an unclaimed suicide*   *NYW*, February 1, 1892.

120 *professor spent July embarrassingly tied up in divorce proceedings*   "Professor Witthaus Must Pay It," *NYTR*, August 3, 1897.

120 *human blood, he declared*   "Human Blood Stains," *BE*, August 23, 1897.

120 *a whopping dredging bill*   "Police Board Meeting," *NYT*, August 19, 1897.

120 *O'Brien lost his own: He was relieved of his post*   "Sleuth O'Brien Bounced," *NYS*, August 31, 1897.

120 *"I have been described in a paper as a 'murderess'"*   "Mrs. Nack Talks Freely to the World," *NYW*, August 6, 1897. NB: The remainder of this scene is drawn from this *World* account of the interview.

14. THE HIGH ROLLER

123   *Mitchell hastily sent for a stenographer*   "Nack's Awful Charge Against His Wife," *NYW,* September 3, 1897.
123   *"She said lots of bad things"*   Ibid.
123   *They were joined by Detective Samuel Price*   Ibid.
124   *"My wife left me in 1896"*   "Murders by Scores Laid to Mrs. Nack," *NYEJ,* September 2, 1897. NB: All but the last line of remaining dialogue in this section is from this *Evening Journal* account.
124   *Dr. Weiss of Tenth Avenue . . . F. W. Werner, quietly assisted*   "Says the Accused Out-Heroded Herod," *NYEJ,* September 3, 1897.
125   *"There is something at the back of that"*   *NYW,* September 3, 1897.
125   *"It's a lie!" . . . "Fool!"*   *NYEJ,* September 3, 1897.
126   SAYS THE ACCUSED MURDERESS OUT-HERODED HEROD   *NYW,* September 3, 1897.
126   *so was the death of John Gotha's ninety-five-year-old father-in-law*   "Mrs. Nack Gains Time," *NYW,* July 13, 1897.
126   *Dr. Weiss claimed to have no idea . . . nor did Mrs. Nack's landlord*   *NYW,* September 3, 1897.
126   *Alois Palm tried rather unsportingly*   *NYEJ,* September 3, 1897.
126   *Even Mrs. Nack's friends faulted her*   "Mrs. Nack's Neighbors," *NYW,* July 4, 1897.
126   *"she was a high roller"*   *NYEJ,* September 3, 1897.
127   *Guldensuppe had kept Gussie from leaving*   *NYW,* September 3, 1897.
127   *Mrs. Nack had gone to one Ernest Moring . . .* hire him to kill her ex-husband "*Journal* Completes Case Against Martin Thorn," *NYEJ,* September 4, 1897.
128   World *reporter ascended the rickety stairs*   "Diploma Mills for Midwives," *NYW,* September 18, 1897.
128   A SCHOOL FOR BARBARITY   *NYW,* September 22, 1897.
128   DIPLOMA MILL FOR MIDWIVES   *NYW,* September 18, 1897.
128   *"Out of 55,000 live births"*   *NYW,* September 3, 1897.
128   *suspicions ran strong that "Madame Restell". . . . had dumped her body*   Reel, *The National Police Gazette and the Making of the Modern Man,* 38.
128   *designated villainess both for moralizing* Herald *journalists and for the American Medical Association*   Srebnick, *Mysterious Death of Mary Rogers,* 86.
128   *state criminalized abortion soon afterward*   Ibid., 85.
128   *laws made it illegal to even discuss*   Brodie, *Contraception and Abortion,* 257.
128   *The better practitioners were often immigrants*   Ibid., 228.
129   *"Their methods are so hidden"*   *NYW,* September 3, 1897.
129   WOMEN FARM, MEN COOK   *NYW,* August 2, 1897.
129   SHE'S PRETTY, EVEN IF SHE IS A LAWYER   *NYJ,* October 17, 1897.
129   *"Really . . . the newspapers are becoming"*   *NYH,* August 9, 1841, quoted in Stashower, *Beautiful Cigar Girl,* epigraph.
129   *another indictment had just been handed down*   "Indicted in Queens," *NYW,* September 16, 1897.
130   *handed over to Undersheriff Baker . . . and slipped out the Leonard Street exit*   "Taken to L.I. City Jail," *BE,* September 16, 1897.
130   *One thousand New Yorkers were waiting*   "Mrs. Nack and Thorn in New Cells," *NYS,* September 17, 1897.
130   *He'd become used to the sound of pile drivers and hammers*   "Nack . . . Cottage" (title partly destroyed), *NYEJ,* September 17, 1897.
130   *"I rented the Woodside cottage"*   Mrs. Nack's Window of Spectres, *NYEJ,* September 4, 1897.

130 *blurted out to* Journal *reporter Lowe Shearon*   "Justice's Bar," *NYEJ,* September 15, 1897.
131 *"That is all rot"*   *NYEJ,* September 4, 1897.
131 *Mrs. Nack had pulled an upper-floor unit*   *NYEJ,* September 14, 1897.
131 World *sent . . . Harriet Hubbard Ayer*   "Mrs. Nack's Own Story of the Killing of Guldensuppe," *NYW,* October 3, 1897.
131 *Ayer was a household name . . . whose cosmetics empire had fallen apart*   "Mrs. Harriet Ayer Dead," *Chicago Daily Tribune,* November 26, 1903.
131 "Must I be locked in?"   *NYW,* October 3, 1897. NB: The remainder of this section is drawn from this *World* account.

15. KLONDIKE WILLIE

134 *Rockaway Ed was a trusty. . . . second only to a "bum boss"*   "Dist. Att'y Youngs Says Journal Gives the Last Link of Evidence," *NYJA,* October 7, 1897. NB: Rockaway Ed's dealings with Nack and the *Journal,* although repeated to some degree in other newspapers, is drawn from this *Journal* account.
135 *writers and artists at the ready to make a copy*   "Mrs. Nack's Strange Letter to Thorn Captured by the Jailers," *NYJA,* October 6, 1897.
135 *the text that would appear in the next morning's paper . . .* "Dear Martin"   *NYJA,* October 6, 1897.
137 *"Where is it?"* Sheriff Doht demanded   *NYJA* October 6, 1897.
137 *The fragments bearing Thorn's writing were reassembled. . . .* "My dear"   *NYJA,* October 7, 1897.
138 *The watch on Thorn's cell was instantly doubled*   "Mrs. Nack Has Lost Hope," *NYT,* October 7, 1897.
138 *"I am sorry." DA Youngs sighed*   *NYJA,* October 7, 1897.
138 *He had tried to induce vomiting . . . hung a picture of a man's disembodied head* "The Soup Was Too Rich," *NYTR,* October 8, 1897.
138 *Mrs. Nack also tried denying the note*   "Nack and Thorn Plan Suicide," *NYH,* October 7, 1897.
139 *the block of brick tenements past the corner of Forty-Second and Tenth*   *Annual Report of the Committee on the Fire Patrol,* 108. NB: All the details of this block except for the mattress shop are drawn from this source.
139 *Mssr. Mauborgne's Mattress Renovating*   *NYT,* classifieds, June 13, 1897.
139 Where's Guldensuppe's head?   "Thorn's Brother-in-Law Sunk the Missing Head," *NYJ,* October 12, 1897.
139 *tantalizing story: that one Frank Clark had heard a boozy confession*   *NYW,* October 6, 1897.
140 *"He often boasted," Clark recalled*   *NYJ,* October 12, 1897.
140 *visit to the ailing forger by the district attorney*   *NYW,* October 6, 1897.
140 Journal *came piling into Menker's hallway*   *YJ,* October 12, 1897.
141 *letter had arrived in Coroner Hoeber's office*   "Did Thorn Admit Murder?" *BE,* August 6, 1897.
141 My dear sir: I cannot   "Hoeber Jumped on Friend," *NYTR,* July 8, 1897.
142 *One claimed that it was* Guldensuppe *who'd been hiding*   "Another Guldensuppe Letter," *NYT,* August 17, 1897.
142 *At least two more claimed that Guldensuppe was alive*   "Letters to Hoeber," *BE,* August 9, 1897; and "Guldensuppe or Edwards?" *NYT,* August 10, 1897.
142 *"I have always believed that he had gone to Europe"*   "Martin Thorn Has Hope," *NYW,* August 5, 1897.

142   Kindly do not believe any of the cards   *NYT,* August 10, 1897.
142   *Yet another missive, sent by Mrs. Lenora Merrifield*   "Guldensuppe Case Stirs Up Cranks," *NYEJ,* August 13, 1897.
142   Guldensuppe is alive, and taking revenge on Thorn   *BE,* August 9, 1897.
143   *"The police do not expect to see Guldensuppe"*   W. R. Hearst, editorial, *NYEJ,* July 3, 1897.
143   *Evangelina Cisneros, the pretty eighteen-year-old daughter. . . . Hearst preferred the latter explanation*   Ibid., 317.
143   *another* Journal *operative—the hotshot reporter Karl Decker—to Cuba*   Whyte, *Uncrowned King,* 325.
143   *Disguised with a sailor's outfit and a cigar*   Ibid., 328.
143   *EVANGELINA CISNEROS RESCUED BY THE JOURNAL*   *NYJ,* October 10, 1897.
143   *A NEW IDEA IN JOURNALISM*   *NYEJ,* October 3, 1897.
143   *offensives against a gas trust and crooked paving contractors*   Procter, *William Randolph Hearst,* 101.
144   *"Every one will sympathize with the* Journal's *enterprise"*   Whyte, *Uncrowned King,* 330.
144   *"The newspapers of your country"*   Creelman, *On the Great Highway,* 187.
144   *"It is epochal"*   W. R. Hearst, editorial, *NYJA,* October 13, 1897.
144   *a fine profusion of ads . . . the Lady Push Ball Players*   advertisement, *NYEJ,* September 4, 1897.
144   *"Organize a great open-air reception"*   Creelman, *On the Great Highway,* 171.
144   *Rooms were hired at the Waldorf, reservations made at Delmonico's*   Whyte, *Uncrowned King,* 332.
145   "scooped every day of its existence"   Ibid.
145   *THE PAPER SUFFERS AN EXCESSIVE STATESMANSHIP*   telegram, October 27, 1897. Pulitzer Papers, container 2.
145   *firing of a reporter for using the word "pregnant"*   Morris, *Pulitzer,* 379.
145   *MAKE SALARIED ARTISTS*   telegram, November 16, 1897. Pulitzer Papers, container 2.
145   *I REALLY DON'T EXPECT TO BE IN NEW YORK*   telegram, October 29, 1897, ibid.
145   *Brisbane, who jumped ship for the* Journal   Morris, *Pulitzer,* 334.
145   Brooklyn Eagle . . . *a curious development in Germany*   *BE,* October 13, 1897.
145   *"reputable merchants of Hamburg," were departing for New York*   *BE,* October 15, 1897.
145   *GULDENSUPPE ALIVE?*   *BE,* October 14, 1897.

16. CORPUS DELICTI

149   *A thick fog blanketed the Hudson*   *NYT,* November 6, 1897.
149   *"The* Fürst Bismarck *has been sighted"*   "Looks in Vain for Mrs. Nack," *NYEJ,* November 5, 1897.
149   *Hamilton Fish was on board*   "A Young Wheelman Hurt," *NYT,* November 6, 1897.
149   *one Josephine Vanderhoff had turned up*   "No Bail for Martin Thorn," *BE,* July 19, 1897.
149   *Edwards's minister visited to view the pickled* "Didn't Know Guldensuppe," *NYT,* August 28, 1897.
150   *they immediately identified the abandoned valise*   "Edward's Satchel Murray Says," *NYTR,* August 29, 1897.
150   *explain the enigmatically marked-up slates*   "Murrays Identify Valise," *NYT,* August 29, 1897.

150 *daughter examined the corpse's hands*   Ibid.

150 *Chicago trial had concluded for the infamous sausage-maker Adolph Luetgert*   *NYT,* October 22, 1897.

150 *nothing but five bone fragments*   "On These Five Bones Hang Luetgert's Fate," *NYEJ,* October 10, 1897.

150 *Thorn eagerly read the wire reports*   *NYEJ,* November 5, 1897.

150 *No Carl and Julius Peterson were listed*   "Ready for the Thorn Trial," *NYTR,* November 7, 1897.

151 *Open twenty-four hours a day*   Rovere, *Howe & Hummel,* 126.

151 *When seventy-eight brothel madams were arrested*   Ibid., 6.

151 *loud green and violet waistcoats*   Ibid., 16.

151 *defended 650 murder and manslaughter cases*   Ibid., 5.

151 *"You cannot prove a* corpus delicti*"*   *NYW,* October 12, 1897.

151 *DA's office laughed Howe off*   *NYT,* July 13, 1897.

151 *The notion had originated with Lord Chief Justice Sir Matthew Hale*   "Proof of the Corpus Delicti Aliunde the Defendant's Confession," 639.

151 *revived in America in 1819 after the Boorn brothers case*   Ibid., 646.

151 *combination safe filled with coal*   Rovere, *Howe & Hummel,* 25.

151 *staff amused themselves by serving one another*   Ibid., 27.

151 *they'd found nothing in the desks*   Ibid.

152 *"I cannot see how the District Attorney can get around the identification"*   "Mrs. Nack Offers to Confess All," *NYW,* October 12, 1897.

152 *Danish preacher Soren Qvist*   Warren, *Famous Cases,* 14. NB: Warren's account of Soren Qvist, along with a number of nearly identical ones published in English in the late nineteenth century, is curiously lacking in specific dates—and may indeed be drawing its information from an earlier Danish fictionalization of the case, the 1829 novel *The Rector of Veilbye.* That tale, though, is drawn from an apparently factual account of a 1626 case.

152 *"Then there was the Ruloff case"*   "Dredging for the Head Hopeless," *NYEJ,* October 7, 1897.

152 *two hapless detectives on the next steamer to Hamburg*   Carey, *Memoirs,* 51.

152 *secretly paying a witness to move to Japan*   Rovere, *Howe & Hummel,* 51.

152 *blaming a stabbing on the man's four-year-old daughter*   Ibid., 69.

152 *"Well . . . when you see Guldensuppe walk"*   "Thorn's Victim Rebuilt," *NYEJ,* July 23, 1897.

152 *carpenters added extra benches*   "Heavy Demand for Seats," *BE,* November 7, 1897.

153 *They'd spent nearly two hours shifting tables*   *BE,* November 7, 1897.

153 *he had a table custom-built for the case*   *NYEJ,* November 5, 1897.

153 *galleries were saved for sketch artists*   "Ready for the Thorn Trial," *NYTR,* November 7, 1897.

153 *Sheriff Doht was flooded with ticket requests*   *NYEJ,* November 5, 1897.

153 *being converted into a newsroom*   *BE,* November 7, 1897.

153 *housewives . . . hung Room for Rent signs*   *NYEJ,* November 5, 1897.

154 COURT TO PRINTING PRESS   *NYEJ,* November 6, 1897.

154 *prosecution of a recent Columbia graduate*   "College Man Confesses Crime," *NYW,* November 9, 1897.

154 *murder trial of a man who gunned down a police officer*   "Traced by a Timepiece," Ibid.

154 *husband driven mad by his wife's incessant whistling*   "Whistling Drove Him Mad," Ibid.

155 *"Martin Thorn is the same as any other man"*   Editorial, *NYEJ,* November 9, 1897.

155 *"Every day there will be some fifty different pictures of scenes"* "Murder Pictures," *NYT,* November 7, 1897.

155 *hundreds of potential jurors . . . waited* "Five Jurors to Try Thorn for His Life," *NYEJ,* November 8, 1897.

155 *Harriet Ayers was easy to spot . . . as was novelist Julian Hawthorne* "Thorn on Trial," *NYP,* November 9, 1897.

155 *gray-haired janitor shuffled up* *NYEJ,* November 8, 1897.

155 *police captain read that morning's newspaper* "Thorn's Counsel Happy," *BE,* November 9, 1897.

155 *district attorney was balding and bespectacled, wearing an off-the-rack suit* "The Trial of Martin Thorn," *NYCA,* November 8, 1897.

156 *"He's dead"* *NYEJ,* November 8, 1897. NB: With the following exception, the remainder of this scene is drawn from this account.

156 *lottery wheel with slips of paper bearing jury-pool names* "Thorn's Trial Opens," *NYME,* November 8, 1897.

157 *"That is not Mr. Blomquist"* "Thorn's Jury Selected," *NYT,* November 9, 1897.

157 *"How long have you lived in this country?"* *NYEJ,* November 8, 1897.

157 *they had interviewed Blomquist* "Thorn's Life Is in the Balance," *NYH,* November 9, 1897.

157 *"Have you an opinion"* *NYEJ,* November 8, 1897.

158 *"I think he's guilty"* *NYT,* November 9, 1897.

158 *Another two men confessed that they were over seventy* *NYH,* November 9, 1897.

158 *the judge had to empty the room out twice* *NYT,* November 9, 1897.

158 *a bell rang out lunchtime* *NYEJ,* November 8, 1897.

158 *all the local establishments were out of food within minutes* *NYH,* November 9, 1897.

158 *peremptory challenges, he admitted to reporters, were following a pattern* "The Thorn Jury Completed," *NYTR,* November 9, 1897.

158 *"I'm going at every talesman with extreme care"* *NYH,* November 8, 1897.

159 *first approved juror was a retired oysterman named Jacob Bumstead* *NYT,* November 9, 1897.

159 *appeared to be counting the gaslights* *NYEJ,* November 8, 1897.

159 *"Thorn is a very average specimen"* "Martin Thorn's Trial Begun, with Singular Celerity," *NYW,* November 9, 1897.

159 *They had run through sixty-four candidates* *NYH,* November 9, 1897.

159 Press *journalist had wickedly spread the rumor* "Thorn on Trial," *NYP,* November 9, 1897.

159 *"This . . . is magnificent"* "Testimony Begun in Trial of Thorn," *BE,* November 9, 1897.

17. COVERED IN BLOOD

160 *Long Island Rail Road's special jury car* *NYH,* November 9, 1897.

160 *held ordinary jobs* "Link by Link Thorn's Chain Is Forged," *NYEJ,* November 9, 1897.

160 *a warning sign from the sheriff* "Thorn on Trial," *NYP,* November 9, 1897.

160 *The farmers had stayed up . . . playing cards* *NYH,* November 9, 1897.

160 *puzzling over the newfangled electrical switches* "Thorn in the State's Toils," *NYH,* November 10, 1897.

161 *janitor was still sweeping out clouds of dust* *NYEJ,* November 9, 1897.

161 *precious white slips that read "PASS ONE"* "Life Against Life, Lie Against Lie," *NYW*, November 11, 1897.

161 *only just gotten over a neck rash* *NYEJ*, November 9, 1897.

161 *flower in Howe's lapel* *BE*, November 9, 1897.

161 *"About a half-pint of diamonds"* "Thorn Jury Discharged," *NYT*, November 13, 1897.

161 Herald *man was keeping track of the betting pools* *NYH*, November 10, 1897.

161 *anonymous note that warned* Ibid.

161 *sitting with a handkerchief atop his bald head* *NYH*, November 9, 1897.

161 *"Hear ye! Hear ye!"* "Rapidly Nearing the Supreme Test," *NYET*, November 9, 1897.

161 *"This is one of the most remarkable crimes"* *NYH*, November 10, 1897. NB: The remainder of this section is primarily drawn from the *Herald*'s transcription.

162 *air in the room had already grown foul again* *BE*, November 9, 1897.

163 *picked out some friends of his in the gallery* *NYT*, November 9, 1897.

163 *signing autographs at just fifty cents a pop* . . . The Headless Body Murder Mystery *NYET*, November 9, 1897. NB: This is title #771 (1897) from the very popular Old Cap. Collier dime-novel series. Dime novels were only haphazardly preserved, so that there is currently only one known surviving copy, at the University of Texas at Austin.

163 *"Where were you shortly after 1 o'clock"* *NYEJ*, November 9, 1897.

163 *"like a ghastly pack of cards"* "Mrs. Nack Has Confessed," *NYT*, November 10, 1897.

164 *"Is this the part of the body found by you?"* *NYEJ*, November 9, 1897.

164 *One* Telegram *writer dryly observed* *NYET*, November 9, 1897.

164 *"He is a good little boy"* "Mrs. Nack Has Confessed the Murder," *NYW*, November 10, 1897.

164 *"Was there any one else there"* *NYEJ*, November 9, 1897. NB: The remainder of this section is drawn from this *Evening Journal* account, except as noted.

165 *corner seat in the jury box was right next to the exhibit table* "Mrs. Nack Has Confessed the Murder," *NYH*, November 11, 1897.

165 *looked like he was about to turn green* "The Thorn Jury Completed," *NYTR*, November 9, 1897.

166 *Isaac Newton . . . failed to see anything funny* *NYT*, November 10, 1897.

166 *"Did you see these three portions together"* *NYW*, November 10, 1897. NB: The remainder of this section is drawn from this account, except for the Aimee Smith exchange noted below.

168 *"Do you remember the case of . . . Aimee Smith?"* *NYH*, November 10, 1897.

168 *first four pages of tonight's issue would be devoted to the case* *NYEJ*, November 9, 1897.

169 *Spanish overture to President McKinley* "Cabinet Like Spain's Reply," *NYT*, November 10, 1897.

169 *vote by the Georgia legislature* "Voted 91 to 3 Against Football," *NYP*, November 9, 1897.

169 *"Dynamite Dick" had been gunned down* "Dynamite Dick Shot Dead," *NYT*, November 10, 1897.

169 *"Interest in the case is not wholly"* *BE*, November 9, 1897.

169 *"We will disprove"* *NYEJ*, November 9, 1897.

169 *betting on Thorn now ran at roughly even odds* *NYH*, November 10, 1897.

169 *Barberi had been the first woman ever sentenced* *NYT*, July 16, 1895.

169 *already been turned into a Broadway play* Morgan and Van Doren, *Italian Americans*, 320.

169   *Barberi was a free woman, sitting in the gallery right beside the lawyer*   "Mrs.
      Nack Saw Thorn with a Dirk Knife," *NYEJ*, November 10, 1897.
170   *"What are you* doing *here, anyway?"*   *NYW,* November 10, 1897.

18. CAUGHT IN THE HEADLIGHT

171   *Mrs. Nack's lawyer was followed*   *NYH*, November 10, 1897.
171   *a melodrama set in Chinatown*   "The First Born a Hit," *NYT,* October 6, 1897.
171   *Friend walking purposefully away, leaving before*   *NYH*, November 10, 1897.
172   *wake up everyone from Captain O'Brien*   *NYT,* November 10, 1897.
172   *to Sheriff Doht*   *NYW,* November 10, 1897.
172   *Howe's house on Boston Avenue . . . darkened and quiet*   "Mrs. Nack Confesses,"
      NYTR, November 10, 1897.
172   *a reporter secretly on his payroll*   Rovere, *Howe & Hummel*, 35.
172   *during big cases he worked out of the Park Avenue*   *NYH*, November 10, 1897.
172   *immense cast-iron castle painted a blinding white*   Korom, *American Skyscraper,* 77.
172   *"Yes, I've heard the news"*   *NYH*, November 10, 1897.
172   *Another knock came at the door . . . a* World *reporter*   *NYW,* November 10, 1897.
172   *"I had the* most perfect case"   *NYH*, November 10, 1897.
172   *counsel . . .* for Nelson Weeks   *BE*, April 20, 1897.
172   *body in the Aimee Smith case had* not *been quickly identified*   *BE*, March 9, 1897.
173   *Newton was in direct charge of the Thorn case's body parts*   *NYT,* November 10,
      1897.
173   *"I cannot understand one thing"*   *NYH*, November 10, 1897.
173   *Californians and even Londoners woke that morning to the news*   "A Murderess
      Tells Her Dark Secret," *Oakland Tribune*, November 10, 1897; and "The New
      York Turkish-Bath Murder," *Pall Mall Gazette* (London), November 10, 1897.
174   *men in the crowd sprinted . . . women, slowed by their long skirts*   "Life Against
      Life, Lie Against Lie," *NYW*, November 11, 1897.
174   World *reporter dubbed it the Flower Garden*   Ibid.
174   MRS. NACK HAS CONFESSED THE MURDER   *NYW,* November 10, 1897.
174   *Thorn went pale and stiffly passed the newspaper*   "Mrs. Nack's Story Told,"
      NYT, November 11, 1897.
174   *"Augusta Nack," announced the court clerk*   *NYEJ*, November 10, 1897.
174   *smoothing her skirt as she sat*   "Mrs. Nack's Awful Story Told," *NYP,* Novem-
      ber 11, 1897.
174   *Her appearance, the* Times *sniffed*   *NYT,* November 11, 1897.
174   *"My name is Augusta Nack"*   *NYEJ*, November 10, 1897. NB: I have drawn
      from different news reports as indicated for the testimony that follows. Many of
      the physical gestures and tone of voice, however, are drawn from the particularly
      detailed rendition given in the November 11, 1897, report in the *New York Press*.
175   *transfixed spectator . . . nearly toppled over*   *NYW,* November 11, 1897.
175   *"Wanted his head?"*   "Story of Murder Told by Mrs. Nack," *BE*, November
      10, 1897.
175   *"He came one evening in my house"*   *NYEJ*, November 10, 1897.
176   *"I told Guldensuppe that he should come with me"*   *NYW,* November 11, 1897.
176   *"I had the key, and I went inside"*   *NYEJ*, November 10, 1897.
176   *not another sound in the room save for the furious* scritch scritch   *NYP,* Novem-
      ber 11, 1897.
177   *"He had a bottle of ammonia"*   "Thorn's Trial Is Postponed," *NYET,* Novem-
      ber 11, 1897.

177 *"Here is a photograph"*   *NYEJ*, November 10, 1897.
177 *favorite diamond pendant*   "Passed Away Very Suddenly," *BE*, September 2, 1902.
178 *"Mrs. Nack. . . . You have told us"*   *NYEJ*, November 10, 1897.
179 *"How long did this frightful love continue?"*   *NYH*, November 11, 1897.
180 *"You prepared to go Europe, didn't you?"*   *NYEJ*, November 10, 1897.
182 *"Mrs. Nack, don't you remember"*   *NYH*, November 11, 1897.
183 *"a scene of disorder in the court room"*   "Mrs. Nack Tells Her Story," *NYCA*, November 10, 1897.
183 *collapsed in a far corner of the jury box*   *NYH*, November 11, 1897.

19. SCYTHE AND SAW

184 *gathered around the Garden City Hotel billiard table*   "New Jury to Try Thorn," *NYT*, November 12, 1897.
184 *crowds scoured the floors . . . and locals pointed out the chairs*   "Thorn Confesses His Part in the Murder," *NYEJ*, November 11, 1897.
184 *"Yes, yes, yes—no, no, no"*   "Thorn Trial Ends; Jury Discharged," *NYEJ*, November 12, 1897.
184 *his rose-and-scarlet scarf . . . diamond-encircled moonstone*   "Thorn Jury Discharged," *NYT*, November 13, 1897.
184 *the size of an egg*   *NYEJ*, November 12, 1897.
184 *"The gallery was nearly full of Long Island folks"*   *NYT*, November 13, 1897.
185 *Howe jokingly shook a fist*   "Thorn's Trial Is Postponed," *NYET*, November 12, 1897.
185 *"Larsen had a very narrow escape"*   "Thorn Juror Under the Knife," *NYH*, November 12, 1897.
185 *In the Cancini case of 1857, he noted*   *NYEJ*, November 11, 1897.
185 *"You! You insignificant little imp!"*   "Jury Discharged in the Thorn Trial," *BE*, November 12, 1897.
186 *"This . . . is the case of my life"*   *NYT*, November 13, 1897.
186 *cheers and congratulations from his staff*   "Thorn's Trial at a Standstill," *BE*, November 11, 1897.
186 *"a damnable spider"*   "Thorn Eager to Testify," *NYT*, November 14, 1897.
186 *"From my first interview I found him* saturated *with chivalry"*   "New Trial for Martin Thorn," *NYH*, November 12, 1897.
186 *million-dollar operation in breach-of-promise cases*   Rovere, *Howe & Hummel*, 77.
186 *John Barrymore, because he didn't give a damn*   Ibid., 95.
186 *"She is the biggest liar unhung"*   *NYEJ*, November 11, 1897.
187 *"Mrs. Nack admitted that she herself had cremated Guldensuppe's clothes"*   "Mrs. Nack Identifies the Saw," *NYEJ*, November 17, 1897.
187 *stern, bespectacled Bronx landlady named Ida Ziegler*   "Lawyer Howe's New Witness," *NYT*, November 21, 1897.
187 *"On one Sunday. . . . I believe it was prior"*   "Thorn's New Witness," *NYW*, November 21, 1897.
187 *the accused barber had been left unshaven. . . . barber showed up at Thorn's cell with manacles*   "Thorn Handcuffed Getting a Prison Shave," *NYW*, November 20, 1897.
188 *Howe associate led a short impresario and a willowy actress*   "Anna Held Meets Thorn—A New Trial and Jury," *NYW*, November 12, 1897.

189 *THORN CONFESSES HIS PART IN THE MURDER* *NYEJ*, November 11, 1897.
189 *women's fashion plates with actual photographed faces* "An Advance View of Striking Autumn Fashions," *NYW*, August 29, 1897.
190 *Pulitzer anxiously telegraphed from Maine* Telegram, December 15, 1897. Pulitzer Papers, container 2.
190 Evening Telegram *ceased publication altogether* "Evening Telegram Suspends and Resumes," *NYEJ*, November 22, 1897.
190 "All the News That's Fit to Print" Campbell, *The Year That Defined American Journalism*, 70.
190 COCAINE PHANTOMS HAUNT HIM *NYEJ*, November 22, 1897.
190 *one could also find all these headlines* *NYH*, November 22, 1897.
190 *far more column inches on crime and accidents than other cities* Baldasky, *Commercialization of News*, 155.
190 *"The two stories of Nack and Thorn have reached an equilibrium"* W. R. Hearst, editorial, *NYEJ*, November 12, 1897.
191 *They tallied some 1,147 letters* "Three New Jurors and a New Judge for Thorn," *NYEJ*, November 22, 1897.
191 *latest ad for the Eden Musée waxworks* advertisement, *NYT*, November 20, 1897.
191 *THE INVASION OF NEW YORK* *NYJ*, November 14, 1897.
191 *THE STORY OF MY LIFE* Ibid.
192 *Augusta Nack was quietly led out of her cell* "Mrs. Nack Has an Outing," *NYS*, November 15, 1897.
192 *"Can you point out the place?"* "Digging Ends," *NYEJ*, November 15, 1897.
193 *"Did you find the saw?"* *NYS*, November 15, 1897.
193 *lost his job at the Astoria Model Bakery* "Nack Lives in Dread," *NYW*, November 13, 1897.
194 *"What do you think of the strange course"* "Mrs. Nack Tells New Secrets," *NYEJ*, November 13, 1897.
194 *newspapers gloated after word of her failed carriage trip* "Thorn Denies That He Is a Jailbird," *NYH*, November 16, 1897.
194 *laborers worked with scythes to clear* "Find Saw as Mrs. Nack Said," *NYEJ*, November 16, 1897.
194 *rusting eighteen-inch surgeon's saw—a Richardson & Sons model* "Thorn's Saw Is Found," *BE*, November 16, 1897.

20. A WONDERFUL MURDER

195 *Malwine Brandel clutched a bouquet . . . begging Sheriff Doht to let her inside* "Women Who Watch the Trial with Morbid Interest Tell the Journal Why," *NYJ*, November 25, 1897.
196 *the de rigueur accessory of the trial—opera glasses* "Mrs. Nack Again on View," *NYS*, November 25, 1897.
196 *Tessie . . . from Greenpoint* *NYJ*, November 25, 1897.
196 *Maddox on the bench—the last judge having excused himself* "Five Jurors Chosen to Try Thorn," *BE*, November 22, 1897.
196 *"I go to the Tombs to sing"* *NYJ*, November 25, 1897.
196 LOOK MORE INTELLIGENT THAN THE FORMER LOT *NYP*, November 23, 1897.
196 *two farmers, a florist, a property agent, an oyster dealer, and fully seven builders* "Twelve Men Chosen to Try Martin Thorn," *BE*, November 23, 1897.
196 *Clara Nunnheimer. . . . A fresh-faced and beaming* "Thorn's Trial Continues," *NYT*, November 25, 1897.

196 *"Do you recall the 25th of June?"*   *New York v. Thorn*, 142.
197 *Nor could he rattle a thirteen-year-old girl*   Ibid., 174.
197 *"kind of diagonally across from Mr. Buala's property"*   Ibid., 156–57.
197 *"Did you ever see William Guldensuppe naked?"*   Ibid., 75. NB: The revelations regarding the identification of Guldensuppe by his "peculiar" penis occur solely in the trial transcript; no other source of the time even dared to hint at them, instead referring to his being identified by his "finger."
198 *"He had very* peculiar *privates"*   Ibid., 82.
198 *"The most peculiar thing* was *his penis"*   Ibid., 87.
199 *"A* very *peculiar penis"*   Ibid., 101.
199 *fruit jar, sealed with red wax*   "Saw Martin Thorn at Woodside House," *BE*, November 24, 1897.
199 *"something looking much like small sections of tripe"*   *NYT,* November 25, 1897.
199 *"Has that changed its appearance?"*   *New York v. Thorn*, 103.
200 *"Church—or golf?"*   "Thorn Jurors at Golf Contest," *NYET,* November 25, 1897.
200 *the Garden City had been designed by Stanford White*   Waldman and Martin, *Nassau, Long Island*, 62.
200 *One juror . . . stuffed buckwheat pancakes into his pockets*   "Hot Cakes in His Pocket," *NYEJ*, November 23, 1897.
200 Church, *a stout minority of five argued*   *NYET,* November 25, 1897.
200 *Hundreds milled about, hoping to gain an audience*   "Four Thanksgivings Behind Bars," *NYW,* November 26, 1897.
201 *"I can say . . . that I really knew what Thanksgiving is today"*   "What Thorn Told Captain O'Brien," *NYEJ*, November 25, 1897.
201 *"Show your passes!"*   "Gotha Betrays Thorn to the Jury," *NYEJ*, November 26, 1897.
201 *"It's a disgrace to have women in attendance"*   "Human Flies at Thorn's Trial," *NYW,* November 27, 1897.
201 *"To show crime in its vulgarest"*   W. R. Hearst, editorial, *NYEJ*, November 11, 1897.
201 BRAZEN WOMEN AND BAD AIR   *NYW,* November 27, 1897.
201 *"more offensive than ever"*   "Mrs. Nack Held as Trump Card," *NYP,* November 27, 1897.
202 *and so, the press pool surmised, was Herman's new wardrobe*   *BE*, November 27, 1897.
202 *"Just a crazy barber"*   *NYP,* November 27, 1897.
202 *Sullivan identified the bullets*   *New York v. Thorn*, 340.
202 *NYPD pistol instructor noted that their caliber matched*   Ibid., 346.
202 *Detective O'Connell, the former plumber*   Ibid., 351.
202 *Thorn smiled at the sight of his old friend*   *NYEJ*, November 26, 1897.
202 *Thorn's informant looked puffy and tired*   "Gotha Repeats Thorn's Story," *NYET,* November 26, 1897.
203 *"I asked him if he done the murder"*   *New York v. Thorn*, 299. NB: The remainder of this section is drawn from the trial transcript.
205 *Howe was thunderstruck*   *NYW,* November 27, 1897.
205 CROWD MAY BREAK RECORDS   *BE*, November 28, 1897.
205 *attorneys were making a pilgrimage*   "All Eager to Hear Thorn," *NYT,* November 29, 1897.
205 *"No women"*   "Martin Thorn a Good Witness," *NYET,* November 29, 1897.
205 *Scores of women promptly laid siege*   "Thorn's Bid for Life," *NYW,* November 30, 1897.

206 *"I have been watching them"*   "Thorn's Story Told, His Life at Stake," *NYH*, November 30, 1897.
206 *women who had gotten in under the pretense*   "Thorn Testifies in His Own Behalf," *BE*, November 29, 1897.
206 *"The killing of Guldensuppe germinated"*   "Thorn Talks for His Own Life," *NYTR*, November 30, 1897.
207 *"In a long career in the court"*   "Jurors Paled at Thorn's Grewsome Evidence," *NYJA*, November 30, 1897.
207 *"Will Your Honor pardon me if I sit down"*   New York v. Thorn, 369.
208 *Howe rose and walked to the jury box*   *BE*, November 29, 1897.
208 *Then the defendant leveled his gaze squarely at the twelve men*   "Thorn's Account of the Murder," *NYEP*, November 29, 1897.

21. MRS. NACK'S OFFICE

211 *Hearst even joked*   W. R. Hearst, editorial, *NYEJ*, November 26, 1897.
211 *$60,000 windfall*   "Patrick J. Gleason Dead," *NYT*, May 21, 1901.
211 *her lucky piece of coral*   "Luetgert Predicts Thorn's Conviction," *NYW*, November 24, 1897.
211 *carried a rabbit's foot—a present from his wife*   "Fears Thorn's Collapse," *NYW*, November 23, 1897.
211 *"The case for the people was complete without her"*   *NYH*, November 30, 1897.
211 *"Where do you live?"*   New York v. Thorn, 387.
212 *her voice small and precise, free of artifice*   *NYW*, November 30, 1897.
212 *"Do you remember"*   New York v. Thorn, 387.
212 *"Is that all your evidence?"*   *NYH*, November 30, 1897.
213 *"I ask . . . that the jury be permitted to view the bath tub"*   New York v. Thorn, 495.
213 *Thorn . . . wasn't interested in joining them*   Ibid., 501.
213 *While a private trolley was requisitioned for the jurors, reporters jockeyed*   "Martin Thorn's Case Is in the Hands of the Jury," *NYEJ*, November 30, 1897.
214 *He hadn't allowed his charges to read . . . "nothing but hotel menu cards"*   "Fight for Thorn's Life Is On Again," *NYH*, November 24, 1897.
214 *Good Thing Club*   "Thorn Jurors' Bright Idea," *NYH*, November 29, 1897.
214 *genially hazed their police escort by loading his rifle with blanks*   "Thorn Will Say the Woman Did It," *NYH*, November 28, 1897.
214 *referred to as Mrs. Nack's Office*   "Thorn Confesses It All," *NYT*, December 1, 1897.
214 *"All off here for Woodside cottage!"*   "Thorn's Fate in Jury's Hands," *BE*, November 30, 1897.
214 *The place had hardly changed*   *NYT*, December 1, 1897.
214 *shooing gawkers to a perimeter*   *NYH*, December 1, 1897.
215 *Sullivan busily threw open the shutters*   "Thorn's Life in Jury's Keeping," *NYET*, November 30, 1897.
216 *Judge Maddox hadn't yet finished his cigar*   *NYEJ*, November 30, 1897.
216 *tugged down on his pin-striped vest*   Ibid.
217 *so loud that the chandeliers jangled*   *NYJA*, November 30, 1897.
217 *"Now, as to your visit to the cottage"*   *NYEJ*, November 30, 1897.
218 *"Remember that the scenes of this day will never"*   *BE*, November 30, 1897.
218 *"Put these things together in a mosaic"*   *NYEJ*, November 30, 1897.
219 *it was 2:25*   *NYEJ*, November 30, 1897.
219 *a single black-veiled woman nearly hidden*   "Thorn Found Guilty," *NYTR*, December 1, 1897.

220   *"So long as Mr. Howe kept in a sphere above the actual evidence"*   "The Jury's
Declaration at Thorn's . . . " (title damaged), *NYJA*, December 1, 1897.
220   *"It is not believed that he cut* himself *up"*   editorial, *BE*, November 27, 1897.
221   *reporters could make out raised voices*   "Jury in Three Hours Finds Thorn
Guilty," *NYJA*, December 1, 1897.
221   *poring over the intercepted jailhouse correspondence*   "Martin Thorn Convicted,"
NYS, December 1, 1897.
221   *"Remove your hats!"*   *NYT*, December 1, 1897.
221   *"Gentlemen of the jury, have you agreed upon a verdict?"*   "Jury Finds Thorn
Guilty of Murder," *NYH*, December 1, 1897.

22. THE SMOKER TO SING SING

222   *"I suppose Howe will get a new trial"*   *NYH*, December 1, 1897.
222   *wrestling with his adopted mutt*   "Thorn Sentenced to Die In January," *BE*,
December 3, 1897.
222   *"I had no motive to kill Guldensuppe"*   *NYH*, December 1, 1897.
222   *"Martin!" his sister sobbed*   "Martin Thorn Is Breaking Down," *NYW*,
December 3, 1897.
223   *"It doesn't make any difference to me"*   *NYH*, December 1, 1897. NB: The remainder of this scene is drawn from this account.
224   *"I am smoking a cigar"*   "Howe Calls Doht a Liar," *BE*, December 1, 1897.
224   *Garden City Hotel dutifully filed*   "Thorn Trial Expenses," *NYS*, December 3,
1897.
224   *Detective Sullivan's fruitless trip to Hamburg*   "Mrs. Nack May Escape Death,"
NYW, December 2, 1897.
224   *the entire cost of the case might balloon to $40,000 or $50,000*   "Luxurious Thorn
Jurors," *NYT*, December 3, 1897.
224   *hotel bill consisted of the usual pettiness*   "Thorn Jury Bill Edited," *BE*, January
13, 1898.
224   *The jury was incompetent to render a verdict*   "The Thorn Jury Wine Bill,"
NYT, January 8, 1898.
225   *"I saw no wine drunk"*   "Thorn Jurors Swear They Had No Wine," *BE*,
January 9, 1898.
225   *"Prisoner, arise"*   *BE*, December 3, 1897. NB: The remainder of the scene is
drawn from this account.
226   *Thorn sat up on his jail cot*   "Thorn Taken to Sing Sing," *BE*, December 4, 1897.
226   *he turned to his dog*   "Martin Thorn in Sing Sing," *NYET*, December 4, 1897.
226   *two inches of slush and snow*   "Thorn Must Die Within Five Weeks," *NYW*,
December 4, 1897.
226   *Thorn slid on the ice*   "Almost Fell Twice," *NYJ*, December 5, 1897.
227   *crowd was pressing on Thorn and his two jailers*   *NYET*, December 4, 1897.
227   *"They all want to see you"*   "Thorn's Vanity Betrayed Him," *NYW*, December
5, 1897. NB: The remainder of this scene is drawn from this account.
228   *a piano maker's wife had thrown herself*   "The Suicidal Mania," *NYT*, May 13,
1881.
228   *man recently arrested for assisting a high diver's illegal leap*   "Jumped from the
Bridge," *NYT*, July 5, 1897.
228   *employee had once run off with the florist's wife*   "Mrs. Spengler Went Wrong,"
NYT, September 9, 1892.
228   *burnished oak coffin*   "Guldensuppe's Body Buried," *NYTR*, December 6,
1897.

229 *his right hand laid upon his breast*   *NYT,* December 6, 1897.
229 Journal *women's page reporter who visited her on Christmas Day*   "Mrs. Nack's Christmas Present to Thorn," *NYJA,* December 26, 1897.
230 *"head devil" of the case*   "Maudlin Sympathy," *BE,* December 6, 1897.
230 *"They should place her in the electric chair with Thorn"*   "Mrs. Nack May Escape Death," *NYW,* December 2, 1897.
230 "Imagine Santa Throwing an X-Ray"   Bloomingdale's display ad, *NYW,* December 5, 1897.
230 FIRE IN A MATCH FACTORY   *NYH,* December 4, 1897.
230 *proposal to put bike racks on trolley cars*   "Brooklyn Trolleys May Carry Cycles Next Season," *NYJ,* December 10, 1897.
230 THOUGHTS PICTURED   *NYH,* November 28, 1897.
230 FISH CHOWDER POURS   *NYJ,* December 15, 1897.
231 *the Prophecy Prize*   "What Do You Think Will Happen in the Year 1898?" *NYJA,* December 19, 1897.
231 *"Poor Martin." Gussie sighed*   *NYJA,* December 26, 1897. NB: The remainder of this section is drawn from this account.

23. A JOB FOR SMITH AND JONES

233 *windowless walls on three sides*   *NYW,* December 5, 1897.
233 *"bathing in a search-light"*   Molineux, *Room with the Little Door,* 21. NB: Though an erstwhile work of fiction, Molineux's book is well worth finding for its account of life on Sing Sing's Death Row—namely, because he was a convicted poisoner sent there just a couple of years after Thorn. Molineux's conviction was one of the next great "newspaper trials" after Thorn's, although he was later released after a retrial.
233 *Thorn had already devoured* The Old Curiosity Shop   *NYT,* December 6, 1897.
233 *Sutherland was a West Indian in for shooting his wife*   "Died in the Electric Chair," *Sun* (Baltimore), January 11, 1898.
233 *warden stopped by with a message from Howe*   "A Stay for Martin Thorn," *NYT,* January 1, 1898.
234 *Hadley was not as fortunate*   "Went to His Death Cheerfully," *NYW,* January 11, 1898.
234 *"I could never eat off* that *table"*   "Ghastly Vanity Fair," *NYW,* January 16, 1898.
235 *salesrooms on 125th Street magically transformed*   "May Go To-Morrow," *BE,* January 13, 1898.
235 *in the reconstituted parlor was a suite*   *NYW,* January 16, 1898.
235 *"a low cut"*   "Mrs. Nack's Effects," *BE,* January 16, 1898.
235 *the plain and melancholy wooden bed of Guldensuppe*   *NYW,* January 16, 1898.
235 *dime-museum men . . . Luetgert's sausage vat*   "Would Exhibit Luetgert's Vat," *NYJ,* December 24, 1897.
236 MURDER DEN A KLONDIKE   *NYEJ,* January 14, 1898.
236 THE FAMOUS STOVE   *NYW,* January 16, 1898.
236 *handed at the entrance—business cards*   *BE,* January 16, 1898.
236 *"Those are terrible things my husband told"*   "Mrs. Nack's Story," *BE,* January 18, 1898. NB: The remainder of this scene is drawn from the *Eagle's* interview.
237 *appeals piled up*   "Calmly Martin Thorn Awaits His Fate of Death," *NYW,* July 28, 1898.

237 *"This is good news"*   "Martin Thorn to Die, and He Is Glad of It," *NYW,* July 31, 1898.

238 *found one hundred dead rats*   "Dead Rats in the Ventilators," *BE,* May 29, 1898.

238 *Howe had claimed a mistrial*   "Trying to Save Thorn's Life," *NYT,* July 29, 1898.

238 *bill was cruelly knocked down to $127*   "W. F. Howe's Cut Down," *NYT,* June 19, 1898.

238 *Howe talked grandly to the press of taking the case to the U.S. Supreme Court*   "Martin Thorn Must Die," *NYW,* June 8, 1898.

238 *"Take all your clothes off, Martin"*   "Murderer of Guldensuppe, Martin Thorn, Will Pay the Penalty and Be Killed Today," *NYW,* August 1, 1898.

238 *a crisp dress oxford*   *NYW,* July 31, 1898.

238 *There were five condemned prisoners*   *NYW,* August 1, 1898.

239 *"I want my books"*   Ibid.

239 *snare a coveted title from the prison library*   *NYP,* August 2, 1898.

239 *chat across the cell walls with the other prisoners*   *NYW,* August 1, 1898.

239 *"Have you seen your mouse yet, Thorn?"*   "Thorn Dies in the Chair for Guldensuppe's Murder," *NYEJ,* August 1, 1898.

240 *Sage was bustling around his office, making preparations*   *NYEJ,* August 1, 1898.

240 *only twenty-eight observers were allowed*   *NYW,* July 28, 1898.

240 *Hearst had deployed Langdon Smith*   *NYEJ,* August 1, 1898.

240 *famed as the country's fastest telegrapher*   "Answer No. 96," *American Mercury,* May 1926, 114.

240 *Haydon Jones, the* World's *own speed artist*   "Martin Thorn Pays the Penalty of Murder in the Electric Chair," *NYW,* August 2, 1898.

240 *scooped up by Pulitzer's crew from the* Mail and Express   Armes, Ethel, "Haydon Jones, Newspaper Artist," *National Magazine* 26 (1906): 151.

240 *his favorite Blaisdell pencil*   Ibid., 148.

241 *room was reminiscent of a small chapel*   *NYW,* August 2, 1898.

241 *"Gentlemen . . . you will oblige me"*   "Thorn Met Death Calmly," *NYS,* August 2, 1898.

241 *"the tentacles of an electrical octopus"*   *NYEJ,* August 1, 1898.

241 *"By these lamps . . . we will test the current"*   *NYW,* August 2, 1898.

242 *"The hour has come"*   *NYP,* August 2, 1898.

242 *long black rubber sash was stretched across his face*   *NYW,* August 2, 1898.

242 *"Christ, Mary, Mother of God"*   *NYEJ,* August 1, 1898.

243 *"like an overheated flatiron on a handkerchief"*   "Martin Thorn Dies in Abject Terror," *NYH,* August 2, 1898.

24. A STORY OF LIFE IN NEW YORK

244 *MARTIN THORN GOES CALMLY TO HIS DEATH*   *NYET,* August 1, 1898.

244 *THORN MET DEATH CALMLY*   *NYS,* August 2, 1898.

244 *MARTIN THORN DIES IN ABJECT TERROR*   *NYH,* August 2, 1898.

244 *WOMAN MEDIUM COMMUNES WITH THORN*   *NYW,* August 2, 1898.

244 *O'Neill was a surgeon with the New York School of Clinical Medicine*   *Medical Times and Register* 35–36 (1898): 185.

244 *sponges had dried out, causing a burn hole*   "Thorn Met Death Calmly," *NYS,* August 2, 1898.

244 *nitroglycerin, strychnine, and brandy*   *NYW,* August 2, 1898.
245 *Kemmler had been left still breathing*   Brandon, *Electric Chair,* 177.
245 *O'Neill bent over and rested the stethoscope*   *NYW,* August 2, 1898.
245 *"The law requires post-mortem mutilation"*   O'Neill, "Who's the Executioner?"
     185.
246 *"the prostitution of science"*   "Electrocution," *American Medico-Surgical Bulle-
     tin* 21, no. 21 (November 10, 1898): 999.
246 Evening Journal *lavished attention that night*   *NYEJ,* August 1, 1898.
246 *front-page attacks on crooked dealings*   "The Journal Stops," *NYJA,* December
     3, 1897.
246 *stoked his paper's capacity*   "The Journal's Presses—Past, Present and Fu-
     ture," *NYJ,* December 5, 1897.
246 THE WORST INSULT   "The Worst Insult to the United States in Its History,"
     NYJ, February 9, 1898.
246 *"Have you put anything else on the front page?"*   Morris, *Pulitzer,* 339.
247 WAR! SURE!   "War! Sure! Maine Destroyed by Spanish," *NYEJ,* February 17,
     1898.
247 THE WHOLE COUNTRY THRILLS   "The Whole Country Thrills with War Fever,"
     NYJ, February 18, 1898.
247 "Remember the *Maine*! To hell with Spain!"   Procter, *William Randolph
     Hearst,* 118.
247 HOW DO YOU LIKE THE JOURNAL'S WAR?   Stevens, *Sensationalism,* 97.
247 *offered the U.S. military $500,000*   Procter, *William Randolph Hearst,* 122.
247 *now rocketed up to . . . a million and a half*   Bleyer, *Main Currents,* 378.
247 *"war news was written by fools for fools"*   Turner, *When Giants Ruled,* 135.
247 *ran news of the death of one Colonel Reflipe W. Thenuz*   "The World Confesses
     to Stealing the News!" *NYEJ,* June 9, 1898.
248 *newspaper publisher tearing around Havana Harbor*   Churchill, *Park Row,*
     131.
248 MUST FIND THAT FLEET!   *NYEJ,* May 28, 1898.
248 *summer dessert tips for homemakers*   "Even Ice Cream and Confectionary Are
     Now Made to Suggest War," *NYEJ,* May 28, 1898.
248 *taking some Spanish prisoners of war*   Procter, *William Randolph Hearst,* 130.
248 *spotted at the Battle of El Caney*   Ibid., 129.
248 *Eden Musée was busy adding a score of patriotic*   advertisement, *NYT,* August
     14, 1898.
248 *its baggage car disgorged a plain pine box*   "Curious Crowds Look on the Cof-
     fined Face of Martin Thorn," *NYW,* August 3, 1898.
249 *worries that freak-show promoters might try*   "Took Amperes to Kill Thorn,"
     NYP, August 2, 1898.
249 *A thousand disappointed spectators had appeared*   "Thorn Met Death Calmly,"
     NYS, August 2, 1898.
249 *A dozen policemen from the Twenty-Seventh Precinct*   "Martin Thorn Body Bur-
     ied in Calvary's Consecrated Ground To-Day," *NYH,* August 2, 1898.
249 *undertaker barred the door*   *NYEJ,* August 2, 1898.
249 *his head still bore red electrode marks*   *BE,* August 2, 1898.
249 *brother-in-law leaned over for a word*   *NYEJ,* August 2, 1898.
249 *luxuriant display of lilies of the valley*   "Thorn Met Death Calmly," *NYS,*
     August 2, 1898.
249 *"Probably a woman"*   *NYEJ,* August 2, 1898.
249 *"Mrs. Nack?"*   *NYH,* August 2, 1898.
250 *inmate #269 at Auburn*   "Mrs. Nack Is Now No. 269," *NYW,* January 20,
     1898.

250 *a three-inch-thick oak door*   "How Mrs. Nack Will Spend Her Term in Auburn," *NYW,* January 16, 1898.

250 *spent her day in the prison's sewing room*   *NYW,* January 20, 1898.

250 *Word was leaking out*   "State Control of Midwives," *Buffalo Medical Journal* 48 (1898): 131.

250 Journal *pounced on a damning discovery*   "Mrs. Nack Has Money in Realty," *NYEJ,* August 11, 1898.

250 *sardonic inscription of* AUGUSTA NACK, SURGEON   "Bright Editorial," *San Antonio* (Texas) *Daily Light,* March 13, 1900.

250 *"Epidemic Hypnotic Criminal Suggestion"*   "Epidemic Hypnotic Criminal Suggestion," *Massachusetts Medical Journal* 21 (1901): 512.

251 SECOND GULDENSUPPE CASE   *NYT,* October 9, 1899.

251 *third* [Guldensuppe case]   "Zanoli, Queer Man of Tragedies," *NYJA,* December 11, 1897.

251 *fourth* [Guldensuppe case]   "Murder and Butchery," *NYT,* February 9, 1898.

251 *fifth* [Guldensuppe case]   "Like Guldensuppe Murder," *NYT,* June 11, 1899.

251 *a woman's leg was found*   "Another Ghastly Find," *NYS,* October 10, 1899.

251 *her chest washed ashore on Staten Island*   "Torso of the Body Found," *NYS,* October 11, 1899.

251 *NYPD threw 200 detectives on the case*   *NYS,* October 10, 1899.

251 *Moses Cohen, the "C" newspaper*   "Murder Still His Mystery," *NYT,* October 13, 1899.

251 *captain of the barge* Knickerbocker   *NYS,* October 10, 1899.

251 *"would have appealed to Sherlock Holmes"*   "The Influence of Sherlock Holmes," *BE,* October 11, 1899.

251 *Prospect Place coal cellar of Alma Lundberg*   "New Clue in Murder Case," *NYT,* December 4, 1899.

251 *other clues proved to be the usual nonsense*   "Police at a Standstill," *NYS,* October 13, 1899.

252 *"the Great American Identifier"*   *NYT,* October 19, 1899.

252 *cuts precisely matched those on Guldensuppe*   *NYT,* October 13, 1899. NB: Although the crime was officially unsolved, police afterward believed that the victim was Kate Feeley, who went missing after answering a newspaper ad for employment. Max Schmittberger, later the chief police inspector for the NYPD, voiced the suspicion that William Hooper Young—later convicted of the 1902 murder of Anna Pulitzer—was the perpetrator. (See "Mrs. Pulitzer Is Buried," *NYT,* August 24, 1902.)

252 *a novel,* Three Men and a Woman   "A Strong Book by an Iowa Author," *Cedar Rapids* (Iowa) *Daily Republican,* June 10, 1901.

252 *"The death of Guldensuppe preyed"*   "Nack Brooded," *Lowell* (Massachusetts) *Sun,* June 23, 1903.

252 *346 Second Street sat vacant*   "For Use as a Wine-Shop," *BE,* March 19, 1899.

253 *thrown the Bualas' baseboards into a bonfire*   "Relics of Murder Burned," *NYTR,* March 24, 1899.

253 *turning them into a jaunty pair of scarf pins*   "Personal Chats," *Muncie* (Indiana) *Morning Post,* May 4, 1898.

253 *"We have already put one haunted house"*   "Join to Rout Ghosts," *NYTR,* May 21, 1904.

253 *only to die of rabies*   "Dog Dealer Dies of Rabies," *NYT,* February 12, 1910.

253 *preserving the bathroom upstairs*   *BE,* March 19, 1899.

253 *Piernot ran half-naked and screaming*   "Saw Guldensuppe's Ghost," *NYT,* December 1, 1900.

25. CARRY OUT YOUR OWN DEAD

254 *A tall, long-haired artist* "Mrs. Nack Set Free, Met Here by Mob," *NYT,* July 20, 1907.

254 CUT HIS THROAT BY ACCIDENT *and* SHE HEARD VOICES *NYJ,* July 19, 1907.

254 *story of a Civil War vet in Central Park* "Talks War to Tots and Kills Self," *New York Evening Mail,* July 19, 1907.

255 MRS. NACK SET FREE *NYEJ,* July 19, 1907.

255 *a train crewman stopped* "Mrs. Nack, Free, Centre of Mob on Arrival Here," *NYW,* July 20, 1907.

255 *"I am glad to be out"* "Mrs. Nack Free, Denies Identity as Murderess," *NYH,* July 20, 1907.

255 *the platform boiled over with hundreds of people* "Great Crowd to See Mrs. Nack," *NYS,* July 20, 1907.

256 *"Get away from me!"* "Mrs. Nack Free, Denies Identity as Murderess," *NYH,* July 20, 1907.

256 *"We are friends of yours"* *NYW,* July 20, 1907.

256 *Ranks of tripod cameras lying in wait on Lexington Avenue* *NYS,* July 20, 1907.

256 *"Keb?"* *NYW,* July 20, 1907.

256 *police station where she'd been interrogated was gone* "The Passing of No. 300 Mulberry St," *NYT,* September 21, 1902.

256 *the courthouse and the jury's hotel were both burnt out* "Garden City Hotel Burned," *NYTR,* September 8, 1899.

257 *she'd had to pay the driver six dollars* "Mrs. Nack, Unwelcome Patron at Hotel, Leaves," *NYET,* July 20, 1907.

257 *"I suppose I shall find things a great deal different"* *NYH,* July 20, 1907.

257 *Manny Friend, had been gone for three years now* "Emanuel M. Friend, Lawyer, Dead," *NYT,* November 2, 1904.

257 *English child of a brothel keeper* "Central Criminal Court, Sept. 20," *Times* (London), September 21, 1854.

257 *forging admission tickets* "Bow Street," *Times* (London), November 4, 1848.

257 *clerk in Blackfriars* "Central Criminal Court, June 17," *Times* (London), June 19, 1854.

257 *convicted in 1854 of impersonating* *Proceedings of the Old Bailey, Eleventh Session 1853–4,* September 20, 1854, Case No. 997, 1193. NB: While it has been suspected since at least Rovere's biography that William F. Howe had a criminal record in the United Kingdom, I am the first to discover the specific offenses and records. They seem to have also remained quite unknown in Howe's own lifetime. The revelation that Howe was the child of an accused madam, noted in the *Times* of London account of September 21, 1854, has also been previously unknown to biographers.

257 *emerged to reinvent himself across the ocean* Rovere, *Howe & Hummel,* 21.

258 *Hotel Markwell, where the manager recognized her* "Mrs. Nack Confesses!" *NYEJ,* April 20, 1907.

258 *Wilson Mizner . . . whose lobby sign read* CARRY OUT YOUR OWN DEAD Johnston and Marsh, *Legendary Mizners,* 66.

258 *"I got those knocking down dames"* Ibid., 113.

258 *signed in as "Mrs. A. Ross, Buffalo"* *NYEJ,* July 20, 1907.

258 *"I have had enough misery for one woman"* *NYW,* July 20, 1907.

258 *"I am selling this story"* "Mrs. Nack Tells of Life in Prison," *NYT,* July 21, 1907.

258 *"Remarkable Photograph"* *NYEJ,* July 18, 1907.

258 *Hearst's paper was now more squat and squarish* *NYEJ,* January 5, 1898, and

July 22, 1907. NB: Although most newspaper histories cite the 1920s as the beginning of the tabloid (along with some brief nineteenth-century forays), in reading issues of the *Journal*, it struck me that the paper was already moving in that direction years earlier. Measuring them shows that indeed it was: The height/width ratio on an 1898 issue is roughly 1.4, while on the 1907 issue it is 1.25.

258   *an outright tabloid format would be "the 20th Century newspaper"*   Lee, *American Journalism, 1690–1940*, vol. 3, 274.

258   *crude wooden-type letters that were seven inches tall*   Winkler, *Hearst: A New Appraisal*, 107.

259   BUILDING FALLS; 40 KILLED   *NYEJ*, July 18, 1907.

259   WOMAN KILLS MAN IN UNION SQUARE   *NYEJ*, July 22, 1907.

259   *fascinated by the notion of sending armed zeppelins*   editorial, *NYEJ*, July 20, 1907.

259   MRS. NACK CONFESSES!   *NYEJ*, July 20, 1907.

259   *money to move back to Germany*   "Mrs. Nack Will Go to Live with Old Mother," *NYW*, July 21, 1907.

260   *she wasn't sure where to start looking*   *NYT*, July 21, 1907.

260   *"This . . . is worse than prison"*   *NYW*, July 21, 1907.

260   *One year later, a call came*   "Mrs. Nack Calls at the Tombs," *Syracuse Herald*, September 6, 1908.

260   *"brutal" place of "wanton waste"*   "Finds Gross Cruelty in Auburn Prison," *NYT*, April 28, 1913.

260   *"You do not have enough to eat"*   *NYET*, July 20, 1907.

261   *"I would like to get a place"*   *Syracuse Herald*, September 6, 1908.

261   *Judge Smith*   "Justice Smith's Funeral," *NYT*, April 1, 1906.

261   *Judge Maddox went on to state supreme court*   "Judge Maddox Buried," *NYT*, March 16, 1916.

261   *Youngs, the case was followed by a plum promotion*   "Col. Wm. J. Youngs Dies," *NYT*, April 2, 1916.

261   *urge the adoption of an alternate-juror rule*   "Change in the Jury System," *NYT*, January 30, 1900.

261   *only took another thirty-three years*   "Extra Jurors Bill Signed by Governors," *NYT*, May 2, 1933.

261   *testifying in major murder cases*   "Dr. R. A. Witthaus, Poison Expert, Dies," *NYT*, December 21, 1915.

261   *view stomach membrane . . . dazzling crystals of arsenic poisoning*   Blum, *Poisoner's Handbook*, 84.

261   *"inheritance powder," as it was dubbed*   Ibid., 79.

261   *under an ultraviolet light, that was chloroform poisoning*   Ibid., 23.

261   *it would also turn yellow for mercury poisoning*   Ibid., 110.

261   *charged the city a dizzying $18,550*   "Molineux Experts' Charges Over $50,000," *NYT*, August 10, 1900.

261   *his heirs would later claim*   "Dr. Witthaus's Will Attacked in Court," *NYT*, September 22, 1916.

262   *evidence ruined by drunk and incompetent coroners*   Blum, *Poisoner's Handbook*, 5.

262   *bribed with, say, a nice gold watch*   "Admits Trying to Bribe Juror," *Los Angeles Times*, April 29, 1908.

262   *the coroner's job was abolished altogether*   "What Coroners' Exit Means," *NYT*, December 9, 1917.

262   *promptly dubbed "Guldensuppe's head"*   "Guldensuppe's Head?" *NYT*, October 30, 1910.

262 *Price, rose to become one of the most recognizable detectives* "Police Capt. Price Dead," *NYT,* January 9, 1914.

262 *O'Brien . . . went on to address the bewildering rise of automobiles* "Ex-Inspector O'Brien Dead," *NYT,* July 3, 1913.

262 *first head of the NYPD's newly formed Homicide Bureau* "Arthur Carey, 87, Ex-Inspector, Dies," *NYT,* December 14, 1952.

263 *teaching the homicide course* "Detective School Faculty Announced," *NYT,* February 24, 1923.

263 *had become a standard procedure* Cole, *Suspect Identities,* 152.

263 *"In a murder case there is no one obvious clue"* Carey, *Memoirs,* 51.

263 *It was a warm June evening* "Bundled Up Body, Dismembered, Found in Street," *NYW,* June 11, 1909.

264 *head was discovered under the Brooklyn Bridge* "Murdered Man, Found Mutilated, Had Love Affair," *NYW,* June 12, 1909.

264 VICTIM CARVED UP LIKE GULDENSUPPE *Hartford Courant,* June 12, 1909.

264 CASE MOST PUZZLING SINCE GULDENSUPPE *NYEJ,* June 11, 1909.

264 *Scores of detectives tracked the distinctive oilcloth* "Beheaded and Dismembered Victim of Murder Was Samuel Bersin, a Decorator," *NYH,* June 12, 1909.

264 *murdered by a jealous husband. . . . robbed for his diamond rings . . . rivals for the hand* "Murdered Man Found Mutilated, Had Love Affair," *NYW,* June 12, 1909.

264 *Sammy was a Russian Jewish anarchist* "Jean Pouren Case Now Figures in Bersin Murder," *NYW,* June 15, 1909. NB: Despite all the attention that it drew, the Bersin case remained unsolved.

264 *"Mrs. Nack has taken the name of Augusta Huber"* "Murder Case Recalled," *Oshkosh* (Wisconsin) *Daily Northwestern,* March 4, 1909.

264 *she was in bankruptcy court* "Mrs. Nack in Trouble Again," *NYT,* July 13, 1909.

265 *Still working the streets of New York* "Old Morgue Inadequate," *Pittsburgh Press,* August 8, 1915.

265 *empty cabernet bottle* "Mrs. Nack May Be Indicted," *NYT,* July 6, 1897.

265 *stabbed while naked* *NYT,* June 28, 1897.

266 *"I last saw her"* Van Wagner, *New York Detective,* 15.

EPILOGUE: THE LAST MAN STANDING

267 *"the first of the great newspaper trials"* "Winchell on Broadway," *Mansfield* (Ohio) *News Journal,* September 12, 1946.

267 *a venture into writing novelty songs* *Catalogue of Copyright Entries, part III: Musical Compositions* (Washington, D.C.: Library of Congress, 1915), 930.

267 *Ike White, went on to expose dozens* "Isaac White Dies, Noted Reporter, 79," *NYT,* September 25, 1943.

267 *Hawthorne landed in prison* "Julian Hawthorne, Dead on Coast, 88," *NYT,* July 15, 1934.

267 Journal *had burned through about $4 million* Morris, *Pulitzer,* 344.

267 *He and Hearst met . . . and negotiated a deal* Ibid., 355.

268 *their resulting agreement went unsigned* Ibid., 359.

268 *came to admire the sober reliability of the* New York Times Ibid., 418.

268 World*'s proprietor was rehabilitated* Bleyer, *Main Currents,* 351.

268 *"a Coney Island of ink and wood pulp"* Palmer, *Hearst and Hearstism,* 120.

268 *Patterson's founding in 1919 of the New York* Daily News Nasaw, *The Chief,* 321.

268   *runs for mayor, then governor*   Winkler, *Hearst: An American Phenomenon*, 191.

268   *inevitably for president*   Bleyer, *Main Currents*, 384. NB: He never made it to the White House, but a few suspected Hearst of depriving a previous holder of the office. In 1901 his penchant for brash content backfired spectacularly when a poem by Ambrose Bierce that wished William McKinley dead ran right before the president's actual assassination. Hearst had to patriotically tack "American" to the *Journal*'s name—making it the *New York Journal American*—to set that one right.

269   *"a lark and a triumph"*   "The Hearst Boom," *Nelson* (New Zealand) *Evening Mail*, November 15, 1906.

269   *"Ah well, we were young"*   Procter, *William Randolph Hearst*, 97.

269   *That man was Ned Brown*   "Ned Brown Dead; Writer on Boxing," *NYT*, April 26, 1976.

269   *"Being a newspaperman gave you stature then"*   Liebling, *Liebling at* The New Yorker, 166.

270   *evicted from his apartment*   "Most Important Possession," *Sarasota Herald Tribune*, May 22, 1973.

270   *the case files had been destroyed years earlier*   "Queens to Destroy Noted Crime Files," *NYT*, December 7, 1949.

270   *reporter picked out a yellowed evidence envelope*   Edward Radin column (no surviving headline), *St. Petersburg Times*, July 13, 1949.

ACKNOWLEDGMENTS

It was years ago that I first chanced upon an 1897 article about some faked murder relics found in a sleepy neighborhood of Queens. From that peculiar beginning came this book—but it couldn't have been written without the love, patience, and encouragement of my wife, Jennifer, or the inspiration of my sons, Morgan and Bramwell. My great thanks also go to Marc Thomas for all his help in the twenty-first century while I was off traveling in the nineteenth.

I am especially grateful to the John Simon Guggenheim Memorial Foundation; the generous support of a Guggenheim Fellowship was vital in the creation of this book.

My many thanks as well to my agent, Michelle Tessler, and my editor, John Glusman; their wise guidance in the book's early stages led to my pursuing New York's newspaper wars as a key part of this story.

Finally, this book is deeply indebted to many librarians. My particular thanks go to the staffs of the New York Public Library, the Library of Congress, Portland State University, and the Multnomah County Library. The soul of this book is probably in room 100 of the NYPL, where I found many of the thousands of newspaper articles I used from the case, and where many more stories slumber and wait to be found. When I first stopped by to see the famed NYPL "Librarian to the Stars," David Smith, he had a surprise for me: "You just got me in time," he said. "I'm retiring in a couple of days." And so he was. I suppose I was his last new author and new book in a four-decade career of assisting everyone from Jimmy Breslin to Colson Whitehead. I hope that this book does his old library proud, and that he gets some good beach weather for reading it.

ILLUSTRATION CREDITS

Frontis: Is Any One You Know Missing?: *NYJ*, June 29, 1897. Courtesy of the Library of Congress.

Page 1: Body diagram: *NYJ*, June 28, 1897. Courtesy of the Library of Congress.

Page 43: Martin Thorn and Anna Held: *NYW*, November 12, 1897. Courtesy of the Library of Congress.

Page 91: "Mrs. Nack, Murderess!": *NYEJ*, June 30, 1897. Reproduced by permission of the New York Public Library.

Page 135: Mrs. Nack's letter: *NYJA*, October 6, 1897. Courtesy of the Library of Congress.

Page 138: Thorn's letter: *NYJA*, October 7, 1897. Courtesy of the Library of Congress.

Page 147: "Thorn Denies That He Shot Guldensuppe": *NYJ*, November 30, 1897. Courtesy of the Library of Congress.

Page 209: "Interior View of the Woodside Cottage": *NYEJ*, November 30, 1897. Reproduced by permission of the New York Public Library.

Page 273: "Mrs. Nack Tells Her Own Story of the Amazing Guldensuppe Tragedy": *NYEJ*, July 20, 1907. Reproduced by permission of the New York Public Library.

INDEX

GHOST NIGHT

This Large Print Book carries the
Seal of Approval of N.A.V.H.

GHOST NIGHT

HEATHER GRAHAM

THORNDIKE PRESS
A part of Gale, Cengage Learning

GALE
CENGAGE Learning™

Detroit • New York • San Francisco • New Haven, Conn • Waterville, Maine • London

GALE
CENGAGE Learning™

Copyright © 2010 by Heather Graham Pozzessere.
The Bone Island Trilogy #2.
Thorndike Press, a part of Gale, Cengage Learning.

Thorndike Press® Large Print Basic.
The text of this Large Print edition is unabridged.
Other aspects of the book may vary from the original edition.
Set in 16 pt. Plantin.

LIBRARY OF CONGRESS CATALOGING-IN-PUBLICATION DATA

Graham, Heather.
  Ghost night / by Heather Graham. — Large print ed.
    p. cm. — (The Bone Island trilogy; #2) (Thorndike press
  large print basic)
  ISBN-13: 978-1-4104-2764-9
  ISBN-10: 1-4104-2764-1
  1. Murder—Investigation—Fiction. 2. Large type books.
  I. Title.
PS3557.R198G43 2010
813'.54 dc22   2010025585

Published in 2010 by arrangement with Harlequin Books S.A.

Printed in the United States of America
1 2 3 4 5 6 7 14 13 12 11 10

For Scott Perry, Josh Perry,
Frasier Nivens, Sheila Clover-English,
Victoria Fraasa, Brian O'Lyaryz
and the great and fun folks
with whom I've been on some strange
and entertaining filming expeditions.

KEY WEST HISTORY TIME LINE

1513 — Ponce de Leon is thought to be the first European to discover Florida for Spain. His sailors, watching as they pass the southern islands (the Keys), decide that the mangrove roots look like tortured souls and call them "Los Martires," or the Martyrs.

Circa 1600 — Key West begins to appear on European maps and charts. The first explorers came upon the bones of deceased native tribes, and thus the island was called the Island of Bones, or Cayo Hueso.

The Golden Age of Piracy begins as New World ships carry vast treasures through dangerous waters.

1763 — The Treaty of Paris gives Florida and Key West to the British and Cuba to the Spanish. The Spanish and Native Americans are forced to leave the Keys and move

to Havana. The Spanish, however, claim that the Keys are not part of mainland Florida and are really North Havana. The English say the Keys are a part of Florida. In reality, the dispute is merely a war of words. Hardy souls of many nationalities fish, cut timber, hunt turtles — and avoid pirates — with little restraint from any government.

1783 — The Treaty of Paris ends the American Revolution and returns Florida to Spain.

1815 — Spain deeds the island of Key West to a loyal Spaniard, Juan Pablo Salas of St. Augustine, Florida.

1819–1922 — Florida is ceded to the United States. Salas sells the island to John Simonton for $2,000. Simonton divides the island into four parts, three going to businessmen Whitehead, Fleming and Greene. Cayo Hueso becomes more generally known as Key West.

1822 — Simonton convinces the U.S. Navy to come to Key West — the deepwater harbor, which had kept pirates, wreckers and others busy while the land was scarcely developed, would be an incredible asset to

the United States. Lieutenant Matthew C. Perry arrives to assess the situation. Perry reports favorably on the strategic military importance but warns the government that the area is filled with unsavory characters — such as pirates.

1823 — Captain David Porter is appointed commodore of the West Indies Anti-Pirate Squadron. He takes over ruthlessly, basically putting Key West under martial law. People do not like him. However, starting in 1823, he does begin to put a halt to piracy in the area.

The United States of America is in full control of Key West, which is part of the U.S. Territory of Florida, and colonizing begins in earnest by Americans, though, as always, those Americans come from many places.

Circa 1828 — Wrecking becomes an important service in Key West, and much of the island becomes involved in the activity. It's such big business that over the next twenty years, the island becomes one of the richest per capita areas in the United States. In the minds of some, a new kind of piracy has replaced the old. Although wrecking and salvage are licensed and legal, many a ship

is lured to its doom by less than scrupulous businessmen.

1845 — Florida becomes a state. Construction begins on a fort to protect Key West.

1846 — Construction of Fort Jefferson begins in the Dry Tortugas.

1850 — The fort on the island of Key West is named after President Zachary Taylor.

New lighthouses bring about the end of the golden age of wrecking.

1861 — January 10, Florida secedes from the Union. Fort Zachary Taylor is staunchly held in Union hands and helps defeat the Confederate Navy and control the movement of blockade-runners during the war. Key West remains a divided city throughout the Great Conflict. Construction begins on the East and West Martello Towers, which will serve as supply depots. The salt ponds of Key West supply both sides.

1865 — The War of Northern Aggression comes to an end with the surrender of Lee at Appomattox Courthouse. Salvage of blockade runners comes to an end.

Dr. Samuel Mudd, deemed guilty of conspiracy for setting John Wilkes Booth's broken leg after Lincoln's assassination, is incarcerated at Fort Jefferson, the Dry Tortugas.

As salt and salvage industries come to an end, cigar making becomes a major business. The Keys are filled with Cuban cigar makers following Cuba's war of independence, but the cigar makers eventually move to Ybor City. Sponging is also big business for a period, but the sponge divers head for waters near Tampa as disease riddles Key West's beds and the remote location make industry difficult.

1890 — The building that will become known as "the little White House" is built for use as an officer's quarters at the naval station. President Truman will spend at least 175 days here, and it will be visited by Eisenhower, Kennedy and many other dignitaries.

1898 — The USS *Maine* explodes in Havana Harbor, precipitating the Spanish-American War. Her loss is heavily felt in Key West, as she had been sent from Key West to Havana.

Circa 1900 — Robert Eugene Otto is born.

At the age of four, he receives the doll he will call Robert, and a legend is born, as well.

1912 — Henry Flagler brings the Overseas Railroad to Key West, connecting the islands to the mainland for the first time.

1917 — On April 6, the United States enters World War I. Key West maintains a military presence.

1919 — Treaty of Versailles ends World War I.

1920s — Prohibition gives Key West a new industry — boot legging.

1927 — Pan American Airways is founded in Key West to fly visitors back and forth to Havana.

Carl Tanzler, Count von Cosel, arrives in Key West and takes a job at the Marine Hospital as a radiologist.

1928 — Ernest Hemingway comes to Key West. It's rumored that while waiting for a roadster from the factory, he writes *A Farewell to Arms*.

1931 — Hemingway and his wife, Pauline, are gifted with the house on Whitehead Street. Polydactyl cats descend from his pet, Snowball.

Death of Elena Milagro de Hoyos.

1933 — Tanzler removes Elena's body from the cemetery.

1935 — The Labor Day Hurricane wipes out the Overseas Railroad and kills hundreds of people. The railroad will not be rebuilt. The Great Depression comes to Key West, as well, and the island, once the richest in the country, struggles with severe unemployment.

1938 — An Overseas Highway is completed, U.S. 1, connecting Key West and the Keys to the mainland.

1940 — Hemingway and Pauline divorce; Key West loses her great writer, except as a visitor.

Tanzler is found living with Elena's corpse. Her second viewing at the Dean-Lopez Funeral Home draws thousands of visitors.

1941 — December 7, "a date that will live

in infamy," occurs, and the U.S. enters World War II.

Tennessee Williams first comes to Key West.

1945 — World War II ends with the Armistice of August 14 (Europe) and the Surrender of Japan, September 2.

Key West struggles to regain a livable economy.

1947 — It is believed that Tennessee Williams wrote his first draft of *A Streetcar Named Desire* while staying at La Concha Hotel on Duval Street.

1962 — The Cuban Missile Crisis occurs. President John F. Kennedy warns the United States that Cuba is only ninety miles away.

1979 — The first Fantasy Fest is celebrated.

1980 — The Mariel Boatlift brings tens of thousands of Cuban refugees to Key West.

1982 — The Conch Republic is born. In an effort to control illegal immigration and drugs, the United States sets up a blockade

in Florida City, at the northern end of U.S. 1. Traffic is at a stop for seventeen miles, and the mayor of Key West retaliates on April 23, seceding from the U.S. Key West Mayor Dennis Wardlow declares war, surrenders and demands foreign aid. As the U.S. has never responded, under international law, the Conch Republic still exists. Its foreign policy is stated as, "The Mitigation of World Tension through the Exercise of Humor." Even though the U.S. never officially recognizes the action, it has the desired effect; the paralyzing blockade is lifted.

1985 — Jimmy Buffet opens his first Margaritaville restaurant in Key West.

Fort Zachary Taylor becomes a Florida State Park (and a wonderful place for reenactments, picnics and beach bumming).

Treasure Hunter Mel Fisher at long last finds the *Atocha.*

1999 — First Pirates in Paradise is celebrated.

2000–Present — Key West remains a unique paradise itself, garish, loud, charming, filled

with history, water sports, family activities and down-and-dirty bars. "The Gibraltar of the East," she offers diving, shipwrecks and the spirit of adventure that makes her a fabulous destination, for a day, or forever.

PROLOGUE

South Bimini
September

The sound of the bloodcurdling scream was as startling as the roar of thunder on a cloudless day.

Vanessa Loren immediately felt chilled to the bone, a sense of foreboding and fear as deep-seated as any natural instinct seeming to settle into her, blood, body and soul.

So jarring! It brought casual conversation to a halt, brought those seated to their feet, brought fear to all eyes. It was the sound of the scream, the very heartfelt terror within it, which had been lacking during the day's work.

The ocean breeze had been beautiful throughout the afternoon and evening; it seemed almost as if the hand of God was reaching down to gently wave off the last dead heat of the day, leaving a balmy temperature behind as the sun sank in the western horizon with an astonishing palette

17

of crimson, magenta, mauve and gold.

The film crew had set up camp on the edge of the sparse pine forest, just yards away from the lulling sound of the ocean. The Bahamian guides who had brought them and worked with them had been courteous, fun and knowledgeable, and there was little not to like about the project, especially as night fell and the last of the blazing, then pastel, shades faded into the sea, and it and the horizon seemed to stretch as one, the sky meeting the ocean in a blur.

A bonfire burned with various shades from brilliant to pale in the darkness, and the crew gathered around as it grew dark. South Bimini was sparsely inhabited, offering a small but popular fisherman's restaurant and little more, unlike the more tourist-friendly North Bimini, where numerous shops, bars and restaurants lined what was known as The King's Highway in Alice Town.

They had taken it a step further than South Bimini, choosing to film on one of the several little uninhabited islands jutting out to the southwest. One with a name that had greatly appealed to Jay.

Haunt Island.

A long time ago, there had been a pirate

massacre here. Over the years, truth and legend had merged, and it was this very story that Vanessa had used in her script for the low-budget horror film they were shooting.

So infamous years ago, Haunt Island was currently just a place where boaters came now and then. An island filled with scrub and pines, a single dock and an abundance of beach. Out here, tourism wasn't plentiful — the terrain remained wild and natural, beloved by naturalists and campers.

There had been more people in their group, but now they were down to ten. There were Georgia Dare and Travis Glenn, the two actors playing the characters who remained alive in the script; Jay Allen, director; Barry Melkie, sound; Zoe Cally, props, costumes and makeup; Carlos Roca, lighting; Bill Hinton, and Jake Magnoli, the two young production assistants/lighting/sound/ gophers/wherever needed guys; their Bahamian escort and guide, Lew Sanderson; and Vanessa herself, writer and backup with the cameras and underwater footage.

It was all but a wrap. The historical legend filled with real horror that was sure to be a box-office hit on a shoestring budget had been all but completed, and they'd been winding down, crawling out of their tents to enjoy the

champagne, laughing and lazing against the backdrop of the sunset and the breeze.

And then the sound of the scream, so much more chilling and horrible than any sound Georgia Dare had managed to emit throughout the filming.

Until that moment, Vanessa Loren had enjoyed the project. It was simple enough — a low-budget horror flick that actually had a plot. She had written the script. In addition, she and Jay were financially committed to the project, which made them both willing to work in any capacity. She was ready to do instant rewrites as needed because of the actors and the environment, and she could film underwater shots and even pitch in as second camera for many of the land shots.

Jay, the director, was planning on making a bundle; he was counting on the success of such films as *The Blair Witch Project* and *Paranormal State.* Vanessa and Jay had known each other forever, and had both gone to film school at NYU. He'd contacted her while she was working back in Miami after she'd gotten her master's degree at the University of Miami. He'd talked the good talk on getting together and finding a few investors to finance a really good low-budget flick.

Luckily, she had just been nicely paid for work she had done writing and filming an advertisement for dive gear. It had been one of the few projects she had worked on that hadn't been rewritten by a dozen people before coming to fruition — and it had been a sixty-second spot.

Jay agreed with her that if they were going to do the project, an independent endeavor, it had to be done really well. However, they were also looking for commercial success. So the script was well written but also included the usual assortment of teen-slasher-flick characters — the jock who counted his conquests with scratches on his football helmet, the stoner guitar boy, the struggling hero, the popular slut coming on to the hero and the good-girl bookworm. So far, two characters had been killed in the water, two had disappeared from the boat — and two had to fight the evil, reborn pirates on land and sea and somehow survive until help could come to the patch of sand where they'd been grounded in the Atlantic.

The scream.

Vanessa had been sitting by the fire, sipping a glass of champagne and chatting with Jay, Lew and Carlos. They'd broken it open just a few minutes earlier, taking a minute

to relax before they all gathered to cook dinner over the fire and the camp stoves they'd brought and finish off the rest of the champagne.

At the scream, she, like the others, stopped what she was doing. They looked at one another in the eerie light produced by the flames in the darkness, then bolted up and started running toward the sound.

Vanessa was in the lead when Georgia came tearing down the beach toward them. Vanessa caught the young woman, trying to hold her, trying to find out what had happened. "Georgia! Stop, stop!" Georgia Dare, a stunning twenty-one-year old blonde, stared at her with eyes as wide as saucers. "Georgia, it's me, Vanessa. What's wrong?"

"Nessa . . . Nessa . . . oh my God, oh, no, no . . . !"

Georgia started to scream again, trying to shake Vanessa's hold.

"Georgia!"

By then, everyone had come, bursting out of their camp tents, forgetting whatever task they had been involved in.

The others gathered behind her while Jay came forward. "Georgia, damn it, what the hell kind of a prank is this?" he demanded. Once, Georgia had tried to pretend that a

stunt knife was real and that she'd been stabbed by a woman from the Retirees by the Sea trailer park back in the Keys.

"The bones, the bodies . . . they are alive, they don't like us, they're going to kill us . . . they're angry . . . we'll all die!" Georgia blurted.

"Damn it, I've had it," Jay said with disgust, turning away. Most of the others did the same.

Vanessa didn't. Georgia was shaking violently. *And that scream! The sound of that scream still seemed to be chilling her blood.*

"They're going to kill us all. Kill us all," Georgia said. Her eyes fell directly on Vanessa's then, and she was suddenly as strong as a sumo wrestler, breaking free from Vanessa's hold and gripping her shoulders instead. "They're real! They're going to kill us, don't you understand, we have to get out of here! They're coming out of the sand. I saw them . . . the arms, the hands, the skulls . . . I saw them, coming out of the sand."

"Georgia, Georgia, please, stop it. Hey, come on, we're filming a horror movie, remember?" Vanessa asked gently. "The guys probably set up some of the props to scare you," She frowned suddenly. "What

23

were you doing alone, way down on the beach?"

"Travis and I . . . Travis and I . . . Travis is gone."

Travis Glenn was the male lead, an exceptionally beautiful if not terribly bright young man.

"Okay, where is Travis?"

"Gone. Gone. The pirate took him."

"The pirate?"

Georgia shook her head. "Maybe he wasn't a pirate. I didn't see him very clearly. But he was evil — he was like an evil shadow, skulking in the darkness. Travis was yelling, and he went after the shadow. He was mad. He thought you all were playing tricks. And then this monster came out of the sand, but he wasn't right, he seemed to jerk around, like his bones were put back together wrong. And he took Travis and I started screaming and ran."

Jay came back, hands on his lean hips, chest glistening in the darkness. "Slap her! Nessa, don't look so damned concerned. She's jerking us around and it isn't funny. Damn you, Georgia. Look, I realize this isn't anything major-budget, but the crew has worked hard and everyone is tired — and you're acting like a complete bitch! It's just not the time for practical jokes. Slap

24

her, knock her out of it, Vanessa!"

Vanessa glared at him and shook her head. Georgia wasn't that good an actress. She had disagreed with casting the young woman, but she had looked phenomenal on film.

"Let's go down to the beach and see what scared her," Vanessa suggested. She looked back at Lew, a big, broad-shouldered Bahamian man who had been one of their guides. "Do you think there's anything down at the beach, Lew?"

"Sand," he told her.

"Let's go see."

Georgia jerked away from her, shaking her head vehemently. "No, no, no! I am not going back there. I am not going back!"

Carlos Roca, their lighting engineer, came toward them. He'd been close to both actors, and Georgia liked him. Vanessa did, too. He was a nice guy — even-tempered and capable. He took Georgia's hands. "Hey, hey. I'll stay here with you, and we'll sit by the fire with the others while Lew, Jay and Vanessa go check it all out. How's that?"

Georgia looked up at him. Huge tears formed in her eyes and she nodded. "Travis is dead," she told him. "Travis is dead."

Jay looked at Zoe, who worked with the props, makeup and buckets of stage blood

25

they'd been using. He glared sternly at her, then turned to Bill and Jake, the young production assistants, earning credit from the U of Miami. "Hey, you guys didn't rig anything, did you — any practical jokes?"

Zoe looked at him with incredulous disdain. "No. No, we did not."

Jay looked from face to face and was obviously satisfied with the chorus of denials.

"All right, we'll check it out," Jay said.

"Yes, yes. Come on, let's do this," Lew said with his pleasant and easy Bahamian accent. "We'll find Travis and see what's going on. Miss Georgia, you're going to be just fine, honey."

But Georgia shook her head. "Travis is dead," she repeated.

"I'll light some torches from the fire," Lew offered.

"I don't believe we're doing this," Jay said, tired and irritated as they started down the beach. "I made a mistake in casting, that's for sure. We're filming a legend, a horror flick, for God's sake. She's letting it all get to her. This is crazy."

Lew chuckled softly. "Ah, yes, well, that's the way it is with American slasher flicks, eh? Two young people drink and wander off into the woods or the pines to make love, and then the monster comes upon them.

26

They are mistaken. This is Bimini. There are no monsters."

Vanessa stopped. They had come to the edge of the beach. A pine forest came almost flush with the water after a rise in the landscape.

"Nothing," Jay said. "There's nothing out here at all."

Vanessa raised her torch to look around. She froze suddenly. There was nothing there now, but just feet from her, the sand looked as if it had been raked, and it was damp as well, as if someone had dumped buckets of water twenty feet inland from the shore.

"Look," she said.

"Someone was playing a joke on her — on her and Travis, maybe," Jay said. He swore. "We've got one more day of filming to tie up loose ends, and I guess it's natural that someone just feels the need to play practical jokes."

"But where is Travis?" Vanessa asked.

Lew was hunkered down by the disturbed sand. "Interesting," he said.

"What?" Jay asked.

"It does look like something burst outward from the sand — more than it looks as if someone were digging in it," Lew said. "As if it erupted, and was then smoothed over."

"We work with great props and special-

27

effects people," Jay said dryly. "Let's get back. I'm tired as hell. Someone has to have some kind of sleeping pill Georgia can take."

"I'm not sure she should be taking a pill —" Vanessa began.

"I am," Jay interrupted her. "I need to sleep tonight!"

"I'll take Georgia in with me," Vanessa volunteered. She surprised herself. She hadn't disliked Georgia; she just found the woman to be a little . . . vapid. But that night, she felt sorry for her. Georgia had dropped out of high school, certain that an actress didn't need an education. She'd spent several years working as a model at car and boat shows, and Jay had discovered her because she'd gotten a local spot on television promoting a used-car dealer. Vanessa had to admit that Georgia might not be the most talented actress she knew, but she had been professional and easy to work with. She was pretty sure that Georgia had never gotten a lot of support from her parents or anyone else.

She also knew that she had been lucky. She had been raised by parents who had cared more about their children than anything else in life. Her mother and father had been avid historians, readers, writers and divers, and they had done everything in

their power to put their two children through college. She loved history and she loved diving. Her actual forte was in script writing, but in Hollywood, that was a difficult route, with scripts being rewritten so many times that you seldom recognized your own work at the end, and you seldom received credit for a project, either. It had been necessary, in her mind, to learn cameras as well, and with her background, underwater work was a natural. She was driven and she was passionate about her work, so she'd jumped at the chance to work on this movie when Jay called her.

Jay loved horror movies, and they had loved each other forever. Not as boyfriend and girlfriend — they had known each other since grade school in the small town of Micanopy, Florida. He had a chance with this movie, and she wanted him to have his chance. She wanted this chance for herself, too.

She had said from the beginning that she was in only if she got her own tent.

But tonight she'd bring Georgia in with her and be a mother hen.

Carlos had been settling the young woman down; the two were sitting by the fire with large plastic cups — Vanessa was pretty sure they contained something a lot harder than

champagne. As Vanessa, Jay and Lew returned, Georgia jumped to her feet, staring at them. "See? See? I told you!"

Jay took Georgia by the shoulders and tried to be calm and reassuring. "Georgia, all I can think is that Travis is playing some kind of a trick on you, sweetie."

"No, no! You have to go look for Travis!" Georgia said.

"I guess we should," Vanessa said quietly.

Jay stared at her with aggravation. "Look for him? Oh, please! You know damned well that Travis is the one who played this ridiculous joke, or he's in on it! And there's nothing there, Georgia. No hands, no skulls, no monsters. Georgia, you've got to get some sleep. I need some sleep."

"No, no, I saw it!" Georgia said, shaking her head in fear. She glared furiously at Jay. "I have to get out of here. I won't stay here!" she insisted.

"You've got to be joking!" Jay declared irritably. "Georgia, you were touting used cars, for God's sake! This could make you the new scream queen!"

Georgia was obviously terrified beyond caring. "I don't care! I don't care if I spend the rest of my life as a waitress. I have to get off this island — now. Now!"

"It's dark!" Jay reminded her.

30

"Hey, hey, it's all right, we're fifty miles from Miami, and we've got a good speedboat. I can take her in and be back to help with any follow-up or backup shots that we need tomorrow," Carlos offered.

"What if we need *the actress?*" Jay demanded. "I haven't looked through the sequences we shot today."

Carlos looked at Vanessa. "If Nessa doesn't mind, she's the same height and build and has long blond hair. She can fill in."

"Yes, yes, Vanessa can fill in! You can be my stunt double!" Georgia said enthusiastically.

"For joy, for joy," Vanessa murmured. But she was still disturbed by the young woman's absolute terror. Georgia was ambitious. Was she really so terrified that she would walk away from what could be a big break for her?

She realized that everyone was staring at her.

"Sure. Whatever is needed," she said dryly to Jay. Of course she would do it. They both had a lot of hard work — not to mention their finances — tied up with this.

"I'll be back in the morning," Carlos promised. "Look, seriously, it's what? Seven-thirty, eight o'clock now? I can make Miami

31

in a few hours. I'll get a night's sleep and head back by five or six tomorrow morning."

It was agreed. In another hour, Carlos and Georgia were off.

Vanessa found herself sitting by the fire with the others, sipping champagne once again, though it had lost its taste.

"I still think we should look for Travis," she said.

Zoe let out an irritated "tsking" sound. "That jerk! He's out there somewhere, laughing at everyone, and not caring that he's put a real bug in the production."

"And messing with the props. When he walks up laughing and swaggering in the morning, I think we should give him a good right hook," Barry said.

Silence fell.

"Hey, we could sit here and tell ghost stories!" Bill suggested.

They all glared at him. Apparently, no one was in the mood.

For a while, they did reflect upon the many disappearances and oddities that had occurred in the Bermuda Triangle, but even that didn't last long.

It was only nine-thirty when Vanessa opted for bed. She lay awake, watching the patterns of the low-burning fire playing upon

32

the canvas roof of her tent. She thought about the ridiculousness of filming the movie — the hours of getting the characters into makeup and how, to save money, they had all taken on so many different tasks. Jay and Carlos had played the vengeful pirates, coming out of the sea, and she had supplied some of the sound effects and acted as the kidnapped and murdered Dona Isabella.

Her script was honestly good, based on history and legend. Once, the Florida Keys and the Bahamas had been areas of lawlessness, ruled by pirates. An infamous pirate captain, Mad Miller, and his mistress, Kitty Cutlass, had gone on a wild reign of terror, taking ship after ship, or so legend said. Then all had gone wrong. They had taken a ship bearing the beautiful and rich Dona Isabella. They had sunk her ship, killed most of the crew and, presumably, planned on ransoming Dona Isabella. She had been sailing from Key West to Spain, back to her wealthy husband, when she had been taken. But nothing had happened as planned. Legend said that Kitty Cutlass killed Dona Isabella in a fit of rage, and on Haunt Island, Mad Miller went *really* mad and massacred the remaining crew and many of his own men. Finally, his pirate ship had sunk off Haunt Island, caught in the venge-

ful winds of a massive storm. Vanessa had based her script on the legend, doing what research she could, with contemporary teenagers finding themselves victims of bitter ghosts risen from the sand and the sea. As a screenplay, the story provided amazing fodder for the imagination. Filming had actually been fun. There had been some amusing accidents along the way, but none that had caused any harm. Bill had fallen into one of the buckets of blood, and Jake had come bolting up out of the water once, terrified of a nurse shark. She liked the people she was working with, and so, for the most part, it had been enjoyable. A crash shoot — all of it done within three weeks. And Jay was right — it could hit big at the box office.

She still felt disturbed and uneasy, although she wasn't alone. The tents were no more than a few feet apart. Jay, who had been bunking with Carlos, was next to her. Bill and Jake were on her left side. Lew, as secure a figure as anyone might ever want to meet, was just beyond Zoe.

But she was still afraid. It was as if Georgia's gut-wrenching scream had awakened something inside her that knew something was coming, something that she dreaded.

At eleven o'clock, she was still staring at

the canvas. She didn't have anything really strong to help her sleep, but she decided on an over-the-counter aid. In another half an hour, she was asleep.

It might have been the pill. She slept, but she tossed and turned and awakened throughout the night. And she dreamed that Georgia was standing in front of her, giant tears dripping down her cheeks. "I told you, I told you there were monsters!"

Georgia's image disappeared.

She dreamed of giant shadow figures rising over her tent and of seaweed monsters rising out of the ocean, growing and growing and devouring ships, boats and people, and reaching up to the sky to snatch planes right from the atmosphere.

She awoke feeling better, laughing at herself for the absurdity of her dreams.

She didn't believe in seaweed monsters — sea snakes, yes, sharks and other demons of the real world, but seaweed monsters, no.

When she had nightmares, they were usually more logic-based — being chased in the darkness by a human killer, finding out she was in a dark house alone with a knife-wielding madman.

It had been Georgia. Georgia and that terrifying scream.

She blinked, stretched and rose. Taking

35

off the long T-shirt nightgown she'd worn, she put on a bathing suit, ready to hit the beach. There were showers in the heads on both boats the crew had been using, the *Seven Seas* and the *Jalapeño.* Of course, one boat wouldn't be back until Carlos returned. It was a bright and beautiful morning, and she felt that a good dousing in the surf would be refreshing.

She stepped out of her tent. The morning sun was shining, but the air retained a note of the night's pleasant coolness. The sea stretched out before her, azure as it could only be in the Bahamas. Jay and Zoe were already up, and one of them had put the coffeepot to brew on the camp stove.

"Morning!" Jay called.

"Morning!" she returned. "How long till coffee?"

"Hey! As fast as it brews!" Jay told her.

Zoe giggled. "What? Did you think this film had a budget for a cook?"

Vanessa walked on out to the water. It was delightful; warm, but not too warm. So clear she could easily see the bottom, even when she had gone out about twenty-five feet from shore and the depth was around ten feet. The current of the Gulf Stream was sweeping the water around to the north; she decided to fight it and swim south, then let

it bring her on back offshore from the camp-site.

She swam a hard crawl, relaxed with a backstroke, worked on her butterfly and went back to doing the crawl, and then decided that she had gone far enough. She had angled herself in toward shore, so she paused a minute, standing, smoothing back her hair.

It was then that she looked toward the shore.

She would have screamed, but the sound froze in her throat.

She stood paralyzed, suddenly freezing as if she were a cube of ice in the balmy water.

The bones . . . the bodies . . .

Georgia's terrified words of the night before seemed to echo and bounce in her mind.

Then she did scream, loud and long. And she found sense and logic, amazingly, and started shouting for the others to come.

The bones . . . the bodies . . .

They were there. There was no sign of the boat, but Georgia Dare and Travis Glenn were there — in the sand. Their heads, eyes glaring open, were posed next to one another, staring toward the sea. Inches away from each, arms stretched out of the sand as well — just as props had done in the film-

ing. It was as if they desperately reached out for help as the earth sucked them down, leaving only those pathetic heads, features frozen in silent screams.

Jay had reached the scene. He was shaking and staring, in shock and denial. He shouted. "Travis, what is this, damn it! Georgia — no! No, no, no! Where is Carlos? What kind of a stunt is this?" Jerking like a mechanical figure, Jay went to touch the actor's head, as if he could wake him up or snap him out of whatever game he was playing.

The head rolled through the sand. The body wasn't attached.

Jay himself began to scream.

Frozen still, shaking from a sudden cold that threatened never to leave her, Vanessa remained just offshore. She didn't move until Lew had gotten the authorities, until a kindly Bahamian official came and wrapped a towel around her shoulders, and led her away.

1

Before him, frond coral waved in a slow and majestic dance, and a small ray emerged from the sand by the reef, weaving in a swift escape, aware that a large presence, possibly predatory, was near.

Sean O'Hara shot back up to the surface, pleased with his quick inspection of Pirate Cut, a shallow reef where divers and snorkelers alike came to enjoy the simple beauty of nature. It was throughout history a place where many a ship had met her doom, crushed by the merciless winds of a storm. Now only scattered remnants of that history remained; salvage divers of old had done their work along with the sea, salt and the constant shift of sands and tides and weather that remained just as turbulent through the centuries.

It was still, he decided, a great place to film.

He hadn't opted for scuba gear that day — it had been just a quick trip, thirty minutes out and thirty back in, early morning, just to report to his partner, David Beckett, so they could talk about their ever-changing script and their plans for their documentary film.

Because Sean was an expert diver, he seldom went diving alone. Good friends — some of the best and most experienced divers in the world — had died needlessly by diving alone. But a free dive on a calm day hadn't seemed much of a risk, and he was pleased that he had taken off early in the morning. Most of the dive boats headed out by nine, but few of them came to Pirate Cut as a first dive, and it wouldn't get busy until later in the day.

And out in the boat, he wasn't exactly *alone*.

Bartholomew was with him.

Climbing up the dive ladder at the rear of his boat, *Conch Fritter,* he tossed his flippers up and hauled himself on board. His cell phone sat on his towel, and the message light was blinking. Caller ID showed him that he'd been called from O'Hara's, his uncle's bar.

"I thought about answering it, but refrained."

Sean turned at the sound of the voice. Bartholomew was seated at the helm of the dive boat, feet in buckle shoes up on the wheel, a *National Geographic* magazine in his hands.

Bartholomew was getting damned good at holding things.

"Thank you for refraining. And tell me again, why the hell are you with me? You hate the water," Sean said, irritated. He pushed buttons on his phone to receive his messages, staring at Bartholomew.

"Love boats, though," Bartholomew said.

Sean groaned inwardly. It was amazing — once he hadn't believed in Bartholomew. Actually, he'd thought the ghost might have been one of his sister Katie's imaginary friends. He realized he either had to accept that she was crazy or that there was a ghost. At that time, Sean couldn't see or hear Bartholomew.

But that had been a while ago now. While solving the Effigy Murders — as the press wound up calling them — he'd ended up with his head in a bandage and stitches in his scalp.

It was the day the damned stitches had come out that he'd first seen the ghost —

41

as clearly as if he had physical substance — sitting in a chair next to the hospital bed.

Sean listened to his messages. The first, from David Beckett, asking him what time he wanted to go out. Sean grinned. David was in love — and sleeping late. Sean was glad, since it seemed that his old friend was in love with his sister, Katie, and she was in love with him. They'd both seen some tough times, and Sean was happy for them.

The next message was from his uncle just asking him to call back.

He did so. Still, he didn't learn much. His uncle just wanted him to come to the bar. Sean told him it would take him about forty-five minutes, and Jamie said that was fine, just to come.

"So what's up?" Bartholomew asked.

"Going to the bar, that's all," Sean said. He was curious. Jamie wasn't usually secretive.

"Can you keep a hand on the helm? Bring her straight in?" Sean asked Bartholomew as he brought up the anchor. Securing it, he added, "Jeez, am I crazy asking you that?"

Bartholomew looked at him with tremendous indignation.

"Really! That was absolutely — churlish of you! If there's one thing I know, it's a lazy man's boat like this!"

Sean grinned. "I'll be in the head in the shower for about fifteen minutes. That's all you need to manage."

"It'll be great if we pass the Coast Guard or a tour boat!" Bartholomew cried.

Sean ignored him. He just wanted to rinse off the sea salt — his uncle had him curious.

He showered, dried and dressed in the head and cabin well within his fifteen minutes. In another twenty, he was tying up at the pier.

Duval Street was quiet.

As he walked from the docks to O'Hara's, Sean mused with a certain wry humor that Key West was, beyond a doubt, a place for night owls. He was accustomed enough to working at night — or even partying at night — but he was actually more fond of the morning hours.

"What do you think Jamie wants?"

Sean heard the question again — for what seemed like the tenth time now — and groaned inwardly without turning to look at the speaker. *Imagine, once he had wanted to see the damned ghost!*

Oh, he could see Bartholomew way too clearly now, though when he had first come home to Key West — hearing that David Beckett was in town and worried for his

sister's safety — he had come with his longtime fear for Katie's mind. She had always seemed to sense or see things. But that had been Katie, not him.

Bartholomew had apparently wanted to be known, though at first he proved his presence by moving things around.

Then Sean had seen him in that damned chair in the hospital room. Now he could see the long-dead privateer as easily as he could see any flesh-and-blood, living person who walked into his life.

He cursed the fact.

He had never believed in ghosts. He'd never wanted to believe. In fact, he'd warned Katie not to ever talk about the fact that she had "strange encounters" or had been "gifted" or "cursed" from a young age. The majority of the world would think that she should be institutionalized.

He wasn't pleased that he saw Bartholomew. Now he had the fear that he would one day wind up institutionalized himself.

And he was far from pleased that the dapper centuries-old entity had now decided to affix himself to Sean.

"I will not answer you. I will never answer you in public," Sean said.

Bartholomew laughed. "You just answered me. Then again, we're hardly in public, you

know. I think the whole island is still asleep. Besides, you're a filmmaker. An 'artiste!' People will happily believe that you are eccentric, and it's your brilliance causing you to speak to yourself."

"Right. Don't you feel that you should go and haunt my sister?" Sean asked.

"I believe she's busy."

"I'm busy," Sean said.

"Look, I'm apparently hanging around for something," Bartholomew said. "Others have gone on, and I haven't. You seem to be someone I must help."

"I don't need help."

"You will, I'm sure of it," Bartholomew said.

Sean kept walking.

"So what do you think he wanted?" Bartholomew persisted.

"I don't know," Sean said flatly. "But he wanted something, and that's why I'm going to see him." He cast a glance Bartholomew's way. The privateer — hanged long ago for a deed he hadn't committed — was really quite a sight. His frock coat and stockings, buckle shoes, vest and tricornered hat all fit his tall, lean physique quite well. In his lifetime, Sean thought dryly, he had probably made a few hearts flutter. Sadly, he had died because of the death of the love

45

of his life, and an act of piracy blamed upon him. However, after haunting the island since then, he had recently found a new love, the "lady in white," legendary in Key West. When they filmed their documentary, Sean meant to make sure that he covered Bartholomew's case and those of his old and new loves.

He'd heard once that ghosts remained on earth for a reason. They wanted to avenge their unjust deaths, they needed to help an ancestor or they were searching for truth. There were supposedly ghosts who were caught in time, reenacting the last moments of their lives. But that was considered "residual haunting," while Bartholomew's determination to remain on earth in a spectral form was known as "active" or "intelligent" haunting.

Bartholomew had been around for a reason — he had been unjustly killed. But Sean couldn't figure out why he remained now. His past had been aligned with David Beckett and his family, and Sean had to admit that Bartholomew had been helpful in solving the Effigy Murders, all connected to the Becketts.

Maybe he had stayed because of the injustice done to him and because he still felt that he owed something to the Becketts.

All Sean knew was that he had been Katie's ghost — if there was such a thing — and now he seemed to be with him all the time.

Sean liked Bartholomew. He had a great deal of wit and he knew his history. He was loyal and might well have contributed to saving their lives.

But it was unnerving from the get-go to realize that you were seeing a ghost. It was worse realizing that the ghost was no longer determined to stick to Katie like glue, but had moved on to him. He was a good conversationalist — and thus the problem. Sean was far too tempted to talk to him, reply in public and definitely appear stark, raving mad upon occasion.

Ghosts were all over the place, Bartholomew had informed him. Most people felt a whisper in the breeze, sometimes a little pang of sorrow, and if the ghost was "intelligent" and "active," it might enjoy a bit of fun now and then, creating a breeze, causing a bang in the dark of night, and so on. Katie had real vision for the souls lurking this side of the veil. So far, thank God, he'd seen only Bartholomew, and maybe a mist of others in the shadows now and then.

Sean had been damned happy before he'd "seen" a ghost at all.

Pirate Cut, he noted mentally. A good

place to begin shooting. They hadn't known in Bartholomew's day that the reefs needed to be protected. They had brought their ships to the deep-water plunge just off the reef many times. Bartholomew knew for a fact that the legend about the area was true — ships of many nations had foundered here in storms, been cut up on the reefs and left to the destruction of time and the elements. But there was treasure scattered here, treasure and history, even if it had been picked over in the many years since.

It would also make for beautiful underwater footage. The colors were brilliant; the light was excellent. And it was near the area where Bartholomew had allegedly chased and gunned down a ship and murdered those aboard. Falsely accused, in the days after David Porter's Pirate Squadron had been established, he had been hanged quickly, and it had been only after his unjust death that his innocence had been proven.

It was a good story for a documentary. Especially considering the events of the recent past, when a madman had decided that it was his ancestor who had been wronged and that the Becketts were to pay.

The whole story needed to be told, and it would.

And perhaps, if he managed to get Bar-

tholomew's story out there, with any luck Bartholomew might "see the light" and move on to the better world he believed he would find.

It was true that Bartholomew was not a bad guy and that, if he were flesh and blood, he'd be great to hang out with. But with Katie engaged to David Beckett now and basically living at the Beckett house, it seemed that Bartholomew was really all his.

And no way out of it — it was awkward. Disconcerting. And he was starting to look as if he walked around talking to himself. So much for an intelligent and manly image, Sean thought dryly.

"Bartholomew, please, stop talking to me. You're well aware that I look crazy as all hell when people see me talking to you, right?" Sean demanded.

"I keep telling you, you're an artist. And a true conch," Bartholomew said. "Born and bred on the island. Tall, with that great red hair, good and bronzed — hey, fellow, a man's man as they say," Bartholomew told him, waving a ringed hand in the air. "Trust me — you're masculine, virile, beloved and — an artist. You're allowed to be crazy. And, good God, man — this is Key West!"

"Right. Then the tourists will have me arrested," Sean said.

They'd reached O'Hara's, toward the southern end of Duval. Sean cast Bartholomew a warning glare. Bartholomew shrugged and followed Sean in.

Sean walked straight up to the bar. Jamie O'Hara himself was working his taps that day.

"Hey, what's up?" Sean asked, setting his hands on the bar and looking at Jamie, who was busy drying a beer glass.

It was early in the day — by Key West bar standards. Just after eleven. Jamie, when he was in town, usually opened the place around eleven-thirty, and whoever of his old friends, locals, or even tourists who wandered in for lunch early were served by Jamie himself. He cooked, bussed and made his drinks, poured his own Guinnesses — seven minutes to properly fill a Guinness glass — and he did so because he liked being a pub owner and he was the kind of employer who liked people, his employees and his establishment. He could handle the place in the early hour — unless there was a festival in town. Which, quite often, there was. Starting at the end of this week, he'd have double shifts going on — Pirates in Paradise was coming to town.

At this moment, though, O'Hara's was quiet. Just Jamie, behind the bar.

Jamie was the perfect Irish barkeep —
though he had been born in Key West. He,
like Sean's dad, had spent a great deal of
time in the "old country" visiting their
mother's family — O'Casey folk — and he
and Sean's dad had both gone to college in
Dublin. Jamie could put on a great brogue
when he chose, but he could also slip into a
laid-back Keys Southern drawl. Sean had
always thought he should have been an actor. Jamie said that owning a pub was nearly
the same thing. He had a rich head full of
gray hair, a weather-worn but distinguished
face, bright blue eyes and a fine-trimmed
beard and mustache, both in that steel-gray
that seemed to make him appear to be some
kind of clan chieftain, or an old *ard-ri,* high
king, of Ireland. He was well over six feet,
with broad shoulders and a seaman's
muscles.

Jamie indicated the last booth in the bar
area of the pub, which was now cast in
shadow.

He realized that someone was sitting in
the booth.

He couldn't help but grin at his uncle.
"You're harboring a spy? A double agent?
Someone from the CIA working the Keys
connection?"

Sean knew that bad things — very bad

51

things — could happen, even in Key West, Florida, "island paradise" though it might be. He'd seen them. But someone hiding in the shadows seemed a bit out of the ordinary.

Jamie shrugged and spoke softly. "Who knows why she's sitting in the dark? She's a nice kid. Came in here, I guess, 'cause the world seems to consider it neutral ground or something. She heard about you and David and the documentary you two are going to film together."

Sean frowned. "We've had ads in the papers for crews for the boats and the filming. David and I have been setting up for interviews at his place."

"What do you want from me, son, eh? She came in here, knowing I was related to the O'Hara looking to film about Key West and her mysteries. I said yes, and she asked if there was any way she could speak to you alone."

"She's applying for a job? Then she should go about it just like all the others and ask for an interview," Sean said, annoyed. He couldn't really see the woman in the corner, but he thought she seemed young. Maybe she was trying to secure a position by coming through the back door, flirting, drawing on his uncle's sympathies.

"I don't think that it's work she's looking for, but I don't know. She's pretty tense. She wanted to know about the recent business down here — you know, all the nasty stuff with the murders — and she was mainly wanting to know, so it seemed, how you all coped with the bad things going on. Like, frankly, were you a pack of cowards, was it really all solved by the police, did I think that you were capable people — and did you really know the area."

"Oh, great. She sounds like someone I really want to hire!" Sean said.

Jamie laughed. "She's not that bad — she was dead honest in the questions she asked me. She didn't use the word *coward,* that was mine. There's something I like about her, Sean. Talk to her. She seems tense and nervous — and somehow, the real deal." His uncle leaned closer to him. "There's some mystery about this girl, and yet something real. Talk to her. Oh, and by the way, she is really something. She's got every diving certificate, advanced, teacher, you name it. She's gotten awards for her writing, and oh — hmm. She happens to have amazing blond hair, giant blue eyes and a shape to die for, nephew. Check it out. Go ahead. What's the matter, boy, scared?"

Sean looked at his uncle in surprise and

laughed. Scared? No. He was at least in-trigued. Couldn't hurt to talk to the woman. He and David were anxious to get started on their project because it was important to both of them — and it was also what they were best known for in their separate ca-reers. But they were discussing just what bits and pieces and stories they would use for their documentary. Bartholomew's situ-ation was a must, Robert the Doll was a must, and the bizarre, true and fairly recent history of Elena and Count von Cosel was also a must. It wouldn't be Key West if they didn't touch on Hemingway and the writ-ing connection. And there had to be pirates, wreckers, sponge divers and cigar makers, and how the Conch Republic became the Conch Republic. But as to exactly what they were using and what they were concentrat-ing on, they were still open. They hadn't made any hard-and-fast decisions yet, but since David was home and planning a wed-ding with Sean's sister, they had decided that, at long last, they should work together. Friends in school who hadn't seen each other in a decade, they had both gone the same route — film. Once the tension and terror of a murderer at work in Key West had died down, David had decided he was going to stay home awhile. That had a lot to

do with the fact that he was in love with Sean's sister, Katie O'Hara. But David was a conch, too — born and bred in Key West from nearly two generations of conchs. David belonged here.

Sean had stayed away from home a lot, too. But now he was excited about the idea of working with David — and working on a history about Key West and the surrounding area, bringing to light what truth they could discover that lay behind many of the legends. One thing had never been more true — fact was far stranger than fiction. But as he knew from living here, fact could become distorted. Tourists often asked which form of a story told by a tour guide was the true one. He and David meant to explore many of the legends regarding Key West — and, through historical documents, letters and newspapers of each era, get to the heart of the truth. Fascinating work. He loved his home. Key West was the tail end of Florida, an oddity in time and place. An island accessible only by boat for much of its history. Southern in the Civil War by state, Union by military presence.

Bartholomew suddenly let out a soft, low whistle, almost making Sean jump. He gritted his teeth and refused to look at the ghost.

"Pretty, pretty thing!" Bartholomew said. "I'd have been over there by now, not wondering if there was some secret agenda behind it all!"

Somehow, Sean refrained from replying. He even kept smiling and staring straight at his uncle.

"Are you going to stare at the shadows? Or are you at least going to let the girl have her say?" Jamie demanded. "I'll bring coffee," he added.

"I know where the coffee is, thanks, Uncle," Sean said. He came behind the bar to pour himself a cup, trying to get a better look at the woman at the booth.

She was waiting for him. There was no looking at her surreptitiously — she was staring back at him. She was still in the shadows, but his uncle seemed to be right about one thing — she was stunning. She had the kind of cheekbones that were pure, classic beauty — at eighty, she'd still be attractive with that bone structure. Her hair was golden and pale and simply long, with slightly rakish and overgrown bangs. He didn't think she spent a lot of money in a boutique salon; the shades of color had come from the sun and the overgrown, rakish look was probably because she didn't spend much time getting it cut.

She was dressed more like a native than a tourist — light cotton dress with a little sweater over her shoulders. Down here, the days were often hot, tempered only by the ocean and gulf breezes that were usually present. But inside, it could be like the new ice age had come — because of the heat, businesses were often freezing. Jamie kept his swinging doors to the outside open sometimes — it was a Key thing. Trying to be somewhat conservative in the waste of energy, the air blasted in the back, not near the front.

Coffee in hand, he walked back to the booth at last. "Hi. I'm Sean O'Hara. We're doing interviews tomorrow and the next day at the old Beckett house, because, I'm assuming you know, it's a joint project between David Beckett and myself." He offered her his hand.

She accepted it. Her grip was firm. Her palms were slightly callused, but they were nice, tanned. Her fingers were long and she had neat nails, clipped at a reasonable length rather than grown out long.

Her eyes were steady on his.

"I'm Vanessa Loren," she said. "I have real experience and sound credentials, but that's not exactly why I'm here, or why I wanted to meet with you here."

He shrugged, taking a seat opposite her in the booth.

"All right."

She suddenly lifted both hands and let them fall. "I've actually practiced this many times, but I'm not sure where to begin."

"You've — practiced?" Sean asked. "Practiced an interview for a job?"

She nodded. "I've practiced trying to explain. This is really important to me."

"All right. Start anywhere," Sean said.

She lowered her head, breathing in deeply. Then she looked at him again. "Unless you've been under a rock, you must have heard about the Haunt Island murders."

He blinked and tried to remember. He'd been filming in the Black Sea two years ago, but he had heard about the bizarre murders. Members of a film crew had been gruesomely slain on an island just southwest of South Bimini. Though uninhabited, the island belonged to the Bahamas.

He hadn't moved into the booth and hadn't left room for Bartholomew. However, the ghost had followed him to the booth, and leaned against the wall just across from them.

"Yes, I heard something about the murders," he said carefully.

"I was with the film crew," she said. "One

of my best childhood friends was the director, and I was the scriptwriter. We both put money into the venture, and we were doing double duty. When I say low budget, I mean low budget. But we had it together — we knew what we were doing, and we worked incredibly hard. The film wasn't going to win an Oscar, but we had hopes of having it picked up by a national distributor."

"Don't know much about that," Bartholomew said sorrowfully, as if he were part of the conversation.

"You were making a film, and people were brutally killed," Sean said, ignoring Bartholomew. He didn't want to feel sympathy for her. Sadly, there were a number of unsolved mysteries that had little chance of being solved. He vaguely remembered some of the newspaper articles his sister had e-mailed him at the time — a lot of people were chalking the tragedy up to the mystery of the Bermuda Triangle. "What are you trying to tell me, or ask me?"

She took a deep breath. "It's really all the same area — the same area you're doing a documentary on. Do you know how many boaters go from the Intracoastal, South Florida, say Fort Lauderdale and Miami, out to Bimini and then on to Key West?" she asked. "Or vice versa. We're all con-

nected here."

"I know that," he said, feeling oddly irritated. "We always intended to do a documentary on the area."

"This is a story that shouldn't just be included, it should be the main focus," she said somberly.

"Why?"

"Because it's an unsolved mystery. And there's a killer or killers out there."

"Sadly, there are many killers on the loose at any given time. I'm not sure what we can do for you. David and I are not law enforcement," Sean said. "And if we were, Haunt Island is still the Bahamas."

"It doesn't sound as if law enforcement has had much luck yet," Bartholomew interjected.

"I was there when it happened," she said quietly. "The truth must be discovered."

"But we're just doing a documentary," Sean protested.

"You're doing a documentary on history — and oddities and mysteries. You'll never find a better mystery," she said flatly. "I admit, the script was written for what would basically be a teenage-slasher-type flick," she said. "But it was based on history. Key West and Bahamian history."

He shook his head. "All right, I'm still get-

ting lost here. You were filming a movie based on history, but it was a slasher film? Low budget? A historical slasher film? You're talking big money there."

She shook her head. "Not with the people we had working with us. The new digital age has helped a hell of a lot. And we had easy access to costumes — we bought most of them here, some from the shop on Front Street, and some at Pirates in Paradise. We refitted one of our boats, and with a little digital finesse, we had a pirate ship, which could become pirate ships. We knew what we were doing — I'm talking about people with real degrees in film and real experience — and more. It was our project."

"I'm listening. Tell me more."

"You're from here and you're working on history," she said. "You must have heard of the *Santa Geneva* — and Mad Miller and his consort, Kitty Cutlass, and the murder of Dona Isabella."

He nodded slowly. He knew the legend. All Key West kids knew the stories about pirates in the area. They made great tales at campfires. "A piece of pirate lore," he said.

"Yes, and if you're following pirate lore, you should be following that story. It was past the Golden Age of Piracy. It was after David Porter came here to clear out the

61

pirates. There were still Spaniards living here, naturally. Dona Isabella was a wealthy woman, with homes in Madrid and Key West. She was married to Diego, a very wealthy Spanish merchant. She was kidnapped off a Spanish ship, the *Santa Geneva*. They say she was never ransomed because Mad Miller, the pirate, fell in love with her — and because of that, she wound up dead. Some say that Mad Miller murdered her in a frenzy, because she loathed him. Some say that Kitty Cutlass, furious over her lover's adoration for another woman, was the one to kill her. At any rate, she supposedly wound up dead in the company of the pirates. It's thought that she survived until the pirates reached Haunt Island, where they might have drawn in for ship repairs. Some of Mad Miller's men then massacred the remaining crew members of the *Santa Geneva,* and members of their own crew who were in revolt over what had happened. Thus the name, obviously, Haunt Island, and the legend."

"I still don't see —" Sean began.

"Dona Isabella lived in Key West. Her ship, a Spanish ship, left from Key West. The pirates raided her in American waters. Off of *Key West.* Mad Miller came from Key West. Let's see — Kitty Cutlass began as a

prostitute in a shack on Duval. Mr. O'Hara, this is an amazing story that has everything to do with the documentary you want to film. You're a fool if you haven't already thought of using the legend — and the truth of what happened to the members of our film crew," she said.

All right — that was aggravating. But there was something desperate in her voice that kept him from entirely losing his temper.

"Okay, Miss Loren. You have a good story. What, exactly, is it that you want? I've told you, we're not any form of law enforcement. I can't go over to the Bahamas and just solve your mystery for you."

She inhaled again, staring at him. She let out a long breath of air. She seemed to physically square her shoulders, as if seeking strength and resolve.

"I know that, and . . ." She paused, wincing. "Look, I'm sorry. I'm just passionate about my feelings on this. First, I need you to hire me. I'm good — really good. I swear. You can check all my references," she said.

"I would definitely do so, no matter what," he said.

"I'd bet good money that she has excellent references," Bartholomew said.

Sean locked his jaw, determined not to turn, or respond to the ghost in any way.

63

"No one is hired unless David and I agree," he said to Vanessa.

"That is certainly understandable," she said. Again, she paused. "I know all about David Beckett, as well. I know that he was once accused of murder, and I know how desperate he was to find the truth. And the truth was discovered. I can't believe that he wouldn't understand how I feel, or be sympathetic to my cause."

Sean felt tension steal through his body. The Effigy Murders had been bad, very bad. He still felt they were all recovering from the terrible things that had happened. He still had scars beneath his hairline.

David would be sympathetic, he knew.

"Go on," he said quietly.

"Then — I think you need to make me your assistant. I'm excellent at managing a schedule, and I can write a scene, narrative, interview questions, anything you need, at the drop of a hat. I know you do a lot of your own scheduling and writing. That's why I say *assistant.* I went to film school. When needed, I can handle any kind of a camera. I'm fit so I can tote and carry. The filmmaker in you must see what there is here — a legend that remains a mystery, historical and contemporary. You can look for the *Santa Geneva,* you can really follow

64

the path of those who came before you. And if you leave out piracy, and the stamping out of the pirates, and the supposed massacre on Haunt Island, you're doing a disservice to everyone."

He leaned back. "If this is such a great documentary, why don't you do it yourself?" he demanded.

She leaned back, biting her lower lip. "Well, for one, I don't have the kind of money you need for a documentary. And . . ."

"And?"

She leaned forward. "Look, I'll work cheap. I'll work harder than anyone you ever imagined."

He leaned back, shaking his head. "I'd like to help you, I'd really like to help you. But it seems as if you're chasing something, and I'm not — I'm not what you're looking for. If these murders haven't been solved, you need a private investigator. You need —"

"Have you ever tried to look for a private investigator who specializes in water, legends and boats?" she asked irritably.

He hesitated for a moment. "Look, from what I understand, every agency possible was involved in that case. If there are no clues, there are no clues."

"No one wanted to follow through on the

legend — or the history," she said, exasperated.

He felt his fingers tense around his coffee cup and he stared at her. "You're trying to tell me that pirates returned to massacre your friends?" he asked.

Something about the tightening in her lips and the way that she stared at him caused him to feel as if he should be ashamed — as if he had spoken out of turn.

But he hadn't. And he couldn't explain to her that he knew what ghosts were capable of doing, and what they weren't. As a matter of fact, he knew a few of them. . . .

"That's not what I'm suggesting at all," she said.

"Then?"

"I — don't know, exactly," she said, looking away. "Here's the thing. We've had this movie stowed since it happened. But . . . people know about it. I'm afraid we'll get an offer from a major distributor. My partner would gladly sell. I don't want to sell — not unless I can get some justice for those who were involved. I don't want to make money on sensationalism, on something . . . something unsolved. I've gotten Jay to agree that I can try one more time to discover the truth."

"I —"

"Please. Please just tell me that you'll consider doing it?" she asked.

He stared at her, not knowing what to say.

No. A flat-out no would be a great answer. He and David hadn't set anything in stone as yet, but . . . no. This one had to be a no. They both had their individual exemplary careers, they knew what they were doing. They could write themselves.

"I'm sorry. I just don't think my partner will agree," Sean said.

"Will you ask David Beckett?" she queried stubbornly.

He smiled. "Will you quit asking if I talk to him and he says no?"

She smiled. "You're — Look, I know I'm asking a lot without much to offer. But I am really good at what I do, and if you give me a few weeks, I promise, I'll help to make anything you want to do come out as brilliantly as possible. I'll be slave labor, I swear."

"I don't want slave labor."

"I'll be the best damned assistant you've ever had," she swore.

"Take her up on it!" Bartholomew said. "Hell, my boy! Take her up on it just for the pleasure of having her upon your wretched little boat."

"I'll talk to David," he said.

67

"You really will. And . . . and if he's hesitant, if there's any chance, will you let me try to persuade him, as well?" she asked.

He forced an even smile. *No, just say no!*

He asked himself if he would be so torn, so tempted, if the person asking him wasn't this young woman, not just beautiful, but . . . strong. So confident in her ability that she would swear she could make his work the best ever.

Ability.

The way she looked.

The sound of her voice.

The mystery involved. Yes, he knew the damned legend. And hell yes, he was curious.

"Look," he began.

But she wasn't looking at him. She was looking at the door. She let out a little cry of surprise and gladness.

Sean swung around. His sister had just come in the door.

He looked at Vanessa Loren.

Ah, hell.

Hell.

The young woman knew Katie. He should have figured.

He stared back at her, irritated, and suddenly certain that it was all over.

"You know my sister," he said.

She glanced at him while rising. "Yes, I

68

know Katie. I've been on a few dive boats with her, and of course, I bring friends in here for Katie-okie when I'm down. . . ."

She started to head out to see Katie. He set his fingers around her wrist, drawing her back.

She didn't jerk away, but then his hold was pretty firm. Those huge, cornflower-blue eyes of hers lit on him.

He smiled coldly. "You know my uncle, too, don't you? And my uncle knew just who you were and what you wanted."

"I've met Jamie before, yes," she admitted. "Katie can explain it all to David, if you don't want to, but I know that she'll convince him that I'm right. I came to you first, because Katie told me that David had said all the major decisions were going to be yours, so if you just agree —"

He stood, releasing her wrist.

"I don't like being played," he said flatly. "Good day, Miss Loren."

She didn't call after him.

Bartholomew did.

"Sean! Oh, come on, Sean. I can help you with this, I was around when it all happened," the dapper buccaneer cried to him. "Sean, oh, do come on! If I were flesh and blood, I'd be on this like a mosquito at a topless bar! Sean!"

69

Sean passed Katie near the doorway. "Hey, sis," he said, kissed her cheek, and kept on going.

They'd all just survived near death. They had dealt with total insanity.

He would have to be insane himself to get into something like this again.

"Mr. O'Hara!"

She had followed him out. The lithe and dignified Miss Loren had come rushing out, and now she stood on the sidewalk, staring after him.

Despite himself, he paused.

She walked to him, her chin high. "I never meant to play anyone," she said. "I'm just desperate for help. You don't understand," she said.

"I think I do," he told her.

"No, no, you don't. I have reason to believe that someone must find out what happened, not just for those who were killed, but . . ."

"But what?"

"Other things have happened. Bad things. Not involved with filming, but with other boaters who disappeared near Haunt Island."

"The sea can be huge and merciless, Miss Loren. And sadly, throughout history, many

70

a boat and ship have disappeared without a trace."

"There's more to it. I know there's more to it, and I'm afraid."

"Afraid of what?"

"I'm afraid that if the truth isn't discovered, more people will die. That there will be blood and death . . . a massacre again, and maybe this time, here, in Key West."

2

Vanessa walked back into O'Hara's, trying to feel as if she hadn't just been crushed in a major defeat.

Katie was sitting at the bar, talking to her uncle. She watched Vanessa as she came up and took the stool next to her. Vanessa had known Katie forever, or so it seemed. They'd met when Katie's school had brought a group of Key West students up to dive the springs and Vanessa's school had been hosting the week of camp. She wasn't sure if she'd liked her at first, being ten and wary of kids who came from cool places like Key West. But she'd been paired with Katie, who had an exceptional voice, for the talent show, and Vanessa had been her harmony and backup act, and they'd won the grand prize — two new regulators for their scuba equipment. That had begun the friendship. Of course, they'd been kids living almost four hundred miles

away from one another even if it was the same state, but they'd kept up as much as possible, visiting one another at their respective colleges and meeting whenever they could.

By the time they had been able to get together in Key West, or anywhere in the Keys, Sean had been gone most of the time, so it really wasn't that strange that she'd never had a chance to meet him before.

It seemed odd that the O'Haras could so clearly resemble one another and yet look so different. When she'd asked Jamie O'Hara what Sean looked like, he told her that Katie was Sean in a dress. That wasn't true at all. Sean was very tall, three or four inches over six feet, with a linebacker's shoulders. Katie was slim and willowy. While Katie had auburn hair, Sean's was lighter, though with the same streaks of red. Katie's eyes were a hazel green while Sean's were more of a golden color. He had almost classic features, just like Katie, but he looked like a man who had braved the wind many a time, and his jaw leaned toward the square side.

Maybe that had just been because he'd been talking to her — and she sensed that she'd irritated him.

"Maybe I should have mentioned first that

73

I knew you both," Vanessa said dryly to Katie.

Katie smiled and swirled a stirrer in her coffee cup. "Ha-ha. Perhaps he's feeling as if we're ganging up on him! Oh, well, Sean is just being — Sean. He'll get over it. Really, I think the lure of the mystery will get to him, once he thinks it all out. I think." She looked at Vanessa with concern. "But . . . are you sure you should be doing this? Maybe you should just leave it all alone."

"You know I can't do that — you know you couldn't do that! Hey, I've talked to people around here. *You* plunged headfirst into finding out what had happened in David's past, a pretty dangerous occupation, so I heard," Vanessa said.

"Yes, but I didn't realize at the beginning that there were going to be more bodies," Katie murmured. "And David was determined."

"All right, then, let me put it this way — could *you* just forget about it? Katie, I saw that poor girl the night she disappeared — and wound up dead. She was terrified. There was something on that beach. Other people go over there still, despite what happened."

Katie frowned. "But nothing has hap-

74

pened since, right?"

"Not on Haunt Island," Vanessa said.

"What happened otherwise?" Katie asked.

"In two years' time? I don't know everything, but I'm suspicious every time I hear about any bad things happening. I know about one boat that disappeared in that area. A charter boat on its way to Bimini about a year ago. Disappeared, as in vanished."

"Things don't really disappear in the Bermuda Triangle," Katie said. "It was just that for years, we didn't know what had happened. But they found the planes that went down years ago, after World War II. They finally found them. No one knows why they went down, but they certainly have educated theories. So a charter boat didn't really *disappear* — it's out there somewhere."

"Well, one of Jay's boats disappeared," Vanessa said flatly. "It disappeared — and Travis and Georgia were found dead on the beach."

Katie looked at her sympathetically. "The Bahamian authorities, Florida State authorities, and even the FBI got in on the investigation, Vanessa. There's a problem with the ocean — when things go down, they may go down miles. There are storms, there are

75

currents. There were no clues on the island."
She cleared her throat. "They, um, never
found the rest of the bodies, right?"

Vanessa shook her head. "I'd say they
actively investigated for months . . . maybe
even a year. The torsos, hips and legs were
never found. God, I can't even believe I'm
saying that!"

"But there was a suspect, right? Carlos . . .
someone?"

"Carlos Roca," Vanessa told her. "But he
was a good guy. A friend."

"Okay, so, no matter how you might think
that he was a good guy, and even if he was
a friend, you have to admit, Vanessa, it does
appear as if Carlos had already killed Travis, and that when he said he'd take Georgia
back to Miami, he was lying. What he did
was kill her, get the boat down the beach,
find where he'd stashed Travis's body, and
stage the heads and arms. Then he stole the
boat and dumped the rest of the bodies into
the ocean. Oh, Vanessa, I know you don't
want to believe that. But there's no other
explanation."

"Carlos would have popped up somewhere. And the boat would have been
found."

Katie let out a long sigh. "Nessa, the boat
could have gotten into trouble — and it

might have sunk. And Carlos might have gone down with it. God knows where he might have tried to go from Haunt Island. But that boat's out there somewhere. I don't know about the bodies anymore — fish are ravenous little creatures, really — and not so little, often. Time, salt water . . ."

"Isn't David's cousin, Liam, a detective now? Could he know something?" Vanessa asked.

"Yes, I talked to him after you called me. He was never in on that investigation. He'd heard about it, of course, but he didn't have anything to do with it."

Jamie O'Hara strode down the bar to where the two of them were sitting. "Don't you be worrying, Miss Loren. If I know my nephew, and I think I do, he'll come around."

Katie arched a brow at Jamie. "Uncle Jamie, don't go getting her hopes up, hmm?"

Jamie winked at Vanessa.

"You think he'll come around, too, don't you, Katie?"

Katie frowned. Then she sighed. "Yes, I started on David this morning, so . . . well, we'll see. But, Vanessa, I don't want you to be so — obsessed. I know my brother and David, and I know that they're fascinated by mysteries like this, but . . . you have to

understand," she added quietly. "David came home determined to discover the truth behind a ten-year-old murder case because *he* had been accused of murder."

"Yes, I know," Vanessa said. She'd read all about the insanity that had first driven David Beckett out of Key West, and then home. Naturally. She had been friends with Katie O'Hara for years. She had read every word in the papers when the case had been solved, and that had brought her back here. Key West had two of its own native conchs — David Beckett and Sean O'Hara — about to embark on a film project that would bring to light many of the mysteries that surrounded the area throughout the decades and even centuries. David Beckett had a military background, and Sean O'Hara had filmed in many dangerous places, had received a great deal of defensive training and certainly knew how to take care of himself. Beckett also had a cousin who was a detective with the Key West police. They were the right people to at least explore the waters, and the story, and make her feel at the very least as if she were doing all that she could to find out just what had happened to Georgia, Travis — and Carlos Roca.

"Oh, I mean, David's a great person!"

Katie said, quickly defending the love of her life. "You have to understand, it's not that he wouldn't care, or that he wouldn't be horrified — but he's not FBI, a cop or any other kind of law enforcement." She brightened suddenly. "Hey, I'll set up a meeting with Liam. I mean, if Liam gets into it, maybe he could help us out."

"That would be great — thanks, Katie. I'd like to meet him and hear what he thinks, because I'm sure he had to have heard about it, at least when it was all taking place."

"Well," Jamie said, "well and good. Now you can't sit here in the bar, moping about all day. Go enjoy the fall. Beautiful days we've got going here now. Days that are the kind that bring people south. Get — get out of bar, go and do something."

"Hey, I know that my friend Marty — big-time into pirates — is getting ready for his booth and show for the Pirates in Paradise performances this year. Let's go give him a hand — he loves to talk pirates. I bet he knows all about that pirate you were using for your horror movie, Mad Miller. And I can almost guarantee you he knows about Kitty Cutlass and Dona Isabella, too."

"Katie," Vanessa said, "I did tons of research. And I love the history — love it!

— but we're talking about people murdered just two years ago."

"But you were filming history, right?"

Vanessa grimaced. "Well, history — fractured beyond belief — that we were using for a slasher flick."

"So I'll call Liam. We'll have dinner. We'll have him over to the house."

"David will be there, right? I mean — you are living with David at the Beckett house, right?" Vanessa asked her.

"David will be on your side," Katie said. "I'll call while we head over to Marty's."

"How do you know that you'll convince David to be on my side?" Vanessa asked.

Katie laughed. "I can be very persuasive. No, all kidding aside, they should agree to follow your mystery. It's good film. They'll be delving into piracy, the founding of the area — and something that's contemporary and horrible. People like justice and a satisfactory ending. No one can bring the dead back to life, but there is something to be said for closure. We don't feel that we failed those who died if we can figure out a riddle and bring a killer to justice."

"I may have you do all the talking," Vanessa told her.

"It will work out," Katie said.

Vanessa wasn't at all sure that she believed

80

Katie, but she had to keep trying. She had exhausted other possibilities. She had plagued many law-enforcement agencies, and people had been kind and they had said the right things. But the case, though open, was not being actively investigated. Her only recourse was filmmakers — and those with a preplanned budget and a plan. *And* a wealth of knowledge about the history of the area.

"Great," Vanessa said. She smiled at the elder O'Hara behind the bar. "Thank you, Jamie. Katie, let's go play with the pirates."

Clear air turbulence in the Bermuda Triangle.

That was one of the main causes listed on a number of the flights — major commercial flights and smaller, private craft — that had plunged a thousand feet or more or had trouble in the last few decades.

There were other losses, however. A number of disappearances in the area known as the Bermuda Triangle. It wasn't officially an area at all, and had only become so in latter history — the U.S. Board of Geographical Names didn't recognize it as a place with a name at all. Superstition ruled a lot of what people believed about the area, and it had a doppelgänger on the other side of the world

called "the Devil's Sea" by Japanese and Filipino people.

The most widely accepted scientific explanation for the strange events in the area had to do with magnetism. In the Bermuda Triangle, magnets might point "true north" in contrast to "magnetic north," which had to do with circumnavigating the earth. The compass variations could be as great as twenty degrees, which would definitely cause havoc when attempting to reach a destination.

Sean leaned back in his computer chair, studying the screen.

The next theory had to do with gas — gas from the sea itself. Subterranean beds shifting due to underwater landslides could cause a vast leakage of methane gas. An Englishman from Leeds University had proposed the theory as late as the 1990s that the weight of the gas in the water could cause a ship to sink like a rock and also that the gas in the air could cause instantaneous combustion of a fuel-filled jet in seconds flat. Boom.

The first odd occurrence went all the way back to Christopher Columbus, who, along with several of his men, reported mass compass malfunctions, a massive bolt of fire that suddenly fell from the sky into the sea

and then strange lights on the horizon — all in the area of the Bermuda Triangle.

Switching from site to site on the Internet, Sean had to admit that he found what he was reading fascinating.

But from magnets and gas, the theories went off into other realms, ones he was certain he couldn't buy himself.

Aliens. Apparently, the belief that aliens were responsible for the disappearances was more widespread than he'd wanted to know. Some people believed that extraterrestrials had brought down a massive ship hundreds of years ago. That ship was down below the ocean floor. Sometimes the aliens were angry and destructive. Sometimes, to perform their evil deeds in their evil laboratories, they would send out their own vessels to snag ships or planes and bring them down below the surface.

Some people believed that they made trips to earth only now and then to snatch planes from the sky and ships from the sea.

Another theory had to do with the lost city of Atlantis. The psychic Edgar Cayce, who passed away in 1945, had claimed that he — and many other people — were reincarnated residents of the doomed Atlantis. He said that the city had not been in the Old World at all but near Bimini, in the

83

Bahamas. The people had been highly advanced and used fire crystals for their power — fire crystals that had gotten out of hand and exploded, thus causing the sinking of Atlantis. There were still fire crystals deeply embedded in the ocean, and their power surged sometimes, causing ships, people, planes and debris to disappear. He prophesied that Atlantis would rise again in 1968 or '69.

In 1968, the Bimini Road or Bimini Wall was discovered — a rock formation of rounded stones beneath the sea near North Bimini that definitely bore the appearance of an ancient great highway. Some geologists argued that it was a natural highway; others were convinced that it might have been a manmade structure dating back three to four thousand years.

Sean had seen the Bimini Wall, and it was fascinating, but he wasn't a structural scholar, so he couldn't determine if the wall had been there forever, lurking beneath sand and the elements, or if it had been man-made.

He didn't believe that Cayce had once been a citizen of the fabled Atlantis.

Another man had put forth a crystal theory — Ray Brown. While diving in the area in 1970, he had gotten cut off from his

84

friends. He'd found an underwater cave. The cave had been extraordinary. He'd seen a pyramid formation against a beautiful aquamarine light. Obviously, some higher intelligence had been at work in the cave, creating the light, the formation and the smooth workmanship within the cave.

He'd found a crystal sphere in the pyramid, and taken it. When he'd left the cave, he'd heard a voice telling him to get out and never to return.

Sean sat back, shaking his head, puzzled. If he'd ever found such a cave, he'd have partners and film crew down in the water before he ever came out of it.

Ray Brown didn't do that.

He didn't tell the world about his remarkable experience.

He brought his crystal to a psychics fair in Phoenix in 1975.

If his cave had ever been discovered or the secret of the crystal divulged, Sean didn't know about it, nor, going from site to site to site on the Internet, could he find any mention of it — the cave, that was. There was mention only of the crystal.

Behind him, Bartholomew sniffed.

"God! Would you not read over my shoulder?" Sean asked.

Bartholomew ignored the question.

"They are referring to the Gulf Stream. They are referring to an area that, even in my day, was one of the most heavily traveled sea passages in the world. The current is always five to six knots, storms rise up constantly out of nowhere, and statistically, it would be almost impossible for things not to happen in the area. Ah, but absurd things do happen. So is there a Bermuda Triangle? Or is it just the natural state of the world?" he queried.

"I believe that you're right about the fact that the sea can be dangerous, the Gulf Stream can be treacherous and human beings can make errors. There was a case just a few years ago where seven fishermen were out. The captain had sailed the waters more than thirty years. They left on a clear day, and a rogue wave overturned the boat. They weren't five nautical miles from shore, but after the wave hit, the boat overturned. Two died and five were found alive. If the five hadn't been recovered, it would have been another case for the Bermuda Triangle, because no trace of the fishing boat was ever discovered and they were in relatively shallow waters, close to shore, when it happened. I don't believe in crystals or aliens. Who knows? Maybe a city was sunk thousands of years ago — I've been places where

they know that one day the volcanoes beneath the surface will blow — and old islands will go down and new ones will be formed. Hawaii will sink — hell, one day, Florida will sink. That's the planet. But as far as people being *murdered* by the Bermuda Triangle, crystals, aliens, or even a subspecies of humanity with gills — I don't believe it for an instant."

Bartholomew laughed. "That from a man carrying on a conversation with a ghost!"

Sean glared at him.

"Hey!" Bartholomew protested. "I'm just pointing out that there is more in the world than what most people are willing to see or accept. But frankly, I'm with you. I don't believe in aliens — not from other planets. Oh, there may be life out there, but I have a feeling that life might be fungi or sponges. And no one sees the future — except for God. I've been around a very long time. I've been able to observe quite a bit. Like the fact that you're thinking about all of this because you've spent the day on the computer."

"Is there no one else you can go haunt?" Sean asked him. "Where is your beautiful lady in white?"

Bartholomew waved a hand in the air. "I'll see her later."

A ghost, yes. He was talking to a ghost. Not his fault — he blamed that on Katie! So he was talking to a ghost, and calling others absurd!

"Ghosts are different," Bartholomew said, as if reading his mind. "We *were,* we lived and breathed. Energy doesn't die — and we are the result. Most human beings have a religious or spiritual belief, and if you believe in what you don't see, as in God, then it's not such a stretch to believe that souls exist. And we all know that even among the living, some people can communicate and some can't. But I do agree with you. The perpetrator of the evil deeds surrounding the film crew was not the Bermuda Triangle, the power of a crystal or a little green man popping out of the ocean. There's a live person, homicidal, organized and possibly psychotic," he finished.

Sean stared at him, hiding a smile.

"I have spent some time in the police station, obviously," Bartholomew said. "Actually, it's quite something. People are always saying 'I'd just love to be a fly on the wall.' Well, that is one thing about departing one's earthly form. I am able to be a fly on the wall."

"Ah, so you're an expert now on all things law enforcement," Sean teased.

"No, I'm gifted at listening to other people — and you may never know when you need the services of an excellent eavesdropper."

"Point noted, thank you. Isn't it time for high tea, or something like that?" Sean asked.

"I'm off to find my dear beauty in white," Bartholomew said. "Be nice to me, Sean O'Hara — I believe I'm still here to watch out for you, so you just may find that you need me!"

Bartholomew walked to the door, and disappeared through it.

Sean turned back to the computer and keyed in the name *Vanessa Loren.*

"Fascinating!" Marty said to Vanessa. She and Katie had joined him at his house on Fleming Street. It was what they called a "shotgun" house, built with a long hall or breezeway, so that if the front and back doors were both open, you could fire a shotgun and the bullet would run right through the house. Basically, the plan was to keep the air going through the house at all times, since it had been built long before air-conditioning became a customary feature in homes in the hot, subtropical climes of the Keys.

Marty seemed like a very nice guy. Vanessa

had actually seen him before, stopping in at O'Hara's for Katie's business, Katie-oke. O'Hara's was always pleasant and laid-back, and a lot of locals planning acts for different festivals, private parties or any such ventures spent time there. The bar had the kind of comfortable feel that worked for locals and tourists alike. Vanessa hadn't met Marty formally before, but she'd seen him do a good job with a pirate bellow in a rollicky sea shanty.

His house was decorated to fit the man. There were a number of ship's bells, ships in bottles, old figureheads, anchors and other paraphernalia from the past set up around the house; he was a collector of books, music, logs, parchments, deeds, old money and more. The place was eclectic and comfortable. Vanessa thought that he must have a small fortune in the place as far as the value of some of the antiques would go, but it was still comfortable and casual.

"Fascinating!" Marty repeated, then he looked sheepish and rueful. "Oh, that's terrible, that's really terrible of me to say. I'm so, so sorry about your friends, of course. And I suppose it all did terrible things to the futures of those who survived. But that it all happened when you were working on

a movie about Mad Miller and Kitty Cutlass . . . I've always been intrigued by the tales of people that have come down to us. History. People make it so dry. This date and that date. It's not dates schoolchildren should be remembering — it's the people. History should be like a reality show — or *Oprah.* No, *Jerry Springer.* People love the weaknesses, the cruelty and sometimes even the honor of others!"

"Maybe an enterprising person will get it together that way one day, Marty," Katie said.

"Aha!" Marty told her happily. "That's exactly what I'm doing at the fort this year. An interview with a few of our notorious pirates and their consorts. You have to come. Better yet, you could be consorts, harlots, barmaids —"

"I have to work, Marty," Katie reminded him.

"I'm hoping to be working," Vanessa said.

Marty sighed, disappointed, and studied Vanessa. "Have you not worked for the last two years — since the incident on Bimini?"

"No, no, I've been working, Marty. I'm doing all right. You know the commercial for the new underwater camera that any two-year old can use? I wrote it."

Marty shuddered. "All those two-year-olds!"

"It was fun, actually. We shot in a lovely private pool, and the kids were really adorable," Vanessa assured him.

Marty still looked at her worriedly. "You okay down here? Where are you staying?"

"She's got a perfectly good room at my house or with David and me — she won't take either," Katie said.

"I'm just down Duval, perfect location, a little room for rent above one of the shops," Vanessa told him. "And I'm quite happy."

"But what if you're not safe?" Marty asked.

"I'm right on Duval, in the midst of the tourist horde. There's someone up just about all hours of the night, and the cops are out in droves. I'm safe. Look, I've been bugging police and anyone else you can think of for two years — whatever happened, happened. It's sliding by, and that's why I'm so concerned. This killer might lie dormant for a long time, then swoop down on another group of unsuspecting boaters."

Marty stood. "Well. Just in case you didn't come across this in your research, I have something to show you."

He walked over to the large buffet where a ship's dining bell held the central posi-

tion. Reaching behind it, he pulled out a framed picture. He turned to her with pleasure in his eyes. "Dona Isabella!" he told her.

Vanessa walked over to study the picture. It was a pen-and-ink drawing of a woman in an elegant gown circa the early eighteen hundreds. Her hair was loose, curling around her shoulders. The artist had captured the beauty of the woman, and something more — something that was partly flirtatious and might also be cunning. She could see that the sketch had been titled "The Mystery of a Woman."

"How do you know that this is Dona Isabella?" Vanessa asked.

Marty smiled, proud of his acquisition. He opened the frame, showing the old parchment on which the portrait had been sketched, and the signature of the artist. Len Adams had sketched the picture, and he had written, "Dona Isabella at Tea with a Friend, 1834."

"I've had it authenticated, of course," Marty said. "Len Adams is known down here — his pieces are coveted. He died very young of tuberculosis, so he doesn't have an extensive body of work. He came here because he was dying in the north. He died anyway. But he sketched many wonderful

portraits."

Vanessa was fascinated by the picture, and suddenly felt guilty about her slasher-film script. Of course, in the movie, Dona Isabella had been the victim of Kitty Cutlass, quickly in the film, and quickly out. It had been Kitty Cutlass who'd returned from her watery grave to join with the ghost of Mad Miller to wreak murder, mayhem and havoc upon the unsuspecting teens sailing to Bimini and on Haunt Island.

"Oh, girl, you're one after my own heart!" Marty said, appreciating the way she looked at the picture. "I'll copy it for you — won't be the original, but you'll have the beauty anytime you choose. Poor thing! So lovely, such a coquette and so tragically young to be a victim." He looked at Vanessa. "Boy, that would be something, wouldn't it? What if your people were killed because the ghosts of Mad Miller and Kitty Cutlass are out there, cruising between Key West and Bimini, right into the Triangle, alive through some wild magnetic source?"

Vanessa stared at him.

He gave her a tap on the shoulder. "Joshing with you, girl. But if you want more pirate history, you come on back here anytime, all right? And if you need anything at all, you come to see me. I'm like a Key

West structure, an institution, always here, and I wouldn't be anywhere else in the world."

She thanked him, and she and Katie said goodbye.

"Do you think that the murders might have had something to do with the story you were filming?" Katie asked as they walked. "No, wait. We'll wait until we all get together, and then we'll talk about it. I don't want to make you repeat it all over and over."

They stopped in front of the Beckett house and Vanessa looked up at the grand facade. "So you're living in the Beckett house!" Vanessa teased.

Katie shrugged. "Life is pretty bizarre, just like death."

"So it seems," Vanessa agreed.

Katie opened the front door with a key and they stepped into the hallway. She paused. "I guess they're already here," she said. They walked through the large parlor, through the kitchen and to the back porch, handsomely furnished with white wicker and plush jungle-colored cushions. There were three men there already — not just the two tall, dark-haired men Vanessa assumed to be Liam and David Beckett, but Sean O'Hara, as well.

They all stood as Vanessa and Katie came into the room.

She envied Katie, who walked comfortably up to David Beckett and slipped an arm around him. There was something nicely sure and confident in the motion, and more so in David's smile of response. They were happy.

David and Liam shook hands with Vanessa and were pleasant and cordial. Sean, of course, she had already met.

He waited quietly.

Then the awkward silence fell at last.

"Why doesn't everyone sit, and I'll get some drinks and snacks," Katie suggested.

Great! Vanessa glared at her, feeling as if she had suddenly been thrown to the wolves. *But she was the one who wanted help!*

She sat stiffly, folding her hands around her knees as she looked at the three. "Perhaps this is way out of bounds. But I don't know where else to go from here."

"Start at the beginning," David suggested. "Sean has told us what you want us to do — but start back at the beginning, the film shoot you did, everything that happened that night and everything that happened after."

Vanessa decided to start out looking straight ahead, and then she decided to

speak as naturally as possible and not avoid anyone's eyes. "I've loved Key West since I was a child, since my father first brought me down here. When my friend Jay Allen came to me saying that he wanted to make a film, the first thing that came to my mind was the story of Mad Miller, his mistress, Kitty Cutlass, and the murder of poor Dona Isabella. Everything went fine, and we were down to a skeleton crew — Georgia and Travis, the last characters who remained alive, Jay and myself, of course, two young production assistants, Bill Hinton and Jake Magnoli, and Barry Melkie, our soundman. Zoe was everything as far as props, costume and makeup, with the help of Bill and Jake. Oh, and of course, Carlos Roca. Lew, our Bahamian guide, was there, too. That night, we had just about wrapped, and I was by the fire . . . Jay was there, I'm not sure who else at first, but everyone was just winding down. Suddenly, Georgia came screaming down the beach — she'd seen heads sticking out of the sand, arms. She described a scene that was the exact one in which we found her and Travis the following morning."

"You found Georgia and Travis?" David asked.

She nodded gravely.

"You found the bodies?" Sean asked.

"I did," Vanessa said. "Lew and Jay came quickly down to the beach, then the others . . . and then the Bahamian authorities."

"Let me see if I've got this straight, though," Sean said. "Georgia and Travis were found dead. Georgia had been running down the beach. Where was Travis?"

"No one knew," Vanessa said.

"Then why didn't you look for him?" Sean asked.

"Frankly, we thought he was part of a huge prank being pulled on Georgia. Jay was aggravated with him. We did go down the beach — Lew, Jay and I — and there was nothing there. Except —"

"Except?" Liam asked.

"The sand where we later found the two had been churned up. It looked as if maybe there had been something stuck in the sand."

"And that didn't bother you?" Sean asked.

"We were filming a horror movie. We thought that someone was playing an elaborate prank, and, as I said, that Travis was involved in the prank. I'm afraid that a lot of pranks are carried out on film sets," Vanessa said evenly. She took a deep breath. "Anyway, Georgia was in terror — she wasn't going to stay on the island. She was

having an absolute fit, so Carlos said that he could take her into Miami and head back first thing in the morning. We all thought it was best. But Georgia and Travis were found on the beach, and Carlos and the boat disappeared."

"I'm not sure there's much of a mystery there," Sean said. "Apparently, Carlos stole the boat after he killed the two."

"I don't believe it, not for a minute," Vanessa said. "The police, the Coast Guard, the FBI — every known agency looked for the boat and Carlos, but it was as if they had vanished. What you don't understand is that Carlos Roca wasn't capable of doing something so horrible. He was one of the most gentle people I've ever met."

"I wasn't in on the investigation, but I do remember it," Liam said. "And I'm sorry to tell you this, but most of those law-enforcement agencies believe that Carlos Roca did murder the two young people and steal the boat."

"I don't care what they believe!" Vanessa said.

She was surprised when Sean said, "Of course, there's another scenario. Someone else hijacked the boat, someone who might have already taken Travis. That person either killed Carlos first to take control of Georgia

or had Carlos knocked out somewhere. Then did the grisly deed on the island and dumped Carlos in the Atlantic."

David leaned forward. "Okay, here's the curious part — where was Travis? Had he been killed and his body hidden? And was it possible for someone to have killed him, hidden his body and managed to go after Carlos and Georgia in the boat, get back to the island without being seen, find the one body, stage the gruesome death scene, and then get rid of Carlos? And how, with the alarm that must have gone out, could they have gotten away with the boat? Everyone in the Bahamas, South Florida and all of the Caribbean would have been on the alert."

"Well, stealing the boat, gassing it up, changing it — that seems the easiest part of it," Sean said.

"I agree with you — where Travis was when the whole thing started would be a nice piece of the riddle."

"Dead," Vanessa said softly.

"Probably dead, but where? And how was he killed, and then not found until later?" Sean mused.

"These are the questions everyone has asked time and time again, and they haven't found the answers. But they aren't people

who know the legends, know the area —"

"Snacks and beer!" Katie announced cheerfully from the hallway.

She set nachos with steaming cheese and other ingredients on the coffee table and passed around the tray she carried with ice-cold beer bottles.

Vanessa accepted a beer with a gaze that said both "Thanks" and "How could you have left me alone in here?"

Katie smiled. "I know you all," Katie said, sitting, "and there isn't a better mystery out there!"

"I have a lot of work to do now," Liam said. "And it's a bad time, a very bad time, at the station."

"Nothing has been decided," Sean said.

"We've all agreed to talk about it. We've talked about focusing on a number of mysteries and legends, but we haven't decided what our focus is going to be," David said. "It's Sean's decision. I am gung-ho on the idea of pooling our resources and working locally, but Sean's been doing the budget, mapping and research, so it's his decision."

"Yes, but if you're thinking about the story, I ought to be on the trip," Liam said. He looked at Vanessa. "It hasn't occurred to you to be afraid? The killer or killers were

never caught. They might still be out there," he said.

"Afraid?" she asked softly. "I still have nightmares. I see Georgia alive and screaming, and I see the heads and the arms sticking out of the sand. I remember being terrified of the dark for nearly a year. And then I got very angry, and I finally figured out that I'd probably have nightmares for the rest of my life if I didn't do something to discover the truth. I think the killer is a coward — he worked in the dark, at night. I think there has to be a way to stand against him. That starts with finding him — and when he's found, I don't care if they give him life or the death penalty, just so long as he can never do anything so horrible to anyone else, ever again."

She stood up. They were going to agree, or they weren't.

"I'll let you all talk," she said. "Katie knows where to find me. Thank you for your time."

Afraid? Yes, she'd been so afraid. . . .

Her only fear now was that they would say no.

The *Happy-Me* sat off the coast of Bimini in shallow water. Jenny and Mark Houghton and their friends Gabby and Dale Johnson

had planned on camping on the beach, but they had gotten lazy. They hadn't tied up at the dock because they'd kept the boat in the shallow water, and talked so late that the sun had gone down.

Both retired, the couples motored the short distance to Haunt Island several times a year.

Gabby and Dale had gone to bed, Mark was still topside and Jenny was humming as she put away the last of the dishes. They'd dined on spaghetti and meatballs, heated up in the microwave.

She was startled to hear her husband call her name. "Jenny!"

She nearly dropped the dish in her hand, it had been so quiet. She set it on the counter and hurried up the ladder to the deck. For a moment, it struck her that they might as well be alone in the world. Entirely alone. There were a few stars in a black-velvet sky, and it seemed that there was no horizon, the sea melded with the sky. The lights of the *Happy-Me* were colorful and brave against the night — and pitiful, as well.

"Hand me the grapple pole there, quickly, Jenny," Mark said, leaning over the hull and staring into the water.

"What?"

She was concerned. Mark had been given a clean bill of health after having suffered a heart attack on his seventieth birthday, but he thought himself a young man still, at times. And he was acting like a crazy one now.

"That one," he said, spinning around. There was a grappling hook on a long pole set in its place in metal brackets against the wall of the cabin.

"But, Mark —"

"Please, Jenny, please — there's someone in the water!"

She heard it then: a gasped and garbled plea for help.

While Mark continued to stare into the water, Jenny reached for the hook, almost ripping it from the wall to bring to Mark.

He stuck it out into the water, calling out, "Here, here, take this, we'll get you aboard!"

"Ah!" he murmured. Jenny saw that someone had the pole and that Mark was managing to pull the person closer to the boat.

"The flashlight, get a flashlight!" Mark said.

Jenny turned to do so. As she did, she heard another gasping sound, and within it a little cry of terror.

She spun around.

The sound was coming from Mark.

Because someone . . . *something* . . . was rising from the sea.

It couldn't be. It was a bony pirate, half-eaten, so it appeared, in rags. Bones and rags, and it was laughing. . . .

"No!" Jenny gasped herself.

The *thing* reached out and grabbed Mark around the neck. It lifted him and tossed him overboard. Jenny started to scream in protest, horrified for Mark, her companion, friend, lover, husband for all of her life.

And then . . .

In terror herself. For her own life.

Because now the *thing* pulled a sword. A fat sword. Maybe it wasn't a sword. Maybe it was a machete. Maybe it was . . .

Her last conscious thought was, *What the hell does it matter what it is?*

It swung in the night.

She never managed to scream. Her windpipe was severed before she could do so. She dropped to the deck, her head dangling from the remnants of her neck.

"Quickly," said the one to the other, joining him on board. "Quickly. The other two, before they wake up!"

The deck was drenched as they walked across it and down the ladder to the cabin below.

Gabby and Dale never woke up.

105

For a while, the *Happy-Me* rolled in the gentle waves of the night, beneath the velvet darkness of the sky.

Then it sank to a shallow grave.

3

Vanessa had the dreams again that night.

They had started the night on the island when Georgia had talked about the monsters, left the island with Carlos — and wound up murdered with her head on the sand.

For the first weeks after the incident, they'd come frequently. They would start with her being Isabella, rising from the sea in her period gown, covered with seaweed.

Vanessa had agreed to play the small role of Isabella, and the day when they had filmed her in the costume had turned out to be fun — after she'd calmed down from being aggravated. There she had been in that gown, floating — a corpse that had come to the surface, about to open its long-dead eyes — and they were supposed to have been filming from beneath her. But in the middle of the shoot, they'd gotten distracted by a school of barracuda, and

she'd looked up at last to see that the boat was far away and there was no sign of the others. She was a good swimmer, but the seas were beginning to rise and the gown was heavy. She lay there cursing them, then called out, hoping someone on the boat would hear her.

The boat had come around at last with Jay and the others on board. They'd been thrilled with their footage of the barracuda — which usually left people alone, unless they had something on them that sparkled and attracted the attention of the predators. Incredulous, she'd asked if they'd gotten the shots of her, floating in the water. Oh, yes, they'd done so. Then, seeing her face, Jay had been entirely contrite, and everyone had tripped over themselves trying to appease her for the afternoon.

But in her dreams, she didn't see Isabella as herself. She saw her dead, murdered, empty sockets where her eyes should be, yet seeming to see, face skeletal and pocked with the ravages of the sea, bits of bone and skull peeking through decomposing flesh. The woman stared at her as if she were the enemy, and all around her, huge black shadows seemed to form, and they were made of seaweed and *evil*.

Then she was alone on the beach at Haunt

Island, and they were coming after her, and she didn't run because there was nowhere to go to escape the darkness and evil, she simply stood there, staring at them, as they seemed to grow larger and larger and come closer and closer, and she could smell the rot of flesh and a stagnant sea and she could almost feel the salt spray of the ocean.

Right before they embraced her, she awoke with a start.

For a moment she was disoriented in the darkness of her room. Then she heard a whistle from below her window, the wheels of a late-night taxi going somewhere and the laughter of the few drunken revelers still on the street, and her eyes adjusted to the darkness. She was in her little studio room atop the bathing suit and T-shirt shop on Duval Street. A glance at the faceplate of her phone told her that it was just about 2:00 a.m.

She stared at the ceiling for a while, angry with herself. She wasn't afraid of ghosts or sea monsters. Someone real and alive had happened upon the island. A real person had killed her friends — and she just couldn't believe it was Carlos. Carlos was probably dead. She hated the fact that everyone *assumed* that he'd been the killer, when he probably died trying to protect

109

Georgia from whatever sick maniac had come upon them. It was chilling to think that the killer had to have been on the island with them when Georgia had first screamed, when they had all thought that Travis was fine somewhere, laughing at the cruel joke he had played on Georgia. They should have looked harder for Travis that night.

And yet, who would have really suspected anything? They were a large enough group. They'd been enjoying the shoot, and even the pristine isolation of Haunt Island.

She probably lay there for hours, and then drifted off.

Vanessa's phone rang at 8:00 a.m. She knew, because the jarring sound caused her to bolt up, and she saw the time immediately. She fumbled to retrieve it from the stand next to the bed and answered breathlessly.

"Yes?"

"Vanessa?"

She felt as if her heart stood still for a moment. The voice sounded like that of Sean O'Hara.

"Yes?"

"Are you awake? Sorry if I woke you."

He wasn't one bit sorry, she thought.

"I was awake," she said. So she was lying. She wasn't sure what she had said or done

exactly that had seemed to raise a barrier of hostility within him — other than that she did want him to take his project and turn it to her purpose.

"Ready to let me see your stuff?" he asked.

"Pardon?"

"Diving, filming," he said. Was there a touch of mockery in his tone? Was he amused that she might have thought that he meant something else?

"Of course. Anytime. Does this mean that —"

"It means I want to see if you're as good as your credentials," he said flatly.

"Of course. Where do you want me, when, and with what equipment?"

"I have equipment. You probably want your own regulator and mask."

"Of course. What about cameras?"

"Mine are excellent quality."

"So are mine."

"Let's see if you know my equipment, and my methods," he said. "And if I hire you, it's going to be as my assistant, remember? Hauling, toting. But . . . it won't hurt to see what you can do with a camera. You never know when you may need some backup."

"All right."

"Meet me at the dock in half an hour. My dive boat is the *Conch Fritter*. I'll be setting

111

her up."

"I'll be there," she promised.

For a moment she couldn't afford to waste, she just sat there, staring at her phone. He hadn't agreed.

But he hadn't said no.

And in the water, she could prove herself.

She blinked, then shot out of bed. She had thirty minutes to shower, find a suit and run down the seven or so blocks to the boat docks.

And there had to be a cup of coffee somewhere along the way.

Vanessa Loren was all business when she arrived at the dock precisely on time. She was wearing a huge tank-type T-shirt over a bathing suit and carried a dive bag in one hand, a large paper cup of coffee in the other. Her hair was swept back in a band at her nape and she was wearing large dark sunglasses.

"Hand over the bag," he said politely.

"I can manage," she told him.

She could. Without needing a handhold of any kind for balance, she made the short leap from the dock to the deck with amazing dexterity, never in danger of losing so much as a drop of coffee — not that the

112

company didn't serve its coffee with A-one lids.

He shrugged as she landed. "Suit yourself. Want to grab that line aft?"

"Sure."

Bartholomew leaned casually against the rail, arms crossed over his chest. "She's got quite the physical prowess, and yet she's light and sleek as a cat. I say, hire her on! Trust me, the women of my day were seldom adept at working on any ship. Ah, this is but a boat. There you go."

Sean wanted to tell Bartholomew that there had been a number of famous and infamous women working upon pirate ships, but since Bartholomew was indignant at the term *pirate,* he'd deny it. And he knew that Bartholomew was going to goad him all afternoon.

He refrained from replying.

He went to the fore to release the front line and she scurried to release the one aft. He didn't speak to her as he guided the *Conch Fritter* out of the harbor.

Bartholomew, however, kept up a running conversation.

"Ah, what a lovely day. Truly lovely day! Calm seas, a beautiful sky and just the tiniest kiss of autumn in the air. I do remember this reef — we forced a few Spaniards into

113

her sharp tentacles, we did. Glorious sailing! Oh, and by the way — you do know that this is the area where Mad Miller supposedly attacked the *Santa Geneva* and kidnapped Dona Isabella. Alas, the ship upon which she sailed sank to the bottom of the sea with the nasty, evil creatures upon the pirate ship, Mad Miller's flagship, slicing up many a man as he begged for mercy, cast into the water, drowning!"

Slicing them might have been a mercy, if they were drowning, Sean thought, but he kept silent.

As he cleared the channel, Vanessa came and took the companion seat by the helm.

"Ah, but she looks lovely there!" Bartholomew commented.

She did. She was relaxed, enjoying the wind that whipped around them as they sped through the water. The *Conch Fritter* wasn't new, but she was a thirty-eight-foot Sea Ray custom Sundancer, and Sean loved her. She did twenty knots with amazing comfort — she wasn't going to outrun a real powerboat by any means, but she could move. The cockpit was air-conditioned and equipped with two flat-screen TVs, and there were three small sleeping cabins, the captain's cabin at the fore and two lining the port and starboard sides. There was a

small galley and main cabin as well, and the helm sat midway through the sleek design with a fiberglass companion seat that offered plenty of storage. He'd had her outfitted with a helm opening and an aft boarding ladder with a broad platform, and portside and starboard safe holds for dive tanks.

"Yes, yes, you love your boat," Bartholomew said, rolling his eyes. "And she is a thing of beauty! But then again, can anything rival the gold of that young woman's hair, the sea and sky that combine in her eyes?" he asked with an exaggerated sigh.

Sean thought, *I will not look at you, you scurvy spectral bastard.*

"Where are we going?" Vanessa asked above the hum of the motor.

"Pirate Cut — it's a close, easy dive," Sean said.

"We don't even need tanks," she commented.

"Ah, she knows the reef!" Bartholomew said. "Frankly, it seems that everything this young woman has said to you is true."

"If you want to stay down and film we need tanks and equipment," Sean said pleasantly to Vanessa.

She flushed and looked away, but it was obvious that she knew the reef, and prob-

ably knew it fairly well.

She did. She knew exactly where they were going, and how long it was going to take to get there. When they were still five minutes away, she stood and dug into her bag. She worked with a dive skin, not a suit, but a skin, light and not providing warmth. He actually liked a skin himself — a skin protected a diver against the tentacles of small and unseen jellyfish.

But he hadn't brought one.

By the time he'd stopped the motor and dropped anchor, she had on her skin and dive booties. Dive booties could be good, too, he had to admit. He'd brought neither his skin nor booties, but he didn't always wear them. She'd attached her regulator to a buoyancy-control vest and tank — the one next to the tank he'd prepared for himself. She wasted no time.

"What are we using?" she asked him.

He opened his storage container. He loved his equipment; he could spend hours perusing new camera equipment on the Internet.

He had many makes and models of video and still cameras, lighting systems and sound recorders, though often sound was added after shooting. He chose a Sony that day, with a Stingray Plus housing.

"Want help with your BCV and tank?" he asked.

"Nope, thank you."

He'd worked on dive boats growing up; tanks were heavy, it was easy to go off balance with them. Most people didn't mind help rising with them.

He let her go on her own.

She buckled into the vest and rose carefully, her mask on her head, her regulator ready. She proceeded carefully to the edge, slipped her regulator in her mouth and entered in a smooth backward flip. She had managed the weight on her slim body without any difficulty. All right, so she was trying to be one of the guys, not a hindrance, not someone on a crew who couldn't manage basic tasks.

She surfaced, and he handed her the camera equipment. She removed her regulator and asked him, "What am I filming?"

"Something artistic," he told her. "And I'm right behind you."

She nodded, but she wasn't waiting around at the surface. She could handle the camera housing fine while releasing air from her BCV. She sank below the surface.

"What a woman!" Bartholomew said. "Why, if I were only flesh and blood . . ."

"But you're not," Sean told him.

He hurried into his own gear and followed in her wake.

Pirate's Cut was a beautiful place to dive. The water was clear, and visibility was amazing. Staghorn coral rose and wafted in the movement of the water, while torch and pineapple coral in dazzling shades grew around it. Tiny fish darted here, there and everywhere, while a large grouper, at least three hundred pounds, decided to swim at her side.

It did make for beautiful filming. She shot the coral with the tiny fish and panned slowly around to the giant grouper.

There was a drop-off near the shallow area of the reef, and she followed it down; she knew that the ocean went to no more than a hundred feet at the drop-off. She eased down about another twenty feet, aware that Sean was near her then, watching her. He came to her, motioning for the camera. She frowned behind her mask but handed it to him. He indicated her side, and she saw that the giant grouper was still following her, like a pet dog. She shrugged and swam slowly alongside the fish while Sean took footage. She reached out and stroked the side of the fish. He circled her — hoping for a handout, she was certain. Divers must

have recently come to the reef with food to encourage the creature to come near. It was amazing that he hadn't wound up on a dinner plate himself.

He lingered a little while longer, and then swam off.

Sean returned the camera to her. She decided to go to the bones of the old sunken ship that was assumed to be the *Santa Geneva*. She'd been a wooden-hulled ship and had broken up, however it was that she'd gone down. She was really nothing but wooden bones now, since the sea had caused the disintegration of most of the hull. Vanessa still loved the wreck. It was possible to imagine the size of the ship, where the masts had been, the hold, the cabins, the quarters.

She looked through the camera as she neared a section of the remains.

She almost choked, and started in the water.

Through the lens, she saw a figurehead.

Impossible. The figurehead was long gone.

She looked again, and for a moment, she could have sworn that she was seeing a woman's face — and the sleek lines of a beautifully crafted figurehead.

She blinked, and it was gone.

She moved the camera away for a moment

and lowered herself down to the ruins. She shook the image of the figurehead and filmed the length of the ruins, taking in the fish, the barnacles growing on those sad bare bones that remained.

Something crusted rose from the bed of sand on the floor of the ocean that held the wreck. It was just a dot on the sand, but through the lens, it seemed to be something. Vanessa moved down and reached out, gently swishing sand from the object. She wasn't sure what it was, it was so encrusted, but it was odd, so she picked it up.

Sean was behind her. He eased himself down on his knees and she showed him what she had discovered. He took the camera from her and pointed upward. He was ready to surface.

They had moved a good hundred feet from the boat and stopped at thirty-three feet to pressurize. Sean reached the dive platform and ladder before she did. He set the camera down on the platform and threw his flippers on board as she grasped hold of the platform. The sea rocked around them, but Sean ably drew himself up and turned to reach for her. She hesitated only briefly and then accepted his hand, throwing her flippers up as well and climbing up the ladder.

They came through the little custom hatch to the deck of the Sea Ray and he spun her around without asking, unlatching her tank.

"I'll get yours," she said.

He didn't protest but accepted her help and stowed the tanks. He came back to her and asked for the object she had picked up from the ocean floor.

He turned it around and around in his hand. "I have friends to take this to," he murmured.

Vanessa felt a sudden, eerie sweep of air around her. She spun around, looking for . . .

Something.

But there was nothing around her.

Still, she was suddenly cold. She could remember the figurehead she had seen through the camera lens with a frightening clarity — since it hadn't really been there. And now . . .

This. This chilling sensation that . . .

They weren't alone.

Sean looked at her suddenly. "What's wrong?" he asked her.

She shook her head. "Nothing. A goose walked over my grave, I guess. What do you think it is?"

"A coin . . . or a pendant. I think you've found a real relic," he told her.

"Really?"

"Well, we could find out it's a 1950s Timex or something . . . I don't know enough to take a chance trying to get the ocean crust off it, but as I said, I have friends who do this professionally. We'll bring it to them. I'm driving in. Want water, beer, soda? They're in the cooler, over there, portside. Help yourself."

He pulled down the dive flag and drew in the anchor — it was automatic, all he had to do was push a button. The Sea Ray was definitely nice.

He went to the helm, starting the motor, taking the wheel. She still had the crazy feeling that they weren't alone, that the air was charged.

She grabbed a couple of bottles of water out of the cooler and hurried back to the companion seat.

"So — did I pass inspection?" she called to Sean, more to start a conversation than because she was really ready for an answer.

He didn't reply; he was looking straight ahead with a small smile on his face. The wind had ruffled his hair, he was in board shorts and nothing else, and his chest was gleaming bronze and powerfully muscled. She was startled to feel a stirring of admiration or something worse, even — attraction.

It was the smile, she thought.

He reached for sunglasses, and leaned casually against the captain's seat rather than sitting.

She eased back in the companion chair, tired from the night before. She closed her eyes and allowed herself just to feel.

The figurehead had seemed so real . . .

Her eyes flew open. She almost bolted out of the chair.

The figurehead! The figurehead with its beautiful face . . .

The same face she had in her own possession, her copy of the artist's rendering of Dona Isabella.

4

Vanessa Loren knew how to work and how to move. She seemed familiar with every aspect of equipment and the importance of rinsing off their dive gear and his camera rigging as soon as they got back to the dock. When they were done, she slipped her oversize T-shirt back on and looked at him expectantly.

"Tell her she's hired," Bartholomew said. He was stretched out on his back on the aft seat, hands crossed behind his head, hat over his eyes, as if he still needed to shade them from the sun. One leg dangled over the other in lazy comfort. "Tell her that she's hired, and you're doing the story. You know you're going to do it. She's a scriptwriter, she knows cameras, she knows boats, and she sure seems to have a great work ethic. Not to mention great legs as long as a yardarm and . . . well, nothing wrong with the rest of her, either."

Sean ignored Bartholomew. He smiled at Vanessa. "You know we'll do a background check," he told her.

"Go for it," she said, looking off into the distance. She seemed distracted.

He nodded. "Oh, the object you found — I'm going to take it to friends who have a small shop on Simonton — they usually work privately, but they have a little storefront. It's called Sunken Treasures. You're more than welcome to take it yourself, if you prefer. You discovered the piece."

"I trust you to take it — I'm not after treasure," she told him. Her hair was still damp; her eyes seemed the most brilliant blue he had ever seen, filled with honesty. There was something as she stood there, her answer to him filled with trust and disinterest, that seemed to catch at his throat. Or his heart.

Or, admittedly, other parts of his anatomy. Even wet, she was stunning. And yet beauty itself never created such an appeal. Maybe it was her energy or vitality. Or the way she seemed filled with warmth and vibrant, sleek movement — even when she stood still. He wanted to step closer to her, as intrigued by the woman as the mystery she brought.

He stepped back.

"All right, but you'll know where it is," he told her.

She smiled. The smile seemed a little distant. She looked around him and seemed confused, then shrugged, as if returning to the subject. "Thanks. I'll, uh, talk to you later, then?" she asked.

"Yes. I'll talk to you later," he assured her.

"Thank you."

She was sincere.

And yet it was odd. She still seemed distracted as she walked away. Sean watched her go, puzzled.

"She senses me — that's what's going on," Bartholomew said, rising and adjusting his hat. "She's got the sense — it's not developed, but she's got something. I know — trust me. I spent a few of my early years in this rather awkward state playing tricks on people. There are those who will never sense a thing, and there are those who always get a feeling . . . but don't really know what it is. She's gifted, I'd say."

"Wonderful. She's tracking a murderer — seriously, that's what she wants to do — and you're doing your best to make her jump at every whisper of breeze," Sean said.

"Excuse me! I don't really have much to do with it. Well, maybe I do. I mean, ghosts can make an effort, as you know . . . but I

wasn't doing anything."

"That's not exactly true — since you talked a blue streak all day. Now I have to think over some things."

Bartholomew shrugged. "But you know you're going to work with her."

"It's not just my decision. David has to decide on this, as well."

"David's going to do whatever you want to do."

"The point is, really, there's nothing new that we're going to discover. Say Carlos Roca did it — he's long gone. Say someone else did it — that someone has managed to change the boat so that no one would ever recognize her, and they're probably living in Brazil by now," Sean said.

"You know better than anyone that it's never too late to seek the truth," Bartholomew said.

"Bartholomew, you're like an old fishwife. Quit nagging. The story is intriguing. I have to see how I'm going to fit it in with the rest of the history we want to put out there — touching on enough, creating a story line —"

"You were creating a documentary about legends and mysteries in this area. Fits right in," Bartholomew said.

"Hey, look — isn't that the lady in white?"

Sean asked, pointing toward the center of Mallory Square. There was no one there, but Bartholomew looked. He glared at Sean. "She has a name, you know. Lucinda, Miss Lucinda Wellington — Lucy."

"Well, it's just damned adorable to see you so smitten, my friend," Sean said.

Bartholomew shook his head. "You won't distract me. Lucy and I have a lovely relationship. We walk every afternoon through the cemetery, strolling and reading the headstones. And sometimes we stroll down Duval and observe the tourists. Ah, I can smell the rum, so it seems, at times. But, Sean O'Hara, God knows why, it seems I'm here still to help you, and my beautiful lady in white, dear Lucy, seems glad enough to be with me."

"Great. Just great. Well, why don't you go see if she's in the cemetery now. I'm going to take a shower and then bring whatever that encrusted piece is that Vanessa found over to Jaden and Ted."

He left the ghost on deck and went down to the *Conch Fritter*'s head. Twenty minutes later, he headed to his friends' shop, curiously flipping the thing — trinket or treasure — in his hand.

Back in her room, Vanessa showered for a

128

long time, luxuriating in the heat of the water, trying not to think. She emerged, and, convincing herself that she was over-tired and suffering from the nightmares again, she went to the dresser and stared at the copy of the likeness of Dona Isabella that Marty had given her the day before.

She'd never heard that any ship had sailed with a figure head carved as a replica of Dona Isabella.

Of course. There was no figurehead. She was exhausted, and she'd spent the morning trying to prove that she was more efficient than the Energizer bunny.

She dressed quickly and looked at the time. One o'clock. She realized that she was starving and still really exhausted. Okay, she was pretty sure that she'd pulled the morning off quite well — she'd been efficient, she'd gotten good footage, the giant grouper had certainly allowed Sean to get some good footage of her with the fish, and she'd discovered something at the bottom of the ocean, where the ship had wrecked and broken up nearly two hundred years ago.

She could take a nap.

Food and a nap.

And maybe a drink to help her relax. She was just a few feet away from the Key West

Smallest Bar. Food, something good and stiff and a long nap.

She had imagined the figurehead in the water. But, really, if she thought about it, if she was going to imagine images, maybe in her mind the poor martyred Dona Isabella was trying to help her, she wanted the history known, she wanted the world to know what horrible villains Mad Miller and Kitty Cutlass had been.

Sleep.

And she would quit seeing things.

And with any luck, she wouldn't dream.

Sunken Treasures was located on Simonton. The proprietors, Jaden Valiente and Ted Taggart, were friends of Sean's from school. They'd lived and worked together for years without choosing to marry, but they seemed happy, had no children, kept five cats in the small store, and appeared pleased with every aspect of their lives. They never fought, which was nice, since Sean was good friends with both of them. He'd traveled so much working that he hadn't been home much since high school, but when he was in Key West, with the two of them, it was as if he had never left.

"Hey!" Jaden said, looking up from her workstation as he entered. Ted was across

the room at an identical station. They were both equipped with bright, twist-neck lamps, bottles with all kinds of solutions and brushes with varying degrees of bristles. The shop was decorated with old broadsides and sailing paraphernalia from every century and decade. It was eclectic and had one showcase — where they displayed the reproduction pieces that they made, much more affordable than the real items that could be purchased many places in the city.

Jaden looked at him through magnifying glasses that made her eyes appear huge. They were warm brown eyes, and she had curly brown hair past her shoulders that gave her the look of a new age hippie. Ted had the same look — he was wearing a Grateful Dead T-shirt and he also had curly brown hair that he wore long, a curly brown beard and mustache and an easygoing smile.

"Nice to see you in our neck of the woods. We usually have to go to karaoke down at O'Hara's and warble out an old Cream number to get to see you, Sean," Ted said, grinning.

"Speak for yourself. I do not warble, I sing delightfully off-key," Jaden said. "What's up?"

"A young woman diving with me this morning made a discovery," Sean said.

131

"Oh? What?" Jaden asked, coming around from her workstation.

Sean produced the piece. "Right now, God knows, it could be anything, but . . . this kind of growth and debris upon it, whatever it is, it looks as if it has been out there awhile."

Jaden took it from him, studying it. Ted came around, as well. "Looks old," he said.

"Is it a coin?" Sean asked.

"Looks more like a medallion . . . a brooch? Where was it found?" Jaden asked.

"Pirate Cut," Sean told her.

"That's where the *Santa Geneva* went down under pirate attack," Ted said. "Other ships, too. The water is so deep and then the shallow reef juts up — caught lots of ships over time."

"We were diving over the bone structure — what's left — of the *Santa Geneva*," Sean said.

"Cool!" Jaden looked at Ted with a pleased smile. "This really could be something."

"I'd have thought that, over the years, almost everything of any value had already been brought up," Sean said.

"For shame, Sean O'Hara!" Jaden said. "The sea is ever a cruel mistress, and you never know what's been found and what hasn't — especially over time. I'll get on it

right away," Jaden promised. "And carefully!"

"I knew you would," Sean told her.

"It would be spectacular if this were a documented piece of jewelry!" Jaden said enthusiastically.

"Did you get any of it on film?" Ted asked him.

"Yes, some of the discovery."

" 'Cause you're going to work with David Beckett and do a really cool documentary, right?" Ted asked. "Wow — and you start off by finding a treasure from the *Santa Geneva*. Lord, do I love that story!"

"Romantic in an icky kind of tragic way," Jaden agreed.

"Gorgeous Dona Isabella captured, her ship sunk in Pirate's Cut!"

"Apparently when Mad Miller attacked the ship, he swept Dona Isabella from it first. And of course, he was supposed to be asking her husband for a ransom," Jaden said. "But he fell in love with her."

"And infuriated Kitty Cutlass!" Ted said dramatically.

"The ship was blown to smithereens, most of the crew killed in the water, but some of them taken prisoner as well for slave labor," Jaden said.

Looking at them, Sean shook his head and

smiled. "You two should take it on the road. You're very dramatic."

"Well, who knows what really happened?" Jaden asked with a shrug. "All that is fact is that Mad Miller did attack the ship and he did kidnap Dona Isabella. And Kitty Cutlass was madly in love with Mad Miller. I mean, supposedly, Mad Miller was in love with Kitty Cutlass, so why kidnap Dona Isabella unless it was for ransom, and she had a rich husband, and whether they were living apart or not, he would have paid the ransom, just for the sake of his pride. But, no — Dona Isabella is murdered, some say *by* Kitty Cutlass, and the crew of the *Santa Geneva* who were taken prisoner rather than murdered or left to drown at the site were then massacred on Haunt Island. Oh! And those other murders took place on Haunt Island just about two years ago — now, there's a story for you, Sean.

"Hey, who were you with?" Jaden asked him curiously. "Who is the 'young woman'?"

"Her name is Vanessa Loren. And, yes — I see you're starting to frown. If you were following the newspapers when members of the film crew were killed on Haunt Island, you heard the name. She was one of the survivors."

"Whoa — wow!" Ted said. "Man — per-

fect. Why, you have an excellent story going there. Hey — what is she like? How did she wind up here?"

"My God, I can't even imagine how horrible that must have been — not that we haven't had our share of our own absurdities around here lately," Jaden said. "Whoa, whoa, whoa! Did she come to see you on purpose?"

"Yes," Sean said.

"Can't wait to meet her!" Ted told Jaden.

"Now, wait —" Sean said, frowning.

"Oh, come on. We're not going to say anything to her. We won't embarrass you!" Jaden protested.

"It's not that — I just can't imagine she really likes being quizzed constantly on what happened. It must have been pretty — horrifying."

"Ah, but you two have something in common. You were almost killed by a madman," Ted pointed out.

"But Sean's madman was caught — and no one knows what happened to the other," Jaden said. "Oh, it is a mystery! I'd love to know what happened on that island. Most people, of course, think it was that fellow who was supposed to take the actress home. . . . Rodriquez . . . Rod . . ."

"Roca. Carlos Roca," Sean said.

"What does she think?" Ted asked.

"I'm dying to see what she looks like!" Jaden said.

"Just be nice when you meet her," Sean said. *He was defending her. Well, these were his friends, but they were professing some intrusive curiosity.*

"And you might have found a relic. Like Ted said, 'Wow, cool!' " Jaden said happily.

"You know what some people think?" Ted asked, nodding sagely.

"What?"

"It's the Bermuda Triangle," Ted said, as if it were fact.

"Ted, ships get lost, planes go down, and many so-called victims of the so-called Bermuda Triangle have been found. Ships have sunk."

"Aha! But throughout the years, they've found ghost ships out there, too. Ships with absolutely nothing wrong with them — but no one aboard. Hey, come on! You can order DVDs from the educational channels on the Bermuda Triangle," Ted argued.

"The Bermuda Triangle did not decapitate two people and leave their heads and arms in the sand," Sean said.

"Ugh. Scary!" Jaden said.

"Who says that there isn't some form of really vicious creature making its home in

the Triangle?" Ted asked. "They're finding new species of fish constantly — things like the megamouth shark that was supposed to be extinct. They *know* that giant squid exist, but they know almost nothing about the habits of the creatures," he said triumphantly.

"A giant squid didn't do it either, Ted," Sean said.

"Ah! But what happened to the boat? If there's an explanation, go ahead — you find it!"

"A half-dozen law enforcement agencies, including the Coast Guard, couldn't find it — I'm not so sure I'm going to," Sean said.

"And what about the killer? If it's a man, he's out there somewhere. Or, like I said, he's a victim of the Triangle. The Bermuda Triangle harbors some form of evil, and that evil got into the man, and then the man killed the actor and actress."

"You sure it wasn't aliens?" Sean asked dryly.

"Evil aliens living in the Triangle!" Ted agreed.

"I don't think that Sean's accepting any of your theories, my love," Jaden said. "Sean, before he starts to argue UFOs, I suggest you get out of here. I'm going to get right on this piece — I'm really excited,

137

it just might be something unique and historic. I'll call you later, okay?"

"Be good to that young woman," Ted advised. "Poor thing!"

"Yes, be kind," Jaden admonished.

They were staring at him like a pair of proud parents on prom night. "I'll do my best," Sean said. He offered a grimace, waved and left the shop.

Key West was a small island. Pretty soon, everyone would be talking. And like Ted, most people liked to believe there was *something* about the Bermuda Triangle. Or aliens.

As he headed out, his phone rang. It was Liam Beckett. "I've checked out everything possible on your Miss Loren."

"She's not exactly *my* Miss Loren," Sean protested.

"Well, she came to you," Liam said. "Anyway, she appears to be everything that she claims on paper. She went to college, and she's worked on prestigious projects since. Apparently, she invested about fifty thousand dollars into filming the movie and her partner, Jay Allen, did the same. But it doesn't seem that she's in any financial trouble — in fact she was recently very well paid for a project. I have a list of her work, some of which can be pulled up on You-Tube."

"I don't know why I had you do extensive work on her background," Sean said. "I didn't think that you'd find anything."

"She's the real deal, so it seems."

"Thanks."

"So?"

"So?"

"So, if you're doing this — I want in on it. I have to apply quickly for the time. Hey, you two are going to need me. Yeah, yeah, you're tough guys, but I'm a cop, and three of us who completely trust each other are better than two. You need me," Liam repeated.

"You were always invited, whatever the end choices. I just didn't think that you could get off with everything that has gone on lately."

"Oh, no. I'm there," Liam said. "I'll see you later."

"You will?"

Liam laughed. "Katie-oke at O'Hara's. David sips a beer and munches on conch fritters every night she works, as if he's still afraid to let her out of his sight."

Yes, I understand that feeling. So why am I even considering doing this?

Because he knew, too, what it was like not to know the truth, to mistrust your best friends and wonder as the years rolled by.

"You are going to be following the route of the film crew, aren't you?" Liam asked.

He wanted to protest again that he wasn't working alone, that the business venture was between him and David Beckett.

But David had already handed the decision over to him.

"Yes," he said simply. "I'll see you later tonight."

He headed over to the Beckett house; that afternoon, they were interviewing for positions for the shoot.

One, he knew, was already taken. Two. Liam was in, as well. And if they were all going, well, then, he could guarantee that his sister would be with them, as well.

There would be two boats, as always planned.

It occurred to him that the film crew who met the tragic and traumatic fate had also started out from Key West with two boats. Wasn't that the point? He mocked himself.

They were re-creating history. Seeking the truth.

And they were probably fools.

But, he determined, they'd be fools who came on the journey aware and alert — and well armed.

The Smallest Bar in Key West was very

small. Vanessa had gotten to know several of the bartenders, and they were nice — even when she just wanted to order a soda or a bottle of water. She was certain that they knew who she was — her picture had been in the papers and on the news.

The afternoon had gone well. The warm shower, food and the Irish car bomb the bartender had suggested had done a number on her and she'd slept like the dead for almost four hours. Once she awoke and thought about the night, she didn't want to be alone and she didn't want to sit by the phone waiting to see if Sean was going to call her.

She decided to head south on Duval for O'Hara's. Katie should have been setting up the karaoke by then. Not that she had to set up much — it was her uncle's bar, and nothing was going to happen to any of her equipment there.

As she walked down the street, she knew that many of the shopkeepers and servers at outside restaurants watched her as she went by. Just another reminder that people would not quickly forget her face, or the story that was associated with it.

Such gruesome murders did not occur without a great deal of sensationalism.

She wondered sometimes if whoever had

killed Travis and Georgia — she didn't believe for a minute that it had been Carlos Roca — had relished the attention that the killings had brought. The police had questioned both her and Jay about their enemies. To the best of her knowledge, she didn't have any. Nor did Jay. They had led simple lives, gone to college, gone out into the world, worked really hard and survived. That had come from a lot of twenty-hour days at film school, but they had paid off. She knew she was lucky, too; she knew the water, thanks to her father.

Ah, her father! As far as her parents knew, right now she was just in the Keys with Katie. She knew they wouldn't be happy if they knew what she was doing — trying to retrace the steps she had previously taken and find out if there was an answer anywhere. Maybe, if she had convinced Sean, they would find nothing. But she would have the satisfaction of knowing that she had tried everything that was in her power to find out the truth.

When she reached O'Hara's, she found that Katie and David were seated at the bar. Katie was ready to go when the time rolled around, and she was snacking on conch fritters with David and sipping a soda. The two were in deep conversation when she arrived.

She wondered what they were talking about — they shut up the moment they saw her.

David Beckett stood politely, offering her the stool next to Katie. She tried to tell him to sit, but he wouldn't, so she thanked him and sat down. "I hear we're on," Katie said happily.

"We are?" Vanessa asked.

"Sean called and asked if I was sure it was a direction I willing to go in — and I must say I'm intrigued. We've had Liam studying what information he can from various sources, and it is one of the most disturbing mysteries of recent time," David told her.

Katie looked at Vanessa with triumph. She had an "I told you so" look in her eyes.

"We started interviewing for researchers and our film crew today," David said.

"And how did that go?"

David grinned. "Sean said that not one of the people we saw had your credentials. But some seemed okay. We actually have a number of friends who are top-notch, but most of them are already committed to projects — it's tough, even for the best people, so when something is up, you commit fast. And I admit, we didn't set this up ahead very far, which might have helped in that area."

"I'm still sure you can find the people you

need," Vanessa said.

"Oh, yeah. But it would have been easier to hit the folks we know — and whose work and work ethic we know," David said.

"Everyone has to start somewhere," Vanessa said.

"That's true, and now I have to go to work," Katie said. "I'm counting on both of you if it's a dead crowd," she added.

Vanessa smiled and shook her head. "A group number!" Katie said.

There were about twenty people in the bar when Katie started up, singing a number with a friend of hers, Clarinda, who was also one of the night servers at O'Hara's. The two sang a country number that was beautiful and sexy. By the time they finished, other people were walking in the door.

"I don't think that she's going to have any problem with this crowd not getting up," Vanessa told David.

"Probably not. We're off the hook. Oh, and she's trying to get Clarinda to get up enough confidence to take it over when she's not here," David said.

"Oh?"

David smiled. "You don't think we'll all be going on this excursion without Katie, do you?"

Vanessa smiled. "So it's a done deal?" she asked.

"It seems to be so," David told her. "I heard about your dive today — and that you might have discovered a relic of some kind."

"Hopefully. And hopefully, it is a real relic, and not a watch lost recently that encrusted quickly," Vanessa said.

"I don't think so," David said, "Sean has a good eye for things like that. The sea can play games, that's for certain, but anyone who has grown up diving down here has found something lost from a boat from some period of time — he'd probably know if it was just a twenty-year-old barnacle crustation."

"I found it awfully easily."

"The current is always moving and the sand is always shifting," David reminded her.

She faced the doorway where, in ones, twos and threes, others were now coming into the bar. She saw Marty and he waved to her as he headed up to Katie and her computer area to request a song.

"Ah, good, Marty is here. We'll be getting a good sea shanty," David said.

She smiled at him and noted the door again.

She stiffened where she sat at the stool,

dead straight.

She didn't believe it, didn't believe that she was seeing the man who was walking in.

A man obviously looking for someone.

Her.

5

Sean arrived at his uncle's bar around nine-thirty. Katie-oke was in full swing.

He saw David at one of the high-top tables in the rear of the karaoke area and came to sit by him at one of the free bar stools. There was one left; Bartholomew sat in it as if he and Sean had come in together like any friends out for a drink together.

David acknowledged Bartholomew's presence with a nod. He could hear Bartholomew at times and see his faint outline at certain times, too. Sean didn't think that David had any kind of a sixth sense, but Bartholomew had become so entwined in the events that had nearly cost all of them their lives that David did have a sense of him. It was often a relief for Sean to be with his sister and David, who knew about Bartholomew's presence. That way, when the pirate goaded him, he could reply without appearing to be talking to an

imaginary friend.

"Liam here yet?" he asked.

"Not yet. But I talked to him after you did. Seems he's in on this one way or the other," David said.

"Which is great — having a skilled cop with us cannot be bad," Sean said.

"You really think that we might have trouble?" David asked.

"Two people were murdered, maybe three, when they were making the film. I think that the only rational explanation is that Carlos Roca was the killer, and that he's out there somewhere. But will he come after our crew? Probably not. He got away with murder — and a good boat. I don't think he'd come back. Is there the possibility of something going wrong, such as idiot drug smugglers, human traffickers? Sure, always. We both know that. So it's good to have a cop along. We can watch each other's backs. Yeah, I like that," Sean said.

"The pickings seemed slim today at the interviews," David said.

Sean shrugged. They had talked to a couple of "possible people." He wished he could have Frazier, from Key Largo, but he was working on a *National Geographic* project. There were other friends he'd known for years and years. Of course, they

could delay the project. But now, he didn't want to.

"We'll be all right," David said. "You know Katie is coming. And she can help with lights, sound . . . cameras. She says she hung around you enough when you first got into it, and we've been out doing some fooling around filming on the reefs since we decided to do this."

"Two and two," Bartholomew said. "Always close enough to be in easy vision, that's the way to do it."

David gazed in his direction. "And which boat will you be on?"

"Whichever appears to be more comfortable. Or, perhaps, more in danger," he said.

"You'll leave Lucinda, Lucy — your lady in white — for that kind of time?" Sean asked Bartholomew. He realized, oddly enough, that as much as he didn't want to be "haunted," he did think it was a good thing that Bartholomew was ready for the trip.

"Can't leave you folks alone. And who knows, maybe Lucy will be up for the voyage. Though she does hate the water. And boats," Bartholomew admitted.

"A long time to be away," Sean noted, mumbling so that only David could hear him.

149

Bartholomew slowly lifted an aristocratic brow. "Time is irrelevant, my dear boy. You must remember, Lucy and I have both been drifting these streets for many, many a year now. We'll be fine with a few weeks apart — as they say, absence makes the heart grow fonder." He frowned. "Alas, you should be worrying about a living vision of grace and beauty!" Bartholomew said gravely, looking toward the booths in the bar area.

"What?" Sean turned to stare.

Vanessa Loren was seated in one of the booths, oblivious to his presence — and all else, including the slightly inebriated college student attempting a rap number on stage. She was facing a man; Sean could see shoulders and a head of dark hair. She was speaking passionately, and seemed to be upset.

"Who is it?" Sean asked David, frowning. "I didn't know Vanessa was in here."

"I don't know who it is, and you didn't ask about her. We were talking. She saw that fellow in the doorway and excused herself, telling me it was an old friend she was surprised to see."

"Really?" Sean said.

So who was the guy?

Yeah, right, and what was it to him?

That morning she had attracted him. In

150

fact, he realized, he was more than attracted, and he didn't want to be. He wanted everything professional, every single decision he made. But she had slipped into him, mind, soul and substance, since he had first seen her sitting here in O'Hara's, and he wondered if that was why he had wanted to fight anything she had to say to him — it was far safer, it was far more *professional* not to be attracted to an employee, especially when employment started out with such a story.

All right, face it, he didn't want her bothered by anyone. All right, in all honesty, he wasn't sure what he wanted, but he didn't want her there with anyone else.

He had no right to feel that way — he still barely knew her. A day of diving did not a long-term friend make, nor did standing near her, realizing just what a chemical mystique she possessed, give him the right to go interrupting her conversations with other men.

He stood. He suddenly felt as if he were a jealous boyfriend, irked that his girlfriend was flirting with someone else. Ridiculous feeling — but she had pursued him, determined on her course of action. And people *had* been murdered. He'd agreed to what she wanted — he did have a right to find

out why she appeared to be so disturbed.

If she was happy speaking with an old friend, fine. But if she wasn't, well, she had appealed to him for help in one way already.

Even as he approached the booth, he didn't think that this was anyone with whom Vanessa had an intimate relationship. They were on opposite sides of the booth. Her hands went from the table to the air as she spoke but never touched his. When he was speaking, she sat leaning back, arms crossed over her chest, and she seemed annoyed.

He reached the end of the booth. The man was talking, but he fell silent when Sean arrived and started to get up. He was about Vanessa's age, tall, well built and well bronzed, as if he spent a lot of time in the sun.

Sean set a hand on his shoulder. "Sit, sit, sorry, I didn't mean to interrupt a conversation. I just came by to say hello to Vanessa."

"Hello, Sean," Vanessa said, her voice tight.

"Sean — Sean O'Hara?" the man asked.

"Yes. And . . . you are?"

The young man stood quickly, offering his hand. "Jay. Jay Allen."

Jay Allen.

Producer, director and the man who had lost a small fortune because of the murders

on Haunt Island.

"Please, sit down, please, please, join us," Jay said.

Vanessa didn't seem to want to have anyone — more specifically him — join them. Her jaw was set at a rigid angle and she stared at Jay as if her eyes were vivid blue daggers.

He was definitely going to join them.

Vanessa didn't move; she didn't look away from Jay and she appeared rigidly angry. Sean slid in beside Jay as he scooted to the inside edge of the booth.

"Frankly, I'm here to apply for work — with you," Jay said.

Sean thought that Vanessa kicked Jay under the table.

"Oh?" Sean asked.

Jay nodded. "I heard that Vanessa was down here and that there were filmmakers about to embark on a historical documentary. I was working — filming tourists while they played with dolphins — in the Bahamas."

"I see," Sean said.

"I'm — Honestly, I know everything — or at least something about everything — from shooting, lighting, sound, editing, you name it. Seriously, ask Vanessa. Oh, and I have a boat. It's got some equipment. I can work

anything on any vessel you've got, my diving certificate is a master's and I wash dishes," he said. "I've directed, but don't worry — it's not an obsession. I can take direction, as well."

Jay seemed earnest. It was just too bizarre — him being here, right after he had agreed to film in the direction Vanessa had petitioned.

Or maybe it wasn't bizarre at all. Vanessa was here. Maybe she'd been elected to be the one to get under his skin and get it all going.

He stared at Vanessa. Obviously, she knew what he was thinking. Or she had known exactly what his thoughts might naturally be once Jay had shown up.

"I didn't know Jay was coming in," she said flatly.

"Sure," he said.

"Hey, look, I just arrived with a tremendous amount of hope," Jay said. "I went down like a lead balloon in all that, you have to realize."

"Two — possibly three — people are dead," Vanessa said sharply.

"Oh, of course! I mean, that's the most important part of all this, the really tragic part," Jay said. "And they deserve justice. And if Carlos is innocent and out there

somewhere . . . alive, well, we owe the truth to him, too, right? And if he did murder poor Travis and Georgia, and he didn't get swallowed up by the Bermuda Triangle, he deserves to go to prison. Or be executed. The whole thing *screams* for answers, don't you agree?"

"Answers, yes," Sean agreed. "Whether there's a prayer in hell that a set of film-makers could get the answers, I don't know."

"I'm good, I swear, ask Vanessa," Jay said.

"Vanessa?" Sean asked politely.

"He's good. He knows boats and he can dive," she said, still not facing Sean. Her cheeks seemed flushed.

"I'll take it all under consideration," Sean said. "And, of course, discuss it with my partner."

He started to rise.

"Please. Please consider me," Jay said. He sounded humble. Sincere.

And desperate.

"I can't tell you what it means to me. Honestly — yes, yes, other than the dead — this didn't affect anyone as badly as me. I can't tell you . . . I still spend my life wondering," Jay said.

Sean shook his head. "There's not even a real suggestion that we can find any an-

swers," he said.

"Please," Jay repeated.

"I'll discuss it with the others," Sean said. He left then, aware that Vanessa's eyes were following him as he walked across the room.

He hadn't realized that Bartholomew had been behind him until he felt the pressure when the ghost bumped into him.

"Such a skeptic!" Bartholomew said.

"Sorry, I don't like it."

"Don't like what?" Bartholomew demanded.

"I decide to go her way — and suddenly her old friend is here, asking for a job."

"She didn't know he was going to come here," Bartholomew said.

"Are you sure?"

"She seems honest. I don't think she knew."

"Either that, or she was just hoping to use David and me as saps."

"Ouch. There's a chip on your shoulder, my friend. Wait — better call it a boulder."

"I intend to be careful," Sean said.

"So — what is there to be so careful about? I'd say that it's natural. If you'd been involved in something like that and you heard that someone was doing anything that touched upon the mystery, wouldn't you jump it on it like a starving tick on an Irish

wolfhound?"

"A starving tick on an Irish wolfhound?" Sean repeated.

"I make my point — and if you tell me no, I'll call you a liar of the worst kind."

"All right, yes, I'd be after anything that could get me close again," Sean admitted. He paused. His sister was singing an old Beatles number, giving all due honor to the Fab Four. He paused, clapping, and watching David clap, watching the pleasure on his face. The world seemed so strange. David Beckett was seriously in love with Katie. It was nice. It was the kind of thing you had to admire — and envy.

He gave himself a mental shake. He'd had his share of relationships, most of which had ended decently, and he was long past the stage where he understood anyone who tried to hook up with a stranger in a bar purely for the purpose of sex. But somehow, looking at his sister and David, he felt a strange sense of emptiness he'd never known. He'd liked his life; come and go as you please, come and go anywhere in the world. Appreciate family and old friends, and look for new adventures. But now . . .

He took his stool back at the high-top table with David.

"So?" David asked.

"That is Jay Allen — the director of the movie that went so astray," Sean explained.

"Ah, the plot thickens," David said.

"He thinks it's strange that Jay just appeared," Bartholomew said, rolling his eyes. He jumped up suddenly.

"What? What is it?" Sean asked sharply.

"Lucinda lingers just outside. You'll excuse me . . . ?" Bartholomew asked.

"Why doesn't Mistress Lucinda just come in?" Sean asked. "Damn, Bartholomew, the way you jumped up . . . I thought something had happened. Invite the lovely and ethereal Miss Lucy in."

He shuddered. "Good God, she'd never!" he said.

"Wait — are you insulting my uncle's establishment?" Sean teased.

"No, you're forgetting that such an establishment as O'Hara's didn't really exist in my lady's day. Quite frankly, there was a house of disrepute on this very corner back then, and it was certainly no place where Lucinda would come. That's why she wanders so much. Of course, she knows that it's not a house of prostitution now, but still . . . memories will linger."

With a touch to his hat, he was gone. Sean watched him. Out on Duval, a rather staggered trail of tourists was wandering by.

Oblivious to them, Bartholomew met his Lucy, his lady in white, in the street. He took both her hands in his own and looked down into her eyes, laughing at something she said. The tourists continued to move on by . . . smiling, chatting to one another, unaware of the tenderness that went on beneath their noses. One young woman paused and looked in their direction, and then smiled. The young man at her side paused as well, asking her what she saw, what made her smile, so it appeared. She shrugged and replied, stood on her toes and briefly kissed his lips, and then kept moving.

Sean saw Liam beyond the door. Like the young woman, he paused, as if sensing something there. But he didn't see the ghostly duo. He shrugged and came on in. He took the seat Bartholomew had vacated.

Liam knew about Bartholomew. One night, they had tried to explain. Liam tried to believe them; he just couldn't. He didn't see Bartholomew, or hear his voice. He didn't show his skepticism, but Sean knew it was there. Liam seemed to think they were victims of a shared hysterical hallucination, but he didn't voice his thoughts or his doubts.

"How's the hiring going?" Liam asked

159

them both. Clarinda came by then, asking them what they'd like. Sean ordered a Guinness, wondering if the dark mellow tones would lighten his mood. Liam opted for one as well, musing that it sounded good when Sean ordered it.

"We met some folks who are possibilities. I'd take one Frazier Nivens over the six people we saw today, but he's working," Sean said.

"You're doing all right though, really," Liam argued. "You've got me and Katie — and Vanessa. David and you, and you'll be fine with a few more people. I'm not great, but I'm a solid backup guy on the boat and I can hold an extension and boom arm when you're recording on deck — good muscles for that. I did it enough for both of you when we were kids and recording backyard bands and some of our great oceanic discoveries like old work boots. And I can haul anything you need in the water."

"Hey, Liam, we're thrilled with you going. Hate the idea of you taking time off now, though," David said. "It's such a bad time."

"You know you are always wanted," Sean assured him. "And I've just had another applicant."

"Someone in the bar?" Liam asked.

Sean indicated Vanessa Loren's booth.

"Jay Allen — Vanessa's friend, and the director of the ill-fated film shoot."

"Ah," Liam said. "And what are you thinking?"

"I don't know," Sean said. "I'm irritated in a way — it's kind of like Vanessa was sent in as a vanguard, and now he's here."

"Send in beauty, and then bring the beast?" Liam asked dryly.

"She pretends to be — or is — unaware that he planned on coming," Sean said.

"And it may be the truth," David told him.

"I don't like the idea of being used," Sean said.

"Liam, want to be in charge of another background check?" David asked his cousin.

Liam grinned. "Way ahead of you guys. I checked out everyone on that film crew. I even did cursory checks into the one or two day jobbers they took on in different locations, and the other four cast members. Jay Allen appears to be clean as a whistle. Got through school with excellent marks — and perfect attendance, for whatever that is worth. He's never been arrested, pays his bills on time and works out of Palm Beach most of the time now — that's where he has his office. He directed segments of a historical series set up in Virginia, chronicling the men in the Civil War. And he won

an award for editing. He's got good reports from every employer. They say that he is imaginative, dedicated and responsible."

"And no corpses turned up anywhere else he worked, right?" Sean asked.

"No. The movie project collapsing caused him to fall into a steady decline, though, I'm afraid. He lost his personal savings, obviously — just like Vanessa," Liam said.

"But she's doing all right?" Sean asked.

"Yes — maybe because she wasn't the director of the project. Who knows why certain people wind up suffering and others don't?" Liam said.

"Okay, say we take on Jay Allen. It might not be a bad thing," David said. "If we've agreed we're following this trail, why not?"

"Give me a timetable, and I'll get it all legit through the Bahamian authorities," Liam said.

"I'll set up a schedule tomorrow," Sean said. "We'll take Jay Allen on with us, mainly because I'd like to interview him when we get to Haunt Island but also because I'd like to have a lot of footage edited on a daily basis, seeing how we're moving on. It will be great if it's not something we have to do ourselves, since it's so time-consuming. I'd like to start with Marty, dressed up in his pirate best, telling

the tale of the *Santa Geneva,* Mad Miller, Kitty Cutlass and poor Dona Isabella. That will explain Vanessa's script — and the quest we're heading out on, to find the truth. Marty is a great character. He can also tell some of the pirate lore and history in general without becoming dry — or downright boring."

"It sounds like a plan to me. Set it up," David said.

Sean saw Vanessa and Jay stand; they headed together over to the table where Liam, David and Sean were sitting together. "David, Liam, this is Jay Allen. He and Sean just met. He's applying for work on the project."

Her voice was clear, but there was no emotion in it. She was angry and covering it up.

Jay offered his hand. The introduction was acknowledged.

"I'm heading on out for the evening. I hope you'll consider me for your crew. I truly can never explain just how much this project means to me," Jay said.

"We may find nothing. We may just rehash the same old, same old," David said.

"I'd like to be aboard, just for my own peace of mind, retrace every step — and see if there wasn't something of importance that

we never gave to the police," Jay said.

His words sounded reasonable, and they would certainly appeal to David.

"Well, like I said, I'm out of here," Jay said. "I'm at Paradise Inn, and —" he paused to write a number on a cocktail napkin "— this is my cell number."

"Plan on meeting us here tomorrow at one o'clock," Sean said. "We're going to do an interview with a friend who's an expert in pirate lore and Key West history. I'm going to have you edit the footage and we'll see what we get."

Jay brightened and grabbed Sean's hand, pumping it. "Great. Great. You won't regret it, I swear. I can stand in as well, in almost any capacity. Whatever you need. Thank you. Thank you." He looked around the table, animated, humble and grateful. "Thank you, thank you all." He turned to Vanessa. "Nessa, want a walk back to your place?" he asked her.

She shook her head. "You're south, I'm north. I'm fine. But thanks. I'm going to hang around a few more minutes," she told him.

"Nothing is too far south or north around here, you know," Jay said.

"I'm fine, really. Thanks."

Jay nodded to her, and nodded toward the

table again. He backed away. "My equipment or —"

"Ours, thanks," Sean said.

Jay nearly knocked into a table as he left, still looking at them all the while, as if they would change their minds if he didn't. Finally, he was out the door.

David had already risen to drag a chair over to their table for Vanessa.

When she sat, David said, "Well, this is interesting."

She shook her head. "I had no idea he knew anything about this, or that he was anywhere nearby at the moment."

"Right," Sean murmured.

"So," Liam said quickly, "you two are old friends?"

She nodded. "Micanopy is not a big place," she said. "We went through twelve years of school together — I've known him since I was four or five. He is a good filmmaker, and he's serious when he says that he'll do anything, anything at all. That's why our initial project had seemed so exciting. It was mainly our money, and we were willing to do what it took to get the movie made. And it is true, he's excellent at editing. He has the instinct for it, which, in my mind, at least, is one of the hardest parts of any production. Slow, hard, tedious — and

amazingly important to a final project. Honestly, I admit, I was angry that he suddenly showed up and wanted me to . . . introduce him to you all, but . . . he is good."

She sounded so damned honest. Sean didn't know why he still felt a strange twist inside. He wanted to trust her. Maybe he wanted to trust her too much.

She hadn't left, Sean knew, because she had felt the need to talk to the three of them. Was she protesting too much?

"Would you like a drink?" David asked her.

She shook her head. "Thanks, no. I'm going to head out, too. I just wanted to . . . I wanted to talk to you for a few minutes, try to explain."

"It's fine. We'll see what he's worth on the project tomorrow," David said.

"Do you want me to come, too?" Vanessa asked.

"No, that's not necessary," Sean said quickly. "You proved your ability today." He stood. "I'll walk you back," he told her.

She smiled. "That's not necessary. I've walked Duval alone a . . . a zillion times. I'll be fine."

"I wasn't going to because it was necessary. I was going to walk you down because I wanted to," Sean said.

"All right, then, sure. I'll just say good-night to Katie."

She walked to the stand. A man of about sixty was onstage. He was doing a damned good Sinatra imitation with his version of "Fly Me to the Moon."

She kissed Katie on the cheek; Katie looked up and waved to Sean. She was smiling. He walked to the computer area himself and kissed his sister on the top of the head. "Tomorrow, kiddo," he told her. "Ready?" he asked Vanessa.

She nodded.

They walked through the high-top tables in the karaoke area and said good-night to David and Liam. "Can you grab the tab?" Sean asked David.

"Got it. I'm not too worried — I know the owner," David said.

Sean waved a hand and walked Vanessa out.

The south end of Duval was quiet as they walked along. Down by the inn where Vanessa was staying, there would still be activity at Sloppy Joe's, Captain Tony's, Rick's, Irish Kevin's and maybe a few more. It would probably be a mild crowd though. On Friday and Saturday nights, it was a wild crowd. When any of the festivals was going on, anything went.

"I really didn't know anything about Jay looking to join on," Vanessa said.

"Yes. That's what you've said. Several times."

"But you don't believe me," she said flatly, turning her blue eyes on him. The woman really looked like a damned angel. Her hair was like a halo, blond, and bleached lighter by the sun. Not really an angel. She wasn't delicate, he had learned that by watching her in action. She was really just about perfect. Too perfect. He felt jealous, though he barely knew her. He wanted to strangle Jay Allen because he seemed to be so close to her. He wanted to know if — in the years of their *friendship* — they had ever been intimate. Information he had no right to. He barely knew her.

He wanted her. She was gorgeous, she was sensual, she was lithe, athletic. He was imagining far too much about her.

That meant he had to stay the hell away.

"Look, it's not that I don't believe you, it just seems all too opportune," he said. "But my partner agrees that it's interesting, and we'll see how Jay does tomorrow."

"I should be there," she said.

He shook his head. "Let's see how he stands on his own, okay?"

"All right."

They were coming closer to the northern end of Duval, where revelers were still out. Too many people for a real conversation. All seemed to be having fun — a few were inebriated.

"Watch out," he murmured. A group, nicely dressed and not composed of teen-agers, seemed to be having a bit of a prob-lem navigating the streets. He thought a tall stout man was about to run into Vanessa. He took her hand and pulled her out of the way.

She laughed. "Thanks."

"Here we are," he said.

She nodded. "The stairway is up the back, through the garden gate." She rummaged in a pocket for her key.

"I'll walk you around," he said.

"All right, thanks."

They passed through a little walkway. It led to the back. There was nice foliage along the way, but the inn was basic, just some rooms over a storefront. No charming tables and chairs outside, no pool, nothing but ac-cess to the rooms.

Sean knew that it was filled with spring-breakers and bachelor and bachelorette par-ties.

"I'm surprised you chose this place," he told her. "It gets awfully loud."

"I wanted the loud," she said.

"Oh?"

"And the activity — cops around most of the time, lots of people at all hours."

"Are you afraid?" he asked her, frowning and setting his hands on her shoulders.

"No, I'm not really afraid. But I like people and noise."

He nodded. "All right. But you do know my sister well, so it seems. She owns the house we grew up in, though I'm living there now and Katie has moved in with David. Both places are huge. You're on the project now. You're welcome to come stay at either."

"Thank you." It seemed there was a slight tremor in her voice. "I thought I should stand on my own until we get going with this."

"Your choice," he told her.

"Thank you." She looked at him for a long moment. He found that he really was in love with her eyes. Other assets as well, but her eyes . . .

The moment grew awkward. He pulled his hands away and shoved them in his pockets. "All right. I'll talk to you tomorrow, then."

"Actually . . ." she began, and then hesitated.

"Actually, what?" he queried.

"Well, I am your assistant, and a writer. I have a list of interview questions. I wrote them up, assuming you'd be interviewing an expert on the pirate era, and with Pirates in Paradise gearing up, it seemed to make sense. And Marty is amazing. I mean, it's your project, you have your own questions, and once Marty gets going, but . . ."

"I'll take your questions," he told her.

"I'll be right back," she told him. She turned the key, entered the hallway and ran up the stairs. She returned within a minute flat, an envelope in her hands.

He grinned. "You are on the ball," he told her.

"I swear, we're good at what we do. I'm good at what I do. Honestly."

"I believe you." He cleared his throat. "I'm still waiting to hear back from Jaden and Ted."

"Of course. Um, well, see you then."

The door was still ajar. He opened it for her, and she entered the hallway. He watched as she ran up the stairs. The door closed behind her, and Sean pushed it so that it would close firmly and lock. He turned away and headed for his own place.

He barely knew her.

If he'd admitted it to himself, that didn't

171

matter. He wanted her to be everything that she seemed. He wanted to know more about her. Everything.

Two people had died. Maybe a third.

And the mystery was intriguing. The only way to really understand it, to try to figure out what *could* have happened, was to follow the same trail.

They would do so.

Two boats.

He'd make sure that Vanessa was on his.

And that Jay Allen wasn't.

That night, it was the heads.

Vanessa was sound asleep, and the world was pleasant and dark, and then the darkness began to lift. She was walking along the shore, and it was beautiful, pristine white sand, the ocean in all its glorious shades of aqua and blue, light and deep. She heard the sound of the waves and felt the sand and the pleasant wash of the waves over her toes.

And then she reached them. Georgia's head, with her arms in front of her, stuck out of the sand, and Travis's head, his arms in front, as well.

"Vanessa, see! I told you I wasn't lying!" Georgia said angrily.

"And I don't play bad practical jokes on

people," Travis said. "Why didn't you all look for me, why did you just assume I was being an ass?" Travis demanded.

"Oh!" Georgia said. Her arms moved in the sand with the exclamation, and she pointed down the shore. "They were having champagne. They were celebrating. And they all got mad at me! Then Carlos . . ."

"Then Carlos what?" Vanessa cried out.

"Carlos . . . Carlos . . ." Georgia said. "I don't know. Come help me. Oh, wait. I can't get out of here. I have no legs. I have no torso. Why didn't you believe me, Vanessa, why didn't you believe me?"

"Be careful. They'll get you, too," Travis warned. He blew a lock of his hair out of his eyes. "They'll get you, too."

"And you can be with us, just heads, talking heads, sitting in the sand," Georgia said.

"We have arms," Travis reminded her.

"Yes, we have arms," Georgia agreed, and they both waved their hands in the air.

"Be careful, Vanessa, be careful, you need the truth, or you can join us . . . heads and arms and hands, hands and heads . . . here, in the sand."

"In fact," Travis said, "you need to come closer and closer. . . ."

She awoke with a start. She was shaking,

173

clammy with sweat. She inhaled on a deep breath and wondered if the nightmares would ever stop.

It was day. She glanced at the cheap alarm on the bedside table. Almost 9:00 a.m. She would get up, walk down to the Internet café, read some e-mails and drink lots of coffee. A shower would be wonderful, so wonderful now.

She ran her hands over the bed as she pushed herself from it. She frowned as her hands went over something gritty.

Sand.

She jumped out of the bed. There were a million explanations for it. She'd spent the day diving. There was dirt and sand everywhere.

The pile on her bed was pristine and white.

With a shout of irritation, she whisked it off the bed and to the floor, and hurried into the bathroom.

There were tons of explanations. . . .

Yeah, right. The explanation, ridiculous and horrible, that came to her mind was simple and sad. Georgia and Travis were haunting her. They blamed her for not doing more. They . . .

They needed the truth, justice, closure.

Somehow, she had to give it them.

174

Before she became nothing more than a head and arms in the sand herself.

6

One o'clock rolled around and Sean, Jay and David went to film at Marty's place. Marty told them that they didn't need to pay him for an interview on his love of pirates and the sea, but they insisted and he shrugged it off. He seemed pleased enough to meet Jay, and he was more than helpful as they set up for the shoot in his eclectic house. When they were set, Sean did the questioning, admitting to himself that the questions Vanessa had written were excellently phrased and led Marty quickly in the right direction.

David filmed, Jay was recruited for lighting, and Marty was assured that it didn't matter if he made mistakes or wanted to go back, it was fine. The footage would be edited.

It went well. Marty was a natural showman, and if any man looked like an old pirate, it was Marty. He talked about the

early days of Key West — the very early days, when the Calusa Indians were around, through the Spanish period, the English period, the Spanish period, and then the days when Florida — and Key West — became a territory of the United States. He knew his piracy and could trace it through the sixteen, seventeen and eighteen hundreds — and he could even tell hair-raising tales of modern-day piracy.

Sean led him to talking about the attack on the *Santa Geneva,* Mad Miller and Kitty Cutlass.

"Ah, well, there's a story!" Marty said, his eyes blazing. "Mad Miller was born and bred on the island, just like his paramour, Kitty Cutlass. Kitty was a saloon girl, right on Duval Street, and let me tell you, they were rough places back then, shacks, they were. Some say she was a sweet girl gone bad, and some say she was born pure evil. Mad Miller was working a rich man's merchant vessel when he turned it around and made her a pirate ship. He managed to take a gunboat down and steal her cannons, then reworked the merchant ship into a fine pirate vessel with twenty guns. Now, it's said that the early days were good days — Mad Miller would blast a merchant ship or any enemy ship to smithereens, but he'd always

pick up the survivors, and he never kidnapped a soul for ransom, just left them all beached somewhere. Ah, but then the battle of the sexes began! There's always a woman, right? In any story. Except in this story, there were two. Key West had barely become an American territory, Admiral David Porter had just begun his campaign with his Mosquito Squadron to clear out the pirates, when Mad Miller and his crew came upon the *Santa Geneva*. Relations with Spain were doing fine — God knew, enough Spaniards were still living here. Now Dona Isabella was a great beauty of her day. Black eyes, black hair, fair skin, white bosom and wasp waist, and she lived a fine life of society right around the Southern tip of Duval — the house is long gone now, though a fine residence still stands where it once was. She was married to Don Diego de Hidalgo, a man highly respected in his native Spain, where he chose to reside most of the time. Dona Isabella had just left Key West to return to Spain — her husband wanted her back with him — when Mad Miller and his crew lit out after her ship, said to carry great riches upon it. But it seemed that Mad Miller suddenly changed his ways — he took a number of the surviving crew captive, but it's said that his men slashed to death those

178

in the water who were begging to be saved. From the point of the attack — near Pirate Cut and the Pirate Cut reef — Mad Miller sailed off to his safe harbor at Haunt Island, a nearly desolate islet off South Bimini. There it's said that Mad Miller and his crew massacred the survivors — even the beautiful Dona Isabella. Of course, much of what we suspect is theory, since no one knows what really happened. But there were rumors among other men of unsavory repute that Mad Miller had gone insane with desire for Dona Isabella and that Kitty Cutlass, in a jealous rage, had murdered her. Mad Miller then left Haunt Island, ready to attack more ships, but it wasn't to be. He met his demise not at the end of a hangman's noose but in the midst of the fury of the Atlantic. A hurricane came through, and Mad Miller's ship was sunk with all aboard, and all his treasure. This is known because another ship caught in the weather made it back. The hazardous conditions prevented any type of rescue operation, and frankly, since the ship that reported her foundering was a part of the Mosquito Squadron, it's likely that the men watched her go down with laughter on their lips — when they weren't fighting to stay afloat themselves!"

Marty stopped speaking and looked at

Sean and then David and then Sean again.

"Wonderful. You were great, Marty."

"Yeah? Really?" Marty asked.

"Wonderful!" Jay said. He looked really pleased. "Marty, you're so damned good, it's going to be easy for me to appear to be the world's most talented editor. When I'm done, you'll see what I can do. You're going to love the final footage."

"I know it's going to be good," David said.

"One more thing, Marty. Will you do one of your sea shanties for us?"

"A privilege, boys, a privilege!" Marty said. He went for his old guitar in the corner. "Should have a squeeze box, really, but this will do."

"Give us a chance to move the lights and the camera around a bit," Sean said. Marty nodded happily and practiced strumming his string and tuning the instrument.

"Ready," Sean said. "And we can film several takes, so you're under no pressure."

Marty grinned, strummed and sang.

"Oh, the sea, she is my lady,
E'er my lady true,
For the lady t'was my lady
Back upon the shore"

Marty strummed the last chord, set the

guitar down and grinned.

"Cut," Sean said. "Perfect!"

"Great," David agreed.

"Should we do another, for safety's sake?" Marty asked anxiously.

David glanced at Sean and shrugged with a grin.

"Sure, we've got the time, the people, and you — you're an amazing intro, Marty," Sean said.

Marty was pleased. He blushed. He picked up his guitar again, explained that it was an old sea shanty his father had taught him, one that had come down from old pirating days.

The next take was even better. Marty was just warming up.

They spent a while longer there, letting Marty go over a few facts and figures from history and the area, and then they wrapped it up.

While they packed the equipment, Jay asked, "Can I get started immediately on the footage, show you just what you'll be getting?"

Sean hesitated, wondering what his problem was with Jay. Of course, he knew. Allen was close with Vanessa Loren. He was being unreasonable.

"Yes."

"I'll go back now —"

"Go to my place. I've got the equipment set up that you need," Sean said.

Jay nodded with pleasure. "You won't be disappointed."

"If that comes out well enough, you'll be wanting to take some shots at the setup for Pirates in Paradise, down by Fort Zachary Taylor," Marty said. "Costumes, knives, swords, reproductions of all kinds. Pirate food and grog. Hey, everybody wants to be a pirate. Everybody wants to be Johnny Depp in *Pirates of the Caribbean,* huh?"

They all agreed that Johnny Depp had done wonders for piracy, and then left the house at last. David went on to find Katie, and Sean took Jay Allen to his house, to the back, where he had his computer set up with all the software Jay might need.

And where he found Bartholomew, reading the screen — and pushing the keys.

"What the hell?" Jay murmured.

Sean reached over and pushed the escape key and then keyed in for his film system.

"You might have just said 'move,' " Bartholomew said. "Or, more politely, 'Bartholomew, old fellow, I need the computer now. Would you mind?' "

Sean didn't respond.

"You're good to go," he told Jay.

"You'll see, you'll see — and you'll want me more than you ever expected," Jay promised, sitting down to get started.

"Go for it," Sean told him.

"You're not going to watch over my shoulder, are you?" Jay asked.

Leave this guy alone in his house?

"Don't worry — I'll be here, looking over his shoulder!" Bartholomew assured him.

Sean lowered his head to hide a smile. It was perfect. He could leave and yet know every single thing that went on in his house while Jay was there.

"Actually, no. I need to see a few friends," Sean assured him.

"Okay, I'll lock up," Jay told him. "When I'm done. I'll leave it in a 'Marty' file for you to find when you get back."

"Great," Sean agreed. "All right, then. I'll call you if I don't see you."

He walked to the door. Bartholomew had taken another chair, at the table, his feet plunked upon it. He was watching Jay Allen with narrowed eyes.

When he headed for the door, Jay called him back. "You really don't know how much I appreciate this opportunity."

Sean nodded, and left.

With the door closed, he smiled. Bartholomew could be a true pest, an annoyance,

183

taunting him when a response would make Sean appear to be totally insane.

But the old pirate/privateer was actually a damned good guy.

Oddly enough, a damned good friend.

Vanessa didn't want to stay in her room at the inn, and she had been sincerely un-invited to be involved in the day's shoot with Marty. She had decided to go explore down by the grounds at Fort Zachary Taylor, wearing a bathing suit beneath a cover-up dress, and force herself to stay calm and away from anyone with the name Beckett or O'Hara.

The main events of Pirates in Paradise weren't taking place yet, but Vanessa learned from the first "pirate" she encountered that the booths would be starting to open the next day with eager, friendly vendors — all in pirate attire, of course — and that the first parties would take place that night. She was invited to come — he'd get her in free. She thanked him, said that she wasn't sure and explored a lot of the merchandise.

At one booth, she found a beautiful display of reproduction jewelry. As she looked through the pieces she was impressed. The booth carried pen-and-ink drawings of various ships, lists of their manifests, the pirate

"code of honor" and many more bills of lading and other pieces of the past, all historic copies.

She started when she looked up after studying one case to see that the picture above it was of Dona Isabella. Or at least it was a likeness similar to that which Marty had given her.

The girl attending the booth, a pretty young thing who looked to be no more than a teenager, came before her smiling. She was in a corset, skirt and big billowing blouse, with a tricorn hat perched atop her head.

"She startles everyone," the girl said. "Dona Isabella, I mean. What a gorgeous creature — to die so sadly. Do you know the story?"

"Yes, actually, I do," Vanessa told her.

"She's supposed to haunt a lot of places, you know. Pirate Cut for one — a few divers swear that they've seen her! And, let's see — she haunts the south end of Duval Street, where she supposedly lived. And Haunt Island, of course. I mean, what would Haunt Island be without a few haunts?"

Vanessa smiled. She didn't want to talk about Haunt Island.

"What's this?" she asked, pointing to the piece in the display case that had drawn her

attention. It was a jeweled pendant, a mermaid studded with various precious stones.

"Oh, this is a reproduction of one of Dona Isabella's necklaces. Beautiful, isn't it?" She giggled. "There was description of it in the ship's manifest. There were always three manifests, you know. One for the ship's owner, one on the ship and one left with the dockmaster's office from the original embarkation point of a ship's journey. This pendant was in the manifest — well, not *this* pendant, it's a reproduction, of course — and, as you can see, Dona Isabella is wearing it in this picture, which is another copy, of an oil painting that hangs in a museum in Spain."

"It's gorgeous. Truly, absolutely gorgeous," Vanessa said.

"And more reasonable than you would think. Okay, truthfully? It's done in ten carat — if I'd had my say, it would be fourteen carat at the very least. Eighteen for such a piece would be closer to the original. And the jewels — that really looks like a ruby, but it's a garnet. And that's not a sapphire, it's blue topaz, and the yellow stones are citrine."

"How much?" Vanessa asked.

The girl smiled and told her. The piece

was more than affordable. Vanessa bought it.

She looked at an exhibition that was going to be on food, and she glanced through the costume racks, remembering when the world had been bright, when she had done so with high excitement, thinking that she and Jay were about to produce their first full movie. That was then, this was now. She walked around and saw some excellent outfits — should Sean and David want them for anything — then moved on to the beach.

It was a decent day, even though they were into fall. The air temperature was still rising to eighty-five, and the water at the shore was only about ten degrees cooler. She'd grown up in the chilly freshwater springs of north Florida, so it was a lovely temperature to her.

She lay on the sand, slipped on her sunglasses and watched the waves.

She tried not to think about the fact that she was ready to kill Jay. She could remember the look in Sean O'Hara's eyes when he had met Jay, when Jay had said that he was applying for work. She looked like the agent sent in to scope it out.

What was, was.

Except that she needed the truth more than Jay.

She needed to silence the nightmares.

To keep from thinking too much, she headed into the water. She swam awhile, working her muscles, then ambled back toward the shore, watching a father play with his children — a boy of about ten and a little girl, around five — and as she walked, not paying attention, she crashed into someone. A hard body. She stepped back awkwardly and quickly apologized. Hands shot out to steady her.

It was Sean.

"Hey," she said.

"Hey, yourself. You're hard to find," he told her.

"Well, I would have been easier, if I'd known you were looking for me."

He smiled. "I called."

"Oh — my phone is with my towel and bag, on the shore."

"Ah."

"So — you were looking for me. How'd the filming go?" She realized she was shivering. It was getting later than she realized; the sun was beginning to sink, and while the temperature was still far from cold, being wet made her shiver.

He arched a brow to her. "Not that badly, trust me, no need to shake."

She laughed. "Sorry, I'm suddenly freezing."

"Then let's get out and get you a towel."

"It's a good plan," she said.

She hurried ahead of him and found her towel. He had worn cutoff chinos into the water, and just the edges were wet. He reached for the polo shirt he had thrown on the sand near her things and skinned it over his head. She towel dried quickly and slid on her dress, and still she was shaking.

"Ah, you know what you need?" he asked, taking her discarded towel and wrapping it around her shoulders and rubbing them.

"Dry clothing?" she suggested.

"A hot toddy — and Irish whiskey. I know where they make the best."

"Would that be a place south on Duval known as O'Hara's? I hear that it's a real hangout for actual locals — conch-type people — and that the tourists crash in sometimes, wanting to hang with the locals," she said with a smile.

"That's the place," he agreed.

He was pleasant and easy, charming, in fact. She wondered how she would have felt about him if they'd met on different footing. If she'd just come in with Katie somewhere and it had been, oh, Vanessa, you've met my brother, Sean, right? No, after all

189

these years, imagine. Well, anyway, then, Sean, this is Vanessa, Vanessa, Sean.

She had chosen their meeting. Katie had offered to introduce him. She hadn't wanted friendship to be a part of it. Maybe she had made a mistake. What did it matter? She was getting what she had set out for — another chance to discover what had happened. At the very least, a chance to feel that she had done everything in her power.

"So, seriously, how did it go?" she asked.

"Brilliantly. Better. I don't know if I would have thought of having an intro with Marty if I hadn't wanted to see what Jay could do. And Marty was wonderful. He's a natural before the camera, and he absolutely loves his history, so it was all great. Jay is editing now."

"He brought all his equipment?"

"No, he's at my house."

She was silently impressed — with Jay. She was surprised that Sean would trust a stranger with his work system, and she said so.

"You left him — at your house — alone."

"Yes."

"You're a trusting soul."

"Hardly."

"But?"

She started to sink in the sand while tak-

ing a step. He took her hand. The feel was a jolt. A nice one. She liked the scent of him, too. Ocean and . . . him. Clean and fresh.

She didn't want to feel so attracted.

She didn't want to break free from his hand.

She walked casually, thanking him.

"I looked around at costumes today. This is really one of the best places to purchase. A lot of the retailers have researched the period thoroughly. They have great poet's shirts, vests, jackets, hats, corsets, blouses, skirts — you name it. Oh! I bought a piece today. A replica of one worn by Dona Isabella," she said.

He nodded and continued walking.

The vendors had covered up their wares; some were still around, chatting, eating sandwiches and keeping a firm eye on their goods, while others were off, trusting in hired security.

"I drove down here. Let's get to my car," Sean said.

They hurried along, Sean still holding her hand. He unlocked the car and opened the passenger-side door for her.

It was a car she might have expected for him, and she liked it. A Jeep. New enough, but not brand-new, a car that could go just about anywhere. It fit Sean very well, down-

to-earth, utilitarian, and somehow, though anyone could buy the car, it seemed rugged and sensual and masculine.

She really had to stop her mind from wandering in that direction.

It was difficult. A St. Nicholas medallion hung from the rearview mirror, and she wasn't surprised to see that he honored the patron saint of the sea. An O'Hara's sticker was on the front windshield, low, on the passenger side. The rear of the Jeep was filled with a stack of neatly piled clothing, as if he had just been to the laundry, though she wasn't sure why he would go out since she was certain that the house — which had actually been bought by Katie — had a washer and dryer.

He saw her looking at the stack of clothing. He winced. "I suck at it so I take it to the Laundromat to get it done for me. I've had too many white and beige things wind up an ultrafeminine shade of pink."

Vanessa laughed. Good God, she found even that endearing.

"Let me see your piece," he told her.

She dug in her tote and took out the box that carried the mermaid pendant.

He took it and stared at it, and then at her.

"What?" she demanded. Something about

192

the way he looked at her made her shiver.

"I just saw this same piece," he told her.

"Oh? Did you go by the vendors?" she asked. Her voice seemed faint.

And hopeful.

He shook his head slowly. She thought she knew his answer before he spoke, and she was oddly afraid without knowing why.

"This is the piece you found at the shipwreck site the other day. Where the *Santa Geneva* went down. It's — it's the exact piece," he said at last.

They were at O'Hara's, where they had run into Katie and David. Sean had gotten Vanessa the promised Irish coffee. It was delicious. At O'Hara's, there were equal parts Irish whiskey and Drambuie in with the coffee, along with a generous dollop of real whipped cream. The night was pleasantly cool with a southwesterly breeze, making the hot drink perfect.

She was still in her bathing suit, and the damp and the salt and the sand were irritating, and she was certain that her hair looked like windblown spiderwebs. If they were all about to take part in filming on boats and at sea, she supposed, they should all get accustomed to one another in wet and scraggly mode.

"Well, if it's the original, eighteen or twenty-four karat, with rubies and sapphires, it's worth a mint," David said.

"I imagine," Sean agreed.

"What will you do with it?" Katie asked.

"Do with it?" Vanessa said blankly. "Well, I don't actually see it as mine. I was on a trial run for the film when I happened upon it. I don't know — it should be in a museum, I guess. It's confusing, though. It should really belong to Sean and David, I think. Isn't that the way it works when you're working for someone? Like Mel Fisher had all kinds of divers, but the finds were his — right?"

Sean laughed. "After he fought the state for a decade," he said. "But he won. Nowadays, in territorial waters, it's twenty-five percent to the state. The rest is yours. Jaden was beside herself with excitement when she called me. She says that it's stunning. I haven't had a chance to get over and see it in person yet. All I have is the picture she sent to my phone. She and Ted had a party tonight, so she locked it up tight. We'll go and see it in person in the morning."

"Wonderful," Vanessa said. She wasn't sure it was wonderful at all. She wished that she hadn't found it. She could only imagine the terror of the woman who had worn it.

By legend, Dona Isabella hadn't died on the ship — she had been murdered with the others on Haunt Island, probably by Kitty Cutlass. In the movie script, she'd written in a spectacular scene of the beauty floating in the water. It was unlikely that had been the case — Dona Isabella's bones were somewhere beneath the sands of Haunt Island.

Kitty Cutlass had most probably perished in the storm.

"Yes, that sounds fine," Vanessa said.

"Oh my God!" Katie said. "You don't sound excited. Vanessa, that's a real historical find. It's amazing. I've been on those reefs all my life. I found an old boot and a high school ring from Miami High, class of '75. Hey, this is . . . treasure!"

Vanessa smiled and nodded. "I've got to get to work," Katie said. She rolled her eyes.

"I'm going to go to Sean's and see what Jay has done with the footage we took this morning," David said. "Katie . . . do you mind? I'll be back before you close."

Katie laughed and touched David's face tenderly. "I worked here long before you came back, my love. But, hey, I do appreciate walking home together, so thanks."

She went off to introduce her show; a blonde girl was waiting impatiently to sing.

"So let's head down to my house," Sean said.

"Well, I'm off to shower and change," Vanessa said, slipping from her stool. She paused. "Thank you, Sean, the Irish coffee was delicious."

"Glad you enjoyed it," Sean said, standing, as well. "Don't you want to see the footage? I put some together from the dive, as well."

"Sure, but . . ." She grimaced, indicating what she was wearing. "I really need to shower and change."

"That's easy enough. We'll walk by your place, and I'll wait for you."

"No, no, that's all right. It will take me a few minutes."

"Not a problem," David assured her.

"Sure — we haven't looked in the T-shirt shop windows for a while," Sean said, but he was smiling. "Actually, Irish Kevin's has a great band. We can hang out and listen, and when you're ready, head to my place."

"You're forgetting something," she told him.

"What?"

"Your car."

"It's fine here. I'll get it in the morning. There won't be anyplace to park on lower Duval. I've left it before — it will be fine."

196

Duval was crazy at night, with many people dressed up. Open containers were legal in Key West, and many a pirate and his dame walked about with their grog in a leather-bound drinking vessel of some kind or another. Some looked great and truly played the part.

"Hey, we wouldn't be hard put to find extras, if we were filming a smashing pirate scene," Sean said dryly.

"It's happened every year for about a decade," Vanessa said. "No surprise there."

"One of the parties is happening," David said. "I think it's down on Mallory Square, but I'm not sure. It won't be in full swing for a while."

"And hopefully, we'll be out of here by then," Sean said, grinning.

"Hey, I think it's great. They do reenactments and all kinds of cool historical stuff. Kids can come to it, and face it, Key West isn't always kid-friendly," Vanessa said.

"Excuse me — I was a kid here, and I came out just fine," Sean said.

"I grew up here, too. So we stayed off Duval growing up," David said. "We had the water. Boats, the sea, diving. What more could you ask?"

They reached Vanessa's place. When Vanessa ran up to shower and change, Sean and

David walked across the street to Irish Kevin's. She would find them there when she was ready.

She showered and shampooed, and though she was in a hurry, she discovered that she was determined to be thorough. She shaved her legs, dried her hair with the blow-dryer and despite herself, opted for makeup. She chose a knit dress that was both casual and slinky, and though appalled at her choice, she went for heeled sandals.

Dressing up as if out on the hunt, she mocked herself.

It wasn't her — it wasn't the way she lived.

And yet, that night, it was.

Impatient at last, she gave her hair a last brush and hurried out. As she crossed the street, whistles followed her from the tiny bar next door. She blushed and was glad.

The two men were hanging at the entrance to Irish Kevin's — the music could be heard clearly from there. The band *was* good, playing something from Three Dog Night that she hadn't heard in years and years but sounded absolutely great.

"Shall we?" Sean said, seeing her.

David whistled. "What a transformation."

She laughed. "Thank you."

Sean cleared his throat. "Yes, you look great. But transformation? David, are you

implying that she doesn't look great wet, in sand, with ratty hair?"

"Not in the least. And I'd have never said *ratty* hair," David protested.

"Hmm. You're right. I do apologize!" Sean said.

She grinned. "Thank you both, I'm pretty sure. Should we go and see if Jay is still at your house?"

They agreed. She walked between the two of them as they traveled the short distance from Duval to the O'Hara house.

Vanessa remembered it well. She had stayed here with Katie many a time.

It hadn't changed much, though Katie had added a few little touches that made it her own. There were new seascapes on the walls, light, new upholstery on the furniture that still seemed to fit the Victorian period of the house, and there was a new entertainment center with a flat-screen TV in the parlor. Walking into the house was comfortable. She'd spent good times there.

"You know my house?" Sean asked her.

"I spent a lot of nights here," she said.

"Pity. And I never knew," Sean murmured.

"Hey! You're back!" Jay called from the rear of the house, once an open porch, then a screened porch, now a glassed-in family room.

They headed toward the sound of Jay's voice.

The rear of the house *had* changed. It was all Sean O'Hara's now, with several screens set up, a large computer, camera equipment here and there, microphones, booms and more. Jay was in a twirling office chair at the computer.

"Nessa, old gal, you've made it with the boys! I'm so glad. This is great stuff, great!" Jay said enthusiastically.

"He's shy, never toots his own horn," Vanessa said dryly.

"Let's see it," Sean said.

Jay hit a key that sent the film to the largest of the screens in the room. They moved around to perch on chairs to watch. As she took a seat on the divan by the back of the house, Vanessa felt a chill sweep through her and something almost like a gentle touch on her arm. She looked around, certain one of the men was near her. But Sean was perched on a stool and David had taken the wicker wingback chair to her far right. Neither was anywhere near her.

And Jay was at the computer chair still, arms crossed over his chest.

Vanessa had to admit that the footage was fantastic. Marty was an amazing subject and storyteller, and Jay had the editing just right.

It ran approximately three minutes, with an extra twenty seconds of the old pirate historian playing his sea shanty. In all, it was fabulous footage.

"Well?" Jay demanded.

"You're good," Sean said.

"Yes, very good," David agreed.

"Am I hired? Please?" Jay begged.

Sean was still staring at the screen, though it was dark. "Yes," he said. "You're hired."

Jay let out a yelp of joy. He sprang from the chair and came to Vanessa, pulling her from her seat, swirling her around the room. "Thank God, thank God!"

She didn't share his elation. She felt her cheeks redden, and she nodded.

Sean rose, ignoring the two of them. "This is what we got the other day," he told David. He hit a few keys. Sean narrated what had been shot, and she knew that, beyond a doubt, she would watch the documentary even if she had nothing to do with it. His voice was a captivating tenor with the right inflection at every moment. There was footage she hadn't even realized he had taken as she set her mask and slipped off the side of the boat. Her shots of the reef with the brilliant fish flashed by as he explained the wrecks and the delicacy of the reefs, along with the dangers they had, and still did, cre-

ate. There was footage of her with the grouper as he talked about the wonder of the reef today — and then went into the sinking of the *Santa Geneva* as she was beset by pirates. He talked about the legend, about the film crew, and how they had chosen, in presenting unsolved mysteries, to focus on the legend of the *Santa Geneva,* Mad Miller, Kitty Cutlass and the sad plight of Dona Isabella. That legend had given rise to many others.

"Wow. You did that just shooting with the two of you?" Jay said. "Hey, what am I talking about? I was doing a motion picture with a small crew that did extra duty as stunt doubles!"

"You're a walking wonder, Jay," Vanessa said, teasing him, and yet, she realized, her tone was dry. She was still angry with him. He shouldn't have just shown up. He should have called her.

But then again, she had barged in. No, she had set up an appointment. Jay had used her.

"I am a walking wonder, Nessa," Jay said, grinning. But then he sighed. "I just wish I knew what had happened."

"All right," Sean said. "Tomorrow, we'll get together and go through everything you did from the time you came to Key West to

start filming. Since this was planned as a documentary, there's an outline and a list of shoots, but no actual script. Things will change now, some, but I don't want to make the changes until you've given me your story from start to finish."

Jay nodded gravely. "All right."

"We might make another dive where the *Santa Geneva* went down, too," he said.

"Hey, you're the boss. Bosses," Jay said, looking from Sean to David.

"What now?" Vanessa asked.

Sean smiled. "Dinner. No one has had any."

"Oh, man, great idea. I'm starving," Jay said.

David rose and said, "How about Turtle Kraals? Tourists are out, but it's a guaranteed relaxed atmosphere and it's on the water."

"Sounds good to me," Sean agreed.

They walked the back streets down to Turtle Kraals and the docks. The air was pleasantly cool and the walking was beautiful. She was next to Sean, who was somewhat quiet, while Jay walked next to David, talking enough for everyone.

"Beginning to end," he said. "You know what I remember, clearer than anything? Just how annoyed I was with Georgia. If I'd

only known . . . if we'd only looked for Travis. But we weren't expecting anything. I'd been on Haunt Island dozens of times. Boaters come and go. And of course we did everything by the book, notifying the Bahamian authorities, even hiring Bahamian tour guides just to keep everything legit. And that on our budget. I still can't figure it, I just can't figure it. I didn't see any other boats during the day. I know that most of the authorities believe that Carlos Roca killed Travis earlier in the day, and killed Georgia when he pretended he was going to take her home. Why? I can't begin to fathom. And why stage the bodies in the way that he did? None of it makes any sense. You'd think there had been a ghost," he said with disgust.

Then, oddly, he jumped and spun around.

"What the hell was that?" Jay demanded.

"We're in front of you," Vanessa reminded him.

"Must have been the wind," Sean said, still walking and not looking back.

"That was one hell of a wind," Jay said.

"Oh, we get those now and again down here," David said.

They walked on and arrived at the restaurant. Sean knew the right people. He smiled and chatted with the hostess, and they

wound up with a perfect table, one that overlooked the water of the historic seaport. It was a pleasant place, named for something not so pleasant, really. It was where turtles had once been stored until it was time for them to be sent to whatever restaurant or manufacturer or distributor of turtle soup and turtle steak was ready for them. Nowadays, turtles were protected, and the wildest events here that included the reptiles were the turtle races held on certain days of the week.

They ordered, and Vanessa excused herself, saying she wanted to look at the moon over the water. She walked out and realized someone was behind her. She turned to see that Sean had followed her. "Beautiful night," he said. "Perfect weather. Calm seas and a full moon."

"Yes, perfect," she agreed.

There was a silence between them for a moment. It wasn't awkward, and yet Vanessa knew he was about to say something. And he did.

"You know, there's something underneath everything here. On the surface, what happened was a horrible, gruesome tragedy, a heinous crime. The kind that couldn't be repeated. But now we're about to go the same route. Have you ever wondered if the

person — or persons — responsible might find out what you're doing, be afraid that you know something and come after you?"

She inhaled deeply. "I did my best to convince you to make your film following our route. But it might have been the wrong thing. If you're afraid in any way —"

He shook his head impatiently, interrupting her. "I'm not afraid. We've been on a dangerous route before. I'll have myself, David, Liam and maybe a few other people I know well and trust with my life. I'm worried about you. All right, I don't think you ought to be in that room on Duval Street. Yes, it's Duval, yes, there are cops around. If you don't want to stay at my house — or Katie's house — go and stay with Katie and David at David's house."

"It just . . . it would be awkward, either way," she murmured.

"I can ask Jay to stay, as well," he said.

She spun around to look at him. "Hey, I can honestly be the perfect gentleman," he told her.

"Must you always be?" she asked him.

He arched a brow and smiled. She looked quickly away, wondering what she had been thinking to speak so rashly. She stared at the water. "Good God, I'll be on a boat again with Jay. I love him, he's a good

friend, but he drives me crazy when the contact is constant!"

As she stared into the water, images seemed to form within it. As she looked, it rippled.

Fish. Fish were always moving about.

But it wasn't a school of fish moving. Something seemed to be rising, coming to the surface. She wanted to grab Sean's hand and find out if he saw it, too, but she seemed to be frozen in place. She knew what it was.

The image of the figurehead. The figurehead that bore the facial features of Dona Isabella.

She turned away from the water. "All right," she said. "Thank you. I'll stay at your house. I appreciate the offer. I'll move in tonight, after dinner, if that's all right with you."

He seemed startled by her sudden change of mind. He looked at the water.

And saw nothing.

"Perfect," he said softly. "Shall we go in? Food is probably about ready."

She nodded, looking up at him with her wide, beautiful eyes. They caught the opalescence of the water and sky and seemed especially hypnotic. He cleared his throat. "I'm going to give Liam a call and see what

your other friends are up to now," he told her.

"What? What friends?"

"Your crew from your movie shoot."

Her brows shot up. "You're going to hire us all on?" she asked.

"Well, we're following the trail that you and Jay and your crew followed for the movie. I thought we should use everyone who was involved in the film shoot."

She blinked and nodded.

"Is there something wrong?"

She shook her head. "No, I think it's brilliant. But it's not as if we were all the best of friends. We worked well together but I had never met Bill Hinton or Jake Magnoli until the shoot. I've known Barry and Zoe through different projects during the years, but . . . I'm sure, though, that Jay would have information on how to reach them."

"Don't worry about it. Liam will find them."

"Okay," she said.

"Great. We'll get on it."

She still stared at him, wondering why she felt quite so paralyzed that night.

"Are you all right?" he asked her. "Seriously? Do you not want the others —"

"Oh, no! Of course I do," she said.

He smiled.

She gave herself a shake. Something didn't seem to be boding well for her, but she didn't understand her feelings of dread. She tried to shake them off.

"Food!" she said. "I think I need food."

He slipped an arm around her shoulders and led her in.

And the feel of him was good.

7

The scream awakened Sean like a bolt out of the blue.

He had been sleeping soundly, glad to have Vanessa under his roof. He didn't know why he was suddenly worried about her sleeping in what should have been a fairly safe haven, but maybe it had been recent events here that had gotten him so worried. And maybe he was looking for something closer. Ass. Any fool in his right mind would want more. She reeked of beauty and sensuality.

Just having her in the house was some kind of a strange primitive pleasure.

But the scream ripped him from any thoughts except the possibility of danger, and he tore out of his own room and down the hall to where she slept in Katie's room.

"Vanessa!" He turned the light on, seeking whatever threat she faced.

But there was nothing there. She was up

on her knees, staring into the sudden light, blinking furiously. She was more than decently clad in a massive cotton T-shirt, and he didn't hesitate to rush to her, slide onto the bed and take her shoulders, shaking her slightly, bringing her focus to him.

"Vanessa, what? What happened?"

She didn't reply for a minute. Then her eyes focused on his and a flood of color filled her cheeks.

"Oh, God! I am so sorry. I never thought that I . . . that I screamed aloud," she said.

She was shaking. He pulled her toward him, leaning her against him where he sat on the bed. "It's all right. What? A nightmare?"

"It used to always be the same. Now it's changing. First, I just saw the heads in the sand. Then they began talking to me. Asking me how and why I let it happen. Travis wants to know why we didn't even look for him. Georgia wants to know why we didn't believe her when she screamed about monsters . . . and now . . ."

"Now?"

"Now, on top of Travis and Georgia, I keep dreaming about Dona Isabella. It makes me think that I am losing it and I certainly had no right coming here and getting you and David involved. Except that,

of course, I don't think these nightmares will ever stop if . . . if there can't be an answer somewhere out there."

"Hey!" He found himself smoothing back her hair. "It's all right. I understand. And David and I aren't coming into this blindly. We know what happened. We consider ourselves worthy of the task, honestly. We're good at what we do, and we know how to defend ourselves. Liam is a cop, and he's coming. We'll stack the decks with the right people, Vanessa."

She looked up at him. "How? You were saying that you weren't getting exactly what you wanted, so many of your friends were already involved in projects."

"It will happen. I'm going to try to recruit old Marty, and maybe even Jamie. It will be fine. Tomorrow, we'll do some more shooting on the reef with the four of us working and see how it falls out."

"Lew will come to the beach again. He was there, and he saw," she said.

"Lew . . . ?"

"Our Bahamian guide," she said.

"Of course," he said. "David has already sent ahead to the Bahamian government, getting film permits and letting them know our location plans. We'll soon need a list of the crew, though I believe he's submitted

certain names already. . . . Listen, about your screaming . . ."

"Yes?"

"Never be afraid if you scream in the night here. We've had our share of fear and dread, and there's nothing to be ashamed of when it regards fear," he said.

He wanted to melt into her being suddenly. Those eyes. Huge and blue and staring so trustingly into his.

Great. When holding her made every sexual instinct in him scream away in silent agony.

Yes, come to my house, it will be perfectly safe! he mocked himself.

She smiled.

"Do you want me to stay here? Until you fall asleep?" he asked her.

"Oh, I really couldn't ask you to do that," she said, offering a small laugh. "And I'm sorry. It is embarrassing. I am competent! And you'll never believe that if I keep screaming in the middle of the night."

"Apples and oranges," he assured her.

She smiled again. "Stay," she said.

"Your wish, my command," he told her. "Well, for tonight, anyway."

That brought a true smile to her lips. She crawled up to one side of the bed. "Really awkward, huh? I was about to plump the

pillow, asking you to come up. But that would be rather . . . oh, God, the whole situation is very . . ."

He laughed. "Premature. That's all. Quite frankly, every time I see you, I'm more under some kind of a spell. I'm fascinated with your knowledge and talents. And there's the simple fact that you love the water as much as I do. Then again, it could be how beautiful you are. God knows, you're probably vibrant and vital when you sleep. Stop me if there's someone in your life and I'm going on ridiculously," he said.

"There's no one in my life. Dating is really out of the question when you're the wrong kind of screamer," she said dryly.

He laughed and moved up to the pillow. He drew her head down on his chest. "Sleep, my dear, in comfort, I hope. You're safe from the evils of the world — and me — for the night."

"I think you might be too good to be true," she whispered.

"Oh, nothing is that good, and certainly not me," he assured her gruffly.

He smoothed her hair. It felt like silk.

He felt her breathing against him. Felt her warmth, her form, close to his.

A sense of longing filled him. Not just the burning need for sex she could create.

Longing. For something more.

Tonight, he would be content.

Thank God, she didn't scream again. Waking, Vanessa opened her eyes and realized that she was sprawled atop Sean. For a moment, she didn't dare move, and then she did so. He was awake, watching her. She flushed and winced.

"I'm so sorry. Did you sleep all right?" she asked him.

"Beautifully," he assured her.

"Thank you for staying with me."

"My pleasure."

"Sure."

"Well, it could have been greater pleasure," he teased.

She grew serious. "I didn't ask last night, what about you?" she asked him. "Is there any involvement in your life?"

He shook his head. "I haven't been home that long. Before, I moved too much. The Black Sea, the Great Barrier Reef. Loch Ness. The Great Lakes. The Bahamas."

"You've really been everywhere," she noted.

"Everywhere — and nowhere," he murmured. He rolled over and rose. "I'll put coffee on. Are you a breakfast person? I'm a decent cook — that's what happens when

you live on boats half the time. You get desperate and learn how to cook."

"But no laundry, eh?" she teased.

"Hey, I packed enough for what I needed. Laundry was done onshore. Eating is a necessity on a daily basis. So, you a breakfast person?"

"Sure, only I help cook," she said.

He nodded. "Actually, there's already coffee on. Programmed it last night. I'm going to jump in the shower. Help yourself whenever you're ready."

"Thanks."

He left the room. Vanessa walked into her own bathroom and met her reflection in the mirror. She was still flushed. She washed her face, brushed her teeth and thought about the shower.

Then she thought about the night.

She thought about his words, and about the way he had behaved.

She winced, hesitated, caught her breath.

He was everything she wanted, as well. Yes, he was gorgeous, tall, bronzed, well muscled, with his striking, rugged and intriguing face. Classical features. Golden eyes. But it wasn't just the tempting pull of his equally sculpted build.

It was the sea. The things he loved. The way he behaved. Even his bark when he was

angry. Even the way he looked at her when he was wary, skeptical. It was in his movement, in his words.

She didn't step into her own shower. She walked down the hall, knowing which room was his from days gone by. She listened and heard the sound of the water flowing in his shower.

"Sean?" She tentatively pushed open the door to his room and walked through it. The bathroom door was ajar and the water was flowing.

She stepped closer. "Sean?"

The shower curtain jerked open and he looked out, alert and anxious.

"What's wrong?"

"Nothing, nothing!" she declared quickly. So much for being a femme fatale with a casual and sensual style.

"I — oh, God, I'm not at all good at this. I thought that maybe . . . we could shower together. I mean the way that you were speaking last night, it didn't seem quite out of the question," she said.

His shoulders eased. A broad smile slowly creased his features and he looked down for a moment, and then back to her.

"The shower will work better if you come in naked," he told her.

She laughed, breathless and more than a

217

little nervous. She slipped from her panties, drew the huge T-shirt over her head and walked over to join him. Unabashedly, he looked her up and down.

"Well, since bathing suits leave little to the imagination, I can't say that I haven't noticed the infinitely fine attributes you possess. But reality is far superior to anything I imagined."

"Where on earth did you get your language skills?" she demanded.

He pulled her under the spray beneath him. The water was warm and delightful. His body was pure fire and magnificent against hers.

"You don't like my language skills?" he asked.

"No, no, they're fine! Lovely, really," she assured him.

"Maybe I should stop speaking," he said. He did so, pressing his lips down upon hers. The touch was electric, and his kiss was perfect, gentle, tasting at first, his mouth molding to hers. And then, as their bodies crushed closer together, it deepened to something forceful and coercive, volcanic in the rush it created within her. Or maybe it was the molten-steel feel of his body, the rise of his erection against her lower abdomen. All she knew was that what she had

218

started so tentatively was now urgent. While the warm water coursed around them, she felt a buildup of arousal within her that seemed insane and yet so wonderful she wanted to experience it forever.

Their hands moved upon one another. They found the soap, used it, lost it, crashed into one another finding it again. Suds covered them, making their flesh slick and sleek, and then the water rinsed off the suds, and they were together again, just holding each other for a moment beneath the spray. She laid her head against his neck and felt the throb of his pulse. She felt his hand slide down her hip, between her thighs. He lifted her, with the water still sending out spray and steam; he held her high, then brought her down, guiding her down on him. She wound her arms around his neck and her legs around his waist, and he balanced against the fiberglass of the shower as he eased completely into her, his eyes on hers. Then he began to move.

She didn't know if it was him, if it was the simple fact that they were there, just as they began, with the pounding sound, water and steam, but nothing had ever seemed more erotic to her, and the way that he moved was an arousal unlike any other. She clung to him, arched and writhed to his lift and

fall, and gave herself over to the pure carnal rawness of the experience. Far too soon she realized that she was burning and frantic and climaxing. She felt a final great thrust from him, shuddered, and eased slowly down on him, but he held her against the fiberglass until the sound of the water was just that again and the spray and the mist kept them warm, even as they cooled.

His lips found hers again, wet, hard, wonderful. He kissed her deeply, her wet hair entangled in his fingers.

He groped for the faucet at last, stopping the spray. Still nearly on top of her, his lips just inches away, he said, "Try and get me out of bed at night, hmm?"

"I think that you're quite lovely in bed, actually," she said.

"I hope you'll think I'm even lovelier now."

She nodded.

"Towels," he said.

"Pardon?"

"I'll get towels."

"Oh, yes, that would be lovely, too."

He stepped from the shower and produced two towels, large towels, with sailing motifs. She wrapped hers around herself and stepped out into the bedroom. His private quarters were neat. He had books stacked on his bureau, most of them sea charts, or

books on great sailing ships, some on diving, and one or two fiction. His furniture was solid mahogany without Victorian carving, more in an old west Mission style. It was a personal place, too, though. Not just bare. There were pictures of dive trips and sailing and foreign shores. On the dresser, too, sat a family photo: Katie and Sean, their mother and father. It was a wonderful room. Probably because she had just decided sex with Sean was wonderful, everything in the world about him was wonderful, as well.

"How's the room?" he asked. "Am I passing muster?"

She laughed. "The room, let me see. Solid, manly furniture. Good photos. Good reading material. Sparse and neat — belongs to a man, most obviously, accustomed to tight spaces on a boat. It's really unbelievable that he still messes up his laundry, but hey, in the list of could-be faults, that is quite a small one."

"What about the bed?" he inquired.

"Oh, definitely macho. Studly, even. A lovely bed. Something I'd actually love to try out tonight."

"Why wait for tonight?" he asked her.

Why wait?

Words coming from his lips were as arous-

ing as the most provocative touch. . . .

And it would be rather senseless at this point to argue the feeling . . .

She turned into his arms. Towels were lost. What was lost from the steam and spray of the shower was found in slow discovery, touch after touch, complete intimacy. There was the wonder of finding every little scar and wound upon his body, learning where it had come from — a dive into shallow water when he had been a kid; a cut from a catfish, oh, so dumb and he knew it; the only fight he'd gotten into in junior high, and, of course, she should have seen the other guy. There was so much laughter, so much sensuality as she kissed each little wound, as he returned the questionnaire, as they lay entwined until the touches and kisses became breathless and ever more predetermined and purposely provocative, hot and wet and aimed at erogenous zones. They melded together again, holding still for that perfect moment as he thrust deeply into her, then letting basic instinct come into play, the renewed desperation for fulfillment. The sheets became entangled and damp, and still they lay locked together, ever moving, writhing, arching, until the sweet moment of climax burst upon them, and they fell into one another's arms, damp,

depleted, sated and smiling breathlessly. Vanessa listened to the thunder of his heart as it slowed and felt her own, and they seemed to meld, as well.

She rolled away from him and jumped to her feet, heading for the door.

"Hey!" he called.

"We have to start the day," she replied.

"So we do — but we could lie here a moment quietly, couldn't we?" he asked.

She caught the door frame and looked back at him. "Maybe you could," she said softly, and ran out, heading for the shower in Katie's room.

When the water came down on her this time, it came with the memory of joining him, and she burned beneath the water, both amazed and glad for what she had done, and yet horrified. She wasn't sure what had possessed her, but she was certain she had never done anything that had felt more perfect and right as it had progressed. It was new, it was magnificent, and all that she wanted to do was be with him, hear his voice and the laughter, and discover again and again how easy it was to lie with him, what an absolute wonder it was to get to know him.

It was crazy. She had just seduced the man who was more or less her employer, a good

friend's brother and someone with whom she was about to embark on a strange mission. Not good.

Oh, yes, good, very good, but . . .

He was showered again and dressed for the boat when she came down. Coffee had brewed and there was a cup waiting for her by where he sat at the counter, perusing the newspaper. He signaled to it as he saw her. "I just talked to David. He's gotten hold of Jay, and we're going to do some more footage at Pirate Cut. Are you a vegetarian?"

"What? Um, no."

"Good. Bacon is in the microwave and I'm about to put the eggs on. We have about half an hour, then we meet them down at the docks."

"Okay, sounds good," Vanessa said.

He stood and walked around to the oven, tested his fry pan and poured the egg mixture into it, then added chopped onions, peppers, mushrooms and tomato.

"So, you are a cook," she said.

He turned to her. "And you might pop that bread in the toaster, if you like."

"Aye, aye, captain."

"Ah, such a reply is necessary only on a boat!" he teased.

Vanessa popped the toast into the toaster. As she did so, she had the strange sensation

that something cold passed behind her.

And Sean was looking in that direction, frowning.

"Is there a draft in the house?" she asked.

He shrugged. "A ghost — so I've been told."

Vanessa smiled. "Really?"

"It's actually a very old place, you know. But I think there was a structure here before, long, long ago, when the pirates were at their heyday. Real butter? Or the fake spray stuff?"

"What?"

"Which do you prefer?"

"Real butter."

"In the refrigerator. I heard it's not really that bad for you unless you consume the whole stick."

"All things in moderation, so they say."

He added cheese to the omelets while she got the butter and spread it on the toast. There was orange juice in the refrigerator, and she poured a glass for each of them. He directed her to the microwave as he flipped the omelet, slid it onto a plate and separated it to slide half onto a second plate. They set it all on the counter and took their seats again.

"Do you have a copy of your original script with you?" he asked her. "The script

you wrote for the movie."

"Sure. It's still in my computer," she told him.

"Can you give me a rundown?"

"We started from Key West, with three couples meeting up to take a trip out to Haunt Island. The usual college-age crew — Jay was hoping to reel in the seventeen-to twenty-one-year-old crowd. There was the good girl, the one you liked, the nerd . . . you know, the usual slasher cast. We had permits, of course, and filmed them getting together at the dock. They went diving at Pirate Cut, and they made fun of the story of Dona Isabella, and drew up silly pictures of Mad Miller and Kitty Cutlass. Then they did this ridiculous thing, like a game of Bloody Mary, but they called up Mad Miller. The first death occurs when one of the kids sees a woman floating in the water and goes to help her, but when he turns her over, her face is skeletal and eaten away. When he shrieks and tries to get away, the sea ghost of Mad Miller drags him down, cutting him up in the water. We're talking true teen-slasher flick," she said, grimacing apologetically.

"I understand someone trying to break in — and make a living," Sean said. "Many a director has cut his teeth on a slasher flick,

and some have made very respectable livings on that alone." He seemed thoughtful as he munched on his toast. "Go on."

"Well, the rest on board are terrified, of course, and they try to perform a ritual that will let the poor murdered Dona Isabella rest — and send Mad Miller and Kitty Cutlass to hell. One by one they end up dead as the boat limps toward the closest land — Haunt Island. Of course, the heroine, Georgia Dare, is something of a scholar and she discovers that Haunt Island was where everyone was massacred. In the script, Mad Miller and Kitty Cutlass come after them, but Georgia and her boyfriend — Travis, of course — find a way to raise the massacred dead, and they come to life and destroy Mad Miller and Kitty Cutlass, and then sink back into the sand. Simple, basic — some history, some ridiculous witchery, even if I did write it myself — good, gory teen fare."

"What schedule did you follow filming?" he asked.

"I have that in my notebook, too. Oddly enough, most of the scenes were in order, and that was because we were so cost-conscious that we didn't want to pay actors when we didn't need them," Vanessa explained. "Obviously, we filmed the scenes at

Pirate Cut first, and then we filmed at a few of the reefs up by Key Largo, and then made our way over to South Bimini and finally Haunt Island. When Carlos and Georgia left on the night she was killed, they were supposedly heading straight for Miami."

"And you don't believe that Carlos Roca was a brilliant psychopath, pretending to be a great guy and savoring all the possibilities when Georgia went nuts and wanted to go home?" Sean asked.

"No. If he were that good an actor, he would have been in front of the camera, would have been there for years, and garnered a few Oscars," Vanessa said with certainty. "But here's the thing, of course — he's gone. He can't defend himself. I don't know what I really even think that we can get out of this, but Carlos is another reason I'd so desperately love to find the truth. He might be a victim, too, and stand accused for this in the memory of his family and loved ones. It isn't right."

"We may do this and wind up with nothing more than an interesting documentary that merely gives rise to more questions," Sean warned.

"It's more than anyone else is doing right now," she said.

"True. But, objectively, I can't blame the Coast Guard, the Bahamian police, the FBI or any other law-enforcement agency. They've hit a brick wall. It's impossible to drain the ocean — by today's technology, at any rate. I'm sure that all over the Southeastern United States and at Caribbean ports, people are still on the lookout for the boat."

"Right — and how hard do you think they're looking now? People forget, and they move on. Other crimes happen. It's sad, but true," Vanessa said. "And by the way, you do make an excellent omelet."

He grinned. "Yep, I do dishes well, too. It's only the laundry thing that escaped me. But how about you clean up for me, I'll get David on the phone, gather some supplies and meet you down at the dock. We'll get your buddy Jay out there as well today, and I'll interview both of you while we're on the *Conch Fritter.*"

"I'm great at dishes," she assured him.

He set his in the sink. He carefully kept his distance from her. He wanted the day to be productive. At this moment, touching her would be counterproductive.

It was a beautiful day. Calm seas, bright sun, cool air.

Jay was called upon to act as cameraman, though David and Sean set up the shot. They spoke about beginning their documentary. They were both excellent speakers, and it was a really good and casual segment, explaining that they were going to follow the legend and speaking about the events that had occurred on the recent film shoot. They talked about the fact that Vanessa was Katie's friend and had come to them, and how they were they hoping to shed some light on the mystery.

Sean then repositioned himself and the camera so that he in turn could interview Jay about the film. Sean explained to David where he would want sea charts and other visual aids edited in, and they all seemed to be getting along quite well.

Katie had come on board with David, so there were five of them out. When they were ready to go into the water, Katie determined that she was just going to lie in the sun — she was tired. It was a busy time at O'Hara's, and she was trying to make sure that Clarinda would be ready to take over for her when they set out through the Bermuda Triangle for the Bahamas.

On film again, Sean explained that they were looking for good footage of the "bones," or the wreck field of the *Santa*

Geneva. Over the years, with storms and currents, wreckage could move for miles. The initial sinking or breakup of a ship could begin the process, and time could keep it going into eternity. The site was fairly shallow, and it was popular with divers; you would think it had been picked clean by salvage divers in the eighteenth century, and yet still more relics had been found in the present, including the mermaid pendant Vanessa had discovered.

Jay paired up with David, and Vanessa naturally paired up with Sean.

It was cool in the water, but Vanessa's skin was still enough for her. Sean and the other men also opted for skins.

Vanessa was thrilled that the sea was clear that day and the visibility was amazing. She hovered with Sean just below the surface, trying to capture the enormity of the spread of the wreck over the years, and the size and shape of the ship itself. Overlays could be edited in that would describe the *Santa Geneva* when she was afloat — and how she had been blasted by the pirate ship and came to sink and break up, forced onto the reef now known as Pirate Cut.

The ship had sunk north to south, and it was actually from a position of about five feet below the surface that Vanessa discov-

ered she was getting the best long shot of the bones of the ship. It was amazing to see the shape and tragically disjointed outline of what had once been a regal and majestic sailing ship. She moved slowly and smoothly over the bones of the wreckage, keeping a straight sweep of the site, and then panning in slowly to show what divers saw as they got closer. If it wasn't known that a great ship had gone down, a diver might have explored the wreckage for a long time without knowing what it was when he got too close.

She adjusted the zoom, and it was then that she saw something from the periphery of her eyes.

The figurehead.

A chilling sensation burned through her as cold and hot as dry ice.

She drew the camera away and looked down at the site. The *Santa Geneva* seemed settled, at peace, in her sunken graveyard.

How many had died in this area? The pirates had given the ship a vicious cannon salvo; they had boarded to kill and maim with cutlasses and pistols, and kidnapped Dona Isabella for the ransom she would bring. Those who had fought, who had perished in the water, were here somewhere, now long gone, flesh eaten, bones bleached and dis-

articulated, food for the creatures of the sea. Ghosts and memories were all that remained.

Vanessa looked through the lens again.

And there she was, hazy at first, seeming to look up from jagged coral and sand, the myriad of fish in their amazing colors — and the remains of the deck of the *Santa Geneva* far below.

Vanessa wanted to scream but knew she'd choke, spitting out her regulator. She wanted to give a swift kick with her flippers, burst up the few feet to the surface, leave the water and never come near the reef again.

But it went against everything she had been fighting to do!

Maybe she had let it all play on her mind too much; the nightmares were always tearing into her life, and she wasn't crazy at all, she was simply finding ways to seek and find anything that she could.

The image of the figurehead was probably some other minor clue that went into the fantastic computer of the human brain and manifested in an eerie manner.

She had to believe that, and she had to follow the figurehead, because, so far, it had led her to a mermaid pendant, and it might lead her to . . .

She couldn't let it scare her. She had to

believe in a logical explanation.

She kicked, and her body surged into the depths rather than surfacing.

She was about fifty yards west of where she had found the locket. She eased more air out of her BCV to settle on the bottom. It seemed that she was near the body, or actual remaining structure of the wreck. Jagged and beautiful coral rose to her right — the drop-off pitched to a hundred feet and then two hundred feet to her left.

She began to move the sand, not knowing what she was looking for. There wasn't a spark of light — the reflection of the sun on an object — or anything to suggest that she would make a find.

She felt Sean come down near her, concerned — she had made a swift descent, but they were still no more than fifty feet down.

He tapped her shoulder.

She looked at him and smiled, and returned to her task of shifting sand.

Her heart skipped a beat and thundered. After several minutes, she touched something. Something hard.

She turned. She could see Sean's eyes behind his mask. He was staring at her with great concern. She caught his hand and brought it down to the sand.

He felt what she felt. He still frowned, but he seemed incredulous, as well.

He began working in the sand. She carefully set the shoulder strap of the camera around her and began to dig, as well.

Whatever they had discovered, it was large. A fair amount of work brought them to realize that they had found the top of something. It was about five feet by three, and appeared to go deeply into the sand. With what they had — their hands — they weren't going to be able to dig it out.

Sean motioned to her that they needed to surface. She nodded.

He went up first on the dive ladder; she knew that he did so should she need help with the weight of her tank. She was good, though, and seldom needed help, but she allowed him to steady her as she climbed up. Katie came aft where they stood, helping each other remove their tanks and vests.

"I was about to come after you," she said sternly. "David and Jay have been up — they're in the cabin. David was convinced you knew your air consumption. . . . I guess you did."

"We found something," Vanessa told Katie breathlessly.

"What?" Katie asked.

"Ah — something?" Sean said, smiling.

"As in? A cannon? An anchor? A big fish?" Katie asked, exasperated.

"I don't know," Sean said. He went over to the ice chest for water, brought out two and tossed one to Vanessa. "We have to go back down. I have two blowers. I don't know if it will be enough, but it will definitely help. Whatever it is, it's buried deep. I honestly think it's a treasure chest. To the best of my knowledge, gold and jewels have been brought up many times, but treasure chests . . . I think only one or two have ever come up. This is buried. It's like it sank into the sand, and because of that, it's preserved. It's the right size, and it seems that it was wood, covered in leather. I believe the leather is disintegrating, but the chest is very solid. Lead-lined maybe. I've got to tell David." He paused, turned, took Vanessa's cheeks between his hands and kissed her quickly on the lips.

Katie stared with surprise.

Sean, oblivious, headed for the cabin.

Katie stared at Vanessa. "I guess you two are getting along all right."

Vanessa nodded. She felt something at her back and swung around, but no one was there. Katie, watching her, looked guilty suddenly.

"Is everything all right?" Katie asked.

"Yes, of course. This boat just gets . . . strange drafts, I guess," she said.

Katie gasped suddenly. "A treasure chest! Do you think he's right?"

Vanessa shook her head. "I don't know. It's something — it's hard."

"How did you find it?"

"Digging in the sand."

"How did you know where to dig in the sand?" Katie asked.

"I don't know. Something just led me there."

"Wow. Like . . . something led you to the mermaid pendant?"

Vanessa shrugged, wishing that Katie wasn't looking at her so probingly. "I don't know — I really don't."

Katie nodded, frowning. The three men appeared, coming from the cabin. "New tanks, all of us, and two blowers . . . if it's heavy, we're probably going to need some kind of winch and tackle," David said.

"I think we should go for it now," Sean said. "This could be the find of the century. All right, the *Atocha* was probably the find of the century. But . . . no. We go for it now. We can set up a winch. We're talking fifty feet down. I have enough rope to set up a winch. Katie may not be able to handle it alone. . . . Four of us will go down and set

it — and someone will come back."

"We'll take the blower first?" David asked.

Sean grinned. "Yeah — we'll make sure we do have something," he said. "But we do. I know we do. The pendant Vanessa found was real — it belonged to Dona Isabella. Jaden said it's a beautiful piece. I don't know exactly what we've got — or what Vanessa has. Rule of thumb is twenty-five percent to the state, but every find is subject to maritime law, and we are in Florida waters. Let's go down —" He paused. "Vanessa? You good for a second dive?"

"Of course."

Sean secured his portable blowers and checked that they were clean and ready for use, murmuring that it had been a long time since he'd had them out.

Within minutes, they were diving in, one by one, David and Sean carrying the hand-held blowers, which looked like vacuum cleaners. Sean had a keen sense of direction and led the way, never glancing at his compass. When they reached the object, David and Jay ran their hands over it.

Sean motioned Jay and Vanessa out of the way and he and David went to work on opposite sides of the object. Little by little, they began to create wedges.

Sand flew in a fury.

Then both turned the blowers off and waited.

Sand settled.

And there it was. It still needed a great deal of digging to come free, but it was evident that they had indeed made a discovery.

It was a chest. A pirate's chest.

A treasure chest.

8

David wound up working with Katie on deck. Vanessa helped, but Jay and Sean seemed to have a system for rigging the rope around the chest, and she hovered within easy call if they beckoned for her assistance. Eventually, the sand was dug out enough; rope was gotten around the chest, and Sean tugged on the rope, letting David know it was time to work the winch.

They guided the chest as it began a slow and careful ascent to the surface.

When they breached the water, there were several hectic moments as they moved as quickly as they could to board the boat, shed their gear and guide the heavy chest aboard, as well.

When they were finished, they all collapsed on the deck. Jay began to laugh; it was contagious. Then there were high fives all around, and David went down and broke out the beer.

"Not to ruin this party, but we still don't know what we have," Katie pointed out.

"True," Sean said. He ruffled his sister's hair. "It's treasure. Come on, be a ray of sunshine, huh?"

"I'm not so sure I like treasure," Katie said, frowning. "Well, it's Vanessa's treasure."

Vanessa shook her head. "It's a group treasure, whatever it is!" she said.

"You found it," Katie reminded her.

Sean had gone to the chest. The old, encrusted lock that held it closed was firmly in place. It seemed to be sealed as tightly as if the long-ago owners had welded it shut.

"We can break the lock, but I don't think that's going to help. The damned thing is heavy as hell — and it looks like they might have welded it or something. They wanted it to be sealed, watertight," he said.

"We can take it to Jaden and Ted. They'll know the best thing to do," David said.

"They'll know, yes," Katie said. "And we should be getting back in. We're going to lose the sun any minute. And I have to go to work."

Sean smiled. "Are you afraid of the dark, Katie? You never were. Work! You work all the time. You can be a little late. This is a treasure chest."

"Yes. I know it's a chest. I'm so excited. But we're not going to open it here," Katie said.

Vanessa realized that she, too, wanted to be back onshore. There was something about the trunk that suddenly made her feel uncomfortable. It was wet, dark with age, still covered in sand, but the lock, encrusted, seemed somehow ominous. She felt ridiculously superstitious. Someone had locked the trunk carefully. They had sealed it.

For a reason.

What the hell was in it?

Yes, it did look like it belonged in a Robert Louis Stevenson novel. Or in Mel Fisher's museum. It was dome-topped and handsome, even in its current state. Maybe it was just the way Katie was acting.

Vanessa wished that she had never found it.

The strangest thing was that she wasn't certain she felt the same way as Katie. Katie seemed scared. Vanessa wasn't certain that she was scared. Yes, yes, she was scared. The chest was . . .

An instrument . . . of something else?

Ridiculous. None of them even knew what was in it.

"We'll head in right now," Sean assured his sister. He seemed puzzled by her re-

action and paused to give her a hug. "It may be treasure," he said.

"And it may not," she told him. She waved a hand in the air. "Maybe it's documents. A captain's log, something like that."

"To me, that would be a greater treasure," Sean said.

"Pieces of paper?" Jay queried glumly.

Sean laughed. "Come on, you must know the value of that kind of paper."

"Yeah. Historic!" Jay said. "I say it's going to be pieces of eight! Gold and silver ingots. We know the *Santa Geneva* sank there. And she had come from Columbia to Cuba — and to Key West to bring Dona Isabella and others back to Spain. There had to have been great treasures on the ship!"

"I say that it's going to be gold and silver because the damned thing is heavy as hell," Sean said.

Katie moved back by Vanessa. She waved a hand in the air. "Boys, boys! Bring this boat back in — or I'll take the helm!"

Sean grinned at her and started the engines.

Vanessa glanced at her. "He doesn't want you driving his boat?"

"Oh, he'd let me, but I hit the dock once. It was rather an expensive error," Katie said. She tried to grin. The grin failed.

Sean, David and Jay remained excited. Sean was at the helm, but David and Jay hovered with him. They gestured as they spoke, all enthusiastic.

Vanessa jumped off the boat quickly to help with the ties when they arrived at the dock. By then, she didn't even want to be on the boat with the chest. It was ridiculous, but she felt uneasy. It was so stupid! She didn't usually let herself behave so ridiculously. Even when they had found the bodies of Travis and Georgia . . . or what had remained of them, she hadn't been uneasy. She had been horrified, and then angry. They had been so young. They had been so cruelly robbed of their lives. And someone was getting away with it.

She was tired. Certainly, that was it.

As if reading her mind, Sean looked over at her. "You all right?"

She nodded. "Hey — I'm going to run back to the inn and get the rest of my things."

"I'll meet you there."

"Are you two coming by tonight?" Katie asked. "I'm going to change for work."

"I'll be home soon," David promised, pausing to kiss her, smiling and smoothing her hair back.

"Boys, boys — take your time. Vanessa

and I will be fine," Katie assured him. She looked at Vanessa. "We can walk part of the way together."

"Perfect," Vanessa said.

She was on the dock; Sean was on the boat. He smiled at her. "I won't be all that long, really. I'll come to the inn and get you. We definitely need a big drink at ye olde family bar tonight!"

She was glad to see him so enthusiastic.

Jay was staring at her, too. He gave her a thumbs-up, glad because she was proving that the two of them were worth something.

"What do you think our problem is?" Vanessa asked Katie as they started toward Front Street.

"I don't know — weird, isn't it? I was as excited as anyone when we started — then it came aboard. Creepy. Hey, we are probably idiots. If that thing is filled with treasure, even after the state gets hold of it, we'll be in nice shape."

"Katie, all of us are working. None of us is desperate for a treasure. Okay, maybe Jay. He went through a serious funk after . . . after everything with the movie went so badly. He didn't work a lot. I think he's been working lately, but . . . not doing what he wants. Underwater weddings, scuba trips . . . just enough to keep going. He

thought we would have been in the big bucks once the movie went to a distributor. But then it was all so horrible . . ."

"Well, we'll leave it to the boys," Katie said, rolling her eyes. "And Jaden and Ted have worked with some of the most amazing finds. Treasure after treasure. They'll get it unsealed without compromising anything. Now, that is amazing! Sealed and preserved. We need to be happy."

"Sure," Vanessa said. She wrinkled her face in perplexity and stopped to stare at Katie. "It's absurd. I was excited. Now I'm not. What made the difference?"

"I don't know . . . I don't know. Maybe we should go back tomorrow to see Marty — he'll be getting his shows going and all by now. We'll get him to talk about Dona Isabella. Maybe that will help us somehow."

"I did a lot of research — I was nuts about the legend. It was so tragic. I'm not sure what else Marty can tell us," Vanessa said.

"Can't hurt, right?" Katie said.

"Can't hurt," Vanessa agreed.

She was surprised when Katie wrapped her arms around herself, shivering. "Sorry — goose bumps. I'm glad Sean is coming back for you."

"I'd be fine," Vanessa said. She was glad, too.

"Come into Katie-oke. That'll make you feel normal!" Katie assured her.

Vanessa nodded. She and Katie hugged quickly, then went their separate ways.

She was glad to head down Duval. The tourists and bright lights helped her shake her feelings of unease.

She was surprised when she hesitated as she neared her inn and decided she'd like a break instead of going right inside.

She walked onto the patio restaurant next to the shop and decided that she'd like one drink. There was a small empty table and she sat at it. Despite the fact that it was busy, a waitress came her way fairly quickly, and she opted for a whiskey with cola.

Her drink came and she sipped it, watching the activity. Yes, Pirates in Paradise was happening. A trio, dressed as pirates, was playing back at the small bandstand.

She smiled, closed her eyes for a moment and sipped her drink. She opened her eyes, feeling more relaxed and focused on taking in her environment.

The next table was filled with would-be pirates. It was fun to see the different ensembles. Women were fond of the corsets — which could be bought on Front Street or on the grounds of Fort Taylor. The skirts were in a multitude of colors and lengths.

Despite the fact that Key West pirates most often appeared to be very authentic, a few women were in short, sexy costumes from well-known short, sexy costume manufacturers.

Some wore them better than others.

Everyone seemed to have a good time, though.

As she casually surveyed a group at a nearby table, a woman turned toward her.

She was a wench.

A well-done wench.

She was a pretty woman with strawberry-blond hair that was wild and curled down her back. She wore no hat of any kind. Her blouse, beneath her corset, was billowing and a shade of off-white that looked to be unbleached cotton. Her skirt was long, but with ties that could hike it up so that it wouldn't constantly sweep the ground.

She looked a bit tired, a bit worn.

And she looked right at Vanessa.

Vanessa smiled in return.

The woman's mouth moved as she spoke. She was saying something to Vanessa. The beat to "Joy to the World" was pounding in the distance, and there was a great deal of conversation and laughter all around them.

And yet Vanessa thought that she heard her.

"It's not what it seems. Help me, I'll help you."

She was a stranger; it couldn't be what she was saying. Frowning, Vanessa rose, ready to walk over to the woman and introduce herself, prove that she was saying something else.

She stood. A heavyset man in a giant frock coat walked between the tables.

Vanessa knew that he didn't see her; politely, she gave way.

But as she headed for the other table, she stopped. The chair where the strawberry blonde had been sitting was empty.

Vanessa looked around; she had to be somewhere nearby.

She would just ask the people where their friend had gone. The chair she had vacated was quickly filled by the man in the giant frock coat. She approached the group, who looked at her with friendly smiles.

"Hello?" said one of the women, her smile open and generous.

"Hi, all. You look great," Vanessa told them.

"Thank you," the man in the giant frock coat said. He stood. "Care to join us? This is great for us — we're having the time of our lives. Jessy — that's my wife over there — teaches high school history, so for his-

tory buffs, this is just cool."

"Can we get you a drink?" another woman asked politely. "I'm Gena, Jessy's sister."

Introductions went around.

"No, thank you so much on the drink. Actually, I was looking for your friend. She was trying to tell me something, and I couldn't hear her," Vanessa explained.

"Our friend?" Jessy asked. "We're all here. Oh, I mean, we're meeting all kinds of new friends — this is like grown-up costume-party fun right along with a fabulous learning experience! Like minds and all that. But . . . our whole group is here."

"There was a woman . . . sitting here," Vanessa said. "A strawberry blonde."

They all stared at her.

"Oh!" Gena said suddenly. "I think I might know who you mean, but I'm afraid she isn't our friend."

"Who are you talking about?" her sister asked.

"Oh, she was around . . . I don't know who she is," Gena explained. "But she sure looked great! Kind of like a prostitute of old. I saw her, but she wasn't one of our friends."

"She was sitting right here," Vanessa said.

They all looked at her blankly, probably regretting that they had asked her over.

At least Gena had seen the woman, too.

She smiled and rose. "Ah, well, I must have been mistaken. Thank you — and have a wonderful time!"

They assured her that they would.

Vanessa turned around, returned quickly to her own table and set money on her check. She picked up her drink, drained it and left. She really needed to wash off the salt. She wanted to shower.

She wanted Sean to come back for her. She wanted to be with him.

"There's something wrong with it," Bartholomew said flatly, crossing his arms over his chest. "Can't you tell? Both Katie and Vanessa reacted to it — and you should trust Katie's very acute sixth sense!"

"Well, genius, you were around when it all happened. You tell me what's wrong with the trunk!" Sean said. He was aggravated. What was the matter with all of them? It was the find of a lifetime. He wanted to be excited about it. In fact, he realized, he'd been so damned excited, they hadn't filmed any of it, except when Vanessa had first found the damned thing.

"I was around at the time, yes. I didn't run in the same circles as Dona Isabella. I knew that she was a beauty — I saw her in

the streets. She was surrounded by servants. She had a grand house. Her husband never came from Spain, and she controlled all his properties here. Now, I did meet Mad Miller, and in my mind, he wasn't so mad. And Kitty Cutlass . . . well, if she went crazy and killed a bunch of people, it was only because she was madly in love with Mad Miller. But this trunk . . . you found it away from the ship?"

"Not far from the debris field. It wasn't on coral — or in the remains of the ship. But I don't know what you think that means. Debris travels. It can spread out for miles — you know that." Sean paused and looked toward the dock. David and Jay were there; they had called Jaden and Ted, and the couple was coming with their truck to bring the chest back to their place of business. They would study and analyze it and figure out how to open it with the most integrity toward the chest itself and whatever just might be inside. Ted also knew a great deal more about reporting finds to the state and the legal filing that needed to be done.

"I don't like it, I don't like it, I don't like it," Bartholomew said.

"What's not to like about the possibility of a cache of historical coins?" Sean asked.

Bartholomew shook his head. "You don't need to make a fortune. You're a lucky man. You do what you love for a living, and you make a good living at it."

"That from a pirate," Sean moaned.

"Privateer," Bartholomew said irritably.

"You're right — I don't need a hoard of riches. It's not that, Bartholomew. I believe in learning about the past — I believe in museums. I believe in finding out the truth about what happened, and every little clue gives us something more on that end. What's bothering you? What do you feel?"

"I'm a ghost. I don't feel. Well, not really," Bartholomew said.

"You're certainly ready at all times to give an opinion."

"Actually, I do have a . . . oh, all right, I have a feeling. But I don't really understand it. Is it Pandora's box?" Bartholomew asked softly. "I don't think so. But it is something . . . that may change things. Does that make any sense?"

"It may change the way we look at the past," Sean suggested.

Bartholomew shrugged. "I think your friend onshore is already counting his riches," he said.

Jay stood with David, still gesturing, excited.

As Sean watched, he saw Ted and Jaden arrive with their truck. A fair group of tourists and locals had formed in the parking lot beyond the restaurant and the docks, all looking anxiously to see what was going on.

"They're here!" Jay called, spinning around to make sure that Sean had heard him.

Sean nodded. David and Jay returned to the boat, hopping onto the deck. Now that it was out of the water, the chest was manageable, just awkward, especially with three of them. But Ted came hurrying from the passenger side of the truck, leaving Jaden to maneuver it as close to the end of the dock as she could.

"Cool! Cool, oh my God! Cool!" Ted announced, jumping on the deck of the *Conch Fritter.* "Every man to an edge. We'll get her to our place. I can't wait, I can't wait. I want to keep it in a mist until we see how it will do out of the water. This is amazing. Cool, cool, cool!"

They hunkered down, the four of them. Between them, the weight didn't seem that bad. Sean estimated that whatever was actually inside the chest weighed between a hundred and a hundred and twenty pounds.

They moved easily enough with it — moving quickly. They got it onto a tarp Ted had

stretched out over the bed of the truck.

"Sean, your find, you go with Ted," David said. "I'll hose down and secure the *Conch Fritter*. Then I'll head straight over."

"Sure. I'll help David," Jay said without enthusiasm.

David laughed. "No, go with Sean. Never mind — stay with me. We'll both get there faster."

"Yeah, let's do it!" Jay said.

Before Sean could crawl into the cab, Jay was racing back to the *Conch Fritter*.

Sean slid in next to Jaden, leaning forward between the driver and passenger seats. She gave him a kiss on the cheek and grinned. "You are on a roll!"

"Vanessa is on a roll. I have no idea how she found it," he said.

Ted climbed in and slammed the door. "Drive, woman, drive!" he said.

In a matter of minutes they were back at the shop. They didn't have to worry about weight or statistics; Ted and Jaden had carts and ramps, and they quickly had it down, still on a tarp, in one of their temperature-controlled rooms where the air was heavy with moisture.

Jaden and Ted looked over the trunk and discussed the best way to attack it. Obviously, they didn't have a key, and if they

did, the lock was probably too degraded to open with it. They did, however, have a friend who was a locksmith.

He was called.

They were going to have to wait.

If they were going to have to wait, Sean wanted to bring Vanessa back.

"All right, I'm going to call David," he told Ted. "I'll run and grab a quick shower, stop by for Vanessa, and we'll all meet back here in an hour. How's that?"

"An hour?" Ted said. He loved the old, treasure and a mystery.

"Ted, we have to wait for the locksmith," Jaden reminded him.

"We could just need a little oil," Ted said hopefully. "You know what works wonders? Olive oil, not that I was really thinking about olive oil on this. WD-40."

"We'll do it right. Run on, Sean. I'll chill some champagne!" Jaden said happily.

Vanessa told herself that she wasn't afraid of her own room. She was. She didn't want to be alone anymore. She just wanted to go back to Sean's. She'd get the rest of her things later.

She showered fast, scrubbed her face, towel dried her body and her hair, dressed in an A-line knit dress and sandals and ran

back down the stairs. The sun was setting, and it would be dark soon. She was glad she was on Duval Street — and that pirates and wenches and drunken frat boys were plying the sidewalk.

She headed into the little bar again but ordered a soda. She could still feel the warmth of the whiskey and didn't want to appear to be as inebriated as the frat boys. It was while she was there, idly sitting on one of the four stools in the place and watching the crowd, that she nearly choked and fell off.

She wasn't seeing any kind of an apparition.

No one dressed in pirate attire.

To her amazement, Zoe Cally and Barry Melkie, props, costumes, makeup and sound on their ill-fated film, stood in front of the Irish bar, drinking beer, deep in conversation.

She jumped up and ran across the street. "Hey!"

Zoe turned to look at her. She was a pretty girl, small and delicate, with large brown eyes and light hair. She smiled, and the smile was bright and welcoming.

"Vanessa!" Zoe cried with pleasure.

"Hey, you!" Barry said. He picked her up to give her a huge bear hug. He was a big

man, about six foot three and well muscled, in his midthirties.

Barry set her down, grinning as broadly as Zoe. "This is unbelievable! How cool. We were just talking about you and Jay, and thinking that we should call you."

Zoe laughed. "We were talking because we read an advertisement. There are these guys planning a documentary on weird stuff in Key West and environs," Zoe said.

"I know, I know!" Vanessa said. She started to speak again, but Zoe interrupted her enthusiastically.

"Imagine our surprise when *they* called us!" Zoe said.

"Hey, let me buy you a beer, Vanessa," Barry said. "We'll explain."

Vanessa explained how she and Jay were already working with Sean and David. "Sean just called you and my Lord, you got here quickly!" she said.

Zoe giggled. "We were close. We got here last night."

"And guess what? I mean, I think this was all really supposed to happen. I have already called the kids," Barry said proudly.

"The kids?" Vanessa said.

"The kids — our kids, our grad students. You know, both those bozos managed to graduate and get work, can you imagine?"

Barry asked.

Vanessa felt her heart sinking. "You mean Bill Hinton and Jake Magnoli?"

"Well, of course, what other kids did we work with?" Zoe asked, confused.

"Vanessa, come on, let me buy you a beer," Barry said.

"I — I can't right now. I'm waiting for Sean," Vanessa explained.

"And Jay?" Zoe asked, grinning.

"And Jay," she said.

Zoe smiled. "I am so glad. I'm so glad we were already heading here. This is going to be so important, so cathartic, for all of us. We were there! We saw Travis and Georgia. Vanessa, you of all people must understand how we feel!"

"Of course," Vanessa agreed softly.

"This is an amazing opportunity. We've all been ripped apart by nightmares. We've all been like zombies since it happened," Barry said.

"And you're happy, right?" Zoe asked. "You want to work with us again? We were all giving our hearts to that project of Jay's!"

"Of course I'd want to work with you again. I came at Sean O'Hara full blast, but then Jay showed up, and I had no idea Jay was coming, but it *looked* as if I had planned a way to wheedle everyone in," Vanessa said.

259

"I'm thrilled now that they're fascinated by the whole project and want all of us to be crew — and to be interviewed."

"Oh, so cool. So great," Zoe said.

"Do they know that you're here yet?" Vanessa asked.

"Don't think so," Barry said.

"We wanted to do some catching up and all. We've been on separate projects," Zoe said. "We've all been on separate projects, I guess."

"Yeah. Why don't you do some catching up with us?" Barry asked Vanessa.

"I can't right now. But Sean will be glad to hear that you're here in Key West and that you're gung-ho with their plan. Look, there's a bar called O'Hara's down on the other end of Duval. Show up down there around ten o'clock and I'll introduce you."

"All right, sounds great," Zoe said.

"Okay, later," Vanessa said.

Zoe slipped her arm through Barry's and they headed off, waving. Vanessa wandered back across the street to the patio restaurant.

She felt acutely uncomfortable, and she wasn't sure why. After all, Sean had said just last night that he'd ask Liam to get hold of the others.

She ordered another drink.

There were the key words. *Just last night.*

And they were already here.

Well, it made sense, really. She had desperately wanted to reach Sean and David when she had heard about their project and that they were hiring crew. So . . .

To her surprise, she had to call out to Sean to stop him from heading around her building to the stairs to the upper stories. He had showered and changed into jeans and a short-sleeved cotton shirt, so he had evidently been home.

"Hey!" he said, surprised to see her waiting for him at the bar.

"Did you open the trunk?" she asked anxiously.

"Not yet. Jaden and Ted wanted to call a locksmith, so I decided the group should get together for the grand opening. David and I are partners and Katie is his . . . well, those two will wind up married, and she's my sister. You discovered the chest. And Jay — well, as I said, *you* discovered the chest, and you brought Jay in."

"I didn't bring Jay in," Vanessa protested. She winced inwardly. She was aggravated. Sean kept speaking casually, but it was apparent that he *believed* that she had brought Jay in on the project. Jay was her friend, but she *hadn't* brought him in on the project. "I didn't mean that in a bad way," she said.

261

"I've known him forever. He is a good friend. But I didn't bring him in."

"Well, it would hardly seem fair to exclude one person who was on the *Conch Fritter* today, would it?" Sean asked her.

Vanessa smiled. The more she was with him, the more she *liked* him. Which was good, of course. The sexual attraction was so strong, but really liking someone was . . . important.

Did he really like her? Would he do so if he knew that she saw strange things in the water? He knew about the nightmares, of course.

But she had been through an enormous trauma. Any psychiatrist would say so.

"So let's head on over to the shop!" he said.

"All right," she said, but she pulled back a minute, her hand on his arm. "Wait. Zoe Cally and Barry are here."

His eyebrows shot up with surprise. "Wow. I just asked Liam to try to reach them last night."

"They were coming here to ask you for work," she explained.

"So where are they now?" he asked. His eyes were narrowed, and he was staring at her strangely. Maybe he was just staring at her, and she felt guilty. She shouldn't feel

262

guilty. She hadn't done anything.

"I told them to come to O'Hara's tonight," she said.

"All right. That was definitely fast. Let's go see about the trunk."

He slipped an arm around her shoulders. He frowned, and she turned, certain there was someone behind her.

But there was no one.

As they walked, the sun sank completely, and the majestic colors that had filled the western sky faded away. A misty gray followed the sunset, twilight, with darkness coming quickly.

She had never been afraid of the dark.

She was glad of Sean's arm around her shoulders.

And for how long would that be? she wondered. *He didn't seem to be the type of man who would want a woman long who was afraid of the dark, afraid of her own shadow, afraid of being alone in broad daylight.*

She was uncertain about her feelings regarding the trunk. She knew that Sean was excited, and she wanted to feel the same way. The odd thing was that she was now feeling more confused than ever. At first, she had felt that the object was . . .

Evil.

Now, she wasn't sure.

Object. Inorganic. Not good or evil!

They came around the corner and headed to the front door of the shop. Sean knocked, since it was closed for actual business, and Jaden came around to let them in. She didn't seem disturbed at all, but excited.

"They haven't opened the chest!" she said. "Ricky — he's our locksmith — he got the old lock open without destroying it. David and Ted are breaking the seal. Oh, lordy, lordy, this is exciting! I've never, never seen anything like it! Oh, and Ted called a maritime lawyer he knows, so the claim is being filed. It's amazing! Just the chest is amazing!"

Vanessa smiled. "Wonderful."

"Let's get in," Sean said. He looked at Vanessa. "Hey, I don't know your dousing secret, but it's unbelievable. The trunk, and its contents, are yours."

She shook her head. "Hey, I'm one of the crew. I'm grateful that we're doing this. I remain in your debt."

He touched her face. "No debt," he said softly. "No one forced my hand — I chose to set off in your direction, and I think it's going to be a great decision."

She nodded.

"Let's go!" Jaden urged.

They walked on through to the workroom.

Ricky was working extremely carefully with crowbars, small hammers and chisels.

Katie was standing back with Jay. Her arms were crossed over her chest. She tried to offer a cheerful smile as they arrived.

"Oh, while they're finishing up, Vanessa, you haven't even seen the piece you found the other day!" Jaden said.

She went over to a wall safe and spun the lock. She brought out a piece set in a bed of velvet and brought it to Vanessa to show it to her.

Vanessa smiled and looked.

It was the mermaid. The mermaid of which she had bought a copy the other day, the pendant that had hung around the neck of Dona Isabella.

This one was, however, far more ornate. Emeralds blazed from the eyes, rubies adorned her scales. The mermaid was large and heavy, and the gold in the workmanship was rich and deep.

"Here," Jaden said.

"Oh, I don't really want to touch it," Vanessa said. "Sticky fingers — body oils, whatever!" she explained quickly. "Funny thing — I purchased a copy from one of the pirate vendors the other day, and I saw the picture of Dona Isabella wearing the pendant."

"It really is a museum piece," Jaden said.

They were all startled by a sudden jerking sound — and a very strange sound, an expulsion of air as soft as a sigh.

Ricky moved back.

A mist of time escaped the trunk, was visible for a split second, and then evaporated into the air.

"Think there might have been a dangerous buildup of gas?" Ted asked. "Wow, sorry, a little late for me to think of that."

"Crank up the air purifiers," Sean suggested. "But I don't think anything lethal just escaped."

"We can lift the lid," David said.

"Go for it," Sean said.

"Vanessa?" David said, looking at her. He smiled. "Your discovery."

She shook her head. "You and Sean are leading the adventure."

Sean stepped forward and shrugged at David.

They each reached for a side of the lid. And lifted.

They were both dead silent, staring downward into the chest.

"Well, well, come on, what is it?" Ted demanded.

Still, neither man moved. Ted went rushing over and looked down, as well. "Holy

shit!" he exclaimed — his voice filled with horror, not wonder.

"What?" Katie asked weakly.

Jay walked up next. He clapped his hand over his mouth and turned away.

Vanessa knew from Jay's reaction that it was bad. She steeled herself and walked forward and looked down into a chest.

At first she didn't realize what she was seeing.

And then she did.

The chest contained the oddly mummi-fied and distorted remains of a human body. The clothing remained; the head was at an awkward angle. A hat still sat upon a skeletal head. The skin was dark and stretched over the frame, and the fabric of the clothing was stained, probably by the body fluids that had oozed from the corpse soon after death.

The eye sockets were empty.

And yet they seemed to stare and tear into Vanessa's heart.

All she could remember at that moment were Sean's earlier words.

The trunk, and its contents, are yours.

9

"It's Dona Isabella," Marty said knowingly.

"It can't be Dona Isabella. She wasn't killed until the pirates reached Haunt Island," David said. "According to legend, at any rate. Although, frankly, everything about what happened is legend — after the pirate ship attacked the *Santa Geneva*."

"We'll have to wait, and that's all there is to it — hope that the forensic anthropologist can help us," Sean said.

"It wasn't a treasure," Jay said mournfully.

"If the body sheds light on history, the find is a treasure," Sean said.

They were gathered at O'Hara's. The trunk and body were locked in the workroom at the shop, and they were all lined up at the bar.

Vanessa was next to Sean. He had worried about her at first — neither she nor Katie had seemed thrilled about the discovery from the start. But oddly enough, once

she had seen what was in the trunk, she had seemed more relaxed. Maybe she had somehow intuited that they weren't going to bring in a stash of silver and gold, and maybe she felt that, this way, eventually, Dona Isabella would get the funeral she deserved — belatedly — and that there would be some kind of finality for someone, at least.

She had been fine in the showroom, and fine on the walk here. She had applauded and laughed with the rest of them when they had come in to the sounds of a singer doing a version of a Denis Leary number that was tawdry to say the least, but very well done.

Now, at the bar, she was nervously drinking a Scottish single-malt whiskey.

"Maybe the legend has been all wrong — maybe Dona Isabella survived the massacre and was later murdered and tossed over the remains of the *Santa Geneva*," Jay suggested.

Sean looked at Vanessa. She didn't seem to be listening.

"Maybe it's not Dona Isabella, but Jim Morrison of the Doors," he said, touching Vanessa's hand.

She started, and looked at him. "Well, of course, that's a theory," she said.

He smiled. "A penny for your thoughts. A gold cob, rather," he said.

She arched a brow, opened her mouth and shut it. She tried to speak again. Before she could, Jay exclaimed, "Why, as I live and breathe. Hail, hail, the gang's all here!"

Sean spun around on his stool. Four people had just come into O'Hara's. There was a tiny, pretty woman; a tall, broad-shouldered and all-around big man; and two more men who appeared to be in their early twenties, average in height and size, both with sun-bleached brown hair.

"Your crew?" Sean asked Vanessa.

She nodded. "Zoe Cally, Barry Melkie, Bill Hinton and Jake Magnoli. Jake is taller and tends to slouch, and he's no relation to Bill, though they do look kind of like two peas in a pod, in a way. Barry is the really tall guy, and Zoe is the woman. Obviously."

"I didn't know that they were all here," he said.

"Neither did I. But Zoe and Barry told me earlier that they'd gotten hold of the kids."

He knew the names. He'd looked up what he could find on the film crew and the events that had occurred around the filming. She had mentioned the names as well, telling him what she had seen and experi-

enced the night of the murders.

"I had no idea that Bill and Jake were already here," Vanessa added. "They had heard about your documentary, too. Before you had Liam find them all and call them, they all planned to come and try to get work with you."

Sean was surprised to feel irritated.

This was so . . . pat.

He'd thought they'd have to hunt the crew down. He looked over at Vanessa, and he wondered if he hadn't fallen into what she wanted as easily as any idiot.

Jay was by David. He looked stunned, and he stared at Vanessa. "Hey, wait, I didn't even know those guys were in Key West," he protested.

"Vanessa did," he said.

There must have been something in his voice that accused her — or else she felt guilty about the situation.

Because she had planned it all this way from the beginning, and he had walked into it just the way she had intended all along?

It was probably a good thing that he'd never wanted to be an actor.

His face apparently gave away his thoughts. Vanessa was up in an instant, but she didn't turn on him first. She looked at Jay, and then at him.

"Damn you, Jay, don't you understand? They think it was set up that you showed up down here, too." She stood tall and angry, and tossed a length of her hair over her shoulder as she spoke. "What? Are you all suddenly the KGB or the CIA? Why does something have to be a setup? Why isn't it obvious to you all that something absolutely horrible happened? Two people were murdered. Maybe three. Two people we knew well — we'd been working with them for weeks. *We* found them, *we* saw them dead in the sand. Is it so odd that, hearing about your project, this group has all found its way to you?"

David was staring at Vanessa, surprised. He turned to Sean. "I thought you had Liam try to reach the rest of the crew."

"I did," he said.

Vanessa flushed. She winced. "I don't know how everyone managed to be here so quickly. I'm sorry. I . . . Oh, never mind. It is going to work out best this way."

By then, the group was coming their way, having seen Vanessa and Jay. Zoe Cally came forward with a huge, trusting smile.

As if she hadn't any inkling they might not be wanted.

"There are large tables out back in the patio area. We'll head out there," Sean said.

"We'll go talk where we can hear."

A would-be soprano was belting out a number from *Phantom* that was far out of her range and it seemed to him to be nothing more than a very loud screech at the moment.

He headed out back, waving to the others to follow him.

Clarinda, Jamie's favorite server and Katie's close friend, stopped him as he headed out. "Sean, should I set you all up out there? Do you want dinner and drinks, and should I be steering other people away?"

He paused, feeling a break in his temper at last. "Yeah, thanks, Clarinda, that would be great." Come to think of it, they hadn't eaten.

The contents of the chest had made them all forget the fact that they hadn't had dinner.

She smiled sympathetically and moved on; Clarinda would have known, from Katie, what they had discovered in their "treasure" find.

He walked on out to the patio. It was typical Key West, lots of shrubs and trees surrounding Cuban tile flooring and wooden tables, some round, some square, some oblong. Umbrellas over the tables shaded

them from heat during the day and were enough shelter against rain when it was light. He stood by the table, waiting.

The group began to trail out, Vanessa in the lead. Once they could hear, she began the introductions.

There was a large crowd outside by then, so it seemed. Vanessa, Jay and the film crew, himself, David, Jaden and Ted. Jaden and Ted were quiet, watching, as if they were suddenly part of an unexpected reality TV show.

Vanessa was quiet after the introductions, taking a seat at one of the long, oblong tables.

"You all know what we're planning on doing, right?" Sean asked.

"Yes!" Barry said. "It's great. We're so pleased. We were all going to ask you guys for work anyway, and then we talked to your cousin, Liam, and he explained that you wanted those of us who were involved to talk about what happened on camera. But we can help you enormously in other ways," he said.

"Great," Sean said. "I'm sure you all work well together. And that's great. But what we really want is to get each one's perspective of what went on at Haunt Island."

Zoe began speaking quickly. "We're so

grateful for this opportunity."

Clarinda came out in the midst of it all.

"Okay, guys, let me get your orders in. The place is getting busy," she said.

Beer seemed to be the main order for the night, and O'Hara's offered a vast variety. There was confusion as people took seats so that she could take food orders.

Sean wound up at the head of the table at one end, David at the other. They did resemble some kind of strange patriarchs in a ragtag family.

"We've already started filming," Jay told the newcomers excitedly. "And guess what? Vanessa found a corpse!"

"A corpse?" Zoe demanded, staring down the table at Vanessa.

"We thought we had a treasure chest. It was a corpse," Vanessa said.

"Well, it was a chest — it just wasn't filled with treasure," Jay said. "It held a corpse. But you know what? We think it might be Dona Isabella."

"We don't know anything yet," Jaden protested softly. She joined the discussion with enthusiasm. "We don't know anything, really, but the preservation is remarkable. Somehow, when the poor woman was murdered and stuffed in the chest, she became mummified. The chest was sealed, as if . . .

as if . . . oh, I don't know. Maybe someone felt remorse and wanted to see that she was preserved in her tomb in the sea. It's eerie. She's all there . . . clothes and all, and she's at an strange angle . . . neck broken, at least that's what it looks like."

"Dona Isabella? I thought she died during the massacre on Haunt Island, or if not, when the pirate ship went down southwest of the Bahamas," Zoe said.

"Everything about Mad Miller, Kitty Cutlass and Dona Isabella is pure speculation, really," Vanessa said. "There were one or two survivors who actually made it to shore when the *Santa Geneva* went down. They were the ones who told of the pirate attack. The *Santa Geneva* was accosted, there was some kind of communication between Mad Miller and her captain, and then the *Santa Geneva* was fired upon. Before she sank, the pirates boarded, cutting down the crew and kidnapping Dona Isabella. We know, too, that there was a massacre on Haunt Island, because the Bahamians found the remains. They knew that the pirate ship had come there, and that it had sailed. We know that it went down in a hurricane, because it was seen by an American ship when that ship barely survived the same storm. In fact, sailors swore that the

pirate ship went down when a massive burst of fire flared in the sky. If the Bermuda Triangle had been labeled the Bermuda Triangle back then, it might have taken the blame. They called it an act of God. At least they didn't think that aliens came down and swept up the pirate ship."

Zoe giggled. "Well, if aliens came down, they missed poor Dona Isabella's treasure-chest tomb. Hey, I know debris travels, but not that far. The *Santa Geneva* went down off Key West, and the pirate ship — however it went! — perished off of South Bimini and Haunt Island. So the story is all wrong somewhere along the line."

"If that *is* Dona Isabella," Vanessa said.

Jay laughed, pretended a shiver and let out an "Oooooh! Well, of course, it has to be Dona Isabella. And her evil is rising — that's why you two were afraid of the chest."

"I wasn't afraid of the chest," Vanessa said, her tone aggravated.

"Right," Jay said with a shrug.

Food came. The conversation changed to where everyone was staying on the island — Bill and Jake had taken rooms at the Banyan while Barry and Zoe were in the guesthouses on Duval, a couple blocks down from where Vanessa was staying.

Everyone talked about different projects.

Barry admitted that he had looked up information on David and Sean and been impressed with their separate bodies of work. The evening wore on, then Jaden and Ted called it a night, promising to call Sean and David the minute they heard from Tara Aislinn, the woman who was coming down from the University of Florida, the forensic anthropologist they had reached who was fascinated by the find and delighted to come down and examine the body in the chest.

Before the group broke up, Sean said, "David and I are going to do some planning tomorrow. We'll call you when we're set with the decision on when to leave."

Bill and Zoe decided to roam Duval and Barry went back to his room. Jay asked Vanessa if she wanted a walk down the street; he was tired and leaving. To Sean's surprise, she stood and agreed.

David and Sean stood, as well. Vanessa came around the table and gave David a kiss on the cheek. As she neared him, Sean saw that her eyes were sharp.

He stopped her and asked, "What's that look for?"

She shook her head and said softly, "You think that I set this up. You still say that I brought Jay in all the time, and I saw how suspicious you were earlier."

"Admit it, Vanessa. They were all here already."

"Admit it?" she inquired, her voice rising.

"Admit that . . . it all looks suspicious."

"Whatever it looks like, it isn't. And I guess I want more faith. You stared at me tonight as if you were suddenly certain that I'd planned the entire thing, our old crew taking over your project."

"That's not true," he said. "Yes, it's strange, but —"

"You're a liar."

"We can talk," he said.

She shook her head. "No. Not tonight. I need some time. We can talk tomorrow. Tonight, well, tonight I need to take a look at everything that's gone on."

He was hurt, angry — and baffled, still feeling himself to be the injured party. He was doing exactly what she wanted.

But he wasn't ready to throw it all over, and he wasn't thinking about the project.

Vanessa . . .

The ego in him wanted to shrug and tell her that it wouldn't be necessary to talk about anything intimate, if those were her feelings.

But he realized, too, that she must certainly have her own pride.

And he knew, too, that "talking tomorrow" was better than a real break. He'd give her

the space she needed.

He was startled as she walked on by him, waiting for Jay. She was truly upset.

Jay gave David a cheery good-night and shook Sean's hand. "What a day, eh?"

"Yeah, what a day."

Jay hesitated. "Honest to God, this wasn't any kind of a setup."

"I never said that it was," Sean told him.

Jay shrugged. "I saw the way that you looked at Vanessa."

Lord. Were his suspicions — his thoughts — really that apparent? Even Jay had read his expression.

"You're mistaken," he lied.

Jay shrugged.

Vanessa was waiting for Jay on the sidewalk. He joined her, and Sean watched as they started north on Duval together.

"Well, that was interesting," David commented.

"I'm sorry — doesn't it feel a bit weird to you? First Vanessa shows up, pitching her slant to our project, then Jay. Then we think that it might make for a really interesting piece and put out a call to find the rest of the crew, and almost *instantaneously* they all show up?"

"Yes and no," David said. He shrugged. "Maybe they did all hear about it and

280

contacted one another. I don't find it all that odd if they did. Trust me, I know. Events can change your life and haunt you day after day."

David Beckett had once stood accused of murder — if not by law, in the minds of many people who had heard what had happened.

Sean let out a long breath.

Back then, he and David had been friends. Close friends. And he hadn't known what to believe. All he had known was that he had wanted to get away from home, and for years and years he had traveled, staying mainly away from home. Knowing the truth about the past — even though he had not been directly involved, like David — *had* changed everything.

And it was true, too, that he had returned home in all haste when he had heard that David Beckett was here. And then he had been glad as hell, because he had found that David and his sister had become a duo.

"Honestly, I don't care one way or another," David said. "Here's what I care about — Liam doing background checks on them, finding out their work schedules — or with the young ones, their graduation status — whether they've really got the credentials they claim, all that. Parking

tickets are okay — I get enough of those myself. But nothing else."

Sean shook his head. "I don't know."

"Yes, you do. You know that you're more intrigued by this now than ever," David said. "And hell, Vanessa Loren is like a damned dousing rod. One day, a pendant. The next, a chest. With a body. Let's face it, we're in it now."

"Have you talked to Marty? And Jamie? Are they in?"

"They were in from the beginning, too. I say we get Liam on the background checks and plan to head out soon. I'll warn Katie."

"All right," Sean said.

She had just walked away.

Clarinda came out to finish clearing the table. "Hey, this is really getting wild, huh? All these people — and a body!" She shivered, placing empty glasses on her tray.

"It's a very old body, Clarinda," Sean said.

Katie came out the back door and strode toward them. Sean and David had taken their chairs again — at opposite ends of the long oblong table.

"Well. I guess you two scared everyone off," she said. She frowned and looked at Sean. "Where's Vanessa?"

"She went to her room."

Katie's brows shot up. "What did you do

282

to her?"

"Not a thing. She chose to go home," he said, irritated. He didn't feel like explaining himself to his sister. Somewhere in his mind, he recognized the double standard — he had felt like a pit bull when he had first found out about David and Katie.

"You must have done something," Katie persisted.

He stood. "Katie, you and Jamie set me up with her — under false pretenses."

"What?"

"You didn't mention that she was a friend of yours — you had Jamie call me in to talk to her, and you knew all along what she wanted," she said.

"Hey, hey, let's not have a sibling war here," David protested.

"No war," Sean said. "All I know is that Key West is suddenly hosting a whole crew of people — who, incidentally, were all on that island when the murders happened — and it all started with your friend, Miss Loren, and now she's mad at me for what I consider a perfectly reasonable question about how it all came to happen!"

"You probably accused her — basically — of being a liar," Katie said.

"I did not," he said.

"Then you implied that she was a liar."

"Who are you related to here?" Sean demanded.

"Never mind. I'm going to go and get some sleep. We'll talk in the morning. Oh — Katie, sign the bill to me, will you, please. And make sure that you —"

"Take care of Clarinda. Of course."

"Good night," he managed, waving to the two of them.

As he walked the back way to his house, he wondered if he had been unreasonable.

But there was something everyone did seem to be forgetting.

Those six people had been on Haunt Island when Georgia and Travis had been murdered, decapitated and chopped into pieces.

Filming a horror movie that had turned very real.

Jay was cheerful as they walked. "You seem to have some kind of a regular homing beacon for finding things on that wreck. Wonder who the body is. Think it could really be Dona Isabella?"

"I don't know. And I don't care right now. I'm exhausted." They had reached Vanessa's inn. She gave him a hug and a kiss on the cheek. "We'll talk tomorrow, all right?"

"Okay, kid. Sleep well." He started away

and turned back. "Hey, Nessa."

"Yeah?"

"Love you, kid. As a friend, you know."

She laughed. "Love you, too. Good night."

Upstairs, Vanessa was glad that her room was on Duval, and that she could hear the faint sounds of music, laughter and conversation. She turned on the lights, wondering if she had done the right thing or not. She cared about Sean, she was attracted to him in a way she might never have been to anyone before, but he had looked at her with suspicion when all four of the others had walked in.

And he had been the one to say that he wanted them all!

Even if they hadn't known each other long, they had known each other *well,* and it was disturbing to her to know someone that well and not be trusted by him.

They might have gotten together too heavily and too fast. They needed the night apart.

And she was right; she was not apologizing for what she didn't do.

That didn't change the fact that her room seemed impersonal and cold. Nor that she felt incredibly alone, which didn't usually happen to her. Normally, she liked her own company.

She couldn't change things, and she was exhausted. She changed into a giant T-shirt, scrubbed her face and teeth and headed to bed.

She turned off the lights and tried to listen to the revelry from Duval Street.

It wasn't enough.

She turned on MTV — music and videos. The two just might lull her to sleep.

She did fall asleep. And for a while, it was wonderful.

And then the dreams came again.

There was Georgia Dare's head and sand.

Georgia's lips were moving. She was talking.

"Oh, please! Listen. If you'll just pay attention! You know now that I wasn't being silly and hysterical and there were no jokes being played!"

One of Georgia's disarticulated arms moved in the sand; she waved her well-manicured fingers in the air.

"Listen . . . pay attention, oh, please, Vanessa, you can do it!"

"Please!" Travis begged, his mouth moving. He moaned as his head rolled in the sand.

"There's nothing I can do!" Vanessa protested.

She felt as if she were in a wind tunnel

then, being sucked away from them. She was out on the sea, and then she was in the water, and she had a camera in her hand.

The figurehead appeared before her. It seemed that it, too, had arms, and that the head was real and the entire thing was an animate object — a person.

She saw the face on it that she had always seen.

That of Dona Isabella.

The figurehead was smiling and beckoning to her.

She protested, speaking, or telling the figurehead how she felt in her mind, she wasn't even sure.

"No. I don't want to find more bodies."

"But you want the truth," the figurehead said to her.

"There should be justice."

Suddenly, the image of the face began to change. It morphed, and it seemed that its cheeks struggled to stay cheeks.

Brows became higher and more arched and changed again.

The nose and mouth went through transformations.

The figurehead had changed. It held a different face. But she knew that face, too.

She had seen it that afternoon. She had seen it on the woman who had tried to talk

to her. The pirate woman who had been sitting at the table on the patio.

The woman who had disappeared.

"Stop, please, stop, you're being led, you must take care, you don't understand the innocent!" the figurehead told her.

Then she thought she heard a terrible laughter.

"I'm trying to help you! I have helped you. Listen . . . listen . . . listen . . . your friends have pleaded with you, you must listen. Once you didn't pay heed."

The face on the figurehead began to morph again.

Then she saw . . .

The horrible, mummified, darkened, distorted and decaying face of the woman they had found in the sunken chest.

10

"Here's another one," David said. He tapped on his computer screen. "Another incident that might prove that what happened to the film crew wasn't so bizarre. Bring up the *Herald,* December twentieth, last year."

Sean typed in the key words and waited for Google to bring up the paper and the date, and glanced over at David. They were working together at the Beckett mansion, computers at opposite ends of the table, maps and charts spread out between them.

"Any particular page?"

"Front page. You can't miss it."

David's eyes quickly scanned the bold-type headline. "Modern-Day Pirates at Work? Islanders Claim Devil's Play."

"Ah, I see," Sean said. He read the article aloud.

"On December tenth, a charter boat,

the *Delphi,* captained by Tom Essling, an experienced seaman, USN, disappeared while on route to the Bahamas. Captain Essling left Fort Lauderdale, Florida, on December tenth with his first mate and wife of thirty years, Sharon Biddle Essling, and four passengers for a cruise down the Keys due south and southwest, with stops at Islamorada and Key West. As per plan, Captain Essling docked in Key West for a two-day stay, and began his journey east and across the Straits of Florida, an area that's also known as the New Bahama Channel, the body of water that connects the Gulf of Mexico to the Atlantic and continues eastward, beginning the Gulf Stream and separating Florida and the Keys from the Bahamas, the Great Bahama and Little Bahama banks. The length of the straits extends for more than three hundred miles and enters through the region known as the Bermuda Triangle. The width is 60 miles in areas and approximately 100 in others. The greatest depth of the channel has been sounded at 6,000 feet.

"On December 18, all contact with the charter boat was lost soon after the *Delphi* sailed due east of Miami, approach-

ing the southern Bahamas. Relatives were concerned because the captain excused himself in the middle of a phone call and never came back on. None aboard answered cell phones, and radio contact could not be made. American Coast Guard and Bahamian officials began a search that continued with daybreak. Many speculate that the Bermuda Triangle has taken more victims, while others rationalize that traffic has been heavy through the straits since the beginning of the passage of Spanish treasure fleets, has always been heavy, naturally accounting for more misfortune. Until early in the nineteenth century, the region was constantly plagued by pirates, a rising concern among seamen and carriers as piracy resurges in contemporary times, even within such heavily traveled waters."

Sean glanced at the sea chart spread out on the table between them. He stood, glancing at his computer, checking latitude and longitude on the charter ship's last known location.

"This disappearance — last contact with the boat was right about where the Mad Miller's pirate ship went down, right where

the pirates met their demise," Sean told David.

"Interesting. I thought I had another, but they caught the culprits. Idiots pirated another charter boat and threw the crew overboard. They wanted to hijack it to Cuba. They didn't realize it needed gas," David said, shaking his head.

"Maybe," Bartholomew mused, twirling a lock of ghostly hair — great hair at that — as he leaned against the table, "there is something to be said for the Bermuda Triangle. Maybe it emits . . . evil," he suggested. "Evil creates a vortex, and men become mad in that vortex, and begin to rip one another asunder."

"Bartholomew, Mad Miller's ship went down in a storm," Sean reminded him.

"I believe that something happens in that area," David said. "But I don't think it's evil oozing out of the earth. There is a scientific explanation."

Bartholomew studied his fingers and said dryly, "Yes, of course. And I'm here — through the effects of man's science. You see me, some people don't. Ah! There's a genetic trait that allows certain eyes to pick out roving ectoplasm in the air!"

Sean sat back in chair, nearly grinning. "Bartholomew, you may have something

there. It is possible that some people are born with something within their genes that we haven't discovered as yet."

Bartholomew threw his hands into the air. "Something that can be developed? Such as a talent? My friend, ye of little faith, who could not see or hear me for the longest time? Ah, trust is something that cannot be touched, either, and you needed proof rather than trust your own sister for a very long time. Everything is not science, indeed, it is not, my ever wary and doubting friend. Take faith — faith is belief in the unseen. If you have any kind of faith, you already believe in the unseen. We all believe in good — and trust me, I believe in the evil that lies in the hearts of mankind! Anyway, here's what throws me. I knew Kitty Cutlass, and I knew Mad Miller, and yes, Mad Miller turned to piracy, but the legend that has come down about him is pure bunk — which I've told you. If he slaughtered men in the water and murdered Dona Isabella in a rage, it would be a surprise to me. And Kitty! The most naive harlot I ever did come across!"

"Naive harlots can be jealous and vengeful," Sean commented.

"True, maybe," Bartholomew said.

"You saw the chest — tell me something,

Bartholomew. Was that Dona Isabella? You may not have known her as an acquaintance or even a friend, but you saw her around town," Sean said.

"We did not socialize," Bartholomew said. "I spent my time with the English and Americans, while Dona Isabella was the elite of the remaining Spanish society. But yes, I saw her."

"So?"

"So?" Bartholomew shuddered. "I didn't stare into the chest, my good fellow! That was a horrendous sight, what was once life . . . so heinously destroyed and mangled and . . . ghastly! And if I had stared and stared, the way that the decay had set in and the bones had mummified and the fabric of the clothing had clotted with blood and ooze . . . I'd not have recognized my own dear mother!"

"Have you heard any more from Jaden and Ted?" David asked Sean. "When is the forensic anthropologist due?"

"Later today, I believe," Sean said. "I talked to Ted earlier — a Dr. Tara Aislinn is due in with her colleague, Dr. Latham. I believe they're planning on bringing the body back to a lab in Gainesville. They have the facilities for all the testing they want to do. They're extremely excited, they can find

out about dental hygiene, diet, health, parasites — all manner of information."

"You saw today's paper?" he asked Sean.

Sean nodded.

Neither of them had accepted an interview, and to Sean's knowledge, neither had Katie, Jay or Vanessa. But it had been apparent yesterday that they had made a discovery, and there was an article stating that local divers had found a historical artifact and the object was under investigation now.

That afternoon, one of them would take an interview so that the concept that they were "treasure hunting" would not be taken out of context.

David's cell phone rang and he picked it up. He listened for a moment and looked at Sean, nodding.

He hung up.

"That was Liam. They checked out — the film crew, that is. The two grad students, Bill and Jake. And Barry Melkie has worked for several major motion-picture companies, and Zoe, though not as well-known, has certainly had an excellent employment record. There's not so much as a night in jail, a dismissed charge or a single mark."

"They're just seeking truth," Bartholomew said.

Sean started to speak, but he could have sworn that he heard Bartholomew mutter, "Dumb ass!" just beneath his breath.

"What was that?" he demanded.

"Pardon?" Bartholomew said innocently.

"You just called me a dumb ass!"

"Did I? I didn't mean to speak aloud, which, sadly, in most cases, with most people, I actually don't," Bartholomew said.

Sean rose and approached Bartholomew. "Is it possible you could go haunt someone else for a while?"

"Of course. There seems nothing I can do about the fact that you — behave like a dumb ass."

Sean let out a groan of aggravation. "Because?"

"That young woman did nothing to you."

"Wow, excuse me. Are you missing the fact that two people were heinously killed?"

Bartholomew looked away. "Yes, there is that. But you know that she had nothing to do with that."

"And how do I know that? Maybe she was the murderer, maybe Jay is a maniacal killer — maybe one of the others," Sean said.

"They were there," David agreed.

"But do you really believe that bringing them all in was some kind of a setup?" Bartholomew said. "If so, you are certainly

296

thinking and behaving as — a dumb ass."

"Bartholomew —" Sean began.

"Yes, yes, fine! Remember, my friends, you may need me. But for now, I'll go haunt someone else!" Bartholomew responded, aggravated. Shoulders high, posture proud, he strode through the room — and through the front door.

"They check out," David said to Sean, when Bartholomew was gone. "So what do you want to do?"

"Two boats," Sean said. "Which is what we've always planned, *Conch Fritter* and Jamie's *Claddagh.* Jamie can captain his own boat, and he's a hell of a dive master. Katie and you with Jamie, and I'll take Ted and Jaden, and we'll bring Marty along, as long as he's still interested, and, of course, Liam. Four of us on each boat. We'll split up the six from the original trip."

"You think that they were involved in a conspiracy — all of them — to kill their leading couple and leave them outrageously staged in the sand?"

"No. But two people died. Somebody killed them."

David shook his head. "There have been a lot of disappearances and bad things happening out in that area — we've just dug up reports of several that occurred in the last

couple of years. And it's not like there's one bad guy out there. There are probably a lot of less than honest people plying a pirating trade in the straits. Drug runners, people who smuggle cargo, taking them for whatever they might have, to get them into the United States. Whoever committed the crimes may be long gone, killing people in the streets of Venezuela for all we know."

"Those two weren't just murdered," Sean argued. "They were displayed. They were displayed in a way that played into the movie being made." He hesitated. "As if someone didn't want the movie made? God knows — but whatever did or didn't happen, I think we need to keep the original six split up."

"Agreed," David said. "So when do you want to head out?"

"Day after tomorrow. I want to revise the original shooting schedule and make sure that we have both boats stocked. And —" he hesitated and shrugged "— I want to spend some time at the shooting range with Liam — it's been a long time since I shot at something with anything other than a camera."

"You really think we'll come across trouble?" David asked.

"I really want to be prepared — hell, in

the last few years, from what we've seen, too many charters and pleasure boats have been lost. Even without what happened with the film crew, I think it might have been a nice wake-up call to be ready — for anything," Sean said.

His cell started ringing. He picked it up. Liam was on the line.

"Is David with you?" Liam asked.

"Yes."

"Anyone else?"

"No," Sean said.

"Put the phone on speaker, will you, please?"

He did so.

"I don't know if this means anything or not," Liam said. "But I have a report on my desk about another boat that has disappeared — with all four aboard. She's called the *Happy-Me*. She's a thirty-footer that can sleep six, top-of-the-line radio, sonar, all that. She was owned by a retired couple, Jenny and Mark Houghton, who were traveling with another couple, Dale and Gabby Johnson. They were headed out for a couple of weeks, stopping different places. They had notified the Bahamian authorities that they'd be visiting a few different ports in the Bahamas."

"How long have they been missing?" Sean asked.

"A couple of days," Liam told him.

"There's still the possibility that they're fine, that they had trouble, that they're on an island, waiting for a search party," David said.

"There's the possibility. But the couples' children have been calling every law-enforcement agency in the area. One of the daughters says she knows that her parents are dead. They *never* failed to check in," Liam told them.

"Are there search parties out there?" Sean asked.

"Of course," Liam said. "Coast Guard, Bahamians, volunteer rescue societies. But there's been no sight of the boat or any survivors. Of course, it might have no connection with Haunt Island as well, *but* Haunt Island was on their agenda."

"Thanks, Liam," Sean said. "We were just reading about another disappearance in the area. A boat called the *Delphi*."

"The *Delphi* went missing a year ago," Liam said. "So, two years ago, the film crew is attacked. Last year around the same time, a boat goes missing. And now another."

"There have been other boats that have vanished," David pointed out.

"Right. But these two went down some-where near Haunt Island," Sean said.

"If this one is down — we don't actually know that yet," Liam said.

Sean was thoughtful.

"So?" Liam asked.

Sean looked at David. "So I say that we really have to be prepared for anything and keep our eyes open at all times."

"Did you hear anything about the body in the chest yet?" Zoe asked Vanessa.

Vanessa shook her head. She and Zoe were down by Fort Zachary Taylor, cruising through the many booths the vendors had set up near the "pirate" campgrounds.

"Not yet. I believe that the person Jaden contacted is on the way down but is plan-ning on bringing the body back to a lab at the university," she said. They were at a booth that displayed books — some old rare, and very expensive, and some copies — sea charts and maps. One large map that included the Gulf of Mexico, Caribbean ports, Florida and the Bahamas was hung on a supporting beam of the booth. It was large and glass-encased, and Zoe paused, looking at it and shivering. "I think I'm crazy myself!" she said. She followed a path from Key West, up around the islands to

Miami, and then across to Bimini. "That's it — that's our route. Look at all the little red crosses on it! Those are all ships that have gone down or disappeared over the last decades — and centuries! I think I'm crazy, wanting to do this. No, I have to do this. I can't wait to actually sleep again."

Vanessa was silent. *Yes, she still had to do this, too. But now . . . she felt a strange numbness. She didn't date easily; she didn't fall for people . . . she wasn't good at accepting a casual drink. She had never gone out and slept with a man on a first, second, or even third date. But she had felt something about Sean, as if there were something real and deep that made intimacy heady and natural, and something that should have . . .*

Should have been allowed to mature into more. She felt ridiculously empty and alone, and something inside her ached, and she still felt that she had to hold the distance, because it was wrong not to be trusted, and worse to want someone so badly that she might not care. . . .

She realized she was staring blankly at the chart, lost in her thoughts, which had nothing to do with shipwrecks, when she heard her name called.

"Vanessa!"

She turned around to see that Katie was

302

hurrying toward her through the crowd.

Katie — dressed up in pirate attire that appeared authentic and still attractive. She wasn't dressed as a wench — no heaving bosom above a low-cut shirt and corset — but more like a man, in breeches, buckled boots, a poet's shirt and frock coat, and an over-the-shoulder holster that carried several pistols and ammunition, while the broad leather belt wrapped around her hips held a sailor's cutlass.

Vanessa laughed, seeing her. "Wow! You look great. What's up?"

"I need you. Hey, Zoe, how are you?" she asked, acknowledging Zoe.

"Fine, thanks. And you do look great. I costume people, and I couldn't have done better," Zoe said.

Katie rolled her eyes. "This is Pirates in Paradise. You have avid historians around here. Vanessa, Marty sent me out to ask you to come and be a part of the program."

"What?" Vanessa said. "Katie, I don't know anything about what they're doing, I'd be a bump on the log, and it would just be . . ."

"Oh, don't be silly, Vanessa!" Zoe said, enthused. "Come on, you've played a monster, a corpse and . . . and a body a zillion times. Why not find out about it?"

"Come on!" Katie drew her along. Vanessa did her best to lag. She liked being behind a camera. She loved being the eye that found the visions.

But Katie was determined. They came to Marty's booth, and he greeted her with a huge kiss and was pleased to meet Zoe. "It's the trial — just respond as you would if you'd been arrested," Marty said. "Ah, come now, I did tell you girls that I might need some help."

"Whose trial? If it's Anne Bonny and Mary Reid, I don't know enough of the history —"

Marty shook his head. "Look, everyone knows that a body was found, and everyone knows that Sean and David and crew are about to set off to explore the Mad Miller legend. It's a mock trial, and you're going to be Kitty Cutlass — and you just respond however you feel you should. It's based on the premise that Kitty Cutlass was saved."

"But Katie is a performer — she'd make a far better Kitty Cutlass," Vanessa argued.

"I'm the narrator," Katie said. "Oh, come on, Vanessa. It will be fun. It will take the . . . well, it will occupy your mind while we all . . . wait."

"But —" Vanessa began.

"Oh, come on, please!" Zoe said. "I'll help

get you all set. Marty, are there costumes somewhere?"

"Great — just go down the path there to my friend Sally, the one dressed up as Queen Isabella. She'll give you everything that you need."

Despite her protests, Vanessa soon found herself dressed up as Kitty Cutlass. She was not given a chaste costume like Katie's. She was in a low-cut blouse with flaring white sleeves, a workaday corset and a billowing skirt and petticoat. Zoe arranged her hair so it was halfway tied high on her head, but with curling blond tendrils around her face.

She did not get any kind of holster — she had been stripped of her weapons.

She got handcuffs.

A large area of park had been set up for readings and theatrics; there was a modular stage, simple, with a judge's bench and just a few stark wooden pews, and a box for the defendant. Vanessa was surprised to see Jamie O'Hara dressed up as the judge, sitting behind the bench. Marty himself was the prosecutor, Katie the narrator and, apparently, she didn't have a defense attorney.

She was led through the crowd by a couple of Marty's cronies. She was stunned to see that a full audience had gathered around and that, while they awaited the

beginning of the mock might-have-been trial, they were chatting, arguing amiably amongst themselves and giving their opinions. There were avid-eyed children lined up and seated Indian-style before the stage.

Katie introduced the situation in her little speech, and then explained what might have happened had Kitty Cutlass, a woman who was a known accomplice of Mad Miller and accused of the murder of Dona Isabella, been saved from the sinking of the pirate ship and brought in to face the music — the law!

Vanessa, rudely cast into the little box on the stage, almost jumped when Marty began his prosecutorial tirade of her horrible crimes.

Listening to him, she suddenly found herself ready to enter into the game. She didn't interrupt him; she waited until he was done and denied everything, assuring him that every shred of evidence he had against her was hearsay, circumstantial and in no way proof of any evil deed she might have performed. She had been guilty of loving Mad Miller, and nothing more. And they were wrong about Mad Miller, too. He had never been a murderer. Rather, he had been a man drawn to the life, eager for the rewards of the trade, but a man without a

shred of bloodlust in his body.

As she spoke, she looked out at the audience at various times, demanding that they give an opinion. It had all been made up, conjured out of thin air, because every single *fact* that they were bringing forward was nothing more than speculation.

Jamie O'Hara raged from behind the bench that he would give the prisoner a chance — he would listen to thoughts and recommendations of her peers since the prosecution had failed woefully in bringing forth the burden of proof.

As she looked out then, Vanessa froze.

Many men were dressed as pirates. Many women were wenches, ladies and female pirates, and even the children in the crowd were in various stages of fun costume dress.

But there was one man standing behind the proceedings. He had a rich, full black beard and a headful of curly, almost ink-black hair. He was a tall man, and sturdy and strong. He had been watching from behind a group to the far rear, close to a row of merchants, which ended at a large growth of pines that grew raggedly before giving way to the white sands of the beach.

Her jaw dropped.

She'd never seen him with long hair or a beard.

But she knew him.

It was Carlos Roca.

His eyes, she was certain, met hers across the distance.

She cried out, ready to run after him.

But, of course, everyone thought it was part of the theatrics. She nearly shouted his name, but refrained, and when she tried to burst out of the box, Jamie O'Hara thundered his gavel on the bench, and Marty's friends came rushing up to secure the prisoner in the docket.

She flushed, angry, feeling ridiculously desperate, and yet . . .

She didn't want to shout his name.

And . . .

He was gone. Where he had stood, there was another man. Another pirate, quite a dandy of a pirate, really. This one had really rich long hair, queued at his nape, and he wore a cocked and sweeping plumed hat. His frock coat was brocade, his stockings and breeches were amazingly authentic. His face was aristocratic and handsome, and he was frowning at her as if she had truly lost her mind.

"What say you?" Jamie O'Hara roared.

"Guilty! I believed her until she tried to run!" a boy cried from the front row.

"Guilty! And sentencing for pirates, be

they men or women, is that they be hanged from the neck until dead!" Jamie O'Hara roared with glee.

She felt blank, numb and disturbed. Had she been mistaken? Had she seen Carlos because . . .

Had she seen him because of this charade, because she wanted to see him, she had admired and cared about Carlos, and . . .

Her jaw fell open. The man who had taken his place seemed to be staring straight into her eyes, as well. He stiffened.

And seemed to disappear, as if he were fog.

Her knees felt like rubber. The world around her seemed to be a fog. She was going to pass out!

Good God! She didn't pass out. She wasn't the kind to be afraid of her own shadow, she had faced nightmares and the tricks the mind could play again and again. She wasn't weak, and she wasn't going to fall apart.

"Wait!" she suddenly shouted, remembering all that she could of pirate history.

To her surprise, everyone went still. The audience was dead silent.

"I cannot be hanged at this time. I plead my belly!" she announced.

"Brilliant!" someone in the crowd said.

And there was laughter, and then applause.

"Well, then, we shall see! Sentence to be carried out when the condemned is delivered of her child, and so be it!" Jamie announced. His gavel slammed down again, and the charade was over. Marty hugged her and told her she was great, and Katie and Jamie were grinning proudly at her. Audience members greeted them all, asking pirate questions, and she stood and listened and spoke, and wasn't sure what she said, or what she heard.

She was searching the audience.

She didn't see Carlos Roca.

Nor did she see the "pirate" who had seemed to disappear into thin air.

Eventually, she made it back to Queen Isabella's costume booth and the little makeshift tent where she had changed. Back in her clothing, she came out to find that Katie and Zoe were deep in conversation with Marty.

"I just talked to my brother. He and David spent a lot of the day working, looking up all kinds of things and planning what they want to do. It's a go with a schedule — the crews are all set. We'll be heading out on two boats, Sean's and my uncle Jamie's. Jamie is coming, of course, captaining his boat. Marty is coming, Liam and I, and

Sean and David and Ted and Jaden. And your six, Vanessa. You and Jay, Barry, Jake, Zoe and Bill. We'll set out the day after tomorrow."

"Oh, Vanessa!" Zoe said, throwing her arms around her. "This is wonderful. Maybe . . . maybe we'll figure things out!"

"Most likely we won't," Vanessa said. She didn't know why she was now being disparaging. This might well be their only hope, considering the fact that no one else was still actively investigating and they all knew that there were still dozens of unanswered mysteries. "I mean, we can only go through the motions, and try to remember every little thing, and see if there isn't something, some clue somewhere, that everyone has missed. And still, we may not find what we're looking for . . . or even the kind of peace and closure it seems that we're all hoping to find somehow."

"But we may!" Zoe argued. "I'm so excited. I'm going — I'm going to go and find Barry and let him know when we're leaving right away."

"Okay, great," Vanessa said. "And I guess you're in touch with Bill and Jake somehow? Better let them know, too."

"I'm on it!" Zoe said happily.

"Ah, for me?" Marty said, his eyes spar-

kling. "A chance of a lifetime! On the trail of one of the most infamous pirate tales ever!"

Vanessa tried to smile for him.

She had come here for this. And now . . . now she wasn't sure about anything.

Katie turned to Vanessa. "Sean wanted to speak to you. I told him you were changing and that I'd have you call him."

Vanessa nodded. Her heart seemed to take a little leap, and she wanted to kick herself. He probably wanted to give her a list of rules.

"Sure. But, Katie, I'm going to head back to my room for a bit first — too much costume and makeup for me. I need a shower. Oh — thank you," she said.

"Thank me?" Katie said, laughing. "See, you are a ham, and you didn't even know it. You were great."

Vanessa shook her head. "No. Thank you. For influencing David, for introducing me to Jamie — I'm not sure I broached it all right with your brother, but this . . . well, if anything can be discovered, I think that this is the crew to do it."

Katie grinned happily. "Sure. And hey, I'm on this adventure, too!"

Adventure . . .

Vanessa wasn't at all sure she saw it that way.

With a wave, she headed out of the park, leaving all the pirate booths behind her. As she watched, she searched the crowds.

Had she imagined them both?

Many a big tall man with dark hair *might* look like Carlos Roca.

And in the midst of would-be pirates, imagining another pirate . . .

Face it: she wasn't getting enough sleep.

It was a long walk back to her room, but Vanessa was almost glad of it. She needed to walk, to stride, to burn more energy.

She needed to call Sean.

She wasn't ready to do so.

Reaching Duval and starting toward the north end, she realized that she was looking in shops and bars. She couldn't shake the belief that she had seen Carlos Roca.

But if Carlos was alive, then . . .

Did that mean he had murdered the others?

As she neared her inn, she glanced across the street at a group of "pirates" gathered in front of the Irish bar across the street.

One relaxed against the door frame, watching the band, listening to the music. He had dark hair. He was the man she had thought had to be Carlos Roca.

He looked at her. He looked straight at her.

It was Carlos Roca. It had to be Carlos Roca. It was his face.

He turned and disappeared into the bar.

11

"Carlos, no! Wait, stay! It's me, Vanessa!" she cried. She raced across the street. It seemed that pirates had spread across the place, and she tried to excuse herself and wend her way through big frock coats, big hair and bigger hats. She made her way through the bar, searching faces to see Carlos's once again.

But she walked all way through to the emergency exit, and he wasn't there. She burst into the kitchen, only to be shown out. The place was ridiculously crowded, and she realized he might have walked out through the gift shop, slipped through another wall of pirates when she wasn't looking.

At last she gave up and walked her way through the pirates once again to the street.

She walked across, and straight into Sean.

He was standing in front of her inn, lean-ing against the wall, as if he had been there

for some time. He seemed curious that she had come from the Irish bar, and was probably impatient, as well.

"I've been calling you," he said.

"I'm sorry."

"I'd have thought that you might have been more interested in everything going on. Especially as far as getting ready to head out — with your friends all involved now."

"Look, Sean, they're my friends, but not my *friends.* Jay, yes, I've known forever. And I like the others, but I didn't bring them here."

"I'm not holding any of it against you," he said.

"How magnanimous," she murmured, looking away. She wanted to shout that she thought she had seen Carlos Roca. She might have been wrong. And if she'd seen Carlos, everyone would decide that, since he was alive, he was guilty. Until she saw him, really saw him, she couldn't say anything.

What if he was guilty? What if he had seen her, and knew that she had seen him? What if? He had seen her, he had looked straight at her before disappearing.

"Is that all?" she asked him. "It's been a long day, and I'd really like to take a shower, if you'll excuse me. I'll be ready to work

whenever you need anything, but for now . . ."

She started to walk by him. He blocked her path. She looked up and was surprised to see that his golden eyes were opened wide and that everything about him was just slightly awkward. "Vanessa . . . I'm not good at this. And I'd like you to understand how things looked. . . . I'm sorry."

She was startled by the apology. It was amazing, coming from him under the circumstances.

Maybe he just missed the sex. But then again, so did she.

And still . . .

"I don't lie, Sean," she said stiffly.

"I didn't accuse you of lying."

"Well, yes, actually you did."

"I . . . I'm sorry. Okay, I'm not good at this . . . I don't know what else to say," he told her. "I'll ask you again, see it from my side."

She nodded and smiled slowly. "Just say that you know that I don't lie, and that you'll believe in me in the future. That will work."

"I know that you don't lie. I'll believe you in the future," he said, his smile broad.

"Thank you," she said softly. They stood there for a moment, looking at one another,

317

not quite touching, and yet . . .

"I played a pirate about to be hanged today," she told him. "I really need a shower."

"Okay."

"You're not moving."

"You haven't invited me up."

"Come on up."

Maybe showers were destined to be something special between them. And maybe there was something that was just right, amazing, or the intangible bit of animal magnetism, chemistry, or whatever it was that made one person choose another over others. There was nothing awkward in her room, and there was no pretense between either of them. When she walked into the shower, she knew he was behind her. She turned into his arms, euphoric with the feeling that he was there, hard-bodied, rock-solid, vibrant, hot and real. Thoughts and fears left her mind for excruciating moments as she simply lost herself in the beauty and urgency of touch, running her hands down the wet sleekness of his flesh, his sex, along his spine and buttocks, and feeling the deep thrust and hot persistence of his kiss, his tongue and his hands upon her.

They made love with the rush of the water

and then, still enwrapped and absorbed in one another, they found towels and made their way to the bed. Once there, he started with a kiss again, hovering over her, golden eyes burning into hers, and then that kiss, his mouth on hers, and then moving to her throat, where he paused, feeling the thunder of her pulse, and moved on, sending a streak of lightning through her as he teased a breast and trailed his kisses onward again. His caresses were slow, a touch of agony in the midst of exhilaration and wonder. He touched and teased, drawing to a point of complete intimacy, and she twisted and writhed until her frantic energy and demand brought him back to her, and they locked together in a storm of frenetic energy that brought her to a point of climax after climax, shuddering in his arms.

He held her close then, murmuring, his kisses tender.

Eventually, their bodies cooled. Their hearts beat at normal rates, and the ragged sound of their breath was no longer a cacophony in the room.

He held her against him and then groaned softly. "Strange. I don't want to get up. I'm starving, and there are things to do, and I don't ever want to leave this bed."

She laughed. "Of course you do. Eventu-

ally, you'd get bored here."

"When the sun froze over," he told her.

She stroked his face. "That was good. That makes up for your rather stilted apology."

"Excuse me, that was real and heartfelt."

"We could order food to be brought here," she said.

He nodded and turned from her for a moment, staring at the ceiling. "We're supposed to go over to Ted and Jaden's workshop — the doctor of forensic anthropology arrived, and she's been studying the trunk as we found it. She'll give us what she can before she does all the tests on the body. Anything in the sea that long — even mummified, as the body appears — is very fragile."

"Of course," Vanessa said. She hesitated, wondering why she was so uneasy about the trunk.

Pandora's box? If so, it was already open.

And yet, it hadn't been something actually *evil* that she felt, just as if the chest was going to be a catalyst, and she wasn't sure if she liked what it might cause to come about.

"Do you not want to come over there with me?" Sean asked.

"No, no, of course I want to come," she said.

"Then I guess we have to get moving." He stood, his back to her. "You know, I think you should get the tail end of your things out of here for good."

She rose as well, coming around to look at him. "You want me to come over because I'll be safer? Or because you want me there?"

"I'd say both, and that's pretty obvious," he said. She smiled.

She was glad to be invited.

Ecstatic, actually!

And it was true that she didn't want to be here alone. She had horrendous nightmares, she saw figureheads in the water, and on top of that, she kept thinking that she saw Carlos Roca and an unknown pirate who looked at her — and then faded into the air.

Really. They were going to have to lock her up soon.

"It's late," he said huskily. "Let's grab pizza downstairs and then get over to Ted and Jaden's."

Dr. Tara Aislinn was in her midfifties, an energetic and enthusiastic woman who greeted Sean and Vanessa with real warmth. Her colleague, Ned Latham, was more subdued but apparently just as eager to be

there. They had studied the chest and the victim within but hadn't taken the body from the chest. They had come down in their van and, with permission, of course, would be moving the chest and the body to the lab in Gainesville.

Liam and David had come and gone, Sean discovered. They were late, of course, really late, but in his mind, that was fine. He hadn't been in a serious relationship in a long time; he didn't think he'd ever been in a relationship where he'd felt so lost and empty when it seemed that it had ended. David and Liam were capable, as were Jaden and Ted, and he knew that he'd never understand half of what the scientists could learn from the body, so everything had gone in the right direction without him.

"David is calling the media and letting them know what it was you brought out of the water," Jaden told him.

"What exactly is he telling them?" Sean asked.

Dr. Aislinn laughed softy. "Just that we have arrived and are taking the chest and the body, and that we believe that the chest is early eighteen hundreds, and that a unique set of circumstances have preserved the body of a woman who died in the early eighteen hundreds, as well. More details will

follow after we have conducted out tests."

"And what can you really tell us?" Sean asked.

"That she's *not* Dona Isabella!" Jaden burst out.

"What?" Vanessa said.

"Come, come, I'll show you," Dr. Aislinn said. "Dr. Latham, if you'll assist me?"

They walked over to the chest and Latham carefully opened it and offered Dr. Aislinn a set of latex gloves from his pocket. After pulling them on, she reached in and touched the woman's bodice. "This is cotton, and if you'll notice — it's difficult to see with the staining. If you'll hold the flashlight up, Dr. Latham? — that's home sewing. Dr. Latham, the hands if you will? I can't draw them out — we'd break up the mummy — but you'll note the nails. They're chipped and broken, and not the nails of a lady. Whoever this woman was, she didn't grow up in the lap of luxury. From what I've learned about this story, your Dona Isabella was supposedly killed on Haunt Island — or she went down with the ship in the storm. I don't know who this is, but it's not a lady of the time."

"Can you date the corpse to a certain age?" Sean asked.

"Not without a more comprehensive

examination," Dr. Aislinn said. "But . . ." She shrugged. "My guess? Between twenty and thirty. I'm going to need X-rays of the teeth and skull, the hips — all those things help establish age. However, I think you've found a pirate's wench, perhaps a poor girl traveling as a maid or a servant."

"We hope to be able to give you a great deal more," Dr. Latham said.

"I'm sure you're disappointed that it wasn't a chest of gold doubloons, but this is just an amazing scientific find!" Dr. Aislinn said. She looked at Vanessa. "It's extraordinary. I heard you also discovered the pendant — the exquisite mermaid pendant — that Ted showed me earlier. You're quite an amazing woman, Miss Loren. You might have missed your calling as a salvage diver or treasure seeker!"

To Sean's surprise, Vanessa's smile seemed forced and her face seemed pale.

"Oh, I rather like what I do," she said.

"How did you find these relics?" Dr. Latham asked.

"Beginner's luck," she said with a shrug. "And I wasn't looking? I don't know."

"Well," Dr. Aislinn said. "You have made an absolutely amazing discovery here. The mermaid pendant, of course, is beautiful. But the body! We can't thank you enough.

We're delighted to be doing the research!"

"Wait!" Ted said. "You didn't tell them the most gruesome part yet." He looked at Sean and Vanessa and shook his head. "I mean, we know that the pirates could be violent. And what with the story of Haunt Island, it shouldn't be surprising."

Jaden said, "Horrible, just horrible. But — of course, long over now."

"What?" Sean demanded.

"At first," Dr. Aislinn said, "I thought that someone must have cared for this young woman deeply. Most of the time, those who died at sea were wrapped in shrouds — if that! — and sent overboard. This young woman was sealed in a chest. I thought that we'd discover that the cause of death had been consumption or the ravages of some other disease. But look at the neck — that's not just decayed fabric there, or a shawl or scarf or any other such object. She was strangled. That's the fabric with which she was strangled. I'm not sure what it is yet. We'll know when we take a sample."

"She was murdered," Vanessa murmured.

"As you said," Sean noted, "violence was common, I'm afraid."

"Yes, but it's curious," Dr. Latham commented. "Pirates blew one another to bits with cannons. They slashed with swords and

cutlasses, and they shot one another with their pistols. It's unusual that they would have strangled a woman."

"She must have made someone very angry," Jaden said.

"It's going to be just fascinating to try to discover just who she was!" Dr. Aislinn said. "Of course, I understand all of you are heading out soon to start filming — a most fascinating documentary, I must say! But I'll be in touch constantly by cell phone, and you can reach me anytime you like."

"Thank you," Sean told her.

"So," Ted said, "we're packing her up — the chest and the mummy — in the university van tomorrow morning. Tara and Dr. Latham are leaving then. But Jaden and I are about to take them out for a night on the town, Key West–style. Can you join us?"

Sean didn't have a chance to reply.

Vanessa spoke quickly. "Oh, thank you, and I hope you'll forgive me. It's been a long day, and I didn't get a lot of sleep last night, I'm afraid. But hey, you guys — take them to O'Hara's. They'll have a great time there."

"O'Hara's?" Dr. Aislinn said, grinning and looking at Sean.

"It's my uncle's place, and you will have a great time," Sean said.

"Sean, I'm sorry, I'm really exhausted, but you, of course, are more than welcome to join them," Vanessa said quickly.

She seldom looked vulnerable; for some reason that night she did. Sean felt a surge of tenderness, wanting to make sure that she was safe and warm and protected at all times.

"Sorry, all, and forgive me, too. These have been really long days. My uncle's place has good food, reasonable drinks, and my sister is doing karaoke tonight. It's a bit of a walk down Duval," he said.

"Well, I do love walking, and I don't get down here nearly enough!" Dr. Aislinn said.

Sean and Vanessa left, thanking them again. As they walked down the street, he took her hand — it was crowded that night. Girls were out in skimpy outfits and wench attire; some men were still in pirate costume while others were in jeans and T-shirts. It was Key West. A little cool that night for anything so simple as body paint, but anything might have been worn along Duval.

Vanessa was quiet, and she still seemed disturbed. "What's wrong?" he asked her.

She made a face. "The body is creepy. I'm glad they're taking it to Gainesville."

"It's not really creepy. It's another mys-

tery. We — *you* — found a pendant, which did belong to Dona Isabella, at least according to historical sketches. Then, we — *you* — find a body in a chest, and it proves *not* to be Dona Isabella. That's interesting. I don't remember anything about a maid traveling with her, though, of course, a woman of her stature probably did travel with a servant. Ah, maybe Mad Miller threatened her by killing the maid, and then gave her something of a decent burial. Or, God knows, maybe Kitty Cutlass did the deed."

Vanessa shrugged. "I don't know. We'll have to see what they discover. Both of those doctors seemed fascinated and thrilled, so it was an incredible discovery."

She was silent.

"Hey, you all right?"

"Of course."

"You're the only person who makes incredible finds who seems depressed by their talent. The pendant . . . well, I can see that as a fluke. But none of that chest was showing above the sand. How in hell *did* you become so certain there was something there?"

She paused and stopped walking and stared at him. "You really want to know? If

you make fun of me now, I'll never forgive you."

"I will not make fun of you."

She took a deep breath, her eyes sharp on his. "I keep thinking that I see a figurehead in the water. I dream about it, actually. It's scary and creepy. It has Dona Isabella's face."

He felt his lips start to twitch and remembered he had promised not to make fun of her.

"I see," he managed to say.

"You don't believe a word," she said.

"I'm not saying that!" he protested quickly. He started walking again, eager to get to his home on Elizabeth Street before he somehow managed to lose her once again. "Here's what I think," he said, still holding her hand, and swinging their arms easily between them as they walked. "The story goes that poor Dona Isabella was kidnapped from her transport to Spain by Mad Miller and his pirates. She was forced to Haunt Island and either murdered by Mad Miller or Kitty Cutlass, or still a prisoner — probably one who was raped and abused — when the pirate ship went down in the storm. So you see the face of Dona Isabella because you feel such sympathy for her. And it would be natural that

329

you see the face in the water — as a figure-head — when you are instinctively honing in on something. How's that?"

"Psychology 101?" she asked dryly.

"The mind can do amazing things," he told her. "Then, face it, you've had horrible nightmares since your friends were murdered on Haunt Island — and you found them. There are all kinds of wonderful defense mechanisms in the mind."

"What if the spirit of Dona Isabella is lurking in the water?" Vanessa asked. "Or . . . worse! What if Mad Miller is a decayed old pirate like Geoffrey Rush in *Pirates of the Caribbean*?"

He laughed.

Then he realized that she was serious.

"I remember one time, when Katie and I were small, and we were at the old cemetery, bringing flowers to the grave of one of my mom's friends. Katie was acting nervous. My dad told her that the dead were the safest people in the world — that they couldn't hurt anyone. He told her that she had to learn to be very smart and wary and savvy — it was the living who hurt one another."

She nodded. "Of course. I didn't think that Mad Miller or Kitty Cutlass rose out of the sea to kill and dismember Georgia and Travis."

"Of course not. It's sad to say, because I know you liked him, that most probably Carlos Roca was responsible."

She seemed to start, and to shudder.

He set his arm around her and pulled her close.

"Hey, sorry!"

"It's all right," she murmured. "I just — I doubt it. All right, I know that there have been horrible serial killers who had neighbors who had sincerely believed they were just nice, quiet people. But I knew Carlos. And I don't think so — no matter how it looked."

They had reached the house and he opened the door, drawing her in. He locked the door and asked, "Do you want something to drink? A shot of . . . something. Kahlúa and cream, cup of tea, water, cola, soda . . . ?"

She laughed. "Hmm. Tea and whiskey."

"The old Irish remedy for anything that ails you," he said. He walked into the kitchen and put the kettle on. As the water boiled, he tried to casually look around the house for Bartholomew. The ghost was nowhere to be seen.

Probably out with his lady in white, Lucinda, the new love of his life.

Probably still angry with him.

331

That was all right; he didn't want to be haunted that night.

The water boiled. Vanessa got out two cups and he procured the tea cups and the whiskey. When both were prepared, he suggested, "Let's take them up to bed."

She nodded. "Works for me."

He meant to have a little finesse. Give her a few minutes, watch a bit of a late-night comedy. But they were still too new to one another. Once they had shed their clothing, they made love. He couldn't bemoan his lack of subtle courtesy, because she was so passionate, so urgent, and completely and erotically seductive. She seemed to come beneath his very skin. It was one thing to feel the ultimate in climax and satiation. Sex was instinct, it was breathing, it happened all the time. But it was something else to feel the wonder when he lay with her after, something else to feel that nothing in the world could ever be so complete, so fulfilling . . . even so necessary.

They drank their tea then, cold, and though she kept drifting to sleep at his side, she would awake again and again with a start.

He found the remote and at long last turned on a late-night talk show. The noise seemed to soothe her.

332

She slept next to him as if he were a bastion against the edge of eternal darkness.

Waking with Sean was amazing; she had felt his body and warmth throughout the night, and she had slept deeply. She opened her eyes and felt wonderful. He had been on his stomach at an angle, and she had been sleeping against his back. Great back, broad shoulders, long clean lines, bronze flesh. She drew her finger down the length of his spine delicately, waking him immediately.

He woke well, too. It was all so new and amazing, of course. He turned and took her into his arms, a wicked look in his eyes, and they made love to start the day.

Afterward, Vanessa headed to Katie's room to shower and leave Sean in his own space, and once she was dressed, she came downstairs and to the back of the house where he'd set up his office. He was there already, telling her that coffee was poured and that when she was ready, they'd go over the shooting schedule and she could tell him anything that she thought he might have missed.

Walking into the kitchen while reading the schedule that Sean had printed for her, she stopped, stunned — as if she'd been hit by a brick.

For a moment — just for a moment — she thought that she saw the pirate again. Tall, lean, dashing, rich black hair, plumed hat, standing thoughtfully by the dining-room window, staring out at the day.

She saw him in such detail!

And then he was gone.

She blinked. There was nothing there. Sun streaming in played on the dust motes in the air.

She hurried over to the coffeepot and poured a large cup. She nearly scalded her throat in her hurry to drink it down.

Now she was seeing things nearly on an hourly basis. And after such a miraculous night of deep and undisturbed sleep.

Sean walked into the kitchen to pour himself more coffee. He frowned, looking at her. "What's the matter?"

"Nothing."

"Really? You look — scared."

She smiled. "With you in the room? Never," she said with a laugh. She walked over and hugged him and drew away quickly. "I had another thought that we might add in on your schedule."

"Right," Sean said, smiling. "What scene would you add?"

"Jay and me at night, walking down to where we saw nothing. Where I found the

bodies the next morning. Very descriptive without being gruesome."

"I like it. Write it in. Obviously, we'll film hours that we'll wind up editing out, but any scene that you think might enhance the project, just tell me."

Vanessa lowered her head and smiled. It was amazing that he might have hurt her so much and made her so angry — and that, as far as a working relationship went, he was completely confident and comfortable. He knew what he wanted; he knew where he was going. It occurred to her then that they both wanted the same thing. She hoped they made an excellent documentary that was engrossing and made others think, as well.

Until that moment, she realized, she'd been thinking of her own agenda.

The phone rang, causing her to nearly jump out of her skin.

Sean arched a brow to her. "Hey, telephone. It's a landline — remember those? Granted, we don't use them much anymore." He walked over to answer it.

She couldn't be so jumpy. They would lock her up — before they could even get to the project.

Sean answered the phone. He frowned and reached into his pocket. "Sorry, forgot

to plug it in last night." He glanced at Vanessa and smiled. "I got distracted," he said.

Then his smile faded. "You're kidding!" he said.

He listened again.

"I'll be right there," he said.

He hung up and stared thoughtfully at Vanessa.

"What?" she demanded.

"The body was stolen."

"What?" she repeated.

"I'm heading out to meet Liam. I won't be long. The body was stolen out of the university van. The problem is, no one knows when. They'd packed it up this morning, and Doctors Aislinn and Latham were at a Cracker Barrel in the middle of the state when they decided to check to make sure that the chest wasn't moving around too much. Well, it wasn't moving. It was gone."

"Someone stole the body out of the van?" she repeated incredulously.

He nodded.

"Who in the hell would want to steal a mummified body?" she demanded.

"Here's my question," he said. "Who in hell would even know that it was there to be stolen?"

■ ■ ■ ■

Liam was in his office, filling out paperwork. He looked up the minute Sean came in and glumly waved toward a chair on the other side of his desk.

"Anything?" Sean asked him.

"Nothing — this may be worse than the damned Bermuda Triangle. Most of the time, we can't even find a stolen car, and then we find them half the time because they have LoJack, but they're stripped. But this isn't a car we're looking for, it's a chest with a body in it! This is going to be impossible. They don't know when it happened. They had just left a Cracker Barrel in the center of the state when Dr. Latham decided to check on their cargo. So — they'd stopped for breakfast in Florida City. The van might have been broken into then. It could have happened when they pulled off a few times along the way. So, it might have been stolen anywhere from Key West to Orlando. They believed that their cargo was safe — who tries to steal a corpse?"

"Is there anything we can do?" Sean asked.

"We have reports filled out and sent around the state," Liam said. "They've dusted for fingerprints. The lock was sprung

with a pick, but that doesn't really help any. The door could still be secured, so it doesn't mean that the chest was stolen later than earlier." He shook his head. "Someone must have thought it was a treasure chest."

"There was an article that ran in the paper this morning — David talked to a reporter last night, and I believe it went around on the wire and on the Internet. The article announced that it was a body that had been found."

"Maybe the thieves weren't on the Internet, and God knows, they probably didn't read the newspaper, either," Liam said. "The officers here are livid, of course. Keys police tend to be very territorial — they take the theft personally. She was *our* creepy old body, the way they look at it. They'll be doing everything they can, searching for anything suspicious. Obviously, you need a reason to stop people and search their trucks or vans, but we're good and subtle around here — learned a lot from the drug traffic. Someone may just find the chest somewhere — I mean, once they've discovered they haven't any gold, silver or precious gems, they may just abandon the chest."

Sean shook his head. "I don't think so," he said.

"Why?"

"I don't know. I think that the body was stolen on purpose."

"What? By gang members? Like some kind of initiation? If we have a large clan of devil worshipers down here, I don't know anything about it," Liam said.

"I don't think it was gang members or devil worshipers. I think it was someone . . . I don't know. Someone involved, somehow," Sean said.

"And recently, two unexplained disappearances," Liam said.

"We may be getting into something very bad."

"Well, I am a cop. It's the kind of thing I'm supposed to be doing," Liam said dryly.

"Are you set for tomorrow?" Sean asked.

"I am — shifts covered for two weeks," Liam told him. "Why?"

"I'd like to go for some target practice sometime before tomorrow."

"Target practice?"

"It's been a while for me," Sean said.

"You are really expecting trouble," Liam said.

"Hey — now a nearly two-hundred-year-old body has been stolen. Yes, I guess I am expecting trouble."

"And you still want to proceed?"

Sean hesitated. "I think I feel now more than ever that we have to," he said. "Maybe stealing the body was someone's idea of a prank. And maybe there is something here that we're not seeing — but maybe we're close, and there was something we weren't meant to discover. I don't know. Not much makes sense yet. But yes. With what and who we have — hell, yes, we have to move forward now."

While Sean was gone, Vanessa continued to study the schedule, adding in notes and suggestions. She liked reviewing his work, and going over all the notes he had made about supplies, lighting and editing in the scenes that would go with the narrative.

She rose at one point, realizing that they'd had coffee but not breakfast. Now it was nearly lunchtime, and she was hungry.

She heard the sound of the air-conditioner kicking on as she walked to the kitchen. It might be late fall, but the day was growing warm. The sun was bright outside, casting the dancing rays of rebounding sunlight into the room to play with dust motes in the air again.

She froze again.

He was there again.

Someone by the window. Someone in

pirate attire.

She nearly screamed. She felt again the weakness of her legs buckling.

At first, her mind raced in a somewhat rational direction.

Carlos. It was Carlos Roca. She had seen him, and he was real, and she was wrong, and Sean was right, and he was guilty of murder, and now he had come for her.

But it wasn't Carlos.

It was the pirate — the dandy pirate.

The tall, striking fellow with the sweeping hat and brocade coat. The one she had seen yesterday, and then briefly again just this morning.

She would blink, and he would go away. He wasn't real. He was her mind playing tricks.

Really no. She was seeing things.

But she blinked, and this time he remained. She realized that he was staring at her with equal consternation. He jumped up, his eyes locked with hers, and gasped.

"Oh my God!" he cried.

She was hearing things, as well as seeing them. Not just a figurehead through a camera lens. Oh, no, this was much worse. This was a walking, talking pirate ghost.

In her room.

She let out a weak scream.

341

He let out a weak scream.

Her mouth worked hard.

"Mad Miller!" she gasped.

"Good God, no!" the apparition replied in horror.

Replied. It was talking to her, the images talked to her now, even when she was awake.

She fell back against the door, her hand flying to her throat.

"You're not there," she gasped out.

"My God! You can see me!" he cried. "You can really see me!"

Her knees were really buckling now. And he seemed to be fading in and out, and she wasn't sure what she saw, or what she heard.

"Who are you?" she demanded.

"A friend, I swear. All right, I'm dead, I'm a ghost — but I'm a friend, honest to God, please don't scream again!"

She didn't.

So much for being strong. So much for being the kind of woman who just didn't *pass out.*

She slumped against the wall and sank to the floor, entering a sweet world of darkness and silence.

12

As he headed back to his house, Sean tried not to dwell on the stolen corpse. He called different suppliers, making sure that everything was set for them to leave in the morning. He had a few calls to make, since they needed everything from diving supplies to film, memory cards, backup equipment and groceries.

David called to let him know that he and Jamie were at the dock and that things were coming as promised.

He tried calling Vanessa, but she didn't pick up.

She was at his house — locked in.

But he found himself hurrying. He didn't know why the theft of the body disturbed him so much. Liam had been right — it had probably been some kind of a prank. Or, God knew, maybe an eccentric collector had decided that he just had to have a mummified murder victim from the early eighteen

hundreds.

Still, as he neared his house, he was almost running. It occurred to him that he'd been gone a long time. Liam had not been able to leave the station then — he'd been tying up his paperwork and transferring his work-load to other detectives throughout the day in preparation for taking his vacation time with Sean and David and the crew.

An hour at the range had been good. He'd always had a clear eye and a steady aim, but since guns weren't in his workaday world, he hadn't carried one in a long time.

The day's events at the fort and beach would be drawing to a close, but there would be parties, lectures and "pirate" entertainment as the night arrived. Once again, pirates and their consorts would be roaming the streets. At the moment, it was one of the most beautiful times of the day; there was nothing like a Key West sunset. The bright sunlight gave way to a gentle, pale yellow, and the brilliant blue of the sky overhead became a silver-gray. Then the sun started down, and it seemed that the horizon and everything around was shot full with a palette of unbelievable colors, from deep magenta to the most delicate pink, shim-mering gold to gentle rose. It was most amazing to watch the sun set over the water,

but to Sean, the colors were still visible, and the colors were what created the beauty.

The brighter shades were just giving way to violet, silver and gray when he reached his house. Once there, he bounded up the walk and fitted his key into the lock, calling Vanessa's name.

In the foyer, he paused, calling her name again.

Vanessa was there. She walked to the foyer from the center of the house and the kitchen and dining-room area.

She stared at him with immense eyes that seemed to accuse him of the foulest of heinous deeds.

"Sean," she said.

He noticed that she had shampooed her hair and that she was wearing a white halter dress that showed off the tan of her skin.

"Are we going somewhere?" he asked.

"Oh, yes. Bon voyage party at O'Hara's. All of our friends will be joining us," she told him. "It will be Katie's last night for now, so she's going to be there in case Clarinda needs her. David said as long as we're all ready and aboard by ten we'll be fine . . . oh, and Marty has turned his booth over to his friend for pirate fest — you have been gone awhile. Did you learn anything?"

"No. The police barely know where to

start searching for the chest. I went — I went to target practice with Liam."

"We're having guns aboard?" she asked, frowning.

"Think about it. Yes," he said.

"Well, we don't have to leave right away. Come in and sit down and let's talk for a minute, shall we? Sit, please. Can I get you something? It is your house, of course. Thank goodness, the choices here are much broader than what I have up in my room. Beer? Wine? Soda, soda and whiskey, or whiskey. Rum! That's right. It's a pirate drink. Strange, I've had this growing affection for a good stiff drink from just about the time I arrived here."

She was definitely behaving strangely, and yet she certainly seemed stone-cold sober.

He followed her to the dining room. He noticed that Bartholomew was there. He was seated at the dining-room table. He looked at Sean with a guilty expression.

Sean frowned, feeling a sensation of dread.

"I'll take a beer," Sean said. "But I can get it myself."

"No, no, let me. Sit," she said.

He took a chair at the end of the table. Bartholomew — for once — was silent.

Vanessa set a beer in front of him. She had taken one for herself, and walked

around to take a seat at the other end of the dining-room table.

"Sean, I mentioned to you that I see a figurehead — with Dona Isabella's face on it — in the water, and it leads me to things beneath."

"Yes," he said slowly. Carefully.

She learned toward him, eyes snapping with light and anger.

"You hypocrite!"

"What?"

"You tell me everything is a trick of the mind — when you live with a ghost!"

He was certain that his jaw fell. Then, of course, he gave himself away by staring at Bartholomew. She saw him! She saw Bartholomew.

"What a jerk!" she told him. "You might have mentioned your pirate friend to me!"

"Privateer," Bartholomew said, but weakly.

"You see him," he said, his voice just as pale.

"Yes, and he nearly gave me a heart attack. You should have told me. When I saw him, I thought that he might have been Mad Miller —"

"That was terribly insulting," Bartholomew interjected.

"How was I supposed to know?" Vanessa

347

snapped to him. She wagged a finger at Sean. "You should have told me!"

He opened his mouth but no sound came. He cleared his throat and tried again. "You would have thought that I was crazy."

"Really? That's great. Instead, I've been thinking that I'm crazy."

"You can see him — clearly?" Sean asked.

"She's far more perceptive than you'll ever be," Bartholomew said.

"Thank you so much," Sean said dryly.

"You want everything to be black and white," Bartholomew said. "You want science and explanations."

"There is probably a science to everything," Sean said. He looked at Bartholomew. "We just haven't figured it all out yet."

"I hope not — I hope something is left to a — a dimension of faith, or the next world, be it Heaven or Hell," Bartholomew said earnestly. "God forbid someone discovers how to force a soul to stay on this earthly plain."

Sean looked from Bartholomew to Vanessa. "You hear him clearly, too?"

"Perfectly. Actually, we had a lovely discussion this afternoon. He's been around watching out for me a great deal of the time. I kept feeling as if there were . . . something. Of course, I didn't believe in *ghosts*," she

said. "But now . . ."

"Oh, please," Bartholomew said. "You are not all sharing a mental experience, or conjuring the same imaginary friend."

Vanessa smiled and laughed easily. "No. Now I know," she told him. She spoke to him fondly.

Well.

"You . . . should have told me that you . . . that you knew there might be some things that were — unexplainable," Vanessa said. "It would have helped me a lot."

He got up and walked around the table to her, taking her hands. "Vanessa . . . trust me, if I hadn't thought that . . . well, seriously, you know . . . *most* people can't see Bartholomew."

"Frankly, I was stunned," Bartholomew said.

"I — think we're at a point where we need to trust one another," Vanessa said.

He kissed her gently on the lips. "Yes, but you must understand —"

"Oh, yes. I do. Just as you really need to understand that I came here not knowing that Jay and the others would show up — and that when you think about it, it's not odd at all," she said solemnly.

He pulled her to her feet. He smoothed her hair back. "I'll never doubt you again,"

he said softly.

"Oh, good God," Bartholomew said. "I thought we were going out."

They both turned to look at him.

"Never mind. I'm going out." He looked at them, shook his head and made a tsking sound. "I shall see you when you get there."

Vanessa wound her arms around Sean's neck and kissed him. A few minutes later, he told her huskily that if they were going to leave, they needed to go. And they did.

O'Hara's was insane that night, inside. People had heard about the excitement of finding a pendant from the ill-fated *Santa Geneva* that had once graced the neck of Dona Isabella, and then the discovery of a body in a chest — and the theft of the body in the trunk. For a while, as everyone arrived, they stayed inside, but when they had all gathered at last, Jamie suggested the patio, a private area in the back, and they all agreed.

Everyone in their group who would be heading out the following day was there.

Clarinda was doing her first night as a karaoke hostess, and despite her innate shyness, she was doing very well.

They could hear the singers and the music faintly, and the night was typically beauti-

ful, not really cool but not hot.

Vanessa sipped a Guinness, enjoying the taste and leaned back against Sean, oddly relaxed. She'd seen a ghost.

And the ghost had proved to be real, or a real mass hallucination. Apparently, Bartholomew had actually been Katie's ghost and helped out in David's time of trouble; though Liam wasn't really in on actually seeing and conversing with the ghost, he knew there was *something*.

And as crazy as it sounded, she wasn't frightened anymore — she was in awe. It was actually something of a dream come true, actually conversing with someone who had lived almost two centuries ago. He had told her his own sad story, which had connected bizarrely with David's, and then he had told her that somehow, he knew it just wasn't right for him to leave yet — follow the light to wherever it might bring him — because he felt he was still needed on Earth. Which was really fine now, because after years and years and years, he had finally met the lady in white, his Lucinda, who had been a lonely figure walking up and down Duval and haunting the cemetery for years — afraid to reach out to others. Bartholomew had no explanation as to why some people had a sense of something, and some

actually saw ghosts. Some saw particular ghosts and not others and, of course, there were plenty of ghosts to be seen! The streets of Key West were often riddled with ghosts; after all, people had been dying there forever.

Bartholomew hadn't come to O'Hara's with them; he was determined to join the film project, and so he would spend the night with his beautiful Lucinda.

Vanessa was leaning against Sean. They sat at one of the benches horse-style and it was easy and comfortable to lean against his back.

Sean and David had spent some time delineating duties for each member of the crew and assigning boats. Then Sean lifted his beer. "To success — and safety!" he said.

They all toasted.

The conversation turned to the chest Vanessa had discovered — and the stolen mummified body.

"What if," Jay said, thinking as he went, "what if . . . what if it was Dona Isabella? The anthropologist might have been wrong. Maybe they dressed her up in peasant garb. Maybe she broke free herself, and was going to come after everyone in . . . revenge for what happened to her?" he asked, wide-eyed.

"Jay!" Vanessa snapped. "That's . . . ridiculous. Mummies don't come to life, and why would Dona Isabella want revenge on anyone living? You're talking as if you're plotting out another horror movie, and we're doing a documentary."

"It would be a great and creepy premise," Barry said.

"A sequel!" Zoe said.

Vanessa glared at her. "There isn't going to be a sequel — there was never really a movie. Therefore, you can't have a sequel."

"Well, actually . . ." Jay said.

Vanessa felt her muscles tighten up with tension. It had been a nice night — thus far. Sipping Guinness, munching on O'Hara's specials such as Shillelagh Sticks — rolled and baked corned beef in pastry — and Tam O Shanters — something like sliders. Such a nice night. She'd been so amazed — and pleased — about Bartholomew. She'd been so happy to be with Sean.

And now . . .

"Jay, what are you talking about?" she demanded.

He flushed, and lifted his hands uneasily. "I've had a call from a rep with a national distributor. He thinks we have a surefire hit — especially with everything else that went on."

Vanessa sat up, staring at Jay. "Jay — our lead actors were murdered."

"Bad things have happened before and movies have still come out and been very successful — and it was really a wonderful chance for fans to say goodbye," Jay said, defending himself.

"When the leads were murdered?" Vanessa asked icily.

"I'm sure somewhere along the line, yes . . . but think of the real things out there! Poor Heather O'Rourke of *Poltergeist* died very young — and they've used her scenes in tacky advertisements! When they filmed the *Twilight Movie* years ago, a star and two children were killed, and it aired. People said goodbye to Bruce Lee, Brandon Lee, Heath Ledger and many more actors when their movies aired after their deaths."

Vanessa felt Sean holding her back, but she stood anyway, walking over to Jay. "That would be the height of bad taste, and I put my money into that film, too, and I won't allow it."

"That's great for you — you've hit jobs that pay well. I need to make some money, Nessa," Jay pleaded.

"Jay, it's wrong."

Sean stepped into it then. "Well, the surviving members of your crew are here,

354

Jay. Why don't you find out how they all feel?"

Bill spoke up first. "All right, I was more or less a lowly production assistant on the shoot. But . . . I liked Georgia and Travis. And they have family living now. Family — who might be hurt."

Barry cleared his throat. "I don't know what I feel. Georgia wanted to be a star. And she survived in the movie. She might be happy."

"Yeah, Georgia was sweet. Dumb, but sweet," Zoe said. "But Travis . . . Travis was a jerk."

"Zoe!" Bill gasped, horrified.

"Hey, I'm sorry — it's horrible that he died the way he did, yes. But was he a nice guy? No!"

"My money was in it, Jay," Vanessa said. "And I say no."

Jay inhaled and stared at her. He exhaled and took a long sip of his beer, and looked at her again. "What if we find out what happened?" he asked.

"What?" she said.

"We all came here. We heard about Sean and David and their project, and we all came here. Doesn't that mean something? We all care, we were all horrified. Vanessa, I own the majority share — fifty-one percent."

355

"You slimy basta —" she began.

"Wait, please!" Jay said. "Let's see what we can discover on this documentary project. And then, if there's really a story to be told about what happened to us, it would only be right to release the movie that we filmed."

Sean leaned forward. "Jay, if you want to throw threats around, you'll note that David and I own this particular project."

Jay's jaw fell. He hadn't thought that he might get kicked off the new project.

Sean smiled pleasantly. "We didn't draw up any contracts."

"I'm not threatening anyone. I'm just . . . I'm just mentioning facts," Jay said.

"And so am I," Sean told him politely.

Jay looked at Vanessa pleadingly. "Will you think about it when this project is done?"

The conversation had been bouncing between them with everyone there staring at them. She didn't want to get into a huge fight with Jay that would naturally begin to involve all the others. The whole project could become an antagonistic disaster by the morning. She didn't want any hostility on the trip or involved with the filming.

For a moment, Vanessa felt the silence that fell among the group.

"You're right," she said. "Let's see what

happens on this trip. If we find out some-thing new about what happened, if there is a prayer of solving the murders, then I'll think about it. But if we find nothing at all and their deaths remain mysteries, Jay — please. Let's shelve it."

Jay looked at her, then looked away. "All right."

"Promise," Vanessa insisted.

"I promise," he said dourly.

There was a silence again. Then Katie stood, raising her glass. "Here's to great camaraderie and a wonderful work experi-ence. Here's to tomorrow!"

Again, glasses clinked, and they all toasted one another. The joy of the evening had faded, though, and soon, one by one, they were taking leave.

As they walked home, Sean told Vanessa, "You know, I can fire his ass now, if you want."

She looked at him and flashed a smile. "No, Jay is good. And he promised, and he is my friend."

"He's your broke friend, it sounds like. And in a way, he has a point. I agree with you, but he has a point. Here's the thing that I'll say in his defense — he didn't try to cash in on a tragedy. He had invested his life's savings into that movie. He didn't rush

out and try to give it to anyone right after it happened."

"You think he's right?" Vanessa protested.

Sean shook his head. "Me? I don't think I could do it — not when both of the victims were so young, not when they had family still living." He slipped his arm around her. "*Titanic* the musical played on Broadway. I thought that a musical based on such a horrific event was in terrible taste. Katie wanted to see it, so the family went. And it was actually something that I wound up enjoying, that gave a certain honorable memorial to many of the people involved. Much better than the movie!" he told her, smiling gently.

"Sean — this was a slasher flick."

"I know. Anyway, let's get home and get some sleep, shall we?"

They didn't get to sleep right away. They made love again, and it still seemed so amazing and new, and there was still so much they had to learn about one another. When she drifted to sleep, she was warm, secure and comfortable, and being with him seemed like a bastion against the world. It was ridiculous to think that she could actually fall in love with anyone so quickly, and yet, in the time they had known one another, she had come to realize that now she

couldn't imagine a time without him. She had let her pride stand in the way once — he had been a jerk — but he had proven himself, coming to her, and she thought that finding the right relationship had been as hard in the past for him as it had been for her, none of which mattered, because when she was with him, feeling his warmth and the vibrant pulse of his heart so near to hers, she didn't envision the future beyond tomorrow.

She should have slept as sweetly and deeply as she had the night before.

But the dreams came again, though they took a different twist.

She was back at O'Hara's, sitting on the bench at the patio, and Jay was speaking again.

"What if the mummy came to, and broke out . . ."

Then she was walking down Duval, and it was odd, because no one was there.

She was alone.

And then she wasn't.

The streets were filled with pirates. She told herself that naturally the pirates were there. Pirates in Paradise was happening, and there were events to the last minute, and even then, some people stayed and dressed up, loath to get back to reality.

But they weren't real pirates.

They were ghosts.

Ghosts existed.

They walked along, some in a hurry, some strolling together. Some talked and teased with wenches, some joked with one another. They strode, they swaggered, and one limped on a peg leg. They paid her no heed.

Then she heard carriage wheels. They seemed to come slowly, ominously. The sky blackened and a chill fog sprang out from the sea. The mist whirled in shades of gray, and the clip-clop of the horse's hooves came ever more slowly.

She turned, aware that the carriage was coming to a halt, and that it was coming to a halt near her.

Or perhaps it was coming for her.

A woman, an elegant woman in silk and high fashion, stepped from the carriage, her every movement in slow motion. She looked straight at Vanessa, and Vanessa knew her. She knew the mermaid pendant the woman wore around her neck, and she knew the face — she had seen it on a figurehead that had led her to strange discoveries beneath the sea.

"You must help. You must listen. You must find the truth," the woman said. She smiled at Vanessa, and produced a hatbox. She

opened the hatbox, and lifted something.

It was Georgia Dare's head.

"Vanessa!" Georgia cried to her pathetically.

Dona Isabella let the head fall back into the hatbox. She looked around her. Vanessa did the same. The pirates on the street were changing. They seemed to turn into black ooze. They cried out and screamed, and seemed as if they were moving in a black, malevolent mass toward the woman and the carriage.

The wind began to whip up. Vanessa knew that she had to wake up; the evil pirates were coming for Dona Isabella, but she was in their way.

"Here, here!" came a cry.

She turned.

And it was the mummy. The mummy from the pirate's chest.

The face was leathered and dark and decayed. The hands were bony, with dead skin stretched out over them far too tightly. The clothing was stained and ripped, and the eye sockets were empty, nothing but black stygian pits.

"Come, come!" the mummy cried.

Her jaw fell open in horror. The bony fingers were coming closer and closer to her.

"No!" she whispered.

"Yes!" Someone was behind her. She felt the presence and spun around in terror.

The street was still dark; the carriage bearing Dona Isabella away was beginning to move. It was still in slow motion, yet it was trying so hard to pick up speed. Dona Isabella was running now from the wrath of the pirates. She sought escape, as she hadn't found in the past.

Vanessa thought that she should have leaped into the carriage.

Because now she was caught between the mummy . . .

And the living, breathing man behind her.

Carlos Roca. She stared at him.

"Am I seeing you? Are you dead? Did you kill them, Carlos, did you have us all fooled?" she demanded.

He stood there, frozen in silence.

"I am alive," he told her. "And I am innocent."

He looked at the black shadows. "Come with me!"

"Come, come quickly!" the mummy begged.

She spun around. The mummy was there. So pathetic. So sad.

"Vanessa, you know me!" Carlos said.

Yes, she knew him, and he was there. Was he really alive, and was he running, too, or

was he part of a black swirling mass of ooze and evil that was winding slowly down the street, ready to devour her . . . ?

"You don't understand," the mummy said.

And the dead, leathered fingers, bones sticking out, nearly touched her. . . .

She screamed.

And awoke.

And Sean was with her, holding her in his arms, smoothing back her damp hair, whispering words of assurance.

She felt the terror of the dream slip away from her, and she felt the strength of his arms. She ceased to shake and she turned him. "I'm so sorry . . . I didn't think . . . when I was with you . . ."

He touched her face. "I'm not the monster in the dream, right?"

She laughed shakily. "No."

"Then it's much better to have nightmares with me than without me, right? Although," he admitted, "these nightmares seem to plague you so cruelly, a therapist might be in order."

"I had a therapist once," she said. "It didn't help."

He rocked with her in silence for a minute, then said, "Then somehow, we have to find the truth. Catch a killer. And put the past to rest."

■ ■ ■ ■

The morning was a whirlwind of activity. There were dozens of air tanks that needed to be stowed, and though David had overseen the loading of the boats with grocery supplies, ice, film, memory cards, cords, computer needs, batteries, flashlights, flares and every conceivable necessity, they all had their personal gear to stow, as well.

Jamie had David and Katie, Liam, Barry and Bill and Jake aboard the *Claddagh.* Sean had Vanessa, Jay, Ted and Jaden, Marty and Zoe aboard the *Conch Fritter.*

And Bartholomew, of course.

The boats would follow one another through the day, hugging the Intracoastal up to Jewfish Creek, and heading out to the Atlantic at Key Largo. David and Barry would take turns with the camera during the day on the *Claddagh* while Sean, Jay, and Vanessa would trade off on the *Conch Fritter.* They would drop anchor that night southwest of Miami, and in the morning start filming at the first reef where the previous crew had begun their offshore work. Sean felt that he had had enough of Pirate's Cut and that they should start filming in other areas. He had the Marty footage and

the footage that Vanessa and Jay had already shot at Pirate Cut.

The first day was easy; it was getting to know the boat, the equipment and one another.

The boats met up at about 4:30 p.m., and tied on together — Sean wanted footage taken on board that night. He and David took turns in front of the camera, describing the voyage and their plans, and the film taken would be edited in with the shots they'd taken of leaving port that morning.

Jamie O'Hara had a portable barbecue grill that extended from the boat's hull, and that night, the *Claddagh*'s crew was responsible for dinner. While Jamie and David barbecued, Katie and Bill prepared salads and green beans. Barry kept the camera going as they cooked and the group settled around to eat.

He took beautiful shots as the sun fell.

Vanessa enjoyed dinner; they all piled aboard the hull and deck of the *Claddagh* for their first major meal together, and she sat back with Katie, enjoying the light sway of the boat in the still night. That morning, the nightmare had all but faded away, and yet she was left to wonder if she had really seen Carlos Roca, if her dreams weren't some kind of a warning.

And if she should tell Sean that she had seen him.

But everyone seemed to think that he had to be guilty. If she told anyone else at all — even Sean — and he appeared again somewhere, someone might shoot to kill.

She had to have imagined Carlos.

Except that she hadn't imagined a dead pirate.

Odd, but true.

And Bartholomew was there. He hadn't come across to the *Claddagh.* He stood at the bow of the *Conch Fritter,* just looking out over the sea. She wondered what he was thinking or feeling, or if — without flesh and substance — he couldn't feel, and yet she thought that he could. She decided then that the soul had to consist of both intelligence and the heart, and it was rather sad, because pain could then remain long after death.

Marty played his guitar and sang on deck, and Katie joined him. Bill and Zoe engaged in a game of chess. Jamie, Liam, David and Sean closed themselves away in the cabin of the *Claddagh* for about an hour, planning and charting, and when they were through, Vanessa was ready to return to the *Conch Fritter* and head into bed.

It was nice to sleep with the captain, she

decided. The master cabin very comfortable. Marty was given the convertible couch in the main cabin, while Ted and Jaden were portside and Jay and Zoe were in the slim bunks on the starboard side.

Vanessa went to bed by herself because Sean took first watch on the *Conch Fritter* while Liam took first watch on the *Claddagh.*

Watches were in four-hour shifts. As she curled comfortably into the master cabin's bed, Vanessa realized that the schedule for watch duty included everyone — but someone in Sean's group would be on one of the decks at all times.

Did he distrust someone he had hired on? she wondered. Or was he always that careful and wary?

She thought about Jay wanting to sell their film; a major distributor could mean really decent money, and she knew that he needed the money — and that he still had dreams of producing and directing his own films.

It just disturbed her.

She stared at the small table by the bed that held a reading lamp. She noticed that there was a newspaper there, beneath one of Sean's books. She glanced at the book and noticed that it was on the numerous wrecks in the area. She pulled out the news-

paper beneath it.

The headline on the page read, "Missing!"

Beneath it was a picture of two couples standing on a dock. They wore white casual boating clothes and hats, and they were all older, attractive people with happy smiles.

Sean had told her about more disappearances. Disappearances in the area. She scanned the article. Both Mark Houghton and Dale Johnson were experienced captains. They loved traveling together, and though they had made more distant trips, they were sun and warm-water people and set off every couple of months together to tour a part of the Caribbean.

They enjoyed camping on Haunt Island.

She winced and set the article down. She'd been so busy lately that she hadn't seen anything on the disappearance. Of course Sean had known about it.

There had always been disappearances. But now this. A year after the *Delphi.*

Two years after the murders of Travis and Georgia.

She closed her eyes and tried to sleep.

A while later, she felt Sean crawling in beside her, and she sidled up against the warmth of his naked length and lay awake for a very long time.

The sun was rising in the east.

It was almost morning, almost time for their first dive as a complete crew.

She wondered if she was afraid.

No, Vanessa thought. She wasn't afraid of diving. She wasn't afraid of figureheads in the water, or even the absurdity of her dreams.

She was afraid of reaching Haunt Island.

13

The dive that morning was beautiful and uneventful. They went down to several of the wrecks on the Shipwreck Trail in Biscayne National Park. Reefs were beautiful, and though modern technology helped, ships and boats still had to be wary. The *Alicia*, built in Scotland, had slammed into the Ajax reef and the outline of the ship hosted a massive ecosystem of brilliantly colored fish, rays, nurse sharks, groupers and more. It was a beautiful wreck to film, and it was one that Vanessa had filmed before. They had shot scenes of their characters off enjoying themselves before they had stumbled upon the legend and the horror of the ghosts who had come back to tear them to shreds.

That afternoon, they docked at Dinner Key in Miami, since they would begin the voyage across the straits — in the Bermuda Triangle — to reach Haunt Island in the

morning. They had a late lunch at Monty's on the water, and after, Sean announced that they were all welcome to do what they wished as long as they were aboard and ready to leave again first thing in the morning.

Vanessa was surprised when Sean suggested that she and Katie and whoever else wanted to should explore the area, go to a club, do something enjoyable.

He didn't tell her what he had planned. She decided to ask him point-blank — they were supposed to be trusting one another.

"So? Where are you going, what are you up to?" she asked him.

Sean hesitated. "I'm off to see a Coast Guard friend of Liam's," he told her.

"I should come," she said.

He shook his head. "He's told us that they didn't get anything."

"Then why are you seeing him?"

"Because I'm hoping to trigger something. Spend the afternoon and evening with Zoe and Katie — and whoever you wish. Jamie won't leave his boat, and Marty has determined that he's going to keep watch over the *Conch Fritter.* Ted and Jaden have some friends to see. So . . . Katie will stick with you like glue," he said.

She frowned. "I don't need to be careful

371

here, do I?"

"You need to be careful everywhere," he assured her. "Just stay in public places, and call me if anything disturbs you at all. At all — okay?"

As the others left one by one, Jay told Vanessa, "I have an idea."

She groaned. "I don't think I want to hear any more of your ideas."

He grimaced. "There's a beautiful little park just north of here, and it has great views of the bay and bridges and downtown Miami. I'd like to take some footage of you there, talking about the time we spent in Miami, and how this had been Georgia's destination the night she — died."

She started to protest. Katie was at her side. "Actually, it doesn't sound like a terrible idea," she said. "We can grab a cab and get there while it's still daylight. And it's not the Keys, but it's a beautiful day, and it should be fine footage. I'll go with you," Katie assured her.

"And I'll come," Zoe said.

"Hey, Barry, Ted — Bill. What are you doing tonight?"

"There's a theater up the street," Bill said. "I thought I'd take in a movie — okay, and do some barhopping in Coconut Grove."

"Barry?" Vanessa asked.

He smiled. "The barhopping sounded good to me, too."

Jake told them, "I'll come with you. I guess we need two cabs, though."

"No big deal, it's right down the street," Jay told them.

They left the restaurant and easily hailed cabs.

The park was beautiful. There were wide-open spaces, and areas for volleyball, little pavilions for picnics and separations that were composed of overgrown trees and rich foliage. Beautiful bougainvillea crawled over the pavilions, and majestic oaks vied with palms. They were on a deepwater channel, but the view of the water was spectacular, and as they arrived, the colorful lights of downtown Miami were just beginning to grace the skyscrapers in the distance.

Jay found the perfect place for her to stand. She was on a small mound with bougainvillea and the richness of the foliage to her left as she faced him while a view of the water, the bridge and downtown were just over her shoulder.

Jay set her up where he wanted her and gave her directions. She told him that they hadn't come up with any kind of a script and he told her just to talk. She'd seen Sean do it, easily and naturally, and she tried to

emulate what he did. Actually, it was easy. She just talked.

"One more time," Jay told her. "And . . . action."

She started to talk.

She looked at Zoe, who smiled at her with a thumbs-up gesture. Katie nodded, as well.

The sun was setting in the west, away from the water. The sky was beautiful and the night was balmy. She looked toward the foliage near the entry of the park, and she fell silent.

There he was.

He was in jeans, a T-shirt and a wind-breaker. His hair was long, but he had shaved the beard.

Carlos Roca.

He stood on the path, watching her.

He beckoned to her.

But then he saw the others start to stare at Vanessa in her sudden, still silence, and twist to see what had caused her reaction.

He turned his back and moved quickly down the path to the right, into the conceal-ment of the rich foliage.

"Vanessa, I just wanted one more take!" Jay said. "What's the matter with you?"

Vanessa ignored him.

And ran after Carlos Roca.

■ ■ ■ ■

They met Andy Jimena at the yacht club where the Coast Guardsman kept a membership. It was beautiful, on the bay, and afforded a view of a host of sailboats and pleasure craft. Jimena was an experienced officer who had been with the patrol boat asked in by the Bahamian government. He was fifty, graying and still as sturdy as a rock.

He and his crew had arrived on the island late in the afternoon after the heads and arms of the murder victims had been found onshore.

"I don't know how much I need to tell you all about the way the sea and the sand can hide evidence, or how deep the channel can be in places and how wind and weather can wreck anything on the sand. I'm telling you, here were the problems — the sand on the beach by the victims was dead dry. There were no prints. No footprints whatsoever. Obviously, someone put those bodies there. We found some smashed bracken nearby and further inland, so I'm assuming that Travis was murdered earlier, and that the killer was either Carlos Roca and he came back with Georgia, killed her, too, cut up the bodies and escaped in the night, or

— there had been someone else on the island, that person had a boat, maybe something really small, got in, killed Travis, pirated Carlos Roca, killed him and the actress, and went back to pose the bodies."

"What about the people on the island?" Sean asked him.

Jimena shrugged. "They all looked as if they were shell-shocked. Lewis Sanderson, a Bahamian national and guide, was with them, and he was in control but equally horrified. The tents the film crew slept in were all near one another. Apparently, they'd been working all day, work was over, they were about to split open some champagne, and Georgia came down the beach screaming. Sanderson said that he walked down the beach with Jay Allen and Vanessa Loren and that they found nothing — except that someone had been digging in the sand, right where the heads and arms were found later. We searched the shoreline and the surrounding water. We sent out divers. We never found the rest of the bodies, Carlos Roca or the boat. Bahamian officials questioned everyone on that island, and although it's a sovereign country, the Bahamians invited the FBI in and their men questioned everyone involved, as well."

"So what did you believe in the end?"

Liam asked him.

"Let's see . . . one woman told me that alien monsters lived in the Bermuda Triangle and that they rose from the depths to kill. But that's not what I believe. I believe that the most logical answer is that Carlos Roca killed the actor — Travis — and came back to camp and behaved normally. Then he left with the girl, killed her, came back and staged the scene — and disappeared himself. It might have been hard for him at first. But there are a lot of places where you can go by boat, and I don't care how any government or law-enforcement group tries — there are just miles and miles and miles of coast around here, along Florida and in the Caribbean. It's possible to disappear. And after a few years, he could establish a new name, and eventually, people would forget to look for him."

"What about the others on the island?" Sean persisted. Jimena frowned, having answered the question once.

"We're working with what was left of that crew now. I'd like to know what you thought of all of them — and if you think it was possible that whoever carried out those murders had an accomplice," Sean explained.

Jimena arched his brows. "Well . . . I suppose it's possible. It seemed to me that they

were all in reach of one another, but . . . I suppose you'd have to ask them all if they're really certain they were all together at the times when it occurred. I know that when the investigations took place, no one suspected the survivors of being guilty."

"That doesn't mean that they weren't," David said quietly.

"Well, no, of course not. All I can tell you is that it was . . . clean, if that makes sense. There were no mounds of drying blood. There were no footprints, no fingerprints, and there wasn't a murder weapon to be found, and they had to have been chopped to pieces. We searched for the boat and never found it. If you're out with that crew and you're the least bit suspicious, well — I'd keep one hell of a good eye on them." Solid, experienced man that Jimena was, he shuddered. "That was one hell of a scene on Haunt Island. One hell of a scene."

Soon after, they left Jimena, thanking him for his help.

"I think there's something we should start doing," Sean said as he, David and Liam headed back.

Liam looked at him sharply.

"I've charted a number of recent disappearances. I think we might want to make another chart and do some comparisons.

378

You're the only one with the contacts to do it, Liam," Sean told him.

"All right. What am I doing?" Liam asked.

Sean explained.

"Vanessa! Vanessa!"

It was natural, of course, that the others ran after her.

She ignored them at first, running as fast as she could to the path, and then frantically searching the smaller trails among the foliage, hoping against hope that she would find Carlos, that he would be alive and real, and ready to tell her the truth about what had happened — including the fact that he was innocent.

But Carlos was nowhere to be found, and she was left on a path, frustrated and breathless.

A twig snapped behind her and she jumped, suddenly aware that the sun had fallen, she was in the midst of bushes — and she was supposed to be careful and wary.

She spun around.

It was Jay.

He was angry.

He held the camera at his side. It slapped against his leg.

"What the hell are you doing?" he de-

manded.

He took a step toward her. In her life, she had never been afraid of Jay. She reminded herself that she had known him forever. He was the little kid her own age who lived down the street.

But she stepped back.

Jay started to lift the camera. She had the bizarre fear that he was about to crash it down on her head.

But Zoe came running down the path, crashing into Jay's back. And Jake was right behind Zoe.

"Hey!" Jake said, trying to defuse the situation. Apparently, Jake realized that Jay was really angry.

"Vanessa!" Zoe gasped.

Katie came running from the other direction. She was armed.

She held a giant stick in her hand.

"Vanessa, oh, thank God!" Katie breathed.

"What in hell were you doing?" Jay demanded, still angry.

She opened her mouth. She didn't want to tell anyone about Carlos. Especially not Jay. Not at that moment.

"I was imagining things," she said. "Silly. Ridiculous. I — I thought I saw Dona Isabella standing here."

"What?" Jay exclaimed.

Zoe gasped. "What?"

"It's ridiculous. I'm a little unnerved, I guess. Finding a corpse, finding out the corpse was stolen. I'm sorry, guys, really, I saw a lady standing here and thought it was Dona Isabella. Actually, I scared the poor woman half to death. She was a young Cuban woman, strikingly beautiful, just like Dona Isabella," Vanessa said. The lying was coming too easily, but then, she had thought once that she'd seen Dona Isabella, or she did see her often, her face carved as a figurehead, in her dreams . . . Maybe reality and imagination were blending so that the line was barely there anymore, this lie was coming so easily.

"Oh, Lord, oh, Lord!" Zoe exclaimed, horrified.

Maybe she should have said that she'd seen Carlos Roca. Jay was staring at her as if she was crazy, and Zoe looked terrified.

"Look, I'm sorry, I ruined your brilliant idea. It's getting really dark, they must be about to send the rangers in to close this place, and I want to get back to the boats," she said.

Jay looked at her and then sighed. "Well, the first take was good. And when you took off, I wound up with some fantastic shots of the sky. But get a grip, girl!"

"Dammit, Jay, just give me a break, okay?" Vanessa asked. She cursed herself. Surely she could have thought of a different lie! One that wasn't — supernatural.

"Oh, God, oh, God!" Zoe said.

"Hey, there's a cute little restaurant bar just down from Dinner Key marina — we'll go and indulge in big stiff drinks and feel better all the way around!" Jake suggested.

Vanessa didn't want a drink. She wanted to be away from all of them. Except for Katie.

But Katie wanted peace and happiness all the way round. "One big stiff drink apiece," she said. "We'll have a long day tomorrow. One big friendly drink."

"And Vanessa will start seeing little green people, aliens in the Bermuda Triangle," Jay said.

Jake punched Jay in the arm — not hard, but soundly. "Jay, stop!"

Jay stared at Jake. He had a superior, angry look in his eyes for a moment. The look seemed to say *Hey, I'm a director/ producer, I'm the boss.*

But Jay wasn't a producer/director on this shoot.

He let out a breath suddenly. "Jake, thanks — I needed that," he said with a laugh. "Vanessa, I'm sorry. I was just — You looked

so beautiful there, your hair kind of floating in the breeze, with the lights and the bridge and the foliage. And it was forlorn, it had . . . oh, well. I'm a great editor. I'll make it work, and Sean and David will love it."

He was Jay again. The Jay she had known forever. She felt silly, being afraid of him.

"Let's get that drink," she said.

They had fun. Vanessa was pleased that she hadn't insisted she was going back.

The bar was composed of a small number of tables with palm-frond shelters over them, their waitress was nice, and a single guitarist played and sang.

When they returned to the boat, Marty was on deck, taking his guard duty very seriously.

"Ahoy, who goes there?" he demanded.

"It's us — we're back," Vanessa told him. She was capable of jumping down to the deck, as were Zoe and Jay, but Marty rose, ever the gentleman, to help them on board.

"Are the guys back yet, Marty?" Vanessa asked.

"Jaden and Ted came back half an hour ago, and they're both in bed. Sean, Liam and David are still out, but they'll be along soon, I warrant," he said cheerfully. "I'll be right here, right here on deck, if you need

me, though."

"Thanks, Marty," she told him. "I guess I am calling it a night. Good night, Jay."

"Good night, Vanessa," Jay said. "I'll hang out here with Marty a bit, I guess." He was silent, looking at her. "Good night," he said again, and then, his back to Marty, he mouthed, "I'm sorry. I'm really sorry."

She smiled and nodded. "See you in the morning."

In the master's cabin, she started. Bartholomew was next to the bed, one ghostly buckle-shoe foot upon it as he stood in a Captain Morgan stance. He gave her a start, and she thought again that she was having trouble with reality and fiction or imagination.

He was a ghost, he was real. As real as a ghost could be. Others saw him.

He was glaring at her.

"What?" she murmured.

He shook his head, and then wagged a finger at her.

"I followed you today," he said.

"You did? Well, that was . . . nice of you? Or nosy of you?" she asked.

He sighed, set his foot on the floor and walked to her. It was odd. She could feel him. At first, she had thought that he was cold. A cold breeze.

But now she thought that he offered a strange warmth. She saw his eyes, and he was concerned. Bartholomew liked her. She was glad.

She would have liked him.

"Vanessa, I don't know what you're thinking, but you have to tell Sean the truth," Bartholomew said.

"What truth?"

"That Carlos Roca was in the park, following you. At least, I think that's who it is. And he was in Key West, too, at the pirate festivities. He's been watching you — and following you," Bartholomew said.

Vanessa gasped. She sank down on the bed in the cabin, and Bartholomew sank down beside her.

"He's real," she whispered.

"Yes," Bartholomew said.

"Real — and alive?" Vanessa asked.

"The man was no ghost. Trust me, sadly, I know," Bartholomew said. He sighed. "Obviously, I can tell Sean and David, because they have a right to know. But I really don't like telling tales when it's someone else's business. But people were killed. They might have been killed by Carlos Roca. The man might be stalking you. You might be his next intended victim. Vanessa, this is scary. Terrifying. And I think

you've suspected that he's out there. Why haven't you told Sean?"

She was about to answer when she heard Jay's voice, whispering to her from just beyond the door. "Vanessa? Is something wrong? Are you all right?"

"Fine, Jay!" she replied in a loud whisper. "Fine — I was singing, that's all. Sorry!"

He laughed. "Now you're singing! Night, sweetie."

"Night!"

Vanessa waited until she heard him move away and then she whispered to Bartholomew. "I just can't believe it. I really can't. What if Carlos is trying to reach me because he is innocent, because he needs my help, because he suspects or knows what really happened?" she asked.

"You still need to tell Sean. Look, there are other lives at stake here," he reminded her.

He touched her cheek with a ghostly hand. She thought that she could feel the warmth and tenderness. "I'm going topside, help old Marty keep watch," he said.

She nodded. He stood and looked at her.

"I'll tell him," she said.

He nodded, and disappeared through the door.

Sean was surprised and glad when he arrived back on the boat to find that Vanessa was awake. She stirred when he quietly entered the cabin and stripped down to join her in bed.

"Hey," he said softly.

She smiled in the dim light that filtered through from the dock.

"You aren't on guard duty," she said.

"Ted is taking a turn," he told her. "Had to get Marty to get some sleep," he added dryly. "Did you have a nice night? What did you do?"

She studied him carefully. "We went to a park. Jay took some footage. Let's see, Bill and Barry went bar-hopping, but Zoe, Jay, Jake, Katie and I went to a park. Jay had an idea for a scene, and he's all excited. He thinks you're going to like it."

"I probably will. He's good."

She was still searching out his eyes. He smiled and kissed her lips. She drew the covers more tightly around her and she frowned, trying to understand her sudden reticence with him.

She let out a deep, pent-up breath. "Sean, I saw Carlos Roca."

"What?" He sat up, staring at her, trying to fathom her eyes in the shadows.

"Actually, I had just *thought* that I'd seen Carlos, but . . . Bartholomew was with us, following us, and he said that it was Carlos Roca."

"So the man has been hiding in Miami," Sean said, "hiding in plain sight." He started to rise.

"Sean, wait. Where are you going?" she asked.

"To notify the authorities," he said.

"But what if he's in hiding — because he's innocent?" Vanessa asked.

"Vanessa, if he's innocent, he'll be able to prove it."

"How? We both know that he looks guilty as hell, and that innocent men do go to prison," she argued.

He stared down at her and shook his head sadly. "Vanessa, I have to notify the authorities. If he's been living here —"

"He hasn't been living here," she said.

"What? How do you know? Did he accost you?" he asked, coming down beside her again, drawing her to him. "Did he hurt you, did he threaten you, did —"

"No, no, no. I never got close to him. But he was in Key West."

He eased away, trying to study her face

again. "You saw him in Key West, and you didn't tell me?" he asked her.

"I didn't know that I had seen him. I *thought* that I might have seen him," she said. "But then, God knows what I see anymore!"

"So he is following you," Sean said.

"I don't know that. And if he is, I swear, I think it's because he needs help."

"Vanessa, what happened to the trust thing that was supposed to be going on between us?" he asked her softly.

"I do trust you. I just know how you feel."

He nodded slowly. "You wouldn't have told me now — except that Bartholomew saw him, too."

"Your *ghost*," she reminded him dryly.

He stood. He reached for his jeans again. "Sean —"

"Vanessa, I'm really sorry. The authorities have to know," he told her. He walked to the deck. Ted was leaning back on the aft cushions, watching the stars — and the dock.

"What's up?" he asked.

"A Carlos Roca sighting," he said. "I'm going up to radio the Coast Guard and let the police know that the man was seen in Miami."

"Roca?" Ted sat up straight. "Do you

389

think . . . Wow. Do you think he'll come after the rest of that crew?"

"Ted, we're traveling the way we are just to make sure we don't have trouble and that no one can take us by surprise. But if you're worried about you and Jaden, I can leave you here and you can get a rental car to take home."

"No. No," Ted told him. "We're on this. We've discussed it. We're with you all the way. And I'm ready. Trust me. I'm ready." He showed Sean that he had a speargun down by his side. "I know how to use this faster than a winking eye, and you know it."

Sean nodded. "Yeah, I know."

He radioed the Coast Guard first, and then called the police, and then David. Bartholomew was seated in the companion seat, aware of Ted just below.

"She told you," Bartholomew said.

Sean nodded.

Bartholomew looked out at the water, at the various boats docked at the public marina. "You had to know," he said.

"Yep."

"I'll be on deck," Bartholomew said.

Sean smiled. "Thanks."

He went back down, telling Ted that he'd spell him in three hours.

He went back to his cabin.

Vanessa's eyes were closed. He didn't think that she was sleeping, but he lay down beside her without touching her.

A moment later she spoke in the darkness. "You called the police?"

"Yes."

She was silent, staying on her own side of the bed. He didn't press the matter. He had done what he had to do, even if he understood that the man had been her friend and she believed in him.

But everyone on that island had been her friend. She trusted them all.

And the more he thought about it all, the more he learned, Sean didn't believe that there had been someone in a boat who had slipped onto the island, killed Travis, gone after Carlos Roca and Georgia, killed Georgia, dismembered two bodies, and escaped with the boat and Carlos Roca, who was now miraculously alive and well.

That was too suspect.

Someone in that film crew had been guilty. Someone knew more than they were saying. And with the violence and brutality of the murders, he doubted that it was someone who had killed only once, for a purpose. That someone had killed before, had probably killed again, and would keep killing. It seemed likely that maybe that person was involved in

391

a murder conspiracy with Carlos Roca.

"I'm sorry," Sean said.

"So am I," she said.

He smiled. "Are you sorry that I called the police — or sorry that you didn't tell me earlier?"

"Both," she said after a moment.

He rolled toward her and reached for her, pulling her into his arms. "Please understand. It's a dangerous world out there," he said softly.

"I know," she told him gravely.

He nodded. He wasn't sure what else to say. He kissed her. And then he knew that he'd have to leave soon enough, take his turn on guard duty.

He made love to her, slowly, tenderly, and she responded, making love in turn, her kisses gentle, her whispers soft . . . her movement fluid. They winced together at one point — it was a boat, and they were trying to be quiet, and they were, but . . .

They lay together afterward, and the boat rocked gently, and he heard a distant bell.

"I don't think that it will matter that I called the Miami police," he told her.

"Why not?"

"Because I think he's already out there. Carlos Roca knows where we're going, he knows our route, and he knows we're

392

headed for Haunt Island.

"And he's already on his way."

14

"Let's head straight on over, set up camp on the island and work backward from there," Sean suggested. He and David had met at the breakfast bar near the marina. He opened the book he kept on their schedule with relevant sea charts and maps. "We're clear with the Bahamian authorities, and I started doing calculations on what I could find regarding the current at the time, the time of year and the storm — and I think that once the pirate ship started to take on water and break up during the storm, it would have been forced out of the deep water where it was always assumed to have sunk, and that the debris field would stretch out not far from the first drop-off to the southwest of Haunt Island."

"I like the logic of getting there, setting up a base and moving on from Haunt Island," David said. "You like the split that we have of people? Yesterday was the first

time it seemed you didn't trust everyone with us."

"I don't. I don't trust anyone right now."

"Especially Carlos Roca? And you really think that Vanessa saw him — and that it was him?"

Sean shrugged, looking toward the marina. "There are just so many factors in this situation that make no sense. I'm going to try to get Vanessa to take me through it all again, step by step, from earlier in the afternoon *before* Georgia Dare came running down the beach. The thing is, I don't think that one person could have done all this. I think that if Carlos was guilty, he had to have had an accomplice. If he wasn't guilty, two people had to be involved. Yes, it's possible that there was a boat at anchor near the island that was hidden from view behind palms or foliage or even the curve of the shoreline. But the thing is — *why?* Don't you think that someone must have had a reason — no matter how psychotic — to butcher bodies and leave them on display?"

"There's the outside chance that an islander, dismayed with what they were doing on Haunt Island, lay in wait, and that the murders were because of outrage over mak-

ing a film based on the massacre," David said.

"Yes, there's an outside chance," Sean agreed. "I know that Liam ran everything he could on Lew Sanderson, the Bahamian guide who was with them."

"The man is squeaky-clean. He's worked with dignitaries from around the world. He's a family man, married twenty years, two children, and known for helping out in times of distress, such as doing volunteer road work and clearance after storms. His neighbors love him — he's an open book, so it seems," David said. He drummed his fingers on the breakfast table. "I think your idea of matching up people and places over the last two years is a good one, and I know that Liam is on the computer now. It doesn't seem possible to me that someone could commit such a horrible crime, then go back to a normal life as if nothing ever happened."

"That's my point. And I still say . . . I don't know, we're missing something, and I think it has to do with the *why,* and if we could just figure that out, we'd discover the *who.*"

David leaned back, shaking his head. "Well, there are plenty of theories. First, chalk it up to the Bermuda Triangle. Sec-

ond, it *is* called Haunt Island."

"We both know that a ghost — or even ghosts — didn't commit those murders."

"Agreed — I'm just throwing out the theories," David said.

"Right," Sean agreed. "Third theory — modern-day pirates, cleverly plotting. They committed gruesome murders and stole a boat and dumped Carlos Roca's body overboard. But now Carlos Roca has been seen, so that theory is out. Okay, fourth theory. It was Carlos Roca, and he had friends — modern-day pirates — in on it. Fifth theory, Carlos was innocent, and he was hit on the head and is walking around suffering from amnesia. But that's unlikely, considering the fact that there was an intensive manhunt going on for him after it first happened. Sixth theory — someone on the film crew was in on it with Carlos Roca. That's why he's alive and well, it's how he managed to stay 'missing' all this time, and it's why he seems to be following us now."

"We're still back to why," David said. "All those people had good careers. What would make a professional with no record whatsoever suddenly commit murder?"

"That's something we have to find out," Sean said. "It's going to be interesting, though. All of us so close together. And

that's how we're going to stay. The film crew — or at least the majority of it — wasn't expecting anything bad to happen. They were working. They were in a place that was a pristine hangout for boaters. There was no reason to expect anything. And we know damned well that bad things happen. So . . ." Sean hesitated. "Maybe Katie should stay here, in Miami," he said. "I asked Ted last night . . . but he wants in."

"Katie won't go back — you know your sister," David said. "Look, I really think that we're dealing with cowards here. The whole company wasn't killed. Travis was probably taken by surprise. And as far as Carlos and Georgia and the boat . . . well, any way you look at it, it was one man who was the surprise, or was taken from the back in the dark. We'll be all right. Marty and Jamie are fierce old pirates, we've got Liam, you and me. Once we're on the island, we'll have perimeter, with one us on guard at all times, maybe two of us. So here's the thing. We do it or we don't. And at this point, I say we do it."

Sean nodded and called for the check.

It was a beautiful day for the trip across the straits from Miami to Haunt Island. The boats moved parallel across fairly calm seas,

the sky was a pristine blue with only a few puffs of white clouds, and the sun shone down brilliantly throughout the day.

Seated in the companion seat, Vanessa was glad enough to laze the time away. Marty took the helm several times, and Jay and Sean spent the hours filming the voyage. Sean did a few minutes on the straits, the proximity of the Bahamas to Florida, and how the voyage would have been different in the eighteen hundreds when the wind played such an important role in travel. They pointed out the area where Mad Miller's pirate ship had supposedly gone down, and Sean gave his calculations on the currents of the time, estimating that the debris field had to extend farther than it had often been presumed.

Vanessa was roused for a few moments to do a two-minute take on her research regarding Dona Isabella, Mad Miller and Kitty Cutlass, and how they had followed the same path when they had been making the film.

She was surprised when Sean filmed Jay, asking him about his feelings on the distribution of the film. Jay sounded sincere when he said that he believed that Georgia and Travis would have wanted it shown — they had been actors, after all — and that he

hoped they could find the truth, see that the murderer was punished and be able to distribute the film feeling that they had justice and closure at last.

Jay's speech seemed heartfelt.

From her comfortable perch, a warm poncho around her shoulders against the chill of the wind, Vanessa observed Sean's questions as he interviewed Zoe and Jake, wanting to know everything that had happened on the island the day that Georgia and Travis had been murdered. Jake had been in charge of props, and he explained that it was easy to understand why they had all dismissed Georgia's fears — any one of them might have played a prank.

When she had come screaming down the sand, he had been in his little tent, getting ready to come on out and share the champagne.

Zoe talked about her love of the period costumes and relayed the story about the afternoon when they'd dressed Vanessa up as a deceased Dona Isabella and gotten a bit carried away, forgetting that she was floating in the ocean in heavy materials. She had last seen Travis that afternoon, when they had filmed the scene in which help had come to the island at last. She, too, had been in her tent, pleased with the film and

hoping for great distribution and big notches on their résumés for future work.

Vanessa noted that Bartholomew was silent, watching their destination before them and listening intently to the interviews. He seemed thoughtful.

They arrived at the island at just about three that afternoon.

She rose and went aft, watching as they came upon Haunt Island and trying to remember when she had been there last. Now it all seemed such a blur. The island appeared lovely and tropical, totally benign in the bright sunlit day. She had thought she would feel something. She had thought that she'd be afraid. She wasn't. It was just an island.

Lew Sanderson was standing at the end of the dock, waiting to greet them. He waved a welcome and caught the ties as the *Conch Fritter* drew in first. Vanessa hopped to the dock and was enveloped in a huge hug by the big man.

It felt good.

The *Claddagh* pulled into the dockage behind the *Conch Fritter.* Vanessa and Lew caught her ties, and soon everyone was standing on the dock. Lew greeted those he knew and met those he didn't, and the next two hours were spent setting up camp on

the island. There was nothing terribly rustic about camping on the island; the tents were large, the camp bunks were not uncomfortable, they had an impressive barbecue area and a battery-operated coffeemaker, not to mention that showers could be had back at the boats — they were well supplied.

By the time all the work was done, they were exhausted, and Vanessa thought that they might have forgotten that terrible things had happened here. They had all seemed to work very well together, hauling boxes and bags to the beach, setting up the tents and then, when all was done, digging a pit and starting a fire on the beach. Sean had brought a good supply of torches as well, and as darkness settled, their area of the beach was still aglow. The sea remained calm and easy and the sound of the waves was lulling. She was amazed to enjoy the glow and the company as they worked together and finally sat down to a meal.

She, Jay, Sean and Barry had taken turns with cameras during the day, documenting their setup. She forgot that Barry was still filming as dinnertime rolled around — Zoe in charge that night, supervising Bill fondly as she barbecued hot dogs and hamburgers and warmed baked beans in a huge pot, and announcing — with a smile for the camera

— that she also had spinach so that they could make certain the meal was healthful. They had to keep up their strength, of course.

Then they sat by the fire, eating. It seemed relaxed. But Vanessa was aware that five people had subtly been changing an important position throughout the day. Guard duty. As Sean took a seat beside her, she saw that his uncle Jamie was standing at the perimeter of the group, watching the dock, the sea and the foliage. He was wearing a windbreaker, and she thought there was a bulge beneath his arm. Jamie was carrying a gun.

If there was tension within their group, Lew Sanderson didn't seem to know it. He entertained them with a Bahamian tale about a talking raccoon, and they all laughed, and then he told them another story, his face dark and mysterious as it was caught in the glow of the fire. "They say we are in the Bermuda Triangle, but long before it had such a name, the people here knew that there was something special about the air. The earth herself is mysterious, and as man has come to learn all about technology and science, he has often forgotten that no matter how far we go, we are dots in the universe, and the universe itself

403

is a mystery. Now, you know, my ancestors who came to these islands came as slaves, and they brought with them a certain magic that belonged to their ancestors. They were open to the world, open to life and death, and aware that all things were not to be seen. Nowadays, we claim that there are underwater forces here. There are the currents, there are the wicked wonders and destruction of the storms and hurricanes that ravage the area. Ah, yes! There are magnetic forces in the earth as well, and they cause confusion, the horizon itself can trick a pilot or a captain. But my people believed that there were gods and devils that dwelled on earth, between the realms of life and death. Forces, for good and for evil. Ki-andra, the sea god, once appeared as an ugly thing in need before two sisters. The first spurned him and married a handsome man. The second felt pity, fed him and married him, and went to live with him in his fine kingdom in the sea, bearing many children. The handsome man the sister married proved to be a *kishi,* an evil devil or demon. She had a child with a human head and a hyena head, and in the end, her husband devoured her. Her spirit remained, evil and bitter, and when Africans came here, many believed that what we call the Bermuda

Triangle now was where the first sister's bitter soul came to dwell and that now, while the sea god Kiandra and his wife seek to save those who travel the sea, the evil sister's influence can make men crazy, can make the evil dead within the ocean rise and cause all kinds of havoc. There are those who believe that the magnetic forces that cause compasses to spin and ships and planes to go astray are merely the toys of the spirit of the evil sister, and that she teases her prey before she kills, just like a great cat of the sea."

Zoe laughed softy, but the sound seemed a little nervous. "Lew! You don't believe that story, do you?"

Lew smiled. "It is a tale, it is a legend. All people have tales and legends, and perhaps they come from a grain of truth." He shrugged. "I do believe in good and evil, and they dwell within all of us."

"On that, I'll have more coffee!" Bill said. He stood, and having been sitting next to Zoe, he asked her, "Zoe, more coffee? You're shivering."

"I admit to being a little nervous," she said.

He smiled at her. "Don't be. I'll protect you," he said.

Watching them, Vanessa smiled. She

405

hadn't realized — though perhaps she should have — that Bill seemed to have a crush on Zoe. Ah, the slightly older woman. She smiled back at Bill. Maybe Zoe had a crush on the younger man, as well. "Thanks," Zoe said. "I'll hold you to that!"

Well, that was good. Zoe would have Bill with her, and she wouldn't be as nervous, and there was always safety in numbers.

"I think I'm just calling it a night," Katie said, yawning. "I imagine we want to start out on a dive pretty early?" she asked.

"Actually, I was thinking just after twelve tomorrow," Sean said. "I want to take some footage with the original film crew, each person talking a bit more about what they did. And we'll take a walk down the beach, see what we see. Maybe discern if another boat might have come in during the night."

"Well, a boat had to have come in — I think," Barry said. He was frowning. "I mean, if a boat didn't come in, it means . . . Carlos . . . or . . ." He fell silent.

The group was silent.

The fire snapped and crackled.

"One of us will be on guard all night, every night," Sean said.

"One of us?" Jake asked.

"One of us who *wasn't* with the original crew," Sean said.

There was silence again. "Well, good night, all," Katie said, and she left the group.

Sean rose and talked to Marty for a moment. The others began to rise and murmur good-nights and head for their tents.

Vanessa realized that Marty was going to bed; that Sean was taking the first watch.

He looked at her and she smiled, nodded and turned to head for their tent. She slipped inside and almost started — she still wasn't accustomed to Bartholomew showing up all the time.

"Sean is on first watch," he said softly.

She sat at the foot of her canvas bunk, smiling. "And you're watching over me?"

He winced. "Hey, I can *watch* over you at least. And I can make a few things happen. I can push buttons . . . I can trip people. I'm not bad at manifestations, but . . ."

"What?" Vanessa asked.

"I was listening to that fellow tonight, the Bahamian, Lew Sanderson," Bartholomew said.

"He was telling a story," Vanessa said. "An African legend."

"Yes, of course. But often . . . well, gods and goddesses, angels and demons . . . it's strange how the world can be so different, and yet so much the same. The Norse had Odin, the Romans, Jupiter, and the Greeks

had Zeus, and he was nearly one and the same. The Christian, Jewish and Muslim faiths recognize one God, but he lives in Heaven with the angels, and the angels often have characteristics that line up with the lesser gods in other religions."

She was startled at first that he seemed so philosophical, but then she realized that he was seriously troubled by Lew's story.

"You're talking about the fact that people here thought the bitter sister's soul haunted the ocean, while many people now believe there's something eerie about the Bermuda Triangle?" Vanessa asked.

He nodded. He stared at her. "Well, I told you — the legend that has come down about Mad Miller and Kitty Cutlass . . . well, there's just something wrong with it. Mad Miller got his name because another fellow was making fun of him one day and called him *mad* because he was . . . well, he was a bit of a fop. He hated blood. And Kitty . . . Kitty was in love with Mad Miller because he was the best thing that ever came along in her sad and pathetic life. You were making a film about them and Dona Isabella. I was thinking that . . . well, obviously, *I'm* still around, and maybe they are, too."

"Bartholomew, we've all agreed that

408

ghosts couldn't have committed the murders," Vanessa said. "I mean, thank God . . . thank God we do have you, because we know what ghosts can and can't do. And I always believed that ghosts stayed behind because . . . they were lost, or they needed help, or justice, or they stayed behind to help others."

"Maybe," Bartholomew said.

"What do you mean *maybe?* You are a ghost!" Vanessa reminded him.

He nodded. "It doesn't mean I have all the answers. Hey, I was a decent fellow in life. I'm a damned decent fellow in death. But perhaps, if you were a bastard in life, you stay a bastard in death."

"You keep telling me that Mad Miller was basically a prissy-ass pansy," Vanessa said with a sigh.

"Yes, I know, though your language is quite colorful," Bartholomew said.

"Sorry."

"That's why I'm perplexed," Bartholomew said. "Ah, well, you had best get some sleep. I think you'll need it in the days to come." He stood. "I'll be near," he promised her.

She smiled, thanked him and bid him good-night.

It wasn't until he was gone and she lay back and watched the fire dancing on the

canvas of the tent that she felt alone and uneasy — and suddenly fully aware of the last time she had lain in a tent on the beach at Haunt Island.

She remembered dreaming first that Georgia had come to her. She had almost heard the young woman's voice in the shadows of the night as tears streamed down her cheeks.

I told you there were monsters.

Then Georgia's image had faded, and she must have seen the shadows against the canvas of the tent even in her sleep, because they had seemed like giant monsters rising from the sea, made of seaweed, forming arms, reaching into the sky.

She sighed and lay awake, and thought that she would do so until Sean's watch was over.

But somewhere along the line, she fell asleep, and she didn't dream. She was vaguely aware of Sean coming into the tent, and she was comfortably aware that she tried to get close to him.

Then she let out a startled little cry — completely unaware that she had fallen.

"Vanessa!" It was Sean's voice, and a light suddenly flared in their little tent. She was on the ground between the two cots. They'd been pushed together, but in trying to get too close, she had wedged them apart.

Sean was stretched out on his own, flashlight in one hand as he smiled and reached for her hand with the other.

She grimaced ruefully. "I suppose I forgot where we were."

"Hey!"

"Vanessa!"

"What's going on?"

There was a chorus of voices just outside the tent. She scrambled up, glad that she had chosen to sleep in an encompassing flannel gown. She pushed open the flap to the tent just as Katie was nervously opening it.

"Vanessa!" Katie said.

David was behind her, Liam was behind him, and it seemed that everyone was gathered outside their little tent.

"You screamed!" Zoe said.

Barry cleared his throat. "Um, it didn't sound like a scream of . . . um, er, happiness."

Sean was behind her then. "Sorry, all."

"I fell off the cot," Vanessa said, aware of the flush that was rising to her cheeks like fire.

"What?" Bill said, and then started to laugh.

"Oh, Lord! You scared us silly," Zoe said, laughing, as well.

"No more even slightly scary stories around the campfire," Lew Sanderson said, shaking his head. "May I suggest you pull the cot mattresses down and leave them on the sand?"

"Great idea, Lew, thanks," Sean said. "Forgive us, folks, and get some sleep."

The good thing was that everyone seemed to be amused. The negative, of course, was seeing just how on edge they had all been.

And probably would remain.

Sean looked down at her, his grin broad. He pulled her into his arms. "Let's get those mattresses down, huh? We'll fold up the bunks — I think we'll wind up with more room."

She agreed. It was really late; they were both exhausted, and aware of the thinness of the canvas that separated them from the others.

And still . . .

It was good to be close. Seaweed monsters were just shadows on canvas, and Georgia Dare did not return that night with tears streaming down her face to plague Vanessa's dreams.

She thought the morning might be bad as well, with the interviews on the beach. But the sun was shining, the day was bright, and

it was hard to imagine that anything horrible had happened in such a beautiful place on such a pristine beach.

They were surrounded by people.

That was good.

Marty and Jamie O'Hara seemed large, wise and imposing, and as she watched the men, naturally taking positions that seemed to guard the group from opposite angles, she realized that they had been asked along from the very beginning because Sean had felt that he needed a security force of those he knew and trusted. They were able seaman, divers and outdoorsmen, but they took no part in any of the filming. They simply watched, interested.

The only one missing during the morning was Liam. Sean told her he was doing some work on his computer on the boat. He didn't mention what. But Liam was a police officer, and he had taken leave at a time when the force was short, and she assumed he was keeping in contact with his colleagues, keeping up on events in Key West.

She was interviewed with Jay, who was matter-of-fact. She spoke about seeing the heads when she had come down the beach. Jay walked to the sand and winced as he told about his disbelief at what they had come upon.

They were all quiet and somewhat mournful when they finished the segment. They walked back to the encampment in comparative silence. Once there, however, everyone set about the business of a light lunch, since they'd head out to the reefs and an afternoon dive soon after. Zoe and Katie went about setting out the sandwich meats, cheeses, lettuce, tomatoes and condiments, but everyone helped themselves, and everyone picked up after themselves.

It was decided that Lew, Marty, Ted, Jaden and Zoe would stay behind to keep an eye on the encampment. They would take out Jamie's boat, the *Claddagh,* because he had recently purchased new sonar equipment, and Sean and David were eager to see if his calculations might be right, if they might find some of the debris from the pirate ship in shallower water.

There was an hour of busywork, coming and going from the *Conch Fritter* and the *Claddagh* as they transferred dive equipment and supplies from one boat to the other, but in the end, once again, it seemed that they all moved smoothly.

As the divers and crew climbed aboard, Vanessa noted that Bill looked forlornly back at Zoe, and that Zoe smiled and waved.

The romance was blooming.

Bartholomew seemed torn. At the last minute, however, he came aboard the boat.

They set out, running slowly due southwest of the island. Sean grew excited at a blip on the screen, but a study of the sea charts showed that it was a World War II ship that had gone down in 1943; at war's end, it was already becoming part of a growing reef.

"Wait," Sean said. "Uncle Jamie, let's bring her around. If there is something here, that could be a reason that it has never been found!"

"Sean, good call — worth an exploration, at least," David said. "That happened with the old British ship *Renegade* in the Bay of Bengal. She had twisted beneath a trawler that went down several hundred years later."

Barry was filming the discussion. "Wow, yeah, we might have found something!"

His excitement was such that he forgot that he was filming.

"Ahem, camera, my friend!" Jay reminded him.

"Let's break out the diving gear and the casements for the cameras," Sean said. "David, obviously, you and Katie. Jamie —"

"I'll be aboard, keeping watch on the line and my boat!" Jamie said firmly.

"You want me on board or in the water?"

Jay asked.

Sean seemed to hesitate for just a second.

He doesn't trust Jay! Vanessa thought.

"What about me?" Barry asked.

"Barry, you're up here, camera ready, with Jamie," Sean said.

Barry frowned. "I —"

"You're the soundman, Barry, and you're good with a camera, too. Be ready when we come up," Sean said.

"Where do you want me?" Bill asked.

"Make it a threesome with Vanessa and me," Sean said. "And, Jake — you tag on with Katie and David."

He had done it again, Vanessa realized — divided the old group. Jamie would watch Barry. Marty was onshore, along with Ted and Jaden, keeping an eye on Lew and Zoe. Liam — David's cousin and Sean's close friend — would be watching Jay. David would have his eye on Jake.

Barry seemed unhappy but resigned. He brightened while the others got into their gear and asked Jamie if he had any fishing equipment.

Jamie scowled. "You'll be catching the divers!"

"No!" Barry protested. "I'll be catching fresh fish for dinner!"

Jamie shook his head but assured Barry

416

he had fishing equipment, but that Barry needed to remember that he was in charge of filming when the divers surfaced.

As Vanessa slipped her mask and regulator on and held the mask in place in order to slip over the hull backward, she noticed Bartholomew. He was standing aft, looking back at the island.

As they descended, the water was clear and beautiful until they reached thirty-three feet and paused to pressurize. Another twenty feet down, and while visibility was still good, the sunlight didn't penetrate as well.

Vanessa saw the hull of the old World War II vessel and followed Sean around the port-side, aware that Bill was keeping pace with her. Sean had the camera, and Vanessa was glad.

It was the camera lens that seemed to play tricks on her.

Sean motioned Bill, instructing him down to the sand where something peculiar seemed to be stuck just beneath the vessel.

It was while they were occupied that Vanessa saw the figurehead.

It was just feet in front of the men. She wouldn't be leaving her partners to follow it, to see if it was real.

To see if it led her to an old treasure again,

a pendant.

Or a dead body.

She moved toward it in the water and realized that it was actually within a torn segment of the World War II ship's hull. No. She wasn't going to follow — not without her fellow divers knowing that she was entering the wreck.

She turned, giving a massive kick with her flippers, only to realize that she was already inside the ship. She moved toward the hole through which she had entered, only to discover that the ship seemed to have shifted; the entryway — the exit! — was no more.

And there was no figurehead to be seen.

For a split second, she nearly panicked.

It had all scrambled her mind; she was going ever-so-slightly crazy — and now it was going to trap her and kill her.

She braced herself, checked her air gauge and her compass, and knew that her partners weren't far away. She moved in the opposite direction from the false lure of the figurehead with the face of Dona Isabella *that didn't really exist.*

The tear in the giant craft was just ahead of her. As she reached it, she saw that the ship had probably been sunk by a torpedo — there was a giant hole extending beneath

its watery graveyard in the sand. And beneath it . . .

There was something.

It looked like a broken shaft of wood. There were clumps and lumps all over it, encrusted in barnacles and sea growth. She reached for it with gloved hands and struggled to pull it free. It gave, but it was heavy.

She banged against the hull of the ship with her dive knife. A second later, Sean came through water toward her, his eyes showing concern through his mask.

She'd never let him know that she had nearly panicked, and thought herself trapped!

She smiled around her regulator and gave him an okay signal. He saw what she had.

He lifted the camera as Bill moved himself through the water to help her grasp the heavy object. He signed to her, and they carried it between them with Sean following. They made their way to the anchor line and moved up to thirty-three feet, waited and moved up again, following the line.

The others had seen them. They begin to ascend, as well.

Jamie was at the dive platform, ready to help them. Vanessa heard Barry say a quick "Oh, shit!" And then he had a camera rolling. Bill climbed out first and shed his tank

and BCV in order to help Jamie shift the piece from the dive platform to the boat. Katie followed, throwing her flippers on board and hauling herself up. Sean was quickly behind her, and she reached for the camera. Soon, they were aboard, and the piece she had found was lying on the stern section of the deck with the group gathered around to stare at it.

"It's a piece of a mast," Jamie said.

"And the clumps?" Barry asked.

Jamie stared at Barry, grinning, and then looked at Sean. "Ted and Jaden will have some work to do tonight. Look at the circular patterns. You've found a stash of coins, my friends. Gold and silver, I'd wager. And if I'm right, and if our experts can clean them and give us some dates, I think we'll find that you're right, Sean. We've come upon a debris field of the pirate ship, if not the pirate ship itself."

Sean turned to Vanessa and pulled her close, planting a huge kiss on her lips.

"You're amazing!" he told her.

She smiled uneasily.

She had followed the figurehead again.

But the figurehead had nearly trapped her that day. Had it been leading her to treasure?

Or trying to lure her to her death?

420

15

"Oh my God!" Jaden cried, delighted with the discovery. "Ted, look . . . it's definitely a cache of coins. I'd say it is a piece of the mast. Maybe the new wreck crushed the old wreck. I think that Sean was right, and that it was a long debris field . . . and still, what's left of the pirate hull might be there . . . it's possible. It's certainly not *impossible!*"

"This is really fabulous," Ted said. "The last time I saw something like this it was . . . wow, it was a display from the *Atocha*." He turned to Jaden. "We can get started. We brought supplies. I can't wait to see the dates on the coins and find out what was on that ship. I can't wait to see the coins. I think there are definitely some cobs attached there — those are bits taken off the gold bars. They could have been stolen from anyone, French, English, Spanish or Americans!" he said excitedly.

They were back on the beach and the

heavy piece of mast with its encrusted treasure lay in the center of a tarp while they gathered around it and stared.

"It's amazing," Zoe breathed, looking at Vanessa. "And you found this, too?"

"More or less. I was diving with Sean and Bill," Vanessa said.

"You really missed your calling," Zoe said.

"Hey, Bahamian or International waters?" Jay asked, looking at Lew.

Lew smiled broadly. "Bahamian! Yeah!"

"Ah, there goes the treasure," Jay said sadly.

Vanessa stepped back, not really thrilled with the fact that she had once again discovered a find in the water. She couldn't help but think about Lew's story — and the things Bartholomew had said.

But . . .

Say there was a ghost that somehow haunted her in the water. First off, why would Dona Isabella, so cruelly taken and murdered, want to cause evil to anyone?

And second, ghosts didn't have the power to do what had been done.

She realized that she had backed out of the group, and she was sorry that Sean was so concerned with safety that they couldn't possibly have a minute alone. Not alone, maybe. But . . . with just Katie and David.

She started as she stood in the back of the group — something had hit her on the back. She spun around and looked down. A tiny pinecone lay there in the sand. She frowned, and then looked up.

Carlos Roca.

She stared at him. He was real. Alive — and on the island. She couldn't begin to fathom how he had followed them so easily.

Unless, of course, he was good at that kind of thing.

She looked at him, at the misery in his eyes, at the pleading within them. She saw that his face had grown gaunt; he looked like a man haunted by a million demons.

He was beckoning to her. He drew a finger to his lips.

She'd be crazy to walk to him in the brush. Alone.

She winced. She wondered if there was such a thing as instinct, and if her belief in the man was actually crazy. After all, he was there.

He hadn't been killed.

She turned, thinking she could grab Katie or someone.

They were all still discussing the coins. Jaden was explaining how many people used something like an electrode to clean such pieces, but they had always had good luck

with certain chemical washes and delicate handwork.

Everyone was staring at the treasure thoughtfully or looking at Jaden.

She hesitated and then took another step back, and another. And when no one noticed her moving at that point, she turned and headed into the brush and the pines.

She had unbuckled her dive knife earlier and shoved it into the pocket of her jeans, and she had her jeans on now. . . .

Right. Like a dive knife could save her against the maniac who had decapitated and dismembered two people!

She entered a tree-shaded trail, and felt as if a mist and darkness gathered around her. It did not; it was just that the sun wasn't penetrating through the pines.

"Carlos?" she said softly.

He stepped out in front of her.

"Jesus Cristo!" he said, and crossed himself. "I have been waiting for you. I have tried so hard to reach you. I need for you to understand."

There had been so much commotion over Vanessa's discovery that they had finally broken to go about different tasks when Sean realized that he didn't see Vanessa anywhere in the group. He saw Katie laying

towels over one of the support ropes for her tent to dry, and he hurried over to her. "Katie! Where's Vanessa?"

"What? Well, she was there with the rest of us, listening to Jaden, and then . . ."

Her voice trailed away and she stared at him with fear in her eyes.

Sean was afraid that she was going to scream or alert the others. He was terrified that she had been dragged into the pine woods and brush, and he quickly looked around the encampment, searching for members of the original film team.

Zoe was with Bill, preparing the barbecue. Barry was showing Jay the fish he had caught that afternoon while they'd been diving — two snappers and a medium-size grouper.

David came over as he searched the group.

"What's wrong?" David asked.

"Vanessa," Sean said.

"I'll help you search."

"No — I'll find her. Make sure that everyone else stays around here, David."

"Right. If you're not back in ten minutes, though, I'll send Liam and Jamie after you."

Sean nodded and hurried back toward the pines. There was a trail — small and overgrown, but it had been traveled recently.

He ran down the trail, afraid to call her

name and afraid not to, his heart thundering. He reminded himself that he was certain that the murders had not been committed by one person alone, that whoever had done it had to have had some assistance.

And they were all back at the beach. All of them except for Vanessa. Lew Sanderson had been there as well, rinsing dive gear with Jamie on the *Claddagh*.

Carlos Roca.

He was alive. He had been in Key West. He had followed them to Miami.

And now he was here. On the island.

And he had Vanessa.

He drew out the .38 Special he had stuffed under his jacket and kept moving as quietly as he could along the trail. Visions of what might have happened plagued the back of his mind.

Vanessa. Down on the sand, beautiful blond hair trailing out over it.

Eyes open with horror . . .

He was about to scream out her name, scream with a desperation that would be heard throughout the island.

He bit back the cry and hurried onward, then paused, listening.

He heard conversation. Hushed. Two people. Whispering. To his right.

He broke through the trees and brush then and burst upon the two of them — Vanessa, perfectly fine, standing in the clearing with her arm on Carlos Roca's shoulder, as if she had been urging him to do something.

He aimed the .38 Special at Carlos Roca's head and said flatly, "I spent time at target practice before the trip. At this distance, I can guarantee a clean shot between your eyes. Step away from Vanessa. Now."

Roca instantly moved to do so.

And Vanessa stepped in front of him, lifting a pleading hand to Sean.

"No, no, please, Sean! Carlos is innocent. He's been desperate all this time. He's been following us — at great risk to himself — determined to keep anything horrible from happening again."

Sean grated down on his teeth, tension bracing his muscles. "Vanessa, get away from him."

"Sean! You have to listen."

"Fine. Carlos, we'll walk back to the encampment. And you can talk to everyone there."

Carlos looked at Vanessa.

"No, Sean, please, no!" Vanessa begged.

He eased the gun down, still ready to lift it again if need be. He didn't want to keep

it aimed at Vanessa.

"Please! Sean!" Vanessa pleaded again, wincing. "Sean — we can't let anyone know that Carlos is here. He's watching . . . watching after us. Sean, listen to him."

"It's one of them," Carlos said quietly and with dignity. "It's one of them. We were barely out at sea when I was attacked at the helm. I never saw who was there. I was struck so hard I went down. I was tossed overboard, and somehow, by the grace of God, the cold woke me up. I was dazed, my head was bleeding. I don't remember much else. I swam. I found a piece of driftwood and clung to it. I came to on one of the small islands, tended by a fisherman's wife. Then, I found out that *I* was wanted for murder. I have a Bahamian friend who got me a false ID claiming that I'm a fisherman from the Dominican Republic. I have been trying to find out what did happen ever since, lying low . . . and studying disappearances in the air and acts of piracy."

"Why should we believe you?" Sean asked, not moving, his voice cold and steely. "Why should I believe that this isn't a game you're playing, that you don't have an accomplice among the crew, and that if I keep the secret that you're here, you won't be waiting for the right time to kill again?"

"You can ask Lew," Carlos said quietly. "I told you, I came to on a Bahamian island. The people who found me were decent people. They contacted him and got him to come to me. He was there to see the fifty stitches in my head. He knows that I'm telling the truth. The night I left with Georgia, one of them either hid on the boat or found a way onto the boat. I was attacked from behind. God help me, the person just wanted Georgia. I sleep at night, still hearing her screaming!"

Sean still stared at Carlos. He saw that Vanessa believed in the man, believed with every fiber of her being.

She had from the start.

If he was innocent, he was a valuable ally on the island. He was the unknown that they could have in their favor.

And if he wasn't . . .

He was aware that Bartholomew was at his side.

"I believe he's telling the truth. I followed Vanessa into the woods. There were tears in his eyes. He pleaded. No man is that good an actor," Bartholomew said.

"Someone was on the boat. When you left, who did you see on the dock?" Sean asked.

"Vanessa and Jay. I saw them both," Carlos said.

"That wouldn't mean that either of them was innocent — they might have been an accomplice to whomever slipped aboard. Or are you certain that they slipped aboard before you left? Could someone have come broadside and slipped on?"

Carlos took a deep breath. "It was night. I was moving slowly."

"You have to make a decision," Bartholomew said. "Someone will be coming after you within a few minutes now."

Vanessa came hurrying toward him. She caught his hand and stared into his eyes. "He's telling the truth. I know that he's telling the truth."

"How?" he grated.

"I know. I know!" she said, slamming a fist against her chest. "Sometimes . . . you *know*."

Sean stared at Carlos over Vanessa's head. "If you're not telling the truth, you're a dead man."

"I am telling the truth. And I am watching. And I am waiting, unknown now, to find out who did this. Because they are here, and they will strike again," Carlos said.

Sean winced and turned, sliding the safety on and the gun beneath his jacket and waistband, and taking Vanessa's hand. When they neared the beach, he slowed his pace

430

and came out of the trees calmly, hoping no one but Katie and David had noticed their absence.

Miraculously, it seemed that no one had. Zoe, Barry, Bill and Jake were standing around the barbecue, chatting excitedly. Jay was staring out at the water. Jamie, Marty, Ted and Jaden were still inspecting the mast and the cache of coins.

Only Liam stood tensely with Katie and David, trying to pretend casual conversation.

"We'll need somewhere alone — guaranteed alone," Sean said quietly. "Liam, how have you been doing on that task I asked you about yesterday?"

"Hopefully, I'll have some information back by the morning," Liam said.

"We're going to need it," Sean told him.

Liam looked at Vanessa, frowning. "What the hell is going on?" he demanded.

"Let's take a walk to the *Conch Fritter*," he suggested. He turned and stared at Vanessa. "All of us!"

She nodded, and the group walked toward the boat.

"Hey!" Barry called after them.

"Yeah?" Sean yelled back.

"Bring another bag of charcoal, will you please?" Barry asked.

Sean nodded.

Aboard the boat, he looked back to shore, assuring himself that the others had remained behind. Then he looked at Vanessa. "Why don't you tell them? You're the one with complete faith."

She stared at him, and then at David, Liam and Katie. "Carlos Roca is on the island."

Liam stiffened. "All right. We'll figure out a way to keep you safe while we flush him out. No one is more fierce at protection than Jamie O'Hara, and between Sean, David and me —"

"No, Liam, no!" Vanessa said. "He's hiding. He's watching out — for us."

"He said he was attacked on the ship, and he knows it had to be by one of the crew. He was struck on the head. He says Lew Sanderson will vouch for all this. He's been keeping his secret all this time. He was tossed overboard, assumed dead or left to drown."

"This is crazy," David said.

"Vanessa, can *Lew* actually be an alibi? You don't know that Lew wasn't guilty," Liam pointed out.

"Oh, please, I can't believe that Carlos is lying." She stared at them all. "Ask Bartholomew! *Your friendly neighborhood ghost*

believes in him. We all know that faith can't be held or seen, and I have faith in Carlos."

"I hope you're right, Vanessa," Liam said softly. "I really hope you're right. If not, you've just fed into the psychosis of a savage murderer."

"Vanessa?" Katie asked.

"I know I'm right."

"I'll tell Uncle Jamie what's going on, and he'll let Marty know," Sean said.

David nodded. "What do you think he's waiting for?" he asked.

"The murderers to show themselves," Sean said.

"And how will they do that?" Liam asked dryly.

"They'll try to find a way to separate someone from the rest — and murder them, as well," Sean said.

Liam nodded. "Somehow, we'll have to find a way to bait them."

That night, Vanessa knew that Sean was still angry with her.

He played his part well in front of others, but she knew. She knew the tension that knotted his body, and she knew the tone of his voice.

It wasn't until they had gone to bed for the night that she realized just how angry.

433

"First you lied to me about him," he told her, keeping his distance, arms locked behind his head as he stared up at their canvas roof. "You lied about seeing him. Then you did the most horrendously stupid thing in the world. You walked off into the woods." He stared at her then. "Don't! Don't even try to get mad at me for saying it was horrendously stupid because you know it was."

"Yes."

"That's all you have to say?"

"I know it was stupid," she said softly. "Sean, I'm sorry."

He shook his head. "Sorry? Vanessa . . . that can't always cut it, you know," he told her.

She fell silent for a moment, aware of his distance. "Want me to sleep somewhere else?" she asked, praying that he would say no.

"I'm angry, Vanessa. Furious. You risked your life, you risked other lives. I'm disturbed about this trust thing we've got going — or not going. But your plan is to walk away anytime it gets rough between us. No. I don't want you to go away — and I don't want you running away from me when I'm right to be angry."

She stared at him, not knowing what to

434

say. She could have told him that she was pretty sure that she never wanted to leave.

But she didn't know if that would be right at the moment.

She eased down by his side and laid her head on his chest.

After a moment, she felt his hand on her hair. And in time, he drew her to him.

That night, she dreamed. In the dream, she was still in his arms. She woke because there was a woman in the tent, standing before her.

She wasn't afraid, and she didn't know why she wasn't afraid.

She had seen the woman before, on a crowded afternoon in Key West, when pirates and wenches were everywhere.

She should be afraid. She was certain that the woman was Kitty Cutlass. Pretty, not quite beautiful. Not dressed elegantly. Worn, tired.

"Please, if you would just understand," she said.

"I think I do," Vanessa told her. "You didn't kill Dona Isabella. Dona Isabella planned the attack. The ship had riches on it that were supposed to go with her to her husband in Spain. She didn't want to go to Spain, and she didn't want her husband. She arranged with Mad Miller that he

435

should attack the ship, but . . . she wanted to control the pirates, and she didn't want you. You were the body in the chest, Kitty. It was you."

The woman, the ghost in front of her, smiled sadly.

"She is evil."

"She is dead now, too, Kitty," Vanessa said. "She died in the storm."

"Evil doesn't die," Kitty said. "You must be careful. Evil doesn't die."

Kitty faded away.

A few moments later, Vanessa awoke. She looked around the tent and realized quickly that there was no place for anyone to hide in the small tent.

She lay back and listened to Sean's breathing, felt his warmth and the pulse of his heart.

She wondered if she had been guessing at the truth all along, and if the figurehead image of Dona Isabella leading her into a trap that day hadn't finally made it clear in her mind.

Then she had straightened it all out in a dream.

Either that, or . . .

The ghost of Kitty Cutlass had been in her tent.

Either way, she felt that it was important

436

that she knew what had happened. Somehow, letting everyone know the truth was going to help them solve the mystery.

In the morning, Sean announced that he wanted to make another trip out to the site where Vanessa had found the broken shaft of old mast with the encrusted coins, but that they'd start out again just after noon — first, they would set up to film Ted and Jaden working with the heavy cache of broken mast and encrusted coins. Ted said he'd be the display hands — Jaden would do the talking.

He and Jaden had freed and cleaned a few of the coins, and Jaden was happy to display them and happy to talk about what they had found and what they had done. "This was someone's personal treasure, I believe, *before* it became the property of the pirate crew," Jaden said, speaking to the camera. "We have a mixture here of gold and silver, and coins that show different mint marks, beneath different rulers. This coin bears a mark showing that it was minted in Peru, and here we have one that is very old, and I'm still working very delicately to see if we still have a mint mark. I would judge it was one of the first coins to come out of the mines of South America. This is why I think

that the pirates didn't actually amass the treasure, but that in sinking the *Santa Geneva,* they happened upon a collection of personal riches belonging to Dona Isabella's husband and traveling back to Spain with her."

Jaden displayed her work and spoke of the patience that was needed. Different people worked in different ways when working with centuries-old salvage, but she had Ted had both grown up in Key West and had worked with Jaden's father, a salvage expert from the time he was a child, to learn their craft.

When they finished with the segment, Vanessa asked Sean if she could put forth a theory. He was surprised, but shrugged and told her that she was certainly welcome to do so.

"Walking along the beach?" Jay suggested.

"Sure," Vanessa agreed.

"We'll use two handhelds?" Jay asked Sean.

"I'll observe on this," Sean said.

Vanessa was aware that the group was mostly together, and that was what she wanted. Marty and Liam were at the boats, and Jamie had remained at the encampment while Ted and Jaden continued to work with the treasure.

But Jay was filming and Barry had the

second camera while Bill and Jake held the light shield. Zoe was hovering, just in case she was needed. David walked with Sean, discussing shots and angles, and Katie followed, curious to hear Vanessa's theory. Lew walked behind as well, arms crossed over his chest. He was watching out for everyone, and watching the terrain around them. Sean hadn't said so, but she was pretty sure that he had found a few moments during the activity of the first filming to casually corner Lew — and demand to know what he knew about Carlos Roca.

It seemed that whatever Lew had told Sean, it had satisfied him.

There had been no call for a manhunt to drag Carlos out of the pine and shrub forest, nor had there been any suggestion that they weren't alone on the island.

She wondered if what she was about to do was crazy, or necessary.

She walked slowly along the beach, almost unaware of the cameras or the reflector shield being wielded by Bill and Jake. "Yesterday," she began, "we made an amazing find. People often wonder why, when a wreck has rested in the ocean so long and we have so much advanced equipment to put to work in the oceans these days, it hasn't been previously discovered. As Sean

O'Hara noted, we have to remember that conditions in the past might have been different, and that the ocean is always shifting and hiding her treasures. What we refer to as the Bermuda Triangle is a busy area where currents and weather are particularly active and where, perhaps, there are major magnetic fields at work. Basically, it's natural phenomena that dictate what happens beneath the waves. Mad Miller's pirate ship was taken down by a force of nature. And the force of nature, over the years, shifted the wreckage, and created a long debris field. Despite sonar, seagoing robots and other technical devices, treasures and wrecks can hide in plain sight. As in this case, the great metal hull of a World War II ship has hidden a great deal of the wreckage. What we have discovered this time is treasure. It's my belief that we have imagined the real story of Mad Miller, Kitty Cutlass and Dona Isabella wrong. We saw what happened as Dona Isabella would have *wanted* the world to see it. She was a beautiful woman, a proud and haughty woman. She lived life as she chose in Key West in luxury. She traveled the Caribbean, and she took on lovers as she chose, all with her husband's riches. I believe that she made a deal with Mad Miller. Somewhere, she met

the pirate. She told him the course of the *Santa Geneva* and what riches the ship would carry. In return, they would split the bounty. It would be assumed that she'd died in captivity — but not until a ransom had been paid. Dona Isabella would then take on a new identity and live richly — without the yoke of her husband's financial power over her — wherever she chose. I can't imagine just what seductive power or force the woman wielded, because earlier, at the site of the *Santa Geneva* wreck, we pulled up a chest that held the body of a murdered woman. The 'treasure chest' of her body was stolen somewhere en route to a lab in Gainesville, but the experts noted immediately that she was not decked out in great finery. It's my belief that Dona Isabella was entranced with the pirate way of life and perhaps with Mad Miller himself. Either on her own — or with his blessing — Dona Isabella murdered the one person who stood in her way in the act of completely subduing the pirate Mad Miller to her total control. In remorse, Mad Miller saw to it that Kitty Cutlass went to the bottom of the sea in a sealed tomb. With Dona Isabella now calling the shots like a true pirate queen, she and the remaining crews of the ships sailed on to Haunt Island,

where the massacre of all those who would not bow down before her took place. She was truly in her power when she and Mad Miller then set sail again, only to sail into the embrace of a massive storm, and a watery graveyard for all aboard. How furious she must have been — furious with God and the heavens. She had at last obtained freedom, power and control — only to fall victim to the revenge of the sea herself. Once, Africans brought to these islands believed that the tempest within this area — now known as the Bermuda Triangle — was caused by the bitter fury of a woman who had not been kind, while her sister had taken pity on a poor and broken man who proved to be a god. The haughty sister married a rich and handsome man who turned out to be a demon who killed her and devoured her. Her fury caused the thunder and waves and strange phenomena that brought down ships and planes. Perhaps, in later years, sailors — pirates, patriots, merchants and pleasure seekers — might well find that same evil spirit rests in the bitter and furious soul of the heartless woman who murdered for power and riches."

She stopped walking, and smiled.

Jay lowered the camera and looked into

her eyes. The reflector shields fell, and Sean came walking toward her, taking her by the shoulders, his grin deep, his eyes admiring.

"Fantastic!" he said.

"Oh!" Katie gasped. "That's brilliant, Vanessa, and you probably got it all right after all these years of us believing that Kitty Cutlass was a murderess!"

"It makes perfect sense," David agreed.

"But wait — I'm confused," Zoe said. "You found Dona Isabella's pendant. That was the first find that you made."

"Yes — I'm sure she purposely lost that pendant, and someone was supposed to have found it years and years before I did. When salvage divers came out to the wreck, they would believe that the pendant was wrenched from her neck in the struggle. Maybe they wouldn't find it, but the seeds were planted for her story — the story she wanted people to believe — to come to light. Of course, this is my theory. I'm not sure that I can prove it in any way, and the body is gone now, but from what Dr. Aislinn said when we did have the body, it seems likely that it was Kitty Cutlass," Vanessa said.

"Oh, Lord, and what a cool bit!" Barry said to her, grinning. "Dona Isabella can be seen as the evil that lurks in the Bermuda

Triangle. I love it!"

"After all these years of man being man, war and devastation, I'm sure a lot of evil energy went down in the ocean," Sean said dryly.

"Evil is in the mind, really, isn't it?" Jay asked.

"And in idle hands, right?" Zoe asked, grimacing.

"Well, in the mind — and in the hands of those it inhabits, I guess," Barry noted, grinning. He frowned and stared at Vanessa. "You're not suggesting that the evil spirit of Dona Isabella came up from the sea to somehow decapitate and dismember Georgia and Travis."

Vanessa shook her head. "Hey — I just put forth a new theory, that's all. A theory. We've always worked on theories and suppositions."

"Fascinating," Bill Hinton said, nodding in thought.

"Creepy," Barry said.

"Ah, but it's all in the mind, really, isn't it?" Jay asked. He looked at Vanessa, frowning. "In an odd way, maybe Dona Isabella was getting her evil revenge. *You* wrote our script, relying on supposed history and legend. Maybe Dona Isabella wanted it all remembered that way."

444

"Why kill Georgia and Travis — if evil ghosts of the past had anything to do with it?" Vanessa asked.

"Hey, I don't know," Jay said, shrugging. He rolled his eyes. "Maybe evil spirits demand sacrifices!"

"Human hands committed murder," Sean said. "Anyway, let's get back to working on what we've begun to find. Light lunch again, and an afternoon dive. That was great footage, Vanessa, great. I loved it. Let's see what else we can find."

While lunch was being prepared, Sean went aboard the *Conch Fritter,* where Liam had been on the computer using his various contacts to try to track the movement of the original film crew in more detail over the last two years when the other two boats disappeared.

"Some of this we knew. Vanessa has been doing commercial shoots. Three of the others, Barry Melkie, Bill Hinton and Zoe Cally, were part of a crew that filmed in the Bahamas. Jay hasn't done as well as the others. He's had a few dry spells in there. So really, anyone could have easily been around when the other disappearances occurred."

"Good to know. I guess it's still not proof of anything. And I'm still trying to figure

445

out *why.* Vanessa's theory on Dona Isabella being in collusion with Mad Miller was fascinating, and rings true, and it had all kinds of motive — for Dona Isabella. I don't see the motive in the killings now — if, indeed, some of these disappearances were caused by the same murderer or murderers who killed Georgia and Travis," Sean said, perplexed. "There was no financial gain, not that I can see. The deaths of Georgia and Travis put Jay into financial difficulty. It's true that the water can be rough around here and that ships have disappeared in the area forever, but other disappearances now might be related. David and I read about the *Delphi.* It seemed it disappeared into thin air, and the boat was captained by an experienced man. There should have been a distress call, something."

"You can't make a distress call if you're taken by surprise," Liam pointed out.

"We could still be way off course," Sean said. "But you're right. And Carlos thought someone was aboard the boat because he was knocked out — taken by surprise."

"If we're not being taken in by Carlos," Liam said.

"I don't think we are." He hesitated. "I think that the man is telling the truth, and that someone with us is guilty. Carlos Roca

446

is convinced someone on the island at the time was involved."

"We're taking a leap of faith to believe in Carlos Roca," Liam noted.

Sean nodded. "Yes and no," he said softly. "Vanessa has . . . something. Like Katie. The thing I always wanted to deny. Until Bartholomew. Now I know that things do exist that we can't see. She has instincts and . . . something. I trust that something."

"Let's hope you're right," Liam said.

Everyone wanted to dive that day. Sean, however, didn't want to leave the encampment alone, nor did he want to leave Ted and Jaden alone to keep guard. In the end, it was agreed both boats would go out that day with Jamie O'Hara remaining topside on his *Claddagh* and David and Katie remaining topside on the *Conch Fritter.*

They followed one another going down, but the World War II vessel was a huge hulk, and they split to follow it around in different directions. Vanessa led, bringing her partners around to the gash in the giant hull that had probably caused its sinking. They began to explore the area, Sean turning the camera on the wreck and then the different divers.

Vanessa realized that they were in an

equipment room, and she began to study the dials and levers on one side of the wall. She followed them to the sandy bottom, where in some places they were on the ocean floor and in others she heard the metallic clink of the vessel's flooring. She kept searching the flooring, aware that her fellow divers were near.

She found an uneven patch in the sand and started carefully moving the sand around it. She grew excited as she realized that she had come across something. There was a piece of something that glittered. She moved more sand and realized that one object was laid atop another. She picked up the first and was surprised to see that it was a knife. It wasn't old; the hilt was wearing and the blade was dull and crusted, but it was a modern diving knife. She slipped it into her belt and looked at the object beneath it. It was long and wedged tightly between the rip in the hull's floor and the sand.

She looked for the others and saw that Zoe was at a hatch, struggling with the door. She swam toward her just as the door gave.

Vanessa ducked the massive sheet of steel that seemed to have some kind of spring; Barry, shooting ahead of her, did not.

She heard the thud as he crashed, head-

first, into the steel.

He shot back, his regulator falling from his mouth. She realized that he was unconscious and hurried toward him, catching his drifting weight and gripping her backup regulator to force it immediately into his mouth. Zoe shot for her, trying to help, but she was panicking and in the way. Sean let the camera fall, suspended, to his side, shooting toward them. He signaled that they needed to surface, which, of course, they knew.

Decompression time had to be taken, but between them, they kept the air going into Barry's lungs and bubbles coming out into the water. When they surfaced, Zoe began to shout, drawing David's attention. He was quickly at the dive platform with Katie, and between them they got Barry's body on deck, stripped of dive gear and wrapped in a towel.

Sean stood over him and looked the ten feet over to the *Claddagh*. The other divers were up, and Liam shouted over to Sean. "What happened?"

"Barry took a beating from a spring-loaded hatch," Sean cried.

"It was my fault. I should have known," Zoe moaned. She was flustered, fluttering over Barry, trying to touch him, whispering

that she was sorry.

"He's got to get to medical care," Sean said. "He might have had some oxygen deprivation, though Vanessa got to him quickly."

"I'll tie up and take Barry on board the *Claddagh.* She's got a bit of speed on your Sunray, Sean. I'll radio ahead and they'll be ready for him in Bimini," Jamie called to him.

"All right," Sean conceded.

"I can't believe I did this," Zoe said.

"Zoe, you didn't do it — the door sprang right when Barry was heading for it," Vanessa said. She glanced at Sean and realized that he thought that Zoe's ministrations might prove to be too much for the poor man. "Barry will be fine. Jamie's boat is fast. We've got him breathing, and he has a weak but steady pulse going."

"Grab the bumpers," Jamie called to his crew aboard the *Claddagh.*

Vanessa and Jay ran to do the same for the *Conch Fritter.* A few minutes later, Barry was aboard the *Claddagh,* and it was agreed that David and Katie would go with him while the rest of the crew came aboard the *Conch Fritter* to head back to the island.

Vanessa watched the *Claddagh* sail away, and she waved to Katie and David.

450

She felt a chill.

They would be all right. They had to be all right. They were close to Bimini, it was still daylight and there were three of them aboard with Barry.

She still felt an ominous sense of dread that something horrible would happen before she saw them again. The sea wind suddenly seemed chill, and when she turned away, she felt the strange sting of tears in her eyes.

16

"Barry could die," Zoe said, watching as the *Claddagh* disappeared into the horizon.

"He's not going to die," Vanessa assured her, giving her shoulders a hug. "It's going to be fine."

Zoe looked at her and tried to smile. "And I didn't find a thing," Zoe said.

Vanessa tried to brighten. "I did."

They all looked at her.

"Well, of course you did," Jay said. "What?"

She looked around at the faces. Sean was just waiting, Liam at his side. Bill, Jake, Jay and Zoe were wide-eyed.

"I don't know," she said.

That wasn't true. She knew that she had found a modern dive knife. Maybe it wasn't indicative of anything — perhaps a diver had lost it. But for some reason, she decided not to tell them all about the knife — just what was beneath it.

"The floor was uneven, and it was all crusted . . . I think it might have been what remained of a sword or a cutlass. I didn't have time to try to figure it out — Barry was hit. But we can find out tomorrow. I know exactly where it is," Vanessa said. She smiled. She was proud of this find. She hadn't seen a ghostly figurehead in the water. She had found it on her own.

She saw that Bartholomew was standing just behind Liam and Sean; he watched her solemnly.

"It might have been German, or fairly modern," she said. "It was impossible to tell."

"We should go back down right now," Jay said.

"No. Not today," Sean said. "Today, we had a member of our crew injured. We'll head back and let the others know what happened, and wait to hear about Barry's condition."

"Oh my God, you are worried he could die!" Zoe said.

"No. He just needs care. But this is it for the day," Sean said. He headed to the helm. Vanessa came and curled up on the companion seat, hugging a throw around her shoulders — she hadn't been able to shake the chill that had seized her as she had

waved goodbye to Katie.

She was anxious to hear that the *Claddagh* had arrived safely in Bimini.

Liam was seated aft.

Watching, she thought.

Watching Zoe, Bill and Jake.

They didn't have far to come in to the island, but she decided that the demand for a freshwater shower on the one boat might be high that night, and she slipped off the seat, telling Sean that she was going to take a quick shower. It was good, though quick. Zoe followed her lead while the guys washed off on the deck, using the equipment hose.

She felt better once she was dressed in jeans and a sweater. And in another few minutes, she heard Sean calling for the ties and the bumpers. They had returned to Haunt Island.

A fire had been built and the barbecue had been set to blaze and dinner put on in their absence. Jaden, busy flipping thin flank steaks, was horrified when she heard about Barry, and Ted had to take the barbecue fork from her hand to save a piece of meat.

"It was an accident," Jay said, "nothing but an accident." He set a hand gently on Zoe's shoulders.

"And he's going to be all right," Vanessa added.

"They'll call soon," Sean said.

Vanessa felt she had to escape for a few moments at least. She murmured something about needing to put a few things away in her tent. She glanced at Sean, hoping that he would follow her.

She started entering the tent. Bartholomew had preceded her entry and was seated on the ground, Indian-style, hands folded prayer-fashion and tapping his lower jaw. He started to rise when he saw her, but she shook her head and sank down beside him.

"I've been thinking all day," he said.

"And?"

"And your theory is right. It has to be. I told you — I knew them, Mad Miller and Kitty . . . and they weren't evil or cruel. Mad Miller must have made a financial agreement with Dona Isabella. She traveled a lot — they could have met at several ports. He was . . . he was soft. Once he had stopped her ship, she took control. She insisted it be sunk, and she murdered Kitty. It all makes sense now."

Vanessa shook her head. "It still doesn't make sense. I kept seeing Dona Isabella's face on a figurehead — she was the one leading me around."

The tent flap opened and they started, but

it was Sean, and evidently he had heard them.

Sean shook his head. "Whatever type of spirit she is, she's been playing with you. She's been leading you. She wanted you to find the pendant, because that lent credence to the tale. That would bring everyone aboard to follow this whole route again. And — just in case it didn't — she then had you find the body. She probably didn't realize that a forensic anthropologist would immediately realize that it was the wrong body."

"But the body disappeared," Vanessa said.

"She led you — and she's leading someone else," Sean said.

Bartholomew nodded.

"Oh!" Vanessa said, and dug into her bag. "I did pick up something today, but no one led me to it. It was in the gap in the ship, on top of the object I was describing." She produced the knife and showed it to Sean. He studied it, rolling it over in his hand and chipping at the crust on it.

"T-B-E," Sean read. "Tom Essling," he said.

"I'm sorry?" Vanessa asked.

"Tom Essling — he was captain of a boat that disappeared in that area just last year. If we further our search, I have a feeling

we'll find his boat, the *Delphi,* too," he said grimly.

"So . . . someone has been pirating other vessels near here. Someone maybe using Haunt Island as their base, as if it's their . . . their home fort," Vanessa said.

"I don't know. It's all supposition," Sean said.

"She's right. I know she's right," Bartholomew said. "But I'm watching . . . I'm always watching, and I can't figure it out yet."

"Well, it has been figured out to this," Sean said. "Someone here knows much more than he or she is saying. Someone is —" He broke off, looking at Vanessa. "A killer, I believe," he said softly.

From outside the tent, they heard Jaden call out loudly. "Dinner, folks, dinner! Come and get it now!"

"Let's go on out," Sean told Vanessa. "We'll keep up all appearances."

As they walked over to the barbecue area, Vanessa asked Sean, "David hasn't called yet. Why hasn't David called?"

"He will," he assured her.

Unless what Barry had done had been an act. Barry was a big man, muscular, powerful. The kind who could wield a knife and a bone saw, if needed. What if he had been

457

pretending the entire event, and he had known that they would save him, bring him to the surface.

And rush him to a hospital.

She began to fear that Barry would suddenly rise, taking David and Jamie by surprise. He would attack from the rear, when they weren't expecting it. He would toss them overboard as he had done with Carlos, and then he would come for Katie. . . .

She clenched her fists, knowing that she was letting her imagination run away from her.

But she was scared.

And she wanted David to call, or Katie, or anyone.

Jaden and Ted tried to be cheerful and upbeat as they doled out dinner. Marty, however, appeared wary and watchful.

Lew Sanderson sat on the beach alone, watching the others as they ate.

Liam stayed on one side of the group and Sean on the other.

When Sean's cell phone started ringing, they all jumped. He answered it quickly, and then breathed a sigh of relief as he looked at the others.

"They are in Bimini, and the doctors

believe that Barry will pull through," he told them.

It seemed that everyone let out a sigh. And then they began to chat with relief, and in a few minutes, they were even joking with one another.

David, Jamie and Katie wouldn't return until the next morning, which meant that Sean had lost three of the people he trusted most for the night.

Lew — he thought he trusted, but he didn't know.

Ted and Jaden he trusted, but they were really scholars, not fighters, though Ted did know how to use a speargun.

Carlos was an unknown element in the whole game.

Still, he had himself and Liam and Marty. And they were guarding a tiny blonde woman and two twenty-somethings who didn't appear to be musclemen.

Maybe there was something he still wasn't seeing. One of the group had been involved, but they'd had outside help.

Everyone seemed tired that night. He told Liam about the knife they had found, and they both knew that they'd be searching for the *Delphi* the next day.

"Tonight?" Liam asked.

"We all stay on guard. Marty, Ted, you

and I. And Lew. But I'm uneasy now, and we'll actually be watching Lew, as well. I'm thinking that when David and Katie and my uncle Jamie return, it may be time to put an end to this. I think a killer is in reach, but I don't want to risk anyone else's life. We need a larger crew — a totally trustworthy crew. Anyway, we'll each take a few hours, and stand guard in threes through the night," Sean said.

"You want some time first?" Liam asked.

"Sure. Thanks. I'd like that," Sean admitted.

Vanessa was already in their little tent. She had seemed chilled during the day, and was wearing her flannel nightdress again. He smiled at her, coming in to zip the flap on the tent.

He came to her, taking her by the shoulders, and she looked up at him expectantly.

"These are really tight quarters," he whispered. "And we are really, really close to other tents, but . . ."

He loved her smile, loved her eyes. "We're very good at whispered conversations," she said.

"There are many ways to communicate, you know."

Her arms wrapped around him. She drew him down with her to the thin mattresses

on the canvas floor of the tent and he reflected that it was really one of the finest beds he'd ever seen. Any bed was fine, if Vanessa was there. He cupped her face in his hands and kissed her slowly, and she slid her fingers beneath his shirt, teasing the flesh of his abdomen, then drawing the shirt up and over his head. They came together again, and she felt his blood begin to burn as her fingers dipped into the waistband of his jeans. She went still as she felt his gun.

"I'm sorry," he whispered.

"I'm not. I'm damned glad you have it. And I'm definitely glad it was a gun. It seemed a very strange place to have such a body part," she teased.

"I'll show you body parts," he whispered.

"Promises, promises . . ."

They quickly grew breathless and winced here and there, pressing their fingers to each other's lips, smiling, laughing, making love just a bit awkwardly and with just a bit of difficulty and yet finding that the smiles, the whispered warnings and the laughter itself made the moment sweeter and more frantic, and even in hushed gasps the moment of climax incredible and shattering. Then they lay together, damp and breathing deeply, hearts thundering, interlocked, and strangely silent.

"You're going out, aren't you?" Vanessa whispered.

He nodded. "I just . . . I . . . I needed this time," he said. He'd never realized that he didn't know how to speak to a woman. Not true, speech had been easy. But he had never intended to become involved, never realized that he could feel that he needed to wake up with someone every morning. He let out a breath and turned to her and just let the words come. "I think I love you," he said.

She smiled. "I think I love you, too."

"I think . . . I think that when this is over you shouldn't leave," he said. "I think that we should both see where this thinking is going. I think the thinking could become certainty."

She brushed her lips against his, and her eyes, so dark and beautiful a blue in the shadows, met his. "I think that I'll be here," she said softly.

He didn't want to leave her; he had to. He knew that he was right, that even if the three of them guarding the place appeared to be overkill, it was necessary.

He rose, reaching for his clothes and dressing quickly in the cramped quarters. Vanessa slipped back into the flannel gown. "I'll come with you."

"No."

"But —"

"Get some sleep. Tomorrow will be a long day, and . . . well, you are distracting," he told her.

"All right," she said softly.

He unzipped the flap on the tent and slipped away.

Despite everything that had happened during the day — or perhaps because of it — Vanessa found herself falling into a deep sleep almost immediately after Sean left her.

For a while, even in sleep, she knew the comfort of the sweet rest.

Then she felt as if she was being touched.

She opened her eyes. It was dark in the tent, though the many torches set into the sand kept the area light enough. Strange patterns and shadows were dispersed between faint lights.

She must have still been sleeping. She could see a face. It wasn't the face that had been on the figurehead, not that of Dona Isabella.

It was the face of the blonde woman, not as pretty, just a little worn. Kitty. Kitty Cutlass.

And her eyes were tinged with worry now.

She was dreaming again, of course.

"Come, come . . . come on. You must leave, please, hurry!" the woman warned her.

She had been sleeping so, so deeply. . . .

She was still struggling to rise when she saw another face.

Zoe's. Zoe was shaking her and half sobbing, very softly. "Vanessa, you have to come. Quickly."

Vanessa sat up instantly. "What's wrong?"

"It's Bill . . . he's . . . Please, you can't wake the others. You can't let . . . you can't let Lew see us. You have to come quickly. He knows something, and if you let out the alarm, Lew will come and kill him. Please, Vanessa, hurry! Be silent."

Tears streamed down Zoe's delicate cheeks. "All right, all right, Zoe. We have to get to Sean —"

"Yes, but after you see Bill. You'll have to make Sean understand!"

She slipped quietly out of the tent with Zoe, her heart racing. *Lew? She had trusted him! He had a family, little children . . .*

She crept low, but they had barely gone a few steps before she heard Sean's voice.

"Hey. What's going on?" he asked.

Zoe stared at him without speaking.

"Sean," she said softly. "You need to be quiet and not raise an alarm."

"What's going on?" Sean repeated.

"Zoe —"

"Zoe's tired of waiting and being pushed around," Zoe said flatly. Her voice was deep and coarse and dry, and not her at all.

Sean drew his gun but not quickly enough. Vanessa felt the steel prod of Zoe's weapon at her back. "Set it down, Sean. Shooting Vanessa will be a piece of cake."

"Zoe, what do you think you'll accomplish?" Sean asked her.

"Satisfaction — and her rewards," Zoe said.

"But you can't get off this island alive," Sean argued.

"Put your gun down, Sean. I'm good with weapons. This is a Magnum .45 — Vanessa's entire chest will burst out in your face, and it will be all your fault," Zoe said.

"Shoot her, too, Sean," Vanessa said. "She intends to kill me in the end anyway!"

They could both sense Zoe's delicate finger on the trigger. Sean set his gun on the ground.

"Now step out of my way," Zoe said. "Vanessa and I have a little business together."

By then, the others had come running.

Ted with his speargun, Liam with his police revolver. But Zoe was calm and

resolved. "Put the weapons down. I cannot tell you what it will look like if I fire into Vanessa's flesh and blood and bone!" She said the last with relish.

Liam held on to his gun for a moment.

Suddenly, he stiffened.

"Down, my friendly neighborhood cop," Bill Hinton said. "Set it down, come on now, good cop! Zoe, go on, take her. I've got the situation here."

"Hell, no!" Liam said. He spun quickly, but not quickly enough. Bill Hinton brought the butt of his gun down on Liam's head with a savage vengeance and turned to shoot at Marty's foot. Marty, stunned, let out a roar of pain and fell to the sand.

"I said to drop all the weapons!" Bill thundered. He turned his gun on Jaden. "She'll look great with a shattered kneecap!"

The entire group was still. "Take her, and I'll be right behind," Bill said, his voice bizarrely gentle as he spoke to Zoe.

"Hey, I'll be all right," Vanessa said. "We're just going for a little walk in the woods."

Her heart was racing. She saw the trapped fury in Sean's eyes, and she was afraid that he'd wind up dead in the sand himself if she didn't defuse the immediate situation. "Please, stand back," she begged Sean. "I'll

be all right."

She wasn't going to be all right. She couldn't believe that Zoe — who had cried in fear of what she had done to Barry that day — could be this person. But she had been fooled — Zoe was petite, delicate. Zoe was a murderess, apparently. And she had probably managed to spring the door on purpose, knowing it would bring a weakening of the ranks.

Zoe dragged her into the trail where she had first traveled to find Carlos.

Zoe meant to kill her, just as she had killed Georgia Dare. It wasn't for money. It was because she had become strangely . . . *possessed.*

Sean made a dive into the sand, rolling to retrieve his weapon.

In all honesty, he wasn't sure if he would make it or not.

But it didn't matter.

Just as Bill started to rage at him, his attention distracted as he tried to take aim at Sean, something came leaping from the tent behind Liam's prone body — something! A whir of motion and of fury.

Sean got his hands on his gun just as Carlos Roca brought Bill down to the ground. Bill twisted, trying to aim his gun

467

at Carlos Roca's face.

Sean fired, as carefully as he could, praying that his aim would be true.

It was. Bill Hinton screamed in agony as his hand exploded and his gun went flying. Carlos Roca did not find mercy at that cry of pain. He slammed a bone-crunching fist into Hinton's face, and the cry was cut off cleanly. Hinton was out.

"Jesus!" Jaden cried, almost sinking to her knees, then rising, going one way, and then the other, not certain whether to see to Liam or Marty first.

"Liam!" Ted suggested, and they crossed one another as Ted raced to Marty and Jaden hurried on to Liam.

Jake Magnoli stood in the middle of the group, his jaw wide with astonishment and horror.

"Zoe? Bill?" he breathed.

Jay had been frozen in place. He moved, pacing, looking at Sean. "She's crazy. She's got to be crazy. She's got Vanessa. Why Vanessa?"

"We've got to hurry, track them, run . . . !" Lew Sanderson cried.

"No! No, we have to track them, but she can't see us," Sean said. "She'll kill. I know she'll kill. We have to take her by surprise." He looked up. Bartholomew was at the start

of the trail. He looked at Sean, and he began to run into the darkness of the pines.

"She can't hear us, she can't see us!" Sean said. "Carlos . . . come. Lew and the rest of you, stay here. Help Liam and Marty. Call for the authorities!"

He ran toward the trail, his heart thundering.

Zoe? Zoe Cally? The little bitty blonde . . .
The little bitty bloodthirsty blonde.

"All right, I admit to being incredibly confused," Vanessa said, trying to keep her voice calm and her words conversational. "I did figure out the truth behind Dona Isabella, right? What I'm trying to understand is how on earth you came to be so . . ."

"Crazy?" Zoe asked. "I'm not crazy. She's here. She *is* the power of the sea. Eventually, she'll reward us, and we'll live like royalty within her realm!"

"What are you talking about? She made you kill people. You ruined your own work with the movie —"

"Oh, right! The only people who would have made money on that movie were you and Jay," Zoe said. "While Dona Isabella . . . you must understand. She thrives on blood, she needs so much blood in the sea. Souls are good, too, but she really likes a good

machete massacre."

"She thrives on blood?" Vanessa said. "Zoe, when did you start this? How? Why?"

"How? I was chosen, don't you see? I knew the legend, good God, we all knew the legend. I used to love to come here and wonder what it was like in my own mind. And I sat here once and she came to me, and I knew. I knew what she wanted. She needed to be fed lots of blood. Then there was a bit filmed here for one of the history channels . . . let me see, that was four or five years ago. Bill was playing a bit part, and I saw that he would have loved to have been a pirate. It was so easy then. . . ." She broke off, laughing softly. "We had to learn, of course. We started with a girl who was diving here . . . a Bahamian. We didn't really know what we were doing and it was a very messy murder, but luckily, no one was around. And I'm so good with costumes and makeup, when the film that you and Jay were doing came up, well . . . it was just brilliant. Wonderful! We became pirates. Travis was easy. We terrified him before we killed him. And then we got on board the boat when Carlos tried to take Georgia away. Oh, it was so much fun. And the more blood Dona Isabella got, the more power she had, the more power she gave to us! But

you! You went and found the trunk. That was very tricky, because we had to pretend to be just hanging around Key West while we caught up with that doctor and her assistant and stole it back, then got a boat and dumped it back out at sea . . . but we're wonderful at getting rid of things in the sea. The sea is merciless, don't you agree?"

"A year ago, you killed the people on the *Delphi.* And you just killed more people, those retired people, on the *Happy-Me.*"

Zoe appeared indignant. "Dona Isabella needed her strength for this." She smiled. "Sometimes you have to seize your chances when they appear. Picking off retirees on boats that are just anchored here? Now and then you can have fun. You can do the whole pirate thing. Ghosts rising from the sea in flesh and blood with machetes!" She smiled, so proud of herself. "All you need is a place to run, excellent diving abilities and sheer talent. Oh, Vanessa! Murder is really ridiculously easy. The tricky part, always, was pulling off the crimes and then being back to appear to be innocent as hell. Actually, the hardest night was when we both had to slip out of our tents to catch up with Georgia and Carlos when they left that night. Catch up with them and get back into our own tents so we could wake up in horror and

come see what had happened, what was lying on the sand. But it was wonderful!"

Zoe might have been describing an incredible trip abroad, or a loving sexual encounter. She appeared ecstatic.

Vanessa tried to keep her talking.

"Zoe, you need to stop now. I'll help you. If not, you'll wind up arrested. You may get the needle instead of life in prison," Vanessa warned. She could still feel the prod of the gun so sharply against her back.

"No. Dona Isabella will protect me," Zoe said. "Won't you?" Zoe smiled slyly at Vanessa, then looked to her side.

Vanessa looked, too.

And there she was. The ghost of Dona Isabella, haughty, proud and cruel, and highly amused as they walked through the pines.

"You," Vanessa said, "will surely rot in all the fires of hell, and soon."

Zoe looked shocked. "You see her?" she demanded.

Dona Isabella looked furious. She spoke with a sultry voice, pleasantly, despite her words. "Zoe will kill you slowly, Vanessa. Slowly. You will bleed into the sand and into the sea."

Zoe looked distracted for a minute. "Where's Bill?"

"I'm sure he's dead," Vanessa said. "You

think those men just let a boy playing with a gun stop them?"

The nose of the gun pressed harder.

Vanessa realized that they were coming through the trees to the other side of the island. When they reached the sand, she thought, she would be in trouble.

The moon was out, and they neared the water. She could hear the waves, the sound lulling. They were about to break through the trees.

They did.

To Vanessa's surprise, they came to a sudden halt. "Ah, well, if it isn't the Spanish whore of all time!" came a voice.

Bartholomew. The ghost was awaiting them.

"Pirate scum!" Dona Isabella said. "Go — out of my way. Push through him. Just push through him. He is nothing but a mass in the air."

"As you are," Vanessa said.

She was stunned when the ghost swung about, when she saw hands of mist come toward her and encircle her throat. She felt the pinch . . .

And then she refused to do so.

"You bitch! You let her go!" Bartholomew said.

Zoe let out a little cry, thrusting Vanessa

473

forward so that she fell onto the sand. She lifted the gun, but her hand was shaking as Bartholomew pitched himself at Dona Isabella and the spirits went flying downward in the night in a mist of white and sand.

And just as they did, Vanessa heard something like a whir, a motion so fast it seemed more ethereal than the ghostly specters in the sand.

Sean.

He flew into Zoe so fast, pitching himself from the trees, that she didn't even have a split second to pull the trigger. She fell to the earth, and Jay, behind Sean, swept up her gun. Zoe began to toss and writhe and scream incoherently.

Sean kept her down.

Lew Sanderson walked out of the trail and approached the ghosts locked in combat on the sand. And he began to speak, too, some kind of an ancient dialect, his booming voice rising over Zoe's desperate tirade and screams.

Then Lew's words changed to Latin, and he lifted a cross, speaking the same words over and over. He reached into his pocket. From the sand, Vanessa stared at him, afraid that he had a gun, that he would begin to shoot needlessly at the mist . . .

But it wasn't a gun. It was a vial of water,

and he sprinkled it again and again. . . .

Suddenly, a piercing scream of agony and terror erupted from the sand. Vanessa looked toward the sea. It seemed that her monsters had risen, but they were seaweed monsters of darkness and fire. . . .

Black mist rose like fierce, roiling thunderclouds, seeming both unreal and with substance, a viscous mass that steadily came forward.

Dona Isabella stared at it, screaming in a rage. Words of protest tumbled from her mouth.

It seemed that thunder roared, silencing her.

She backed away.

But it did no good.

The darkness had come for her.

The black, roiling mass washed its way over the shoreline, an unstoppable army of oily shadows, somehow alive and furious, bearing red eyes that spoke of all the demons of hell.

Coming for Dona Isabella.

The mass enveloped her. She screamed and writhed, but to no avail. She became part of the mass, and it ripped her from shore, bearing her back to the water again.

Vanessa blinked. It was over; she was gone. Her heart flew to her throat because

she didn't see Bartholomew, either. All there was to be seen was Zoe, now suddenly silent, almost catatonic.

Lew turned to them. "She is gone," he said simply.

Jay blinked. "Who is gone?" he whispered.

He didn't know what he had seen. Now, as the waves lapped gently again, as the moon rode over the water, Vanessa wasn't sure, either.

Lew Sanderson stooped down by Zoe. "I will take her. She will go to the Bahamian authorities," he said. "And perhaps face charges elsewhere."

Sean left Zoe to Lew.

He walked to Vanessa, caught her hand and drew her up into his arms. He was shaking.

"You know what I think?" he whispered.

"What?"

"I don't need to think anymore. I know that I love you," he said, and he drew her hard against him, still shaking as he held her there.

The remains of the *Happy-Me* were found the following week, and the *Delphi* was found two weeks later. Once in custody, Bill and Zoe seemed to have no problem talking, even though most of the law-

enforcement officials they spilled their souls to thought they were crazy.

It was Dona Isabella. She taught them how to be pirates. She helped them slip aboard boats, kill the crew one by one and make them disappear into the ocean.

The film shoot had been so easy. They had made a point of switching places constantly, so that neither could really be accused. For instance, Zoe had made certain that Bill was working when she took down the *Delphi,* just as Bill had made sure that Zoe was seen at the time he lured Travis out to the sand during the making of the horror movie. Travis! Conceited oaf. He had died quickly and easily. And it was bizarre that the authorities had never found the machete that they had used to cut up the bodies — they had left it hidden in the pine forest on the island. They had sunk Jay's boat — as they sank all the boats, stealing off them little by little. They weren't bad people — they were chosen. They were chosen by Dona Isabella to help her rule the sea.

There were a dozen times when Vanessa wanted to turn to Sean and say, "Did that really happen? Did we see what we saw? Did an evil ghost walk the world just as easily as the pained spirits of those who had been wronged, or who sought to help others?"

She never spoke. Maybe they both knew that the world was composed of good and evil. As Bartholomew had suggested, good men were good men.

And evil men — and women — were evil.

Just how crazy had Zoe become?

And did it make them all a little mad?

They were questions that haunted Vanessa at first. But they weren't about to stop her from living her life, from being with Sean. Barry healed quickly, and Marty was thrilled to walk around with a cane for a while. Liam came to before the authorities even arrived, furious with himself for having fallen prey to a pathetic little bastard like Bill Hinton.

But they had survived, and they had found a certain truth — if not the total truth. No one would really know what had happened on the pirate ship — and man might never really know what had caused hundreds of years of wild weather and strange occurrences in the Bermuda Triangle.

They didn't expect to solve that riddle.

They weren't salvage divers, either. They were filmmakers.

And so they became the filmmakers who worked with the salvage divers who brought up the pirate ship.

Vanessa still had a strange knack for find-

ing treasure. She'd be led sometimes by a gentle presence in the water — a blonde woman who had worked too hard in life, fallen in love with a pirate and been murdered for that love. Kitty Cutlass.

She had feared for Bartholomew that night. But he had joined her later in the confusion on the shore, and he had assured her that he was not going to the place that was now hosting Dona Isabella. He wouldn't say more, just that he was destined for a better end, and that he was actually quite anxious to get back to Key West.

It wasn't long before they had a break and spent time in the city. And it was at dinner at O'Hara's where she saw that Bartholomew was really all right. He had been sitting with them idly at the bar, and then . . .

His Lucinda, his lady in white, came by, and he was gone, hurrying out to the street to meet her, where he held her tenderly in his arms, where their eyes met, and he kissed her.

"Very romantic!" she said, pleased.

Sean pulled her into his arms. "Let's go home," he said softly. "And I'll show you romantic."

She smiled, and slipped from the bar stool.

She turned into his arms. "I don't need to think much at all anymore, Sean O'Hara. I

know. I know that I love you."

"I know . . . that I love you," he said.

And they left the bar, and went home, and made good on their words to each other.

AUTHOR'S NOTE

Key West is known as the Conch Republic; those born there are known as Conchs and those who have been there for more than seven years are known as Freshwater Conchs.

Naturally, in Key West, you're going to come upon many conch offerings. The Bahamians and the Keys' people tend to believe they've both created the same recipes, but you'll find subtle flavor variations wherever you go.

But when in Rome — or the Conch Republic — it's great to try the local dishes. And conch chowder and conch fritters — two very popular uses for the shellfish — can be absolutely delicious.

One thing to remember — conch meat can be tough and rubbery. In any recipe, it's best to bring a heavy-duty meat mallet, and be ready for dicing and grinding!

These recipes may not be low-cal — but if

you've been imbibing a few of the local drink choices, you won't care too much!

KEY WEST CONCH CHOWDER

(8 servings)

Ingredients:
2 cups fresh or frozen conch meat, well
  ground or chopped
4 cups potatoes, peeled and diced
2 quarts water
4 cups diced lean pork meat (bacon may be
  substituted)
1 cup fresh or canned tomatoes, diced
2 small onions, chopped fine
2 cloves garlic, chopped fine
1 green pepper, chopped fine
Salt and pepper to taste
2 tablespoons olive oil
2 tablespoons butter

Directions:
Place conch in half olive oil, half butter,
and heat on low heat; do not brown, just allow to heat. Add potatoes and water and

bring to a boil; reduce heat. In a separate pan, sauté lean pork (bacon) and tomatoes, peppers, onions and garlic until tender. Add to the conch mixture and allow to cook thirty to forty-five minutes, covered, until a creamy texture is reached and conch is tender. Add salt and pepper to taste — and enjoy!

KEY WEST CONCH FRITTERS

Ingredients:
3 cups flour
1 tablespoon baking powder
1 1/2 cups pounded and diced conch
1 clove garlic
1/8 cup minced onion
1/8 cup finely diced red bell pepper
1/8 cup finely diced green bell pepper
2 tablespoons finely chopped parsley
4 eggs (or substitute such as Eggbeaters)
Salt and pepper to taste
(For a spicy Bahamian version, add 1
   tablespoon finely chopped jalapeño pepper
   and a dash of cayenne pepper or a touch
   of hot sauce.)

Directions:
Sift the flour and baking powder together,
mix other ingredients with eggs, then blend
together. Season as desired. (Mild, or with
a kick!) Form fritters, and deep-fry in

vegetable oil until crispy and golden-brown. Great when served with a Key lime mayonnaise. Add some cayenne to the mayonnaise for those who love more spice.

ABOUT THE AUTHOR

Heather Graham is a *New York Times* bestselling author of over 100 titles, including anthologies and short stories. She has been published in more than 15 languages and has over 20 million copies of her books in print.

The employees of Thorndike Press hope you have enjoyed this Large Print book. All our Thorndike, Wheeler, and Kennebec Large Print titles are designed for easy reading, and all our books are made to last. Other Thorndike Press Large Print books are available at your library, through selected bookstores, or directly from us.

For information about titles, please call:
   (800) 223-1244

or visit our Web site at:
   http://gale.cengage.com/thorndike

To share your comments, please write:
   Publisher
   Thorndike Press
   295 Kennedy Memorial Drive
   Waterville, ME 04901

6/3

AUG . '10

Rousseau's vision would know a subtle but complete victory, and the newborn infant—from first opening her eyes until the call of death—would gaze upon and depend on the largesse of the fatherland, knowing nothing else.

Aggressive nationalism also gains as the loyalty of individuals to the family diminishes. The absolute loyalty claimed by the total state can succeed only as it destroys the reality of family autonomy. This was, for example, the inner contradiction of the supposed German National Socialist affection for families. Claiming to support motherhood and family life, the Nazis in practice destroyed the German family in their quest for empire. As historian Claudia Koonz explains in her able work *Mothers in the Fatherland*: "True, publicity exalted the family as the 'germ cell' of the nation, but social policy emptied the household of its members. Eugenic laws interfered with private choices related to marriage and children. The demand for total loyalty to the Fuhrer undercut fathers' authority. As indoctrination supplanted education, youth leaders and teachers rivaled mothers for children's devotion."[8]

The symbolic effort to drive women back to the home, so often associated with the Nazi regime, was actually abandoned in 1938 in favor of the drive for war and conquest: German women were actually forced into factories to serve the war machine. Indeed, Nazism aimed in the end at the elimination of marriage: "[World War II] accelerated Hitler's determination to establish an entirely new social order based on race and sex, with the ideal couple at its core: not a husband and wife, but a soldier and his mother, obedient to Hitler, the patriarch *über alles.*"[9]

For similar reasons, Communism shared this preference for the liberation of the individual from the family. Friedrich Engels, Karl Marx's friend and collaborator, first developed this argument in his 1884 book *The Origin of the Family, Private Property and the*

State. Engels called for the family's end as an economic unit, for elimination of the concept of legitimacy, for "the reintroduction of the whole female sex into the public industries," for the collective care and rearing of children, and for "the full freedom of marriage," meaning easy and unilateral divorce.[10]

Shortly after the Bolsheviks took power in Russia in November 1917, this theoretical assault on the family became real. As the Communist leader Madame Smidovich explained, "To clear the family out of the accumulated dust of the ages we had to give it a good shakeup; this we did."[11] Some parents, "narrow and petty," failed to see the course of history and were "only interested in their own offspring." There was no room in Communist society for this "proprietary attitude." As Alexandra Kollontai wrote: "The worker-mother must learn *not* to differentiate between yours and mine; she must remember that there are only *our* children, the children of Russia's communist workers." Accordingly, children must be raised by "qualified educators" so that "the child can grow up a conscious communist who recognizes the need for solidarity, comradeship, mutual help and loyalty to the collective." And then: "In place of the individual and egoistic family, a great universal family of workers will develop, in which all the workers, men and women, will above all be comrades."[12] Indeed, by 1925, the provision of easy, unilateral divorce—"to be obtained at the [simple] request of either partner in a marriage"—had already undermined many Russian families.

In short, the secular "liberal" vision of Hobbes, Locke, Mill and Rousseau—devoted to freeing the individual from family and religious authority—led *ironically* and *inevitably* to the grander oppressions of the twentieth century, whether in the "total states" of National Socialism and Communism, or in the "welfare states" of Western Europe, North America, and Australia-New Zealand. A philosophical scheme devoted to liberty became, in the end, a blueprint for both the grand slaughters that marked the middle decades of the twentieth century and the public bankruptcies looming in the early twenty-first. Men and women have been "liberated" from meaningful ties to children, parents, and kin, in order to become servants of and dependents on the total state.

The basic liberal error lay at the beginning: the natural unit of society is not, and can never be, the individual. Rather, social order and true liberty depend on recognition of the role of *the natural family* as the fundamental unit, or cell, of society. The philosophical tradition rejected by the liberal mind in the seventeenth century—one extending from Aristotle to Thomas Aquinas—had rested on this premise. The core liberal mistake lay in separating the individual from the natural protections of the family, leaving each person easy prey for the aggrandizing nation.

THE AMERICAN EXAMPLE

The American experience offers another telling example of how this process occurred. In the beginning, the family was at the center of American political concern. It is true that the U.S. Constitution, unlike the basic laws in many other lands, makes no reference to family relations. Even its language is cast in remarkably "gender free" terms, using words such as "person" where the generic "he" might have been expected. Nevertheless, this was not due to a remarkably early outbreak of feminism among the Founders or to an assumption by them that the family is irrelevant. In fact, the family was deeply rooted in what we might call the *unwritten* Constitution of these new United States, in the cultural and social assumptions about the social order that must be present to sustain a free republic.

The Founders agreed with the ancient Roman statesman Cicero that the family household was the seedbed of virtue and of the political state. Historians underscore how the colonists had left the Old World, hoping that America would be a better setting in which to raise their true and precious "tender plants": that is, "a good place to train up children amongst sober people and to prevent the corruption of them here by the loose behavior of youths and the bad example of too many of riper years."[13] Historian James Henretta underscores how late eighteenth-century Americans raised children to "succeed them," not merely to "succeed." Rights and obligations bound together the generations: "The [family] line was more important than the individual; the patrimony was to be conserved for lineal reasons."[14]

In her investigation of the phrase "the pursuit of happiness," found in the American Declaration of Independence, the historian Jan Lewis underscores the true intent of Thomas Jefferson. Most analysts have seen this phase as a fairly insignificant substitution of "happiness" for the pursuit of "property" found in John Locke's earlier list of mankind's inalienable rights. Looking at Jefferson and his fellow Virginians, though, Lewis emphasizes that "it was within the family circle that men and women told each other to look for happiness, and there, if anywhere, that they found it." Noting the tendency of Virginians to romanticize family life, she nonetheless concludes: "Virginians who rhapsodized about the family were creating and reinforcing an article of faith for their society, a belief perhaps more central to their lives than any other. . . . Virginians often found that their ideal of the perfect family was in fact the image of their own family."[15] Along with "life" and "liberty," this pursuit of *family* happiness was at the core of American identity and purpose.[16]

In his provocative book *The Myth of American Individualism*, the political historian Barry Shain shows that "Americans in the Revolutionary era embraced a theory of the good life that is best described as reformed Protestant and communal." The American Revolution, he asserts, had more to do with the defense of "familial independence" than it did with quests for personal liberation. Americans of the founding era, Shain insists, were rooted in agrarian, religious, family-centric communities.[17] These Americans saw family households as the common source of new citizens, the places where the character traits necessary to free government would be shaped, the foundation stones of ordered liberty. Defense of *this society of households* lay with the states and the people. The U.S. Constitution assumed a nation of families. The spirit found in the Bill of Rights, especially in the Ninth and Tenth Amendments, affirmed the rights of the people and the powers of the states as bulwarks against centralized social experimentation.

Since the late nineteenth century, however, the federal government—like all modern governments—has grown massively. The doctrine of *parens patriae*, "the parenthood of the state," spawned the first examples of the American interventionist state, including an intrusive "reform school" campaign and the drive to impose "common schools" on the populace. The Fourteenth Amendment to the U.S. Constitution, initially intended to protect newly freed slaves from retribution at the state level, became instead a legal wedge for the steady expansion of federal authority at the expense of the states, and potentially of the families they had sheltered. Doing particular damage was the right of "privacy," supposedly discovered by the Supreme Court in the "emanations" and "penumbra" of the Constitution in 1965. It spawned rights to contraception, abortion, and sodomy while leveling the authentic rights of all parents, fathers in particular.

A detailed list of court cases would lead to this simple conclusion: the last 125 years might be written as the steady surrender of the Ninth and Tenth Amendments to the growing sweep of the Fourteenth and to the exercise of *parens patriae*. Today, the very size and pervasiveness of the federal government—comprising as it does over 20 percent of Gross Domestic Product and intruding into every aspect of American life—leaves the family vulnerable. The original American plan—leaving family issues to local communities and the states—no longer works in the age of a U.S. Department of Education, welfare spending, Social Security, the federal income tax, the Department of Homeland Security, and federal child care policies.

THE FAMILY IN THE INDUSTRIAL ECONOMY

That tangle of events called the "industrial revolution" also disrupted the family. Before the industrial revolution, before the rise of great cities, virtually all humankind lived in family-centered economies. The family household was the center of most productive activity. In the United States, circa 1800, about 90 percent of the free population were farmers. Most of the remaining 10 percent were family-scale artisans and shopkeepers also maintaining home gardens, family cows, and flocks of chickens. Each family raised most of its own food, made most of its own clothing, provided most of its own fuel, crafted most of its own furniture. Anthropologist Hugh Brody offers a concise summary of life on the family farm: "A family is busy in the countryside. Mother is baking bread, churning butter, attending to hens and ducks . . . preparing food for everyone. Father is in the fields, ploughing the soil, cutting wood, fixing walls, providing sustenance. Children explore and play and help and sit at the family table. Grandma or grandpa sits in a chair by the fire. Everyday is long and filled with the activities of the family. . . . There is a loyalty . . . to the tasks and expertise and duties that each member of the family undertakes . . . . The family in its farm is the family where it belongs."[18]

The industrial principles of centralization and the quest for efficiency tore through this settled way of life. The family household ceased to be the center of productive labor. Centralized factories, warehouses, and offices displaced home workshops, gardens, and storehouses. Cash exchanges pushed aside the altruistic exchanges of the family. Industrialization destroyed the ancient unity of home and work, the natural ecology of the family, which had prevailed for hundreds of generations. Mothers, fathers, and children alike were pulled into the wage-laborer ranks. Family bonds, once the source of economic strength, now stood more as obstructions to the efficient allocation of labor. The individual, unencumbered and alone, was the new ideal worker. As the English essayist G.K. Chesterton, writing in 1919, summarized: "[The family] is literally being torn in pieces, in that the husband may go to one factory, the wife to another, and the child to a third. Each will become the servant of a separate financial group, which is more and more gaining the political power of a feudal group. But whereas feudalism received the loyalty of families, the lords of the new servile state will receive only the loyalty of individuals: that is, of lonely men and even of lost children."[19]

Advertising became another vehicle for implementing this economic revolution. In whetting appetites for more industrially produced goods, it implied that residual forms of family production were inferior, and it drew family members deeper into the brave new world of consumerism. The home economics movement as crafted by Ellen Richards turned science and efficiency into the new household gods, reinforcing the turn to consumerism.

This radical change, too, might be seen as the consequence of ideas and political coercion. As Karl Polanyi argues in *The Great Transformation*, laissez-faire capitalism actually relied on state coercion designed to make human society subservient to the economic mechanism: "*Laissez faire* was not a method to achieve a thing," he wrote. "[I]t was the thing to be achieved."[20] As a later analyst influenced by Polanyi, Robert Nisbet, would explain: "*Laissez faire* . . . was brought into existence. It was brought into existence by the planned destruction of old customs, associations, villages, and other securities, by the force of the State throwing the weight of its fast-developing administrative system in favor of the new economic elements of the population. . . . There is indeed much to be said for regarding capitalism as simply the forced adjustment of economic life to the needs of the sovereign state."[21]

In the new order, the status of marriage altered. In the pre-industrial order, husbands and wives had specialized in their labor according to their respective strengths and skills so that their small family enterprises might succeed. This natural complementarity reinforced their need for each other, uniting the sexual and the economic functions and giving real strength to marriage. Industrial managers, in contrast, preferred the androgynous individual, sexless, interchangeable. In this new order, men and women needed each other less than before. As an institution, marriage weakened.

The status of children also changed. In an agrarian and artisan economy, children—even small ones—were economic assets, parts of small family enterprises. Accordingly, fertility on the family farm and in the artisan's shop tended to be high. In the new order, children were either pulled away into an early—and often dangerous—economic independence (such as little girls tending the spindles in the early textile plants) or became liabilities, left at home by working parents to fend for themselves. Fertility plummeted, as actual or potential parents avoided taking on these new little burdens. Two leading analysts of modern fertility decline, Kingsley Davis writing in 1937 and John C. Caldwell writing in 2003, have both concluded that "the family is *not* indefinitely adaptable to modern society, and this explains the declining birth rate."[22]

REACTIONS: EUROPEAN AND AMERICAN

Indeed, these common products of urban-industrial "modernity"—weakened marriages and low fertility—are another reason for contemporary attention to the family. As Davis and Caldwell imply, the natural family is not an institution capable of drastic change. Rather, it is a set of relationships rooted in human nature: natural (biologically grounded) and universal (found in every healthy human society). In modernity's wake, the critical tasks became—and remain—the defense of this natural family from the negative pressures of "modernity." Specifically, family policy has meant constructing barriers around the home to limit the spread of the industrial principle and its twin, the autonomous individual, to preserve some domain of family autonomy within the coercive modern industrial order.

Early on, somewhat different approaches were tried in Europe and America, although *both* were tied to a common family ideal that would bring at least the mother and children back home. Starting around 1900, Europeans consciously set out to build family policies that would protect marriage and restore fertility to a more natural level. The first intellectually consistent efforts to lay out a family policy drew inspiration from Pope Leo XIII's 1891 encyclical *Rerum Novarum* (*The New Age*). Leo argued that "the present [industrial] age handed over the workers, each alone and defenseless, to the inhumanity of employers and the unbridled greed of competitors." Rejecting the wage theories of both laissez-faire liberalism *and* socialism, Leo called instead for an economy based on "the natural and primeval right of marriage" and "the society of the household." This family-centered economy would rest on the "most sacred law of nature that the father of a family see that his offspring are provided with all the necessities of life" and that women were "intended by nature for the work of the home . . . the education of children and the well-being of the family." This meant that any just wage must enable the father "to provide comfortably for himself, his wife, and children." Men and women stood equal in dignity and basic legal claims, but differed in social function. This goal of a "family wage" received more direct affirmation in Pope Pius XI's 1931 encyclical, *Quadragesimo Anno* (*Forty Years After*). Pius declared that "every effort must be made" to insure "that fathers of families receive a wage large enough to meet ordinary family needs adequately." He gave "merited praise to all, who with a wise and useful purpose have tried and tested various ways of adjusting the pay for work to family burdens."[23]

Inspired by Catholic social teaching, lay political leaders in France, Belgium, and other European lands proceeded to build family policy systems that would shelter families from the negative consequences of industrial organization and liberal leveling. The favored approach became "family allowances" that would recognize the disproportionate burdens carried by laborers with wives and children at home. Christian businessmen began introducing family allowances on a private basis in 1916. The French government passed laws in the early 1920s creating "equalization funds" within industries, so eliminating any incentive employers might have to avoid hiring workers with families. Corporations contributed to these funds on a per capita basis. Besides paying generous allowances for each child in a family, these funds also provided families with marriage loans, pre-natal care, midwives, visiting nurses, birth and breastfeeding bonuses, medical care for children, layettes, and fresh milk. During the late 1930s, these quasi-private funds and programs were absorbed into the French government's emerging social security program. In Belgium, a similar system provided child allowances in a manner favoring larger families: from 15 francs per month for the first child to 100 francs per month for the fifth and additional children. The government also crafted large tax deductions and credits for families with children, built a network of pre- and post-natal child health centers, and provided subsidized housing loans and rent rebates for larger families.[24]

In America, policy construction to protect families took a somewhat different course. To begin with, the label "family policy" was rarely used in a direct way; "child welfare" was the preferred moniker. Nor were there many open appeals to "pro-natalist" goals. Still, the ideal of a "family wage" also came to govern American policy formation. And the American model fostered family formation and fertility even more successfully than the French, Belgian, and other models.

Inspired by so-called "maternalist" reformers such as Julia Lathrop, Josephine Baker, and Florence Kelly, the U.S. Congress created the U.S. Children's Bureau in 1912. Lathrop, named first Chief of the Children's Bureau, laid out the guiding principles for current and future American policy: "The power to maintain a decent family living standard is the primary essential of child welfare. This means a living wage and wholesome working life for the men, a good and skillful mother at home to keep the house and comfort all within it. Society can afford no less and can afford *no exceptions*. This is a *universal* need."[25]

Pursuing the goal of "Baby Saving," the Children's Bureau also set out to reduce infant and maternal mortality and to improve early child care. The Bureau sponsored "Baby Weeks" to promote good mothering. The Smith-Lever Vocational Training Act of 1917 provided Federal funds to school districts to promote education for girls in the "household arts": This was the *first* Federal education program. The U.S. War Department introduced child allowances into military pay in 1917. The Sheppard-Towner Act of 1921, the first true federal entitlement, provided federal funds to the states for pre-natal and child health clinics and visiting nurses for pregnant and post-partum mothers.

The Great Depression of the 1930s was as much a family crisis as an economic crisis. Both American marriage and fertility rates fell sharply during the early 1930s. The New Deal, constructed in response by the Franklin D. Roosevelt administration, expanded the scope of the "family wage" ideal in federal policymaking. For example, the National Industrial Recovery Act of 1934 codified wage scales that paid men up to 30 percent more than women for the same work and that affirmed sex-defined job categories ("men's jobs" and "women's jobs") with even larger pay differentials. The Works Progress Administration, the largest government relief program, "deplored" the employment on WPA programs of women with husbands or dependent children; denounced child day care; and retrained unemployed teachers to teach homemaking and maternal skills. The Social Security Amendments of 1939 provided "homemakers' pensions" to women married to eligible men and generous "survivors" benefits to the widows and children of covered male workers. The National Housing Act created the

FHA mortgage program featuring long-term amortization, a low down-payment, and insurance protection for the lender. Joined in 1944 by the Veterans Administration (VA) mortgage program, billions of new dollars were mobilized for home construction, with over 99 percent of these government-backed mortgages targeted to young married couples. Tax reforms in 1944 and 1948 extended the marriage-friendly benefits of "income splitting" to all American homes and substantially raised the real value of the tax deduction for dependent children.[26]

Linked to these policy changes was a renewed family ethos, rooted in religious faith. Church membership and attendance rose dramatically across the country, as did the construction of new church buildings. The whole ethos of the era became marriage- and family-friendly.

The statistical results were impressive. Between 1935 and 1963, the marriage rate rose by 30 percent, the average age of first marriage fell to historic lows (age twenty-two for men; age twenty for women), the proportion of ever-married adults reached a record high (over 95 percent), and the fertility rate—after falling for 100 years—rose by 75 percent. The increase was particularly dramatic among Roman Catholics, where completed family size doubled. Following the turmoil of World War II, even the divorce rate declined between 1946 and 1960. While certainly not wholly due to public policy, it does seem clear that policy initiatives between 1912 and 1948 *did* affirm and encourage the amazing "marriage-" and "baby-booms" of mid-twentieth-century America.[27]

THE POST-FAMILY WAY

And yet, starting in the mid-1960s, these positive gains quickly disappeared. The "family model" that had undergirded policymaking in both Western Europe and the United States—the breadwinner–homemaker–child-rich family sustained by a "family wage"—entered into crisis. More specifically, a rival view of human nature focused on Rousseau's radical individual came to the fore, with a very different understanding of the human family.

One of the most systematic and influential twentieth century advocates of this new understanding was Alva Myrdal, a socialist and feminist theorist from Sweden, active from the 1930s through the mid-1970s. Her influence spread to America, then globally. A philosophical atheist, she argued that human nature was *not* biologically fixed in a created order. Rather, she believed that family structure was the product of material, environmental evolution. As economic relationships evolved, so must social relationships. A family structure inherited from agrarian times could no longer function in a modern urban environment, Myrdal said. Marriage relationships founded on the biological differences between men and women were no longer relevant to an industrial setting. The family and population crises of the early twentieth century, she insisted, were the product of a social and cultural lag behind economic change. A *new family model* was imperative. "Paid work, productive work, is now a woman's demand, and as such a social fact, which lies completely in line with general tendencies of evolution," she wrote. The so-called "traditional family" was an "abnormal situation for a child," an "almost pathological" state. Instead, "a new parenthood" was needed, one that would be part of "the evolution toward a rationalization of human life." The day care center, Myrdal wrote, not the disintegrating home, represented the new human order. In the former, small children could be rescued from the shallow views of their parents, and reprogrammed for life in an androgynous, cooperative socialist order.[28]

Alva Myrdal's arguments represent an early and relatively coherent version of the general intellectual assault mounted against the family system in Sweden, America, and elsewhere in the developed world. Atheist, neo-Malthusian, humanist, feminist, socialist, Marxist, playboy philosopher—all could agree on a common foe: the breadwinner–homemaker–child-rich home. And starting in the mid-1960s, their assault produced policy effects. The culture of marriage—seemingly strong in the 1950s—waned. "No-fault" divorce statutes further weakened the institutional nature of marriage. Egalitarian economic policies eliminated the vitally important family wage. Population policy refocused on the so-called "population bomb," its advocates calling for dramatic reductions in family size. Day care subsidies grew; "at home" parenting drew scorn. Schools became "substitutes" for the family. Housing policies shifted to favor so-called "new family forms." Pro-family tax codes disappeared in favor of individualized taxation. And welfare systems began to penalize family inter-generational care.

THE DAMAGE

We can assess the damage that has been done. To begin with, children are vanishing. In *every* developed nation in 2005, births were insufficient to replace the existing population. In nations as diverse as Italy, Spain, Greece, Russia, and the Czech Republic, barely half the needed offspring are born. Urban economic powerhouses such as Hong Kong and Singapore have become virtual baby-free zones, as have American cities such as Portland and San Francisco. While babies disappear, the average age of these populations climbs. Schools are shuttered, only to reopen as elder care centers. Already, Europe resembles a vast assisted care center.

Marriage, too, is in decline. Since 1970, marriage rates have generally tumbled in every developed land. Sometimes, as in Scandinavia, cohabitation has emerged as a substitute. In other places, such as Italy and coastal China, male-female bonds of any permanence have simply disappeared. Indeed, some now claim the right to marry others of the same sex, meaning perfectly sterile unions. The image of life and hope—the triad of mother, child, and father—fades around the globe.

All the same, in crisis lies opportunity. The very phrase "natural" implies the potential for rebirth. As Chesterton suggested, the family is the one true anarchical institution, the reliable source of social renewal, the only human group that renews itself as eternally as the state, and more naturally than the state. Recent numbers suggest increases in marriage rates among the better educated and less movement toward divorce.

The Bulwark of Liberty

OUR RESPONSE TO THE SITUATION outlined in the previous chapter focuses on the natural family: its origin, its expression, and its gifts. In this manifesto, we recognize the natural family as part of the created order, imprinted on our natures, the source of bountiful joy, the fountain of new life, and the bulwark of liberty. Identifying the true character of the natural family allows us to draw out principles to guide action.

A PART OF THE CREATED ORDER

Modern debates about marriage and family frequently pit the partisans of biblical revelation against the partisans of science and evolution. We hold that the story of scripture and the evolutionary narrative actually wind up in surprising concurrence over the origin and nature of the human creature.

People of biblical faith—Jews, Christians, and Muslims alike—find the origins of the family chronicled in Genesis 1 and 2. In these chapters of scripture, God establishes marriage as an unchanging aspect of His creation, essential to the very foundation of the divine order: "So God created man in his own image, in the image of God he created him; male and female he created them. And God blessed them, and God said to them, 'Be fruitful and multiply, and fill the earth and subdue it; and have dominion over the fish of the sea and over birds of the air and over every living thing that moves upon the earth'. . . . Therefore a man leaves his father and mother and cleaves to his wife and they become one flesh."[1]

These passages affirm marriage as both sexual ("Be fruitful and multiply and fill the earth") and economic ("fill the earth and subdue it" and "have dominion over [its creatures]"). They also emphasize marriage as monogamous. As John Lierman explains, these passages underscore as well the incompleteness of the individual, as half a person, and the necessary unity of male and female: "A married couple does not fuse or transubstantiate. A married couple reconstitutes the single entity of *adam*, which subsists in male and female and is truly manifested only by male and female in concert. A married couple manifests the image of God."[2]

What does science actually teach? The founders of modern anthropology also held that marriage is an unchanging institution, universal in its basic elements and common to all humanity. As Edward Westermarck explained a century ago: "Among the lowest savages, as well as the most civilized races of men, we find the family consisting of parents and children, and the father as its protector." Marriage bound this family system together, uniting "a regulated sexual relation" with "economic obligations." According to Westermarck, special *maternal*, *paternal*, and *marital* instincts all existed, each rooted in human nature. As he explained, "the institution of marriage . . . has developed out of a primeval habit."

Certainly there were differences in the marriage systems of distinct human cultures. Nevertheless, the fundamental marriage bond did not change.[3] As a later anthropologist, George Murdock, wrote in his great 1949 survey of human cultures: "The nuclear family is a universal human social grouping." He added that "all known human societies have developed specialization and cooperation between the sexes roughly along this biologically determined line of cleavage." Murdock emphasized that "marriage exists only when the economic and the sexual are united into one relationship, and this combination only occurs in marriage. Marriage, thus defined, is found in every known human society."[4] His work pointed to marriage as natural, necessary, and unchanging.

Contemporary scientists implicitly agree. Writing in the journal *Science*, for example, paleo-anthropologist C. Owen Lovejoy argues that "the unique sexual and reproductive behavior of man"—not growth of the cortex or brain—"may be the sine qua non of human origin." The evolutionary narrative indicates that the pairing-off of male and female "hominids" into something very much like traditional marriage reaches back between three and four million years, to the time when our purported ancestors left the trees on the African savannah and started walking on two legs. As Lovejoy concludes, "both advances in material culture and the Pleistocene acceleration in brain development are sequelae to an *already established hominid character system*, which included *intensified parenting* and *social relationships, monogamous pair bonding, specialized sexual-reproductive behavior*, and *bipedality*. [This model] implies that the nuclear family and human sexual behavior may have their ultimate origin long before the dawn of the Pleistocene."[5]

Other new evidence supports this conclusion. Writing in *Evolutionary Psychology*, Ronald Immerman of Case Western Reserve

University reports that from the very beginning, our distinctly human ancestors showed a unique reproductive strategy in which a female exchanged *sexual exclusivity* for special provisioning by a male. Immerman shows that "[t]his sharing of resources from man-to-woman is a universal." Also from the dawn of the human race, it appears that *women* chose *men* because of their skills in *provisioning* and *loyalty*, rather than physical size. Women have bonded to men who reliably returned to the family circle with fresh meat or similar resources. At the same time, the ethnographic "data suggest an independent man [to]child affiliative bond which is part of *Homo* [*sapiens*] bio-cultural heritage." This trait, he notes, is not found anywhere else in the animal kingdom. Immerman again turns to evolutionary selection to explain this bond. Besides looking for reliable providers, women "were simultaneously selecting for traits which would forge a social father: a man who would form attach-ments—bond—with his young and who would be psychologically willing to share resources with those young."[6]

A 2003 paper featured in *The Proceedings of the National Academy of Science* examines the difference in male and female size ("sexual dimorphism") in *Australopithecus afarensis*, a human ancestor said to have lived three to four million years ago. Among mammals [including the apes], sexual dimorphism is most pronounced when sexual coupling is random or where one male accumulates numer-ous females. Dimorphism is least when male and female pair off in monogamous bonds. Contrary to earlier investigations, this new study finds that *Australopithecus* males and females were about the same size, no different than men and women today. This finding implies that this human ancestor was monogamous, with male and female in a permanent pair bond, "a social complex including male provisioning driven by female choice."[7]

True, it would be going too far to say that modern evolutionary theory has converged with Genesis. Important differences remain over issues such as "when" or "how" humankind arrived on earth. All the same, it would be fair to conclude that research guided by evolutionary theory does agree with the author of Genesis that from our very origin as unique creatures on earth, we humans have been defined by heterosexual monogamy involving long-term pair bonding (that is, marriage in a mother-father-child household) and the special linkage of the reproductive and the economic, a linkage in which two become one flesh. According to the scientists, the evolution of marriage occurred only once, at the beginning when "to be human" came to mean "to be marital." Other cultural variations surrounding marriage are simply details. Any "change" is the mark of cultural strengthening or weakening around a constant human model.

IMPRINTED ON OUR NATURES

While the main current of Western philosophy and social science rushed toward new forms of understanding and meaning in the late nineteenth and twentieth centuries, a dissenting school of sociology offered an alternative analysis. The first of these dissenters was the French academic, Frederic Le Play, active in the 1870s and 1880s.[8]

Le Play argued that human behavior did not follow the theoretical schemes of his liberal and socialist contempories. Rather, he identified and sought to explain the close relation between what he called *la famille soudre*—or the stem family—and historical examples of a stable, creative prosperity. This stem family, he insisted, was something more than the nuclear dyad of husband and wife, although this pair bond surely lay at its core. The stem family also embraced extended kin as meaningful, and often guiding, forces in human development. He argued that this family form "by a remarkable favor of Providence has within its very structure the beneficent qualities of the individual and those of association." It rested on ownership of the homestead and of the essential tools for economic life, solid habits of work, adherence to inherited mores, internal self-reliance in crisis, and fecundity through the welcoming of children.

Above all, Le Play insisted that the family naturally retained parental control over the basic education of children. In the stem family, children received their education at home. Even if sent to school, their most important training was moral, an education in character and judgment received by working side by side with parents. In Le Play's stem family system, father and mother also took the role of religious instructors. Properly presented, the religious principles and rules taught to children became habits, not easily broken or undermined by skepticism. Indeed, they acquired a quality of sacredness. Meanwhile, the individual would be absorbed within the family community and learn to rely, not only upon himself, but upon his family as well.

Rather than an historical curiosity, Le Play claimed to find the stem family recurring in all creative periods of human history. He found it among the Jews, the ancient Greeks, the pre-Imperial Romans, and—until recently—most of the European peoples. The stem family, he argued, combined a sense of community with opportunity for individual expression, thus avoiding the stifling oppression of the rigid patriarchal family *and* the egoistic atomism of the modern liberal system. The family is the true "cell of society" and the source of stability, progress, and authentic liberty.

Three twentieth century American sociologists based their efforts on the legacy of Le Play: Carle Zimmerman; Pitirim Sorokin; and Robert Nisbet.

Carle Zimmerman, professor of sociology at Harvard University and the founder of a distinctive American rural sociology, wrote *Family and Civilization*, which traced the course of family structures throughout the globe and across the millennia. In his classic text, *Principles of Rural-Urban Sociology*, Zimmerman followed the modern cultural crisis back to the decay of a vital rural society resting on the family.

In Zimmerman's view, the family farm—defined as "an organization of agriculture in which home, community, business, land and domestic family are institutionalized into a living unit which seeks to perpetuate itself over many generations"—constituted the critical source of social renewal, revitalizing cities that were incapable of self-renewal, either biologically or in virtue. As he put it, "these local family institutions feed the larger culture [with self-reliant and virtuous people] as the uplands feed the streams and the streams in turn the broader rivers of life."[9]

In describing the prospects for family reconstruction, Zimmerman also embraced Le Play's concept of the stem family, renaming it the domestic family. Zimmerman's other great book, *Family and Society*, analyzed in depth "a simple but relatively prosperous family" living in the American heartland. This family "has sufficient food, clothing, and shelter for all basic needs," although its members "have little money [as judged] from our commercial standards and purchase few goods." It is "strongly familistic," he continued, and "highly integrated." The family members "observe local customs rigidly. The home and the hearth are the center of their familistic enterprises." Powerful moral and religious codes govern this family form, reinforcing "regular habits of work," obedience to parents, and thrift. None of the family members are "a burden on the relief funds of the county, state, or federal agencies. On the contrary, the family stands ready to help its absent members." Above all, Zimmerman explains, the domestic-type family is an educational entity: "The family hearth is supplemented by the work of the school, so that the education of the child remains home-centered."

Zimmerman insisted that this domestic family model was not an expression of a dying or transitional past. Rather, the whole body of his work sought to show that it was a pattern of life recurring throughout time and across the globe. Indeed, he insisted that the domestic-type family was, in practice, a viable option for any age, since it provided a true harmony with the realities of human nature. A domestic-family system develops, Zimmerman said, "among all people who combine the benefits of agriculture, industry, and settled life with the commonsense idea of defending their private life from the domination of legislators, from the invasion of bureaucrats, and from the exaggerations of the manufacturing regime." Progress and harmony would only be won, he concluded, by recognizing and reinforcing the domestic-type family as the cell of society.[10]

Zimmerman's colleague in Harvard's sociology department during the 1930s and 1940s was Pitirim Sorokin, born and educated in Russia and expelled by the Bolsheviks in 1921. Like Zimmerman, Sorokin was not content with examining certain small facets of human social behavior. Rather, he sought to synthesize grand changes over time. He described the evolution of human civilizations from what he called "ideational," "idealistic," and "integral" forms to the "sensate" phase, each shift or "transmutation of values" accompanied by great and sometimes terrible crises.

Sorokin also shared with Zimmerman a debt to Frederic Le Play, accepting his concept of the stem family as the most stable, creative, and natural social form. In his best and most accessible book, *The Crisis of Our Age*, Sorokin emphasized the linkage of mounting social turmoil to the shrinkage of family size and the atrophy of family functions. Above all, he identified the family's surrender of the *educational* function as the sign of impending doom: "In the past the family was the foremost educational agency for the young. Some hundred years ago it was well-nigh the sole educator for a vast proportion of the younger generation. At the present time its educational functions have shrunk enormously . . . . In these respects the family has forfeited the greater part of its former prerogatives." To this list of abandoned functions, Sorokin added others:

> [The family] is less and less a *religious* agency, where . . . its place is taken either by nothing or by Sunday schools and similar institutions. Formerly the family supplied most of the *means of subsistence* for its members. At the present time this function, too, is enormously reduced: hundreds of other agencies, including the state and philanthropic institutions, perform it. Other *economic* functions of the family have likewise either dwindled or disappeared. . . . So it is also with *recreational* functions. Formerly the family circle took care of these. Now we go to the movies, theaters, night clubs, and the like, instead of "wasting our time at home." Formerly the family was the principal agency for mitigating one's psychosocial isolation and loneliness. Now families are small, and their members are soon scattered. . . .The result is that the family home turns into a mere 'overnight parking place.'

Sorokin was fully aware, though, that this structure could not stand. The family's loss of meaningful tasks—the move from a "domestic family" structure toward an atomized "sensate" structure—would result in social decay, mounting crime, declining fertility, ever poorer health, and mounting state coercion merely to hold the crumbling edifice together. He concluded in the early 1940s that the Western world had already entered an "extraordinary" crisis, as a corrupt late "sensate culture" gave way to disorder, immorality, and confusion. The only feasible course was to replace "the withered [and sterile] root of sensate culture" by a new cultural order. As he put it: "A transformation of the forms of social relationship, by replacing the present compulsory and contractual relationships with purer and more godly familistic relationships, is the order of the day. . . . Not only are they the noblest of all relationships, but under the circumstances there is no way out of the present triumph of barbarian force but through the realm of familistic relationships." The remedy would be difficult, he acknowledged, but it was the only hope for salvaging life from the darkness.[11]

The third great American sociologist in this tradition is Robert Nisbet, best known as the author of *The Quest for Community* and *The Twilight of Authority*.[12] In the latter volume, published in 1975, Nisbet affirms Le Play's emphasis on the strength of the kinship principle as the key determinant of "every great age, and every great people." "We can," Nisbet says, "use the family as an almost infallible touchstone of the material and cultural prosperity of a people. When it is strong, closely linked with private property, treated as the essential context of education in society, and its sanctity recognized by law and custom, the probability is extremely high that we shall find the rest of the social order characterized by that subtle but puissant fusion of stability and individual mobility which is the hallmark of great ages."[13]

According to Nisbet, the key qualities undergirding family authority have been duty, honor, obligation, mutual aid, and protection, not the "companionship" so emphasized by liberal modernists. Nisbet joins his predecessors in stressing the overriding importance of reintegrating education into a familial framework. He notes that great peoples, resting on strong families, have existed in the past in the total absence of institutions such as the Western world's state schools and colleges. On the other hand, he continues, "we have not yet seen a great people or a great age of history resting on the school or college to the exclusion of those ties and motivations which are inseparable from kinship."

Speaking for the whole intellectual tradition founded by Le Play, Nisbet concludes with a passage of profound importance for us today. "It should be obvious," he says, "that family, not the individual, is the real molecule of society, the key link of the social chain of being. It is inconceivable to me that either intellectual growth or social order or the roots of liberty can possibly be maintained among a people unless the kinship tie is strong and has both functional significance and symbolic authority."[14]

In this summation, Nisbet is altogether correct. The family, when functioning as the *cell of society*, delivers all that is good, precious, and necessary to life as human beings. Through the appropriately labeled "conjugal act," the family is the source of new biological life—children springing up within the matrix of responsible love and care as part of a kinship community and able to grow into stable and productive participants in community life.

So understood, the family also humanizes the incentives and pressures of the modern industrial economy. The family—we must understand—is the primal economic community, where exchanges properly occur on the basis of altruism, charity, and compassion, where the pure socialist vision—"from each according to his ability; to each according to his need"—actually works. At the same time, human beings do have an instinct to innovate and to trade, barter, and specialize in tasks, which serves as a vehicle for economic growth and the creation of wealth. The family, rightly conceived, exists as the critical and only successful boundary between these two economies. It defends the small altruistic economy of the household and kin group from the misapplication of competition and individualism to familial bonds. At the same time, it defends the "market economy" by resisting the misapplication of altruistic socialism on a scale where compassion cannot work because judgments of individual need and character cannot be made. The family, when properly constructed and protected, allows us to have both economic growth and social stability, both efficiency and charity, both competition and compassion, both wealth and altruism.

At the same time, the family is the foe of *all* ideologies, those "isms" or utopian visions at war with human nature: Rousseau's liberalism; Jacobin republicanism; Marxism; fascism; feminism; Nazism; and aggressive nationalism. Claiming, through the biological roots of the order of creation, a first loyalty from individuals, the family denies the claims of every "total" ideological system. This explains, in turn, the hostility these ideologies exhibit toward the family. This small unit is the principal foe of every ideologue, every fanatic out to construct and control "a new humanity." In every case, ambitious ideologues must first destroy family sentiment and family loyalties, inspiring the innumerable political assaults the family unit has experienced since the French Revolution unleashed these evils, fully armed, on human life.

THE SOURCE OF BOUNTIFUL JOY

The most remarkable, and perhaps the most desired, human emotion is joy. While *happiness* can in certain circumstances be something of a steady state and where *ecstasy* is the nearly painful passion of a moment, joy delivers an intense and exultant experience that can last for hours, or days, before it settles into an inner peace.

The English author C.S. Lewis offers deep insight into the nature of joy. In *The Screwtape Letters*, he provides a fictional set of missives from an experienced devil to his nephew, an apprentice tempter named Wormwood. In letter II, Screwtape divides the causes of human laughter into Joy, Fun, the Joke Proper, and Flippancy. "Fun," the senior devil notes, "is closely related to Joy—a sort of emotional froth arising from the play instinct." He acknowledges that Fun can sometimes be used to divert humans from certain tasks that "The Enemy" [God] would like them to perform. But in general, Screwtape laments, Fun is of "very little use to us. . . . in itself it has wholly undesirable tendencies; it promotes charity, courage, contentment, and many other evils."

Turning to Joy, Screwtape confesses that analysts in hell have not yet determined its nature or cause, and adds: "Something like [Joy] is expressed in much of that detestable art which the humans call Music, and something like it occurs in Heaven—a meaningless *acceleration in the rhythm of celestial experience*, quite opaque to us. Laughter of this kind does us no good and should always be discouraged. Besides, the phenomenon [of Joy] is of itself disgusting and a direct insult to the realism, dignity, and austerity of Hell."[15] Understood as an "acceleration in the rhythm of celestial experience,"Joy is indeed the way in which living humans can experience the feel, the taste, and the glow of heaven.

In this world, joy cannot be perpetual, but it is possible for joy to return, over and over again. An essential human project becomes the creation of customs and the preservation of social structures that encourage such bountiful renewal. Such customs and ways of living must give freely and generously. They must be plentiful and marked by abundance; they must be fruitful and multiply.

The natural family is the truest source of this bountiful joy, both in the marital attachment of woman and man and in the gift of marital fertility. The sixteenth century Christian reformer Martin Luther argued that procreation was the very essence of the human life in Eden before the Fall: "Truly in all nature there was no activity more excellent and more admirable than procreation. After the proclamation of the name of God it is the most important activity Adam and Eve in the state of innocence could carry on—as free from sin in doing this as they were in praising God."[16] In Luther's view, the fall of Adam and Eve into sin interrupted this potential, pure, and exuberant fertility. Even so, Luther praised each conception of a new child as an act of "wonderment . . . wholly beyond our understanding," a miracle bearing the "lovely music of nature," a faint reminder of life before the Fall: "This living together of husband and wife—that they occupy the same home, that they take care of the household, that together they produce and bring up children—is a kind of faint image and a remnant, as it were, of that blessed living together [in Eden]."[17]

While finding joy a difficult thing to quantify, social science has long affirmed that the bonds of family, the interconnectedness of marriage and children, serve as the surest predictors of life, health, and happiness. Perhaps this is the meaning of Tolstoy's famous phrase, "All happy families are like one another." In the classic 1897 study *Le Suicide*, sociologist Emile Durkheim tied the "social integration" promoted by marriage and the presence of children to low suicide rates.[18] The relationship remains strong to this day. Recent study of "the very happiest people" shows them to be "enmeshed" with others as members of strong social groups. Even among youth, "the very happy people spend the least time alone and the most time socializing." More notably, "marriage is robustly related to happiness,"[19] as is the presence of children.[20]

The possibility of happiness and joy rests, of course, within a larger matrix of sacrifices, sorrows, foregone opportunities, and trials that also mark family life. Living together in families requires that persons confront and overcome their own selfishness. All the same, it is only through this hard task that the possibility of joy opens on the far side.

THE FOUNTAIN OF NEW LIFE

Europe is dying. So are the once dynamic "Asian Tigers." America is not far behind.

In Germany and Italy, for example, more persons are buried each year than are born: populations are shrinking; and those left are—on average—getting older, much older. Even under fairly optimistic assumptions, Italy's population will fall from 57 million to 41 million by the year 2050. And most young Italians of the future will be children without brothers or sisters, aunts or uncles, or cousins: children, that is, without the bonds of kin that defined Italian social life not so long ago. Russia counts a net loss of 750,000 persons each year. By mid-century, Japan's population is expected to fall by a third.

Indeed, the United Nations itself—long a center of near-hysteria about *overpopulation*—issued a 2000 report entitled "Replacement Migration: Is It a Solution to Declining and Aging Populations?" The document warned that all of the European countries and Japan face "declining and aging populations" over the next fifty years.

Is the situation any different in the United States? Regarding overall numbers, the U.S. population continues to grow at the fairly solid rate of about one percent a year. Yet this growth occurs for two reasons: immigration remains at a high level in America,

with approximately 800,000 legal entrants a year (and a net gain
of another 300,000 illegals); and the out-of-wedlock birth rate has
soared since 1950, to one-third of the U.S. total. If we look strictly
to the marital fertility of U.S. residents, the birth rate has been
cut almost in half since 1960; and the number of births within
marriage has fallen by 35 percent. In short, without immigration
and extra-marital births as compensations, the U.S. would be close
to the same position as Europe's demographic basket cases of Italy,
Spain, Germany, Russia, and Denmark.

Indeed, in all parts of the world, human fertility is declining
sharply. Overall, human numbers continue to grow—the world
reached six billion in 1999—but not because of high birth rates.
Rather, growth comes because of better diets and longer life spans:
what demographer Nicholas Eberstadt calls a "health explosion."[21]
Counting our six billionth soul should have a time for celebrating a great human achievement, not for a new round of grim
journalistic sermons on the tragedy of overpopulation. But such
growth is a legacy from a more fertile past, and will not continue
much longer. The world's total population should start shrinking by
mid-century, with the Western nations far in the lead. As Phillip
Longman shows, even China and India face a fertility crisis. By
2050, "China could easily be losing 20-30 percent of its population
per generation. . . . Meanwhile, India's sudden drop in fertility
means that its population will be aging at three times the rate of
the U.S. population over the next half century."[22] Depopulation,
not a mythical overpopulation, is the problem that nations face in
the twenty-first century.

There appears to be six ways to understand this development.
The first way is as the result of a successful conspiracy. Donald
Critchlow's fine 1999 book *Intended Consequences* shows how "a
small group of men and women, numbering only a few hundred,"

caused a revolution in American policy toward fertility, with reper-
cussions around the globe. This group of wealthy Americans—with
names including Gamble, Pillsbury, Moore, and Rockefeller—believed that war and poverty were the result of unrestrained population growth. And they looked with horror on the "baby booms"
of the 1950s in the U.S., Australia, and parts of Europe, where
the new suburbs filled up with three- and four-child families.

Critchlow shows how the money and influence of this group
twisted popular views of population growth and large families
from being "blessings" into being "dangers." They funded the
research that developed the "birth control" pill. This wealthy cabal
turned U.S. foreign aid into a global population control project.
Their pressure and money spawned domestic U.S. birth control
programs, such as Title x, and the shift in public attitudes toward
abortion. Hugh Moore, Rockefeller, and Ford Foundation grants
also proved instrumental in launching the feminist movement in
the 1960s and the homosexual rights campaign of the 1970s; both
carried out in the name of reducing fertility.[23]

Second, the commercial introduction of the birth control pill
in 1965 and the legalization of abortion in most Western countries in the 1968 to 1980 period resulted in a sharp decline in the
percentage of unwanted births. Among married women in the
United States, the percentage of unwanted births (defined as "not
wanted by mother at conception or any future time") fell from 21
percent in 1965 to 7 percent in 1982. About 40 percent of the fall
in total U.S. fertility between 1963 and 1982 can be explained by
this decline in unwanted children.

A third way to understand modern fertility decline is as one
consequence of the ongoing retreat from marriage. Sweden and the
United States offer two examples of societies that are consciously
dismantling the normative institution of marriage. In the former,

marriage is rapidly disappearing as an institution. In 1966, Sweden counted 61,000 marriages; by 1972, the number had fallen to 38,000; and in the 1990s, to only 25,000 a year. Back in 1960, 44 percent of Swedish women aged twenty to twenty-four were married; by 1978, the number had fallen to 19 percent; today, it is under 10 percent. Taking the place of marriage is unmarried cohabitation. As late as 1960, only one percent of Sweden couples living together were unmarried. By 1970, the figure was 7 percent. Today, the figure is over 50 percent. Some cohabitating couples do continue to produce babies. Yet their completed fertility appears to be less than half of that found among married couples.

In the United States, it is true, wedlock remains popular by comparison. Nonetheless, this country has also witnessed a significant retreat from marriage. The marriage rate for one thousand unmarried women, ages fifteen to forty-four, declined from 148 in 1960 to seventy in 2003, a fall of over 50 percent. Viewed from the other side, the number of never-married young adults has climbed dramatically. Among women in their early twenties, for example, the never-married figure climbed from 28 percent in 1960 to 75 percent in 2003. Even the "remarriage rate" for women who were previously divorced or widowed has fallen off sharply since 1965. The number of reported cohabitating couples in the United States has climbed from 523,000 in 1970 to over 5 million in 2000, a tenfold increase. And American cohabitators are even less likely to have children than their Swedish counterparts.

Fourth, contemporary fertility decline is a consequence of a new set of anti-natalist economic incentives, inherent in the transition from a one-income to a two-income family norm. In "Will U.S. Fertility Decline Toward Zero?", sociologist Joan Huber answers yes: "The most probable long-run fertility trend is continued decline, not just to ZPG but toward zero." [24] Huber argues that it was, ironically, the new demand for female labor during the baby-booming 1950s that undermined prevailing cultural assumptions about a woman's responsibility to care for children at home. During that decade, the rapid expansion of government bureaucracies increased demand for clerical workers, traditionally a female job. Similarly, the baby boom itself ironically stimulated demand for teachers and nurses, also "female" tasks.

More broadly, the very construction of the welfare state rested primarily on hiring women to do tasks (such as child care and education) that had formally been done in the home. These changes coalesced into a kind of revolution, a curious form of feminist socialism: the shriveling of the private home and a massive expansion of the state sector.

Fully politicized, this revolution soon overturned the family-friendly structures found in the economy. Title VII of the Civil Rights Act of 1964, which banned discrimination in employment on the basis of sex, undermined the American "family wage" regime. The real wages of men declined. Housing prices rose as two career families began to outbid traditional families seeking homes. Indeed, feminist ideology in collision with the facts of biological replacement "made the U.S. profoundly anti-natalist."

Huber concludes that the primary long-term effect of women's rising employment has been "to increase the perception that parenting couples are disadvantaged in comparison to non-parenting ones." The "squabble" over jobs and income is not between men and women; rather it is a zero-sum contest between parents and non-parents. Barring dramatic changes, she says, American children will disappear.

The fifth way to view depopulation is through the value-revolution which swept the Western world after 1965, marked by a retreat from religious faith. As Belgian demographer Ron Lesthaghe has shown, recent negative changes in family formation and fertility reflect a "long-term shift in the Western ideational system" away from the values affirmed by Christian teaching (specifically "responsibility, sacrifice, altruism, and sanctity of long-term commitments") and toward a militant "secular individualism" focused on the desires of the self. Put another way, secularization emerges as a cause of contemporary fertility decline.[25]

The new "tolerance" of alternative lifestyles comes close to excluding parenthood even as an option. Dutch Demographer Kirk Van de Kaa notes the paradox that it was the arrival of "perfect" contraception—the birth control pill—in 1964 which, instead of bringing "wanted" children within marriage, produced couples who could live outside of marriage "without fear of unwanted pregnancy and forced marriage"[26] and perhaps subsequently make a "self-fulfilling choice" to bear only one child. The great French historian of childhood Philippe Aries describes "a new epoch, one in which the child occupies a smaller place, to say the least." Between 1450 and 1900, he writes, the Europeans had expanded the place of the child in their civilization. Levels of care improved noticeably, and the period of childhood became something precious. But at the twentieth century's end, Aries described the emergence of a civilization with almost universal pre-marital sex, ubiquitous contraception, legal abortion, and record-low fertility. Aries further concludes that the child's role is likewise "changing today, before our very eyes. It is diminishing."[27]

Finally, demographer John Caldwell emphasizes the role of mass state education in generating fertility decline. Based on research in Africa and Australia, he argues that state mandated schooling serves as the driving force behind the turn in preference from a large to a small family and the re-engineering of the family into an entity limited in its claims. Public authorities actively subvert parental rights and authority, substituting a state morality. Children learn that their futures lie with the modern State rather than the pre-modern family. As Caldwell summarizes, "it . . . has yet to be [shown] . . . that any society can sustain stable high fertility beyond two generations of mass [state] schooling."[28]

THE BULWARK OF LIBERTY

The terrible campaigns against marriage mounted by the Nazis and the Communists, just as the assaults on marriage launched by left liberals and socialists, reveal a common truth: the first targets of any oppressive, totalitarian regime are marriage and family. Why? G.K. Chesterton explains the reason in his powerful 1920 pamphlet *The Superstition of Divorce*: "The *ideal for which* [*marriage*] *stands in the state is liberty*. It stands for liberty for the very simple reason . . . [that] it is *the only . . . institution that is at once necessary and voluntary*. It is the only check on the state that is bound to renew itself as eternally as the state, and more naturally than the state. . . . This is the only way in which truth can ever find refuge from public persecution, and the good man survive the bad government."[29] Or, as he argued in *What's Wrong with the World*: "It may be said that this institution of the home is *the one anarchist institution*. That is to say, it is older than law, and stands outside the State. . . . The State has no tool delicate enough to deracinate the rooted habits and tangled affections of the family; the two sexes, whether happy or unhappy, are glued together too tightly for us to get the blade of a legal penknife in between them. The man and the woman are one flesh—yes, even when they are not one spirit. Man is a quadruped."[30]

Even in its most benign forms, the modern welfare state requires the full surrender of household liberty to the state. As scholars in both Sweden and America have documented, a "post-family" politics has achieved something "truly revolutionary": the near disappearance of private life and a massive expansion of the state sector. Indeed, in both Western Europe and America, the dramatic growth in female employment over the last four decades has been confined to only a few work categories: child care; health care; public education; welfare services; and other government employment. The result is that women as a group are now doing the same tasks as before, but working instead for the state rather than in their own homes. With a certain accuracy, some feminists have labelled this change as the triumph of "public patriarchy" over "private patriarchy." This new arrangement, based on massive state funding, has also allowed new household forms—which could never survive on their own—to thrive, notably the "sole-mother family" effectively married to the state.[31]

Even under the worst of governments, however, families have found ways to survive. During Nazi rule in Germany, for instance, the regime's propagandists made much of the fact that the nation's marriage rate was rising. In fact, there is good evidence suggesting that marriage had actually become an anti-Nazi act. As historian Claudia Koonz explains: "Germans who drove the marriage rates upward may well have sought an *escape* from participation in the Nazified public square."[32]

The Communist experience provides similar example. In a recent article on Uzbekistan during the period of Soviet Communist rule, the author writes: "Only traditional relationships enabled the people to survive the particularly difficult conditions which prevailed throughout the Soviet period. . . . While the sovietization of Central Asian society rocked the religious and cultural foundations of the family, its basic . . . features were preserved." The work of sheltering private society commonly fell to women. As the author notes: "I know of families where the father was a teacher of scientific atheism, while the wife said her prayers five times a day and observed 'ramadan,' so as to (as she put it) atone for her husband's sins." As the Communist regime fell and Uzbekistan regained its freedom, these traditions were still there, allowing husbands, wives, and their children to rebuild a nation.[33]

Another example of familial resistance to state coercion comes from the People's Republic of China. Compelled by Mao Tse Tung to live and work on collectivized industrial farms during the 1950s, the Chinese suffered terribly as the Communists worked to eliminate families as "fundamental habitation and production units." Thirty million died of famine between 1958 and 1961 alone. But Mao's death in 1976 brought policy changes, including introduction of the "family responsibility system." The state broke up collective farms, and families regained use of land according to their size. After meeting a quota, they could consume or sell the surplus farm produce. This system also allowed peasant families to engage in side occupations.

Results over the next fifteen years were spectacular. Farm output and rural family wealth and well-being all climbed sharply. Traditional marriage patterns reappeared after decades of suppression, as did a preference for having many children. In the more rural parts of China, three-quarters of women now wanted at least four children. Indeed, this "family responsibility system" meant rural subversion of the post-Mao leadership's other innovation: namely, the "one child per family" population policy.[34]

Moreover, Dutch scholars have documented that the imposition of Communism on Poland after 1945 did not weaken the family system there. Instead, the oppressive Communist system actually increased family solidarity: "We [found] that the importance of the family increased [under Communist rule], and that—as in

Hungary after World War II, . . . the family increased its role as the cornerstone of society. Political and social suppression can have unexpected positive effects, like the strengthening of the family."[35] As Chesterton predicted, the natural family—"the one anarchist institution"—survived, and even triumphed over totalitarian Communism, one of its great twentieth-century foes.

More broadly, persecution, disaster, even the fall of nations and civilizations cannot destroy the familial character of humankind. "In the break-up of the modern world," Chesterton observed, "the family will stand out stark and strong as it did before the beginning of history; the only thing that can really remain a loyalty, because it is also a liberty."[36]

OUR PRINCIPLES

From this perspective, we draw out principles in *The Manifesto* to serve as a guide to action. These statements also rest on other sources.

To begin with, we draw inspiration from the international movement broadly called Christian Democracy. Encouraged by writers such as Abraham Kuyper, Emmanuel Mounier, Etienne Gilson, and Etienne Borne, we focus on the concept of personalism. Each individual, this approach holds, is a unique, precious, and free moral agent. But the whole person only emerges through relationships with others, in social structures such as the family. As Gilson explained in his 1948 book *Notre Democratie*: "From his birth to his death, each man is involved in a multiplicity of *natural social structures* outside of which he could neither live nor achieve his full development. . . . Each of these groups possesses a specific organic unity; first of all, there is the family, the child's natural place of growth."[37] Such small communities are intrinsic or innate, and always reappear out of the very instincts or nature of man. They also pre-exist the state. The law does not create families; it "finds" them.

We also share this movement's understanding of the political task ahead. The great disorders of the last 150 years can be explained, in significant degree, as a consequence of the weakening of the family, as industrialism promoted by materialistic philosophers (both liberal and Marxist) has stripped away family function after family function. Policy and culture must now work to restore functions to families.[38]

In addition, we share with Christian Democracy an interest in human rights, properly understood. For example, women should enjoy basic civil legal, economic, and political rights, on par with men. Nevertheless, these rights need to be shaped around the natural differences in function that men and women exhibit in marriage and family. This can mean, for example, that motherhood should enjoy special protections and encouragements while fathers should receive a living family wage that enables mothers to remain home with their children.[39]

Finally, we share with Christian Democracy a desire for strong alliances with other faith traditions that also recognize and affirm the natural family. Following the Nazi darkness, the post World War II Christian Democratic movement worked to unite Catholic and Protestant believers and sympathetic others—including Jews and agnostics—in a defense of Christendom as a civilization with religiously infused values.[40] Without compromising our own beliefs, we too seek broad coalitions in communities, in nations, and globally, to defend and encourage the natural family.

Our principles also draw on the "family clauses" found in the Universal Declaration of Human Rights (UDHR). Most importantly, our key term, "natural family," derives from Article 16, paragraph

3, of the UDHR: "The family is the *natural* and fundamental group unit of society and is entitled to protection by society and the state." The origin of this sentence lies in the 1948 debates of the United Nations Commission on Human Rights. The arguments of the man who drafted this sentence, Charles Malik of Lebanon, are recorded in the minutes: "He [Malik] maintained that society was not composed of individuals, but of groups, of which the family was the first and most important unit; in the family circle the fundamental human freedoms and rights were originally nurtured."[41] Or as another advocate, Rene Cassin of France, argued, he "did not think it was possible to disregard human groups and to consider each person only as an individual."[42]

Alongside Article 16, paragraph 3, other clauses of the UDHR merit our support:

Regarding family autonomy, Article 12: "No one shall be subjected to arbitrary interference with his privacy, family, home or correspondence."

Regarding the right to marry, Article 16 (1): "Men and women of full age, without any limitation due to race, nationality or religion, have the right to marry and found a family. They are entitled to equal rights as to marriage, during marriage and after its dissolution." and (2): "Marriage shall be entered into only with the free and full consent of the intending spouses."

Regarding a father's right to a family wage, Article 23: "Everyone who works has the right to just and favorable remuneration ensuring for *himself* and *his* family an existence worthy of human dignity, and supplemented, if necessary, by other means of social protection."

Regarding the protection of motherhood and childhood, Article 25 (2): "Motherhood and childhood are entitled to special care and assistance."

And regarding parental rights, Article 26 (3): "Parents have a prior right to choose the kind of education that shall be given to their children."

We also draw inspiration from the documents crafted by The World Congress of Families (WCF), sponsor of fifteen regional sessions and of global assemblies in Prague (1997), Geneva (1999), and Mexico City (2004). Notably, we embrace the definition of the natural family created in May, 1998 by a WCF Working Group. Meeting in a room dating from the Second Century BC in the eternal city of Rome, the group concluded that

> the natural family is the fundamental social unit, inscribed in human nature, and centered around the voluntary union of a man and a woman in a lifelong covenant of marriage for the purposes of satisfying the longings of the human heart to give and receive love, welcoming and ensuring the full physical and emotional development of children, sharing a home that serves as the center for social, educational, economic, and spiritual life, building strong bonds among the generations to pass on a way of life that has transcendent meaning, and extending a hand of compassion to individuals and households whose circumstances fall short of these ideals.

We also have been inspired by the Declarations of the three World Congresses held to date. Representative of these Declarations, the following key statements from the Geneva Declaration (approved November 17, 1999) strongly affirm the abiding importance of the natural family:

> We assemble in this World Congress, from many national, ethnic, cultural, social and religious communities, to affirm that the natural human family is established by the Creator and essential to good society.

The natural family is the fundamental social unit, inscribed in human nature, and centered on the voluntary union of a man and a woman in the lifelong covenant of marriage.

The cornerstone of healthy family life, marriage, brings security, contentment, meaning, joy and spiritual maturity to the man and woman who enter this lifelong covenant with unselfish commitment.

The natural family provides the optimal environment for the healthy development of children.

The complementary natures of men and women are physically and psychologically self-evident.

The intrinsic worth, right to life and sanctity of life of every human person exists throughout the continuum of life, from fertilization until natural death.

Human society depends on the renewal of the human population; the true population problem is depopulation, not overpopulation.

Parents uniquely possess the authority and responsibility to direct the upbringing and education of their children.

Economic policy, both corporate and governmental, should be crafted to allow the family economy to flourish; what is good for families is good for the economy.

Government should protect and support the family, and not usurp the vital roles it plays in society.

Parents have the right to teach their religious and moral beliefs to their children and to raise them according to their religious precepts.

We include the full texts of the Geneva and Mexico City Declarations as appendices.

— 3 —

The Fundamental Unit of Society

I F YOU COULD CREATE SOCIETY the way you think it should be, what would that society be centered around? The individual? The church? The corporation? The state? Or the family?

Prior to the World Congress of Families II held in Geneva, Switzerland, November 1999, the Wirthlin Worldwide research firm surveyed people on five continents. Those in Europe, Asia, Latin America, the Middle East and Africa, and the United States, representing nineteen countries and varied cultures, religions, and socio-economic backgrounds, formed the survey group. The results cut across these cultural divisions. The Wirthlin team reported widespread support for marriage and family:

> Nearly eight in ten respondents (78%) worldwide agreed that "A family created through lawful marriage is the fundamental unit of society." Almost six in ten (57%) strongly agree with this statement. Only 15% disagree, while 7% are neutral or don't know.

Opinion regarding this statement is so universal that majorities in every region of the world agree. The only region where support is not over 70% is in Europe, where 54% agree and 30% disagree.

Not only do most people acknowledge that the family is central to civilization, they prefer it that way. When presented with the hypothetical possibility of creating their own society and asked to identify which institution would be central components of that society, 64% — including a majority from each region—say they would center their society around the family. Others would center their society around government (17%), the individual (17%), the church (12%), or the business community (10%).[1]

In short, the global consensus is that the natural family is the fundamental unit of society.

Of course, these alternative possibilities exist, each with its own story and claims. Appendix 1 offers an overview of their respective qualities. We consider them here as ideal types.

THE STORY OF THE INDIVIDUAL

A lone man in his own wilderness. He wakes to a morning of his own making. He surveys his environment and sees only possibilities, an extension of dreams from his sleep. The only other person in view is the man in the mirror. The day is his to capture and conquer. There is no one to get in his way. No one to interfere. No one to cast judgment, to impose a threat, to make afraid. Just a lone man with limitless imagination to claim the day.

He will ponder in the still of the morning, "Should I go fishing? Should I build a house? Should I comb my hair? Should I invent a cure for cancer?" The mattress upon which he still sits feels very comfortable. He could just lay the day away. There is no pressure to do anything. He might be tempted to act basely. There is certainly no other person for whom to do anything. There will be no one calling him, no one knocking on the door, no mail to open, no one to impress.

The world he meets he faces alone. He will cry alone and face sickness alone. Life has very little meaning because, for him, life has very little contrast. While he might smile, he will not feel joy. While he might weep, he will not feel sadness. The lone man cannot provide meaning, context, or definition to his life. His perspective is one-dimensional. His ideals, if any, are dull. The lone man might do anything, but he will rarely recognize what he has done.

But even a lone man must survive—his one true purpose in life. He must be fed. He must be sheltered. He must be safe. Furthermore, he might choose to be comfortable, as he has been in the bed of his own making. He begins the day with "must" and then moves on to "might."

Happiness? A full belly. Progress? The sure prospect of a full belly. Safety? Protection from the elements. Comfort? Protection from the elements by degree. And so he ventures out of bed. His quest is simple—what will it take to stay alive today? On a good day, if he is motivated, his quest might include a larger thought— what will it take to stay alive this week? Or, on achieving a degree of comfort, how can that level be maintained?

In an isolated world, our lone man is truly on his own. As if booted singly from a terrestrial Garden of Eden, he looks warily at the trials of a unknown world facing him and sees only a vast nothingness. Or, undaunted, he might instead see unlimited resources and no one preventing him from consuming them. Either way, he is both captain and king of his destiny, not to mention both slave and laborer.

There is a little of the lone man in all of us. It is what makes us selfish, narrow-minded, impatient, prideful, carnal, and otherwise self-absorbed. It also can drive us habitually to get what we need and want out of life. In consequence, any society focused chiefly upon the individual will soon confront a unique set of problems and promises.

While few people actually live isolated from other human beings, the ideology and psychology of atomistic individualism creates social frameworks of isolation. That is, amidst the masses, the atomistic individual is hard pressed to cope effectively day in and day out because at every turn his internal wiring runs contrary to social conformity and function. And even when conformity is in his best interests, he fails to recognize that beyond mere conformity lies cooperation; self-interest simply offers no perspective on such cooperation, let alone the productive values of a working community. Again, he is left to operate within a social framework without understanding its meaning, context, and definition.

Not conforming to the natural order around him nags his individualist psyche. "Why is my approach wrong? Why must I conform? Surely I am not isolated. I have friends and associates—those other individuals who help me get what I need and want out of life. Besides, I am free and they are free and together we are a free people. In fact, our society is both free and prosperous because it is interdependent, requiring all individuals to work toward their own best interests, and cooperative, for without each other we would truly be left a lone man in our own wilderness."

Within this psychological framework he is economic man, if he is anything. This is his obvious strength to a society based on the individual. His survival instinct drives him to care for himself. As an economic creature, he says that when everyone is looking out for his or her own self-interest, such selfish behavior will also serve the interests of others. A man who knows how to build homes needs to eat while another man has food but no home. Their respective self-interests allow them to trade a skill for a commodity and satisfy both needs. This "community of self-interest" seems to have all the answers. It seems to explain all sorts of behavior, social as well as economic. Individuals marry out of self-interest; they commune spiritually out of self-interest; they organize politically out of self-interest; they build societies out of self-interest. The "invisible hand" really seems to work!

So we ask, if everyone is getting what they desire out of self-interest, then why not build a society on the fundamental unit of the atomistic individual? The answer to this question might be surprising to some people; no doubt it will sound as simplistic as its counter-claim. The answer is that such a community of self-interest cannot preserve its freedom, over the long haul.

The individual is incomplete. And a society of individuals is just as incomplete. Contrary to its proponents' claims, a society based upon the individual is not like a puzzle in which all of the pieces come together neatly to complete a picture. When everyone has a different vision, there is no vision. Rather, the picture it creates is vague and chaotic. While this situation offers incentives for every person to work out the possibilities in each new reality, it fails to offer peace, stability, order, and function. It offers its participants a very fragile house of cards built to collapse in the end. All persons become laws unto themselves, self-justified, because every vision has some merit.

The key to understanding individualism's innate weakness is to grasp its innate strength: such individualism is simply a choice, as to how each of us will live in an existence that transcends our individual life. It is a choice of how to be purposeful and how to belong. And this is why we value our individualism so highly—it is the pathway to other possible lives. We value our ability to choose, but to choose something more than the self, not something less. This is especially so as we contemplate building a society.

In a world where the individual is the fundamental unit, people are socially isolated. Culturally, they are narcissistic. Their art and literature reflect their self-absorption—a world of autobiographies and self-portraits—literally reflective but not genuine. Politically, they are very utilitarian or, we might say today, libertarian. As the conservative scholar Russell Kirk once observed, "We flawed human creatures are sufficiently selfish already, without being exhorted to pursue selfishness on principle."

To conclude this brief analysis of how the story of the individual contrasts with the story of the family, let us turn to a geological metaphor. Sand is nothing more than atomized stone. Though substantial in the aggregate, it is no more than the accidental product of stones and shells as they slowly disintegrate.

Individualism as a force is no more than the atomization of the family unit. Individualism is the sand; family is the stone. A society built upon the foundation of atomized individualism will never be able to sustain the weight of human experience. Family is the fundamental unit of society for good reason; it is the stone upon which humans can rely even as waves break upon it. We might think we can build our human institutions from the sand of individualism. But no matter how high we build our sand castles, they dissolve in the first real storm.

THE STORY OF THE CHURCH

The church, meaning here an organized structure focused on the worship of God and the promotion of the faith, is another potential center for social organization. As a reflection or, perhaps, a conduit for the divine, the church can claim special authority. This might even include privileged communication with the Creator.

Relative to individuals, the church can motivate persons toward sacrifice, through the subordination of selfish interests to a common creed. With an ultimate grounding in faith rather than in reason, the church can show a special authority and mobilize its followers toward effective action.

Concerning morality, the church is ideally suited to bring out the good (or at least the better) in all people. It inspires and channels charity and good works, alleviating the needs of the poor, the sick, and the suffering. It creates educational structures that rest on solid virtues and teach wisdom and heritage. By insisting on self-discipline, the church motivates its followers to good health and social stability. As a community of saints, it inspires happiness.

Relative to the economy, the church transcends the narrow views and selfish demeanor of *homo economicus*. The divine economy has a different purpose and structure in which the marketplace is irrelevant and money holds no value. Instead, the church relies on altruism, or selfless giving based on love and duty. Rejecting raw materialism, the church focuses instead on matters of the spirit. In place of money, the church delivers compassion, charity, and personal care.

Regarding order, the church holds to an orthodoxy that changes only slowly, if at all. Adherence to core doctrines alleviates uncertainties, doubts, unhappiness. Rejecting rival truth claims actually frees individuals to live in *their* version of truth, with a certitude that brings inner peace.

All of these qualities reinforce the potential role of the church as the fundamental unit of society. On further examination, though, such a claim falters before the lessons of history, and of scripture itself.

Regarding the latter, the Book of Genesis—sacred to Jews, Christians, and Muslims alike—clearly shows the *family* as pre-existing the church. The creation of humankind in the image of God, "male and female created he them" (Genesis 1:27), the admonition that they "be fruitful, and multiply, and replenish the earth (1:28)," the charge that a man "shall leave his father and his mother and shall cleave unto his wife: and they shall be one flesh" (2:24), and the conception and bearing of children (4:1-2) all occurred well before men "began . . . to call upon the name of the Lord" (4:26).

We also have an historical record of attempts to build a City of God on earth. Many of those that worked for a time were marked by a modest size and geographic isolation: the Massachusetts Bay Colony of the early seventeenth century, and the Amana Colonies of Iowa and the United Order of the Mormons, both founded in the nineteenth century. Such experiments worked, and even thrived, for several generations. Eventually, though, they integrated back into a larger and more complicated social order. In addition, some small experiments in building a City of God ended in apparent exploitation and violence: remember Jonestown in Guyana and the Branch Davidians in Texas.

More important have been efforts to build national or imperial projects premised on a practical union between state and church. The Holy Roman Empire of Charlemagne, the Hapsburg Empire of Charles v, the Ottoman Empire of the Caliphs, and the contemporary Kingdom of Saudi Arabia—all can claim impressive achievements and world-historic influence. And yet, all have proven vulnerable to another force: dissent. The close union of church and state mandates the steady suppression of heresy. In Medieval Europe, violent campaigns targetted the Albigensians, the Hussites, and others. The Ottomans allowed Jews and Christians to exist as tribute-paying communities, stripped of political influence and unable to proselytize. The Saudis prohibit any non-Islamic activity on their soil.

Such structures cannot survive in the modern world. They are incapable of accommodating free thought, innovation, diversity, or real democracy. The Holy Roman, Hapsburg, and Ottoman Empires are gone; the Kingdom of Saudi Arabia now falls victim to its internal contradictions. Indeed, the pervasiveness of organized religion in this world actually proves the unlikelihood of a city of God—too many gods, too many prophets, too many doctrines, and too few like-minded adherents.

All the same, a city of God can and does exist in the family. The family is a perfect home for God. Organized religion then becomes a true complement to society and an effective facilitator of religious expression. Religious expression has no limits, and differences in the ways families express their religious beliefs become strengths for the community. The family provides the best opportunity for religion to flourish—it allows for diversity of belief and encourages communities of belief. It provides a proving ground of faith for children to test religious values and ideals safely.

It is true that religious expression in some families is a hard and austere experience for children. However, the alternative—the lack of any religious experience—usually sends children into an emotional and social tailspin.

The power of religious faith centered in the family comes as no surprise. The family is prior to organized religion. The latter was created, in part, to serve the former. The story of the church recognizes an ordered universe. The family is at the center of that universe. It is the nearest point to heaven in our fallen world.

THE STORY OF THE CORPORATION

Unlike other possible organizing units of society, the story of the corporation is direct, and it comes in two parts: the transaction and the money. To establish the corporation as the fundamental unit of society is to base society's entire existence on the free exchange of goods and services and the quest for wealth. We might be tempted to say at this point that neither purpose is bad in itself, but we should reserve judgment on this point because it will become crucial in discerning exactly why the corporation fails as a fundamental unit.

Like the story of the church, the story of the corporation can be framed by the walls it occupies. It too has its cathedrals and towers, its prophets and seers, its organization and policies. Even so, uniquely different within this particular story is the identity of those it serves. Almost uniformly throughout the world, the corporation is established with a governing board of directors whose sole purpose is to serve its shareholders, and to do so in only one way: to make them money.[2]

It is rather an ingenuous model. Shareholders, the investors and owners, willingly part with their capital and place it in the hands of the board of directors. They do so with confidence because the directors are capable men and women who will care for the operation and maintenance of the business. The shareholders (again, the owners of the business) are not burdened with the day to day management of their investment. They simply turn their money over to the corporation and it serves them. Moreover, the shareholders typically are not liable for anything that goes awry. They risk one thing and one thing only—their money.

But the ingenuity of the model does not stop there. The corporation is a legal person, in some respects independent of its owners. In fact, its owners, even the most important among them, will come and go, die even, and the corporation is structured to outlive them all. A corporation is an artificial person and, in the United States as in most of the Western world, it is protected by due process and equal protection. It has rights.

Its story can be summed up neatly by United States Supreme Court Chief Justice John Marshall:

> A corporation is an artificial being, invisible, and existing only in contemplation of law. Being the mere creation of law, it possesses only those properties which the charter of its creation confers upon it . . . These are such as are supposed best calculated to effect the object for which it was created. Among the most important are immortality and if the expression may be allowed, individuality; properties by which a perpetual succession of many persons are considered as the same, so that they may act as a single individual. A corporation manages its own affairs, and holds property without the hazardous and endless necessity of perpetual conveyance for the purpose of transmitting it from hand to hand. It is chiefly for the purpose of clothing bodies of men, in succession, with these qualities and capacities, that corporations were invented, and are in use. By these means, a perpetual succession of individuals are capable of acting for the promotion of the particular object, like one immortal being.[3]

Immortality: a remarkably solid basis for the future. The corporation has a charter, a purpose, and functions for its associates to fulfill; it is organized and governed strictly through its by-laws. Better yet, it is uncomplicated. All those involved know their roles, for despite a necessary division of labor within the corporation, their varied tasks collectively become one: to make money.

But there is something more to the story of the corporation than just money. This story is incomplete without an understanding of its remarkable allegiance to transactions. Advocates of the corporation often defend this allegiance as essential to the integrity of the free flow of goods and services. Even in competition among its own kind, corporations will stand unified in defense of this free flow. The freedom to transact should not be encumbered. If making money is its primary object, then the ability to transact must be held inviolate. In many respects the corporation represents liberty—the power to transact freely, to work, to make money, and to prosper. Add to this liberty its organizational prowess and a keen argument could be made that the corporation is an ideal basis for an aspiring society.

While the corporation has blessed the economies of men, it would be extremely short-sighted to assume that it has the where-withal to carry the weight of being the fundamental social unit. Indeed, its problems here are many-fold, not the least of which is the counter-social behavior for which it creates incentives.

Withhold judgment for the time about the innate goodness of the corporation's two purposes, maintaining complete freedom of transaction and making money. After all, making money through honest work or trade is a good thing and transactions facilitate it. But the innate goodness of this two-fold purpose does not exist in a vacuum. It must compete with other reasonable purposes. When Milton Friedman said "the business of business is business," he authoritatively sided with the two-fold purpose to the exclusion of others. For instance, the business of business is not promoting social welfare. The business of business is not maintaining a family. The business of business is not even primarily advancing the well-being of its employees and administrators. What the esteemed economist was saying is that the business of business is to make money for the shareholders. In a society so organized, the work of care is done by those who do it for money. Those without money receive no care.

The other half of this dual purpose appears in a similar context. The transaction facilitates the making of money and the freer our transactions, the more money that can be made. It is important to note that for the transaction to maximize its value, it must be completely unrestrained. This is important, for it reveals that the transaction alone is the value, not what is being bought and sold. It recognizes no distinction between oranges and guns, no distinctions between human flesh and poultry. The price of a good or service is a function of a corporate "bottom line," but the real value of anything is whether or not it can be part of a transaction. If distinctions are drawn between commodities, it is not the result of some kind of corporate discernment, only some external proscription. There is no incentive for a corporation to proscribe, for instance, the sale of pornography. It is a commodity like any other to be bought and sold. Such a prohibition must be handed down from elsewhere in society.

Initially we held to the proposition that to establish the corporation as the fundamental unit of society would be to base society's entire existence on the free exchange of goods and services and the quest for money. And then we were tempted to say that neither purpose was bad in and of itself, but that we should reserve judgment. This is why. Like the goodness of the individual, the goodness of the corporation depends ultimately on choice—a choice as to how we will lead and conduct our lives according to purposes much greater than simply making money and trading. However, life itself is about more than making money. Any healthy society will reflect this broader definition of life. As such, the corporation is only a part of this broader life, and certainly not its center.

Were we to place the corporation at the center of our society, we would find ourselves in a world lacking in order, beauty, and grace. We would find ourselves competing with other family members and neighbors in a setting of social Darwinism that would divide rather than unify. Our culture, too, would be fiercely competitive—creating a Marxist portrait of haves and have-nots painted not only on an economic canvas but everywhere—an environment in which money alone made something right, or its lack made something wrong. Politically, we would function in a perverse meritocracy, claiming to reward meritorious achievement but, as in *The Richest Man in Babylon*, only finding a standard in our ability to make and handle money. And imagine our spiritual lives—the profit motive as religious doctrine?

We see the great value of the corporation. It creates jobs, wealth, and many other benefits. We recognize that money is required in this life and that we must have sufficient sums for our needs. We appreciate the liberty afforded transactions within the story of the corporation. We see the value in creating incentives for industry and competition. What we do not see is why these qualities should be the center of our lives and the foundation upon which we build everything else.

The story of the corporation is much too narrow to drive a healthy society. Only the natural family can do that. As much as families can benefit from the wealth generated by corporations, the value of such surplus does not come close to the bounty required for lasting peace and happiness in a context of ordered liberty.

THE STORY OF THE STATE

Try to paint a picture of the state as the fundamental unit of society. Would it look like the *Republic*? *Leviathan*? *Animal Farm*? *1984*?

The Communist Manifesto? Mein Kampf? A Brave New World? Or would its shades and hues be more subtle? Like perfectly planned communities? Government schools? A social welfare program? Public mass transit? The New Deal? The Fair Deal? The Great Society? Or would such a portrait be a series of revolutionary representations? The French Revolution? The Russian Revolution? The Asian genocides from Mao to Pol Pot? Mass starvations in Eastern Europe? The gas and torture chambers in Nazi concentration camps?

Of course, these portraits beg a very important question. Is there one among them, or any other we can recall, that depicts a productive, healthy, peaceful, and joyous picture of community life and personal freedom? And if not, why?

The story of the state should not be confused with the need for government. Purposeful lives require governing, and when formalized, we call such a task government. There is self-government, family government, contractual government, local or neighborhood government, state or provincial government, federal or national government, and even international government. The story of the state actually separates the spiritual from the physical, essence from matter. This story is the tale of a harsh reality—unforgiving, uniform, relentless, given to extremes, and as intrusive as a small piece of stone in our shoe.

This story is not a pretty one, no matter how it is told. But it always begins in the same place—the quest for perfection. And it always ends the same way—in failure. The narrative in between goes something like this.

This abstract state lies in waiting, the would-be servant of the people. It will do no more or no less than what is requested of it. Of course, it is eager to help; it is just waiting to be asked. Not impatiently, mind you. It understands its place, role, and functions perfectly. It would never pretend to assume a responsibility not delegated to it by the people.

However, it does observe the world around it. It sees disorder and chaos. It sees need and want. It sees unhappiness and disease. It sees starvation and poverty, classes and conscience, waste and destruction, greed and envy. It sees the crushing burden of tradition. And it asks why such things must exist? Surely it could be called upon to intercede, to fix what is broken. After all, it has the power to fix anything. So there it sits perplexed, but patient—why are the people not calling on it to help?

It sees that there is and always has been a sinister force behind nearly every social problem. This conspirator against perfectibility goes by many names—agency, free will, liberty—but the state knows it by its most pejorative expression: the freedom to choose, or, simply, choice. It wonders why the people cannot see this self-evident problem. To be able to do what you want to do is to possess exactly the kind of power needed to correct so many problems. Yet, to see that power reduced to the individual whims of the people is inefficient. People could be so much better served by letting the state exercise that power by dictating all decisions. In fact, allowing this control only makes sense; it is efficient.

Alas, the state's patience pays off. Finally, a few people emerge who see the world the way it does. Better yet, they see the value of the state in finding solutions to their various problems. Slowly but steadily come the flow of requests for assistance: "People are much too different. What can the state do to help correct this inconsistency? People are not diverse enough. How can the state encourage multiculturalism? Some people have too much money while others go without the basics of life. What can the state do to correct this inequality? Surely some people are brighter and more intelligent than others. How can the state help the others understand what is good for them? Religiously-based morality is too exclusionary. How can the state rid itself of any such influences? People are not morally sensitive to the circumstances of others. How can the state shape an acceptable public morality?"

The state feels liberated to do what it was created to do. It can help. Very soon, things appear to get done. The problems seem like they are being addressed. The trains run on time. The people are grateful for answers to their problems, especially their money problems. The state is more than happy to step in to fill the inadequacies of the people.

Sooner rather than later, however, the apparent answers begin to fall short. The state struggles with more solutions. Perhaps not enough resources have been allocated to address the problem properly? Perhaps the right operatives were not in place to execute the "recovery plan"? Perhaps the people have not transferred enough authority to government?

Then the real answer emerges. People are the problem. Of course! Perfectibility is not possible so long as people are allowed to choose activities and behaviors that run counter to the quest for efficiency. The state ponders the matter. It faces the ultimate dilemma—how does it effectively deliver to the people complete safety and optimal welfare without the ability to control their lives and decisions?

It is at this point that the story of the state turns ugly. This is the point of the final option—it must save the people from themselves and it must do so with rapidity and force. A helping hand becomes a back hand. The servant becomes the master. The state becomes the fundamental unit of society. The people are now the problem; all will suffer; some must die.

Choosing this path is deceptively easy. After all, the state is only trying to help. And, by the way, the people asked for the help.

The state is only doing what the people asked it to do. The requests were reasonable enough—work for the common good, for decency, for the common man, for the provision of order, and for the unity of the people. We must all live together in peace. This can only be accomplished if the state is allowed to fulfill its purpose, and if people are not allowed to choose their own existence.

This story of the state has been lived and relived, tried over and again with the result always being failure. To place the state as the fundamental unit of society is to dehumanize people. No longer are people the reason for, or the purpose of, life. Perfection becomes the end game—a game lost even before it is played.

THE MIXED UNIT

In answering our initial question—"If you could create society the way you think it should be, what would that society be centered around?"—we might be forced to ask another obvious one. Must we choose just one axis? This is a very reasonable question, reflecting an obvious sentiment. Perhaps there is a more eclectic, menu-driven way of settling upon what combination of center-points actually work best. Why must we be forced to choose one over another? After all, we need each of these organizing principles in our lives. So, if we need the strengths of each, why not craft a blended center-point taking the best from each? What is the result?

Let us define a center-point utilizing the primary strength of each (you can craft a mixed unit however you like using the matrix in Appendix 1): the economic power of the individual (the "invisible hand"), the cultural power of the family (traditional and generational), the social power of the church (communal), the spiritual power of the corporation (yes, spiritual power—the "profit motive"), and the political power of the state (its coercive power).

Immediately, we run into a dilemma. The invisible hand runs head long into the coercive power of the state. And then the communal, or cooperative, sociality of religion, which asks people to care for others altruistically, runs up against the profit motive impelling people to act selfishly. Cut and paste, pick and choose as we might, we consistently face dilemma after dilemma. We discover a world of never-ending and frustrating conflict.

Perhaps this is the way the world is supposed to be, especially within democratic government. The give and take. The checks and balances. The selfishness of the individual held in check by the higher expectations of the Church and the altruism required of family life. The obsessive-compulsive priority of making money through the corporation balanced against the broader priorities of the state. Perhaps it all works out in the end. Perhaps asking for just one center-point is not only unrealistic but unfair.

THE FAMILY UNIT

Actually, it is neither unrealistic nor unfair to demand that we settle on one fundamental unit of society. We are not asking that one path be chosen to the exclusion of all others. The reason that each organizing principle is a viable option is that each is so fully integrated into our lives. We are individuals. We do express religious faith in meaningful ways. We do enjoy work and making money. And we recognize that a modicum of order and submission is required to live safely and peaceably in community.

However, here is our claim.

Every strength of each potential organizing center is maximized through the filter of the natural family as the fundamental unit of society. The unique strengths of the individual are magnified within the context of the natural family. Religious life has greater meaning in this context. Work and earning money are given full purpose. And the state is more effective in its role when families are strong and autonomous. All of the other organizing principles become stronger when we base society on the natural family. The same cannot be said of any of the others.

All facets of life are enriched when we choose the natural family as the fundamental unit of society. Our social life is richer—we experience broad diversity within a context of stable familiarity. Our cultural life is richer—we are better able to take advantage of generational experience and the lessons of tradition. Our political life is richer—strong, autonomous families maximize the best functions of democracy. Our economic life is richer—we work with lasting purpose, cooperatively and altruistically, for others and not just for ourselves. And our spiritual life is richer—we are motivated to become our better selves as we give birth and nurturing to the rising generations.

The natural family is the key to the fullness of life. It does what no other organizing principle can do—it makes everything around it better, it amplifies the best elements of all other institutions. It is the foundation of ordered liberty.

4

Eternal Truths and the Sciences

T HE HEART AND SOUL of *The Natural Family* are those sections telling "the story of the family" and offering "a vision" for our common future. The former looks to a new couple and narrates their life as an archetype. It follows them from the first signs of mutual attraction through marriage, homebuilding, childbirth, parenting, and the grandparent years, to their final rest. The latter section looks to culture and society, and points toward an abundant landscape of fruitful family homes, filled with productive activity and animated by the sounds of many children.

We readily admit that these portraits of the natural family appeal to ideals. They are intended to inspire, to motivate, and to encourage. We hope they fire others' imaginations, as they have fired our own. We especially hope they will turn the aspirations and the dreams of the young toward home- and family-building.

Still, we also ground this story and this vision in the natural world, where their truths are open to study and confirmation by the physical and social sciences. Being "natural" means that the family rests within the created order. It is open to honest investigation, to fair scrutiny. The natural family welcomes scientific inquiry, with the confidence of welcoming a friend.

It is true that during much of the twentieth century the opinion was widespread that social science was hostile to traditional family relations. As one analyst explained in 1917, "the new view is that the higher and more obligatory relation is to society rather than the family."[1] The Swedish economist Gunnar Myrdal also underscored the radical nature of the social sciences. There were, he insisted, no lasting economic or social laws, no "natural" institutions, for the whole of human institutional life was a variable. Moreover, Myrdal held that the scientific analysis of social problems pointed toward the use of *preventive* policies, in which the goal was to prevent social problems, not to cure them after they appeared. He said that such preventive social policy led to a "natural marriage" of the correct technical and the politically radical solution. Accordingly, Myrdal insisted that the social sciences were in fact subversive of the family and other traditional institutions.[2]

This close identification of sociology with radical politics during much of the twentieth century is based on error, on the subordination of true science to ideology. As Robert Nisbet's extraordinary work *The Sociological Imagination* reminds us, all of the great European founders of sociology were actually inspired by socially *conservative* impulses or questions. Auguste Comte, Alexis de Tocqueville, Ferdinand Tönnies, Frederic LePlay, Emile Durkheim, Max Weber, Georg Simmel, Herbert Spencer—all found inspiration, direct or indirect, from the anti-Enlightenment, so-called "reactionary" writers of nineteenth-century France, social critics such as Bonald, de Maistre, Chateaubriand. They were drawn to a new analysis of social order by the great disruptions of the industrial revolution, and by the excesses of individualism.

According to Nisbet, the very unit-ideas of sociology—analysis of family, community, tradition, authority, status, the sacred, alienation—all show "an unusually close relation" with "the principal tenets of philosophical conservatism." As Nisbet concludes, "the [creative] paradox of sociology . . . lies in the fact that although it falls, in its objectives and in the political and scientific values of its principal figures, in the mainstream of modernism, its essential concepts and its implicit perspectives place it much closer . . . to philosophical conservatism."[3]

Accordingly, we expect social science done well and true to reveal the necessary, irreplaceable position of the "natural family." And this is, we argue, the primary finding of the social sciences over the last twenty-five years. In terms of adult well-being, child well-being, and social well-being, the social sciences point to children living with their two natural, biological parents in a married couple home as the ideal setting for healthy, happy, and enriching human lives. *Any deviation* from this model—cohabitation, adoption, divorce, out-of-wedlock birth, remarriage, "same-sex marriage"—raises the probability of negative outcomes.

Let us be more specific, weaving together statements found in the manifesto with the results of scientific investigations.

> *The small home economy remains*
> *the vital center of daily existence.*

Although the relative size of the household sector of the American economy fell steadily from 1930 to 1985, household production in 1985 still accounted for goods and services valued at 28 percent of the value of all goods and services in the market sector of the economy. Indeed, economic analysis shows that the value of home production in 1973 exceeded 60 percent of the typical American family's money income before taxes and 70 percent of the typical American family's money income after taxes. The value of home production ran highest for families with young children. In these families, it was almost equal to the value of money income after taxes. The value of home production was affected only slightly by wives' employment. Analyses performed by economists from the University of Chicago and Stanford University reveal that "the average two-earner family requires about 30 percent more money income to achieve the same . . . standard of living as a one-earner family" because of higher expenditures for "non-durable goods and purchases of services" of the sort that the one-income family does not need because of the productivity of its own home economy. Looking at a similar nation, careful economic analysis reveals that the economic value of home production in Australia in the late twentieth century was approximately the same as that of the market production measured in the official Australian economy.[4]

Husband and wife learn that family and faith are, in fact, two sides of the same coin.

A nationwide Canadian study provides strong evidence that religious faith fosters enduring marriages. Among Canadian couples who attended church services at least weekly, less than one-fifth dissolved their marriages within twenty-five years, compared to almost half of couples who attended church services seldom or never. In fact, survey research indicates that religiosity serves as a better indicator of marital strength than does family development (e.g., number of children or duration of marital union) or socioeconomic position. The researchers view these findings as clear evidence that religion is "a source of strength and vitality for relationships." In another study, investigators trace a strong pattern linking elements of religiosity to positive marital adjustment. In particular, higher levels of "ritualistic involvement," of "religious experience," and of "conservative" religious belief predict higher levels of marital consensus, satisfaction, and cohesion.[5]

Survey data also show a consistent linkage between creedal assent and active church participation on the one hand and marital success on the other. The researchers see "belief, effort, and participation in religion" as a strong predictor of "better marital adjustment, happiness and satisfaction." Taking a broader look, the prominent bioethicist Leon Kass marvels at the mystery of sexual complementarity, a mystery so deep that it offers "an opening to the truly transcendent and eternal" and inspires "awe in the face of life and sex and love and other great powers not of our making," including "the creative powers exercisable through procreative handing down of our living humanity to the next generation." Thirteen leading social scientists identify "a religious or spiritual orientation" as a component of "strong families," a defining aspect emerging in study and after study.[6]

The truly rich family draws on the
strengths of three or more generations.

Grandparents matter. Two pediatricians credit grandparents with giving their grandchildren a "better overall view of human growth and development" than younger teachers could do. Psychiatric evidence also suggests that "the grandparent-grandchild bond is second only in emotional significance to the parent-child bond." Other social scientists have compiled the psychological and sociological research indicating that grandparents do much to give their grandchildren a sense of emotional security and cultural continuity. The researchers stress "the symbolic, indirect, and direct influences of grandparents" on their grandchildren.[7]

Family households, formerly function-rich
beehives of useful, productive work and
mutual support, tended to become merely
functionless, overnight places of rest
for persons whose active lives and
loyalties lay elsewhere.

Historical analysis exposes as a failure the attempt to renew family life by focusing solely on the companionate husband-wife union while allowing continued erosion of the productive home economy. Though cultural enthusiasm for the companionate marriage did foster short-term renewal in family life (from about 1945 to 1960), the lack of any enduring basis for household production within this type of marriage left it vulnerable, allowing the unraveling of marriage and home life between 1965 and 1980. Thus, a conception of the family rooted in shared consumption and emotional support "failed as a meaningful focus of American loyalty and as a bulwark against both the ambitions of the state and the atomizing incentives of the economy." Analysts attribute the decline in the relative size of the household sector of the economy to the movement of wives and mothers into paid employment. Because economists have typically ignored the household sector of the economy, the shift of production from the household to the market has exaggerated real economic growth in recent decades. Cultural and economic analysis also traces the "festering contradiction of modern womanhood" to the "displacement of crafts," which denied homemakers their traditional productive role by converting them into mere consumers. Intergenerational survey evidence further indicates that young Americans are increasingly shifting their loyalties away from the family and home, toward themselves and the state.[8]

Cultural and economic histories also show how Americans, increasingly entranced by science and efficiency, came to de-value the skills of the traditional homemaker. Because of this de-valuation, more and more women became dissatisfied with a home-based social role. Karl Polanyi's classic work of economic history shows how the rise of market capitalism displaced cottage- and village-based enterprises. The self-sufficient household that satisfied most of its needs through its own home-centered labor gave way to the consumer household dependent on cash income to satisfy its needs through money purchases in the marketplace. Pitirim Sorokin also shows that the loss of the home's productive functions—a loss reducing the home to "a mere incidental parking place"—is one of the twentieth-century's most damaging developments.[9]

We affirm that the natural family
is a fixed aspect of the created order,
one ingrained in human nature.

Humankind has been conjugal since its first appearance on earth. Evolutionary anthropologists identify "the two-parent family household" as a defining characteristic of the species. Tracing the course of human evolution, these scientists highlight the importance of the "sex-based division of labor" that established itself within the "productive pair bond," so creating a "dual economy specific to hominids." It was the remarkable success of this dual economy that made possible "a social revolution . . . from a more apelike to a more human way of life." From a different discipline, a mathematical-genetic model offers an evolutionary explanation for the emergence of monogamy. This model predicts that female mating will naturally tend toward a pattern in which each female has all of her offspring with a single mate.[10]

> We affirm that the natural family is
> the ideal, optimal, true family system.

This statement drives to the core of scientific inquiry. For instance, a task force appointed by the American Academy of Pediatrics (AAP) concludes that "unequivocally, children do best when they are living with [two] mutually committed and loving parents who respect and love one another." The AAP scholars stress that children do not enjoy the same advantages in a stepfamily or in a household headed by unmarried cohabiting parents. Scrutiny of data collected in 1999 from a nationally representative sample of nearly forty thousand children (ages six to eleven) and adolescents (ages twelve to seventeen) also reveals that "those living outside of two-biological-parent married families tend to report more behavioral and emotional problems and less school engagement" than do peers living in two-biological-parent married families. The data especially indicate adverse outcomes for children living in households headed by cohabiting couples. Though the distinctively high incidence of problems among young children (ages six to eleven) in homes headed by cohabiting parents can be statistically attributed to economic circumstances, economic variables do *not* account for the high incidence of problems among *adolescents* in households headed by cohabitors.[11]

Similarly, in psychological and academic data collected from 349 young adolescents, researchers find more support for a "family structure perspective" than for any competing theoretical perspective. "For the most part," the authors of the new study remark, "children who lived with their biological parents had fewer behavior problems and better general adjustment in school than children who lived with divorced parents or with mothers who had remarried." The evidence is overwhelming: "Family structure was associated with six of seven indicators of child's adjustment," with children in intact families achieving higher grades and engaging in fewer problem behaviors than peers in single-parent or step-families.[12]

Such results appear time and again. Data from a nationally representative sample of 850 households reveals "a consistent pattern," the intact family provides the best environment for fostering adolescent well-being: "Adolescents whose mothers and fathers are both in their first marriage have the fewest problems with socio-emotional adjustment, academic performance, and global well-being." In a study of delinquency based on a nationally representative sample of more than 20,000 adolescents in grades seven through twelve, researchers at the National Institute of Child Health and Human Development found not only that teen criminality runs lowest among teens from two-biological-married-parent families, but also that levels of parental involvement, supervision, monitoring, and closeness all average highest in these families.[13]

Other researchers assess adolescent well-being in four types of family structures: those headed by married biological parents; those headed by unmarried single mothers; those headed by a biological parent married to a step-parent; and those headed by a biological parent cohabiting with a partner. Not surprisingly, the researchers conclude that "adolescents living in married, two-biological-parent families generally fare better than teenagers living in any other family type." More specifically, adolescents in intact two-parent families are less likely than peers from other family types to be suspended or expelled from school, less likely to commit delinquent crimes, less likely to be reported for problem behaviors at school, less likely to receive low grades in two or more subjects, and more likely to score well on standard tests of cognitive development.[14]

In a similar study, comparative statistical analysis shows that the nuclear family is far more stable than five other household forms—single individual, couple (no children), single parent, other family types, and other non-family types. The researchers calculate that half of the spells that people spend in the nuclear family last for seven or more years. In contrast, other non-family households were "extremely transitory," with a median survival time of less than two years and with less than a tenth of spells in such households enduring more than five years. Median survival times for non-nuclear family types, including single-parent households, were only three to four years.[15]

Given the instability of these family types, it is hardly surprising that FBI and U.S. Census Bureau numbers show that among the nation's white majority, "diversification" in family forms significantly drives up the homicide rate. The researchers speculate that "as white families become increasingly diversified from traditional forms," they are losing their "means of coping" and the "informal social control [necessary] to impede violence."[16]

Similar results emerge around the globe. Comparative ethnography indicates that "virtually all marriage systems across the world reinforce a pair-bonding template." The reason that pair-bonding appears so universally important is that any "unraveling of the pair-bonding template is aligned with a number of serious society dysfunctions" that "place the commonweal at a disadvantage" in comparison with societies based upon marriage and pair-bonding. Using data on the rate of infection with sexually transmitted diseases (STDs) to create a proxy variable indicating the frequency with which men and women move outside traditional patterns of marriage and pair-bonding, researchers have established a strong correlation between STD rates on the one hand and infant mortality, violent crime, and depressed high-school graduation rates on the other. It would appear that "a jettisoning of pair-bonding/marriage . . . reverberates throughout the community in a myriad of negative or adverse consequences."[17]

*All other "family forms" are incomplete
or are fabrications of the state.*

The tension between the natural family and the state is considerable. Two sociologists conclude that government policy has made children an artificial economic asset in the "mother-state-child" family, a family form that multiplies because of state subsidies. A Scandinavian analyst identifies the rise of the welfare state as the development that ended women's dependence upon men in traditional family circumstances. It is the welfare state that mediates transfer payments from men to women outside of the family. And it is the welfare state that effects "a redistribution of jobs between the sexes" by creating a "decided female bias in the public sector."[18]

The effects of state intervention are also evident to the economist Jennifer Roback Morse, who dismisses "the single-parent family" as "the mother of all myths." Some third party, she argues, is always in the background: "The person who appears to be raising a child all by herself has substituted for the other parent some combination of market-provided child care, employment income, and government assistance." A Norwegian social scientist concludes that it was the passage of welfare state policies providing public support for unwed mothers and their children that made non-marital cohabitation—previously rare in Norway—a common household arrangement. "Cohabitation as a way of life and welfare state programs and policies accommodate . . . one another," she writes.[19]

The breakdown of the natural family, and moral and political failure, not "overpopulation," account for poverty, starvation, and environmental decay.

The work of Nobel laureate Amartya Sen provides a framework for showing how democratic governance serves as a protection against famine. Despite its huge population and its vulnerability to drought and food shortages, India has been able to avoid famine because of its political institutions. In contrast, China and Ethiopia suffered terrible famines not because of larger populations but because both countries were non-democratic. *Science* magazine identifies bad government policies—not nature or overpopulation—as the reasons for famine in Sudan and Ethiopia. Both countries need to overhaul national policies that retard the use of new crop strains and to develop adequate transportation and irrigation systems.[20]

Similarly, decades of communist misrule—not overpopulation—produced "ecological devastation" in Eastern Europe and the Soviet Union. The badly polluted air, water, and soil in these regions drove up rates of anemia, tuberculosis, hepatitis, and other diseases. Viewed economically, famine is "a tragic magnification of normal market and governmental failures." Vulnerability to famine is typically the consequence of a weak national infrastructure, government debility, and authoritarian political processes.[21]

Challenging Malthusian orthodoxy, economist Julian Simon marshals evidence that increasing human demand for food leads to technological innovation and therefore to increased agricultural production and prosperity in the broader economy. This dynamic points the analyst "in an optimistic direction with respect to humankind's ability to feed itself despite—or, more likely, because of—population growth." Large-scale economic analysis actually demonstrates that population brings "positive economic effects in the long run, though there are costs in the short run." Even when focusing on the demand for natural resources, Simon identifies technologically-mediated long-term benefits of population growth. Thus, a realistic study of population effects makes population growth a reason for optimism, not pessimism. In *The Ultimate Resource* he also argues that population growth does not necessarily hinder economic development or reduce the standard of living nor lead to environmental degradation. To the contrary, population growth tends over time to increase the standard of living for all, including ecologists. As population growth fosters technological innovation, natural resources become more and more interchangeable and scarcity turns into abundance.[22]

> *We affirm that human depopulation is*
> *the true demographic danger facing*
> *the earth in this new century.*

Russian demographer Anatoly Antonov warns that one of the world's great nations faces "demographic failure" because of adverse trends in family life, trends he sees in other industrialized nations. Demographic disintegration and entropy are fast replacing equilibrium in Russia and other developed countries. A prominent Australian demographer views the mid-twentieth century baby boom as no more than a "partial detour" in the long-term, economically-driven global decline in fertility. Currently depressed levels of fertility reflect the inevitable consequences of a societal shift from traditional "home production whether on the farm or in the house" to modern "extra-domestic or industrial production."

Available evidence offers little support for the view that this period of decline in family life and fertility is over. Indeed, demographers identify a looming "fertility crisis" in the industrialized world, where completed fertility has fallen under 1.5 births per woman in many countries, well below the 2.1 births needed just to maintain a stable population. The "very low fertility" now being measured in various countries (including Spain, Germany, Russia, and Japan) portends dramatic population contraction in the years ahead. Researchers marvel that global media outlets in the United States, Europe, and Japan have accorded the topic "only limited discussion." Demographers indeed wonder if perhaps "people used to living for the here and now may have difficulty appreciating the long-term consequences beyond their immediate horizon." Social analyst Philip Longman warns that rapidly falling fertility rates endanger the economic well-being and political stability of all industrialized nations. He recommends government intervention to create incentives for childbearing.[23]

> *Everything that a man does is mediated*
> *by his aptness for fatherhood. Everything*
> *that a woman does is mediated by her*
> *aptness for motherhood.*

An important thread running through fatherhood literature defines breadwinning as "active, responsible, emotionally invested, demanding, expressive, and measuring real devotion." Many fathers rank "provider" as the most important role a father can play and view providing as "a way to invest in their families." Not surprisingly, the inability to provide leads many men to withdraw from family life. A "consistent pattern" thus emerges in the paternal-involvement literature: namely, "fathers who provide are involved in many aspects of their children's lives; fathers who do not provide disengage from involvement with their children." Similarly, a medical researcher adduces evidence that mothers can, through their maternal nurturance, give their children "a protective factor" in psychological development that neither fathers nor non-parental caregivers can provide. Indeed, when it takes place within marriage, motherhood safeguards good health in ways predicted by "role enhancement" theory. The status of married motherhood thus fosters decidedly "favorable outcomes" for women who take it on.[24]

To the great surprise of the researcher involved, even students completing law and MBA degrees emphasize the primacy of their future family roles as spouses and parents when interviewed about their future hopes. Only a small subgroup of students, mostly female, anticipate creating a surrogate "family" through friendship. Elsewhere, survey data reveal that young Americans in the 1990s were much more committed to marriage and family life and regarded both motherhood and fatherhood as "more fulfilling" than did their counterparts in the 1970s. Though some elements of American culture remain in tension with traditional understandings of family life, it appears that most young Americans still view wedlock and children as "centrally significant and meaningful." Marriage and children may even have become "more valued, desired, and expected" in recent years. Historical investigation also highlights the reasons many American women responded favorably to the La Leche League's understanding of motherhood as "a valid vocation" and as a "liberating career." These women found their sense of social identity in motherhood conceived as "a rewarding job, a job filled with all sorts of satisfactions."[25]

We affirm that the complementarity of the sexes is a source of strength.

When Nobel laureate Gary Becker applies his economic theory to family life, he demonstrates that a successful marriage benefits both the husband and the wife because of a gender complementarity that "maximizes total output because the gain from the division of labor is maximized." Bioethicist Leon Kass, whose perspective reflects both modern science and ancient scripture, marvels at the mystery of sexual complementarity. The marvelous elements of sexual relations—including explosive elements "almost guaranteed to cause trouble"—can be "clothed by culture, and altered by customs, rituals, beliefs, and diverse institutional arrangements." Yet "the elements themselves are none of them cultural constructions, nor is there likely to be any conceivable cultural arrangement that can harmonize to anyone's satisfaction all their discordant tendencies. On the contrary, political and cultural efforts to rationally solve the problem of man and woman . . . will almost certainly be harmful, even dehumanizing, to man, to woman, and especially to children, not least because such matters are so delicate and private, and their deeper meanings inexpressible."[26]

Men and women exhibit profound biological and psychological differences.

The evidence here is vast. Survey data from thirty-seven cultures worldwide, for example, confirm the predictions of evolutionary theory about diverging male-female mate preferences. In all cultures surveyed, women value potential mates regarded as capable of acquiring resources while men value a physical attractiveness indicative of reproductive capacity. Thus, in all thirty-seven cultures, women favored potential mates who were somewhat older than they, while men favored potential mates who were somewhat younger. The monitoring of newborn infants exposed to mild stress reveals significant and consistent sex differences in both behavioral and neurochemical responses. Such sex differences, the researchers note, are clearly "prior to socialization." In fact, anatomists see a remarkable sex difference in the structure of male and female human brains. Sex differences in the splenium of the corpus callosum suggest that the female brain manifests "less hemispheric specialization" than does the male brain.[27]

A very broad and inclusive survey of empirical studies indicates that men and women differ in other significant ways as well. Many of these male-female differences are remarkably consistent and large. One prominent investigator has noted that empirical studies have not only failed to provide the evidence feminists were looking for to discredit stereotypes, they have actually "produced findings that conform to people's ideas about the sexes." Repeated studies have shown that human males consistently manifest greater aggression than human females. Another investigator has reported that men and women differ in the way they attack and solve intellectual problems. The differences reflect the way sex hormones affect brain organization. The neurological evidence thus indicates that from the very start of life "the environment is acting on differently wired brains in boys and girls."[28]

Indeed, the results for seven gender-role surveys conducted between 1974 and 1997 reveal a pattern of "stability" or even one of "increasing sex typing" over this twenty-three-year period. The researchers interpret this pattern as evidence of "predispositions based on innate patterns as posited by the evolutionary model." The differences first manifest themselves in infancy. Observation of newborn infants establishes a consistent sex difference in response to the odor of human breast milk: whereas female infants with no prior breastfeeding experience are consistently attracted to the odor of human breast milk, male infants with no prior breastfeeding experience consistently fail to manifest any such attraction. In cognitive tests administered in Japan and the United States, researchers limn an "almost identical pattern of sex differences," with males in both countries outperforming females in tests of visual-spatial skills and females in both countries outperforming males in tests of verbal ability. The researchers see in their findings a need for "biologically based" explanations of the differences.[29]

An extensive analysis of biological data for various species establishes that males and females—including human males and human females—are biologically predisposed to follow different life paths and to deploy distinctively different tactics during their individual development. In humans, major cognitive differences emerge early in fetal development and are reinforced during puberty. These biological differences affect human sexual behavior, psychology, and gender role identity. Because these biological differences are "not correlated with socialization," it is not surprising that in recent decades of cultural turmoil the evidence indicates "no consistent tendency for sex differences in social behavior and personality to have eroded." Empirical data collected from various countries actually indicate "near universality of sex differences in spatial abilities across human cultures." Evolutionary theorists interpret this pattern as evidence of a sexual division of labor during hominid evolution, as males did most of the hunting and females did most of the foraging.[30]

Surveying evidence gleaned from military and police records, a prominent social theorist concludes that even the most aggressively feminist policies have not erased "the fact that women's bodies are much less suitable [than men's] for engaging in violence or defending against [it]." Because modern technology has not eliminated the importance of this basic biological difference and because "no society can survive without either the use of violence or the threat of it, . . . complete equality between men and women will never be realized." Indeed, investigation of the biological effects of sex hormones makes it impossible to accept the view that gender roles reflect merely social conditioning and strongly indicates that "sex differences in hormone experience from gestation to adulthood shape gendered behavior." It would appear that "gendered social structure is a universal accommodation to this biological fact." One researcher has even warned that if societies "depart too far from the underlying sex-dimorphism of biological predispositions, they will generate social malaise and social pressures to drift back toward closer alignment with biology. A social engineering program to degender society would require a Maoist approach: continuous renewal of revolutionary resolve and a tolerance for conflict."[31]

When a man and a woman are united in marriage
the whole is greater than the sum of the parts.

Applying economic theory to family life, Becker shows that love in a marriage "raises commodity output" and that caring in a marriage raises the couple's "total income" by making part of their output a "family commodity." Government economic data indicates that once men take on the role of breadwinner—a role traditionally defined as complementary to the wife's homemaker role—they become more productive. That is, "marriage *per se* makes [male] workers more productive."[32]

*Ideas and religious faith can prevail
over material forces. Even one as
powerful as industrialization can be
tamed by the exercise of human will.*

Around the globe, we find encouragement here. Survey data show that during the same years (1982 to 1988) that the overall percentage of eighteen-year-old white American females who were virgins fell from 51 percent to 42 percent, the percentage of eighteen-year-old white fundamentalist Protestants who were virgins actually rose from 45 percent to 61 percent. An economic analysis of the social dynamics that obtain in the secular state of Sweden reveals that the presence of church-attending men and women in a Swedish neighborhood significantly reduces rates of abortion, divorce, bankruptcy, and out-of-wedlock births, even among the non-believers who live in these neighborhoods. A team of pediatric researchers identify religion as a primary reason for the remarkably low levels of sexual activity among Hispanic young women: almost 60 percent of the unmarried women surveyed in this study were still virgins, compared to 35 to 50 percent for the general American population.[33]

*We will end state incentives
to live outside of marriage.*

This deplorable situation is well documented. Two sociologists conclude that government welfare policies make married fatherhood particularly burdensome because married fathers must support their own children directly and other men's children indirectly—through taxes paid to cover the cost of the welfare system. Census and vital statistics data for 1980 indicate that the level of public assistance available was "strongly related to African-American family structure" in urban areas, with higher levels of assistance pushing down rates for marriage and marital fertility and reducing the percentage of children residing in husband-wife families.[34]

In data from a nationally representative sample of 6,288 young women between the ages of fourteen and twenty-two, researchers identify evidence that "higher average welfare payments depressed marriage rates among poor women." The analysis suggests that "poor women may have lower rates of first marriage because the availability [of welfare benefits] is perceived as an economically viable potential alternative to marrying an unacceptable mate, especially in the event of nonmarital child-bearing." The researchers add that "the generosity of public assistance may enter women's calculations of the relative benefits of marriage versus singlehood, regardless of whether public assistance is actually received."[35]

Policy analysis suggests that small reductions in welfare translate into small reductions in illegitimacy but that complete abolition of welfare would produce dramatic reduction in illegitimacy. Between 1940 and 1990, the growth of the entire welfare package (not just Aid to Families with Dependent Children but Medicaid, food stamps, and housing subsidies) dramatically parallels the rise in illegitimacy among blacks. One analyst has shown how the welfare-to-work elements of welfare reform have created a mixed combination of incentives and disincentives to marry. Though there is as yet "little evidence of large effects," the Earned Income Tax Credit in particular creates a significant disincentive for employed unwed mothers to marry. Sociological and economic analyses of recent welfare reforms indicates that the termination of Aid to Families with Dependent Children (AFDC) has been accompanied by a decline in out-of-wedlock childbearing, a leveling off or slight reduction in the divorce rate, and a modest reduction in the number of female-headed households.[36]

We will end state preferences for easy divorce by repealing "no-fault" statutes.

The "no-fault" revolution independently damaged marriage. Economist Douglas Allen challenges statistical methods used to demonstrate that adoption of no-fault laws had no net effect on divorce rates. More reliable statistical methods suggest that adoption of such laws pushed the divorce rate higher. Indeed, statistical analysis of historical data establishes that 17 percent of the rise in the U.S. divorce rate between 1968 and 1988 can be attributed to adoption of new laws permitting unilateral divorce. Another study using data from thirty-eight states yields strong evidence that adoption of no-fault drove up the divorce rate in eight of them (including California) and lesser evidence that it drove up the divorce rate in eight more (including New York). In these sixteen states, the adoption of no-fault statutes appears to have increased the divorce rate by 20 to 25 percent.[37]

Scholars at the University of Oklahoma provide statistical evidence that the adoption of no-fault clearly drove up the divorce rate in forty-four of the fifty states, the six exceptions "being directly interpretable because of peculiarities." The overall statistical pattern indicates that adoption of no-fault had "a large effect" on divorce rates.[38]

Family law specialist Lynn Wardle criticizes no-fault not only for its unintended consequences (such as the impoverishment of women) but also for its failure to fulfill the declared intentions of its advocates. While proponents of no-fault promised that its passage would reduce adversarial litigation, Wardle finds that any reduction in hostile litigation over the grounds for divorce has been achieved merely by a "transfer of hostility into other facets of the divorce proceeding rather than [through] any substantial reduction in the acrimony of the proceeding overall." In fact, the enactment of no-fault statutes has "exacerbated the trauma of divorce" for many children and struggling parents, while the legal profession itself has emerged as "the major beneficiary of the no-fault divorce reforms." Lenore J. Weitzman concludes that as a radical change in the way marriage ends, no-fault divorce inevitably "affects the rules for marriage itself and the intentions and expectations of those who enter it." No-fault divorce thus "redefines marriage as a time-limited, contingent arrangement rather than a lifelong commitment."[39]

5

Life, Death, Work, and Taxes

EMPIRICAL RESEARCH reveals the importance of the natural family as we consider questions of health, wealth creation, sexual identity, education, faith, and even taxes. As in the previous chapter, we draw on the lessons of science to affirm the ideals articulated in the manifesto.

> *We will allow private insurers to recognize*
> *the health advantages of marriage and family living,*
> *according to sound business principles.*

Family living delivers improved health, an old actuarial truth. A legal analyst identifies group risk assessment as a type of classification "at the heart of the insurance system." Noting that in a market-based system, insurers have "a strong incentive" to assess group risk accurately, he concludes that insurance classification fosters economically efficient behavior. It is assessment of group risk that explains why life insurance premiums differ for men and women and for smokers and non-smokers. It is assessment of group risk that also explains why auto insurance companies often consider marital status in setting premiums. Indeed, analysis of the pronounced health and mortality advantage that married men and women enjoy over unmarried peers provides a solid risk-exposure rationale for "restructuring Medicare rates so that married recipients pay a lower monthly premium than the unmarried." Since many Americans remain unmarried because of circumstances beyond their control, actual enactment of such a restructuring is politically doubtful and ethically questionable and therefore compels consideration of other political options (such as tax credits helping young married couples with children) for rewarding family behavior that reduces medical costs. Though this analysis does not look at policies for private health and life insurers, it offers a complete justification for such insurers (who operate outside the constraints on public policymakers and who already offer lower life-insurance premiums to women than to men and lower life- and health-insurance premiums to non-smokers than to smokers) to offer premium reductions to married policy holders.[1]

Confirmation of this link between good health and family living can be found globally. For example, survey data for Dutch adults indicate that married men and women enjoy better health than single, divorced, or cohabiting peers. Although positive health habits account for some of married adults' health advantage, more than half of that advantage persists in statistical models that take such habits into account. Researchers theorize that differences in psychological or material circumstances may account for the rest of married couples' distinct advantage in health.[2]

Ohio State medical researchers report finding significantly lower levels of immunizing antibodies in blood samples drawn from divorced and separated individuals than in blood samples drawn from married peers. The impairment of their immune systems leaves divorced and separated individuals more vulnerable to certain physical ailments (including pneumonia and tuberculosis) than are their married counterparts. Two national health surveys conducted in France indicate that married mothers with children at home enjoy the kind of health improvement predicted by "role enhancement" theory. In contrast, single mothers suffer from "very unfavorable outcomes in terms of perceived health and malaise symptoms."[3]

Princeton scholars have examined data from twenty-six developed nations (from Austria to New Zealand and Singapore) to understand the relationship between marital status and mortality. In all of them, "married persons of both sexes experience a marked mortality advantage relative to single individuals." The fact that sickly men and women usually do not marry accounts for only a small portion of the married-single differential in mortality rates. Health records for a national sample of young women indicate that "women who were not married generally had worse health trends than married women." To the researchers' acknowledged surprise, "the health effects of being never married were as harmful or somewhat more harmful than the health effects of being divorced or separated."[4]

We will end the oppressive taxation of family income, labor, property, and wealth.

Tax policy can have a profound effect on family health. Historically rooted analysis justifies tax preferences for married couples and tax penalties for divorce and non-marital cohabitation. Because the pro-family tax principles on which American tax policy was erected in the post-war era were ignored and even attacked by policymakers in the 1960s and 1970s, government increasingly fostered childlessness and divorce. The Tax Reform Act of 1986 only partly remedied the tax bias against married couples with children, particularly one-income married couples. Analysis in 1987 of historical tax patterns highlights how families were hurt between 1960 and 1985 by the remarkable erosion of the value of the personal exemption allowed for by the Federal income tax code. Because of this erosion, the fraction of median income exempt from taxation fell for the average four-person family from more than three-fourths in 1948 to less than one-third in 1983. By raising the value of the personal exemption to $2400 (more than double its 1986 value of $1080), the 1986 tax reform partially remedied this erosion; however, giving the exemption the same relative value that it had in 1948 (measured as a fraction of per capita income) would have meant raising it to approximately $5,600. A Treasury Department analyst identifies this erosion as, "by almost any measure. . . . the largest single change in the income tax in the postwar era." This erosion particularly hurt families with children.[5]

The estate tax is also anti-family. Those who support confis-catory estate taxes on the basis of progressive social theories are ignoring the way such taxes deplete capital accrual by creating disincentives to work and save. Through the estate tax, in fact, government is "'punishing' the Thrifty clan vis-à-vis Spendthrift." The estate tax thus works as "the opposite of a sin tax" and may actually be "a virtue tax" because it "penalizes people who get wealth and then save it for their children." The property tax like-wise acts as "a virtue tax." Economic analysis demonstrates that under almost any set of statistical assumptions, a tax on housing property is "regressive" toward the lower- to middle-income segments of the population. Congressional hearings in 2001 began with an acknowledgment of the "growing consensus that we must provide income-tax relief for married couples." Testimony during the hearing did show how the Bush Administration provided some relief, chiefly by increasing the size of the personal income tax exemption. However, expert testimony also highlighted the failure to help moderate-income couples not eligible for the child tax benefits available to unmarried peers, a failure that creates "very high marriage penalties." Analysis further showed that attempts to reform the Earned Income Tax Credit (EITC) had "not come close to eliminating EITC marriage penalties."[6]

> *We will end taxes, financial incentives,*
> *subsidies, and zoning laws that discourage*
> *small farms and family-held businesses.*

Historical investigation identifies current legal pressures against home-based handicraft work as the legacy of the New Deal crusade against sweatshop-style industrial homework. Though investigator Eileen Boris acknowledges the risk of abuse, she recognizes the powerful appeal of home-based labor as "a merger of home life [and work] that promises unity in a fragmented world." Similarly, because tax policy for farmland encourages absentee ownership, it has helped drive down the number of farmers who are owner-operators. Tax policy has also encouraged farmers to incorporate their farm in order to reduce their tax burden and then to expand after incorporation. Tax policy thus denies benefits to small, unincorporated family farms that are granted to large, incorporated farms. Tax policy has also created various "problems that are unrelated to traditional farm production," problems that can frequently be resolved only with sophisticated tax advice from specialists.[7]

International social analysis identifies the ways in which family businesses benefit society in ways that other businesses cannot. Because those who run family businesses seek more than merely financial profit, they can humanize a free-market economy. Society has consequently suffered as a result of recent adverse pressures driving many family businesses to insolvency. On the other hand, society has benefited through the growth of telecommuting and other technologies favoring at-home labor. Although U.S. census data does show that white-collar home-based workers earn less than their conventional office-based counterparts, researchers adduce evidence that "argues against exploitation" as the reason for this gap. Rather, it appears that home-based workers are willing to work for less because they seek an equilibrium between income needs and family-schedule flexibility.[8]

It is not equilibrium but disruption, however, one researcher highlights when examining state "relocation subsidies" frequently available to large corporations moving into a new community, subsidies unmatched by any subsidies for the smaller family businesses in the area even though these family enterprises are often economically threatened by the corporate move-in. Meanwhile, a high-profile lawsuit highlights claims by small businesses that inducements granted by federal, state, and local governments to DaimlerChrylser to stay in Ohio force them to subsidize the huge corporation. No small family-held business ever receives such inducements.[9]

We will end the aggressive
state promotion of androgyny.

The evidence is overwhelming: androgyny—the negation of male and female—is a political creation, an act of war against human nature. Fourteen years of survey data from undergraduate college students contradicts "speculation" about widespread movement toward gender androgyny. Data indicate that the measurable psychological difference between the sexes has "not decreased over a whole generation of American life." "It is," psychologist Robert Baldwin suggests, "the concept of androgyny which should be called into question." Historical investigation exposes fraud, distortion, and deception in media and government efforts to deny male-female differences. Analysis shows that such efforts derive from ideology, not honest science. Psychologist Alice Eagley sees "a powerful political agenda" at work trying to marginalize, distort, deny, and suppress research documenting important and sizable differences between men and women. Investigation of the biological effects of sex hormones makes it impossible to accept the view that gender roles reflect merely social conditioning and strongly indicates that "sex differences in hormone experience from gestation to adulthood shape gendered behavior." It would appear that "gendered social structure is a universal accommodation to this biological fact."[10]

And yet the campaign to crush sex differences continues. Professional literature for teachers encourages them to socialize children so as to create "an androgynous society" in which there are "no stereotypical behavioral differences between males and females based solely on sex." Teachers are warned about how "adults can box children into stereotypical roles at a very young age" and are therefore guided toward children's books needed for a "non-sexist education." One federally-published guide explicitly stresses "the concept of androgyny" as the key to "a fresh look at sex roles" that will lead to "challenging gender norms." Educators are told to involve children in "reverse-role playing" in family circumstances. And because "free play, after all, means sexist play," educators are to restrict such free play and intervene in it to eliminate the traditional gender roles it might reflect. This guide also informs educators that the campaign against traditional gender roles must be "pervasive in the school setting." Educators must regard parents as a problem if they "undercut" the campaign against traditional gender roles. Educators should work towards a world in which traditional gender roles are "eliminated."[11]

We will end laws that prohibit employers from
recognizing and rewarding family responsibility.

Statistical analysis shows that the "family wage economy"—created by labor leaders and progressives to support family life by enabling a male wage-earner to support a wife and children—proved remarkably stable until the mid-1970s, when the United States began to move rapidly toward "an economy of pure gender equality." Since family life has eroded in the new economic circumstances and since the assumptions on which the old family-wage economy was erected are no longer politically sustainable, one analyst proposes a package of family-based tax breaks that would deliver many of the same benefits as the old family-wage system.[12]

Economic analysis further suggests that rising numbers of young mothers have moved into paid employment because men's wages have stagnated since the 1970s, so creating "economic uncertainty and fear of downward mobility." Indeed, it was precisely "when husbands' wages began to drop [that] young mothers' employment rates increased." But the movement of young mothers into paid employment has created a "work-family dilemma" for families with young children. One researcher sees an "absence of a work-family dilemma" in past decades when Americans saw "husbands earning a family wage."[13]

Historical analysis helps identify one reason for the erosion of the family wage by exposing the way that a dubious alignment of Dixiecrat segregationists and equity feminists added a prohibition against sex discrimination to the Civil Rights Act of 1964. The Dixiecrats, it appears, hoped to kill the entire measure through this change; instead, they damaged the family. This legal change dramatically undermined the family-wage system that labor leaders and progressive maternalists had created to enable a wage-earning father to support his wife and children. The consequences were a higher divorce rate and a lower marriage rate.[14]

We will end discriminatory taxes and policies
that favor mass state education of the young.

Monopolies produce poor results, especially in education. Though wary of policies that would give public money to private schools, an educational analyst finds ample evidence of the need to "break up the complacent consumer-insensitive monopoly relationship that public schools enjoy in relationship to most of their clients." He also acknowledges that, under policies denying parents the option of taking children out of the public schools, parental liberty is "inhibited." An economist provides evidence suggesting that parents might well find better schools for their children in an educational system in which private contractors compete against each other than in the current system in which public schools enjoy a local monopoly. The researcher acknowledges the possibilities for abuse and fraud in a voucher system but cites notable instances of waste and malfeasance in the current order. In any case, parents with free choice in the use of vouchers might well serve as "more effective monitors [of schools' actions] than parents who have no means of rewarding or punishing the [monopoly] schools that serve their children."

Another economist takes the public schools as an example of the economic harms attendant to a monopoly. Relative to private-school teachers, public-school teachers are in the same position as a state-subsidized merchant in unfair competition with merchants receiving no such subsidy. As monopolies, public schools tend to "crowd out" private-school competitors. Consequently, "the market in education has virtually been destroyed," and a large fraction of the money spent in the U.S. on education is "social loss from monopoly."[15]

We will end abuse of "child-abuse" laws.

The campaign to end child abuse too often abuses families. One of the legal authorities who initially led the national campaign against child abuse, Douglas Besharov, presents evidence that child abuse laws are now too vague, too broad, and too easily turned against innocent parents. Coercive state intervention, he argues, should be based on "what parents did, not on what they 'might' do." Specialists in family law and child psychology at Yale University and the Hampstead Child-Therapy Clinic also warn that because even "temporary infringement of parental autonomy" weakens children's trust in their parents and increases their anxiety, state authorities ought "to err on the side of nonintrusiveness" when dealing with cases of alleged abuse.[16]

A legal expert on children's rights finds that too many children are being placed in foster care and too many parents are losing their parental rights because of child-protection systems distorted by "a bias toward over-reporting and over-labeling [of] child abuse and neglect." Because of a "pernicious shift" in public debate, "child protection" now often depends on "the virtue of breaking up families" and advocates of such protection frequently rely on rhetoric suffused with "the connotation that 'pro-parent' is 'anti-child.'" Indeed, analysis of current court proceedings in child abuse cases suggests disturbing parallels with the Salem witch trials of the seventeenth century. In many child-abuse cases, judges are shirking their duty "to distinguish between false and true accusations," as they—like their predecessors in Salem—allow misguided children to reinforce their own "prejudged certainty" of the guilt of the accused.[17]

Children are especially likely to be scripted into modern witchtrial dramas when embittered divorcing parents deploy "sex-molestation charges as a strategy to obtain custody and to achieve revenge against former spouses." A medical expert on child abuse concludes as well that "the permissive reporting aspects of the child abuse legislation" have opened the door to numerous false allegations of abuse, many lodged by "emotionally or mentally disturbed individuals." It is hardly surprising, then, that a California grand jury concludes that a disturbing number of children were being separated from their parents for extended periods because state officials were "determined to err on the side of assuming guilt" and were, consequently, "accept[ing] reports of molest[ation] as true notwithstanding that they may [have been] inherently incredible, made for motives of harm or gain, or the product of years of 'therapy.'" The grand jury calls for a higher standard of evidence in child abuse cases and for a restitution of the traditional presumption of the innocence of the accused.[18]

Human beings are made to be conjugal,
to live in homes with vital connections
to parents, spouse, and children.

The whole of human history, and pre-history, points to the family in its home as normative. Evolutionary theorists interpret the family as a unit that fits naturally within complex human patterns of human exchange and reciprocity, as a unit essential in providing "intragroup solidarity in the context of intergroup competition," and as a social group that allows post-menopausal women to serve as "post-reproductive helpers." A biologically rooted perspective on history suggests that monogamy originated as a consequence of reproductive strategies (called κ-strategies in neo-Darwinian theory) in which parents have few children but invest a great deal of care in these few. Such strategies made monogamy a necessity in the circumstances in which early humans lived, circumstances where "the cooperation of one male and one female [was] required to exploit and defend the resources." This perspective suggests that "human beings probably were never sexually promiscuous."[19]

Though polygyny has often emerged in environments in which rich and powerful men could claim more than one wife, monogamy has over time manifest "competitive advantages" by sustaining agrarian cultures dependent upon family labor and by exerting "a pacifying and stabilizing influence" on males. Interpreting ethnographic patterns in the light of the sociobiological theory of altruism, one anthropologist argues that "the emergence of monogamy in the great majority of human populations" reflects a biologically-scripted genetic logic. That same logic binds together the conjugal pair and their children in a natural unit and discourages promiscuity and adultery. In assessing the harmful effects of a communal child-rearing arrangement in which infant children slept out of the home, psychologists conclude that that the practice was harmful because it was not in harmony with the nature of the human species. The practice of moving infants out of the home and out of maternal care in this way inevitably entails deleterious consequences because it "significantly deviates from the environment of evolutionary adaptedness."[20]

We see that the family model of the 1950s was largely confined to the white majority. Black families actually showed mounting stress in these years.

The family system crafted in America during the 1950s showed surface strength—and serious shortcomings. In a landmark study, sociologist E. Franklin Frazier identifies high levels of family disruption among African-Americans who had migrated to large cities in the early twentieth century, in part because the traditional black churches had lost much of their cultural force as a consequence of the migration. Daniel Patrick Moynihan famously documented the erosion of family life within the African American community, an alarming pattern of family disintegration, and warned of the consequent "tangle of pathology." Moynihan's perception that family decay had "begun to feed on itself" within the African American community was much attacked at the time but is now widely regarded as prescient. Sociologist Charles Murray suggests that during the 1940s and 1950s the growth of welfare benefits for unwed mothers was already being paralleled by a sharp rise in black illegitimacy rates.[21]

The "companionship marriage" ideal of the 1950s,
which embraced psychological tasks to the exclusion
of material and religious functions, was fragile.

The "1950s family model" rested on a frail set of assumptions. Historical analysis exposes as an ultimate failure the attempt to renew family life by focusing solely on the companionate husband-wife union while allowing continued erosion of the productive home economy. Family sociologist Andrew Cherlin locates the shift from institutional marriage to companionate marriage within a broader cultural deinstitutionalization of wedlock. For many Americans, the companionate form of marriage has now given way to "individualized marriage," premised on maximal personal choice and individual development. The newer forms of marriage have proven less durable and more vulnerable to divorce than the traditional form of institutional marriage. Researchers have clarified the reasons for the fragility of companionate marriages focused on mutual communication and spousal support. In post-divorce interviews, men assessed the reasons they had failed in their efforts to build a companionate marriage. Repeatedly, these divorced men identified fundamental gender differences in communication styles as a reason for the marital ruptures. Former wives had tended to be more open and expressive than the men interviewed and had hoped for a communicative reciprocity that did not develop.[22]

The effort to eliminate real differences
between men and women does as much violence
to human nature and human rights as the efforts
by the communists to create "Soviet man" and
by the Nazis to create "Aryan man."

Androgyny demands and deploys an attack on human nature. His-torians Becky Glass and Margaret Stolee trace disturbing parallels between the radical family policies of the Bolshevik revolutionar-ies who created the Soviet Union and the legislative agenda of progressive activists prominent in late-twentieth-century Western democracies. The family policies of the Bolsheviks fostered such intense "social and internal confusion" that Soviet leaders eventually abandoned them. Yet Western elites continue to press for policies that undermine "traditional and stereotypical sex roles for husbands and wives" in the same way that Bolshevik policies did.[23]

We find views against adultery and divorce
in the other great world faiths.

Scholars of religion note that in Islam divorce is regarded as "per-missible but reprehensible" and that in Hinduism "marriage is treated as a sacrament and divorce is not allowed." Though Juda-ism and Buddhism differ remarkably in spiritual orientation and social organization, Hebrew law and Buddhist law (*miswah* and *sila*) contain notably similar moral precepts, including "universal injunctions against adultery." The appendix to C.S. Lewis' *The Abolition of Man* underscores the essential moral unity on this question.[24]

Moreover, we find recognition of the natural
family in the marriage rituals of animists.

In the six ethnic groups that constitute Vietnam's Hanhi-Lolo linguistic group, animism (in several versions) informs the religious attitudes of patriarchal clans in which marriage forges links regarded as important in this world and the next: parents-in-law are important objects of devotion in the ancestor cult. The animism of traditional Taiwanese folk religion has likewise helped to nurture "deep-rooted ideals" that make marriage "a central event in the life course." Among the many rural Taiwanese adherents to this animist tradition, "the continuity of family lineage" is imperative, and co-residence of parents with a married son persists as a common household arrangement.[25]

> *The record is clear from decades of work*
> *in sociology, psychology, anthropology,*
> *sociobiology, medicine, and social history:*
> *children do best when they are born into*
> *and raised by their two natural parents.*

This truth is unassailable. "Marriage," an American Academy of Pediatrics (AAP) task force explains, "is beneficial in many ways," in large part because "people behave differently when they are married. They have healthier lifestyles, eat better, and mother each other's health." The AAP scholars stress that children do not enjoy the same advantages in a stepfamily or in a household headed by unmarried cohabiting parents. In surveys conducted among Houston-area adolescents between 1971 and 1997, teens who had grown up in intact families were much more likely to indicate that they had received "good parenting" than were peers from single-parent or step-parent families. Having grown up in an intact family also was predictive of less psychological distress, better interpersonal relations with others, and more active social participation. Arguing against the view that genetics matters more than family structure in determining children's mental health and well-being, sociologist Andrew Cherlin cites evidence from study of female twin-pairs showing that a "parental separation or divorce increased the risk of major depression for members of a twin-pair by 42 percent, even after making allowances for genetic relatedness." This and other evidence clearly indicate that "divorce indeed has an effect on mental health . . . the variation is not due only to genes."[26]

Survey after survey indicate that children do best in intact families. Researchers find a clear pattern in the behavioral and achievements data for 12,702 young adolescents in Prince George's County near Washington, DC: "Students living with both biological parents changed more positively [during the course of the study period] than did other students." In sophisticated multivariable statistical models, an intact-family structure was consistently predictive of positive changes in the researchers' composite Success Index. Not only did an intact family predict individual success, but it also predicted the overall health of the school-neighborhood-friendship-family context in which young people live. What the researchers call high "joint context quality" exists in the network of school-neighborhood-friendship-family relationships, suggesting that intact families are essential for creating a "social world [that] is ordered in ways that generally favor young persons."

In a study of delinquency based on a nationally representative sample of more than twenty thousand adolescents in grades seven through twelve, researchers at the National Institute of Child Health and Human Development found not only that teen criminality runs lowest among teens from two-biological-married-parent families, but also that levels of parental involvement, supervision, monitoring, and closeness all average highest in these families. Northwestern scholars conclude that young men and women from single-parent and step-parent families significantly fall short of the educational attainments and occupational status typical of peers reared in intact families. The researchers trace the depressed levels of educational and occupational accomplishment found among young adults from intact families to the low levels of violence they experienced during adolescence. Indeed, the violence often experienced by teens from broken homes forms the first link in "a chain of adversity" in which "victimization undermines academic performance, educational attainment, labor force participation, occupational status, and earnings in early adulthood."[27]

Under any other setting—including one-parent . . .

The one-parent household portends large risks for children. After surveying available data, a task force appointed by the AAP expressed deep concern about social trends putting more than one-fourth of all children (26 percent) in homes headed by a single parent, usually the mother. The AAP task force points out that single-parent households have three to five times higher rates of poverty than do two-parent households and that "family income is strongly related to children's health." Moreover, "paternal absence" is predictive of "multiple and sometimes lifelong disadvantages" that go far beyond "health problems" to include "problems with school attendance, achievement and completion; emotional and behavioral problems; adolescent parenthood; substance abuse; and other risk behaviors."[28]

Studies of twins underscore this AAP finding. Data collected for 1,887 pairs of female twins born between 1975 and 1987 provide strong evidence that paternal absence increases the risk of Separation Anxiety Disorder (SAD) for young women. Statistical analysis identifies paternal absence as "an important predictor of all categories of SAD, even after accounting for other risk factors," including socioeconomic disadvantage. As a "rather robust" statistical predictor of SAD, "the loss or the threat of loss of a father figure has important consequences" in the opinion of the researchers, who note that young women suffering from SAD often manifest "impairment in functioning" at home, at school, and in relationships with peers.[29]

The effects of living in single-parent homes are particularly large for adolescents. Nationally representative data indicate that, compared to peers in intact families, teens from mother-only homes suffer from poorer socioemotional adjustment, achieve less in school, and report less favorable global well-being. The researchers identify teens in households headed by continuously-single mothers as "singularly disadvantaged" in their household resources. When researchers at the National Institute of Child Health and Human Development examine delinquency data collected from a nationally representative sample of more than twenty thousand adolescents, they identified family structure as a key predictor of teen criminality: "Adolescents in single-father families report the highest levels of delinquency, followed by those in father-step-mother and single-mother families. Delinquency levels are lowest among adolescents residing with two biological, married parents." The linkage between family structure and teen delinquency persists in a statistical model that takes into account the characteristics of the children (age, ethnicity, gender) and of the parents (education, income, immigrant status).[30]

Researchers identify father absence as a key predictor of early puberty for girls. In data collected from 281 girls participating in the Child Development Project, analysts discern evidence that "girls who were in single-mother homes at age five tended to experience earlier puberty." And unfortunately, "early onset of puberty in girls is associated with negative health and psychosocial outcomes," including "more emotional problems, such as depression and anxiety" and "alcohol consumption and sexual promiscuity."[31]

Surveying data collected from 485 youth surveyed as part of the Iowa Youth Families Projects, researchers identify "a significant increase in health problems . . . during the transition from adolescence to early adulthood" among children reared in single-parent households. "When only one parent is available in the home," the researchers remark, "the adolescent is more likely to experience conduct problems, school failures, a precocious entry into family responsibilities, a more limited education, and early stresses and strains in their work life. This accumulating process of disadvantage produces a consequent increase in risk for poor health." The researchers interpret their findings in light of previous research demonstrating that "social disadvantage in the family of origin contributes to adverse child-rearing practices of parents and in turn partially determines child adjustment problems."[32]

The effects of living in broken homes show up among young adults as well. Examining survey data collected between 1979 and 1994 for 2,846 young men tracked from ages fourteen to thirty, researchers conclude that "youth incarceration risks . . . were elevated for adolescents in father-absent households." Even after controling for household income, for the receipt of child-support payments, and for residential moves, the researchers find that "youths in father-absent families (mother-only, mother-stepfather, and relatives/other) still had significantly higher odds of incarceration than those from mother-father families." Thus, even after statistically accounting for poverty and residential moves, researchers find that sons in mother-only families were nearly twice as likely to be incarcerated as peers from mother-father families. In the simplest statistical model, researchers find that boys who are fatherless from birth are three times as likely to go to jail as peers from intact families. Similarly, in data collected from 10,353 young men and women monitored from ages seven to twenty-three, a

British-American team of researchers find evidence that young people who have experienced a parental divorce during childhood show more emotional problems, achieve less in school, and find themselves in poorer financial circumstances than do peers whose parents remain married. The researchers conclude that parental divorce often puts children of both sexes into "negative life trajectories through adolescence into adulthood."[33]

Younger children also pay a price when parents do not marry or stay married. Analyzing data collected from thirty custodial divorced mothers, thirty custodial divorced fathers, and thirty married parents with children ages six to ten, researchers found—as they expected—significantly higher levels of conduct problems among the children of divorced parents than among peers in intact families. Although the statistical model attributes much of the adverse effects of divorce to the economic and psychological hardships marital breakdown produces, none of these "intervening variables" can fully account for the statistical linkage between family structure and children's problem behaviors. Consequently, the researchers "reluctantly acknowledge" that their findings indicate that "children fare better in married, nuclear families," though they worry that such "provocative" findings are liable to "misuse by advocates of so-called 'family values.'"[34]

In nationally representative data collected from 9,398 Canadian children ages six to eleven, researchers discern a clear pattern: "children from single-mother families are at increased risk of difficulties," evident in psychiatric problems, social impairment, and depressed academic performance. Although the researchers insist (perhaps for reasons of political expediency) that "children from single-mother families develop difficulties for the same reasons as children from two-parent families," these reasons show up "at higher rates among single-mother families"—significantly higher rates. Furthermore, the evidence indicates that while "punitive parenting" sometimes causes social impairment and psychiatric problems among children in intact families, "the presence of hostile parenting in single-parent families is linked with increased psychiatric and social difficulties beyond that in two-parent families." And in broader analysis, "single-mother status on its own has a significant association with all [negative] child outcomes examined." Nationally representative social and academic data for 20,330 students likewise indicate that children from single-parent and step-parent families do significantly worse in mathematics than do peers from intact families.[35]

Poverty is another consequence of family breakdown. Economic analysis of the 1990s shows that during that decade the combined effects of a strong economy and of ever-more-aggressive government efforts to collect child support reduced the poverty rate of households with children by a mere percentage point (from 20 percent to 19 percent). The researcher identifies an increasing number of single-parent families as the reason for the stubbornly high rate for child poverty: whereas only 20 percent of children under eighteen lived in single-parent families in 1980, 25 percent did in 1990, and 28 percent in 1997. As of that latter year, nearly half of female-headed households had incomes that put them in the lowest quintile, compared to only 13 percent of married couples. More than a third of female-headed households were living below the official poverty line in 1997. The researcher warns that, compared to peers living in more favorable circumstances, "Children reared in poverty have poorer physical and mental health, do worse in school, experience more punitive discipline styles and abuse, live in poorer neighborhoods, and are more likely to engage in deviant or delinquent acts." Economic and medical data indicate that the upsurge in the number of single-parent, female-headed households has pushed an alarming number of children into both poverty and ill health. The poverty that is associated with "the loss of the wage-earning power of the absent parent, usually the father," predicts "higher rates of poor health and chronic health conditions in children," resulting in higher hospitalization and mortality rates among affected children.[36]

. . . step-parent, . . .

Unfortunately, even remarriage does little to alleviate the negative effects of family disintegration on children. After surveying available data, a task force appointed by the America Academy of Pediatrics (AAP) expressed concern about the consequences of the remarriage of a divorced parent. For although such remarriage usually improves household income, "it does not necessarily improve the experience for the child. . . . [I]n general, children who are raised in a stepfamily do about as well as do children of single mothers." An international team of social scientists finds statistical evidence that stepfather presence accelerates pubertal maturation in young girls living apart from their biological fathers. Early female puberty creates concern because it is predictive of "more emotional problems such as depression and anxiety, and. . . more problem behaviors such as alcohol consumption and sexual promiscuity." In psychological and behavioral data from a sample of eighty high schools across the country, researchers see a strong correlation between family structure and adolescents' psychological distress. "Anger," report the researchers, "is . . . more common among youth who come from blended and single-parent families compared to two-biological-parent intact families." Predictably, the researchers also find that "youth in blended and single-parent families are more delinquent than youth in two-parent biological families." In the longer term, the researchers discern a pathological pattern in which "males [laden with the kind of anger often fostered by growing up in a blended or single-parent family] in particular tend to move through a sequence of adaptations, [and] from anger to delinquency to drinking problems."[37]

Parental divorce followed by remarriage has negative educational effects as well. Comparative data provide no support for the widespread belief that remarriage improves the academic performance of children of divorced parents. These data, in fact, indicate that "remarriage following divorce has somewhat of a negative impact on the academic achievement of teenage children," with children in stepfamilies scoring significantly lower on standardized test than peers in intact families *and* in single-parent families, the comparative deficiencies being especially large in math and social studies. Indeed, the evidence indicates that *both* parental divorce *and* parental remarriage bring down children's standardized test results. Noting the general reliability of academic achievement as an indication of a child's overall emotional security and mental outlook, the researcher suggests that "remarriage adversely affects a child's psychological well-being and happiness."[38]

. . . homosexual, . . .

The homosexual household puts children at risk. In data gleaned from fifty-two narratives from homosexually-parented children and from forty appeals court cases involving custody disputes between homosexual and heterosexual parents, researchers adduce evidence that children reared by homosexual parents face special difficulties. Among the homosexually-reared children in the fifty-two narratives, 92 percent identified one or more problems with or concerns about the nature of their upbringing. What is more, out of 213 "score problems" in the narratives, 201 (91 percent) were "attributed to the homosexual parent(s)." And in the appellate cases surveyed, 97 percent of the harms were attributed to the homosexual parent by the courts.[39]

Lynn Wardle skeptically critiques the methodology and motives behind sociological research that puts homosexual parenting in a favorable light. He finds evidence that compared to peers reared by heterosexual parents, the children in homosexual households face a disproportionate risk of being sexually molested, of experiencing gender confusion, of becoming sexually promiscuous, of losing a parent through parental separation or death, of sliding into depression, of becoming users of illegal drugs, and of committing suicide.[40]

. . . cohabiting . . .

Cohabitation endangers children. In nationally representative data, children (ages four to sixteen) living with parents who had never married scored significantly higher on a global index of deviant behavior than did peers living with married parents. Children living with single and divorced parents also scored higher in problem behavior than did peers from intact families. An AAP task force concludes that children living with cohabiting parents are generally worse off than are peers reared by married parents. "Cohabitation," remark the AAP physicians, "is more unstable for children than either married 2-parent or single-mother families and tends to produce worse outcomes for children." One of the worst outcomes is that of abuse, which the AAP scholars note has been linked to living "with a mother and a cohabiting boyfriend."[41]

Scrutiny of data collected in 1999 from a nationally representative sample of 35,938 children (ages six to eleven) and adolescents (ages twelve to seventeen) reveals that "those living outside of two-biological-parent married families tend to report more behavioral and emotional problems and less school engagement." The data provide little to reassure those who suppose cohabitation serves society just as well as wedlock: in households headed by cohabiting couples (whether never-married cohabitors or step-parent cohabitors), children suffer from psychological, behavioral, and academic problems at significantly higher rates than are seen among peers living with two biological married parents. Though the distinctively high incidence of problems among young children in homes headed by cohabiting parents can be statistically attributed to economic circumstances, economic variables do not account for the high incidence of problems among adolescents in households headed by cohabitors. In any case, economists find that cohabiting parents spend less of their income on their children's education and more on their own tobacco and alcohol habits than do married peers. The researchers interpret this pattern as troubling evidence that cohabiting parents are less willing to invest in their children's future than are married parents.[42]

. . . or communal households—
children do predictably worse.

Communal childrearing also falls short. In ways predicted by attachment theory, children reared in the communal arrangements of Israeli kibbutzim experienced deleterious delays in their emotional and intellectual development. Psychological analysis of these delays focuses particularly on the psychological effects of communal sleeping, which kibbutzim leaders arranged as part of a communal upbringing that entailed "the collective's taking away from [parents] the lion's share of authority and responsibility for their children's care." The researchers judge the kibbutzim's communal-sleeping practice as "a social experiment in nature that was predestined to fail . . . because it employed sociocultural imperatives running counter to basic human needs."[43]

Other psychological data reveal further harmful effects of the out-of-home sleeping arrangements that were part of communal childrearing in Israeli kibbutzim. This communal childrearing arrangement resulted in "adverse effects on the quality of infant-mother relationships." As a consequence, adolescents reared in this way were "more vulnerable to becoming disorganized/disoriented." The researchers characterize the communal childrearing practice as one that "significantly deviates from the environment of evolutionary adaptedness." To assess the effects of various types of childrearing, researchers compared adolescents reared in communal kibbutzim settings with peers reared in familial kibbutzim settings, with peers reared in cities, and with peers raised in a communal setting as young children but moved to familial arrangements before age six. Those adolescents reared entirely in a communal kibbutzim setting manifest "less competent coping" when faced with separations than did the other three groups of adolescents.[44]

6

Gifts of the Natural Family

MARRIAGE AND MARITAL PARENTING provide incomparable gifts to all human societies. Again, we turn to statements found in the manifesto and to the scientific evidence supporting these ideals and truths.

Married, natural-parent homes bring health, . . .

"Marriage," an American Academy of Pediatrics task force explains, "is beneficial in many ways," in large part because "people behave differently when they are married. They have healthier lifestyles, eat better, and monitor each other's health." National health data also indicate that children of married parents enjoy significantly better health than do children of divorced parents. The same data set shows that "marital status is related to the health status of all the family members, including both parents and children." Writing from another perspective, a University of Maryland medical researcher blames parental divorce for causing or exacerbating various chronic diseases—including cardiac disease—among children. In addition, economic and medical data indicate that the upsurge in the number of single-parent, female-headed households has pushed an alarming number of children into both poverty and ill health. The poverty that is associated with "the loss of the wage-earning power of the absent parent, usually the father," predicts "higher rates of poor health and chronic health conditions in children," resulting in higher hospitalization and mortality rates among affected children. Finally, a team of Harvard epidemiologists identifies the distinctively high incidence of both physical and mental illness among the children of divorced and never-married parents as the reason that these children require pediatric and psychiatric services significantly more often than do children of married parents.[1]

. . . *learning,* . . .

The intact home is best predictor of true learning. In academic data collected from 349 young adolescents, researchers found that family structure is superior to any competing theoretical perspective in explaining children's academic achievement. Children in intact families consistently earn higher grades and engage in problem behavior less often than peers in single-parent or step-families. An Ohio State sociologist adduces evidence that "family structural effects" account for much of the "quite substantial" gaps in academic performance separating minority students from white peers. Because "living with both natural parents is positively associated with academic performance" for all ethnic groups and because fewer minority children than white children live with both natural parents, almost one-third of the black-white differential in math achievement and two-fifths of the black-white differential in reading achievement can be traced to differences in family structure. Allowance for the same factor actually shrinks the Hispanic-white gap in reading achievement to statistical insignificance. In data collected for the 1994 through 1999 versions of the British Household Panel Study, a strong linkage emerged between educational achievement and family structure. Compared to peers from other types of households, adolescents who grew up in households with both biological parents were more than twice as likely at age sixteen to achieve five passing marks on the General Certificate of Secondary Education and at age nineteen to achieve two A-level passes for their academic performance.[2]

. . . and success to the offspring reared therein.

The future of young people is mediated through their homes. In sophisticated multivariable statistical models, intact-family structure consistently predicts positive changes for students as gauged by researchers' composite Success Index. Other scholars conclude that young men and women from single-parent and step-parent families significantly fall short of the educational attainments and occupational status typical of peers reared in intact families. Not surprisingly, then, national income data indicate that young men and women reared by both biological parents earn significantly more in adulthood than do peers from other family backgrounds. Occupational attainment consistently runs significantly higher for the offspring of intact families than for peers reared in other household arrangements.[3]

Science shows that these same homes give life, . . .

Looking at data for a group of industrialized nations in Western Europe, North America, and Eastern Asia, Princeton University scholars found that married men and women lived longer on average than unmarried peers (never-married, divorced, and widowed) in all of them. Though the mortality advantage was greater for married men than for married women, it was significant for both sexes and actually increased in recent decades. Two national health surveys conducted in France provide data indicating that married mothers with children at home enjoy the kind of health improvement predicted by "role enhancement" theory. In contrast, single mothers suffer from "very unfavorable outcomes in terms of perceived health and malaise symptoms." In medical data collected from 7,524 white women age sixty-five or older, epidemiologists uncover strong evidence that marriage lengthens women's lives. Indeed, the researchers identify marital status as "the most consistent predictor" of mortality rates for the women involved in this study. Meanwhile, data collected as part of the National Longitudinal Mortality Study establish that when compared to divorced and single men and women in every age group, married men and women enjoy a statistically significant mortality advantage. Differences in economic background only partly account for this mortality advantage. And scholars at The RAND Corporation and the University of California-Riverside have established a clear statistical linkage between "experiencing parental divorce in childhood and a subsequently increased mortality risk."[4]

. . . wealth, . . .

Families create and share wealth. Drawing on nationally representative data collected between 1968 and 1992, Cornell and University of Washington scholars find a very strong linkage between marital status and income, showing a "substantial marital effect on the likelihood of experiencing one or more years of affluence during the life course." The researchers suggest that the wealth-fostering effect of wedlock crosses racial and gender lines, showing up for both whites and blacks, both men and women. Indeed, in statistical terms "the power of marriage to deliver affluence for women is extremely strong." The researchers see marriage fostering affluence by eliminating some of the household expenses that two single individuals would incur and by making possible "a division of labor that maximizes family income" by "enabl[ing] the partner with higher earnings [usually the husband] to devote relatively more energy and attention to remunerated work." Using nationally representative retirement data from 1992, Purdue economists also demonstrate that "being married has a large effect on household wealth," with unmarried individuals experiencing a 63 percent reduction in total wealth over the life course when compared with married peers. Separated, never-married, divorced, cohabiting, and widowed men and women all have "significantly lower wealth than the currently married," the differential being most pronounced for the separated and never married and least pronounced for the widowed. The investigators reason that marriage fosters the accumulation of wealth because "it provides institutionalized protection, which generates economies of scale, task specialization, and access to work-related fringe benefits, that lead to rewards like broader social networks and higher savings rates."[5]

Indeed, the wealth-creating benefits of marriage mark the best way out of poverty. Parsing data collected in 1995 from a national probability sample of 10,847 women ages fifteen to forty-four, researchers from Ohio State and Penn State Universities adduce evidence that "marriage matters economically": compared to never-married peers, "ever-married women are substantially less likely to be poor, regardless of race, family disadvantage, nonmarital birth status, or high school dropout." Moreover, the data collected by the authors of the new study indicate that "the deleterious effect associated with a disadvantaged family background is completely offset by marrying and staying married (i.e., disadvantaged and non-disadvantaged women who marry have similarly low odds of poverty)." This means that "marriage . . . offers a way out of poverty for disadvantaged women." The numbers bear this out. Married black women are much better off economically than are their single peers. The household net worth of the average married black woman in 1990 was $15,650, compared to just $4,563 for the average unmarried black woman.[6]

. . . and joy to wives and husbands, as well.

Building a marriage, rearing children, maintaining a home—all take effort and sacrifice. The marital bond can also bring disappointment and sorrow. All the same, true happiness and marriage go together. Psychological survey data collected from 3,032 randomly selected English-speaking American adults clearly indicate that the optimal state of mental health labeled "flourishing" is "more prevalent" among the married than among the unmarried (20 percent of the married, compared to 15 percent of the widowed, 13 percent of the never married, 12 percent of the separated, 10 percent of the divorced). In contrast, the mental state that the researcher calls "pure depression" shows up much less frequently among the married than among the unmarried (8 percent of the married, compared to 10 percent of the widowed, 11 percent of the never married, 13 percent of the divorced and 18 percent of the separated). Similarly, the percentage of individuals identified as both "languishing" and being in depression runs much lower among the married than among the unmarried. The researcher concludes that even after accounting for differences in socioeconomic background, married individuals are still more likely than the unmarried to enjoy "very good or excellent" mental and emotional health.[7]

Parsing national survey data, another researcher uncovers evidence that marital status has a strong influence on perception of well-being for both men and women, with "married people report[ing] they were more satisfied in life than unmarried people were, irrespective of gender." Although some theorists have asserted that wedlock benefits men more than it benefits women, this researcher finds that "married women [actually] scored higher than married men on perception of well-being." And in a survey of seventeen nations (including the United States, Japan, Spain, and Norway), married men and women report significantly higher levels of personal happiness than do their unmarried peers. The researchers interpret their findings as "perhaps the strongest evidence to date in support of the relationship between marital status and happiness." Contrary to feminist claims that wedlock benefits only men, the statistical results again show that "marriage protects females just as much from unhappiness as it protects males." And although the men and women in nonmarital cohabitation were happier in this international survey than were single men and women, their happiness still came in at "less than one quarter of [that] of married persons," further suggesting that "marriage protects more against unhappiness than does cohabitation."[8]

Disease, . . .

National health data indicate that divorced parents and their children suffer from significantly poorer health than do children of married parents. The same data set indeed shows that "marital status is related to the health status of all the family members, including both parents and children." National survey data collected between 1979 and 1995 in Great Britain and Sweden show that single mothers suffer from "significantly poorer health than couple mothers" in both countries, with the differential remaining "fairly constant" over the study period. Despite the particularly generous welfare benefits available to single mothers in Sweden, "the health disadvantage of Swedish lone mothers is substantial and is of similar magnitude to that of British lone mothers." Puzzled, the researchers speculate that Swedish single mothers might be suffering from poorer health than married mothers because of "lower access to social support."[9]

. . . depression, . . .

The absence of family bonds is a source of sorrow. Data collected for single and married mothers living in Ontario reveal a clear psychological disadvantage for unmarried mothers. Compared to their married peers, unmarried mothers are "almost three times more likely to have experienced a major depressive disorder." Compared to married mothers, single mothers are also more likely to have experienced an early onset of depression and to have had a recurrence. In a study initially focused on the mental-health effects of work environment, researchers discovered that for both men and women marital status actually predicts resistance to depression more reliably than does the quality of work environment. Among men, the likelihood of a major depressive episode ran an astounding nine times higher among the unmarried than among the married. A similar but less dramatic pattern was documented among the women in the study, unmarried women being particularly vulnerable to dysphoria (a form of depression), diagnosed three times as often among unmarried women as among their married peers. Unmarried men and women in fact suffer from more depression and anxiety than do married peers even when those married peers have experienced as many or more traumatic events in their lives. Furthermore, regardless of gender, unmarried adults feel less in control of their lives than do married peers. Data collected over a sixteen-year period for 1,380 adolescents and young adults show that compared to married peers, unmarried men and women suffer from significantly more depression and alcohol problems. "No social variable," the researchers conclude, "is more consistently related with the distribution of psychopathology than marital status."[10]

> *. . . and early death come*
> *to those who reject family life.*

Historical data from 1,961 male graduates of Amherst College born between 1832 and 1879 provides strong evidence that "marriage improved survival prospects [for these nineteenth-century men] even after controlling for health status in early adulthood." The self-selection evident in the failure of sickly men to marry did not come close to accounting for the mortality advantage enjoyed by the married: wedlock itself clearly lengthened life. Current data collected as part of the National Longitudinal Mortality Study establishes that when compared to married peers, divorced and single men and women in every age group suffer from a statistically significant mortality disadvantage. Differences in economic background only partly account for this mortality disadvantage.[11]

> *Women are safest physically when*
> *married and living with their husbands.*

Women who live with partners in non-marital arrangements expose themselves to real risk. Contrary to the predictions of feminist theory, domestic abuse (verbal, psychological, and physical) occurs significantly more often among lesbian couples than among heterosexual pairs. Surveys indicate that women who have been in both lesbian and heterosexual unions received significantly more abuse in the lesbian relationships. Nearly one-half of lesbians surveyed reported "being or having been the victim of relationship violence." Almost two-fifths of lesbians surveyed admitted having used violence against a partner. The researchers suggest that "the academic community . . . shares some of the blame for ignoring same-sex domestic violence," likely because of "a reluctance to challenge feminist frameworks." Researchers also find that males who cohabit express a distinctively "tolerant view of rape," evidently because they are "more accepting of violence and control" than non-cohabitors. Such attitudes suggest that "cohabiting women are at risk of physical violence" from their partners.[12]

Another researcher finds in national survey data a much higher incidence of domestic violence among cohabiting heterosexual couples than among married couples. Analysis indicates that cohabitors are more violent than married couples in large part because they are more socially isolated than are married peers. Although a pair of researchers began their work hypothesizing that domestic violence would occur less often among cohabiting couples than among the married, they have acknowledged that national survey data dramatically contradicts this hypothesis: compared to married peers, cohabiting women in this study are almost four times as likely to suffer "severe violence." A similar study finds cohabiting women to be almost five times as likely to experience "severe violence." This elevated level of violence among cohabiting couples cannot be accounted for as a consequence of household income, education, age, or occupation. Examining data from 724 randomly selected Buffalo-area women ages eighteen to thirty, researchers similarly find that, compared to married or single peers, cohabiting women are also more likely both to have used illicit drugs and to have experienced Intimate Partner Violence.[13]

Children are best sheltered from sexual,
physical, and emotional abuse when they
live with their married natural parents.

The power of natural parents to protect their children can be stunning. Child abuse data from Canada show that preschool-age children living with a step-parent are forty times more likely to become child abuse victims than are those living with both natural parents. Indeed, sociobiologists identify stepchildren as distinctively vulnerable to abuse, giving substance to the wicked stepmother stories. The evidence indicates that when "given the choice between abusing a stepchild and a biological offspring, [abusers] never abused their own kin." American survey data reveal that single mothers are 71 percent more likely to visit "very severe violence" upon their children than are their married peers. Unmarried fathers are even more likely to act violently toward their children, particularly if they are impoverished. Overall, the researcher concludes that, compared to married peers, single parents are distinctly likely to harm their children "no matter what the economic situation."[14]

Natural family homes are also havens of protection against sexual abuse. Examining survey data collected in 1995, researchers discern an elevated rate of sexual abuse for children not in the care of both biological parents. Among children not living with both biological parents, 7.4 percent were reported to have experienced sexual abuse at some time in their lives, and 2.9 percent were reported to have experienced such abuse within the last year. Among children living with both biological parents, only 4.2 percent were reported to have experienced sexual abuse at some time in their lives, and only 0.9 percent were reported to have experienced such abuse within the last year.[15]

Consequently, American adults are especially likely to report having been sexually abused as children if they were reared in the absence of one of their natural parents. Men are particularly likely to have been sexually abused during boyhood if they were reared by a single mother. Women are distinctively more likely to have been sexually abused during childhood "under all family circumstances except that of living with two natural parents."[16]

Early abuse has long-term educational effects. Northwestern scholars conclude that young men and women from single-parent and step-parent families fall short of the educational attainments and occupational status typical of peers reared in intact families. Apparently, the violence often experienced by teens from broken homes forms the first link in "a chain of adversity" in which "victimization undermines academic performance, educational attainment, labor force participation, occupational status, and earnings in early adulthood."[17]

> *Fusionist conservatism has shown real*
> *economic results in those family businesses*
> *that successfully balance the pursuit*
> *of profit and the integrity of homes.*

Family businesses tend, as one might expect, to be family-friendly. Recent analysis shows how family businesses benefit society in ways that other businesses cannot. Because those who run family businesses seek more than merely financial profit, they can humanize a free-market economy. The large number of family enterprises in

Japan, for example, has helped to foster the benevolence and good-will that modify the effects of the profit motive. The consequence is that Japanese industry is much less of "a cut-throat jungle" than it would be in the absence of these family enterprises. In the family-owned Cadbury company, historians see a flat contradiction to Marxist theorizing about how capitalist employers invariably exploit employees. In this family business, a spirit of "benevolence without autocracy prevailed" in ways that "tempered capitalism" by maintaining good-will and solidarity in an environment in which "workers had the first claim on their employers' benevolence." Business analysts also fail to find evidence of the oft-assumed profit-kinship conflicts inherent in family business. Rather, their investigation reveals that family members working for small family businesses are satisfied with their careers and remarkably committed to their employment. Quite simply, working in a family business offers "more advantages than disadvantages."[18]

Unless guided by other ideals, corporations
seek cheap labor wherever it can be found and
an end to all home production. The whetting
of appetites commonly takes precedence over
family integrity in corporate advertising.

Globalization can be a danger to a family-centered social order. Anthropologists interpret the conversion of the entire world into "a global factory" as a new strategy developed by corporate leaders seeking cheap and relatively impotent labor. American industrial unions have lost much of their former strength because corporations have successfully converted capital mobility into a "new lever" of advantage. Cultural and economic analysis traces the "festering contradiction of modern womanhood" to the "displacement of crafts," which denied homemakers their traditional productive role by converting them into mere consumers in the capitalist market. Business analysts trace the displacement of community-based values to the triumph of exchange-based corporate values that intensify economic competition, so creating areas of high unemployment.

These exchange-based strategies are designed to satisfy shareholders, not to serve the community as a whole. As American and British corporations move many operations to Asia, Eastern Europe, and elsewhere, the middle class has contracted. Indeed, the median income in 1994 of an American family with two children was 33 percent lower (in inflation-adjusted dollars) than it was in 1973. As more and more U.S. corporations "go global," more American workers will lose their jobs even as more peasants in other countries lose their lands to technologically-driven agriculture. U.S. taxpayers continue to subsidize this process through corporate tax breaks. One analyst highlights the ways in which corporate giants are shedding millions of jobs in the United States and outsourcing production to countries such as Bangladesh or India. Corporations are thus shifting income from workers to investors, while shifting costs from investors to communities. Social disintegration—including family disintegration—is inevitable.[19]

> *We point to an inherent dilemma in capitalism:*
> *the short-term interest of corporations in*
> *weak homes and universal adult employment*
> *versus the long-term interest of national*
> *economies in improved human capital.*

The flashpoint here is the employment of mothers. Data collected for middle-class grade school students show that "the more hours that mothers worked, the lower the children's grades and the poorer their work habits and efforts." What is more, "as mothers worked more hours . . . the children displayed less resilience, resourcefulness, and adaptability in the classroom." Another investigation found that "children of employed mothers, regardless of the mother's occupation, have somewhat lower probabilities of graduating from high school and college than do children of nonemployed mothers. The children of the average employed mother also have somewhat lower chances of going to college than do the children of nonemployed mothers." This pattern of educational disadvantage for the children of employed mothers holds for all but the children of very highly placed professional mothers.[20]

Academic data for 13,881 students show that children perform worse in mathematics if their mothers are employed full-time than if their mothers are employed only part-time or not at all. The researcher interprets this pattern as evidence that maternal employment adversely affects "the amount of social capital available to the child." Statistical analysis also demonstrates that a mother's market work has a "significant negative effect" on her children's school performance. The analyst regards this finding as evidence of a conflict between "a market career for women" on the one hand and "enhanced child development" on the other. Indeed, a demographer suggests that the rising level of employment for married women and the concomitant erosion of men's employment status means "the unraveling of America's social heritage."[21]

Movement of married women into wage competition with men also means the end of a family model premised on "specialization and exchange," a model in which women specialized on home production and their husbands concentrated on employment for wages. The new family model based on economic androgyny translates into low fertility and marital instability. Furthermore, economist Jennifer Roback Morse argues that a society full of *homines economici* cannot turn infants into the fully formed and moral adults necessary to sustain a healthy social order. Only the loving family sufficiently transcends economic imperatives to rear adults fit for ordered liberty.[22]

We marvel at fresh inventions that portend
novel bonds between home and work.

Computer-centered work at home portends a better future. White-collar workers who avail themselves of telecommuting technology in order to work at home generally feel they are better able to balance family and work responsibilities than do office-based peers. Many home-based telecommuters feel their arrangement reduces home-work conflicts and allows them to draw closer to their children or grandchildren by spending more time with them, particularly at critical junctures in the day (such as when children first return home from school). Survey and interview data collected from teleworkers employed in three Canadian organizations provide further evidence supporting a "positive" assessment of the impact of teleworking on family-work relationships. The teleworkers in the study report that starting teleworking significantly reduced the number of problems they experienced in managing family time. Finally, survey data from IBM telecommuters indicate that the majority of teleworkers judge their arrangement to be beneficial for family life. Many favor the arrangement because it allows them "to be with their children more frequently and in a wider range of activities."[23]

We are inspired by a convergence of religious
truth and the evidence of science.

A new president of the American Sociological Association hails the emergence of fresh "theoretical intersections" connecting religion and social science, identifying the study of family structures as one of the places that these new intersections hold particular promise. Important pioneering work in the new synthesis of social science and religion can be seen in research by Catholic sociologists who have devoted themselves to methodologies and perspectives that harmonize with the tenets of their faith. Indeed, sociologists of the family are increasingly turning to religion as an interpretive grid for family research, opening "a bright future for religion and family research." Though himself skeptical of religious metaphysics, even sociobiologist E.O. Wilson sees religion serving a vital biological function by reinforcing "allegiance to tribe and family." Thus "God's will . . . coincides with Darwinian fitness."[24]

Today's young people were born into
a culture of self-indulgence, of
abortion, a culture embracing death.

Too many of the young have been indoctrinated in an anti-family worldview. Sociologist Daniel Spicer identifies in the linkage of permissive attitudes toward pre-marital sex, non-traditional gender roles, and abortion, "a web of linked and interdependent deep-seated beliefs." These attitudes are not discrete and separable but rather part of a distinct "worldview." In data collected by an inter-university consortium, researchers identify a pattern connecting feminist attitudes toward gender roles and family life with higher approval of abortion, less support for childbearing, and more approval of suicide.[25]

More than all generations before, today's
young people have known the divorce of parents.

Divorce hits children with particular force. Data collected between 1968 and 1997 shows that the probability of fathers' nonresidence with their children doubled during this period. Caused by rising rates of divorce and out-of-wedlock childbearing, most of the startling rise in the probability of paternal nonresidence occurred during the late 1970s and the 1980s, leveling off since then. Because of some lacunae in their data, the researchers admit that the risk of father-child separation may not have actually stabilized during the 1990s and may actually be higher than their results show. U.S. census data also reveal a dramatic rise in the percentage of children living in a one-parent or a non-parental household. In 1960, just 12 percent of all American children (7.8 million out of 63.7 million) lived in a one-parent or a non-parental home. In sharp contrast, in 2003, 30 percent of all American children (22.1 million out of 73.0 million) lived in a one-parent or a non-parental home.[26]

Today's young people have lived
too often without fathers.

Fatherlessness spreads like a plague. According to the America Academy of Pediatrics, "paternal absence" is predictive of "multiple and sometimes lifelong disadvantages" that go far beyond "health problems" to include "problems with school attendance, achievement and completion; emotional and behavioral problems; adolescent parenthood; substance abuse; and other risk behaviors." The predominance of female-headed households is also statistically "associated with a particular ecology in which children and adolescents do not thrive." This unhealthy social ecology fosters high rates of infant mortality and juvenile delinquency and low rates of academic achievement and high school completion.

Social historian David Courtwright identifies the disappearance of married fathers from the inner city as "the root cause" of the sharp rise in violent crime among young inner-city black males during the latter half of the twentieth century. Because of the "breakdown in the familial mechanisms for controlling young men," Courtwright sees in the modern inner city the very same social pathology which once made America's western mining camps and cowtowns "the most tumultuous region of the expanding nation." But whereas intact marriages and social fatherhood finally came to and pacified the western frontier, they seem to be disappearing from "the riptide of modern history."[27]

For example, the disappearance of fathers pushes more and more households into poverty. As welfare reform moved single parents into employment in a strong economy, the poverty rate in single-parent families fell from 51 to 44 percent, after factoring in the effects of the Earned Income Tax Credit, between 1995 and 2000. The poverty rate remained above 40 percent, however, because of "the biggest underlying source of poverty and insecurity for single-parent families: the family must generally rely on the earning of one person—typically a low-skilled woman—for support." What is more, concerns remain about "what full-time work may mean for children if mothers would prefer to be caring for their children." In the final analysis, "the best solution [to the problems of single-parent families] might be to find a way to reduce the incidence of single-parent families in the first place."[28]

Adolescent boys reared in the absence of fathers are especially likely to end up in custody. In data collected between 1979 and 1994 for 2,846 young men, researchers limn a strong link between youth incarceration risk and father-absence. Even in statistical analyses that take into account household income and residential permanence, sons reared in mother-only families are nearly two times as likely to be incarcerated as peers from mother-father families. The risk that adolescent boys and girls will engage in early sexual experimentation is also affected by family structure on two levels. First, adolescents (male and female) are especially likely to engage in early sex if they are themselves being reared in a single-parent or step-parent home. Second, the likelihood that adolescents will engage in early sex increases as the percentage of single-mother homes in the area rises. The researchers theorize that "the prevalence of single-mother families among friends and classmates and the lack of responsible and successful male role models may socialize youth to view early sexual behavior as expected and of little consequence."[29]

The sense of alarm grows. A pediatrician reports that inner-city children living in households headed by single mothers suffer with intolerable frequency from diseases (such as bacterial meningitis, rheumatic fever, and iron-deficiency anemia), neglect, abuse, crime, and homelessness. Economists at the Institute for Research on Poverty also identify the sharp increase in the number of single-parent families since 1970 ("the great majority" being mother-only families) as a prime reason that "the economic position of the working poor has stagnated or declined" in recent decades.[30]

*Today's young people are the victims of a kind
of cultural rape: seduced into early sexual
acts, then pushed into sterility.*

Two sociologists of the family lament the cultural triumph of the "greedy organism of the self," a triumph fostered by a "therapeutic individualism" legitimizing personal self-indulgence. Inevitably, such a cultural dynamic entails a "devaluation of children" because of the "restriction on one's freedom" that comes with childrearing. This unhealthy cultural dynamic encourages young adults to keep "control over [their] life and [their] time" by remaining childless.

Demographers investigating the "fertility crisis" in the industrialized world see anti-natal pressures in a global economy, which surround potential parents with "the almost limitless temptations of the modern consumerist society" but which endow children with "no immediate economic value [for] their parents." These investigators also emphasize the effects of "post-modern values" that foster non-marital sexuality but not marital childbearing. And these values have consequences. In interviews conducted in 1993, the majority of two hundred women in New England colleges expressed a desire to marry and have a family. In follow-up interviews seven years later, the majority of these women (now approaching thirty) were still single and childless.[31]

7

Introspection and Confession

Two decades after conservative Christians charged into the political arena, bringing new voters and millions of dollars with them in the hopes of transforming the culture through political power, it must now be acknowledged that we have failed. We failed not because we were wrong about our critique of culture, or because we lacked conviction, or because there were not enough of us, or because too many were lethargic and uncommitted. We failed because we were unable to redirect a nation from the top down. Real change must come from the bottom up or, better yet, from the inside out.

Cal Thomas, *Blinded By Might:Can the Religious Right Save America?*, April 1999.

I believe that we probably have lost the culture war. . . . in terms of society in general, we have lost. This is why, even when we win in politics, our victories fail to translate into the kind of policies we believe are important. . . . I know that what we have been doing for thirty years hasn't worked, that while we have been fighting and winning in politics, our culture has decayed into something approaching barbarism. We need to take another tack, find a different strategy.

Paul Weyrich, open letter to the social conservative movement, February 16, 1999.

We have failed. Our side, the "pro-family," "conservative," "traditional" side, has failed in our collective attempt to hold at bay the advancement of organized homosexuality. The "gay rights" movement has proceeded relatively unabated . . . and in precisely the arenas where we, the self-proclaimed political leaders of traditional Americans, have made it a point to engage the problem. We have failed *not* because we are any less intelligent, any less sophisticated, or any less committed than our opponents. . . . It is time we look in the mirror and ask ourselves some tough questions, not the least of which is, what is the world getting for all our investment?

Paul T. Mero, "Where We Stand," *Center Point* paper, The Howard Center for Family, Religion, and Society, June 1998.

THESE JUDGMENTS all came in the late 1990s, during the dot-com investment frenzy, the sex scandals and impeachment of President Clinton, and the unraveling of the Newt Gingrich "revolution" in the U.S. Congress. Do these judgments still hold?

One could possibly paint a brighter picture today. In retrospect, 1996 had brought two important changes in public policy that have had significant effects on the family. Tax reform that year implemented the new child tax credit, then $400 per child; today, it's $1,000 per child. This proved to be a significant step toward protecting family income and autonomy. Congress also embraced welfare reforms which reduced the incentives to out-of-wedlock births that were driving the growth of a fatherless underclass.

The optimist could list other recent positive developments. The "covenant marriage" idea has been implemented in several states, and may mark the beginning of the end of "no-fault" divorce. Steps have been taken to reduce the "marriage penalty" in federal tax law. The administration of George W. Bush has put persons with solid pro-family credentials in key posts at the Department of Health and Human Services and the State Department. U.S. ambassadors to key United Nations committees have largely brought a halt to anti-family initiatives there. Federal judges with apparent pro-family sentiments have won confirmation to key courts, notably John Roberts and Samuel Alito on the U.S. Supreme Court. We celebrate these gains.

All the same, we sense that darker currents are still at work in our time, and that recent victories have done little to counter the deeper sweep of change. In the United States, the marriage rate continues to fall. The proportion of new babies born out of wedlock rises again. Pornography, once confined to urban back allies, now pours into homes through the internet, creating a terrible new kind of addiction. "Family homes," defined by the presence of both a married couple and children, now comprise less than 25 percent of all American households.

Most dramatically, the "gay rights" campaign moves from legal victory to victory. Pro-family successes in state referenda that define marriage as only between a man and a woman obscure the more important change. Homosexuality has won cultural and legal acceptance as a legitimate lifestyle. Homosexuals can adopt children in most states. Schools commonly teach the gay agenda. Sodomy enjoys constitutional protection. Even the proposed Federal Marriage Amendment would allow states to craft registered partnerships for homosexual couples. In Europe, "gay marriage" spreads even into historically Catholic lands such as Spain.

In brief, Western culture still appears to be in decline, affecting the United States and many other nations. Secularization, the sexual revolution, the impact of industrialization, and the pressure of anti-family ideologies have all contributed to this decline. The iconic figures are there: from Charles Darwin and Karl Marx to Havelock Ellis and Sigmund Freud to Margaret Sanger and Margaret Mead to Alfred Kinsey and Hugh Hefner to Alva Myrdal and Paul Ehrlich. The "culture war" is not new. We are simply in a new phase.

Is such decline irreversible? As with radioactive substances, do all cultures possess a half-life? If so, then there would be no such thing as "failure" among those defending traditional culture. They would simply be playing out their pre-determined part. Yet if decline is not inevitable, then success would be defined by more than good deeds or good intentions.

For about thirty years, the contemporary "pro-family" movement has confronted an unrelenting onslaught of immorality, even depravity. The movement has fought tirelessly and valiantly. It has some victories to show for its efforts. And yet, in the larger context, it is losing—*we* are losing.

The Natural Family: A Manifesto rejects the idea of cultural, as much as economic, determinism. It rests on the premise that truths about morality, life, and purpose are unchanging. It holds that men and women—in any time or age—enjoy personal agency. They can make choices. They can strive to be better persons and to build a better culture. Renewal—personal and familial as well as cultural—is possible.

With this said, we believe it important to note certain mistakes within the movement—our movement—that have limited its effectiveness. Believing in the need for introspection, we ourselves confess to these weaknesses; we name no others.

Too often, individual ambitions and squabbles
have prevented movement success.

Authentic cultural renewal begins within individual families and in small communities. It cannot be accomplished through centralized institutions. For example, the educational renewal movement known as homeschooling began in hundreds of American kitchens, not in some grand building in the nation's capital. Showing a vital and pleasant anarchy, this movement has resisted all attempts at centralization, except for mechanisms of common legal defense.

To be effective, the "pro-family" movement needs to be decentralized as well. A presence in national capitols may be the last thing that we need. We should empower individual families to be informed and involved and then let them do their work.

Another error has been to strap our cause on the backs of personalities. A new form of worship spreads and people in the grassroots begin to look up to egos rather than in the mirror. An array of personal fiefdoms becomes the standing temptation. No one person makes or breaks any healthy movement. A victorious coalition is broad-based and equitable in its responsibilities and expectations. Our most successful efforts, such as stopping passage of the Equal Rights Amendment, occurred out in the states and involved legions of able volunteers. Phyllis Schlafly was the historical hero here. And she always acknowledged the more vital role of her grassroots colleagues and friends.

The essential problem is similar to the one faced by America's founding fathers. The "central government" must be capable, but limited. So should the organization of the pro-family movement. National bodies should provide a cohesive worldview and opportunities for learning, networking, and service. Nevertheless, the real work ought to be done in homes, neighborhoods, and small communities. To adapt a phrase, let a thousand initiatives blossom.

A narrowness of vision has led, at times, to a focus on petty questions, while the truly important battles have been ignored, and so lost by default.

Too many times, we have actually become the caricature of ourselves that is painted by our foes: partisan, uncaring, authoritarian, and greedy. In playing the game of politics, we have squandered credibility and respect. We have sometimes allowed the wholly unreasonable to occur in order to appear more compassionate and humane. In defense of "traditional culture," we have too often sounded arrogant, cold, and old-fashioned.

Part of the problem arises from the projection of private lives into public policy. Most people cannot separate the two. Unfortunately, public policy becomes distorted when citizens make their own lives a justification for dubious laws. Thus, someone who has gone through a rough divorce is likely to support divorce reforms designed to make divorce easy. Or a parent with a homosexual child might afterwards support public policies that legitimize or justify homosexuality. We make the same mistake when we project without caution our private religious beliefs onto public life, or when our own rhetoric adopts the language of moral crusade, or where we project our private lives as a public model.

We care that a man and a woman marry and bear children not because we want to impose our opinions on others but because this fosters social health. We are not telling people how to live; we are recognizing public policies that foster happiness, social peace, and prosperity. We are not imposing our preferences on others; we are trying to shape law and policy around normative arrangements justified by time and reinforced by biological and social sciences.

This is not to diminish the need for moral teaching or religious influence in society. To build an argument in terms of public policy or science is actually to enhance moral and religious argumentation. Not all persons think in a religious framework. We must use a language that the non-religious can understand. The burden is on us to help our neighbors understand the truth about the world's natural order, in ways that do not threaten them. Indeed, they should be inspired by our language.

We must also show them the distinction between the ideal and the real. We might, for instance, use a driving analogy. If you want to drive a car, you must follow the rules of the road. We are taught that the safest way to drive is to keep both hands on the steering wheel at all times, remain constantly alert to our circumstances, drive defensively, and obey all traffic laws. In truth, though, few of us live up to these expectations. We may drive with one hand on the steering wheel, talk on a cell phone, or drink a soda. We may exceed the speed limit. Add children in the backseat to the mix, and our falling short of the ideal is magnified once again.

So why do we hold on to such unrealistic expectations? Surely it would be easier to adjust the rules of the road to the actual driving experience? Yet we do not, for the predictable result would be more accidents, more deaths, more misery. Good public policy reflects ideal—not real world—driving behavior.

The same is true for public policy affecting marriage and family. We raise up the ideal of the natural family as dictated by human experience, knowing full well that no one will ever consistently achieve that ideal. When we ourselves fall short, when troubles afflict our family lives, it is not because we are hypocrites. It is because we are human.

This also frames the limits of public policy. The detailed regulation of someone's private life is not a matter of public policy, even when we foresee the trainwreck ahead. We might—and perhaps ought to—try to intervene privately. However, to maintain the delicate balance between personal liberty and community interests, we urge caution in applying the coercive powers of the state in private life.

We in the pro-family movement must understand this caution, even if our opponents do not. As matters of public policy, we care that men and women marry, bear children, and avoid divorce. But we should not care—in terms of public policy—why they marry, or whether they have a proper education about marriage, or (with a few obvious exceptions) how they rear their children, or how they manage their day-to-day conflicts. These are private matters, best left to the freedom we afford families to direct their own destinies.

We must also constantly remember that laws cannot turn around a nation. A good law is a reflection of a healthy culture. While the Supreme Court's decision in *Roe v. Wade* saddled the nation with abortion-on-demand, the truth is that wide sectors of the population welcomed the ruling. Even some prominent Christian conservatives of the era praised the *Roe* decision as a victory for religious liberty. Only Roman Catholic bishops vigorously dissented at the time.

Fighting now for new pro-life and pro-family Supreme Court justices is important, not least in the hope that *Roe* might be overturned. Still, all the pro-life justices in the nation will not overturn that decision if the nation's prevailing morality holds that abortion on demand is justified. The failed, if well-intentioned, efforts to prohibit the production and sale of alcohol in the United States pose a solid, even sobering example here. Our first priorities need to be reinforcing the structures of civil society and renewing a culture of marriage and family.

*Strategic thinking and bold moves that could
transform key debates have been undone by timidity
on the part of leaders and funders.*

We tell a true story here, withholding names. In 1997, two well-respected foundations, founded by well-meaning Christians, gathered dozens of America's pro-family leaders for a private summit to create a unified strategy to combat the encroaching anti-family culture. Many meetings convened over two years. The original gathering of fifty persons was whittled down to an executive committee of eight. Its task was to draft a strategic plan which would then be presented to the larger group and the foundations for approval and action.

Alas, the strategic plan never saw the light of day, let alone implementation. In place of a coherent strategy there emerged a ramshackle arrangement of individual projects. Indeed, the only unified aspect of the effort was a shared glee over the hope and promise of money for the individual projects.

Along the way, the committee *did* consider three revealing suggestions. The first was that the pro-family movement focus on what it stands for, not what it opposes. Over the previous three decades, we had shown what we were against: homosexuality, feminism, pornography, sex education, and so on. We had opposed virtually every cultural shift and modernist innovation. What we had not done very well was to say what we stood for, and why.

This idea was shot down in committee. The sobering fact which several persons alluded to was that pro-family groups raise money because of what they oppose, not because of what they support. The proposed focus on affirming a pro-family culture cut into an array of organizations whose financial health required slaying dragons daily. There is money to be made in dispatching terrible beasts; but little money for affirming a culture in which the dragons could not or would not exist. The situation also demands an unrelenting search for new dragons.

The second suggestion was that the strategic plan adopt the positive theme of the family as the fundamental social unit. This proposal, too, fell like a lead balloon. Astonishingly, the primary objection to it was that the family was not, in reality, the fundamental unit of society. This role, as one committee member felt, and several others didn't disagree, rightly belongs to the individual. (Indeed, this episode suggests a significant philosophical incoherence within the movement.)

The third suggestion was to focus the strategy on influencing parents. Several committee members argued that parents were the real problem. Children, they said, were more conservative than their parents these days. The latter should be avoided. Efforts at change should focus on children, especially where they congregate most often, in the public schools.

To the credit of those behind the conclave, they knew instinctively that the old strategies had not worked and that they were hearing little that was new. To push the process along, the benefactors brought in an outside consulting firm to critique the movement. The firm's report was thorough. It held that (1) we have failed; (2) we have failed for specific reasons; (3) we must change our approach; and (4) many of the participating groups were incapable of changing their approach, and so became part of the problem.

The outside report was largely ignored. The ramshackle plan reappeared. The very patient and trusting benefactors placed seed money in the kitty. Efforts began to find broader financial support for the plan. None appeared. In less than six months, the seed money was gone. Everyone went their separate ways. A golden opportunity was lost.

We believe that any successful collaboration and cultural change will begin with a focus on what we are for, not what we oppose. It will affirm the natural family as the fundamental social unit as its guiding principle. And it will respect the primary role of parents in setting and maintaining healthy family structure.

Sustaining large institutions, rather than encouraging swift and effective agents, has been too common.

Having become acclimated to Washington, D.C., our movement has willy-nilly joined into the culture of contention, of partisanship. The preference is to fight, rather than to win. There must be an enemy, so that we are always right and they are always wrong; so that we are good and they are evil. And since evil cannot be persuaded, the contest can never end.

These pressures grew apparent in the work of the National Commission on Children, active between 1988 and 1991. Created by an act of Congress, the original outlook for a pro-family result from its work was dim. Of thirty-six members, a third would be appointed by the president of the United States, a third by the speaker of the House, and a third by the president pro-tem of the Senate. The latter two posts were held by Democrats, and they filled their twenty-four slots with modern liberalism's first team: the president of the National Education Association; the president of the American Federation of State, County, and Municipal Employees; the president of the Children's Defense Fund; the ambitious governor of Arkansas; and so on. The very liberal Jay Rockefeller, senator from West Virginia, became commission chairman.

The twelve Republican appointees of President Reagan's were generally less well known. And only seven or eight of them could be accurately labelled as in the pro-family camp. All the same, this small group did its homework. Its members attended the numerous hearings and working sessions. They befriended Senator Rockefeller and earned his trust. On several key issues, he even became a convert. When the left-leaning staff produced an early draft "final report" that subtly violated hard-won agreements, he rebuked the staff and told them to get it right. When the Democratic majority finally showed up en masse at the session where the Commission would vote on the final draft, they were appalled by the document they were presented. All the same, the senator took them into a closed room and twisted their collective arm.

The Democrats were appalled that a report they thought would focus on expanding government services for children instead focused on ways to strengthen families and empower parents. As Barbara Dafoe Whitehead of the Institute for American Values later explained: "The National Commission on Children's . . . major public policy proposal does not call for new or expanded services to children. The $1,000-per-child tax credit proposal both affirms parental responsibility and widens parental choice. By putting money into the hands of families themselves, the tax-credit empowers parents, not providers and bureaucrats." She continued: "The commission's 519-page final report is filled with the language of moral values. . . . this is not the official language of insider politics and legislative analysis. It is the everyday language of the kitchen table. . . . It is an important intellectual event that marks a major turn after decades of partisan wrangling over the relationship between cultural values and child well-being."[1]

Alas, as it turned out, others in the pro-family movement preferred a continuation of partisan wrangling. Intense pressure came from one large pro-family group to vote against the Report. Democrats could never do the right thing, it insisted. In order to keep up the intensity on which fund raising rested, there could be no victory. The quarrel was needed—not the win. Similar pressure for similar reasons also came from the White House of President George H.W. Bush. One pro-family commissioner who worked for this administration was told that he would be fired, "cut off" at his knees, and "never work in this town again" if he voted in favor of the Report.

While this story had a happy ending (despite the pressure, the Report won almost unanimous approval; the lone exception was the ambitious governor of Arkansas, who abstained), most others do not. Anyone who has been a lobbyist in Washington, D.C., soon learns the game. Your job security depends on keeping your clients in the hinterland in a constant state of fear: "Terrible things are about to happen here in Washington; only I can save you." The same is all too true for large organizations. Contention, not victory, is what the system thrives on.

Money, particularly "direct mail" money,
has become the measure of too many things.

The virtue of "direct mail" fundraising is that it can provide an organization with a reliable monthly revenue stream. And money, of course, is necessary for the functioning of any effective organization. All the same, it is the writing of direct mail copy that can turn otherwise genial people into the "bigots" that the other side so delights in mocking. Positive messages usually generate a poor return; fear sells.

It is also easy for money to trump mission. Pro-family groups are properly mission driven. But the very logic of direct mail requires that attention focus on the scariest issues, not the more important ones. Keeping the flow of money going can quickly become all-consuming. Mission disappears because it does not pay.

In the search for new funds, organizations sometimes draw in successful business leaders as trustees. Unfortunately, it sometimes happens that these business leaders intentionally put money before mission. That is what they do in their for-profit realm, a priority they fail to reverse in the non-profit domain. These well meaning business people might suppose that if a mission does not pay, then the mission is flawed. In consequence, we witness the push to place money ahead of mission. Ultimately, we see otherwise loyal adherents working unconsciously to undermine some very good organizations.

> *Doctrinal and sectarian differences on important,*
> *but tangential, questions have been allowed*
> *to obscure unity on the central issues of family*
> *and life. Our foes have celebrated as old fears*
> *and suspicions between religious groups have*
> *trumped potentially powerful new alliances.*

In some fundamental ways, America has been blessed by religious peace and cooperation. The religious clauses in the federal consti-

tution ban religious tests for public office, protect the free exercise
of religion, and prohibit the favoring of any one sect over others.
The result has been an astonishing flowering of denominations and
the continued strength of religious belief and behavior, long after
secularism has come to dominate most other Western nations.

All the same, profound divisions continue to trouble efforts
at inter-faith cooperation in defense of the family. Forty years
ago, prominent Baptists and evangelicals applauded U.S. Supreme
Court decisions overturning state laws that had prohibited the sale
of contraceptives (*Griswold*) and abortion (*Roe*). They saw these
laws as "Catholic" issues.

Today, conservative evangelicals and Baptists hold a much more
positive view of Catholic natural law doctrine and have become
aggressively pro-life on the abortion question (the contraception
issues remain more problematic). Other forms of pro-family cooperation between Catholics and conservative Protestants have
grown as well.

On occasions, the collaboration has spread further. During the
1990s, for example, American Catholics and evangelicals joined
in a pro-family coalition at the United Nations that also included
Latter-day Saints (Mormons) and even Muslims. They successfully blocked UN efforts to make abortion and sodomy guaranteed
human rights. The definition of the natural family adopted in
Rome in May 1998, came from a group representing Catholics,
Evangelicals, Lutherans, Mormons, Jews, Muslims, and even a
Unitarian. The World Congress of Families II, held the following
year in November, marked the high point of this cooperation.

Since the events of 9-11, though, this alliance has faltered.
Old suspicions have returned. Theological questions that divide
have taken precedence over the common interest in defending the
natural family.

Our foes are never more cheerful than when old religious bigotries and fears rear up again, sowing discord in the pro-family ranks. Their opportunities for building a post-family order hostile to homes and children are never greater than when religious peoples let those things which divide them triumph over that which unites.

> *The initiative on most questions
> has been left to the other side.*

The pro-family cause also falls prey to an obligatory optimism. The unspoken rule is that we shall never admit failure. We can go down in flaming defeat on an issue, and this obligatory optimism prevents any learning from our mistakes or humble admissions that our approach might have been wrong. Our tendency is to sit back, smile, and say: "What do you expect? We were up against the liberal media as well as [pick your enemy]."

This has led to a false impression of effectiveness. As a consequence of our failure in political efforts, we constantly redefine success. For example, consider where we are on the issue of gay rights. Twenty years ago, the U.S. Supreme Court gave us the *Hardwick* decision upholding state anti-sodomy laws—a huge political victory. A year later, in 1987, we won again with a Congressional prohibition on the use of tax dollars to promote homosexuality.

In 1988, however, the omnibus "Ryan White" bill became law, undoing our victory the prior year. Federal funds to support the gay agenda began flowing. The Hate Crimes bill came next. For the first time, federal law equated "sexual orientation" with traditional suspect classes of people, along the lines of the Civil Rights Act of 1964. Also for the first time, President George H. W. Bush invited homosexual activists to the White House for the signing of the bill. Starting in 1993, the Clinton Administration partly opened the U.S. military to homosexuals ("Don't Ask, Don't Tell"); through regulatory acts, it completely opened the civil service ranks. In 1994, Congress again approved federal funds to support the gay agenda on a 234 to 194 vote (seven years earlier, *only forty-seven votes* were in favor, compared to 368 opposed). Our last redoubt, or line of defense, is now marriage; the chosen vehicle a constitutional amendment to restrict marriage to a man and a woman. Even here, though, we have yet to win even a simple majority in the Senate, let alone the sixty-seven votes needed.

Meanwhile, the U.S. Supreme Court affirmed the enigma of "sexual orientation" in its *Romer* decision, striking down a Colorado measure that had denied special status to homosexuals. A defense of the natural family now leaned toward "animus." Compounding this extraordinary shift was the Court's *Lawrence* decision in 2002, where it held that objections to homosexuality are "irrational." Through the same logic, sodomy became a protected constitutional right.

Many hope that the new "Roberts Court" will make a difference. Perhaps so. We fear, though, that it will at best slow the pace of change and not reverse the broad rights and privileges bestowed on "the gay community" and their diverse sexual allies over the last two decades.

The truth hurts. If we were a business, we would be bankrupt. If we were a sports team, we would be in last place. Obligatory optimism blinds us from confronting our string of losses, and looking for new approaches.

What might make a difference? One model of action that we raise up is the World Congress of Families. It recognizes that the battle in which we are engaged is universal in scale, but requires solutions only found in the hearts of persons of good will. It serves as a rallying center for the world's family systems grounded in religious faith. Confronting the militant secular individualism and the moral anarchy that has swept over the Western world, it fosters an international network of pro-family organizations, scholars, and cultural and political leaders who work to restore the natural family as the fundamental social unit. It affirms and builds a positive united front among the family-centered religious peoples, notably Christians, Jews, and Muslims.

The Congress also works to shift the terms of key public debates, with a focus on what we are for replacing a focus on what we oppose:

- We celebrate the creation of large families as special gifts (instead of "opposing abortion and population control").

- We raise up the Natural Family as the source of social renewal and progress (instead of "opposing new family forms").

- We proclaim religious orthodoxy to be the source of humane values and cultural progress (instead of "opposing secularism").

Another way of explaining the World Congress of Families (WCF) is to clarify both what it *is* and what it *is not*:

- The WCF *is not* a structure seeking to unify the world's pro-family and pro-life organizations under its guidance and control. It *is* a practical effort to build greater understanding and encourage informal networks among family advocates at the national and international levels.

- The WCF *is not* an "ecumenical" campaign seeking to advance its agenda by doctrinal compromise. It *is* a coalition of the most orthodox believers within each denomination, church, or faith group, persons who are the least likely to compromise on their core beliefs.

- The WCF *is not* an effort at crafting "one-world religion." It *is* a venue where religiously-grounded family systems can respond together in a positive manner to the global spread of a militant secularism that threatens the liberties and existence of all vital faiths.

- The WCF *is not* a massive organization with visions of power and permanence. It *is* a project currently coordinated by a small organization; it will continue only so long as it proves helpful to others and to the defense of the natural family.

The record of the first three congresses suggests that this model works. For example, the World Congress has already altered key terms of debate. The phrase, "traditional family," with its aura of "old-fashioned," is being replaced in national and world debates by "natural family," with its aura of energy. This has occurred globally.[2] Closer to home, American groups ranging from the Church of God to the American Legion have formally embraced the new terminology, and have used it as a basis for action.

Changing the terms of debate is the first step toward any moral, intellectual, and political victory. The World Congress of Families model has taken that step.

8

A Natural Family Policy

INSPIRED BY IDEALS, informed by science, our manifesto also lays out an agenda, a platform of action, a true family policy fit for the twenty-first century. While forward looking, our broad scheme draws inspiration from historical figures and proven political foundations.

We look to the example of Louis de Bonald, who stands for us as a hero. He confronted the social extremists of the French Revolution, denouncing proposed reforms that would weaken marriage and encourage divorce. As he explained in his 1801 book *On Divorce*, marriage was "natural" in a particular sense: "[I]t derives from the constitution of our being, of our nature, and is a natural act: for the true nature of man and the real constitution of his being consists in natural relationships with his being's author, and in natural relationships, both moral and physical, with his fellows."[1] He lost the argument in that year. In the wake of Napoleon's defeat, though, he led the successful effort to repeal the equivalent of "no-fault" divorce, restoring authority to the natural family.

We also look to the example of Edmund Burke. He, too, opposed the social radicalism of the French Revolution. He also affirmed the true foundations of ordered liberty, finding them in the web of association that gives purpose and direction to the individual. As he wrote in his 1791 *Reflections on the French Revolution*: "To be attached to the subdivision, to love the little platoon we belong to in society, is the first principle (the germ as it were) of public affections. It is the first link in the series by which we proceed toward a love to our country and to mankind. The interest of that portion of social arrangement is a trust in the hands of all those who compose it; and as none but bad men would justify it in abuse, none but traitors would barter it away for their own personal advantage."[2] These "little platoons" include villages, religious societies, colleges, and neighborhoods. However, it is the family resting on conjugal fidelity and fecundity that forms, energizes, and renews all the others.

We draw inspiration, as well, from the Dutch cleric and political leader of the late nineteenth century Abraham Kuyper. We share his analysis of the legacy of the French Revolution, an event which "proved to be not just a change in *regime* but a change of system, of political organization, of general human *theory*. In place of the worship of the most high God came, courtesy of Humanism, the worship of *man*. Human destiny was shifted from heaven to earth. . . . And *emancipation* became the watchword by which people tampered with the bond of marriage, with the respect children owe their parents, with the moral seriousness of our national manners."[3]

We also share Kuyper's concern over the imperialism of the industrial principle, which—if left to itself—seeks to intrude into all areas of life, including family relations: "So must everything become uniform, level, flat, homogenous, monotonous. No longer should each baby drink warm milk from the breast of its own mother; we should have some tepid mixture prepared for all babies collectively. No longer should each child have a place to play at home with its mother; all should go to a common nursery school."[4]

As did Kuyper, we call on nations to honor religion so as to protect "our standard of human life." We affirm freedom of conscience and religious liberty. We seek the restoration of "organic relations." This need not necessarily be with all the details found in, say, 1788 or 1957. However, it should be "on the basis of the family." And we urge that "the spirit of the Compassionate" fill public life, so that "our legislation may show a *heart* and officialdom some sympathy for suffering citizens; that powerless labor may be protected from coolly calculating corporate power; and that even the poorest citizen may count on the prospect of swift and sound justice."[5]

In addition, our policy prescriptions rest on the closely related principles of federalism and subsidiarity. Federalism dictates that political power should be divided between a central authority and smaller political units, such as provinces, states, cities, and townships. This division of powers marks each entity as both co-ordinate with and independent of the others, so that no one authority can claim the same level of power as found in a unitary state. Subsidiarity has received fullest expression in Catholic social teaching. As Pope John Paul II explained in the 1991 encyclical *Centesimus Annus*: "The 'principle of subsidiarity' must be respected. 'A community of a higher order should not interfere with the life of a community of a lower order, taking over its functions.' In case of need it should, rather, support the smaller community and help to coordinate its activity with activities in the rest of society for the sake of the common good." And at the base of this pyramid of small communities we find, once again, the natural family.

LESSONS LEARNED

Our platform also builds on lessons learned from past episodes of family reconstruction. Notably, we admire the achievements of the American family model in the middle decades of the twentieth century. Between 1935 and 1965, the marriage rate climbed, the marital birthrate soared, the divorce rate fell after 1946, and measures of familial happiness rose. And yet, as noted in chapter 1, this renewal disintegrated over the next fifteen years.

Part of this failure can be attributed to the ideological assaults—feminist, Marxist, neo-Malthusian, "Playboy-ist"—that mobilized against the breadwinner/homemaker/child-rich family model. All the same, we see weaknesses that left the restored American family of the mid-twentieth century vulnerable.

- The new suburban family rested on an assumption of the "companionate" model of marriage, which emphasized psychological tasks such as "personality adjustment" and exaggerated gender roles (for example, the role of the "glamour girl" for wives[6]) to the exclusion of true complementarity and meaningful household functions.

- Homemaking women and adolescents were increasingly isolated in suburban developments without viable central places for the building of healthy community.

- Breadwinning men engaged in long commutes and were often only occasional figures in their homes.

- After 1945, policy-making elites failed to recognize America's mid-century family policy achievements, leaving them vulnerable. Specifically, when the "family wage" concept came under challenge, few were able or willing to defend it.

- African Americans never fully entered the family model of the 1950s, a failure ably dissected in Daniel P. Moynihan's famed 1965 report *The Negro American Family: The Case for National Action.*[7]

- Certain "internal contradictions" within the Social Security system also emerged, including disincentives to bear children and a hostility to direct intergenerational care.

- And the "family wage" scheme of the 1950s proved too rigid to accommodate complex human circumstances.

We need to do better.

Our platform also draws on recent examples of successful family policy. Starting in the *mid-1970s*, for instance, a growing number of American parents—for various reasons—turned to homeschooling. At first, they faced hostile state authorities: some were arrested, and some briefly imprisoned for seeking to reclaim this pre-modern family task. Yet the home education movement grew, and by the early 1990s had regained this natural right in all fifty states. By 2005, over two million American children were in home schools. The educational results have been impressive. More significant, though, are the social effects. Virtually all home-schooled students are in married-couple homes. And 77 percent of homeschooling mothers do not work for pay, compared to 30 percent of all mothers nationwide. Importantly, the fertility of these families is substantially higher than that of other families.

Sixty-two percent have three or more children, compared to only 20 percent nationwide. And slightly over a third (33.5 percent) have four or more children, compared to a mere 6 percent in all homes with children.[8] By rejecting "modern" state education, and by embracing "pre-modern" approaches, these American families have grown stronger and larger.

Second, about twenty years ago America also *re*discovered an alternative to state child allowances and paid parental leave, an approach that has a positive fertility effect. Specifically, after two decades of neglect, the U.S. Congress in 1986 nearly doubled the value of the personal income tax exemption for children to $2,000 per child, and indexed its value to inflation. Repeated studies have found that European child allowances—paid by the state to mothers as a monthly stipend for each of their children—have little positive effect on fertility. However, in the U.S., there is strong evidence of a "robust" positive relationship between the real, after-inflation value of the tax exemption for children and family size. Economist Leslie Whittington has actually calculated an astonishing elasticity of birth probability with respect to the income tax exemption of between .839 and 1.31. This means that a one percent increase in the exemption's real value results in about a one percent increase in birth probability in families.[9]

Why this difference? It appears that allowing families to keep more of what they earn while raising children—that is, turning children into little tax shelters—has a positive, even life-affirming psychological effect on parents that money coming from the state cannot replicate. In any case, a significant increase in overall American fertility coincides with the increase in the exemption's value in 1986. More recently, the rise in marital fertility, starting in 1996, correlates precisely with the introduction of a new, additional child tax credit that year. In other words, pro-family tax cuts appear to work.

Our platform builds as well on relatively favorable cultural conditions. Americans stand almost alone among modern nations as a people bound to active religious faith, and active faith commonly translates into larger families. The American system, which encourages the free exercise of religion while prohibiting the formal establishment of a state religion, has encouraged stronger religious sentiments.[10] At the most dramatic level, some religious communities still on the margins of American life—the German-speaking Old Order Amish found in rural communities in twenty states, the Hutterites in Montana and North Dakota, and Hassidic Jews in New York, Cleveland, and other cities—continue to report average completed family size in excess of six children. In addition, the fertility rate of the state of Utah is nearly twice the national average, reflecting an average of about four births per woman among Latter-day Saints or Mormons. Surveys also show that "fundamentalist Protestants" and traditional "Latin Mass" Catholics who attend religious services at least once a week also record higher total fertility.[11]

Finally, Americans are generally held less hostage to the antinatal dogmas of pure "gender equality" than are the "Swedenized" Europeans. As the University of Virginia's Stephen Rhodes' book *Taking Sex Differences Seriously* reminds us, women and men are hardwired to be different. Denying these differences can only result in violations of human nature, doing particular harm to existing *and* potential children.[12] After decades of work by feminist ideologues to re-engineer human nature, some Americans remain resilient, open to the natural power of gender complementarity. For example, despite massive federal financial preferences and incentives for putting small children in day care, over 60 percent of new mothers avoid returning to full-time work and a third of young mothers still find ways to remain home full-time with their preschool children. And this proportion appears to be growing again.[13] Phillip Longman even sees a "return of patriarchy," rooted in the relative biological vigor of religious peoples.[14] The imperatives of biology, of human nature, are still active in the U.S.

A PRO-FAMILY FRAMEWORK

How might these lessons be applied in public policy?[15]

Marriage Policy

- Governments should re-introduce "fault" into laws governing divorce.

- States should treat marriage as a full economic partnership. In the United States, this would mean reintroducing full "income splitting" in the income tax, as existed between 1948 and 1963. Such a measure would eliminate the most notorious "marriage penalty."

Population Policy

- All governments should recognize that strong families commonly rest on religiously-grounded morality systems, which deserve autonomy and respect as vital aspects of civil society.

- States should welcome large families, created responsibly through marriage, as special gifts to society, deserving affirmation and encouragement.

- All national governments and international entities should underscore that the demographic problem facing the twenty-first century is depopulation, not overpopulation.

Domestic Policy

- Income tax exemptions for children and child tax credits should be greatly expanded, indexed to inflation, and made universally available to families.

- Agencies promoting population control and diminution (such as Title x of the Public Health Services Act in the United States) should be shut down.

Infant and Toddler Care

- State subsidies and credits for daycare should also be available to parents who care for their preschoolers full-time, at home. A tax credit for this purpose should be refundable to those parents without the income to claim the full credit, allowing for a reduction in means-tested government daycare subsidies.

Education of the Young

- Home education should be protected. All relevant governments should reform their compulsory education laws along the model of the American state of Alaska, where any child is exempted who "is being educated in the child's home by a parent or legal guardian." This law precludes registration, reporting, or curricular requirements.

- Educational diversity should be encouraged in ways that reinforce family autonomy and school independence. "Tuition tax credits" are too narrow in their focus, giving no reception to home-educating families. "Vouchers" tend to make private and religious schools dependent on state funds, open these institutions to potential regulation, and subtly erode the virtues of personal and familial sacrifice, which are key to the success of independent schools.

- In place of vouchers, other measures deserve attention:

  - Per-capita child tax deductions and credits, without any link to schooling, should be preferred at all government levels; and

  - New tax credits on all forms of educational expense (including books, fees, tuition, and special lessons) should be created, with an Illinois law allowing a credit of 20 percent on such expenses up to five hundred dollars per year as a model; or

  - All educational expenses (from preschool fees and homeschooling expenses to university tuition) could be treated as an investment in human capital, logically enjoying full income tax deductability.

- To restore educational liberty and neighborhood integrity, all state school systems should be deconsolidated to single-school districts. These public schools, moreover, should be "open." Like an American community college, they should offer their learning and extra-curricula opportunities to all families in the district, but compel none. These schools would again be able to reflect the values of local communities and would have strong incentives to serve the neighborhood and its inhabitants.

Housing

- The need is to refunctionalize individual homes, abandoning governmental biases toward the frail "companionate model" of family home-design and opening urban, suburban, and rural life to a return of the "productive home." In the American setting, specific reforms would include:

  - Abolishing all mortgage underwriting rules that discourage the creation of home offices, home schools, and home businesses.

  - Ending those regulations of the professions—such as medicine, law, dentistry, and accounting—which favor giant institutions and prohibit decentralized learning through arrangements such as apprenticeships.

  - Loosening or abolishing zoning laws and restrictive covenants to allow the flourishing of home gardens, modest animal husbandry, home offices and businesses, and home schools.

Elder Care and the Bonds of the Generations

- True "intergenerational" reform would rebuild incentives that favor both childbearing and family-centered elder care, by restructuring incentives within the Medicare and Social Security systems. With America again as the example:

  - Taxpayers should be granted a credit of 20 percent against their total FICA (payroll) tax for each child born or adopted, a credit to be continued until the child reaches age thirteen. This would mean that a family with five children, ages twelve and under, would pay no FICA tax in that year (but would still receive all due employment credit).

- Taxpayers should be granted a 25 percent credit against their total FICA tax for each elderly parent or grandparent residing in the taxpayer's home.

- For each child born, a mother should receive three years (twelve quarters) of employment credits (calculated at the median full-time income) toward her future Social Security pension.

- A person should also receive one year's employment credit toward Social Security, at the same median income level, if he or she serves as the primary caregiver for an elderly relative residing in his or her home.

- Base FICA tax rates could be raised to accommodate these reforms at a revenue-neutral level (so shifting the tax burden onto those without children and/or refusing to care for their own); or the OASDI tax could be applied to all income and no longer capped off at incomes over $94,400 (as of 2006).

Child Welfare Policy

- All levels of government should protect parental rights in at least two ways: (1) laws and regulations should unequivocally endorse and reinforce the married, two-parent family as the fundamental unit of society, and (2) laws and regulations should unequivocally safeguard against the abuse of state power, particularly when it comes to terminating the constitutionally protected rights of parents.

- Of all the powers the state possesses in child welfare proceedings, the ability to terminate permanently the legal rights of parents is the ultimate and most drastic. Allowing the state to do so on grounds less than parental fault is inconsistent with the constitutional status of parental rights.

- This would mean that the court must find by clear and convincing evidence that the parent or parents have either abandoned, abused, substantially neglected the child or children, or are unfit or incompetent by reason of conduct or condition which is seriously detrimental to the child or children.

Divorce Policy

- Covenant marriage provides an attractive possibility for reform since it is voluntary for the parties involved. However, this also may mean that it is more likely to attract couples with a high level of commitment, whereas some couples who most need legal incentives to make their marriage work will not receive them. Other piecemeal reforms are also attractive, especially those that recognize the severe impact of divorce on children. These tend, however, to focus on modifying the way a divorce takes place, not discouraging a divorce in the first place.

- In the final analysis, only a forthright admission that no-fault divorce is detrimental for couples, children, and society will be truly effective. The corollary of this admission is that fault grounds need to be reintroduced into the law of marital dissolution. This will allow the law to serve as a check on unilateral divorce and ensure that marriages are not dissolved for frivolous or trivial reasons. It will also signal to prospective married couples that the law expects them to take seriously their commitments and that they ought to think deeply and prepare well before marrying. As it shifts cultural trends, it can also provide assurance for children that their families will not be shattered unless they are really at risk. Given research that indicates that, over time, even couples in unhappy marriages will eventually begin to appreciate their partner again and experience a happy marriage, a change in the divorce culture might enhance the individual happiness of adults.

- The best public policy on divorce would reintroduce fault grounds where a marriage is longstanding or where children are involved. Accordingly, irreconcilable difference should not be grounds for divorce if: (1) there are living minor children of the marriage; or (2) the parties have been married ten years or longer; or (3) one of the spouses contests the divorce.

Family Impact Statements

- The increasing complexity and intrusiveness of the law and the increasing fragility of family relations argue strongly for a mechanism that maintains the core unit of society. A family impact statement is an important tool in maintaining this discipline, and is most likely to be successful if it: (1) recognizes the pre-existing nature of the family, (2) includes a normative definition of the natural family,

(3) includes a check on actions that would be unfriendly to the family, and (4) provides tools for assessing whether an action will maintain or undercut the family.

- A two-tiered approach with the enactment of family impact statement legislation and appointment of a commission to assess the impact of current law on the family could go far to ensure that a state is truly "family friendly."

Pornography

- States and provinces should allow divergent and diverse communities to regulate the existence, flow, and content of pornography and obscenity in their own way.

- The simplest way to do this is to increase the penalty for pandering obscenity from a misdemeanor to a felony. Most states only penalize pandering with a misdemeanor, hardly an incentive for prosecutors to spend precious time and resources on protecting communities from obscenity. Increasing pandering penalties from a misdemeanor to some degree of felony would create an incentive for prosecutors, already inclined to attend to these legal matters, to do so.

Taken together, we believe that this policy framework would undergird and encourage a stable, autonomous, child-rich, multigenerational, natual family system.

We can also point to very specific models of legislation that meet our criteria. For instance, the proposed "Parents' Tax Relief Act of 2006" (HR 3080, S 1305), introduced in the 109th U.S. Congress, would:

- Extend the existing child care tax credit to include stay-at-home parents with young children.

- Make the $1,000 child tax credit permanent, index it to inflation, remove income limits on eligibility, and extend the age of covered dependent children to eighteen.

- Eliminate the marriage penalty in the federal income tax, once and for all.

- Increase the personal income tax exemption for children to $5,000.

- Support home-based businesses and encourage telecommuting for parents.

- Extend Social Security work credits and benefits to stay-at-home parents.

We applaud this measure because it recognizes the value of the parental care of small children and expands the child care choices of all new mothers and fathers. It affirms marriage as a public good and restores recognition of the marital couple as an economic partnership. The bill properly affirms the value of children to the nation and responds to the extra economic burdens faced by young parents. This measure seeks to reduce conflicts between workplace and home by making it easier for the home itself to be a place for market labor. And the measure recognizes the full-time mother or father as individuals doing publicly valued work, deserving recognition within the Social Security system.

These approaches also avoid the mistakes of the European model. Most other developed nations provide state child allowances to parents as offsets to the costs of rearing children. As shown earlier, though, this method tends to make families wards of the state and to weaken marriage. In contrast, the "Parents' Tax Relief Act of 2006" uses carefully targeted tax policy measures to enable families to retain more of their *own* earned income while children are in the home. The record shows that this approach supports family formation and strengthens homes.

Viewed from another angle, this bill would also eliminate inequities that have crept into U.S. tax policy. For example, federal law currently gives a generous tax credit, or subsidy, without income limit to parents who purchase daycare. But existing policy gives no recognition at all to full-time parental child care which, social science shows, is predictably better for young children.[16] The "Parents' Tax Relief Act of 2006" would begin to set things right by granting a tax credit of $250 per month for families that make the financial sacrifice to have one parent serve as the full-time, at-home caregiver for children ages six and under. On the one hand, this measure creates a level playing field; on the other, it expands the child care choices of *all* qualifying families.

Second, the infamous "marriage penalty" remains alive and well. The tax cut of 2001 removed this penalty only for the 15 percent tax bracket. The "marriage penalty" still afflicts the majority of Americans in the middle and high tax brackets. The proposed bill would fully eliminate this penalty by making all tax brackets twice as wide for married couples as they are for singles.

Third, the per-child tax relief provided by the existing personal exemption and the child tax credit is inadequate, well below the relief delivered by the exemplary, pro-child Tax Reform of 1948. The proposed bill would raise the personal exemption for children to $5,000 and make permanent the $1,000 per child tax credit and index it to inflation, in order to protect its future value.

Reflecting old assumptions about the need for industrial centralization, federal tax policy still favors large central offices and factories over market labor in the home. This bill would simplify and expand the availability of the deduction for business use of the home and also encourage telecommuting. These are progressive ideas designed to increase family-friendly, home-centered work opportunities in the new information age.

Finally, the American Social Security system fails to recognize the full-time care of small children as real work (even the existing "homemakers" pension has no linkage to children). This is troubling, for there is strong evidence that existing incentives within Social Security discourage the birth of children,[17] even though such new children are in fact needed to maintain the system in the future. This measure boldly faces this problem by granting employment credit toward future Social Security benefits to those parents who make the sacrifices to raise their children, full-time, at home.

THE CALL

Authentic pro-family policy, though, only provides a legal and financial framework for social health and renewal. The flesh, blood, and spirit of a culture animated by the natural family ideal comes from those young persons ready to commit themselves to this vision of life. Accordingly, we conclude the manifesto with a special call to the young, "the ones with the power to make the world anew." They have lived through the disorders of the last several decades, and have witnessed the consequences in troubled or ruined lives. We point them to a different future: "You have the chance to shape a world that welcomes and celebrates children.

You have the ability to craft a true homecoming. Your generation holds the destiny of humankind in its hands. The hopes of all good and decent people lie with you." And we predict their success, for this fresh life is in harmony with human nature and the will of our Creator.

May it be so!

The Geneva Declaration (1999)

We assemble in this World Congress, from many national, ethnic, cultural, social and religious communities, to affirm that the natural human family is established by the Creator and essential to good society. We address ourselves to all people of good will who, with the majority of the world's people, value the natural family. Ideologies of statism, individualism and sexual revolution today challenge the family's very legitimacy as an institution. Associated with this challenge are the problems of divorce, devaluation of parenting, declining family time, morally relativistic public education, confusions over sexual identity, promiscuity, sexually transmitted diseases, abortion, poverty, human trafficking, violence against women, child abuse, isolation of the elderly, excessive taxation and below-replacement fertility. To defend the family and to guide public policy and cultural norms, this Declaration asserts principles that respect and uphold the vital roles that the family plays in society.

THE FAMILY AND SOCIETY

The natural family is the fundamental social unit, inscribed in human nature, and centered on the voluntary union of a man and a woman in the lifelong covenant of marriage. The natural family is defined by marriage, procreation and, in some cultures, adoption. Free, secure and stable families that welcome children are necessary for healthy society. The society that abandons the natural family as the norm is destined for chaos and suffering. The loving family reaches out in love and service to their communities and those in need. All social and cultural institutions should respect and uphold the rights and responsibilities of the family.

THE FAMILY AND MARRIAGE

The cornerstone of healthy family life, marriage brings security, contentment, meaning, joy and spiritual maturity to the man and woman who enter this lifelong covenant with unselfish commitment. In marriage, both husband and wife commit to a life of mutual love, respect, support and compassion. Spousal conflicts that can arise in marriage are opportunities for personal and marital growth, not, as modern cultures encourage, reasons to break the covenant. Divorce is destructive to families and society. Society and public policy should discourage divorce, while taking legal or other appropriate action in cases of intransigently abusive relationships. Steadfast commitment in marriage provides the security in family life that children need. Children also need and are entitled to the complementary parental love and attention of both father and mother, which marriage provides. Communities and religious institutions should care for families and households whose circumstances fall short of these ideals. Social policies should not promote single-parenting.

THE FAMILY AND CHILDREN

The natural family provides the optimal environment for the healthy development of children. Healthy family life fulfills the basic human need to belong and satisfies the longings of the human heart to give and receive love. The family informs the human person's original attitude toward such fundamental matters as identity, security, responsibility, love, morality and religion. In personal and intimate ways that no self-defining entity could, the natural family cares for its children and provides for their spiritual, physical, psychological and moral growth. Policy should promote the definition and permanence in family relationships that create the stability and security in family life children need.

THE FAMILY AND SEXUALITY

The complementary natures of men and women are physically and psychologically self-evident. These differences are created and natural, not primarily socially constructed. Sexuality is ordered for the procreation of children and the expression of love between husband and wife in the covenant of marriage. Marriage between a man and a woman forms the sole moral context for natural sexual union. Whether through pornography, promiscuity, incest or homosexuality, deviations from these created sexual norms cannot truly satisfy the human spirit. They lead to obsession, remorse, alienation, and disease. Child molesters harm children and no valid legal, psychological or moral justification can be offered for the odious crime of pedophilia. Culture and society should encourage standards of sexual morality that support and enhance family life.

THE FAMILY AND LIFE

The intrinsic worth, right to life and sanctity of life of every human person exists throughout the continuum of life, from fertilization until natural death.

Every human life is a gift to the person, the family and society. Loving families cherish and serve all their members, including the weak, aged and handicapped. Taking innocent human life through abortion and euthanasia is wrong; respect for human life demands that we choose the life-protecting options of adoption and palliative care. The destruction of embryonic human beings, lethal human embryo experimentation and abortifacients also involve wrongful takings of human life. All experimentation and research on human beings should be beneficial to the particular human subject. Trafficking in the organs and limbs of aborted children and other human beings, cloning humans and human-genetic engineering treat human life as a commodity and should not be allowed. Animal-human genetic experimentation is a crime against humanity. Policy should respect the inherent dignity of human life.

THE FAMILY AND POPULATION

Human society depends on the renewal of the human population; the true population problem is depopulation, not overpopulation. Many nations are experiencing below-replacement fertility, arising from widespread abortion, birth control, lack of interest in marriage and declining family sizes. People are living longer, increasing the size of elderly populations, while there are proportionally decreasing numbers of taxpayers to support their elders' retirement incomes and health care. Because just governments and creative human enterprise and charity offer the best hope for addressing the problems of poverty, hunger and disease, no country should be coerced to accept policies of "population control." Efforts to assist developing countries should focus on promoting family self-sufficiency, not dependency.

THE FAMILY AND EDUCATION

Parents uniquely possess the authority and responsibility to direct the upbringing and education of their children. By its nature, education is not only technical and practical, but also moral and spiritual. The family is the child's first school, parents the first and most important teachers. Love of community and loyalty to nation begin in the family. The state usurps the parental role when it monopolizes and mandates the educational system, and deprives parents of their intrinsic authority over their children's education. Nor should government schools or health clinics treat minor children's health without parental approval.

School curricula should not undermine the right of parents to teach their children moral and spiritual values. Parents have a duty to their children and to society to provide their children an adequate education. Parents should be free to spend their education resources, including tax money, on the schools of their choice, such as sending them to a religious school or educating their children themselves in the home.

THE FAMILY AND THE ECONOMY

Economic policy, both corporate and governmental, should be crafted to allow the family economy to flourish; what is good for families is good for the economy.

Family economy centers on the pursuit of meaningful employment to fulfill one's personal vocation and to provide for the present and future needs, obligations, and desires of the family -- such as food, shelter, education, health care, charity, recreation, retirement income, taxes and the intergenerational family estate.

Healthy families produce good citizens and workers, competent consumers and innovative entrepreneurs. Employers should allow workers flexible family and maternity leave. Corporate philanthropy and national and international funding for economic development should strengthen the natural family. Such funds should not be used to support organizations whose programs harm the family. Commerce in products that appeal to addictions, such as harmful drugs, gambling and violent and pornographic media, undermine the family and should be opposed.

THE FAMILY AND GOVERNMENT

Government should protect and support the family, and not usurp the vital roles it plays in society.

When the state or its agent attempts to exercise a right or responsibility that belongs to the family, albeit with good intentions to address a vexing social problem, its effect is to undermine and displace the family and make matters worse. Government policies should not create pressure for mothers to enter the workplace when they would prefer to care for their families full time. Government should secure an orderly, lawful and just society that allows families freely and responsibly to: form in the covenant of marriage and bear children, pursue meaningful work, provide for their material and health needs, direct the education and upbringing of their children, participate in charitable, civic and recreational activities, care for elderly family members, build estates for their present and future generations, and practice their religion.

THE FAMILY AND RELIGION

Parents have the right to teach their religious and moral beliefs to their children and to raise them according to their religious precepts. Based on, and consistent with, the human right to religious liberty, families have the right to believe, practice and express their religious views in love. Religious institutions should not accommodate cultural trends that undermine the created nature of the family. One need not hold religious views to recognize that the family is part of human nature and the fundamental social unit. Religious institutions have the crucial cultural-leadership role of affirming that: the natural human family is established in creation and is essential to a good society; life and sexuality are gifts from the Creator, to be enjoyed respectfully and wholesomely; the family is sacred and has the unique authority, responsibility and capacity to provide for its members' education, health care and welfare; and all social institutions should respect and uphold the institution of the family.

CALL TO RESPECT THE FAMILY

We exhort all persons, families, social organizations and governments throughout the world to respect and uphold the institution of the natural human family, in accordance with the principles of this Declaration, for the good of present and future generations.

The Mexico City Declaration (2004)

ON THE WORLD CONGRESS OF FAMILIES

The World Congress of Families was initiated by Allan Carlson, President of The Howard Center for Family, Religion and Society. At the first World Congress of Families held in 1997 in Prague, the Czech Republic, a Declaration affirming the central, vital, and essential role of the natural family was adopted. In 1999, the second World Congress of Families adopted a Declaration of Principles about the Family, now called The Geneva Declaration. It called on people of faith and all men and women of good will to work together to strengthen the natural family as the fundamental social unit of society.

We, of the World Congress of Families III, assembled in Mexico City, from many national, ethnic, cultural, academic, social and religious communities, affirm that the natural family is established by the Creator and is fundamental to the good of the society. We also recognize that since the World Congress of Families II, new issues have arisen that threaten the well-being of the family, <u>and</u> marriage, such as euthanasia, reproductive technology, cloning, and other bioethical issues.

OUR PURPOSE

We address ourselves to all people of goodwill who, with the majority of the world's people, value the natural family. Challenges to the family's very legitimacy as an institution include extreme individualism, easy divorce, radical homosexual activisim, irresponsible sexual behavior, and the reinterpretation and misapplication of human rights. To protect and promote the family and to direct public policy with a family perspective, this Declaration asserts principles and recommends actions that respect and uphold the vital functions that the family plays in society.

THE FAMILY AND SOCIETY

Principle

The natural family is the fundamental social unit, inscribed in human nature, and centered on the union of a man and a woman in the lifelong covenant of marriage. The natural family is defined by marriage, including extended family members, procreation, and adoption. Secure and stable families that welcome children are necessary for a healthy society.

Actions

- Encourage governments to uphold and maintain the natural understanding of marriage.

- Provide special benefits to the unique relationship of man and woman in marriage.

- Recognize that the security of nations and the survival of civilization depend upon the strength of families worldwide.

- Establish an effective information system to compile and disseminate information on family friendly policies.

- Promote research on family issues through specialized institutions.

- Encourage media and other institutions (such as schools and non-governmental organizations) to uphold the above principle.

THE FAMILY AND MARRIAGE

Principle

Marriage, the cornerstone of healthy family life, brings security, contentment, meaning, joy and spiritual maturity to the man and woman who enter this lifelong covenant with unselfish commitment. In marriage, both husband and wife commit to a life of mutual love, respect, support and compassion. Steadfast commitment in marriage provides the security in family life that is needed by children. Children are entitled to the complementary parental love and attention of both father and mother, which marriage bestows. Due to the importance of a child being raised by a mother and a father, social policies should not encourage cohabitation or single parenting.

Actions

- Present marriage as a desirable good for men and women.

- Implement programs to prepare men and women for marriage in order to increase their chances of success.

- Promote measures that aid in the healing of troubled marriages and broken homes.

- Revise laws to encourage commitment to the marriage relationship.

- Take legal or other appropriate action in cases of abusive relationships.

- Encourage media and other institutions (such as schools and non-governmental organizations) to uphold the above principle.

THE FAMILY AND CHILDREN

Principle

The natural family provides the optimal environment for the healthy development of children. Healthy family life fulfills the basic human need to belong and satisfies the longings of the human heart to give and receive love. The family shapes the human person's attitude towards such fundamental matters as identity, security, responsibility, love, morality, and religion. In personal and intimate ways, the natural family cares for its children and provides for their spiritual, physical, intellectual, social, psychological, and ethical growth.

Actions

- Encourage and support mothers in their essential role in caring for their children.

- Recognize the vital role of fathers in child rearing.

- Facilitate adoptions as a means to provide children with a family and to reduce abortions.

- Recognize the right of all children to a father <u>and</u> a mother.

- Support agencies which assist women and families in crisis.

- Strive for a society where all families have access to good homes, health care, and nourishment and opportunities for physical, intellectual and recreational development.

- Encourage media and other institutions (such as schools and non-governmental organizations) to uphold the above principle.

THE FAMILY AND SEXUALITY

Principle

Sexuality exists for the expression of love between husband and wife and for the procreation of children in the covenant of marriage. Marriage between a man and a woman forms the moral context for sexual union. The complementary natures of men and women, both physically and psychologically, are evident throughout the course of human history and in every society. Deviations from natural sexual behavior cannot truly satisfy the human spirit. Culture, society, and government should encourage standards of sexual morality that support and enhance family life.

Actions

- Give unique recognition to the societal benefits of the complementary relationship of man and woman in marriage.

- Take appropriate actions to assist homosexuals in programs of voluntary rehabilitation.

- Encourage media and other institutions (such as schools and non-governmental organizations) to recognize and encourage the unique importance of traditional marriage.

THE FAMILY, LIFE, AND BIOETHICAL ISSUES

Principle

Every human person has intrinsic value throughout the continuum of life from fertilization until natural death. Every human life is a gift to the person, the family and society. Loving families cherish and serve all their members, including the weak, aged and handicapped. Taking innocent human life through abortion and euthanasia is a direct attack on human life and dignity. Respect for human life demands the life-protecting options of adoption and palliative care. The destruction of embryonic human beings, lethal human embryo experimentation and abortifacients also involve the wrongful taking of human life.

Actions

- Protect and respect through public policy the inherent dignity of human life.
- Prohibit by law all forms of artificial manipulation of human life that threaten human dignity, including cloning, in vitro fertilization, abortion, and embryo experimentation.
- Encourage media and other institutions (such as schools and non-governmental organizations) to uphold the above principle.

THE FAMILY AND POPULATION

Principle

Procreation is the key to the survival of the human race. An increasing number of countries are experiencing below replacement birth rates due to misguided population-control programs that promote contraception, abortion, delayed marriages, and the abandonment of the institution of marriage. Demographic growth is an indication of the expansion of human resources that represents challenges and opportunities, not burdens (poverty, hunger, and disease have other causes, including a lack of good will and misuse of governmental resources). These problems can be solved by education, creative social policies, economic development and promotion of family integrity regardless of geographical boundaries, cultural practices and religious affiliation.

Actions

- Make individuals aware of the positive social consequences of parenthood within marriage.

- Provide incentives by the state and educational institutions to promote marriage and support the natural family and pro-life policies aimed at reversing the declining fertility rate.

- In countries with below replacement birthrates, encourage an increase in population to provide a broad foundation to help support the expanded elderly population.

- Allocate public resources to encourage responsible married-couple families to have children.

- Craft an economic system that allows women to stay home and to bear the number of children they desire.

- Affirm that environmental improvement can be compatible with population growth.

- Encourage media and other institutions (such as schools and non-governmental organizations) to uphold the above principle.

THE FAMILY AND EDUCATION

Principle

Parents possess the primary authority and responsibility to direct the upbringing and education of their children, except in clear cases of abuse and neglect. By its nature, education is not only technical and practical but also moral and spiritual. The family is the child's first school with parents their first and most important teachers. The state usurps the parental role when it monopolizes and mandates the educational system and deprives parents of their intrinsic authority over their children's education. School curricula should not undermine the right of parents to teach their children moral and spiritual values. Parents have a duty to their children and to society to provide their children an adequate education. Parents should be free to spend their resources for education, including tax money, on the schools of their choice, such as sending them to a religious school or educating their children themselves in the home.

Actions

- Structure state policy to respect the natural authority and primary responsibility of parents over the education of their children.

- Craft policies that are responsive to parents who need assistance in fulfilling this duty.

- Encourage media and other institutions (such as schools and non-governmental organizations) to uphold the above principle.

THE FAMILY, ECONOMY AND DEVELOPMENT

Principle

The natural family is the fundamental unit in society for economic growth and development. Promoting the dignity of families and respecting their rights are necessary conditions for a healthy and stable society. A nation cannot create true wealth if its policies lead to family disintegration. Policies that promote responsible government, sustain economic growth, care for the environment, and promote cultural harmony must also support the family. The advancement of economic, social, technological and political growth is necessary, but not sufficient for, true human development.

Actions

- Formulate and implement public programs which include the family perspective within all government entities.

- Require evaluations of the impact of public policies on the natural family.

- Empower families to break the cycle of poverty.

- Include the health and stability of the family as an indicator of development.

- Facilitate work conditions that allow both men and women to fulfill their respective family responsibilities.

- Encourage media and other institutions (such as schools and non-governmental organizations) to uphold the above principle.

THE FAMILY AND GOVERNMENT

Principle

Government should protect and support the natural family and not usurp the vital roles that it plays in society. Government policies should not create pressure for mothers to enter the workplace when they would prefer to care for their families full time. Government should secure an orderly, lawful, and just society that allows families freely and responsibly to:

- Marry and bear children
- Pursue meaningful work
- Provide for their material and health needs
- Direct the education and upbringing of their children
- Participate in charitable, civic and recreational activities
- Care for elderly family members
- Provide security for their present and future generations, and
- Practice their religion.

Actions

- Formulate public policies that allow mothers the choice to remain at home and care for their children.

- Make the health of the family the primary focus of international agencies.

- Encourage international agencies to embrace the family perspective.

- Re-examine international laws and policies that may harm the well-being of the natural family.

- Encourage Heads of State and other high governmental officials to issue proclamations affirming the natural family.

- Identify or create international mechanisms to foster cooperation in the interests of the natural family.

- Promote public policies with a clear family perspective.

- Encourage the media and other institutions (such as schools and non-governmental organizations) to uphold the above principle.

THE FAMILY AND RELIGION

Principle

As the primary educators, parents have the right to teach their religious and moral beliefs to their children and to raise them according to their religious precepts. Based on and consistent with the human right to religious liberty, families have the right to believe, practice and express their religious views. Religious institutions should not accommodate cultural trends that undermine the created nature of the family. Religious institutions have the crucial cultural-leadership role of affirming that:

- The natural human family is established in creation
- The family is essential to a good society, and

- Life and sexuality are gifts from the creator to be enjoyed, respectfully and wholesomely.

Actions

- Recognize that the state, its agencies, the media or other entities should not undermine the parents' role in teaching their children a belief system and raising them accordingly.

- Encourage media and other institutions (such as schools and non-governmental organizations) to uphold the above principle.

CALL TO RESPECT THE FAMILY

We exhort all persons, families, social entities, governments, and international organizations throughout the world to adopt the family perspective to craft and pursue realistic targets for action, and to respect and uphold the institution of the natural human family for the good of present and future generations, in accordance with the principles and recommended guidelines of the Declaration adopted at the third World Congress of Families in Mexico City.

Adopted March 31, 2004, Mexico City, Mexico

Notes

Introduction

1   http://www.unmarriedamerica.org/column-one/3-6-06-natural-family-resolu-tion.htm (7/7/06).
2   http://www.pamspaulding.com/weblog/2005/03/natural-family-vs-homo-agen-da.html (7/7/06).
3   http://www.salon.com/politics/war_room/?blogs/politics/war_room/2005/03/17/family/index.html (4/4/05).
4   http://www.whatsupwithkanab.com/blog (7/7/06); "Utah Town's Pro-Family Resolution Sparks Debate," at: www.gopusa.com/news/2006/february/0228_utah_marriageep.shtml (7/7/06).

The Natural Family: A Manifesto

1   Theodore Roosevelt, *Presidential Addresses and State Papers of Theodore Roosevelt. Part Two* (New York: P.F. Collier & Son, [1904?]): 493.
2   Francis Fukuyama, *The Great Disruption: Human Nature and the Reconstruction of Social Order* (New York: Free Press, 1999).
3   Karl Polanyi, *The Great Transformation* (New York: Rinehart & Company, 1944).
4   John C. Caldwell, *Theory of Fertility Decline* (London & New York: Academic Press, 1982): 324.
5   For example: Thomas Hobbes, *De Cive: The English Version* [1642] (Oxford: Clarendon Press, 1983): 42-48, 122-24.

6   As example: Jean Jacques Rousseau, *The Social Contract* [1762] (New York: E.P. Dutton, 1950).

7   Louis deBonald, *On Divorce* [1801], trans. and edited by Nicholas Davidson (New Brunswick, NJ: Transaction, 1992).

8   Edmund Burke, *Reflections on the Revolution in France* (London: J. Dodsley, 1790).

9   G.K. Chesterton, *What's Wrong With the World* [1910] and *The Superstition of Divorce* [1920]; in *Collected Works*. Volume IV (San Francisco: Ignatius Press, 1987): 67, 256.

10 Phillip Longman, *The Empty Cradle: How Falling Birthrates Threaten World Prosperity and What to Do About It* (New York: Basic Books, 2004).

11 Phrases borrowed from David Schindler, The John Paul II Institute, Washington, DC.

12 Jan Lewis, *The Pursuit of Happiness: Family and Values in Jefferson's Virginia* (Cambridge, UK: Cambridge University Press, 1985); and Barry Alan Shain, *The Myth of American Individualism: The Protestant Origins of American Political Thought* (Princeton, NJ: Princeton University Press, 1996).

13 Daniel Patrick Moynihan, *The Negro Family: The Case for National Action* [1965]; in Lee Rainwater and William L. Yancey, eds., *The Moynihan Report and The Politics of Controversy* (Cambridge, MA: M.I.T. Press, 1967).

14 *The Universal Declaration of Human Rights* (Adopted and Proclaimed by the General Assembly of The United Nations, 10 December [1948]: Articles 16(3), 25(1 and 2), 26.

15 See the research abstracts available through "New Research" at SwanSearch (www.profam.org); also, the Family and Society Database at www.heritage.org.

16 C. Owen Lovejoy, "The Origin of Man," *Science* 211 (Jan. 23, 1981): 348.

17 Carle C. Zimmerman, *Family and Civilization* (New York & London: Harper & Brothers, 1947).

1   A School of Despotism?

1   From a statement submitted to authors, April 2005.

2   Thomas Hobbes, *DeCive: The English Version* (Oxford: Clarendon Press, 1983): 42-48, 122-24.

3   John Locke, *Of Civil Government (Second Essay)* (Ann Arbor, MI: Edwards Brothers, 1947): 35-37, 41-44, 51-54.

4   John Stuart Mill, *The Subjection of Women* (Cambridge, MA: The MIT Press, 1970): 22, 28-29, 36-37, 48.

5   John Rawls, *A Theory of Justice* (Cambridge, MA: The Belknap Press of Harvard University, 1971): 74, 301, 462-63, 511.

6   John Jacques Rousseau, *The Social Contract* (New York: E. Dutton, 1950): 44, 15, 27; and an extract from Rousseau's *The Government of Poland*, found in Philip Abbott, *The Family on Trial: Special Relationships in Modern Political Thought* (State College, PA: The Pennsylvania State University Press, 1981): 55-56.

7   Arthur W. Calhoun, *A Social History of the American Family* (New York: Barnes & Noble, 1945 [1918]): 171-72.

8   Claudia Koonz, *Mothers in the Fatherland: Women, the Family, and Nazi Politics* (New York: St. Marten's Press, 1987): 178.

9   Koonz, *Mothers in the Fatherland*, p. 398.

10   Friedrich Engels, *The Origin of the Family, Private Property and the State* (Chicago: Charles H. Kerr & Co., 1902 [1884]).

11   A Woman Resident in Russia, "The Russian Effort to Abolish Marriage," *The Atlantic* (July 1926), p. 1; at http:www.theatlantic.com/cgi-bin/send. cgi?page=http%3A//www.theatlantic.com/issues/2 (6/2/2004).

12   Alexandra Kollontai, "Communism and the Family," *Komunistka* (No. 2, 1920): 8, 10; at http://www.marxists.org/archive/kollontai/works/1920/communism-family.htm (6/2/2004).

13   Barry Levy, "'Tender Plants': Quaker Farmers and Children in the Delaware Valley, 1681-1735," *Journal of Family History* 3 (Summer 1978): 117.

14   James A. Henretta, "Families and Farms: Mentalite in Pre-Industrial America," *William and Mary Quarterly* 35 (Jan. 1978): 20-21.

15   Jan Lewis, *The Pursuit of Happiness: Family and Values in Jefferson's Virginia* (Cambridge, England: Cambridge University Press, 1983): 204-05.

16   See: Allan Carlson, *The 'American Way': Family and Community in the Shaping of the American Identity* (Wilmington, DE: ISI Books, 2003).

17   Barry Alan Shain, *The Myth of American Individualism* (Princeton, NJ: Princeton University Press, 1994).

18   Hugh Brody, "Nomads and Settlers," in Anthony Barnett and Roger Scruton, eds., *Town and Country* (London: Vintage, 1999): 3-4.

19   G.K. Chesterton, *The Superstition of Divorce*; in *Collected Works*, Vol. IV, *Family, Society, Politics* (San Francisco: Ignatius Press, 1987): 259-60.

20   See Karl Polanyi, *The Great Transformation* (New York: Farrar & Rinehart, 1944).

21   Robert Nisbet, *The Quest for Community: A Study in the Ethics of Order & Freedom* (San Francisco: Institute for Contemporary Studies, 1990 [1953]): 247, 257.

22   John C. Caldwell and Thomas Schindlmeyer, "Explanations of the Fertility Crisis in Modern Societies: A Search for Commonalities," *Population Studies* 57 (2003): 241-63.

23   *Two Basic Social Encyclicals* (Washington, DC: The Catholic University of American Press, 1943): 5-11, 15, 55-59, 133-35.

24   See: Hubert Curtis Callahan, S.J., *The Family Allowance Procedure: An Analysis*

of the Family Allowance Procedure in Selected Countries (Washington, DC: The Catholic University of America Press, 1947): 3, 68.

25 Quoted in Molly Ladd-Taylor, *Mother-Work: Women, Child Welfare, and the State,* 1890-1930 (Urbana: University of Illinois Press, 1994): 91. Emphasis added.

26 On the arguably "pro-family" nature of the New Deal, see: Allan Carlson, *The 'American Way',* 55-78.

27 Evidence for the direct positive effects of these innovations on family formation can be found in: Harvey S. Rosen, "Owner Occupied Housing and the Federal Income Tax: Estimates and Simulations," *Journal of Urban Economics* 6 (1979): 263-64; D. Laidler, "Income Tax Incentives for Owner-Occupied Housing," in A.C. Harberger and M.J. Bailey, eds., *The Taxation of Income from Capital* (Washington, DC: The Brookings Institution, 1969): 50-64; Leslie Whittington, "Taxes and the Family: The Impact of the Tax Exemption for Dependents on Marital Fertility," *Demography* 29 (May 1992): 220-22; and L.A. Whittington, J. Alms, and H.E. Peters, "Fertility and the Personal Exemption: Implicit Pro-natalist Policy in the United States," *The American Economic Review* 80 (June 1990): 545-56.

28 Alva Myrdal, "Kollektiv bostadsform," *Tiden* 24 (Dec. 1932): 602; Alva Myrdal, "Yrkes-kvinnansbarn," *Yrkes-kvinnor klubbnytt* (Feb. 1933): 63; Alva Myrdal, *Stadsbarn: En boken deres föstran i storbarnkammare* (Stockholm: Koopertiva förbundets bökförlag, 1935); and Alva and Gunnar Myrdal, *Kris i befolkningsfrågan* (Stockholm: Bonniers, 1934).

2   *A Bulwark of Liberty*

1 Genesis 1: 27-28; 2: 24 (Revised Standard Version).

2 John D. Lierman, "The Family and the Word," *The Religion & Society Report* 22 (June 2005): 9.

3 Edward Westermarck, *The History of Human Marriage: 5th Edition* (London: Macmillan, 1925): 26-37, 69-72.

4 George Peter Murdock, *Social Structure* (New York: The Free Press, 1965 [1949]): 1-8.

5 C. Owen Lovejoy, "The Origin of Man," *Science* 211 (Jan. 23, 1981): 348. Emphasis added.

6 Ronald S. Immerman, "Perspectives on Human Attachment (Pair Bonding): Eve's Unique Legacy of a Canine Analogue," *Evolutionary Psychology* 1 (2003): 138-54.

7 Phillip L. Reno, Richard S. Meindl, Melanie A. McCollum, and C. Owen Lovejoy, "Sexual Dimorphism in Australopithecus afarensis was similar to modern humans," *Proceedings of the National Academy of Science* 100 (Aug. 5, 2003): 9404-09.

8   For the seminal work, see: Pierre Guillaume and Frederic LePlay, *Le Reform Sociale*, Vol. 1, Book 3 (Tours: A Mame et fils, 1887): chapters 24-30.

9   See: Carle Zimmerman and Pitirim Sorokin, *Principles of Rural-Urban Sociology* (New York: Henry Holt and Co., 1929).

10 Carle Zimmerman and Merle Frampton, *Family and Society: A Study of Sociological Reconstruction* (New York: D. Van Nostrand, 1935): 133, 221-37.

11 See: Pitirim Sorokin, *The Crisis of Our Age* (New York: E.P. Dutton, 1941); also Pitirim Sorokin, *The American Sex Revolution* (Boston: Porter Sargeant, 1956).

12 Robert Nisbet, *Quest for Community: A Study in the Ethics of Order & Freedom* (San Francisco: Institute for Contemporary Studies, 1990 [1953]); and Robert Nisbet, *Twilight of Authority* (New York: Oxford University Press, 1975).

13 Nisbet, *Twilight of Authority*, p. 254.

14 Ibid., p. 260.

15 C.S. Lewis, *The Screwtape Letters* (New York: Harper San Francisco, 1942): 53-54. Emphasis added.

16 Martin Luther, *Luther's Works. Vol. 5: Lectures on Genesis. Chapters 1-5* (St. Louis: Concordia, 1958): 133.

17 *Luther's Works. Vol. 5*, 133.

18 Emile Durkheim, *Suicide: A Study in Sociology*, trans. John A. Spaulding and George Simpson (Glencoe, IL: The Free Press of Glencoe, 1951).

19 Martin E.P. Seligman, *Authentic Happiness* (New York: Free Press, 2002): 55-56.

20 For example, see: Myriam Khlat, Catherine Sermet, and Annick LePape, "Women's Health in Relation with their Family and Work Roles: France from the early 1990s," *Social Science and Medicine* 50 (2000): 1807-25.

21 Nicholas Eberstadt, "Power and Population in Asia," *Policy Review Online* (Feb. 2004); at http:www.policyreview.org/Feb04/eberstadt.html (6/10/05).

22 Phillip Longman, *The Empty Cradle: How Falling Birthrates Threaten World Prosperity [And What to Do About It]* (New York: Basic Books, 2004): 11.

23 Donald Critchlow, *Intended Consequences: Birth Control, Abortion and the Federal Government in Modern America* (New York: Oxford University Press, 1999).

24 Joan Huber, "Will U.S. Fertility Decline Toward Zero?" *The Sociological Quarterly* 21 (Autumn 1980): 481-92.

25 Ron Lesthaeghe, "A Century of Demographic and Cultural Change in Western Europe," *Population and Development Review* 9 (1983): 411-35.

26 Dirk Van de Kaa, *Europe's Second Demographic Transition* (Washington, DC: Population Reference Bureau, 1987): 25.

27 Philippe Aries, "Two Successive Motivations for the Declining Birth Rate in the West," *Population and Development Review* 6 (Dec. 1980): 649-50.

28 John C. Caldwell, *Theory of Fertility Decline* (London and New York: Academic Press, 1982): 324.

29 G.K. Chesterton, *Collected Works: Volume IV: Family, Society, Politics* (San Francisco: Ignatius Press, 1987): 256.

30 Chesterton, *Collected Works, IV*, pp. 67-68.

31 Yvonne Hirdman, "the Importance of Gender in the Swedish Labor Movement, Or: A Swedish Dilemma," paper prepared for The Swedish National Institute of Working Life," 2002, pp. 3-5, 10; and Frances Fox Piven "Ideology and the State: Women, Power and the Welfare State," in Linda Gordon, ed., *Women, the State and Welfare* (Madison, WI: University of Wisconsin Press, 1990): 251-64.

32 Claudia Koonz, *Mothers in the Fatherland: Women, the Family, and Nazi Politics* (New York: St. Martin's Press, 1987): 393.

33 Marfua Toktakhodjaeva, "Society and Family in Uzbekistan," *Polish Sociological Reviewi* 2 (1997): 149-165.

34 Li Zong, "Agricultural Reform and Its Impact on Chinese Rural Families, 1978-1989," *Journal of Comparative Family Studies* 24 (Autumn 1993).

35 H. Ruigrok, J. Dronkers, B. Mach, "Communism and the Decline of the Family: Resemblance between the occupational levels of Polish siblings from different gender, generations, political background and family forms." Paper presented at the Seventh Social Science Study Day conference, April 11-12, 1996, The University of Amsterdam.

36 *Illustrated London News*, June 17, 1933.

37 In Mario Einaudi and Francois Goguel, *Christian Democracy in Italy and France* (Notre Dame, IN: University of Notre Dame Press, 1952): 126.

38 Guido Dierick, "Christian Democracy and Its Ideological Rivals: An Empirical Comparison in the Low Countries," in David Hanley, ed., *Christian Democracy in Europe: A Comparative Perspective* (London & New York: Pinter Publishers, 1994): 24.

39 R.E.M. Irving, *Christian Democracy in France* (London: George Allen & Unwin, 1973): 61-62.

40 Noel D. Cary, *The Path to Christian Democracy: German Catholics and the Party System from Windthorst to Adenauer* (Cambridge, MA: Harvard University Press, 1996): 180.

41 From: Johannes Morsink, *The Universal Declaration of Human Rights: Origins, Drafting, and Intent* (Philadelphia: University of Pennsylvania Press, 1999): 255.

42 Morsink, *The Universal Declaration of Human Rights*, p. 255.

3 *The Fundamental Unit of Society*

1 The Howard Center for Family, Religion & Society, "Special Report: Results of a Global Survey on Marriage and the Family." Prepared by Wirthlin Worldwide (November 1999). Some responded with two choices; hence the numbers total over 100 percent.

2   The authors recognize that in the United States and a number of other countries, non-profit corporations exist.

3   *Dartmouth* v. *Woodward* (1819).

4   *Eternal Truths and the Sciences*

1   Arthur W. Calhoun, *A Social History of the American Family: From Colonial Times to the Present* (New York: Barnes & Noble, 1945 [1917]): 165-75.

2   Gunnar Myrdal, "Social politikens dilemma," *Spektrum* 2 (No. 3, 1932): 1-13; and (No. 4, 1932): 13-31.

3   Robert Nisbet, *The Sociological Tradition* (New York: Basic Books, 1966): 11, 17.

4   John Devereux and Luis Locay, "Specialization, Household Production, and the Measurement of Economic Growth," *The American Economic Review* 82 (1992): 399-403. Reuben Gronau, "Home Production—A Forgotten Industry," *The Review of Economics and Statistics* 62 (1980): 408-416. Edward P. Lazear and Robert T. Michael, "Real Income Equivalence Among One-Earner and Two-Earner Families," *The American Economic Review* 70 (1980): 203-208. Duncan Ironmonger, "The Domestic Economy: $340 Billion of G.H.P.," in *The Family: There is No Other Way* (Melbourne: Australian Family Association, 1996): 132-146.

5   T.R. Balakrishnan et al., "A Hazard Model Analysis of the Covariates of Marriage Dissolution in Canada," *Demography* 24 (1987): 398-400; Erik E. Filsinger and Margaret R. Wilson, "Religiosity and Marital Adjustment: Multidimensional Interrelationships," *Journal of Marriage and the Family* 48 (1986): 147-151.

6   Erik E. Filsinger, "Religiosity, Socioeconomic Rewards, and Family Development: Predictors of Marital Adjustment," *Journal of Marriage and the Family* 46 (1984): 663-670; Richard A. Hunt and Morton R. King, "Religiosity and Marriage," *Journal for the Scientific Study of Religion* 17 (1978): 399-406. Leon R. Kass, *The Beginning of Wisdom: Reading Genesis* (New York: Free Press, 2003), 119-121. Maria Krysan, Kristin A. Moore, and Nicholas Zill, "Research on Families," Report on a Conference Convened by the Office of the Assistant Secretary for Planning and Evaluation, U.S. Department of Health and Human Services, 10 May 1990.

7   Robert A. Aldrich and Glenn Austin, *Grandparenting for the 90's* (Incline Village: Robert Erdmann, 1991): 15-20. Arthur Kornhaber, "Grandparenthood and the 'New Social Contract,'" in *Grandparenthood*, ed. Vern L. Bengston and Joan F. Robertson (Beverly Hills: Sage, 1985): 160-165. Thomas E. Denham and Craig W. Smith, "The Influence of Grandparents on Grandchildren: A Review of the Literature and Resources," *Family Relations* 38 (1989): 340-345.

8   Allan C. Carlson, *From Cottage to Work Station: The Family's Search for Social Harmony in the Industrial Age* (San Francisco: Ignatius, 1993). John Devereux and Luis Locay, "Specialization, Household Production, and the Measurement

of Economic Growth," *The American Economic Review* 82 (1992): 399-403. Stuart Ewen, *Captains of Consciousness: Advertising and the Social Roots of the Consumer Culture* (New York: McGraw Hill, 1976): 161-164. Paul C. Glick, "The Family Life Cycle and Social Change," *Family Relations* 38 (1989): 123-189.

9   Glenna Matthews, *'Just a Housewife': The Rise and Fall of Domesticity in America* (New York: Oxford, 1987): 146-171. Karl Polanyi, *The Great Transformation* (New York: Rinehart, 1943), 74-75, 83, 92. Pitirim Sorokin, *Social and Cultural Dynamics: A Study of Change in Major Systems of Art, Truth, Ethics, Law, and Social Relationships*, rev. and abridged ed. (1957; rpt. New Brunswick: Transaction, 1985): 695-705.

10   Duane Quiatt and Jack Kelso, "Household Economics and Hominid Origins," *Current Anthropology* 26 (1985): 207-211. Joel R. Peck and Marcus W. Feldman, "Kin Selection and the Evolution of Monogamy," *Science* 240 (1988): 1672-1674.

11   American Academy of Pediatrics Task Force on the Family, "Family Pediatrics," *Pediatrics* 111 Supplement (2003): 1541-1553. Susan L. Brown, "Family Structure and Child Well-Being: The Significance of Parental Cohabitation," *Journal of Marriage and Family* 66 (2004): 351-367.

12   Cheryl Buehler and Kay Pasley, "Family Boundary Ambiguity, Marital Status and Child Adjustment," *Journal of Early Adolescence* 20 (2000): 281-308.

13   David H. Demo and Alan C. Acock, "Family Structure, Family Process, and Adolescent Well-Being," *Journal of Research on Adolescence* 6 (1996): 457-488. Stephen Demuth and Susan L. Brown, "Family Structure, Family Processes, and Adolescent Delinquency: The Significance of Parental Absence Versus Parental Gender," *Journal of Research in Crime and Delinquency* 41 (2004): 58-81.

14   Toni Richards et al., "Changing Living Arrangements: A Hazard Model of Transitions Among Household Types," *Demography* 24 (1987): 77-85.

15   Wendy D. Manning and Kathleen A. Lamb, "Adolescent Well-Being in Cohabiting, Married, and Single-Parent Families," *Journal of Marriage and Family* 65 (2003): 876-893.

16   Karen F. Parker and Tracy Johns, "Urban Disadvantage and Types of Race-Specific Homicide: Assessing the Diversity in Family Structures in the Urban Context," *Journal of Research in Crime and Delinquency* 39 (2002): 277-303.

17   Ronald S. Immerman and Wade C. Mackey, "The Societal Dilemma of Multiple Sexual Partners: The Costs of the Loss of Pair-Bonding," *Marriage and Family Review* 29 (1999): 3-14.

18   Randal D. Day and Wade C. Mackey, "Children as Resources: A Cultural Analysis," *Family Perspective* 20 (1985): 258-262. Jon Elvind Kolberg, "The Gender Dimension of the Welfare State," *International Journal of Sociology* 21 (1991): 119-146.

19   Jennifer Roback Morse, *Love & Economics: Why the Laissez-Faire Family Doesn't Work* (Dallas: Spence, 2001), 89-136. Natalie Rogoff Ramsøy, "Non-marital Co-

habitation and Change in Norms: The Case of Norway," *Acta Sociologica* 37 (1994): 23-27.

20   Frances D'Souza, "Democracy as a Cure for Famine," *Journal of Peace Research* 31 (1994): 369-373. Ann Gibbons, "Famine: Blame Policy, not Nature," *Science* 254 (1991): 790.

21   Barbara Jancar, "Democracy and the Environment in Eastern Europe and the Soviet Union," *Harvard International Review* 12.4 (1990): 13-18. Martin Ravillion, "Famines and Economics," *Journal of Economic Literature* 35 (1997): 1205-1247.

22   Julian Simon, "The Effects of Population on Nutrition and Economic Well-Being," *Journal of Interdisciplinary History* 14 (1983): 413-437. Julian Simon, *The Ultimate Resource* (Princeton: Princeton University Press, 1981). Julian Simon, *The Ultimate Resource* 2 (Princeton: Princeton University Press, 1996).

23   Anatoly I. Antonov, "Depopulation and Family Failure in Russia," *The Family in America* 15 (July 2001): 1-8. John C. Caldwell, "Demographic Theory: The Long View," *Population and Development Review* 30 (2004): 297-316. John C. Caldwell and Thomas Schindlmayr, "Explanations of the fertility crisis in modern societies: A search for commonalities," *Population Studies* 57 (2003): 241-263. Philip Longman, *How Falling Birthrates Threaten World Prosperity and What to Do About It* (New York: Basic, 2004).

24   Shawn L Christiansen and Rob Palkovitz, "Why the 'Good Provider' Role Still Matters," *Journal of Family Issues* 22 (2001): 84-106. Mohammadreza Hojat, "Satisfaction with Early Relationships with Parents and Psychosocial Attributes in Adulthood: Which Parent Contributes More?" *The Journal of Genetic Psychology* 159 (1998): 202-220. Myriam Khlat, Catherine Sermet, and Annick Le Pape, "Women's health in relation with their family and work roles: France in the early 1990s," *Social Science & Medicine* 50 (2000): 1807-1825.

25   Robert M. Orrange, "Individualism, Family Values, and the Professional Middle Class: In-Depth Interviews with Advanced Law and MBA Students," *The Sociological Quarterly* 44 (2003): 451-480. Arland Thornton and Linda Young-DeMarco, "Four Decades of Trends in Attitudes Toward Family Issues in the United States: The 1960's Through the 1990's," *Journal of Marriage and the Family* 63 (2001): 1009-1037. Lynn Y. Weiner, "Reconstructing Motherhood: The La Leche League in Postwar America," *The Journal of American History* 80 (1994): 1357-1381.

26   Gary Becker, "A Theory of Marriage: Part I," *The Journal of Political Economy* 81 (1973): 813-846. Kass, *The Beginning of Wisdom*, 119-121.

27   David M. Buss, "Sex Differences in Human Mate Preferences: Evolutionary Hypotheses Tested in 37 Cultures," *Behavioral and Brain Sciences* 12 (1989): 1-14. Maryann Davis and Eugene Emory, "Sex Differences in Neonatal Stress Reactivity," *Child Development* 66 (1995): 14-27. Christine De Lacoste-Utamsing and Ralph L. Holloway, "Sexual Dimorphism in the Human Corpus Callosum," *Science* 216 (1982): 1431-1432.

28 Alice H. Eagley, "The Science and Politics of Comparing Men and Women," *American Psychologist* 50 (1995): 145-158. Doreen Kimura, "Sex Differences in the Brain," *Scientific American* (August 1992): 32-37.

29 Lloyd B. Lueptow, Lori Garovich-Szabo, and Margaret B. Lueptow, "Social Change and the Persistence of Sex Typing 1974-1997," *Social Forces* 80 (2001): 1-35. Jennifer W. Makin and Richard H. Porter, "Attractiveness of Lactating Females' Breast Odors to Neonates," *Child Development* 60 (1989): 803-810. Virginia A. Mann et al., "Sex Differences in Cognitive Abilities: A Cross-Cultural Perspective," *Neuropsychologia* 28 (1990): 1063-1077.

30 Linda Mealey, *Sex Differences: Developmental and Evolutionary Strategies* (San Diego: Academic Press, 2000): 11-23, 376-377. Irwin Silverman and Marion Eals, "Sex Differences in Spatial Abilities: Evolutionary Theory and Data," in *The Adapted Mind: Evolutionary Psychology and the Generation of Culture* (New York: Oxford University Press, 1992): 533-579. Martin Van Creveld, "A Woman's Place: Reflections on the Origin of Violence," *Social Order* 76 (2000): 825-846. J. Richard Udry, "Biological Limits of Gender Construction," *American Sociological Review* 65 (2000): 443-457.

31 Martin Van Creveld, "A Woman's Place: Reflections on the Origin of Violence," *Social Order* 76 (2000): 825-846. J. Richard Udry, "Biological Limits of Gender Construction," *American Sociological Review* 65 (2000): 443-457.

32 Gary Becker, "A Theory of Marriage: Part I," *The Journal of Political Economy* 81 (1973): 813-846. Gary Becker, "A Theory of Marriage: Part II," *The Journal of Political Economy* 82 (1974): S11-S26. Sanders D. Korenman and David Neumark, "Does Marriage Really Make Men More Productive?" No. 29 in the Finance and Economics Discussion Series, Division of Research and Statistics, Federal Reserve Board, May 1988.

33 Karin L. Brewster et al., "The Changing Impact of Religion on the Sexual and Contraceptive Behavior of Adolescent Women in the United States," *Journal of Marriage and Family* 60 (1998): 493-503. Niclas Berggren, "Rhetoric or Reality? An Economic Analysis of the Effects of Religion in Sweden," *Journal of Socio-Economics* 26 (1997): 571-596. Robert H. DuRant, Robert Pendergast, and Carolyn Seymore, "Sexual Behavior Among Hispanic Female Adolescents in the United States," *Pediatrics* 85 (1990): 1051-1058.

34 Day and Mackey, "Children as Resources: A Cultural Analysis," 258-262. Mark A. Fossett and K. Jill Kiecolt, "Mate Availability and Family Structure among African Americans in U.S. Metropolitan Areas," *Journal of Marriage and the Family* 55 (1993): 288-302.

35 Diane K. McLaughlin and Daniel T. Lichter, "Poverty and the Marital Behavior of Young Women," *Journal of Marriage and the Family* 59 (1997): 582-594.

36 Charles Murray, "Does Welfare Bring More Babies?" *Public Interest* No. 115 (1994): 17-30. David T. Ellwood, "Anti-Poverty Policy for Families in the Next

Century: From Welfare to Work—and Worries," *The Journal of Economic Perspectives* 14 (2002): 187-198. Daniel Lichter and Rukamalie Jayakody, "Welfare Reform: How Do We Measure Success?" *Annual Review of Sociology* 28 (2002): 117- 142.

37 Douglas W. Allen, "Marriage and Divorce: Comment," *The American Economic Review* 82 (1992): 679-685. Leora Friedberg, "Did Unilateral Divorce Raise Divorce Rates? Evidence from Panel Data," *The American Economic Review* 88 (1998): 608-627. Thomas B. Marvell, "Divorce Rates and the Fault Requirement," *Law and Society Review* 23 (1989): 544-563.

38 Paul A. Nakonezny, Robert D. Shull, and Joseph Lee Rodgers, "The Effect of No-Fault Divorce Law on the Divorce Rate Across the 50 States and Its Relation to Income, Education, and Religiosity," *Journal of Marriage and the Family* 57 (1995): 477-488.

39 Lynn D. Wardle, "No-Fault Divorce and the Divorce Conundrum," *Brigham Young University Law Review* 13 (1991): 79-142. Lenore J. Weitzman, "The Divorce Law Revolution and the Transformation of Legal Marriage," in *Contemporary Marriage: Comparative Perspectives on a Changing Institution*, ed. Kingsley Davis (New York: Russell Sage, 1985): 305-335.

5 *Life, Death, Work, and Taxes*

1 Kenneth S. Abraham, "Efficiency and Fairness In Insurance Risk Classification," *Virginia Law Review* 71 (1985): 403-451. Bryce Christensen, "The Costly Retreat from Marriage," *The Public Interest* No. 91 (1988): 59-66.

2 I.M.A. Joung et al., "Health Behaviors Explain Part of the Differences in Self-Reported Health Associated with Partner/Marital States in the Netherlands," *Journal of Epidemiology and Community Health* 49 (1995): 482-488.

3 Susan Kennedy et al., "Immunological Consequences of Acute and Chronic Stressors: Mediating role of Interpersonal Relationship," *British Journal of Medical Psychology* 61 (1988): 77-85. Myriam Khlat, Catherine Sermet, and Annick Le Pape, "Women's health in relation with their family and work roles: France in the early 1990s," *Social Science & Medicine* 50 (2000): 1807-1825.

4 Ellen Eliason Kisker and Noreen Goldman, "Perils of Single Life and Benefits of Marriage," *Social Biology* 34 (1987): 135-151. Ingrid Waldron, Christopher C. Weiss, and Mary Elizabeth Hughes, "Marital Status Effects on Health: Are There Differences Between Never-Married Women and Divorced and Separated Women?," *Social Science & Medicine* 45 (1997): 1387-1397.

5 Allan Carlson, "Toward a Family-Centered Theory of Taxation," *The Family in America* 12 (January 1998): 1-8. Thomas J. Espenshade and Joseph J. Minarik, "Demographic Implications of the 1986 US Tax Reform," *Population and Development Review* 13 (1987): 115-127. Eugene Steuerle, "The Tax Treatment of

Households of Different Size," in *Taxing the Family*, ed. R.G. Penner (Washington: American Enterprise Institute, 1983), 72-75.

6   Edward J. McCaffery, "The Political Liberal Case Against the Estate Tax," *Philosophy and Public Affairs* 23 (1994): 281-312. Richard A. Musgrave, "Is a Property Tax on Housing Regressive?" *The American Economic Review* 64 (1974): 222-229. United States Senate, 107th Congress, 1st Session, *Easing the Family Tax Burden*, Hearing Before the Committee on Finance, 8 March 2001 (Washington: U.S. Government Office, 2001).

7   Eileen Boris, "Crafts Shop or Sweatshop? The Uses and Abuses of Craftmanship in Twentieth-Century America," *Journal of Design History* 2 (1989): 175-192. Charles Davenport, Michael D. Boehlje, and David B.H. Martin, "Taxes and the Family Farm," *Proceedings of the Academy of Political Science* 34 (1982): 112-121.

8   Bryce Christensen, "For Profit or for Posterity? The Unique Legacy of America's Family Businesses," *The Family in America* 18 (July 2004): 1-8. Robert E. Kraut and Patricia Grambsch, "Home-Based White Collar Employment: Lessons from the 1980 Census," *Social Forces* 66 (1987): 410-426.

9   Richard M. Vogel, "Relocation Subsidies: Regional Growth Policy or Corporate Welfare?" *Review of Radical Political Economics* 32 (2000): 437-457. Robert Weissman, "Corporate Welfare Challenge," *Multinational Monitor* (January/February 2000): 20-26.

10   Robert O. Baldwin, "Femininity-Masculinity of Blacks and Whites Over a Fourteen-Year Period," *Psychological Reports* 60 (1987): 455-458. Allan Carlson, "The Androgyny Hoax," *Family Questions* (New Brunswick: Transaction, 1988): 29-47. Alice H. Eagley, "The Science and Politics of Comparing Men and Women," *American Psychologist* 50 (1995): 145-158. J. Richard Udry, "Biological Limits of Gender Construction," *American Sociological Review* 65 (2000): 443-57.

11   Carol Flake-Hobson, Patsy Skeen, and Bryan E. Robinson, "Review of Theories and Research concerning Sex-Role Development and Androgyny with Suggestions for Teachers," *Family Relations* 29 (1980): 155-162. The National Project of Women in Education, U.S. Department of Health, Education, and Welfare, *Taking Sexism Out of Education* (Washington: U.S. Government Printing Office, 1978). Mary Ellen Verheyden-Hilliard, *Reducing Sex Stereotyping in Career Education: Some Promising Approaches to Persistent Problems* (Washington: U.S. Government Printing Office, 1979).

12   Allan Carlson, "Gender, Children, and Social Labor: Transcending the 'Family Wage' Dilemma," *Journal of Social Issues* 52 (1996): 137-161.

13   Mark Evan Edwards, "Uncertainty and the Rise of the Work-Family Dilemma," *Journal of Marriage and the Family* 61(2001): 183-196. Allan Carlson, *The 'American Way': Familiy and Community in the Shaping of the American Identity* (Wilmington: ISI Books, 2003), 153-160.

14   Carlson, *The 'American Way'*, 153-160.

15   William Lowe Boyd, "Balancing Public and Private Schools: The Australian Experience and American Implications," *Educational Evaluation and Policy Analysis* 9.3 (1987): 183-198. Dick Neal, "How Vouchers Could Change the Market for Education," *The Journal of Economic Perspectives* 16.4 (2002): 25-44. E.G. West, "The Burdens of Monopoly: Classical versus Neoclassical," *Southern Economic Journal* 44 (1978): 829-845.

16   Douglas Besharov, "The Need to Narrow the Grounds for State Intervention," in *Protecting Children from Abuse and Neglect*, ed. Douglas Besharov (Springfield: Charles Thomas, 1988): 62-88. Joseph Goldstein, Anna Freud, and Albert Solnit, *Before the Best Interests of the Child* (New York: Free Press, 1979): 24-25, 136-137.

17   Martin Guggenheim, "Child Protection, Foster Care, and Termination of Parental Rights," *What's Wrong With Children's Rights* (Cambridge: Harvard University Press, 2005): 174-212.

18   Hans Sebald, "Witch Children: The Myth of the Innocent Child," *Issues in Child Abuse Accusation* 8 (1996): 179-186. Frederic N. Silverman, "Child Abuse: The Conflict of Underdetection and Overreporting," *Pediatrics* 80 (1987): 442. San Diego Grand Jury, "Child Sexual Abuse, Assault, And Molest Issues," Report No. 8, 29 June 1992.

19   Jennifer Nerissa Davis and Martin Daly, "Evolutionary Theory and the Human Family," *The Quarterly Review of Biology* 72 (1997): 407-435.

20   David Herlihy, "Biology and History: The Triumph of Monogamy," *Journal of Interdisciplinary History* 25 (1995): 571-583. Umberto Melotti, "Towards a New Theory of the Origin of the Family," *Current Anthropology* 22 (1981): 625-638. Abraham Sagi et al., "'Sleeping Out of Home in a Kibbutz Communal Arrangement: It Makes a Difference for Infant-Mother Attachment," *Child Development* 65 (1994): 992-1004.

21   E. Franklin Frazier, "Urbanization and the Negro Family," in *The Negro and the City*, ed. Richard B. Sherman (Englewood Cliffs: Prentice Hall, 1970): 109-112. Daniel Patrick Moynihan, *The Negro Family: The Case for National Action* [1965] in *The Moynihan Report and the Politics of Controversy*, ed. Lee Rainwater and William L. Yancey (Cambridge: Massachusetts Institute of Technology, 1967), 50-105. Charles Murray, "Does Welfare Bring More Babies?" *Public Interest* No. 115 (1994): 17-30.

22   Allan C. Carlson, *From Cottage to Work Station: The Family's Search for Social Harmony in the Industrial Age* (San Francisco: Ignatius, 1993). Andrew Cherlin, "The Deinstitutionalization of Marriage," *Journal of Marriage and Family* 66 (2004): 848-863. Terry Arendell, "The Social Self as Gendered: A Masculinist Discourse of Divorce," *Symbolic Interaction* 15 (1992): 151-181.

23   Alice H. Eagley, "The Science and Politics of Comparing Men and Women," *American Psychologist* 50 (1995): 145-158. Becky L. Glass and Margaret K. Stolee,

"Family Law in Soviet Russia 1917-1945," *Journal of Marriage and the Family* 49 (1987): 893-901.

24 John L. Esposito, Darrel J. Fasching, and Todd Lewis, *World Religions Today* (New York: Oxford, 2002): 215, 289. Melford E. Spiro, "Religious Symbolism and Social Behavior," *Proceedings of the American Philosophical Society* 113 (1969): 341-349. C.S. Lewis, *The Abolition of Man* (New York: Macmillan and Co., 1974).

25 Nguyen Van Huy, "The Particularity of Popular Beliefs among Ethnic Communities of the Hanhi-Lolo Linguistic Group," *Social Compass* 42 (1995): 301-315. Mei-Lin Lee and T-Hsiung Sun, "The family and demography in contemporary Taiwan," *Journal of Comparative Family Studies* 26 (1995): 101-115.

26 American Academy of Pediatrics Task Force on the Family, "Family Pediatrics," *Pediatrics* 111 Supplement (2003): 1541-1553. Zeng-Yin Chen and Howard B. Kaplan, "Intergenerational Transmission of Constructive Parenting," *Journal of Marriage and the Family* 63 (2001): 17-31. Andrew J. Cherlin, "Going to Extremes: Family Structure, Children's Well-Being, and Social Science," *Demography* 36 (1999): 421-428. Thomas D. Cook et al., "Some Ways in Which Neighborhoods, Nuclear Families, Friendship Groups, and Schools Jointly Affect Changes in Early Adolescent Development," *Child Development* 73 (2002): 1283-1309.

27 Stephen Demuth and Susan L. Brown, "Family Structure, Family Processes, and Adolescent Delinquency: The Significance of Parental Absence Versus Parental Gender," *Journal of Research in Crime and Delinquency* 41 (2004): 58-81. Ross Macmillan and John Hagan, "Violence in the Transition to Adulthood: Adolescent Victimization, Education, and Socioeconomic Attainment in Later Life," *Journal of Research on Adolescence* 14 (2004): 127-158. Jacqueline Scott, "Family, Gender, and Educational Attainment in Britain: A Longitudinal Study," *Journal of Comparative Family Studies* 35 (2004): 565-589.

28 American Academy of Pediatrics Task Force on the Family, "Family Pediatrics," 1541-1553.

29 Nicole J. Cronk et al., "Risk for Separation Anxiety Disorder Among Girls: Paternal Absence, Socioeconomic Disadvantage, and Genetic Vulnerability," *Journal of Abnormal Psychology* 113 (2004): 237-247.

30 David H. Demo and Alan C. Acock, "Family Structure, Family Process, and Adolescent Well-Being," *Journal of Research on Adolescence* 6 (1996): 457-488. Demuth and Brown, "Family Structure, Family Processes, and Adolescent Delinquency," 58-81.

31 Bruce J. Ellis et al., "Quality of Early Family Relationships and Individual Differences in the Timing of Pubertal Maturation in Girls: A Longitudinal Test of an Evolutionary Model," *Journal of Personality and Social Psychology* 77 (1999): 387-401.

32 K.A.S. Wickrama et al., "Linking Early Social Risks to Impaired Physical Health during the Transition to Adulthood," *Journal of Health and Social Behavior* 44 (2003): 61-74.

33 Cynthia C. Harper and Sara S. McLanahan, "Father Absence and Youth In-
    carceration," *Journal of Research on Adolescence* 14 (2004): 369-397.

34 P. Lindsay Chase Lansdale, Andrew J. Cherlin, and Kathleen F. Kiernan, "The
    Long-Term Effects of Parental Divorce on the Mental Health of Young Adults:
    A Developmental Perspective," *Child Development* 66 (1995): 1614-1634.

35 Jeanne M. Hilton and Stephan Desrochers, "Children's Behavior Problems
    in Single-Parent and Married-Parent Families: Development of a Predictive
    Model," *Journal of Divorce & Remarriage* 37 (2003): 13-34. Ellen L. Lipman et al.,
    "Child Well-Being in Single-Mother Families," *Journal of the American Academy
    of Child and Adolescent Psychiatry* 41 (2002): 75-82. Suet-Ling Pong, "Family
    Structure, School Context, and Eighth Grade Math and Reading Achievement,"
    Journal of Marriage and the Family 59 (1997): 734-746.

36 Karen Seccombe, "Families in Poverty in the 1990s: Trends, Causes, Conse-
    quences, and Lessons Learned," *Journal of Marriage and the Family* 62 (2000):
    1094-1113. David Wood, "Effect of Child and Family Poverty on Child Health
    in the United States," *Pediatrics* 112 (2003): 707-212.

37 American Academy of Pediatrics Task Force on the Family, "Family Pediatrics,"
    1541-1553. Bruce J. Ellis and Judy Garber, "Psychosocial Antecedents of Varia-
    tion in Girls' Pubertal Timing: Maternal Depression, Stepfather Presence, and
    Family Stress," *Child Development* 71 (2000): 485-501. John Hagan and Holly
    Foster, "S/He's a Rebel: Toward a Sequential Stress Theory of Delinquency and
    Gendered Pathways to Disadvantage in Emerging Adulthood," *Social Forces* 82
    (2003): 53-86.

38 William Jeynes, "A Longitudinal Analysis of the Effects of Remarriage Follow-
    ing Divorce on the Academic Achievement of Adolescents," *Journal of Divorce
    & Remarriage* 33 (2000): 131-148. Pong, "Family Structure, School Context, and
    Eighth Grade Math and Reading Achievement," *Journal of Marriage and the
    Family* 59 (1997): 734-746.

39 Paul Cameron and Kirk Cameron, "Children of Homosexual Parents Report
    Childhood Difficulties," *Psychological Reports* 90 (2002): 71-82.

40 Lynn D. Wardle, "The Potential Impact of Homosexual Parenting on Children,"
    University of Illinois Law Review (1997): 833-919.

41 Thomas M. Achenbach et al., "National Survey of Problems and Competencies
    Among Four- to Sixteen-Year-Olds: Parents Reports for Normative and Clinical
    Samples," *Monographs for the Society for Research in Child Development, Serial
    No. 225*, 56.3 (1991): 68-93. American Academy of Pediatrics Task Force on the
    Family, *Family Pediatrics*: 1541-1553.

42 Susan L. Brown, "Family Structure and Child Well-Being: The Significance
    of Parental Cohabitation," Journal of Marriage and Family 66 (2004): 351-367.
    Thomas DeLeire and Ariel Kalil, "How Do Cohabiting Couples With Children
    Spend Their Money?" *Journal of Marriage and Family* 67 (2005): 286-295.

43   Ora Aviezer, Sagi Abraham, and Marinus va Ijzendoom, "Balancing the Family and the Collective in Raising Children: Why Communal Sleeping in Kibbutzim Was Predestined to End," *Family Process* 41 (2002): 435-454.

44   Abraham Sagi et al., ""Sleeping Out of Home in a Kibbutz Communal Arrangement: It Makes a Difference for Infant-Mother Attachment," *Child Development* 65 (1994): 992-1004. Miri Scharf, "A 'Natural Experiment' in Childrearing: Ecologies and Adolescents' Attachment and Separation Representations," *Child Development* 72 (2001): 236-251.

6   Gifts of the Natural Family

1   American Academy of Pediatrics Task Force on the Family, "Family Pediatrics," *Pediatrics* 111 Supplement (2003): 1541-1553. John G. Guidubaldi and Helen Cleminshaw, "Divorce, Family Health, and Child Adjustment," *Family Relations* 34 (1985): 35-41. James L. Lynch, *The Broken Heart: The Medical Consequences of Loneliness* (New York: Basic, 1977), 78-80. David Wood, "Effect of Child and Family Poverty on Child Health in the United States," *Pediatrics* 112 (2003): 207-212. Gwendolyn E.P. Zahner and Constantine Daskalakis, "Factors Associated with Mental Health, General Health, and School-Based Service Use for Child Psychopathology," *American Journal of Public Health* 87 (1997): 1440-1448.

2   Cheryl Buehler and Kay Pasley, "Family Boundary Ambiguity, Marital Status, and Child Adjustment," *Journal of Early Adolescence* 20 (2000): 281-308. Vincent J. Roscigno, "Family/ School Inequality and African-American/Hispanic Achievement," *Social Problems* 47 (2000): 266-290. Jacqueline Scott, "Family, Gender, and Educational Attainment in Britain: A Longitudinal Study," *Journal of Comparative Family Studies* 35 (2004): 565-589.

3   Thomas D. Cook et al., "Some Ways in Which Neighborhoods, Nuclear Families, Friendship Groups, and Schools Jointly Affect Changes in Early Adolescent Development," *Child Development* 73 (2002): 1283-1309. Ross Macmillan and John Hagan, "Violence in the Transition to Adulthood: Adolescent Victimization, Education, and Socioeconomic Attainment in Later Life," *Journal of Research on Adolescence* 14 (2004): 127-158. Mary Ann Powell and Toby L. Parcel, "Effects of Family Structure on the Earnings Attainment Process: Differences by Gender," *Journal of Marriage and the Family* 59 (1997): 419-433.

4   Yuaureng Hu and Noreen Goldman, "Mortality Differentials by Marital Status: An International Comparison," *Demography* 27 (1990): 233-250. Myriam Khlat, Catherine Sermet, and Annick Le Pape, "Women's health in relation with their family and work roles: France in the early 1990s," *Social Science & Medicine* 50 (2000): 1807-1825. Ellen Eliason Kisker and Noreen Goldman, "Perils of Single Life and Benefits of Marriage," *Social Biology* 34 (1987): 135-151. Thomas Rutledge et al., "Social Networks and Marital Status Predict Mortality in Older Women:

Prospective Evidence from the Study of Osteoporotic Fractures," *Psychosomatic Medicine* 65 (2003): 688-694. Paul D. Sortie, Eric Backlund, and Jacob B. Keller, "U. S. Mortality by Economic, Demographic, and Social Characteristics: The National Longitudinal Mortality Study," *American Journal of Public Health* 85 (1995): 949-956. Leslie R. Martin, et al. "Longevity Following the Experience of Parental Divorce," *Social Science Journal* 61 (2005): 2177-2189.

5   Thomas A. Hirschl, Joyce Altobelli, and Mark R. Rank, "Does Marriage Increase the Odds of Affluence? Exploring the Life Course Probabilities," *Journal of Marriage and Family* 65 (2003): 927-938. Janet Wilmoth and Gregor Koso, "Does Marital History Matter? Marital Status and Wealth Outcomes Among Preretirement Adults," *Journal of Marriage and Family* 64 (2002): 254-268.

6   Daniel T. Lichter, Deborah Roempke Graefe, and J. Brian Brown, "Is Marriage a Panacea? Union Formation Among Economically Disadvantaged Unwed Mothers," *Social Problems* 50(2003): 60-86. United States Commission on Civil Rights, *The Economic Status of Black Women: An Exploratory Investigation*, Staff Report, Oct. 1990: 96-116.

7   Corey L. M. Keyes, "The Mental Health Continuum: From Languishing to Flourishing in Life," *Journal of Health and Social Behavior* 43 (2002): 207-222.

8   Harsha N. Mookherjee, "Marital Status, Gender and Perception of 'Well-Being,'" *The Journal of Social Psychology* 137 (1997): 95-105. Steven Stack and J. Ross Eshleman, "Marital Status and Happiness: a 17-Nation Study," *Journal of Marriage and the Family* 60 (1998): 527-536.

9   John G. Guidubaldi and Helen Cleminshaw, "Divorce, Family Health, and Child Adjustment," *Family Relations* 34 (1985): 35-41. Margaret Whitehead, Bo Burstrom, and Finn Diderichsen, "Social policies and the pathways to inequalities in health: a comparative analysis of lone mothers in Britain and Sweden," *Social Science and Medicine* 50 (2000): 255-270.

10   Lorraine Davies, "Significant Life Experiences and Depression Among Single and Married Mothers," *Journal of Marriage and the Family* 59 (1997): 294-309. Hilde Mausner-Dorsch and William W. Eaton, "Psychosocial Work Environment and Depression: Epidemiologic Assessment of the Demand Control Model," *American Journal of Public Health* 90 (2000) : 1765-1770. Peggy A. Thoits, "Gender and Marital Status Differences in Control and Distress: Common Stress versus Unique Stress Explanations," *Journal of Health and Social Behavior* 28 (1987): 7-22. Allan V. Horwitz, Helene Raskin White, and Sandra Howell-White, "Becoming Married and Mental Health: A Longitudinal Study of a Cohort of Young Adults," *Journal of Marriage and the Family* 58 (1997): 895-907.

11   John E. Murray, "Marital Protection and Marital Selection: Evidence from a Historical-Prospective Sample of American Men," *Demography* 37 (2000): 511-521. Paul D. Sorlie, Eric Backlund, and Jacob B. Keller, "U. S. Mortality by

Economic, Demographic, and Social Characteristics: The National Longitudinal Mortality Study," *American Journal of Public Health* 85 (1995): 949-956.

12   Donald G. Dutton, "Patriarchy and Wife Assault: The Ecological Fallacy," *Violence and Victims* 9 (1994): 167-182. Lisa K. Walder-Haugrud, Linda Vaden Gratch, and Brian Magruder, "Victimization and Perpetration Rates of Violence in Gay and Lesbian Relationships: Gender Issues Explored," *Violence and Victims* 12 (1997): 173-184. Terry Huffman et al., "Gender Differences and Factors Related to the Disposition Toward Cohabitation," *Family Therapy* 21 (1994): 171-184. Jan E. Stets, "Cohabiting and Marital Aggression: The Role of Social Isolation," *Journal of Marriage and the Family* 53 (1991): 669-680. Kersti Yllo and Murray Straus, "Interpersonal Violence Among Married and Cohabiting Couples," *Family Relations* 30 (1981): 339-347.

13   Jan E. Stets and Murray A. Straus, "The Marriage License as a Hitting License: A Comparison of Assaults in Dating, Cohabiting, and Married Couples," Paper presented at the 1988 Meeting of the American Sociological Association, VB20F. PSS, VB119, 8 July 1988. Maria Testa, Jennifer A. Livingston, and Kenneth E. Leonard, "Women's substance abuse and experiences of intimate partner violence: A longitudinal investigation among a community sample," *Addictive Behaviors* 28 (2003): 1649-1664.

14   Martin Daly and Margo Wilson, "Child Abuse and Other Risks of Not Living With Both Parents," *Ethology and Sociobiology* 6 (1985): 197-209. Joy L. Lightcap, Jeffrey A. Kurland, and Robert L Burgess, "Child Abuse: A Test of Some Predictions From Evolutionary Theory," *Ethology and Sociobiology* 3 (1982): 63-68. Richard J. Gelles, "Child Abuse and Violence in Single-Parent Families: Parent Absence and Economic Deprivation," *American Journal of Orthopsychiatry* 59 (1989): 492-501.

15   David Finkelhor et al., "Sexually Abused Children in a National Survey of Parents: Methodological Issues," *Child Abuse and Neglect* 21 (1997): 1-9.

16   David Finkelhor et al., "Sexual Abuse in a National Survey of Adult Men and Women: Prevalence, Characteristics, and Risk Factors," *Child Abuse and Neglect* 14 (1990): 19-28.

17   Ross Macmillan and John Hagan, "Violence in the Transition to Adulthood: Adolescent Victimization, Education, and Socioeconomic Attainment in Later Life," *Journal of Research on Adolescence* 14 (2004): 127-158.

18   Bryce Christensen, "For Profit or for Posterity? The Unique Legacy of America's Family Businesses," *The Family in America* 18 (July 2004): 1-8. Ronald Done, "Goodwill and the Spirit of Market Capitalism," *British Journal of Market Capitalism* 34 (1983): 462-480. Charles Delheim, "The Creation of a Company Culture: Cadburys, 1861-1931," *American Historical Review* 92 (1987): 14-43. Terry A. Beehr, John A. Drexler, Jr., and Sonja Faulkner, "Working in Small Family Businesses: Empirical Comparisons to Non-Family Businesses," *Journal of Organizational Behavior* 18 (1997): 297-310.

19   Michael L. Blim, "Introduction: The Emerging Global Factory and Anthropology," and Frances Abrahamer Rothstein, "Conclusion: New Waves and Old-Industrialization Labor, and the Struggle for the New World Order," in *Anthropology of the Global Factory*, ed. by Frances Abrahamer Rothstein and Michael L. Blim (New York: Bergin & Garvey, 1992): 1-30, 238-246. Stuart Ewen, *Captains of Consciousness: Advertising and the Social Roots of the Consumer Culture* (New York: McGraw Hill, 1976): 161-164. Andrew Kakabadse and Nada Kakabadse, *The Geopolitics of Governance: The Impact of Contrasting Philosophies* (New York: Palgrave, 2001). Sharon M. Keigher and Christine T. Lowery, "The Sickening Implications of Globalization," *Health and Social Work* 23 (1998): 153-158. David C. Korten, *When Corporations Rule the World* (West Hartford: Kumarian/Berrett-Koehler, 1995): 1-23, 215-220.

20   Wendy A. Goldberg, Ellen Greenberger, and Stacy K. Nagel, "Employment and Achievement: Mothers' Work Involvement in Relation to Children's Achievement Behaviors and Mothers' Parenting Behaviors," *Child Development* 67 (1996): 1512-1527. Matthijs Kalmijn, "Mother's Occupational Status and Children's Schooling," *American Sociological Review* 59 (1994): 257-275.

21   Chandra Muller, "Maternal Employment, Parent Involvement, and Mathematics Achievement Among Adolescents," *Journal of Marriage and the Family* 57 (1995): 85-100. Frank P. Stafford, "Women's Work, Sibling Competition, and Children's School Performance," *The American Economic Review* 77 (1987): 972-980.

22   Valerie Kincade Oppenheimer, "Women's Rising Employment and the Future of the Family in Industrial Societies," *Population and Development Review* 20 (1994): 293-336. Jennifer Roeback Morse, *Love & Economics: Why the Laissez-Faire Family Doesn't Work* (Dallas: Spence, 2001): 3-22.

23   Samantha K. Ammons and William T. Markham, "Working at Home: Experiences of Skilled White-Collar Workers," *Sociological Spectrum* 24 (2004): 191-239. Linda Duxbury, Christopher Higgins, and Derrick Neufeld, "Telework and the Balance between Work and Family: Is Telework Part of the Problem or Part of the Solution?" in *The Virtual Workplace*, ed. M. Igbaria and M. Tan (Hershey: Idea Group Publishing, 1998): 218-255. Jeffrey E. Hill, Alan J. Hawkins, and Brent C. Miller, "Work and Family in the Virtual Office," *Family Relations* 45 (1996): 293-301.

24   Helen Rose Ebaugh, "Presidential Address 2001: Return of the Sacred: Reintegrating Religion in the Social Sciences," *Journal for the Scientific Study of Religion* 41 (2002): 385-395. Darwin L. Thomas and Marie Cornwall, "Religion and Family in the 1980s: Discovery and Development," *Journal of Marriage and the Family* 52 (1990): 983-992. Edward O. Wilson, *Sociobiology: The New Synthesis* (Cambridge: Harvard University Press, 1975): 167-168, 561-562.

25   Daniel N. Spicer, "World View and Abortion Beliefs: A Replication of Luker's Implicit Hypothesis," *Sociological Inquiry* 64 (1994): 114-126. Steven Stack, Ira

Wasserman, Augustine Kposowa, "The Effects of Religion and Feminism on Suicide Ideology: An Analysis of National Survey Data," *Journal for the Scientific Study of Religion* 33 (1994): 110-121.

26   Sanjiv Gupta, Pamela J. Smock, and Wendy D. Manning, "Moving Out: Transition to Nonresidence Among Resident Fathers in the United States, 1968-1997," *Journal of Marriage and Family* 66 (2004): 627-638. U.S. Census Bureau, "Living Arrangements of Children Under 18 Years Old: 1960 to Present," Table CH-1, 15 Sept. 2004, *Families and Living Arrangements*, at <http://www.census. gov/population/www/socdemo/hh-fam.html> (10 June 2005).

27   American Academy of Pediatrics Task Force on the Family, "Family Pediatrics," 1541-1553. Claudia J. Coulton and Shanta Pandey, "Geographic Concentration of Poverty and Risk to Children in Urban Neighborhoods," *American Behavioral Scientist* 35 (1992): 238-257. David Courtwright, *Violent Land: Single Men and Social Disorder from the Frontier to the Inner City* (Cambridge: Harvard University Press, 1996): 240-280.

28   David T. Ellwood, "Anti-Poverty Policy for Families in the Next Century: From Welfare to Work—and Worries," *Journal of Economic Perspectives* 14 (2000): 187-198.

29   Cynthia C. Harper and Sara S. McLanahan, "Father Absence and Youth Incarceration," *Journal of Research on Adolescence* 14 (2004): 369-397. Kathleen Mullan Harris, Greg J. Duncan, and Johanne Boisjoly, "Evaluating the Role of 'Nothing to Lose' Attitudes on Risky Behavior in Adolescence," *Social Forces* 80 (2002): 1005-1039.

30   Margaret McHugh, "Child Abuse in a Sea of Neglect: The Inner-City Child," *Pediatric Annals* 21 (1992): 504-507. Robert D. Plotnick et al., "Inequality and poverty in the United States: The twentieth-century record," *Focus* 19.3 (1998): 7-14.

31   Howard M. Bahr and Kathleen S. Bahr, "Families and Self-Sacrifice: Alternative Models and Meanings for Family Theory," *Social Forces* 79 (2001): 1231-1258. John C. Caldwell and Thomas Schindlmayr, "Explanations of the fertility crisis in modern societies: A search for commonalities," *Population Studies* 57 (2003): 241-263. Michele Hoffnung, "Wanting It All: Career, Marriage, and Motherhood During College-Educated Women's 20s," *Sex Roles* 50 (2004): 711-723.

7   *Introspection and Confession*

1   Barbara Dafoe Whitehead, "What Families Must do for Children," *The Chicago Tribune* (October 1, 1991).

2   See: Chapter 5, "In Defense of the Natural Family," in: Doris Buss and Didi Herman, *Globalizing Family Values: The Christian Right in International Politics* (Minneapolis: University of Minnesota Press, 2003).

8   *A Natural Family Policy*

1   Louis de Bonald, *On Divorce*, trans. and ed. By Nicholas Davidson (New Brunswick, NJ: Transaction, 1992 [1801]): 36-37.

2   Edmund Burke, *Reflections on the French Revolution* (London: J.M. Dent & Sons, 1955 [1790]): 44.

3   Abraham Kuyper, "Maranatha" [Speech to the 1891 convention of the Anti-Revolutionary Party held in Utrecht], in James D. Bratt, ed., *Abraham Kuyper: A Centennial Reader* (Grand Rapids, MI: William B. Eerdmans, 1998): 212.

4   Abraham Kuyper, "Uniformity: The Curse of Modern Life, [22 April 1869]," in Bratt, *Abraham Kuyper: A Centennial Reader*, p. 32.

5   Kuyper, "Maranatha," 225-26.

6   A role described and praised by sociologist Talcott Parsons in "An Analytical Approach to the Theory of Social Stratification," *Essays in Sociological Theory* (Glencoe, IL: The Free Press, 1949): 174.

7   The full text of this report can be found in: Lee Rainwater and William L. Yancy, eds., *The Moynihan Report and the Politics of Controversy* (Cambridge, MA: MIT Press, 1967).

8   Lawrence M. Rudner, "Scholastic Achievement and Demographic Characteristics of Home School Students in 1998," *Education Policy Analysis Archives* 7 (23 March 1999): 7-8, 12.

9   Leslie Whittington, "Taxes and the Family: The Impact of the Tax Exemption for Dependents on Marital Fertility," *Demography* 29 (May 1992): 220-21; and L.A. Whittington, J. Alan, and H.E. Peters, "Fertility and the Personal Exemption: Implicit Pronatalist Policy in the United States," *The American Economic Review* 80 (June 1990): 545-56.

10 Allan Carlson, "Separation and Cooperation: Perspectives from the USA and Europe." Paper for The Cooperation of Church and State Conference, The Centre for Cultural Renewal, Calgary, Alberta, June 8-9, 2006.

11 See: F. Althous, "Differences in Fertility of Catholics and Protestants Are Related to Timing and Prevalence of Marriage," *Family Planning Perspectives* 24 (Sept/Oct. 1992).

12 Steven E. Rhoads, *Taking Sex Differences Seriously* (San Francisco: Encounter Books, 2004).

13 Jane Lawler Dye, "Fertility of American Women: June 2004," *Current Population Reports*, p20-555, U.S. Census Bureau, December 2005.

14 Phillip Longman, "The Return of Patriarchy," *Foreign Policy* (March/April 2006).

15 For a more detailed list of policy prescriptions and their specific justifications, see: Allan Carlson, *Fractured Generations: Crafting a Family Policy for Twenty-First Century America* (New Brunswick, NJ: Transaction, 2006): 135-40.

16   See: "The Child-Care 'Crisis' and Its Remedies," *Family Policy Review* 1 (Fall 2003): 1-159.

17   See: Charles F. Hohm, et al, "A Reappraisal of the Social Security-Fertility Hypothesis: A Bidirectional Approach," *The Social Science Journal* 23 (1986): 163; Isaac Ehrlich and Francis T. Lui, "Social Security, the Family, and Economic Growth," *Economic Inquiry* 36 (July 1998): 404; and Allan Carlson, "Making Social Security Reform Family Friendly," a Family Policy Lecture for the Family Research Council, February 23, 2005.

Index

A NOTE ON THE AUTHORS

ALLAN C. CARLSON is president of The Howard Center for Family, Religion, and Society, and founder of the World Congress of Families. Born 1949 in Des Moines, Iowa, Carlson received his BA, *magna cum laude*, from Augustana College and his PHD in modern European history from The Ohio University. The author of eight books, he has testified on the family before the U.S. Senate and has lectured at universities the world over. He is married and has four children.

PAUL T. MERO is president of the Sutherland Institute. He previously served as executive vice president of The Howard Center for Family, Religion, and Society, where he administered the Second World Congress of Families meeting in Geneva, Switzerland, in 1999. He also worked in the United States Congress, serving two conservative House members from 1987 to 1997. He is a graduate of Brigham Young University. Paul and his wife, Sally, have six children and three grandchildren.

This book was designed and set into type

by Mitchell S. Muncy,

with cover photograph and design by Stephen J. Ott,

and printed and bound

by Bang Printing,

Brainerd, Minnesota.

❧

The text face is Adobe Caslon,

designed by Carol Twombly,

based on faces cut by William Caslon, London, in the 1730s,

and issued in digital form by Adobe Systems,

Mountain View, California, in 1989.

❧

The paper is acid-free and is of archival quality.

50